Politics and Government in Europe Today

COLIN CAMPBELL
Georgetown University

HARVEY FEIGENBAUM
George Washington University

RONALD LINDEN
University of Pittsburgh

HELMUT NORPOTH
State University of New York—Stony Brook

HARCOURT BRACE JOVANOVICH, Publishers

San Diego New York Chicago Austin Washington, D.C.
London Sydney Tokyo Toronto

To: Margaret and Charles Shepherd

Donna R. LaTorre

Sarah

Erick and John-Paul

Preface

We could not have chosen a more exciting period in which to write a book about politics and government in Europe. This time last year (February 1989), Americans were just beginning to realize the immense importance of the steps that most of Western Europe will be taking in 1992 as the European Economic Community moves further along the road toward economic and political union. During the subsequent months of 1989 on into 1990, developments in Eastern Europe loomed so large that they easily overshadowed the momentous process unfolding on the Western side of the Iron Curtain. Indeed, we can no longer take this scar across the face of Europe as given. Communist states have launched the unthinkable—the gradual dismantling of this most evocative symbol of Europe divided.

The exact contours of both post-1992 Western Europe and the liberalization of East Europe remain to be seen. However we have strived to provide the most up-to-date account of European politics and government available in any textbook. Right down to the wire, we have incorporated the most recent developments.

This book focuses on the United Kingdom, France, West Germany, and the Soviet Union. It does this because these are still the four greatest powers in Europe. Italy comes close to membership in this exclusive club. And although Italy rivals Britain as an economic power, Britain merits special attention because it looms much larger in the American consciousness. The original thirteen colonies that formed the United States were British. And, of course, many of America's legal and political traditions derive from British institutions and conventions.

Notwithstanding our focus on the United Kingdom, France, West Germany, and the Soviet Union, we have gone to considerable lengths to provide at least some material on the systems that this book does not cover in depth. We've done this by looking at politics and government in three regions of Europe. Thus, we have included in this volume special chapters on Latin Europe—with treatments of Italy, Spain, and Portugal; Scandinavia—with coverage of Sweden, Norway, and Denmark; and Eastern Europe—with special attention to the dramatic upheaval of Communism throughout this region.

Obviously, the section on the Soviet Union and the chapter on Eastern Europe present the most exciting material in this book. However, the entire volume offers fresh perspectives on recent developments throughout all of Europe. The British section challenges—perhaps with a directness found in no other text—the American tendency to view the United Kingdom as an exemplary democracy. It also offers a critical evaluation of Margaret Thatcher's eleven years as prime minister.

The French section takes pains to demonstrate the degree to which much of contemporary politics and government in France plays out historic divisions and conflicts. However, it tries above all to address Anglo-Saxon prejudices that see France as less democratic and efficient than the United Kingdom. It makes us ask why France—under a Socialist government no less—appears to work so well now.

The section on West Germany concerns the country that will be most directly affected by the changes in Eastern Europe. Indeed, there might well be one Germany not so long after publication of this book. In the meantime, this section tries to discover why West Germany, despite the horrifying legacy of the Third Reich, has emerged as one of Europe's most vibrant democracies.

We begin this book with an introductory chapter that discusses the type of knowledge we seek in the comparative study of politics and government, the development of comparative political science in the United States, and five propositions about contemporary Europe that stem from events over the past decade.

The substantive part of the book is divided into five sections. The first four focus on the United Kingdom, France, West Germany, and the Soviet Union, respectively; the fifth contains three chapters that examine Latin Europe, Scandinavia, and Eastern Europe, in that order. Each country section or regional chapter takes pains to place its analysis in a historical context, to discuss issues associated with political culture, to examine the operation of electoral and party systems, and to assess both the intended and actual functions of formal parts of the governmental apparatus. Further, each of the country sections probes specific policy cases in an effort to provide the reader with a concrete understanding of how the political systems under consideration actually work.

Acknowledgments

It is one thing to derive satisfaction from completion of a book. It is another to recognize that we never would have reached this point without the help and support of many people whose names will not appear on the cover.

Even though we did not ultimately "go" with them, Bert Lummus and Stephen Wayne originally approached us about writing this book. We owe an immense debt for their encouragement and guidance. Drake Bush of Harcourt Brace Jovanovich took us under his wing and calmly prodded us to finish more or less on schedule. Barbara Conover and her colleagues did excellent work as production editors.

Each of us has specific colleagues to thank for their assistance. Colin Campbell owes gratitude to several members of the Department of Government of the University of Manchester where he was a Hallsworth Fellow during 1986–87. He notes especially the support of Roger Williams, Geraint Parry, and George Moyser, and three visiting fellows—Richard Chapman, David Reisman, and Judith Marquand. James B. Christoph provided an exhaustive critique of an initial draft of Campbell's contribution to the book. And Jenefer Ellingston—his assistant at Georgetown—worked tirelessly at the task of stamping out infelicitous writing.

Harvey Feigenbaum wishes to give special thanks for Nicole de Montricher's and Michael Loriaux's detailed comments on his part of the manuscript. Patricia Mann helped immensely as a research assistant.

Ronald Linden gratefully acknowledges the careful reading and helpful suggestions of Donald Kelly of the University of Arkansas as well as the detailed critical comments on drafts by Jonathan Harris, William Chase, and Carmine Storella.

Helmut Norpoth extends his deep gratitude to Chris Soe for his many helpful comments and suggestions. He also thanks Dieter Roth of Forschungsgruppe Wahlen in Mannheim for generously granting access to German polling data.

Since one of your co-authors is a Roman Catholic priest and another—though married—has yet to receive a visit from the stork, we decided not to make a blanket dedication of this book to our "wives" or "children." Instead, Campbell addresses his dedication to an aunt and uncle, Feigenbaum to his wife, Linden to his daughter, and Norpoth to his two sons.

Colin Campbell
Harvey B. Feigenbaum
Ronald Linden
Helmut Norpoth

Contents

11 A Fragmented Political Culture   184

12 Decline, Alienation, and the Organization of Interest   196

13 The Party System as a Moveable Feast   208

14 The State Apparatus   220

III   WEST GERMANY

IV THE SOVIET UNION

V LATIN EUROPE, SCANDINAVIA, AND EAST EUROPE

1

Introduction

Professors teaching courses covering one or another aspect of politics and government in Europe do not have to tell their students that this is an important topic. Maybe things will change in the next few years. However, at this writing—January 1990—Americans find so much coverage in our media about developments in the Soviet Union and other "Eastern" countries such as East Germany, Czechoslovakia, and Poland that they might understandably conclude that Europe has crowded the United States out of the news! On a less sensational level, Western European nations—especially the countries that belong to the European Economic Community (EEC)—have intensified efforts to achieve a greater degree of economic integration. In the EEC, this process passes a milestone in 1992 when members will lift all barriers to trade within the Community. In the build-up, some EEC nations have sought to mark this important event by extracting from fellow members firmer commitments to increased political integration.

You have probably already concluded for yourself that this is a thick book. But Europe is a huge topic. We have sought to put in one volume a manageable proportion of the fundamental material that students should command if they wish to make sense of European politics and government. This chapter highlights the importance of starting with a realistic understanding of the type of knowledge we seek to obtain by studying Europe. It will then point up themes that help make the study of Europe so compelling for anyone concerned about the future of democracy on this continent to which so many of us owe our origins.

WHAT DO WE SEEK TO KNOW BY A COMPARATIVE STUDY OF POLITICS AND GOVERNMENT?

Breaking ground in a new course is not easy. However, some subjects lend themselves more than others to students' making sense of all of the confusing facts. For those students good at memorizing and in possession of strong logical powers, languages can be a snap. Those with facility at storing away

1

what to many would appear to be unrelated details can readily master the declension of nouns and the conjugation of verbs. They can even go far in learning precise usage by memorizing entire expressions. Calculus is bewildering to the uninitiated; however, the adroit reasoner can quickly gain command of equations and their derivation. Chemistry and physics likewise rely heavily upon the student's ability to handle equations; to score well in exams, students of these subjects must also learn how to calculate accurately when rushed.

We do not aim to scare readers into dropping the course for which this book is a text. After all, they might be taking more political science because they have found it easier than other disciplines!

We recognize, thus that many readers might find political science easier than other subjects. Why would this be so if it is difficult to discover a nifty box for every fact and there are a lot of problems that go unresolved? Readers might even have concluded from unhappy experiences with foreign languages, math or one of the natural sciences that their memories and logical powers do not serve them that well. Does this mean that they have taken the line of least resistance—a subject that goes by the name political *science* but, in reality, lacks rigor?

There *is* a science to this discipline. But much of it must build on skills that most students' education left pretty much untutored. American high schools give students a pretty good base in "civics." That is, they provide young people with serviceable knowledge about how the American political system should work—at least, according to the Constitution and the laws of the land. High schools do less well at imparting an understanding of how things actually operate. Further, they generally do very poorly at conveying an appreciation of how political systems other than the American one operate.

This does not mean that American students know absolutely nothing about the world around them, and readers should not despair because their high school provided no formal training on the topic of this book. Most will find, as they read on, that they already know more about politics and government in Europe than they thought. Much of this they will have picked up in the newspaper, on TV or even in conversations with people who know something about Europe. Some will even know a great deal and take to this book like a duck takes to water. Others will find it an uphill struggle at first. However, things that they already knew will eventually come back to them and they will develop a capacity to digest with increasing facility all the new facts.

Whatever their starting points, students will find themselves developing images that will help them absorb all of the detail. Most readers will use the American system as their reference point, and learn how to compare and contrast in their minds.

As they develop their skills, readers will begin to discover more generalized points of reference. They will start getting a notion of how European systems have common traits; they will begin, for instance, to think of France in relation to Britain and West Germany rather than simply to the United States. The comparative examination of many aspects of politics in the Soviet Union might appear more formidable. But, as we will see, things have changed very rapidly in the USSR. Even your authors have had to work overtime to develop new ways of thinking of the Soviet enigma.

Comparative Politics and the Use of Images

Comparative politics is a very old discipline, going back at least as far as Plato, the Greek philosopher who lived from 428 to 348 B.C.

In one of his most important works—*The Republic*—Plato attempted to probe the circumstances under which the just state is likely to emerge and prosper. He employed a wealth of illustrations drawn from his knowledge of the ways in which various Greek city-states functioned as—to use our current expression—political systems. However, he left his real mark through the brilliance of the images he employed to convey his message.

Among such images were those Plato used for his classifications of the different types of people within society. Relatedly, he categorized political systems according to the levels of society that exerted the greatest influence on the actual form that governance took in a given state. Philosopher kings—imbued with wisdom—ruled the ideal or just state. Ambitious men in search of honor—that is, the spirited part of society—dominated in a timocracy. Those for whom wealth served as the driving force established oligarchy. More than a little disdainfully, Plato noted that when the rich degenerate, the poor will seize the opportunity to take control. And the state will soon reflect the tendency of base individuals to yield to the pleasure of the moment.

Importantly for the history of Western civilization, the debate did not end on this pessimistic note. Aristotle (384–322 B.C.) took Plato to task. To be sure, Plato's rich images and adroit marshalling of detail elevated the comparison of political systems to a lofty plane. But Aristotle searched for less rigid approaches to the fundamentals of politics. His tack originated in his view of science. For instance, he had said in *Physics*: "Now what is to us plain and obvious at first is rather confused masses the elements and principles of which become known to us later by analysis." In a word, our images of reality come only gradually, after much observation. They should not be forced. In addition, Aristotle cautioned in his *Ethics,* we cannot achieve the same level of certitude in matters dealing with human behavior and institutions as we might attain in natural sciences:

> Our discussion will be adequate if it has as much clearness as the subject-matter admits of, for precision is not to be sought for alike in all discussions, any more than in all the products of the crafts.

Among Aristotle's many insights, three from his book *Politics* worked an especially profound effect on the way we in the West view governance as related to various types of societies. First, Aristotle did not believe that political systems must adhere to rigid principles in order to achieve justice. Rather he conceived of the political systems as building upon the natural desire to seek moral perfection. The state thus emerged as a natural social organism—like, but infinitely more complex than, a biological organism.

This perception led to Aristotle's second contribution—the assertion that a healthy constitution is one in which all the elements of society have given their assent to and strive for the state's development and survival. And, third, Aristotle concluded, after probing the strengths and weaknesses of various forms of government, that the most practicable political system is one in which the middle class holds the balance of power. That is, those in the middle rungs of society must exceed in strength—both qualitative and quantitative—both the very rich and the very poor. For instance, they must control more aggregate wealth than the very rich and outnumber the poor.

We cannot overstate the importance of Aristotle's image of the state as a social organism to the development of the Western view of politics. Above all, it dovetailed very neatly with the Judeo-Christian understanding of political community. The Jewish tradition portrays God as having chosen Israel as his very own domain. Obviously, this sense of

Aristotle (384–322 B.C.), whose works had a profound influence on the way governance is viewed in the West.

SOURCE: Culver Pictures, Inc.

selection and purpose would affect immensely the way in which the Jewish people would view governance. Under Christianity, Jesus presents himself as sent by God to establish his kingdom here on earth. Jesus used especially powerful imagery in portraying the development of his reign in terms of the growth of the kingdom from utter insignificance—for instance, a small flock or a tiny mustard seed—into a spiritual force that would encompass all nations.

At the time in which Jesus lived, the Roman Empire did dominate virtually all of the Western world. When the empire began to crumble, Christianity filled the vacuum. For much of the Dark Ages (476 to 1000 A.D.), the Church provided the only coherence that Europe enjoyed. The strong, centralized nation-state did not begin to assert itself fully

until well into this millennium. At first, it coexisted with the Church. Indeed, temporal rulers found that the strong kingdom imagery of the gospels provided fertile soil for earthly monarchies. The magnificent Gothic cathedrals, which dominated church architecture from the twelfth through to the fifteenth century, unheisitatingly affirm that the temporal kingdom reflects divine rule. However, the more that kings struggled to consolidate their power, the more they began to steep their appeals in the imagery of the divine rule. For instance, James I of England (1603–25) considered himself a vicar of Christ with absolute authority over his realm.

Coincident with the absolutist phase of the British crown, in the seventeenth century Thomas Hobbes wrote his *Leviathan*. This work, more than any other, ushered in the modern era of thought about politics. Here begins the gradual process whereby political philosophers began to cast aside organic views of the state. Hobbes himself stood Aristotle on his head by stating that individuals' desire for self-preservation, not moral perfection, served as the natural end of the "commonwealth." Much taken by modern physics, Hobbes saw the study of politics as the science whereby the appetite for personal liberty along with dominion over others might be controlled.

Sir Isaac Newton, writing in the latter part of the seventeenth century, confirmed for the natural sciences—especially physics—the dominance that they would enjoy through the next century. Just as human reason had proven itself capable of penetrating to startling new truths about physical reality, it was then thought that reason could decode the essence of politics. In the mid-eighteenth century, Montesquieu, a French political philosopher filled with the new scientific spirit, set about comparing European political systems. He believed that liberty might well derive from proper institutional arrangements more than from some special disposition on the part of a citizenry. His conclusion—in favor of the separation of powers between the executive, the legislature, and the judiciary—worked a seminal influence on the thinking behind the U.S. Constitution.

Ironically, Montesquieu became an advocate of the separation of powers after examining the British political system. Even as Montesquieu wrote, however, Britain had started on the road toward a system characterized by relative unity between the three branches of government. Montesquieu favored the continuation of the monarchical system in France. He believed, however, that an autonomous legislature and judiciary would counter the tendency of French monarchs toward absolutism.

Baron de Montesquieu (1689–1755), whose views on separation of powers influenced the framers of the U.S. Constitution.
SOURCE: The New York Public Library.

The history of political philosophy hardly ends with Montesquieu. In fact, he remains a lesser light beside the likes of Locke (a predecessor), Rousseau, Hegel, and Marx. All of these—and several others—affected European views of political systems much more than did Montesquieu. Yet Montesquieu shaped American images of politics in Europe more than any other writer. Indeed, until the 1960s, American textbooks on European politics still tended to limit themselves to detailed inventories of the relative power positions of different elements of the political system. The almost mechanistic preoccupation with achieving the optimal balance between countervailing structures served as the main concern of American students of European politics.

The Blossoming of Comparative Politics in America

Until the 1960s, American comparative politics was the last field one would expect to set off sparks. Deeply imbued with a mechanistic view of the political system, its practitioners did not stray far from cataloguing the various institutional arrangements for the performance of governmental and political functions. Scholars pursued their research in a legalistic and formalistic way. That is, they dwelt on the prescriptive dimensions to constitutions and institutional arrangements. They did not examine rigorously whether structures actually carried out those specific functions they were designed to perform.

A number of developments made the decline of this approach to comparative politics inevitable. Most decisive were the collapse of the Weimar Republic and the rise of Nazism in Germany in the early 1930s. It became clear that no amount of constitutional engineering could prevent despotism if social, economic and cultural factors favored its emergence. However, a great deal was happening in political science as a discipline as well. Scholars in the field began to consider themselves as *social* scientists. Increasingly, they drew upon the theories and methods of psychology and sociology in framing their hypotheses and conducting their research.

This reorientation of the discipline to social science—beginning in the 1930s and deepening during the 1940s and the 1950s—laid the groundwork for a rush of comparative research in the 1960s. In large part this was owed to a generational transition: The young scholars who had delved into psychology and sociology as graduate students in the 1930s and the 1940s had come into their own as mature researchers.

From the standpoint of images of the political system, nothing short of a revolution had occurred. Once again, the concept of the political system as a living organism began to take hold. Social sciences had developed around biological models rather than those taken from physics. Applied to politics, this meant that purpose or direction takes root in fundamental systemic principles. These amount to more than simply the sum of all the parts. The study of systems entails the search for cyclical processes and inherent goals that govern the shape of political structures and how they perform various functions. Like biological organisms, political systems change according to the phases through which they pass.

David Easton provided the first full-fledged systems theory for political science.[1] With a starting point similar to that taken by Aristotle, Easton cautioned that we had first to look at political phenomena through a "weak telescope" so that we would see the whole system.[2] This is why students of politics have over the ages turned to natural sci-

ences for analogues. In this regard, the utility of viewing politics as involving a system of processes and relationships becomes clear. It highlights the distinction between each "political system" and the environment in which it functions. It therefore defines political life as human behavior that operates within and responds to a system's environment. This enables us to examine political structures and functions in relation to external factors such as social, economic and cultural conditions.

Each system bases its existence on interactions. In politics, these center on what Easton terms "the authoritative allocation of values."[3] In other words, the system takes certain decisions and actions, and individuals accept these as legitimate. The allocative process tends to focus on the persistence of the political system. It tries, in other words, to cope with internal and external stress. Because it is a complex of human relationships, however, the political system exceeds its biological analogue in one crucial respect: It has an innate capacity for self-transformation of its goals, its practices and the very structure of its internal organization. Political systems more than simply adapt to internal and external circumstances; they also consciously partake of the creative act of innovation.[4]

Easton's framework won wide acceptance by students of comparative politics throughout the 1960s and 1970s. It involved three stages of action. First, the environment affects the political system in such a way that the latter becomes crosspressured by demands, many of which conflict fundamentally. There are as well many ways in which the environment supports the system. Together these demands and supports enter the system as "inputs."

Second, within the system itself we find a

---

[1] David Easton, *The Political System* (New York: Knopf, 1953); and *A Framework for Political Analysis* (Englewood Cliffs, NJ: Prentice-Hall, 1965).
[2] Easton, *Framework*, p. 2.

[3] Easton, *Framework*, pp. 49–50.
[4] Easton, *Framework*, p. 100.

David Easton (b. 1917) developed the "systems" approach to comparative politics.

Gabriel A. Almond (b. 1911) greatly influenced the corporative standing of political development.

number of structures and processes. Members of the attentive public and interest groups articulate the various inputs. Parties attempt to aggregate these inputs into coherent programs. Only the executive, including political executives and bureaucrats, legislatures, and courts, can make authoritative responses to various clusters of demands and supports. Finally, these "outputs"—decisions and actions of officials—return to the environment as "feedback."

Despite its widespread use, Easton's framework drew serious challenges from some students of comparative politics. Many believed that—disclaimers notwithstanding—Easton betrayed a conservative bias. He focused on the persistence of the system to an extent that led some to conclude that he took a regime's desire to survive as a common denominator of all political systems. By so lowering its

sights, the model did not seem to invite fundamental questions about the character of a regime.

Gabriel Almond did much to plant systems theory more firmly within a context more open to the prospect of fundamental change. For the concept "persistence" he substituted that of "levels of development." He noted, for instance, that democracy had proved integral to political systems' responsiveness to human needs and, ultimately, sensitivity to general welfare.

Almond believed that rational norms must permeate every level of the political system before true development emerges.[5] Structures

---

[5] Gabriel A. Almond and G. Bingham Powell, *Comparative Politics: A Developmental Approach* (Boston: Little, Brown, 1966), p. 300.

must differentiate roles more clearly, subsystems within political systems must achieve a higher degree of autonomy from one another, and society itself must shed traditional cultures in favor of modern ways of doing things. Indeed, political scientists must facilitate modernizers as they go through the process of discovering in science, technology, education, bureaucracy and open political association a set of ways for fulfilling human capacities more effectively than did their traditional ways of operating.[6]

Karl W. Deutsch, while not denying the superiority of the approach to legalistic and formalistic comparative studies, also objected to system theory's focus on regime persistence. He suggested that political scientists should canvass other analogues to see if these might serve inquiry better than biological models. Citing the paleontologist Pierre Teilhard de Chardin, Deutsch called for a comparative political science that would allow for "genuine evolution." Such a stance would constantly leave analysis open to the emergence of sudden change and true novelty. Importantly, Deutsch saw the political system "as an open-ended process containing the possibility of *self-disruption* or *self-destruction,* as well as a change of goals."[7] Unlike Almond's critique of systems theory, Deutsch's seemed to accept that students of comparative politics must equip themselves to examine regress as well as progress.

Along similar lines, Harold D. Lasswell, a student of American politics who had centered his previous research largely on political psychology, entered the debate. Like Deutsch, Lasswell attempted to place political processes in the context of evolution.

Drawing upon the work of the philosopher Alfred North Whitehead, he set the unfolding of political reality within the frame of the "creative advance of nature" toward "events" that never took place before.[8] The models we employ in analyzing the significance and direction of political events cannot help but take sides.[9] They must show a preference toward the accumulation and distribution within the state of core human values. These include power, enlightenment, wealth, well-being, skill, affection, respect and rectitude.[10]

Notwithstanding the correctives of Almond, Deutsch, Lasswell, and many others, systems theory never really completed the task of settling on an analogue that would exceed the explanatory power of Easton's biological model. Those employing the approach seemed to agree that persistence hardly captured the potential richness of development. However, they could not come to a viable consensus on the other goals by which they should evaluate the performance of political systems.

Two blind spots seemed to impair the systems movement. First, some adherents to the approach placed far too much trust in technology and "rational" procedures. Almond's estimation of the inherent capacity of modernization and democratization to trigger and sustain development serves as the clearest illustration of this defect. He did not seem to entertain the prospect that the developments in participatory democracy, bu-

---

[6] Gabriel A. Almond, "Political Development: Analytical and Normative Perspectives," *Comparative Political Studies,* 1 (1969): 456–463.

[7] Karl W. Deutsch, *The Nerves of Government: Models of Political Communication and Control* (New York: Free Press, 1966), p. 37.

[8] Heinz Eulau, "The Maddening Methods of Harold D. Lasswell: Some Philosophical Underpinnings," *Journal of Politics,* 30 (1968): 3–24.

[9] Harold D. Lasswell, "The Policy Sciences of Development," *World Politics,* 17 (1965): 290.

[10] Harold D. Lasswell and A. R. Holmberg, "Toward a General Theory of Directed Value Accumulation and Institutional Development," in *Political and Administrative Development,* ed. Ralph Braibanti (Durham, NC: Duke University Press, 1969), pp. 356–57.

reaucratization of the state and the secularization of society might reach plateaus —even recede monumentally—in times when political systems undergo especially intense stress.[11]

Since the late 1970s, many European states have rolled back a substantial number of reforms adopted in the late 1960s that were designed to enhance the direct involvement of the people in the policy process. Many planning-oriented bureaucracies that placed immense trust in their ability to make decisions on the basis of rational criteria proved woefully inadequate at addressing the severe economic decline in many European countries during the 1970s. On the right side of the political spectrum, radical politics has begun again to assert itself in Europe to the point where—as is clear in France—neo-fascism has appealed to a significant portion of the electorate. On the left, the rise and continued appeal of movements like the Greens (radical environmentalists) in West Germany and the anti-nuclear groups in Britain suggest that not everyone in Europe has locked arms and marched in unison toward "modernization."

Second, those—such as Deutsch and Lasswell—who pleaded for more comprehensive criteria for systemic analysis than simply persistence or modernization left us with an overwhelmingly difficult task. These authors tried to focus our attention on the inexhaustible potential of political development. They seemed, however, too ready to stretch our horizons beyond the capacity of political science. A fully inclusive view of the political system might take us from political analysis to "metaphysical pathos."[12] That is, we might reach the point where we abandon

the rigor of science in favor of appeals to individuals' beliefs about what human institutions should strive to achieve.

Our own view is that the comparative study of politics and government finds its most salient analogues in the psychology of the human being and the sociology of groups. If adopted, analogies from neither of these realms would allow for anywhere near the specificity that Easton found in the parallels between biological and political systems. We have eschewed, thus, the temptation to limit ourselves to one analogue. Further, we recognize that political science has not covered as much new ground since Aristotle as many people appear to believe. We will not claim greater exactitude in the comparative study of European politics and government than it is capable of producing.

EUROPE AND ITS FUTURE: FIVE PROPOSITIONS

When comparative politics was blossoming in the 1960s, scholars were still wondering just how secure European democracies were. The rise of fascism in the 1930s had shaken the confidence of even the firmest believers in the feasibility of structural checks on despotic rule. Further, the Soviet Union seemed to demonstrate that unchecked state power can arise from the "left" as well as the "right." Spain and Portugal served as reminders that not even Western Europe had rid itself of dictatorships. In addition, two of the region's democracies—France and Italy—did not appear that stable. Finally, deep doubts persisted about the suitability of the German national character for democracy. Scholars found it hard to forget the horrors of Nazism.

Notwithstanding all of these doubts, the comparative politics of the 1960s had not anticipated what would prove to be the overwhelming preoccupation of the discipline be-

[11] Colin Campbell, S.J., "Current Models of the Political System: An Intellective-Purposive View," *Comparative Political Studies*, 4 (1971): 29.

[12] Martin Landau, "Political and Administrative Development," in *Political and Administrative Development*, ed. Braibanti, pp. 334, 346.

gining in the late 1970s and continuing on into the current decade. The focus of comparative politics shifted dramatically from questions about the viability of democracy to profound worries about economic *decline*. Two developments associated with the world economy had provoked this anxiety. First, the two energy crises—in 1973 and 1979—had abruptly impressed upon Europeans a sense of their dependence on reliable and cheap sources of petroleum. Second, European economies, like the American economy, were discovering the difficulty of competing with Japan and other Asian countries for their share of overseas markets.

Can Political Parties Go Bankrupt?

The economic pressures building in the 1970s began to work dramatic effects on the political climate during the latter part of the decade and the early 1980s. In Britain, the Labour government faced a bitter defeat at the hands of the Conservatives. The government had failed in subduing labor unions' demands for the wage increases necessary to keep up with inflation, which had risen above 10 percent. The resulting strikes during the 1978–79 "Winter of Discontent" had left the voters with the impression that Labour had lost its capacity to govern. Changes in France and West Germany lagged behind those in England. In 1981, François Mitterand led the socialists to power. He had pitched his appeal to voters on the argument that the French government had to intervene more concertedly and vigorously in order to reverse the tide of rising inflation and unemployment. West Germany had withstood the economic pressures of the 1970s better than either Britain or France. However, inflation and unemployment began to worry voters there in the early 1980s. In 1982, the Social Democrats, who had controlled the government since 1969, fell to a vote of no confidence, which the electorate endorsed by returning a Christian Democratic government in March 1983.

In each of these cases, the parties that had held governments in the worst part of the economic crisis of the later 1970s and early 1980s have not been able to rehabilitate their images. Even in France, voters, after an interval of *cohabitation* (joint government with a socialist president and a conservative prime minister), appear more willing to trust their economy to the socialists than to the conservatives. Significantly, we find a similar pattern outside of Europe. American voters have now declined two opportunities to forgive the Democrats for the economic debacle occurring under Jimmy Carter's presidency. Canadians renewed the Progressive Conservative mandate in fall 1988 even though the government of Brian Mulroney had made innumerable political blunders. And the Labor government of Bob Hawke in Australia has managed to renew its mandate twice against the Liberals.

Richard Rose and B. Guy Peters anticipated a backlash over the size of government during the late 1970s in their book *Can Government Go Bankrupt?*[13] They maintained that electorates had supported the rapid expansion of government programs in the postwar years because their net impact was to increase the average voter's disposable—that is, after-tax—income. In the 1970s, governments were approaching the threshold beyond which the funding of additional programs would actually bite into disposable income. Simultaneously, sluggish economies, laboring under high unemployment and

---

[13] Richard Rose and B. Guy Peters, *Can Government Go Bankrupt?* (New York: Free Press, 1978), pp. 33–34.

inflation, meant that nations were generating less of the new wealth essential to the gradual enhancement of wage earners' take-home pay.

Rose and Peters thus focused our attention on a deeply transactional perception on the part of electorates about government spending: namely, that governments must offset the added costs of increased spending with economic performances that give voters more disposable income. Rose and Peters did not dwell, however, on the possibility that parties can go into *political* bankruptcy. That is, voters might indefinitely withhold their support from parties whose administrations got the more - government - spending/increased - disposable-income transaction wrong in the late 1970s.

Studies of the motivations behind voters' electoral preferences have increasingly centered on economic conditions. For instance, U.S. scholars have even rejected the view that Ronald Reagan's winning personality and style secured him his second term in 1984. They point up that, in fact, changes in his approval ratings had followed relatively auspicious decreases in unemployment levels and inflation along with increases in disposable income.[14] It appears that George Bush benefited from a similar effect.

Parties that have presided over the economic recovery of the 1980s have been quick to remind voters of how poorly their predecessors did. Certainly, Ronald Reagan and George Bush both adeptly reminded Americans of how bad things became during the "Carter recession." People forget that the worst stages of the economic downturn took place during the first half of Reagan's first term. Evidence suggests that politicians can whip up paranoia among voters by laying all of the blame for economic decline on their opposition.

This has clearly occurred in England. The economic downturn deepened considerably in Mrs. Thatcher's first two years, beginning in May 1979. In fact, voters began to blame Mrs. Thatcher for the nation's worsening predicament.[15] However, the economy started to pull out of its dive by 1981. We must also take into consideration Mrs. Thatcher's handling of the Argentinean invasion of the Falkland Islands in 1982. For those attributing the 1978–79 Winter of Discontent to Labour's pandering to unions, Mrs. Thatcher's steely resolve regarding the Falklands War suggested that she would give equally short shrift to disruptive strikes.

Even data from the 1987 British election still point up the halo effect around the Conservatives, contrasting with Labour's disrepute. Labour campaign polls found voters still extremely skittish about their party's ability to manage the economy.[16] In one survey, 46 percent of respondents believed that Labour's campaign promises would cost too much. Only 18 percent considered Conservative's commitments as extravagant. Fully 56 percent of respondents feared an economic crisis if Labour assumed power.

Such skepticism about a former governing party's competence raises a serious question about the political systems of advanced democracies. A very large literature has developed over the years about "critical elections" in which it appeared that electorates

[14] D. Roderick Kiewiet and Douglas Rivers, "The Economic Basis of Reagan's Appeal," in *The New Direction in American Politics,* eds. John E. Chubb and Paul E. Peterson (Washington, DC: Brookings, 1985), pp. 79–81.

[15] Helmut Norpoth, "Guns and Butter and Government Popularity in Britain," *American Political Science Review,* 81 (1987): 949–59.
[16] David Butler and Dennis Kavanagh, *The British General Election of 1987* (Houndmills: Macmillan, 1988), pp. 134, 248, 258, 273–74.

fundamentally realigned their allegiances from one party to the other.[17] However, we have tended to associate such occurrences with cathartic experiences. The 1930s Depression clearly ranked as an epochal event of this kind.

During the late 1970s and early 1980s, voters throughout Western Europe encountered a prolonged period of *stagflation*—that is, simultaneously high inflation and unemployment. The economic decline fell considerably short of a depression. Nonetheless, the electorates in many Western European countries seem no longer to view the responsible parties as capable of managing the economy. We will see, in the pages that follow, other ways in which the threat of economic decline has substantially altered the way in which democracy operates in several Western European nations. However, one proposition clearly emerges from voters' long memories over who presided during the period of stagflation: **Parties that lose power in a period of serious economic decline—even if this falls considerably short of a depression—will find it difficult to reinstate themselves as a viable option for governance.**

Changes in the Economy Can Transform the Orientation of the State

When we speak of the welfare state, we note that the conventional concept of governance within a nation includes a high value on the promotion and maintenance of social goals such as income support, housing and health. No modern state can withdraw completely from social provision. However, the economic crisis of the late 1970s—along with

the public backlash to ever-growing public expenditure—has led to virtually every European government rolling back the level of social provision to which it commits itself. Relatedly, many European nations have curtailed their involvement in the production of goods and operation of services, such as petroleum products or airlines, through state-owned corporations. We term the withdrawal of governments from state enterprise *privatization*.

Major shifts in what governments do—through either social provision or commercial enterprise—tip us to transformations in the very nature of the state. Focusing on Norway but adducing many points that can be applied to other systems, Johan Olsen traces the contours of these types of changes. Olsen starts by making the point that we should be paying a great deal more attention to the relationship between economic conditions and political leaders' views of what the state should do. In Norway, he maintains, the interval of conservative-center government in the early 1980s reversed the tendency for the government to relate essentially to special interests as embodied in organized groups. Norwegian governments, therefore, had tended to adapt their policies according to the power constellations that formed around various issues.[18]

In large part the approach to government in Norway prior to the conservative-center coalition stemmed from the explosive growth of the welfare state after World War II. The sheer proportions of the expansion of the state required the devolution of a substantial amount of political discretion to the bureaucracy. In turn, this led to the widespread use

[17] V. O. Key, "A Theory of Critical Elections," *Journal of Politics*, 17 (1955): 3–18; James L. Sundquist, *Dynamics of the Party System: Alignment and Realignment of Political Parties in the United States* (rev. ed., Washington, DC: Brookings, 1983).

[18] Johan P. Olsen, "Administrative Reform and Theories of Organization," in *Organizing Governance: Governing Organizations*, eds. Colin Campbell, S.J., and B. Guy Peters (Pittsburgh: University of Pittsburgh, 1988), pp. 233–54.

of consultative mechanisms granting organized interests direct access to governmental decisions. Only these devices could lend political legitimacy to decisions that elected political leaders had delegated to civil servants.

The conservative-center government started the process of privatization and deregulation, which aimed essentially to reestablish the boundaries of the state. The approach went beyond simply making the state smaller. It also tried to reaffirm the traditional view that elected politicians make policy while bureaucrats simply administer the law. For instance, the former would now give more political direction to economists rather than simply deferring to the economists' judgment.[19] Further, they would impose monetarist and free-market views of economics on the grounds that more conventional approaches had not adapted to the times.

Olsen's observations lead to a second proposition that will guide the comparative politics contained in this book: **Perceptions of the role of the state and sectors within it change according to the values that dominate a political system at a given point in history.** The period of economic crisis induced deep fears about financial security at the expense of other societal goals throughout Western Europe. In order to adapt, tremendous pressures built to reorient governmental structures from providing social benefits and producing goods and services to promoting the growth of the economy. The politicians who took over governments in this period had come to believe that economic recovery would prove elusive unless government shrunk and deregulation freed up markets. In short, they sought to reverse the course of governance. Inevitably, this tack has introduced immense changes in the roles of governmental and political institutions.

Are the Aging and Ossification of Nations and Their Institutions Reversible?

It has become an old saw of economics that Germany and Japan lost the battle—World War II—but won the real war—the struggle to capture more than their shares of world markets. As the theory goes, the Allies' destruction of both nations' industrial base during World War II forced both economic systems into modernizing themselves through redesign and reconstruction. On the other hand, Britain and the United States muddled through with piecemeal revamping of their industrial capacities. Especially in manufacturing, the two "victor" nations ultimately found that their plants had fallen so far behind the state-of-the-art facilities in Germany and Japan that the only way out was to shut down. Thus, the emergence of the "Rust Belt" in the American Midwest and "deindustrialization" in the British North point up what happens when nations' manufacturing capacities age and ossify.

Mancur Olson, in his book *The Rise and Decline of Nations*, asserts that the aging process in advanced industrial nations does not stop with closed and rusting plants. It permeates social and political institutions so that government loses its capacity to respond in a timely and effective fashion to economic threats.[20] Olson employs a powerful analogue while making his case. He asserts that political systems can develop institutional sclerosis. That is, so many strong organizations and alliances can make their will felt in

---

[19] Johan P. Olsen, *Organized Democracy: Political Institutions in a Welfare State: The Case of Norway* (Oldon: Universitetsforlaget, 1983), p. 100.

[20] Mancur Olson, *The Rise and Decline of Nations: Economic Growth, Stagflation and Social Rigidities* (New Haven, CT: Yale University Press, 1982), pp. 75–79.

any given issue that the countervailing pressures can clog up the policymaking process. Just as with excessive cholesterol in the human body, the surfeit of powerful special pleaders leads ultimately to the ossification of the main decisional arteries of the political system.

Olson's book dwells on the relative success of West Germany and Japan at avoiding the stagflation—simultaneously high unemployment and inflation—that robbed the United States and Britain of economic growth during the late 1970s and early 1980s. He also notes that even France, though less than a paragon of economic performance, weathered the crisis better than either the United States or Britain.

The logic supporting Olson's argument is convincing. Both formal organizations and secret arrangements dedicated to collective action in an economic sector develop slowly when societies first democratize. In time they take root more readily. And, existing organizations and arrangements tend to persist—even if through inertia rather than vitality. This bias toward survival hinges largely on the stake that group and alliance leaders have in the status quo.

Eventully, the proliferation of organizations and arrangements induces fragmentation of sectors of the economy. For instance, the members of several different unions might work in a single plant. This would contrast with a situation whereby all employees in a factory belong to a single, industry-wide union. With this fragmentation, groups and alliances lose sight of the overall profitability of the sector. Instead, they concentrate their attention on maximizing their share of income and other benefits. The cumulative effect of such strategies makes it increasingly difficult for the sector to obtain optimal economies and output.

In assessing the political and economic systems of Britain, France, West Germany and Japan, Olson concludes that the British case presents a classic instance of institutional sclerosis. Throughout this century, Britain has experienced a lower rate of economic growth than any of the other developed democracies. The country's long experience with stable democracy secure from foreign invasion has provided a perfect breeding ground for the proliferation of collective organizations and secret commercial alliances. Britain experienced much higher inflation *and* unemployment during the period of stagflation than did France or West Germany. It did this, Olson maintains, because both industry and labor continued to seek large enhancements of income even though the economy was straining to achieve any growth at all.[21]

In Olson's view, the experiences of West Germany and Japan contrasted sharply with Britain's. World War II had done more than level the industrial plant of the two countries. It—along with the totalitarian regimes which had provoked hostilities in the first place— had essentially uprooted the organizational and associational life of both nations. After the war, interest groups and commercial alliances in both countries reemerged from scratch. Neither society had, in the 30 years leading up to the economic crisis, experienced the proliferation of special pleaders with narrow appeals necessary for ossification to occur. As a result, both political systems kept in check extravagant demands for shares of income and benefits from production. This became manifest in their relative avoidance of inflation which, in turn, fostered an economic climate in which high employment could be maintained.

Olson suggests that France, though spared much of the war's devastation, mimicked some of the traits of West Germany and Japan. That is, its lack of constitutional stabil-

[21] Olson, pp. 217–18.

ity and of immunity from invasion has, through the entire period of industrialization and democratization, retarded the growth of organizations and alliances. While it did not come through the economic crisis as well as did West Germany and Japan, France's performance exceeded stereotypical views that suggest that the French economy is relatively inefficient.

Do Olson's findings tell us that war must devastate and uproot aging political systems such as Britain and the United States before these societies can overcome ossification? Olson himself envisions the prospect that a gradual process might lead societies suffering institutional sclerosis to change their ways. Such a process would depend on the extent to which other researchers corroborate his findings. It also would require the dissemination of this consensus through the educational system and mass media. That is, the electorates of these nations would have to come to the realization that institutional sclerosis made governments incapable of responding effectively to economic challenges.

It is here that we can find further guidance on treatment of institutional sclerosis in Olson's analogue—the human cardiovascular system. In the case of arterial sclerosis in the human being, we know that individuals can follow diets that dramatically reduce their intake of cholesterol. They might also engage in exercise regimens that help the cardiovascular system avoid ossification through inefficient processing of cholesterol. They might even adopt very stringent dietary practices in preference to medications. That is, they might choose to lower their cholesterol levels through willpower rather than through artificial means that carry undesirable side effects.

The proposition that derives from this human analogue for institutional sclerosis is this: **Though much more difficult than the individual exercise of willpower, political systems can reach the point where groups and alliances recognize that they must radically alter their forms of association.** This book will examine at length the many ways in which the British political system has ossified. It will also note how other European systems have developed less institutional sclerosis or have dealt with it more effectively than has Britain. However, we will not carve our assessments in stone. We might find in the next ten years that in Britain the lesson has finally sunk in and that the political system has begun to transform itself. On the other hand, nations that did better than Britain during the economic crisis might be approaching the phase of their development in which ossification becomes a real danger.

A "United States of Europe"?

Recently Paul Kennedy has studied ebbs and flows in the strength of great powers since 1500.[22] He observes that the standing of nations shifts according to dynamics originating in economic and technological developments. Human beings' "innate drive" to improve their lot depends upon innovation. And, the ways in which societies induce and adapt to change vary greatly according to how they are positioned and how they exploit their advantages.

Nations develop different images of what they want to be. Kennedy calls these "models for emulation." "Trading states" have tried to keep military expenditure to a minimum in order to free their resources for domestic consumption and industrial development. On the other hand, "militarized" economies tolerate levels of defense expenditure that weigh onerously on domestic consumption and in-

[22] Paul Kennedy, *The Rise and Fall of the Great Powers: Economic Change and Military Conflict From 1500 to 2000* (London: Unwin Hyman, 1988). See especially pp. 439, 445–46, 488, 513–14.

dustrial development. They view this as essential to maintaining national security. The classic trading state is Japan; European countries that fall into the category include Switzerland, Sweden, and Austria. The Soviet Union has been the European system that operated a militarized state.

Kennedy argues that we can no longer construe the leading Western European countries—Britain, West Germany and France—as powers per se. Rather, their standing in the world has become inextricably linked with the fate of the rest of democratized Europe—especially as embodied in the European Economic Community (EEC). The United Kingdom and West Germany have to a degree cast their lot for military power with the North Atlantic Treaty Organization (NATO). France and West Germany have entered into an agreement for forward deployment in Germany of French troops. They also have discussed the prospects of a Franco-German army. All three countries operate militarily within Pax Americana. Neither in conventional forces nor in nuclear power could the combined strength of Britain, West Germany, and France withstand determined Soviet aggression in Western Europe.

The dependence of Britain, West Germany and France on one another's forces backed by the military power of the United States has worked a subtle influence on these nations' "models for emulation." Increasingly, their world standing seems to hinge at least as much on their ability to succeed as trading states as to maintain their credentials as military powers. This realization, much more than military integration, has led the three countries and the entire European Economic Community to operate more as a single political system. The effects of EEC membership now pervade both the economic and the political life of Britain, West Germany, and France. In 1992, integration will go a step further with the abolition of all remaining barriers to trade between members of the Community. Already, pressures are building for more tangible political union. This book, thus, recognizes the possibility that **Western Europe has put itself on the course to federal union sometime fairly early in the next century.**

The Soviet Union: A Special Case?

Can the four propositions derived from the West European experience be applied to the USSR, an undoubted European power, but one with a profoundly different political history and culture? An assessment of the "bankruptcy" of parties in the Soviet case means focusing our attention on the very nature and viability of the political system. This is because the Communist Party of the Soviet Union has been for so long the sole governing party, to the point where the distinction between the party and the government has often been lost. Thus, as Soviet leaders recognize, how the party now handles the Soviet Union's own very clear economic decline will determine, not only the future of their party but of politics and government in the country. **For the USSR,** more so than for any of the other major powers treated in this book, **economic and political transformation go hand in hand.**

THE PLAN FOR THIS BOOK

This book divides into five parts. Four of these examine the politics and government of, respectively, the United Kingdom, France, West Germany, and the Soviet Union. The final part will look at European government and politics outside of these four countries. It consists of three chapters focusing on "Latin Europe" (Italy, Spain and Portugal), Scandinavia (Sweden, Norway and Denmark) and

Eastern Europe (the eight countries in Europe, besides the Soviet Union, in which—at least until recently—communist parties ruled without rivals.

Not all of the parts dedicated to specific countries nor the chapters focusing on regions will cover every topic in precisely the same order. However, we have taken care to cover the same issues in each of our considerations. These include: (1) an overview of the current condition of each core nation or region with regard to social, political, economic and international circumstances; (2) the historical antecedents to the current situation; (3) the constraints and strengths of societal culture upon which the political system builds; (4) the ways in which individuals are socialized into their roles as citizens and the degree to which they participate in the political process; (5) the ways in which political parties and electoral processes operate; (6) the functioning of the formal governmental process as embodied in the political executive, the bureaucracy, the legislature and the judiciary; and (7) intergovernmental dynamics within the political system (for example, between the national and local governments) and with other nations (for example, between a member nation and the European Economic Community). In addition, each of the four country parts will examine two policy cases—one domestic and the other involving foreign affairs—that illustrate the ways in which keys issues facing each political system reach resolution or remain intractable.

I

THE UNITED KINGDOM

2

Likely or Unlikely Paragon?

The student reading a textbook like this in the early 1960s would find a glowing report on the United Kingdom. Every other major European power had proven unequal to the task of sustaining uninterrupted democracy during this century. To be fair, France had succumbed to Nazi conquest. Yet, the Fourth Republic—the French constitution from 1945 to 1958—had just collapsed. As for West Germany, Americans held their breath. They feared either Soviet invasion or a re-emergence of the totalitarian reflexes that had led to Nazism. Russia remained so far from democracy that one could scarcely conceive of it as a European nation.

In some respects, Britain even struck observers as excelling the United States as a democracy. Despite sharp differences between their forms of government, Americans feel an institutional affinity with Britain. In part, this is due to the many elements in the U.S. constitutional system that owe their origin to British antecedents. Though a constitutional monarchy, the United Kingdom pioneered the extension of representative and responsible government from the city to the nation-state. Britain lacks a written constitution—including a bill of rights. However, its common law system places strong emphasis on protection of individuals from arbitrary rule.

With this backdrop, American students in the early 1960s often heard their professors speak admiringly about numerous features of British democracy. Students might easily have gained the impression that somehow things just worked better in Britain. The British people demonstrated more "civic culture" than did Americans. They seemed to manifest clearer ideas about what democracy expected from them. John F. Kennedy had to exhort Americans in his 1961 inaugural address to ask what they could do for their country rather than what their country could do for them. Britons seemed to work this out by instinct.

Britain was a lot more than simply a paragon for boosters of democracy. Notwithstanding the ravages of war, some of its industries gave competitors in other Western nations a run for their money, especially in heavy manufacturing. Person-for-person,

British scientists claimed more than their share of Nobel laureates. Oxford and Cambridge universities knew few rivals either elsewhere in Europe or the United States. The compactness of the United Kingdom meant that quality dailies—*The Times* of London, *The Manchester Guardian,* and two Sunday papers—*The Sunday Times* and *The Observer*—reached every corner of the nation. Meanwhile, the majority of U.S. citizens relied on local papers whose diminishing number—which continues to this day—became painfully apparent.

Comparative studies indicated that Britons in the early 1960s did not distinguish themselves as joiners. That is, they lagged well behind Americans in active participation in community organizations, interest groups and political parties. Yet, Americans envied the tidiness of the British system. At the time, the U.S. federal government and many of the states locked themselves in combat over social legislation and civil rights. Britain boasted a *unitary system.* That is, there was no level of government between the nation and the localities, and local "authorities" were creatures of the national government. Further, pressures for greater self-determination in Scotland and Wales along with the civil strife in Northern Ireland had yet to emerge.

Along the same lines, the British party and Parliamentary systems struck many as models of what the United States had missed out on. Many U.S. states were "one-party": Either the Republicans or the Democrats dominated their governments. Scholars described Washington as a four-party system consisting of Congressional Democrats and Republicans and Presidential Democrats and Republicans. Many Americans had become tired of the resulting paralysis—especially those who sought a more activist federal government in the fields of economic regulation, social welfare and civil rights. The two-party system in Britain could not have presented a more stark contrast. The two main parties—Conservative and Labour—both had formed majority governments since World War II. Although they represented, respectively, the right and the left, each broadly supported the intervention of the state, where necessary, in the economic and social realms.

Americans can betray an inferiority complex when dealing with Britons. Nothing would bring this out more than a comparison of how British and American bureaucracies functioned. The former, known as Whitehall, appeared vastly more efficient. At the highest levels, it was run by career civil servants with impeccable taste and discretion. No one would think of doubting their intelligence; they mostly claimed Oxford and Cambridge degrees with high honors. Whatever the abilities of American permanent public servants, the fact remained that much less predictable and reliable political appointees stood at the apexes of bureaucratic power in Washington.

In the early 1960s, Britons did a good job of concealing their decline as a world power. Americans remembered that the United Kingdom had bravely stood alone against the Nazis from the collapse of France till the United States entered World War II in 1941. Even the postwar Labour government came readily to the conclusion that Britain should stay right up there with the big boys. Thus, the Labour cabinet gladly rubberstamped the decision of Clement Attlee, their prime minister, to develop an all-British nuclear deterrent. Even in the painful task of dealing with its dwindling empire, Britain showed much more grace than other fading colonial powers, seeming to recognize the writing on the wall sooner. Institutionally, Britain had left former colonies with better legacies with respect both to parliamentary institutions and to administrative machinery.

Americans also viewed Britain as the head of the Commonwealth of former colonies.

This loose political alliance had a far more significant economic side: Its intricate web of special trade relations preserved for Britain dependable supplies of raw materials and fixed markets for manufactured products.

The United States has not remained static since the early 1960s. It should not surprise us, thus, that the Britain of today looks much different from the one just described above. However, events have occurred less convulsively than in the United States. No prime minister has been assassinated. No political scandals have paralyzed a government, much less forced the resignation of a prime minister—at least, during the past 30 years. No Vietnam-like, unwinnable war agonized the nation and depleted its physical and psychic resources.

Only little things added up to tip the balance toward change more than appears at first blush. A sense of incongruity greets American visitors in London's Waterloo station when they hear martial music piped over the sound system. The bowler hats, swagger-style umbrellas, and pinstripe trousers with black coats scarcely appear among the brigades of commuters; the music provides the only hint of nostalgia for a more glorious past. The streets and pedestrian underpasses, even in "posh" neighborhoods in London, present themselves as extremely dirty and littered. And the frequent intrusion of graffiti makes one wonder if London has headed in the same direction as New York City.

Visitors to Britain in recent years have asked themselves whether there is more psy-

Scenes such as this at London's Liverpool Station are standard fare for rail and underground travelers alike in Britain. Even under Mrs. Thatcher, a series of strikes during the summer of 1989 left countless commuters stranded.
SOURCE: Sygma, New York.

chosis in the body politic than existed in the 1960s. The verbal ramblings of taxi drivers suggest this. For instance, a visitor might hear that Mrs. Thatcher is just what the doctor ordered: "We needed a dictator to tell people what to do." The listener might not think for a moment that Mrs. Thatcher has indeed become a dictator. However, such approving assertions on the part of ordinary citizens make one wonder what has happened to the paragon of civic culture. Indeed, one might even be provoked to look more carefully at the historical legacy upon which the British political system is based.

A NOBLE PEDIGREE, BUT A MIXED PAST

We have an expression, "Age before beauty." In some respects, American commentators have tended to ascribe to the U.K. political system both qualities. Thus, students might come to romanticize the legacy upon which modern British democracy stands. This section offers a brief political history of Britain. It will look at four areas of development toward a full-fledged democracy: Parliament's eventual hegemony over the Crown, the House of Commons's gradual ascendancy over the House of Lords, universal suffrage's incremental triumph over oligarchy, and the welfare state's step-by-step mollification of the social dysfunctions of classic capitalism.

The aptness of adjectives such as "eventual," "gradual," "incremental" and "step-by-step" has caused many commentators to lionize Britain's political history. To be sure, many political systems—not the least of which is that of the United States—have sought to attain the same level of relatively peaceful and nonconvulsive transformation that characterizes much of the United Kingdom's evolution toward democracy.

Indeed, one sometimes discerns among Americans pangs of guilt over the fact that the thirteen colonies, unlike more passive siblings such as the Canadian and Australian colonies, ultimately severed their ties with Britain violently through revolution. We should not forget, however, that Britain moved too ponderously in responding to the legitimate demands of the American colonies. This fact should alert us to the possibility that British gradualism did not always function as smoothly as some would have us believe.

The Emergence of Parliament's Hegemony Over the Crown

The history of parliamentary government in the British Isles takes us back to the Saxon era, which began in the fifth century A.D. Kings and subjects in this period came to accept—with breaches in observance—two conventions concerning their rule. First, kings should consult counsellors on the important matters of state such as making laws or levying taxes. Second, kings alone would initiate such consultations. The counsellors formed no continuous or readily identifiable body. However, they were drawn from the hierarchy of the Church, the nobility, and knights. The latter group consisted of commoners who had distinguished themselves in the service of the king—initially in military campaigns and eventually in the administration of the realm.

After the Norman conquest of England in 1066, events moved to a formalization of the consultative process. The succession of wars, including the costly Crusades, greatly increased the dependence of kings upon taxes. Meanwhile, merchants in cities and towns began to emerge as a monied class in their own right. Kings had to devise ways of extracting funds from them. At the same time, pressures mounted among the merchants for a role in consultative processes.

In 1215, King John, under pressure from

the nobility, acceded to the Magna Carta. This most revered of British constitutional documents established the Common Council of the Kingdom whose consent was now required before the king could levy taxes for his various "extraordinary" needs. This council ultimately became known as the House of Lords. The House of Commons emerged later in the thirteenth century as a less regularized forum for knights' and merchants' deliberations over taxes.

The power of Parliament ebbed and flowed over the next 400 years. In the long run, developments added up to a consolidation of Parliament's role. By the latter part of the fourteenth century, kings served at the pleasure of Parliament. Indeed, Parliament deposed Richard II in 1399. However, monarchs began to reassert themselves by the end of the fifteenth century. The thirty-year Wars of the Roses—civil hostilities that saw the kingdom change hands four times—had disrupted the rule of law. Henry VII, who reigned from 1485 to 1509, felt compelled to convene Parliament only seven times. The notorious Henry VIII, ruling from 1509 to 1547, saw, on the other hand, that Parliament could prove a strong ally in achieving his various objectives. For instance, he resorted to Parliament to legitimize his campaign to achieve the autonomy of the Church in England from Roman Catholicism. Elizabeth I, ruling from 1558 to 1603, followed in this tradition. However, the great military expenses during her rule made her increasingly dependent upon the willingness of Parliament to agree to taxes.

The Stuart period, beginning with James I in 1603, proved to be a watershed for the relationship between the monarchy and Parliament. Taking a cue from their European cousins, the Stuarts attempted to aggrandize their role by invoking a divine right to rule. This included the right to override or ignore Parliament even in the imposition of taxes.

Charles I, who inherited the thrown in 1625, ultimately pressed this notion too far. His contempt for Parliament led to a bitter civil war and his own beheading in 1649. An interval of extreme instability ensued. This included a regime characterized as rule by a Council of State and a military dictatorship presided over by Oliver Cromwell. The period of experimentation came to an end with the restoration of the Stuarts in 1660 under Charles II. However, both Charles II and his successor James II took their dynasty right back into the trap that had snared their ancestors. In 1688, James II fled the country in face of what now stands in British history as the definitive repudiation of the divine right to rule.

This time Parliament left nothing to chance in filling the throne. It enacted statutes in order to expressly limit royal prerogatives. And it placed on the throne William III and Mary of Orange—the son-in-law and daughter of James II. Mary died in 1694. William, who ruled until 1702, eschewed the Stuarts' proclivity for divine aggrandizement.

Two statutes bore special importance in this era. The 1689 Bill of Rights enshrined the powers of Parliament in relation to the Crown. Here Parliament stipulated that the Crown could not enact or suspend laws, raise taxes, or maintain an army without Parliament's consent. Further, it defined the right of free speech within Parliament itself as absolute. The second measure, the 1701 Act of Settlement, set the terms for succession to the throne—including the exclusion of Roman Catholics from the monarchy. It also established that only Parliament could dismiss judges. These enactments, following as they did upon the discredited monarchical legacy left by the Stuarts, ensconced Parliament in a new position of constitutional legitimacy, enabling it, over the next 150 years, to establish unquestioned hegemony over the Crown.

This photograph of a painting by Van Dyck reflects the aggrandizement of Charles I as emperor. The king's absolutist approach to the monarchy led to his beheading.

SOURCE: Kenneth O. Morgan, ed., *The Oxford Illustrated History of Britain* (Oxford: Oxford University Press, 1984), p. 309.

The Rise of the House of Commons

The House of Commons, or lower house, did not become a distinct entity within Parliament until Henry VIII's reign. Before that time, the title "House of Lords" applied to the assemblies of peers that excluded members of Parliament who belonged to neither the Church hierarchy nor the nobility. As a body, the "lords" served as the major pool from which the Tudor monarchs selected their key officeholders. When it emerged as a separate body, the House of Commons based its power on the requirement that it originate tax measures.

The turmoil of the Wars of the Roses weakened the nobility in England, and the tendency for the Tudors to look to the House of Commons for legitimization of its policies further weakened the stature of the House of

Lords. On the other hand, the Stuart monarchs attempted to use the House of Lords to offset the power of the House of Commons. The former had so aligned itself with Charles I that the Council of State, which governed England immediately after the king's execution, abolished the House of Lords. The upper house reconvened (it was not formally reestablished) in 1660. However, the House of Commons soon passed legislation that sought to constrain the lords' power. A 1671 resolution denied the upper house the power to amend a tax. And a 1678 measure stipulated that only the lower house could originate bills involving expenditure of funds.

These actions did not prevent lords from resuming their previous role of providing the pool from which monarchs drew most of their ministers, including the most prominent. Even on this front, however, political expedience often forced monarchs to dip into the House of Commons to fill some key posts. In 1684, for instance, William III constructed a cabinet in which four of nine ministers belonged to a powerful faction of the "Whigs." At that time, the Whigs controlled the House of Commons. Until early in the nineteenth century, struggles between the Whigs and the "Tories" would dominate political life in Britain. The former stood for the rights of Parliament and political reform, while the latter attempted to defend royal prerogatives and the status quo.

The Tortuous Path from Aristocracy to Democracy

Even with the major advances toward entrenchment of parliamentary government during the seventeenth century, Britain remained far from a democracy. Those with significant property holdings dominated both the House of Lords and the House of Commons. Regarding the former, eighteenth-century monarchs created peerages to the point where the association of lords with "nobility" became debased. With respect to the latter, the combined efforts of monarchs and lords preordained that only those belonging to the upper ranks of the propertied or those beholden to the monied stood much of a chance of obtaining seats in the House of Commons. Even candidates for nomination required connections and resources beyond those of the average property holders and merchants. Thus, the nobility still exerted immense influence over the types of people who actually put themselves forward for nomination for seats in the House of Commons. Once official nominees, candidates required the capacity to "buy" votes whenever necessary.

The Industrial Revolution in Britain intervened—beginning in the mid-eighteenth century—to alter radically the distribution of wealth between classes. Eventually, industry and commerce reached levels undreamt of by the traditional elite. A whole new breed of monied individuals arose who became restless under the yoke of aristocratic rule.

The Whigs, who had suffered a reversal of fortunes at the turn of the nineteenth century, began in the late 1820s to mobilize renewed impetus for parliamentary reform. Their attention focused on the abysmal state of representative government in Britain. A large proportion of the boroughs upon which electoral districts were based claimed fewer than a hundred voters. Two constituencies actually housed no inhabitants whatsoever. Meanwhile, communities that had flourished since the Industrial Revolution—especially those in the North—found themselves grossly underrepresented. Indeed, the thriving cities of Manchester, Birmingham, and Leeds sent no members to the House of Commons. The Whigs found fertile ground for the reform movement.

The Whig coalition broke through in 1832

with passage of the Reform Act. Yet, the movement to expand suffrage started modestly. To be sure, it freed up 143 seats from depopulated boroughs and shifted them to expanding centers in the North. It also liberalized the qualifications for the franchise. Now, tenants who rented property worth specific values would qualify for a vote. All told, however, the measures only added just over 200,000 electors to the 400,000 or so who already anjoyed a franchise. An 1867 Reform Act further reduced qualifications for renters. Now an individual male householder simply had to occupy a dwelling for a year and pay the poor tax in order to enfranchise himself. These changes extended the right to vote to virtually all working-class men who headed households in the urban areas. However, it added only about 50 percent to the rolls of rural voters. And the fact that secret ballots were yet to be established meant that electors in the small country areas still followed the cues of the aristocracy in casting their votes.

Parliament approved the secret ballot in 1872. The Representation of People Act of 1884 rectified the imbalances between the urban and rural franchise. In the following year, the Redistribution of Seats Act set 50,000 voters as the desirable population for each electoral district and went a considerable distance toward eliminating multiple member constituencies.

In absolute terms, the two most dramatic increases in the number of eligible voters came as a result of legislation early in this century. The 1918 Representation of the People Act replaced the complex array of qualifications for males with a single six-month residency requirement for the right to vote in a constituency. In keeping with the grandualist approach of the British, however, the same legislation's gesture toward extending the franchise to women stopped short of

The 1867 expansion of the franchise is seen as a leap into the unknown.
SOURCE: The Bettmann Archive—cartoon from *Punch,* August 18, 1867.

those under 30 years of age. Nonetheless the 1918 act increased the electorate from 8 to 21 million. Ten years later Parliament's extension of suffrage to all women 21 years or over expanded the electorate by another 7 million. Like other advanced democracies concerned about the alienation of youth in the late 1960s, Britain enfranchised 18- to 20-year-olds in 1969.

The Inroads of Welfare Provision Against Social Ills

At the time that Britain was developing parliamentary democracy, it also was receiving praise from elsewhere in Europe for the liberties enjoyed by its citizens. Voltaire, for instance, praised Britain to the skies for the relative security of the people from seizure of property, arbitrary arrest and conviction, and restrictions of expression through the press and speech.

In comparison to the lot of those in continental Europe, Britons did enjoy exceptional freedoms. However, much of the solicitousness of the state simply catered to the accumulated claims of a vigorous and ever-expanding middle class. To be sure, they applied to all Britons, that is roughly the same rubrics of judicial process prevailed in criminal cases independent of the social origins of the accused. However, the entire structure defining crimes and punishments clearly placed extreme emphasis on retribution for violations of property. From 1660 to 1819, for instance, Parliament named fully 187 offenses that warranted the death penalty. The vast majority of these dealt with crimes against property. Indeed, attempted murder remained simply a "misdemeanor" until 1803.

The ensuing executions for such a wide range of capital offenses led ultimately to a backlash. Between 1779 and 1788, 531 of the 1,152 who had received death sentences actu-

ally went to the gallows. From 1799 to 1808, only 804 people received capital sentences, and of these, all but 126 won commutations. Increasingly, transportation to penal colonies began to serve as a substitute for hanging as the deterrent against violations of property. Between 1717 and 1776, Britain transported some 40,000 convicts to the American colonies and the Caribbean.

During the eighty years of Australian transportation (1788 to 1868), courts banished some 150,000 convicts to down under. The offenses of some of those on board the first fleet give us an idea of the resolve with which the state sought to discourage crimes against property: A seventy-year-old woman had stolen 20 pounds of cheese; a laborer had appropriated two hens—one live and the other dead; an unemployed woman had pilfered from a kitchen some bacon, flour, raisins, and butter—she went to Australia on commutation of her death sentence for this outrageous crime; a West Indian man raided a garden of twelve cucumbers; a nineteen-year-old young man took a wooden box that contained some linen and five books; and an eleven-year-old boy lifted ten yards of ribbon and a pair of silk stockings. Only a society obsessed with the sanctity of property could expel such petty criminals from their homeland and send them in chains on a seven-month voyage to the edge of the earth.

At the heart of the immense amount of thievery and the absorption of the system with meting out punishments stood the desparate conditions to which laborers and the poor were subjected. Those who accumulated great wealth during the Industrial Revolution did so on the backs of the working class, who became exceedingly vulnerable to swings in the performance of the economy. Most workers lived at a level that usually kept adequate housing, clothing and food far out of reach. Children tended to take employment around the age of six. Not unrelatedly,

Refuge for the destitute, 1843.
SOURCE: R. T. Hilton, *The Workhouse.*

laborers burned out relatively early in their adult years. In addition, some occupations lent themselves to chronic disabilities whose progression preordained untimely curtailment of one's productive years.

All the people who fell out of the labor force with no means of support became a great burden to society—even if they did not turn to crime. During the nineteenth century, however, Parliament and the civil service either ignored poverty or channeled their efforts toward defining it out of existence. This becomes most clear when we reflect upon the great famine in Ireland between 1845 and 1849. During this period over a million people—one of every eight Irish—died of starva-

tion and attendant diseases. Around the same number migrated to England, Scotland, or North America, many against their own will. Tens of thousands of these died either in transit or soon after their arrival, as was the case of some 37,000 of the approximately 100,000 who went to the Canadian colonies in 1847.

The famine had resulted from potato crop failures on the undesirable land where the Irish poor eked out their existence. The Irish, as a conquered people, could make no effective claims on the grain, cereal, and livestock agriculture that thrived on the estates of Ireland's landholders. The latter overwhelmingly either considered themselves as English or had become so "Anglicized" that they bore little or no sense of obligation toward their fellow countrymen.

Throughout the famine, London dithered over issues such as the type of aid that would be given, where foodstuffs would be purchased, who would finance the assistance and who would receive it. Thus, virtually all of the relief that actually reached the poor proved to be too little, too late. Meanwhile, the human suffering approached holocaust proportions—albeit through displacement and starvation rather than direct genocide. In the words of Charles E. Trevelyan, the civil servant who headed the Treasury and fashioned the government's response to the famine, England must leave Ireland to "the operation of natural causes."

The Potato Famine simply serves as the most grotesque instance of official complacence about destitution. The case also points out in bold relief legal structures that effectively hobbled the government in responding to such crises. The first of these, the Corn Laws, strictly limited the importation of agricultural products from outside the British Isles. This policy maintained robust prices for landholders but exacerbated the inability of the poor to afford even minimum sustenance. Even in years when the potato crop succeeded, one in every four Irish would remain seriously malnourished.

Sir Robert Peel, the prime minister at the outset of the Potato Famine, had in fact been looking for an opportunity to move toward repeal of the Corn Laws for several years. The circumstances surrounding the initial signs of serious famine in Ireland allowed him to get a bill through Parliament in June 1846. However, the political backlash immediately resulted in his loss of the confidence of the House of Commons and removal from power. The ensuing confusion and the lagged implementation of the repeal meant that the new trade regime would do virtually nothing to ameliorate conditions in Ireland. However, the repeal paved the way for improved accessibility of foodstuffs to the poor throughout the British Isles in the second half of the nineteenth century.

The second legal structure hobbling the government's response to the Potato Famine similarly curtailed the capacity of the state to address destitution elsewhere in the British Isles. This was the reformed Poor Law of 1834. The legislation evolved from a debate similar to one waging to this day about the poor. While society might willingly assist those "deserving" of assistance, it does not want to throw away money to those who prefer to exploit the system rather than support themselves. The parameters of this debate have changed considerably since the nineteenth century; modern political systems tend more to give the benefit of the doubt to those applying for assistance. Nonetheless, certain segments of contemporary society become outraged over any instances in which the able-bodied receive benefits.

We can understand, thus, why the politicians in the 1830s tried to differentiate between the genuinely needy and the undeserving in the provision of welfare. Their initiatives attempted to negotiate around two seemingly intractable difficulties: addressing the problem of destitution throughout the land, and satisfying taxpayers that assistance programs did not squander their money.

The system selected by Parliament proved as cumbersome to manage as it was parsimonious. The 1834 Poor Law took two approaches. First, it extended the workhouse system whereby recipients of assistance would live and work only in institutions. This prevented the poor from obtaining support and working on the side. Second, it provided that the standard of living within the poorhouse would be kept at the lowest level possible. This assured that the poor would only ask for admittance out of desperation. In the case of the Potato Famine, the mandated channeling of assistance through poorhouses effectively proscribed anywhere near the magnitude of response required in that situation.

The workhouse mentality touched more than just the victims of agricultural and economic catastrophes. It meant that any members of the working class who lost their jobs or earned insufficient money to purchase necessities simply went without. Even as late as the turn of the century, officials rated thousands of working class young men who presented themselves to fight in the Boer War (1899–1902) unfit. They lacked the basic level of physical development and health necessary for military service.

Notwithstanding the gloomy status quo, reformers gradually made advances against the unvarnished capitalism that motivated draconian policies toward the poor. Parliament began in 1833 to restrict the employment of children. From the 1850s, it permitted local boards of health to impose regulations guiding sanitation and require the vaccination of entire populations against certain diseases. In the 1890s, local governments began to provide alternate housing to the unspeakably crowded and filthy tenements in which most urban workers dwelled. A series of statutes beginning in 1870 and ending in 1891 set up a system of free, universal and compulsory elementary education. To an extent, these changes attempted to head off unrest in the increasingly enfranchised working class. However, they also responded to the growing feeling among the more sensitive in the middle and upper classes that *laissez faire* had gone too far.

The dawning of the twentieth century also marked the turning point for the emergence of the welfare state. Parliament, largely in response to the shocking evidence of working

This photograph of a woman and a child in a Glasgow tenement captures the wretched conditions of the poor in the first decade of this century.

SOURCE: Kenneth O. Morgan (ed.), *The Oxford Illustrated History of Britain* (Oxford: Oxford University Press, 1984), p. 516.

class malnutrition found among volunteers for the Boer War, introduced school meals in 1906. Old age pensions and limited sickness and unemployment insurance followed in 1908 and 1911, respectively. Though minimal, these programs departed radically from the workhouse mindset. Both imparted entitlement to specific levels of direct provision outside of institutions.

Two factors quickened the process whereby Britain embraced a limited welfare state. First, the state drew upon the young men of the working class during World War I (1914–18) to an unprecedented degree. This elevated the workers' expectations. They had proven themselves worthy of a higher stake in society. Second, the economy had gone into a sharp decline by 1920.

As unemployment rose exponentially, the government recognized that the working class' sense of greater self-esteem was turning into anger over continued hardship. Through the 1920s, state contributions to the unemployment fund were increased. This allowed provision of benefits beyond those supported by the premiums paid by the employed. In 1927 the government also eliminated tests of means (such as whether claimants had access to the earnings of others or had assets which they could sell), and of "genuinely seeking work." Through the creation of the Unemployment Advisory Board in 1934, it extended unemployment benefits to all without work—even those who had not gained entitlements through payment of insurance premiums.

After World War II, the 1946 National Insurance Act system brought all of the benefit systems for unemployment, sickness, retirement, and maternity under one statute. The 1948 National Health Service Act followed as the final iteration in the evolution of the welfare state. It guaranteed free and universal health care to all Britons.

Both post-World War II statutes took the British considerably beyond the United States in the inclusiveness of social provision. They thus became the objects of envy among those in this country impatient with the reluctance of the U.S. government to go all the way down the road to the welfare state. On the other hand, those Americans who opposed additional programs such as comprehensive health care viewed the British welfare state as an anathema. Thus, they did not hesitate to point to the defects of the British system to prove that "cradle to grave" coverage stifled enterprise and individual initiative.

Both American groups missed a very important point. With the exception of the health care field, the actual benefits and services provided Britons through many of these programs fall considerably short of what Americans eligible for this country's less universal programs receive. This applied even in the mid-1970s, when provision reached its height in the United Kingdom. At that time, the United Kingdom spent a smaller proportion of its gross domestic product (GDP) on

pensions, child allowances, unemployment and sickness benefits than France, Germany, *and* the United States. Its total welfare bill as percent of GDP was eleventh out of the 18 advanced economies belonging to the Organization for Economic Cooperation and Development. With the help of Prime Minister Margaret Thatcher's stringent regime, by 1983 a married man's unemployment benefit declined to 29 percent of national average earnings. This compared most unfavorably with the 70 and 80 percent of per capita income that, respectively, his West German and French counterparts would receive.

AN ANGUISHED PRESENT

Britain established herself in the latter part of the nineteenth century and the first half of the twentieth as almost the epitome of an industrialized society. It maintained a resilient parliamentary democracy, and its vast empire ran relatively efficiently and humanely. By the early 1950s, the signs of decline were manifest to the astute observer. Ten years of engagement in global conflict through two world wars in the span of 31 years had sapped the British spirit, and weighed down domestic enterprise and colonial governance.

The Early Signs Of Decline

Most fundamentally, the two world wars had changed matters too much for Britain to sustain its accustomed role in international affairs and the world economy. The United States and the USSR had established themselves as superpowers in a league of their own. The postwar rebuilding of Western Europe—largely through the auspices of the United States' Marshall Plan—had left Britain's natural economic competitors in a vastly better relative position than prevailed after World War I. In 1958, the European

Economic Community (EEC), which initially included France, West Germany, and Italy but not Britain, emerged. Its success would ultimately convince the United Kingdom of the value of regional economic solidarity. The economic motive for maintaining the Commonwealth, let alone the Empire, was increasingly coming into question.

As often happens in such circumstances, the flaws in the very fabric of British society became more visible. Some have argued that the United Kingdom would have been better off economically if, like Germany, it had suffered the complete destruction of its industrial capacity during the war. Instead, Britain patched up its aging and damaged productive resources and muddled through the 1950s and 1960s, much the same process occurring in the social and political realms.

Certainly, Britain was not the first imperial power to slide down a slippery slope. However, the very nature of British society made it difficult for the country to check what increasingly appeared as historically inevitable. By the early 1960s Britain had chipped away class barriers less than any other major European power. The vitality of the monarchy in Britain does not spell the Camelot that the pageantry of great events such as royal weddings conjure in American minds. Together with the persistence of nobility, the entire monarchical tradition speaks of Britons' undiminished loyalty to privilege.

Education is just one area in which the position of the most advantaged is maintained. To this day, precious few sons and daughters of blue collar workers even aspire to attending university. If they do, the state still does scandalously little to assure that children of the less advantaged can achieve educationally according to their true ability. Meanwhile, private schools, most of which demand very substantial fees, continue their traditional function for the children of the upper classes: Their students obtain a vastly

disproportionate share of the most prized university positions, especially those at Oxford and Cambridge.

Rigidities such as those found in education show their effects in many other corners of social life. In the workplace, these translate into the intractability of management and labor. Britain has made less progress toward worker participation in industrial decision-making than most other Western European nations. Indeed, serious antagonism characterizes relations between management and various elements of the union movement.

The decline and loss of the empire, the failure to revitalize industrial plants and systems, and the persistence of antiquated social barriers and divisions combine to make Britons a defeatist society. Industrial innovators wrestle with a "show me" rather than a "can do" attitude among potential backers and collaborators. Government appears much more concerned about pinching pennies out of university budgets than fostering the research necessary for British scientists to contribute to industrial revitalization. Many gifted young people do not dream dreams because of the obstacles placed before them by the educational system. In a highly elitist social system, even accents can doom the talented to second-class citizenship.

Are Britons Too Passive?

The visitor to the United Kingdom cannot help but note the civility of the people. One cannot even get through a restaurant meal without a succession of "pleases" and "thank yous" which leaves Americans wondering what is wrong—are Americans too perfunctory, or their hosts too servile? Around the fringes, things have changed. It is not pleasant to be on the underground (subway) in London when drunken youths on their way to a football (soccer) match swamp your train. Some neighborhoods appear downright threatening. Yet, reserve prevails in most public behavior. This usually borders on silence in cramped places such as the underground. Most working-class neighborhoods simply appear frumpish—à la 1950s—rather than dangerous.

All of this pleasantness conceals a great deal of hostility. In the 1960s, political scientists believed that Britons demonstrated so much civility because they recognized the intrinsic merits of behaving respectfully and decently. The jury is out right now. Obviously, football rampages and inner-city riots suggest that the canons of behavioral restraint have been eroded; a closer look suggests that many of these were a veneer. Britons were very passive subjects. Beneath the external calm resided deepseated resentments. Only with an understanding of these can observers grasp why trade unions became so militant in the 1970s. The broken silence of other disaffected groups—especially ethnic and racial minorities—also suggests a great deal of pent-up frustration.

The release of profound antagonisms has not confined itself to social groups that have chosen to register their disenchantment. It has become patently clear that the unitary structure of government—that is, the system whereby all political authority originates in London—inadequately accommodates regional differences even in England itself. Where ethnic factors buttress regional loyalties—that is, in Scotland, Northern Ireland, and Wales—the national fabric of the United Kingdom actually has begun to tear.

The case of Northern Ireland has brought especially acute embarrassment to the British. The use of military force and suspension of many civil liberties have left many blots on the democratic copy book of the United Kingdom. The European Human Rights Court has found more infractions of civil liberties in Northern Ireland than anywhere else in the EEC. In English cities, persistent racial strife suggests that British tolerance may have barely been skincolor-deep.

A Flabby Body Politic

Britons do not work very hard at what they do. London commuters still stream out of the underground to 10:00 A.M. Most senior civil servants show up for work around 9:00—an hour and a half after their counterparts in Washington. Even in the nerve centers of government along Whitehall, virtually no lights burn as late as 8:00 P.M.

It should not come as a surprise, thus, that the average citizen does not make much of an effort to participate politically. Yet, it does disturb the observer to see that even activists seem somewhat lethargic. In the height of an election, always call a campaign headquarters before trying to visit it in the evening or on weekends. Chances are you will find it abandoned. And do not expect the plethora of lawn signs that one finds in the United States which at least remind voters that there is an election on. Increasingly, British campaigns have become TV events run from London. The legwork required to blanket a constituency with signs and pinpoint voter support has become passé. Britons, thus, go beyond simply eschewing political involvement. They do not try too hard even when they do take on a political task. Self-starters must buck social conventions against appearing too eager; and all must observe the canons of social deference.

The dysfunctions of a relatively nonparticipatory political society due to lack of energy and legitimacy are disconcerting. In 1982, Mrs. Thatcher's use of the Falklands crisis to reverse her sagging political support demonstrated the degree to which splendid patriotic theater can cover a multitude of deficiencies in executive leadership. Workers' perennial outrage with the government and employers masks the unions' stubborn disinclination to encourage rank-and-file participation in their own organizations. As for the press, tabloid-style alarmism about domestic and world affairs has even invaded "quality" papers such as *The Times*.

A Party System in Transition

Perhaps the widest rips in the fabric of British politics have occurred in the party system. Britain operates a parliamentary government that bases representation on single-member districts. Just as in elections to the U.S. Senate and House of Representatives, the candidates who win the most votes in their constituency take their seats even if they fall short of an absolute majority.

This system operates in favor of one or two dominant parties. Unlike proportional representation, it makes no allowances for small parties, which might attain a significant amount of support across the country—the Liberal party, for instance, drew 14 percent of the vote in the 1979 election. However, such small parties might also fail to obtain the most votes in a substantial number of constituencies—the Liberals won only 11 of the 635 House of Commons seats in 1979.

Since World War II, in all governments but two, one of the main parties—either the Conservatives or Labour—have enjoyed an absolute majority of seats in the House of Commons. The two exceptions were governments formed in 1974 in which Labour, headed by Harold Wilson, lacked the support of a clear majority of MPs. In the first of these, formed in March, Labour emerged 17 seats short of an absolute majority; in the second, formed in October, it squeaked by with a one-seat edge, which it lost in a January 1975 by-election.

An electoral system such as Britain's that allows two parties to dominate has its drawbacks. First, supporters of small parties continually find that their votes do not translate into seats. They may become extremely disenchanted. Second, the solidarity necessary to maintain a united front in the House of Commons means that MPs vote very reluctantly against their party on major legislation. As a result, many MPs frequently find themselves voting against their own convictions and/or the wishes of their constituents.

Of course, the two-party-dominant system has not produced majority governments easily; however, in Britain, it has run more smoothly since World War II than it did before. Of the eleven elections between 1900 and 1935, only six granted a single party an absolute majority of seats.

Cracks in the postwar two-party system appeared simultaneously with the fall of the Conservative government in 1974 and the difficulties of the subsequent Labour government. Many in the Labour Party believed that unions had gone too far in asserting their claims. Besides, many radical fringe movements—dubbed "The Loony Left"—had attached themselves to the party. In 1981, widespread doubts about the direction of Labour took formal shape with the institution of the Social Democratic Party and the defection to it of several Labour MPs, including former cabinet ministers.

The confrontational politics of the 1970s played heavily in the emergence of a fourth party and contributed to the suspension of the tendency among blue-collar and white-collar moderates to shift their support to the party out of office. That is, many voters who might normally have changed their allegiance to Labour have continued to support the Conservatives. This owes in no small extent to the extremism of the far-left elements of the Labour party. A prolonged hesitancy about radicalism could result ultimately in a realignment of potential Labour supporters permanently to the Conservative camp.

New Questions About Old Institutions

The governmental apparatus associated with Britain's parliamentary democracy consists of Parliament—including the monarch; the cabinet; the permanent civil service; and the judiciary. The elective House of Commons and the House of Lords make up the two chambers of Parliament. The House of Lords includes members who take their places by hereditary right, and those appointed for life. It retains a suspensory veto over legislation whereby it can delay bills passed by the House of Commons up to one year.

The cabinet takes in the principal members of government. Other ministers assume executive functions in departments but do not belong to the cabinet. As most departments claim only two or three ministers, they must rely very heavily upon permanent civil servants both for advice on policy options and for day-to-day management. The British judiciary maintains a strong tradition of detachment from politics. This owes partially to the fact that lower court judges attain their positions by appointment rather than by election. The judicial community in the higher reaches of the system plays a very substantial role in determining those who will assume vacancies on the most senior courts.

Many elements of this institutional framework command envy and praise outside of Britain. For instance, American authors have celebrated the efficient operation of the two-party system in the House of Commons, the degree of executive harmony stemming from the cohesiveness of cabinets, the "neutral competence" of the career civil service and the high quality of judicial opinions. Over the past decade, events suggest that foreign commentators had an idealized view of British governmental performance.

At this writing, the cracks in the two-party system have altered appreciably the dynamics of the House of Commons, party discipline has lost some of its force, Mrs. Thatcher's management style has shown up the difficulty of maintaining collegial cabinets in an age when the prime minister can appeal directly to the people, the bureaucracy has begun to reveal clear signs of politicization and demoralization, and judicial decisions increasingly expose the degree to which the courts, while stalwartly independent, habitually side with convention.

Some observers might have exaggerated the width of the fissures in the governmental apparatus; and some of the changes have worked positive side effects or grappled with the inherent dysfunctions in the parliamentary system. For instance, the moderation of party discipline has allowed MPs to strengthen their monitoring of the executive. The emergence of "priministerial" government responds in part to the heightened emphasis of central coordination required by all advanced democracies in order to bring bureaucracy under control. In some respects, Britain's system remains a model for other nations—especially those within the parliamentary fold. However, it lacks the tidiness—largely putative—that it formerly enjoyed.

Unitary, But . . .

Britain resolutely retains its unitary form of government. The failure of 1979 referenda on the devolution of substantial central government powers to Scottish and Welsh parliaments has taken the issue out of the political agenda for the foreseeable future. And Mrs. Thatcher has, throughout the course of her administration, gradually restructured the relations between the central and local governments. The latter now enjoy much less latitude for independent action than they did in the 1960s and 1970s.

It is not always that easy to keep a tight ship. The mere existence of special bureaucratic departments for Scottish and Welsh affairs points up the degree to which the effective handling of regional imperatives requires extensive decentralization of the administrative apparatus. Of course, Northern Ireland presents a case in which administrative decentralization coupled with a separate parliament—now defunct—collapsed under the weight of hostility between Protestants and Catholics. Even with regard to local governments, Mrs. Thatcher has faced defiance from Labour-dominated councils that have bitterly resisted her efforts to limit their activities through stringent fiscal constraints.

Britain's joining the European Economic Community (EEC) in 1973 has further complicated the picture. Now British cabinet ministers must mesh many of their policy stances with EEC positions and initiatives. Some will spend almost as much time in discussions with their opposite numbers in other European countries as they do with their own colleagues in cabinet. Since 1979, Britons have elected MPs to the European Parliament. The European courts of Justice and Human Rights have impinged on the administration of justice in the United Kingdom. Compared to the United States, the EEC remains a very loose federation indeed. However, U.K. membership in this organization has clearly altered the parameters of unitary government in Britain. Increasingly, Britons relate to a center of political authority separate from London. Unlike the United States, this other stratum constitutes *supra*- rather than *sub*-national government.

CONCLUSION

Americans have often labored under a lot of illusions in their view of Britain; it is important to clean out the cobwebs before we launch a detailed examination of the United Kingdom. It probably remains the most important system for Americans to understand —even if simply to derive a comparative grip on the context of their own politics and form of government. It would be a shame for readers to find only half way through this section of the book that their misconceptions— based on others' renderings of a more innocent epoch for Britain—prevented them from comprehending the roots as well as the changes of the past three decades and their ramifications.

References and Suggested Readings

ALT, JAMES. *The Politics of Economic Decline: Economic Management and Political Behavior in Britain Since 1964*. Cambridge: Cambridge University Press, 1979.

DAHRENDORF, RALF. *On Britain*. London: BBC, 1982.

DEARLOVE, JOHN, and PETER SAUNDERS. *Introduction to British Politics: Analysing a Capitalist Democracy*. Cambridge: Polity, 1984.

HARVEY, J., and L. BATHER. *British Constitution and Politics*. London: Macmillan, 1982.

HOLMES, M. *The First Thatcher Government, 1979–1983: Contemporary Conservatism and Economic Change*. Brighton: Wheatsheaf, 1985.

HUGHES, ROBERT. *The Fatal Shore*. New York: Vintage Books, 1986.

NORTON, PHILIP. *The British Polity*. New York: Longman, 1984.

OLSON, MANCUR. *The Rise and Decline of Nations: Economic Growth, Stagflation and Social Rigidities*. New Haven: Yale University Press, 1982.

RIDDEL, PETER. *The Thatcher Government*. Oxford: Blackwell, 1985.

WOODHAM-SMITH, CECIL. *The Great Hunger: Ireland 1845–1849*. New York: Harper & Row, 1962.

YOUNG, HUGO, and ANNE SLOMAN. *The Thatcher Phenomenon*. London: BBC, 1986.

3

The Realm of Transition

History presents us with many lessons. Never to assume that governments and political systems remain stable certainly ranks at the top of the list. Yet, somehow we expect Britain not to change substantially. The preceding chapter has suggested several areas in which much change has occurred. Subsequent ones will examine in greater detail developments in British political culture, socialization and participation, party and electoral behavior, executive and bureaucratic leadership, intra-, inter- and extragovernmental relations, and policy processes, altogether revealing tremendous flux over the past 30 years.

This chapter will provide a broad context for our examination of change in the United Kingdom. It takes the view that the "atmospherics" of the setting for British government and politics have meant a great deal of pitching and yawing as the ship of state plies its course. We will focus on two dimensions of these contextual circumstances. First, we will look at changes in Britain's constitutional system that suggest that the rules of the game have come increasingly under question. Second, we will review the performance of

Britain's economy with special reference to its competitive standing in the world and the internal distribution of wealth and opportunities.

CONSTITUTIONAL UNCERTAINTIES

The United Kingdom, unlike the United States and most advanced democracies, lacks a *written* constitution. It does, of course, have a constitution. Every state must have principles and rules determining the structure of government, its operations and how its authorities—elected and appointed—assume and exercise power. However, no central document specifies the elements of these principles and rules for the United Kingdom. Instead, they reside in acts of Parliament, judicial decisions that interpret these statutes along with the common law, and conventions that effectively enjoy the standing of law. In this context, common law encompasses the British tradition whereby judges take into consideration the legal treatises of great jurists and the successive decisions of courts before rendering a decision. It can come into play both when judges determine the applicability of a specific statute to individual cases and when they make rulings that derive their entire force from custom.

The absence of a written constitution presents especially serious difficulties in the field of human rights. The vast majority of advanced democracies have enumerated the fundamental protections of individuals in one document—for instance, the U.S. Bill of Rights—and enshrined these in their formal constitutions. This practice tends to focus judicial interpretation on one central document enjoying clear paramountcy over statutes, common law, and constitutional conventions. It also provides greater protection against arbitrary majority rule. That is, those wishing to modify the enshrined rights of individuals must, in most advanced systems, garner support appreciably beyond simple majorities of the legislators of the national government.

The British do not find themselves utterly devoid of individual protections against arbitrary action by the government. These simply have not been collected in a single succinct document, much less one enjoying paramountcy over acts of Parliament. Not even the 1215 Magna Carta and the 1689 Bill of Rights satisfy these criteria. The former states a constitutional principle that secured royal assent; the latter is a mere act of Parliament. Both documents focus on the limits to the monarch's powers; first, in relation to the accepted customs of the realm—including what we now call common law—and second, with respect to Parliament.

Notwithstanding this peculiar arrangement, the British system places great stock in what is called "the rule of law": the entire complex of unwritten protections provided individuals in Britain against arbitrary government. These include the following principles: Individuals have a right to legal advice and to full knowledge of the provisions of the law; governments must base their actions on the law and cite specifically what in it has been breached whenever arresting individuals; only an impartial tribunal can establish whether an individual has in fact violated the law; and existing law—not the transient wishes of Parliament or the government—must guide judicial judgment. In theory, the rule of law concept involves a transaction between the government and citizens. On the one hand, it evokes from citizens a high degree of voluntary compliance with specific laws. On the other, it sustains an environment in which individuals feel secure that they will be prosecuted only if they violate the law.

As has become patently clear in some countries, not even an enshrined charter of individual rights can offer absolute protection from arbitrary rule. Thus, we should not ascribe mystical power to written bills of rights. And we should acknowledge that the British constitutional system knows few rivals in the effective protection of individual rights. As we will see, however, Britons increasingly believe that their rights should be protected and preserved in a single document. In addition, Britain's membership in the Council of Europe gives its citizens recourse to Europe's Convention of Human Rights.

The lack of clarity in the distribution of government powers between branches presents itself as another characteristic of Britain's unwritten constitution. In fact, the executive, the legislature, and the judiciary all connect with one another. Convention dictates that members of the cabinet belong to Parliament—either the House of Commons or the House of Lords. This arrangement assures that those exerting executive authority either collectively (in consultation with their cabinet colleagues) or individually (as ministers responsible for the specific actions of government departments) derive their power from the support of the legislative branch.

The *lord chancellor*, a member of cabinet and the House of Lords, presides over the administration of the courts in the United Kingdom, thus serving as a link between all three branches. Finally, the Judicial Committee of the House of Lords, the highest appellate body in the land, overlaps the legislative and judicial branches.

Scholars have noted that the lack of demarcation of the three branches helps make government more efficient in Britain. Some American observers have looked longingly at the British system. Many believe, for instance, that stronger links between Congress and the president in the United States would inevitably result in more coherent policies. Yet, the framers of the U.S. Constitution clearly opted for a division of powers on the grounds that too much continuity between the branches could lead to abuse of authority—especially on the part of the executive branch. They chose to err on the side of checks and balances rather than that of coherence. Experience certainly tells us that British cabinets can rigidly adhere to policies after these have lost the support of the general populace. If it has control of the majority in the House of Commons, the government party need only fear a mandatory election every five years.

No matter how firm its hold on the House of Commons, any reasonable government will partially base its decisions and initiatives on their likely impact on voters reflected in the next election. The system offers no better device for compelling responsiveness to shifts in the electorate's will. Strictly speaking, Parliament includes the monarch as well as the House of Commons and the House of Lords.

For instance, any legislation must obtain the assent of the monarch before it becomes an act of Parliament. Queen Anne (1702–14) was the last monarch actually to veto a piece of legislation. Financial bills need not attain passage through the House of Lords. The House of Commons can overrule the House of Lords on other matters as long as 13 months have elapsed and it reintroduces the measure in a new session. When we add to these points the fact that the courts cannot rule an act of Parliament *ultra vires* (beyond its legal authority), we begin to see the degree to which the power to determine the law of the land resides ultimately in the House of Commons.

This arrangement leaves most observers with the conclusion that the House of Commons expresses the will of the people more authoritatively than any other organ of government. Yet, one should not leap from this observation to the conclusion that sovereignty wholly emanates from the House of Commons. If that were so, this institution would achieve a great deal more than it does in monitoring and checking the actions of ministers and the bureaucracy.

A paradox rests at the heart of this issue. The House of Commons formally plays the decisive role in deeming what will become a law. Yet, the cabinet—that is, the prime minister and the secretaries of the various government departments—determines what the House of Commons will consider. It also governs the implementation of legislation. At the same time, the permanent bureaucracy retains control over the day-to-day functioning of departments. Higher civil servants also use their detailed knowledge of the operation of policies to advise ministers on the most expedient means for fulfilling the political agenda.

Both the cabinet and the permanent bureaucracy function behind a veil of secrecy.

On the grounds that they serve as custodians of the interests of the state, they deliberately conceal much of what they do even from parliamentary surveillance. Thus, the prime minister and cabinet ministers determine what even MPs should know about the actual operation of the executive branch. Party discipline, coupled with a strong tradition of deference, makes it relatively easy for the executive branch to keep detailed information of sensitive matters from MPs on the grounds that full disclosure would damage the state. Party discipline is the tradition whereby British MPs attempt to maintain a united front by not publicly criticizing the leadership of their respective parties. This is usually strongest among MPs belonging to the party from which the "government of the day"—that is, the prime minister and cabinet secretaries—is drawn. MPs from the party that has formed the government will think twice before questioning its performance in a way that might undermine its support.

This entire emphasis upon secrecy and discipline points up a simple fact: The formal paramountcy of the House of Commons disguises a considerable confusion over sovereignty. Everyone gives due obeisance to the principle of parliamentary supremacy. Yet, bureacrats behave very much as the custodians of the secrets of the crown from which they trace their lineage, and ministers work out the parliamentary game plan with minimum consultation of fellow MPs who belong to the government party. In practice, thus, sovereignty divides at least three ways. Permanent officials, clinging to the monarchical legacy, try to exert effective custodianship of the administrative apparatus. Cabinet ministers, invoking their retention of the confidence of the House of Commons, define the contours of the vast majority of measures that will be set before Parliament. The House of Commons technically has the last say. Any substantial shifts in the public

do not normally manifest themselves in legislation unless the cabinet has voluntarily adapted its positions or an election results in a new government party.

A LOOK AT THE PRESSURE POINTS IN THE CONSTITUTIONAL SYSTEM

Obviously, the U.K. constitutional system is a huge topic. Identifying all of the areas where it has experienced special strain goes far beyond the scope of this section. However, we can focus on a few areas that exemplify the ways in which new and unresolved constitutional issues have emerged. These include the following developments: (1) an erosion of party discipline, which has made it somewhat more difficult for recent governments to deliver their legislative programs with the "efficiency" that we normally ascribe to the British paraliamentary system; (2) the decline of the creative dimensions to the adversarial dynamics between the government party and the other parties making up the "loyal opposition"; and (3) the pressures from unfavorable decisions by the European Court of Human Rights along with growing concerns within the United Kingdom about individual protections raise serious questions about whether Parliament should enact a British bill of rights.

The Decline of Party Discipline

We will examine in greater detail in another chapter the degree to which party discipline has declined in the U.K. House of Commons. However, a number of specific cases and several important empirical studies provide clear indications of a substantial shift in the willingness of MPs to adhere to strict party discipline—that is, to temper all public criticism of their leadership and to refrain from voting at variance from their party's

Michael Heseltine—the defense secretary who resigned his post in January 1986 over Mrs. Thatcher's failure to consult him—comes back to haunt her in the form of an unfavorable report by a committee of the House of Commons.
SOURCE: *The Guardian,* July 25, 1986.

official stances.[1] For recent Labour governments—1964–70 headed by Harold Wilson, and 1974–79 lead by Wilson until 1976, when James Callaghan took over—these changes in the attitudes of MPs actually resulted in defeat on several important pieces of legislation. For Conservative Edward Heath (prime minister 1970–74), they produced a near failure on the European Communities Bill in 1972 and forced embarrassing amendments to the Industry Bill.

Even Mrs. Thatcher has occasionally had to weather stiff backbench opposition from her own party. In May 1980, she had to with-

draw a key provision in legislation imposing trade sanctions against Iran. The provision had specified that the measure would apply retroactively. The whips found that enough Conservative MPs opposed the provision that the entire bill might fail to win the approval of the House of Commons. In July 1985 she saw her majority of 140 cut to a mere 17 votes in the wake of a Conservative backbench revolt against raises of up to 46 percent for the most senior civil servants. Fully 48 of her MPs had voted against her—even after the chief whip had cautioned dissenters that she might resign over the issue. In December 1986, her environment minister reversed himself on important elements of a new formula for deciding the size of grants from the national government to local authorities. Some 50 backbenchers had threatened a revolt.

Obviously, the ground rules have changed

[1] John E. Schwarz, "Exploring a New Role in Policy Making: The British House of Commons in the 1970s," *American Political Science Review,* 74 (1980): 23–27; Leon D. Epstein, "What Happened to the British Party System?," *American Political Science Review,* 74 (1980): 9–22; Philip Norton, *The Constitution in Flux* (Oxford: Martin Robertson, 1982).

for the level of loyalty that parties require of their MPs. The exact implications of these developments will become clear in chapter 7. However, three points of overarching importance should be kept in focus throughout our assessment of contemporary British government and politics. First, we can no longer ascribe the degree of efficiency to the British system that it formerly manifested. That is, the benefits associated with the unity between the executive and legislative branches no longer reveal themselves as unambiguously as they did immediately after the war. Governments just cannot get what they want out of their MPs as readily as they could formerly.

Second, events have not spared the opposition parties of a similar depletion of loyalty. In fact, 27 of the 28 MPs who had joined the newly formed Social Democratic Party from its creation in 1981 to the dissolution of the 1979–83 parliament had been elected under the Labour banner. And internal struggles between the left and right of the Labour Party continue to hobble its role as the official opposition.

Third, over the past two decades governments have had to make concessions to MPs' demands for greater scrutiny of executive branch initiatives and administration. The enhancement of the committee system in the House of Commons stands as the major effort at such accommodations. The result is the emergence for the first time in the British Parliament of specialized legislative bodies modeled after U.S. congressional committees. The U.K. variants have a long way to go before they even approximate their American counterparts. However, they have asserted themselves with increasing effectiveness by tirelessly challenging the traditional privileges of ministers and the secrecy of permanent officials. MPs of all political stripes have joined in the task of improving the House of Commons' surveillance of the executive branch.

It is difficult to ascertain exactly where the relaxing of party discipline and the accompanying assertiveness of the House of Commons are taking parliamentary government. The developments do suggest that Americans should exercise a great deal more caution in asserting that British governments find it vastly easier to win their way with Parliament than do U.S. administrations with Congress. Also we perhaps should put less of a premium on "efficiency" in extolling the virtues of the British system. Over the past two decades of emergent assertiveness among MPs, backbench rebellions have actually diverted governments from stances that would have deeply antagonized voters.

Hard Times for Adversarial Creativity

British observers have not all agreed that party discipline of the type that prevailed through much of this century actually served democracy. Some have believed that voting unfailingly with one's party demeans an MP, impinging upon the principle that legislatures derive their legitimacy from the fact that their members serve at the pleasure of the electorate in specified constituencies.

In classic terms, the argument comes down to whether elected representatives serve as *delegates* or *trustees*. If the former, then they must always vote according to the will of the constituents whom they represent. If the latter, they can choose to vote according to other criteria, using representational discretion. This allows them to choose what

---

Your representative owes you, not his industry only, but his judgment; and he betrays, instead of serving you, if he sacrifices it to your opinion.

SOURCE: Edmund Burke, *Letter to his Constituents in Bristol*, 1774.

they discern to be best for their constituency, independent of their assessment of the electorate's will. Such discretion provides the framework in which MPs choose to bow to strict discipline in the interests of their party and the nation.

Despite their growing self-assertiveness, British MPs, unlike U.S. senators and congressmen, still usually fit themselves into the trustee mold. Most justify this on the grounds that their party, in order to retain or gain power, must present a united front. And invoking the received wisdom, they argue that partisan coherence ultimately provides the type of government necessary for effective pursuit of the national interest.

Within the somewhat more rigid format than prevails in the U.S. Congress, the style of political discourse in the House of Commons follows relatively adversarial contours. The prime minister, members of cabinet and MPs in the government party must defend their policies to the hilt. Only reluctantly will they acknowledge defects in the design of legislative initiatives or the execution of existing policies. By the same token, members of the opposition parties must find fault with the government no matter how reasonable its proposals or effective and efficient its handling of the affairs of state.

To the American visitor to the House of Commons, the actual acting out of these adversarial roles might appear to be simply high theater. But many Britons staunchly defend these dynamics, believing that they result in a creative tension whereby the government knows its proposal and administration of policies must withstand even unreasonable criticism. Meanwhile, the opposition finds in the adversarial House of Commons a vital forum for championing the causes of regions, groups, and individuals with grievances against the government.

More important, opposition parties try to turn the confrontational dynamics to their advantage in an overarching strategic process. This involves convincing voters that the government party has done so badly that it does not deserve a renewed mandate in the next general election. In order to win sufficient voters over from the government party, an opposition party must convince them that it will pursue superior policy objectives and run a more effective and efficient government. That is, it must become a credible option in the minds of the voters. Of the opposition parties, only Labour comes close to presenting itself as a viable alternative to the Conservatives. In the elections of 1983 and 1987, the Alliance—an amalgam of the Liberals and the Social Democrats—attained neither the unity nor the number of MPs necessary to seriously challenge the Conservatives.

The case of the Labour Party poses a more serious question with very significant possible consequences for the operation of the parliamentary system in the United Kingdom. Since the late 1970s, Labour has found itself under heavy fire on both flanks. The troubles started with the growing dissent among far-left elements of the party. This contributed greatly to the defections from Labour of the 27 MPs mentioned above who joined the Social Democratic Party after its formation in 1981. The fractiousness of the far left also contributed to the eventual resignation of the party leader, Michael Foot, who served from 1980 to 1983 as James Callaghan's immediate successor.

As suggested by the vast superiority of the 1987 election campaign over that of 1983, Neil Kinnock has managed to restore a semblance of order to Labour. This does not mean, however, that he has reined in the left completely; and the party has in the past few years come under a frontal assault from the Conservatives. This goes beyond the Conser-

If people could be sure that we would never have another socialist government, increasing state control, increasing control of ownership . . . then I think the prospects for this country would be really bright . . . and if only we could get rid of socialism as a second force and have two [parties that] fundamentally believed that political freedom had to be backed by economic freedom . . . I think you could get another realignment in British politics . . . After two more victories.

SOURCE: Mrs. Thatcher in an interview with the *Financial Times*, November 19, 1986.

vatives' incessantly incanting catch phrases such as "Loony Left" to remind voters that Mr. Kinnock still has not gained complete control of his party. It extends to explicit efforts to press the view that the Labour Party no longer should serve as the nation's alternative government party.

A fundamental convention of British parliamentary democracy is that the main party in the opposition is construed as the "Loyal Opposition," it derives its legitimacy from the fact that while advocating different positions from the government party, it strives always to base its criticism on its rendering of the national interest. Now the Conservatives, beginning with Mrs. Thatcher, have increasingly attacked Labour's exercise of this prerogative. They maintain that the advances of the welfare state after the war must be rolled back radically if Britain is to adapt to its transformed economic circumstances. Even the threat of a government sympathetic to "state socialism" will make it impossible for Britain to realize its full potential as an economic power. Labour thus must be supplanted as the alternate party.

Unease about Life Without a Bill of Rights

The growing evidence strongly suggests the need for some sort of action toward firmer

protections of human rights under the British constitution. The building pressures come from both unfavorable decisions of the European Court of Human Rights (ECHR), and recurrent episodes in which the government or the courts in Britain reveal serious insensitivity to the requirements of individual liberties.

Britain has allowed individual citizens to take their cases to the ECHR since 1966. Between the time of its first verdict—1975—and 1985, the court ruled against the U.K. government in 12 of 13 cases. No other European government has suffered so many negative judgments. The cases largely concerned the rights of detainees and prisoners —especially in Northern Ireland; other cases have involved corporal punishment of students, labor rights, homosexual rights, mental health patients, women's rights, freedom of the press and telephone tapping.

Britons who oppose the enactment of an indigenous bill of rights argue that this would undermine the sovereignty of Parliament. Judges would have to apply an omnibus provision enumerating fundamental liberties to each contentious case. This situation would contrast sharply with traditional British perceptions of the judges' roles. They prefer now to view themselves as simply ascertaining the will of Parliament as embodied in legislation addressed to specific areas of law. An overarching bill of rights would place judges in the position of having to reconcile conflicts between an act of Parliament that itemizes fundamental constitutional guarantees, and other statutes. In application of the law to specific cases, they would find themselves in a new predicament: They would doubtlessly have to overrule certain acts of Parliament on the grounds that they did not adhere to the bill of rights.

Notwithstanding the reluctance of many Britons to entrench individual rights in an indigenous bill, the concept of the primacy of

. . . When people come to her door, not seldom accompanied by young children in desperate states and at all hours because, being in danger, they cannot go home . . . the appellant does not turn them away. . . . And what happens . . . ? She finds herself the defendant in criminal proceedings at the suit of the local authority because she has allowed the inmates of her house to exceed the permitted maximum, and to that charge, I believe, she has no defence in law. My Lords, this is not a situation that can be regarded with complacency by any member of your Lordships' House, least of all by those who are compelled to do justice according to the law as it is, and not according to the state of affairs as they would wish it to be.

SOURCE: Lord Hailsham—a senior justice—reflecting in 1977 on the inability of the courts to assist a woman who had taken in battered women in a case in which she was charged with violating crowding restrictions in her boarding house. Cited by Budge and McKay et al., *The New British Political System*, 1985.

acts of Parliament in determining legal cases has lost ground in the past decade. The unfavorable decisions by the ECHR noted above quickened this process. If a European court takes precedence over British courts, one can logically infer that the 1950 European Convention of Human Rights enjoys primacy over any British statutes within its area of competence. However, this conclusion remained only a theoretical possibility until 1987.

In March of that year, a case heard by three Appeal Court judges brought the application of the European Convention of Human Rights directly by British courts that much closer. The case invovled a woman employee's claim to equal wages for equal work. It was a bit tricky in that the company concerned had engaged one man in a group otherwise staffed by women in order to buttress its claim that the women were not being paid less than men in comparable jobs.

The British judges invoked European law

—in this case, Article 119 of the Treaty of Rome—to rule that an industrial tribunal must hear the plaintiff's case. This decision stood in direct contradiction of the 1970 English Equal Pay Act, which prevented such a claim. In a sense, the judges anticipated an unfavorable ruling from the European Court. Their decision paves the way for similar references to the European Convention of Human Rights and the decisions of the ECHR.

Parallel with the increased recourse to European law, a series of cases has made British courts more wary of arbitrary actions on the part of the government. One particularly dramatic case that unfolded from 1986 to 1988 illustrates developments especially well. This involved Peter Wright, a retired member of MI5—the British intelligence and security agency that handles domestic operations. Wright attempted Australian publication of a book detailing supposed treasonous behavior on the part of his former colleagues. Among other things, this entailed evidence that a former head of MI5, Sir Roger Hollis, was actually a Russian spy, and accounts of a MI5 plot to overthrow Harold Wilson by implying that he was a Soviet agent.

In its effort to prevent publication of these allegations, the government faced a long and unsuccessful litigation. To begin, the Australian courts refused to accept its case that Wright had broken his obligation, as a government official, of confidentiality. They also rejected the argument that publication of his book would constitute a threat to national security. In Britain, the government had won a court injunction in 1986 against newspapers publishing the details of the contents of Wright's book.

The government's persistence in pressing the case in Britain backfired. The process followed a tortuous route ultimately ending in failure in a succession of proceedings in several courts. For instance, the head of the High Court's chancery division summarily dismissed the government's charges in June 1987. He did so because the government's arguments, if allowed, "would have subverted the basic principles of civil law and led to unacceptable restrictions on press freedom." When push comes to shove, seemingly arbitrary actions by the government have moved British judges—no matter how reluctant—into employing broad constitutional principles as well as the law in arriving at their decisions.

A TROUBLED ECONOMY

Political scientists talk a great deal these days about governments trying to manage the economics of decline. In other words, they are examining the process whereby mighty industrial powers such as the United Kingdom and the United States have had to cope with a diminished role for their manufacturing sectors. Americans have become familiar with the term "Rust Belt," denoting the areas of the United States in which countless plants have lost their economic viability. The decline has left entire industrial towns blighted and millions of workers out of a job.

Britain has struggled with much more widespread abandonment of manufacturing industries than has the United States. The U.K. economy did not compete well even when the North Atlantic enjoyed relative dominance of the world manufacturing industries. The nation's industrial plant was nearly obsolete. Neither its management nor workers excelled in comparative productivity. Thus, the United Kingdom was not adapting well to the new challenges to North Atlantic economies—especially those from the Japanese and other Asians. Further, the 1973 and 1979 energy crises struck before U.K. North Sea oil was in full flow. All of these factors added up to one seemingly unavoidable outcome. Britain ran the risk of becoming one huge rust belt.

Numerous American columnists, ranging from conservatives such as George Will to liberals like David Broder, wrote stories for their U.S. readership on the 1987 British election campaign. The election itself marked Mrs. Thatcher's triumphant assumption to a third term—an event unprecedented in this century. In unison, the American commentators extolled the success of "Thatcherism" in articles laced with catch phrases and statistics lifted right off Conservative Party campaign literature. Mrs. Thatcher had brought Britain back, they proclaimed. British economic growth had been outstripping that of any other Western European nation. And the government's privatization of several former state enterprises, such as British Telecom and British Gas, had stemmed the tide of socialism. That is, the acquisition of shares in former state corporations by citizens who previously owned no stocks had brought about a surge of "popular capitalism."

One does not like to dampen enthusiasm. However, Britain has a long way to go before it is "back." This section will examine the issue of economic decline and recovery in the United Kingdom. It will first ascertain how the British economy stacks up in comparison to other Western European powers. It will then look at how Thatcherism has differed from the approaches to economic management for other postwar U.K. governments. It will finally assess the effects of Thatcherism on regional and social disparities in the way in which economic goods are distributed in Britain.

The Patient Is Better, but Still Confined to Bed

During the 1987 campaign, the Conservative Party made much of what at first blush appeared to be an astounding set of statistics. Apart from Japan's and Denmark's, Britain's economy had grown faster since 1981 than any advanced nation's. Further, the rise in overall productivity—the average yield from one worker's labor—had outstripped that of any other advanced nation except Japan. In manufacturing industries, productivity actually increased in the United Kingdom more than in any other developed economy in the West.

In assessing the significance of this achievement, one must keep in mind an important omission. Mrs. Thatcher's government began in 1979, *not* 1981. The U.K. economy went into a precipitous decline from the end of 1979 through 1980. Although associated with a world recession, the dive owed much of its sharpness to the policies of the new government. These included an increase of the *value-added tax*—a form of sales tax—to 15 percent, deep cuts in public expenditure, and stringent interest rates designed to harness the money supply. As illustrated by Figure 3.1, the cumulative impact of these economic depressants hit industrial production especially hard.

Having dug a big hole for Britain in 1979, in the 1987 Conservative campaign Mrs. Thatcher was claiming a full reversal of the United Kingdom's economic fortunes. However, statistics from a host of reputable sources, including Lloyds Bank, the National Institute of Economic and Social Research (NIESR) and even the U.K. government Central Statistical Office, all presented a substantially different picture. Between 1979 and 1981, manufacturing output fell in the United Kingdom by 15 percent. This decline resulted in the loss of some 1.5 million jobs. Even by spring 1987, manufacturing remained about 1.5 percent below its level when the Conservatives took over in May 1979. And capital investment—expenditure of industry in its productive capacity—came in fully 17.5 percent below its 1979 level. In fact, the government failed to bring the number of unemployed below 3 million in time for the election. Its efforts fell short despite several changes in the calculation of the figures that made the task of achieving a figure

Figure 3.1 Industrial production in the United Kingdom (percent increase on one year earlier). Based on index of output of the production and construction industries.

SOURCE: *The Economist Diary*, 1988, p. 17.

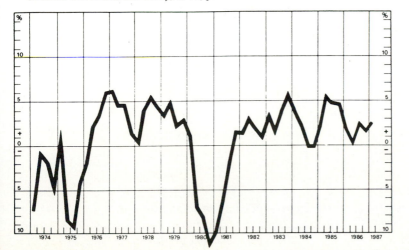

below 3 million much easier than it would have been in 1979. In that year, there were 1.2 million unemployed Britons.

It would come as no surprise, thus, that Britain's actual performance during the entire period of Thatcher's priministership has proved somewhat less robust—in comparative terms—than the Conservatives' 1981 to 1987 analysis suggested. Within the 1979 to 1986 interval, gross domestic product (GDP) and all industrial production, which takes in manufacturing plus other forms of produc-

Figure 3.2   Nation income per person—by countries and by regions (converted to pounds sterling at the average exchange rate for the year concerned).

SOURCE: *The Economist Diary*, 1988, p. 42.

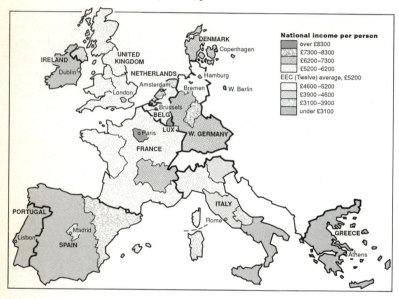

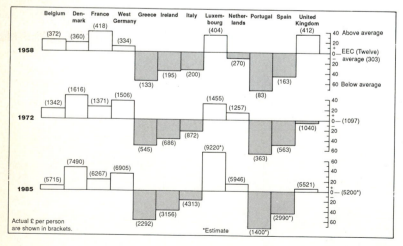

tion, grew 9.5 and 2.75 percent, respectively (NIESR 1987). Both productivity figures attained the 26 percent level in Japan and some 15 percent in the United States. U.K. productivity growth stayed pretty much at its long-term postwar average. This left U.S. workers three times and Japanese, French and West German labor about 1.75 times as efficient as their British counterparts.

Figure 3.2 puts another light on this debate. Notwithstanding the battle between the Conservatives and the opposition parties over whether Thatcherism has worked, Britons still find themselves behind many other Europeans in average income. Most of the United Kingdom maintains the same national income per person as northern Italy and the poorer part of France. West Germans, who trailed Britons badly in 1958, currently remain far ahead. The Italians, formerly far behind the British, have come up quickly. In fact, the Italians, claiming that their "black economy" should be taken into account, now maintain that they have surpassed Britons in per person income. (The term "black economy" refers to the portion of production tax evaders do not report to the government.)

Thatcherism as an Experiment

Whatever her success, Mrs. Thatcher's management of the British economy has departed radically from that of other prime ministers, whether Conservative or Labour, since World War II. This section will explore how the contours of her approach differ from previous approaches. The next section will examine what the early returns from various segments of British society tell us about who has lost and who has gained from Thatcherism.

The consensus that guided British governments from 1945 to 1979 had its roots in developments in the 1930s. In the early part of that decade, *classic monetarism* prevailed.

This view held that only a strong currency could provide sufficient confidence in the economy to foster industrial development. The National Government, a broad coalition consisting of Conservative, National Labour, Liberal National and Liberal MPs, stressed economic policies that influenced only the margins of industrial activity. However, the 1930s did mark a gradual acceptance among political leaders of the need to regulate certain sectors of industry and agriculture. Also, the planning movement, which argued that government had to take a more active role in reconciling industry and the needs of society, took on growing importance.

The theories of John Maynard Keynes entered the picture by the mid-1930s. Economies, Keynes maintained, could fulfill currency stability for extended periods of time without fully utilizing their resources. One of the resources most likely to remain untapped was labor. Such a situation spelled protracted periods of unemployment for many workers. Governments, however, could override such inertia by raising the threshold for equilibrium between prices and demand. Within limits, they could increase expenditure in order to enhance demand. The resulting stimulation of industrial production would reduce unemployment.

To varying degrees, all of the postwar governments before Mrs. Thatcher followed Keynesianism. Similarly, they also embraced both the welfare state and state ownership of key industrial sectors. The 1945–51 Labour government under Clement Attlee greatly increased social services, especially through the creation of socialized medicine under the National Health Service in 1946. Although other public-sector enterprises already existed, the same Labour government had by 1949 nationalized the central bank (the Bank of England), coal, civil aviation, electricity, railways and canals, gas, and iron and steel. Significantly, the Conservative governments that followed Labour from 1951 to 1964 made no substantial efforts to scale down the welfare state. And, they maintained all of the newly acquired public-sector enterprises except trucking, and iron and steel. Labour re-nationalized iron and steel during Harold Wilson's 1964–70 government.

A consensus between the two parties prevailed until the mid-1970s on the two prongs of the interventionist state: social programs and public-sector enterprises. Within a Keynesian framework, this meant that two engines drove successive governments' use of public expenditure to stimulate economic growth. The resulting thrust forced governments of both stripes to claim for the state increasing shares of the gross domestic product (GDP). For instance, the Conservative government under Edward Heath enhanced the state's portion of GDP from 40.5 to 46.4 percent between 1970 and 1974. Even under Mrs. Thatcher, the same figure grew from 44 to 48 percent between 1979 and 1981 in response to pressures for expenditure brought on by a precipitous drop in industrial production and the emergence of double-digit unemployment for the first time since 1938.

The state's seemingly insatiable appetite for ever larger claims upon GDP spawned profound worries about the decline of private enterprise in the United Kingdom. Within the right wing of the Conservative Party, these became especially intense after Edward Heath's total failure to reverse the tide. There emerged a core group of disaffected Conservatives who were intensely dedicated to the idea of reintroducing private-sector market forces to diverse fields of British life that had come under government dominance. By 1974, the movement congealed under the leadership of Sir Keith Joseph, a Secretary of State for Health and Social Security under Heath who had become utterly disillusioned with efforts simply to control the size of government.

The market-oriented Conservatives drew upon a special resource. Under Sir Keith Joseph's leadership, they developed a think tank called the Center for Policy Studies. This highly partisan research organization received the full blessing of Mrs. Thatcher when she assumed the Conservative leadership in 1975. It also began to eclipse the Conservative Research Department as the principal source of policy proposals and analyses for the party's leadership in Parliament. By 1977—two years before the Conservatives returned to power—Sir Keith Joseph won a consensus document from the principal members of the shadow cabinet concerned with economic policy. The Conservative Party had abandoned Keynesianism in favor of *monetarism,* and a centrist position on the role of the state in favor of a market-oriented view.

The Thatcher government's actual follow-through with this ideological shift has proven uneven. This does not mean that the shift has failed to work momentous effects on the distribution of wealth through various segments of British society, as will become clear in the section that follows. To begin, the Conservatives relaxed their monetarist views in 1981 when it became clear that excessively high interest rates had both greatly exacerbated the 1980 decline and made recovery much more difficult. More recently, they secured a pre-election economic boom in 1986 by encouraging a 15 percent deflation in the value of the U.K. pound. This gave British goods added competitiveness in foreign markets.

The residual effects of the 1980 decline—much more than cuts in government expenditure—have made the lot of those on the lower rungs of the socio-economic ladder somewhat worse than in 1979. This is mostly due to the large number of the less well positioned who cannot find jobs. Cuts in government programs have appreciably lowered the level of social security and services such as health and education. However, the Conservatives have stopped short of full abandonment of major social programs. The market-oriented dimension of the Conservative approach thus has manifested itself most clearly in the state divesting itself of corporate assets. This process has involved the selling of shares in such public-sector enterprises as British Aerospace, British Telecom, British Gas, British Airways, Rolls Royce and the British Airports Authority.

Another field where the Thatcher government has not advanced according to plan is taxation. After dramatic cuts in income tax during its first year, the government has taken a cautious approach in this area—despite its belief that cutting down on the drag that the state places on the economy requires radical changes in taxation in addition to simply reducing expenditure in government programs and rolling back the size of public-sector enterprise. According to the Thatcher braintrust, the nature of taxation must undergo transformation, focusing on consumption and, therefore, taking the form of sales taxes such as the value-added tax (VAT). Income taxes, it is felt, operate as disincentives to working *and* saving, while extension of VAT—even to essential goods such as

food—will encourage both. To date, the government has neither grasped the nettle of this potentially unpopular view nor acted further to greatly reduce income tax.

The Costs of Thatcherism

Insofar as the Thatcher government has sought to refurbish British manufacturing, it has failed. Figure 3.3 demonstrates this point dramatically. Manufacturing attracted 20 percent of fixed capital investment in 1970. This figure fell to 16 and 12 percent in 1980 and 1986, respectively. On the other hand, the finance and business services sector has grown dramatically in the portion of fixed capital investment that it attracts. It stood in 1986 at 18 percent, having risen in 1980 to 14 percent from the 6 percent 1970 figure.

This outcome stands to reason. Monetarist policies have kept British interest rates at very high levels in comparison to those of other nations. This makes dealing in pounds—through the London financial houses—an especially attractive proposition. It does not mean that foreign investors have chosen to put their money into British manufacturing. The government's withdrawal from state intervention in industry has also involved the dismantling of incentive systems that might

Figure 3.3   Gross fixed capital investment in the United Kingdom
(£ million at 1980 prices).
SOURCE: *The Economist Diary*, 1988, p. 18.

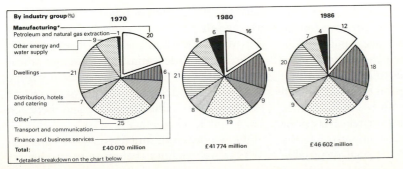

have funneled more funds into manufacturing. In this regard, the tax cuts at the outset of the government did little to spark investment; they simply put extra cash in upper- and middle-class pockets. Government failed to provide structures whereby a substantial part of this extra money would end up in manufacturing.

Notwithstanding all the excitement over "popular capitalism," tax cuts and the privatization of public-sector enterprises have worked no clear effect on the distribution of wealth in the country. According to statistics released in 1986 by the Board of Inland Revenue (the equivalent of the U.S. Internal Revenue Service), the Thatcher years have actually seen an abrupt halt to the gradual deconcentration of personal wealth that had prevailed since the war. For example, the proportion of wealth held by the richest 5 percent of the population stood at 56 percent in 1966. It dropped to 52, 44, and 39 percent in 1971, 1978 and 1980 respectively. Between 1982 and 1984, it held steady at 39 percent.

Perhaps more distressing is the evidence that Thatcherism has deepened divisions within the United Kingdom. The service sector gravitates toward the Southeast of England. The explosive expansion of the banking and finance sector in London reflects this trend especially vividly. Meanwhile, heavy manufacturing industries have traditionally operated in the northern regions of England more than in the southern ones. As these have remained depressed, regional disparities between the North and the South have tended to take on added significance. Figure 3.4 illustrates the extent to which unemployment has taken a much greater toll in the North of England, Wales, the West of Scotland, and all of Northern Ireland than it has in the South.

Table 3.1 demonstrates the relatively poor standing of every region in comparison to the South East in terms of personal disposable

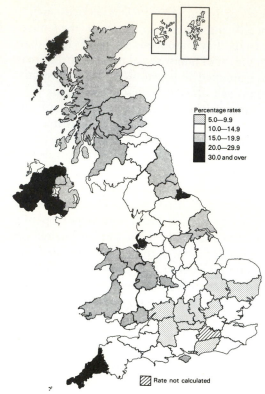

Percentage rates

5.0—9.9
10.0—14.9
15.0—19.9
20.0—29.9
30.0 and over

Rate not calculated

Figure 3.4   Unemployment rates in the United Kingdom (January 1987).
SOURCE: Central Statistical Office, 1987 (*Regional Trends 22,* London: Her Majesty's Stationery Office).

income. To cite the worst case in England proper, the North's average personal, disposable income was 1,234 pounds per head—366 pounds less than Greater London's—in 1975. In 1985, the gap had widened to fully 1,297 pounds. Put another way, average disposable income in Greater London was 3.26 times the 1975 level in 1985, whereas the differential for the same indicator in the North was 3.18. Disposable income in Greater London had grown from 20 to 23 percent above the U.K. average between 1975 and 1985.

We will leave a more detailed examination of regional electoral behavior until chapter

Table 3.1   Per Capita Disposable Income

	£ per Head				£ per Head Index UK = 100
	1975	1983	1984	1985	1985
United Kingdom	1,331	3,664	3,924	4,235	100.0
North	1,234	3,447	3,558	3,919	92.5
Yorkshire and Humberside	1,241	3,457	3,505	3,923	92.6
East Midlands	1,278	3,579	3,877	4,066	96.0
East Anglia	1,252	3,655	3,946	4,244	100.2
South East	1,467	4,073	4,402	4,725	111.6
Greater London	1,600	4,472	4,800	5,216	123.2
Rest of South East	1,371	3,811	4,143	4,407	104.1
Southwest	1,274	3,675	3,953	4,152	98.0
West Midlands	1,350	3,367	3,681	3,997	94.4
Northwest	1,297	3,481	3,762	4,074	96.2
England	1,349	3,712	3,981	4,291	101.3
Wales	1,231	3,273	3,410	3,778	89.2
Scotland	1,288	3,622	3,866	4,181	98.7
Northern Ireland	1,110	3,070	3,307	3,538	83.5

SOURCE: Central Statistical Office. 1987. *Regional Trends 22*. London: Her Majesty's Stationery Office.

five. However, we should not end our discussion of key changes in the economic context of British politics without pointing out the degree to which regional disparities have begun to reveal themselves in deeper electoral cleavages between the North and the South. In the 1987 election, the South West, South East and East Anglia only gave six of their

Neil Kinnock, the Labour leader, and David Owen and David Steel, the Alliance leaders, look on forlornly as the South steams off in the aftermath of the 1987 general election.

SOURCE: *The Guardian*, June 13, 1987.

176 seats to either the Labour or Alliance parties. As one might expect from its greater social diversity, London yielded 26 of 84 seats for the opposition parties. The border areas split their tickets. West Midlands and East Midlands produced 67 of 100 seats for the Conservatives. Further north, the North West and Yorkshire/Northumberland gave Labour a slight edge with 69 of 127 seats. Meanwhile, the North, Scotland, and Wales all gave overwhelming support to Labour. The increases in Labour's vote over the 1983 election in the North West, Yorkshire/Northumberland, the North, Scotland, and Wales exceeded five percent in each case.

CONCLUSION

This chapter focused on the context of British government and politics. It has dwelt on two issues. First, it has outlined the nature of the British constitution. Second, it has examined economic conditions in which the political system operates. With regard to both contextual dimensions, this chapter has highlighted ways in which relatively dramatic developments have triggered processes of change that call for adaptation within the political system.

In our treatment of the constitutional context, we saw that the British political system operates without a written document defining structures, powers, and rights. Thus, many ambiguities surround the actual legitimacy of various conventional doctrines that guide the operation of the political system.

Recently, serious questions have emerged about three elements of the constitution. First, the erosion of party discipline has threatened the ability of British government to maintain the high level of efficiency for which it became famous. However tentatively, the elements of a separation of powers between the executive and legislative branches have taken root. Access by MPs to

forums—notably special committees—that put government policies under closer scrutiny has strengthened this tendency.

The decline of party discipline has undermined the ability of the opposition parties to maintain the unity necessary to preserve their status as the "Loyal Opposition." The Conservative Party has seized upon this weakness. Along the way, it has raised questions about the future viability of the socialist Labour Party both as the "Official Opposition" and as the aspiring government party.

Finally, the wider European constitutional context—including the European Convention of Human Rights—has begun to impinge on the British judiciary, especially its preference for narrow legal interpretation and its deference to the sovereignty of the British Parliament. In addition, Britain has come off as less than a paragon in protection of human rights. The two developments have provoked discussion of the desirability of a written guarantee of human rights.

The examination of Britain's economic context reveals the degree to which the country has fallen behind other advanced Western systems, especially in industrial performance. This state of affairs has had serious consequences for the average Briton's standard of living. Mrs. Thatcher's revolutionary economic policies have tried to redress the situation. Her policies have contributed to an economic boom in the southern regions of the country. However, they also have exacerbated the divide between the economic performance and well-being of the South as against the North of England, Scotland, Wales, and Northern Ireland. That Britain stands a chance of regaining lost ground in its competition with other economic powers is heartening news for those in the South. Yet the gap between their prospects and those of Britons not in the South injects a critical item for the political agenda during the third Thatcher term and beyond.

References and Suggested Readings

ARNDT, H. W. *The Rise and Fall of Economic Growth*. London: Longman, 1978.

BACON, ROBERT, and WALTER ELTIS. *Britain's Economic Problem: Too Few Producers*. London: Macmillan, 1976.

BIRCH, ANTHONY H. *Representative and Responsible Government*. London: Allen and Unwin, 1964.

BUDGE, IAN, and DAVID McKAY et al. *The New British Political System: Government and Society in the 1980s*. London: Longman, 1985.

DREWRY, G. *Law, Justice and Politics*. London: Longman, 1975.

EPSTEIN, LEON D. "What Happened to the British Party System?" *American Political Science Review* 74 (1980): 9–22.

HARVEY, J., and L. BATHER. *The British Constitution and Politics*. London: Macmillan, 1982.

KEEGAN, WILLIAM, and RUPERT PENNANT-REA. *Who Runs the Economy? Control and Influence in British Economic Policy*. London: Maurice Temple Smith, 1979.

———. *Mrs. Thatcher's Economic Experiment*. Harmondsworth: Penguin, 1984.

KAVANAGH, DENNIS. *Thatcherism and British Politics: The End of Consensus*. Oxford: Oxford University Press, 1987.

NORTON, PHILIP. *The Constitution in Flux*. Oxford: Martin Robertson, 1982.

———. "Behavioural Changes: Backbench Independence in the 1980s." In *Parliament in the 1980s*, ed. author. Oxford: Blackwell, 1985.

SCHWARZ, JOHN E. "Exploring a New Role in Policy Making: The British House of Commons in the 1970s." *American Political Science Review* 74 (1980): 23–37.

STREET, H. *Freedom, the Individual and the Law*. Harmondsworth: Penguin, 1963.

4

The Limits of British Political Culture

The preceding chapter examined the context of the British political system, focusing on the constitutional and economic settings. This chapter looks at the building blocks of British politics: individual citizens. More precisely, it will assess the nature of the British citizenry.

Healthy democracies do not run on institutions alone. They require committed individuals to operate them. Most obviously, they depend on political leaders capable of maintaining balance. Leadership consists of one part exertion of authority and another part responsiveness to the public one seeks to serve. At the same time, democracies require the support and the participation of ordinary citizens. If the chemistry between the general public and the political leadership goes wrong—or never adequately develops—then the latter will find it extremely difficult to reconcile authority and responsiveness.

When we talk about the nature of a citizenry we really open three issues. One of these is overarching; the other two show how authority and responsiveness reflect the vigor of the ties between the political leaders and the public. The first we call *political culture*.

The others we call *socialization* and *participation*.

If you were arrested in London, chances are that the police constable would behave in a surprisingly respectful way. He probably would not use a gun—even if he was one of the rare policemen who actually carries one. While there are lapses in demeanor, he would be unlikely to rough you up or use abusive language. Indeed, if he got into a discussion with his station about you on his car radio he might even go out of his way to use courteous terms such as "citizen" when mentioning you. Probability does play a role here. The constable might behave differently depending on your skin color, your dress, your accent, whether you had a vehicle and if so, whether it was a battered Volkswagen Beetle or a sleek new Jaguar. Your and the constable's behavior, however, would remain within significantly tighter parameters than those which prevail in the United States.

The above scenario illustrates an underlying concept of political culture. The hypothetical situation evokes substantially different behavioral expectations in a British setting than it does in an American one. Therefore we speak of political culture as distinctive to each nation. When a killer opens fire on innnocent passersby in the United States we are alarmed at the immense violence existing in this country. However, we likely would not consider the occurrence surprising or attribute it to an external influence. This is not the case in the United Kingdom. Such incidents happen rarely, and when they do, they strike a much deeper horror in the public consciousness. More to the point, commentators tend almost invariably to interpret such events as inspired by and mimicking U.S.-style social pathology as depicted by American television and movies.

The term *political culture* refers to a complex array of attitudes, beliefs, values, and skills predisposing citizens toward various types of political behavior. Even though we know an individual well, we can never predict with total certainty what he or she will actually do in various circumstances. By the same token, we cannot unerringly forecast political behavior. Still, the waters of national character run deep; and anyone who professes to know about the politics of a country surely must have become acquainted with the accumulated record of its political psyche.

The sections below focus on various dimensions of British political culture. Along the way, they will examine patterns in political socialization and participation. The former topic concerns the transmission of political attitudes and values between generations. The latter measures the ordinary citizen's attention to and direct invovlement in the political process.

DEFERENTIAL POLITICS

In 1959, two American scholars, Gabriel A. Almond and Sidney Verba, headed up an interview study of political culture in Britain. Their work formed part of a cross-national project including the United States, West Germany, Italy, and Mexico. When they reported their findings, the authors concluded that Britain was a *deferential* political culture. To understand what they meant, we should look briefly at their classification system.

To ascertain the nature of a political culture, you must examine the orientations of the citizenry to various dimensions of the political system. The dimensions include: (1) the system as a broad phenomenon—its history, size, location, power, constitutional characteristics, and so on; (2) the "input" elements of the system—the organizations and the elites that determine the shape of government policies; (3) the actual "outputs" of government—the substantive nature of government policies and the vagaries of delivery and enforcement; and (4) perceptions of the place of individual citizens as participants in the political process. The orientation to the dimensions of the political system fall under three categories: (1) cognition—how much individuals actually know about the individual dimensions; (2) affect—their favorable or unfavorable feelings toward them; and (3) evaluation—their considered judgments about them.

Three types of political culture emerge from this framework. A *parochial* culture is a primitive society in which the average individual has little knowledge of any of the dimensions of the political system. A *subject* culture is a traditional political society whose citizens are benignly aware of a pervasive phenomenon identified as the political system and who are conscious of its benefits, taxes, and regulations, but who fail to influence its policies; in short, they are politically passive —they see themselves more as subjects than as full-fledged citizens. A *participant* culture is an advanced democracy in which individuals reveal strong orientations toward all four dimensions of the political system.

When Almond and Verba designated Britain as a deferential political culture, they did not mean to diminish its standing as an advanced democracy. Rather, they simply employed the concept to reconcile two potentially contradictory findings. Britons interviewed in 1959 reported reasonably robust levels of participation in their political system, yet they maintained a very strong deference to the authority of the state. The authors argued that in some respects this situation was preferable to that in the United States. Americans, they believed, demonstrate a penchant for criticism and participation bordering on the meddlesome. The deferential culture hypothesis rests, of course, upon inferences about the inculcation of political orientations and individuals' attitudes toward political participation. These require closer scrutiny.

Almond and Verba interviewed over 900 Britons as part of their research project. From these, they selected five case histories to illustrate the dominant clusters of orientations found in their sample. However, a lot has changed in Britain since 1959, as we learned in chapter 3. It is doubtful that the "deferential British participant" will dominate the future.

To some extent, the British political culture represents a more effective combination of the subject and participant roles. . . . The development of the participant orientation in Britain did not challenge and replace the more deferential subject orientations, as was the tendency in the United States. Despite the spread of political competence and participant orientations, the British have maintained a strong deference to the independent authority of government.

source: Gabriel A. Almond and Sidney Verba, *The Civic Culture,* 1963.

To illustrate this analysis, Almond and Verba chose from their respondents an archetypical deferential participant. This person belonged to the working class but supported the Conservative government. He generally spoke favorably of government and politics. And he was inclined to believe in the efficacy of his participation in the political system. In itself, this profile fit a longstanding tradition among certain segments of the working class and did not warrant special comment.

Several other features of the profile raise flags for the inquiring mind in light of developments since 1959. Specifically, we should ask how it stands up to the recent decline of the economy in the North and the related deepening cleavage between the Northern and Southern electorates which was manifested in the 1987 general election.

The subject, "Mr. H," worked as a unionized baker in a large industrial city in the North. He had eight grown children all of whom worked hard and made their way— all the sons found careers in skilled trades. Mr. H noted himself how different this was from when he started out. Then there was no assurance that a person would find security even if he or she had ability and worked hard. Mr. H viewed the central government very positively. He also believed that the local government was equally effective.

If we could track down Mr. H's eight children, what would we find? Have they kept their jobs through the decline of the North? What are their own children doing? Have they found their ways into careers offering the same promise of security that their parents have? What do the parents and the children think about the central government—the political leadership, Parliament, and the bureaucracy—now? In the great battle between the central government and the local authorities waged under Mrs. Thatcher, which side have they taken? Obviously, we cannot ask these questions of Mr. H's descendants. However, we can probe more recent studies of British political culture to discover any shifts or changes in the deferential society.

POLITICAL SOCIALIZATION

Political socialization includes the inculcation of political orientations and values. It may begin as soon as a child becomes conscious of the outside world. It certainly intensifies during the school years. And it may well continue into early adulthood.

The very nature of the deferential culture suggests that political socialization normally shapes budding British citizens into loyal "subjects." This section examines the various contexts in which political socialization takes place. Along the way, it will be alert to developments since the early 1960s that suggest political socialization operates differently in Britain from the way it did when Almond and Verba studied it.

Given the span of years in which political socialization takes place, we must allow for the fact that various settings work their effects on the development of a child into a full-fledged citizen. Among these, the family, the educational system, social class and where one grows up merit our closest attention.

Family

If much of political socialization takes place in childhood, then family background is one of the strongest factors determining a citizen's political views. How much of table conversation in a particular family centers on politics? If a great deal, we can expect those children to absorb political ideas and learn how to express these much earlier than their peers. Are members of the family politically

active? For instance, do they involve themselves in campaign work or attempt to influence political decisions? If so, the children will tend to see such involvement as a natural part of citizenship. Are the parents deeply partisan? Then their children will probably adopt stronger party loyalties than children from nonpartisan homes.

All of these features are manifest in the families of most democratic societies. Britain is singularly distinguished from the United States (and other democracies) in the degree to which class consciousness is passed on to the next generation. Unlike Americans, Britons do not tend to expect that their children will experience upward mobility. In fact, many working-class parents actively discourage their children from aspiring to occupations that would elevate their socioeconomic standing.

Several studies have revealed these patterns. David Butler and Donald Stokes found in a 1970 survey that only 20 percent of respondents had experienced upward mobility. Less than 10 percent had lost socioeconomic standing. Another study that compared the earnings of residents of York in the 1970s with those of their fathers in the 1950s yielded a very high correlation.[1]

Richard Rose's assessment of the party identification of respondents in the 1974 British Election Survey points up two ways in which family experiences prove immensely durable. He looked at several potential influences—both formative and contemporary—on voters' preferences. He found that fathers' class and parents' party preference accounted for over 50 percent of the party preferences of the respondents.[2]

---

[1] Philip Norton, *The British Polity* (London: Longman, 1984), p. 18.

[2] Richard Rose, *Politics in England: Persistence and Change* (Boston: Little, Brown, 1986), p. 174.

Education

Several distinctive elements of the British educational system merit close scrutiny here. The first of these is that the Britons receive their education in politics less formally than do Americans. Thus, primary and secondary schools do not uniformly require that every student receive at least some explicit training in "civics." Much of the material that falls within the compass of politics and government comes to students only indirectly as "history." Indeed, even contemporary history courses sometimes cut off at the turn of the century.

In the United Kingdom advanced secondary school students specialize as they progress toward the final years of their education. At this stage, many British students might not even list a liberal arts selection among their courses, let alone one dealing substantially with government and politics. Universities proved loath to acknowledge "political science" as a separate degree. In fact, most political science departments go by the name "politics" or "government." Oxford still grants a catchall degree called "philosophy, politics and economics." The program's critics claim that it offers a classic "jack of all trades, master of none" curriculum.

To say that education in politics and government occurs informally does not imply that it fails to take place entirely. Britons who seek quality coverage of current affairs may choose between three national newspapers that maintain a standard exceeding U.S. papers. In fact, only the New York Times even comes close to a comparable role in the United States. Both the government-owned British Broadcasting Corporation and the private Independent Television Network provide strong, in-depth coverage of the news. And their documentaries enjoy a loyal following among viewers who wish to maintain a high level of information about public affairs. Further, numerous quality magazines such as The Economist, the New Statesman and New Society maintain strong followings among those especially attentive to politics.

Relying on these informal vehicles for imparting political knowledge, maintaining affective support of the system and providing assessments of major issues still leaves the United Kingdom in a somewhat precarious situation. In the first place, children do not normally avail themselves of such resources until they have entered their teens; thus, they can develop seriously erroneous views of their political system. For instance, British children frequently carry the illusion into their teens that the Queen, rather than the prime minister with the support of Parliament, rules the country. Further, overreliance upon the media as the political educator can leave the children of the masses far behind those of the elite. Most Britons read atrocious tabloid newspapers rather than the quality press. With four TV channels to choose from, one can find at least one light entertainment alternative to more serious public-affairs programs.

The inherent elitism of British education presents a major obstacle to the informal transmission of knowledge of, affection for and evaluation of the political system among the lower classes. To this day, those in the highest socioeconomic brackets tend to send their children to fee-paying schools. Although called "public schools," these institutions remain fiercely private. They employ social as well as academic criteria for admission, and charge as much as the equivalent of $10,000 for a year's tuition, room and board.

On the other hand, state-supported secondary education has gone through a period of turmoil over the past two decades. Until the 1960s, local education authorities ran two types of institutions: "grammar schools," which selected only the very

Table 4.1 Tabloids and "Middle-Brow" Papers
Outsell Quality Newspapers by Far

Daily Papers	April-Sept 1987	April-Sept 1986	% Change
Sun	4,021,122	4,035,117	(0.3)
Daily Mirror	3,130,734	3,114,453	0.5
Star	1,239,699	1,331,301	(6.9)
Daily Mail	1,794,458	1,777,147	0.1
Daily Express	1,675,070	1,773,708	(5.6)
Today	326,281	—	—
Daily Telegraph	1,171,291	1,136,029	3.1
*Guardian	472,648	522,947	(9.6)
*Times	446,790	478,404	(6.6)
*Independent	325,830	—	—
*Financial Times	299,036	253,180	18.1
Sunday Papers			
News of the World	5,021,366	4,881,644	2.9
Sunday Mirror	3,001,732	3,012,586	(0.4)
Sunday People	2,905,273	2,989,535	(2.8)
Sunday Express	2,222,031	2,236,070	(0.6)
Mail on Sunday	1,772,381	1,591,112	11.4
*Sunday Times	1,234,398	1,126,730	9.6
*Observer	772,532	765,579	0.9
Sunday Telegraph	732,808	675,937	8.4

SOURCE: The Audit Bureau of Circulations, September 1987 figures for daily or Sunday circulation as reported by *The Guardian*, October 26, 1987.

* Denotes quality newspaper.

brightest students, and "secondary moderns," which took everyone else. An exam called the "11-plus exam" separated the fliers from the plodders at the age of 11. The strategy of offering an exceptionally high caliber of education to a select few led to many grammar school graduates finding their way to Oxford and Cambridge universities and, eventually, into the establishment.

The verdicts from the 11-plus exam did not allow for late bloomers. In fact, many educators began to worry that the nation might well be denying itself a great deal of talent by such an early and severe separation of the gifted and the average. The Labour Party introduced comprehensive secondary schools when it controlled the government from 1964 to 1970. These merged the grammar and secondary modern schools with a view to allowing students to reach their optimal level at their own pace.

The Thatcher government has taken a dim view of the effectiveness of these institutions. It has launched upon a major drive to encourage superior comprehensive schools to separate themselves from local educational authorities and to charge fees. This initiative might satisfy parents and teachers who long for the former grammar school system. However, it appears to move even further than the former model from the idea that the state owes every child a reasonable chance to develop fully at his or her own speed. Under the Thatcher scheme, the United Kingdom will revert to the situation in which it employs strongly nonegalitarian criteria for ascertaining which students will avail themselves of the educational opportunities requisite for leadership in society.

Social Class

Class consciousness has a discernable influence on British politics. Recent studies suggest that the proportion of the population identifying with a specific class has remained pretty much the same between the mid-1960s and the mid-1980s, with around 50 percent of respondents in surveys associating themselves with a class. In the same interval, however, the proportion of manual workers who placed themselves in the working class has declined from 46 to 39 percent.[3] Scholars offer several reasons for this slip-

[3] Ian Budge and David McKay, *The Changing British Political System: Into the 1990s* (2nd ed.: London: Longman, 1988), p. 79.

page. The most commonly invoked argues that class-based inequalities and conflicts of interest in Britain have always competed with patriotism in the consciousness of the less advantaged. The strongly deferential nature of Britons allows for a situation in which concern for the national interest—as defined by the ruling elite—serves as a strong counterweight to pursuit of class-oriented goals.

The higher standard of living in Britain since World War II is another major factor in the lessening of class divisions. The broad consensus between the Conservative and Labour parties over the mixed economy and the welfare state certainly shifted the tenor of political debate in the 1950s and 1960s from fundamental issues to details. As a result, voters—especially those at the border between the classes—switched their party preference more easily.

A number of developments over the past two decades diminished the influence of class within the political system. The spate of strikes and battles over government attempts to limit wage increases during the 1970s revealed many gaping holes in the politics of consensus. Mrs. Thatcher saw herself as ringing the death knell on the old order by appealing for a new politics of commitment. This approach has worked electoral miracles.

Some doubts arise as to the ultimate impact of Thatcherism. Will it lead eventually to a polarization of the British electorate? The 1987 general election results suggest that the country has indeed divided sharply between the North and the South. The former, of course, has gone against the national mood and repudiated Thatcherism. In this regard, some studies of the sectors of the populace that maintain deep class-based antagonisms prove instructive.[4] Strong working-class sen-

---

[4] Ian Budge and David McKay et al., *The New British Political System: Government and Society in the 1980s* (London: Longman, 1985), pp. 84–85.

Margaret Thatcher

SOURCE: Hugo Young, *One of Us* (London: Macmillan, 1989).

Mrs. Thatcher is the first post-war political leader to declare openly her hostility to consensus politics. In a prepared speech in 1979 she compared herself to the Old Testament prophets who did not say "Brothers, I want a consensus." Instead, she proclaimed the importance of conviction and principle in politics—as if these were incompatible with consensus. In 1981, from Australia, she replied to criticisms from Mr. Heath that she was abandoning consensus politics: "For me, consensus seems to be the process of abandoning all beliefs, principles, values and policies." Some part of the explanation for this hostile reaction is that she realizes that it is a code-word for criticism for her own political style and policies. More importantly, the consensus protected a set of policies and values and a style that she has wanted to abandon.

SOURCE: Dennis Kavanagh, *British Politics: Continuities and Change*, p. 55.

timents have persisted most among those occupying traditional manual jobs in narrow-based industrial areas. Moreover, if the "ambience" of a community remains "working class," the relationship between voters' occupations and their electoral preferences intensify.[5] All of this suggests that the growing rift between the North and South partially masks class-related antagonsims.

Region

It is perhaps too easy to think only of Scotland, Northern Ireland and Wales when considering the significance of region in British political socialization. Each of these jurisdictions remain culturally distinctive, a fact the British government has partially accommodated by delegating responsibility for the administration of many government programs to the Scottish Office, the Northern Ireland Civil Service and the Welsh Office. Indeed, the administrative practices in some fields such as law and order, education and health care vary greatly in the three areas. Of course, Northern Ireland continues to be a special case due to the deep divisions between its Protestants and Catholics on whether the territory should remain in the United Kingdom or become a part of the Republic of Ireland.

In the rest of Britain, factors other than economic decline work their effects toward deepening regional differences. For example, the influx of Irish migrants, beginning with the Potato Famine in the late 1840s, tended to center on Glasgow, Liverpool and Cardiff as ports of entry. To this day, Irish Catholics constitute a highly significant cultural and political force in Glasgow and Liverpool and their surrounding communities.

[5] W. L. Miller, "Social Class and Party Choice in England: A New Analysis," *British Journal of Political Science*, 8 (1978): 257–84, as cited by Budge and McKay et al., 1st ed., p. 82.

The North of England also experienced a considerable influx of Eastern Europeans—especially after the various persecutions during this century. This has further strengthened the influence of Roman Catholicism in the area. West Indian, Pakistani and Indian immigrants have also gravitated to industrial cities and the smaller textile-producing towns of the North. With the economic decline centered in this region of the country, religious or racial barriers exacerbate the frustration caused by deprivation due to economic stagnation.

Race

The British have not become as sensitive to racism as Americans have. Even in polite company, Britons frequently make Irish immigrants the butt of their humor. In fact, one periodically sees articles and books developing the view that such diminution is healthy. As the arguments go, every nation has to have another people to whom they feel superior, and many of the jokes, it is said, base themselves on the real-life quirks of the Irish.

As for blacks and East Indians, many Britons persist in using offensive terms such as "Negro" and "colored" when referring to nonwhites. It remains best during a taxi trip not to mention any topic such as crime, unemployment or the appearance of neighborhoods that the driver might construe as touching on race. As often as not, cabbies will seize the opportunity to present a diatribe about how the immigration of nonwhites has ruined Britain. It will become clear that they simply have assumed that if you are white you must share their views. One sees in the newspapers—even in the quality press—and on television—even on the state-run BBC—an astonishing amount of racial stereotyping, much of it so blatant that it would arouse

"It's from your brother Samir. He is doing very well in England. Unfortunately he has not been allowed into the country yet but they have kept him waiting such a long time at Heathrow he has opened a small corner shop . . ."

Stereotypical cartoon appearing in *The Guardian* on October 16, 1986, when U.K. Immigration Service was detaining entire flights of passengers from the Indian subcontinent in an effort to crack down on illegal immigration.

angry protests from whites and nonwhites in the United States.

Part of the difficulty rests in the tremendous influx of nonwhites since the 1950s. In 1951, only one-fifth of one percent of the population was nonwhite. Since then, immigration from the Commonwealth gradually led to heavy concentrations of nonwhites in urban and industrial centers. In the 1950s, any members of a Commonwealth country or colony in the Empire could invoke their status as "British subjects" and settle in the United Kingdom. Even with the imposition of increasingly stringent immigration rules and procedures, nonwhites residing in the United Kingdom reached 4.6 percent of the population by 1985. This remains an insignificant figure by American standards. Yet, it has caused alarm—in many cases, overt racism—among those Britons who view their society as "white."

The race issue raises a number of important questions associated with political socialization in the United Kingdom. Successive governments have struggled with two related strategies. First, they have tried to control the influx of nonwhites. Here the more benevolent regimes have viewed this task as limiting the flow to a manageable level. This, presumably, would allow time for Britons to get used to the notion of their being a multiracial society. It would also assure that state and market machinery for socializing immigrants would not become swamped. Second, they have tried taking a harder line by adopting policies that attempt to stem the flow as much as possible.

The assumption of either strategy does not necessarily follow the dividing line between Conservatives and Labour. However, the Conservatives under Mrs. Thatcher have tightened access the most. Labour has proved somewhat more accommodating of nonwhites in its own policies and organization than have the Conservatives.

A new dimension has entered racial politics since the beginning of the Thatcher government. The "uncaring" image of the prime minister has made her a target for blame over racial unrest. This became particularly the case in 1981, when riots broke out in some 27 heavily nonwhite urban areas in the country. These and other such occurrences have stemmed from a volatile cocktail with three ingredients: deep alienation among nonwhite youths, resentment among young unemployed whites, and aggressive—bordering on hostile—policing of nonwhite neighborhoods. Insofar as Mrs. Thatcher fails to pur-

The carnival of "love and peace," organized each year by the West Indian population of London, ended in August 1976 riots. Six hundred people, three hundred of them policemen, were injured, and there were sixty arrests.

SOURCE: Sykes/Sigma.

Alarmist portrayal of black activists in a cartoon appearing in *The Independent* on May 5, 1987, when Neil Kinnock was struggling with pressures for recognition of black sections in the Labour Party.

HANDS ACROSS BRITAIN?

sue policies that might alleviate these conditions, she continues to stir the racial pot.

POLITICAL PARTICIPATION

As noted above, Almond and Verba distinguished between subject and the participant-oriented citizens. The former take in knowledge, affection for, and favorable evaluations of the political system—whose existence looms as an overarching reality—and the specific actions of the government. Participant-oriented citizens possess the same three characteristics, with the additional belief that they can contribute to the political process and avail themselves of channels for influencing their government.

In designating Britain as a deferential political culture, Almond and Verba stressed the fact of less participation in the United Kingdom than in the United States, but more subject orientation. Britons do not place the same demands on government for participation that Americans do. As a result, British channels available for influencing government have lagged behind those in the United States. The U.K. apparatus connecting the public will and the government lacks the multiplicity of forums, the refinement of advocacy skills and the relative democratic pluralism of the U.S. system.

Of course, Almond and Verba conducted their research in the late 1950s. The tumultuous 1960s and 1970s and the polarization between the North and the South that followed have led some scholars to expect that the deferential culture might have waned in Britain. Yet the available evidence does not suggest that subject orientations have declined significantly in the United Kingdom over the past three decades. Nor do they suggest that major shifts have taken place in Britons' views of political participation.

In this regard, we should keep in mind the deep historical roots of the deferential political culture. Even within this century, males and females who fell short of the property requirement were denied the vote until, respectively, 1918 and 1928. Until 1948, university graduates and owners of businesses enjoyed the privilege of an extra vote. We cannot expect a nation—especially a gradualist one like Britain—to be rapidly transformed into a participatory culture when it held off so long the most elemental requisites of electoral egalitarianism.

Britons remain significantly deferential. Notwithstanding their adverse economic conditions in comparison with much of the rest of Europe, in several polls taken in the 1970s the British registered greater satisfaction with their circumstances than did citizens in other Western European countries.[6] In one mid-1970s survey, only around 20 percent of respondents said that they would engage in civil disobedience.[7] The same study also discovered that citizens overwhelmingly support strong actions against protestors, including stiff jail sentences.[8] Britons also grant unusual legitimacy to the police. A 1982 survey of popular confidence in major institutions in the United Kingdom, United States, France, West Germany, and Italy revealed that the police enjoyed the highest trust—except in the United States, where they ranked second behind the military.[9] But the 86 percent of Britons with a high regard for

[6] Richard Rose, "Ordinary People in Extraordinary Economic Circumstances," in *Challenge to Government*, edited by author (London: Sage, 1978), as cited by Dennis Kavanagh, *British Politics: Continuities and Change* (Oxford: Oxford University Press, 1985), p. 48.

[7] Alan C. Marsh, *Protest and Political Consciousness* (London: Sage, 1978), p. 118, as cited by Kavanagh, *British Politics: Continuities and Change*, p. 48.

[8] Marsh, *Protest and Political Consciousness*, as cited by Rose, *Politics in England: Persistence and Change* (Boston: Little, Brown, 1986), p. 124.

[9] Rose, *Politics in England: Persistence and Change*, p. 135.

the police outstripped the comparable figure for citizens of the other countries by, respectively, 10, 22, 15, and 18 percent.

On the other hand, Britons thought the least of institutions through which citizens can conceivably influence public affairs. Only Italians gave less credence to the legislative branch than did Britons. And Britons disclosed lower esteem for the press than did respondents in the other countries. The 26 percent in Britain who registered confidence in trade unions fell seven percent short of the comparable U.S. figure and fully 10 percent below that for France and Germany.

Slippage on Several Fronts

A number of features of the British political system suggest that participation has fallen off over the past several years. The whole move toward devolution of some central government powers to Scotland and Wales collapsed after the failure of referendums on that issue in 1979. The proposals called for separate assemblies in Edinburgh and Cardiff that would pass legislation fitting within the devolved powers.

The Welsh referendum lost by a huge margin. The Scottish vote carried by a slim majority, with 51.6 to 48.4 percent in favor. However, the terms of the referendum stipulated that a majority of eligible voters must support devolution before it takes effect. All this has not spelled the end of frustrated national aspirations for Scots. A 1987 Mori survey taken for Scottish Television indicated that 47 percent of voters continue to support devolution, while fully 33 percent want outright independence. Scottish rejection of the Thatcher hegemony does not help much either. In the 1987 election only 10 of Scotland's 72 seats went to the Conservatives. This turn of events even left the government scurrying to find five Scots capable of filling the ministerial posts in the Scottish Office.

A separate Parliament in Belfast, called Stormont, operated in Northern Ireland from 1921 until its suspension in 1972. This body enacted legislation in a host of fields in which various Irish ministries administered the affairs of state. The *line departments*—those with direct responsibility for the operation of government programs—included Home Affairs, Development, Education, Agriculture, Commerce, and Health and Social Services. Of course, acts of Westminster took precedence over those of Stormont in all fields. And Stormont was prohibited from involving itself in legislative areas that remained under the direct control of Westminster.

The events of the late 1960s and early 1970s made the devolution of legislative authority to Northern Ireland unworkable. The Catholic minority simply refused to remain under the sway of the Protestant majority. The fact that the latter outnumbered the former two to one made it highly unlikely that the transition to some legislative institution with built-in safeguards of effective representation for Catholics would occur rapidly. Thus, Whitehall has run the province directly since 1972.

Beneath the question of political participation in Ireland lies the economic one. Catholics find it extremely difficult to participate in the economy through meaningful and adequate employment. In 1987, the unemployment rate for Catholics remained twice that for Protestants, bringing the total jobless rate in Northern Ireland to over 20 percent. Increasingly, Irish-Catholics in the United States have encouraged American investors to withdraw their funds from Northern Irish subsidiaries that do not observe the "McBride Principles"—a series of guidelines for eliminating job discrimination against Catholics. Partially in response to the McBride movement, Whitehall tightened its own sanctions against Northern Irish firms that practice discrimination in fall 1987.

Defense Secretary Roy Mason, with the army in Belfast, in August 1975.
    SOURCE: Bernard Donoughue, *Prime Minister* (London: Jonathan Cape Inc., 1987). Courtesy of Press Association.

While a great deal of ambiguity has always surrounded devolution of authority to the provinces, local governments in the various parts of Britain have until recently enjoyed a relatively high degree of legitimacy.[10] To an extent this owes to the association of local government with the Conservative and Liberal parties. During various Labour administrations since the war, local governments became vehicles of resistance to the socialist tendency to centralize policymaking and standardize programs.

Mrs. Thatcher's approach to local government has revealed that the Conservatives perhaps lacked a dedication to local government in itself. We find, in fact, that the current Conservative government has displayed a penchant for centralization that increasingly resembles the mindset of Labour in the bygone era. However, Mrs. Thatcher's efforts toward centralization differ from Labour's in two important respects. First, while Labour governments have had expansive perspectives on the role of local governments in the furtherance of social welfare and the standardization of services, Mrs. Thatcher has taken an extremely restrictive view. Second, the Thatcher government has experienced a great deal more success at imposing its will on local authorities than has any Labour government.

Mrs. Thatcher has achieved her great success through political maneuvers that have altered the constitutional position of local authorities.[11] As a result, the viability of these institutions as outlets for political participation has diminished immensely. The steps in-

[10] George W. Jones, "The Crisis in British Central-Local Government Relationships," *Governance: An International Journal of Policy and Administration*, 1 (1988):165–67.

[11] Jones, 171.

clude the following: (1) the Conservatives have shifted the effective locus of authority in the unitary state from Parliament to "the government," meaning the cabinet, thereby enabling it to force conformity from local authorities even in the absence of express legislation; (2) they have placed statutory limits on the discretion of local authorities, thereby reducing the local authorities to the handling of administrative matters as distinct from policy issues; (3) they have sharply curtailed the latitude for local authorities to determine their own expenditure levels; (4) they have abolished elective councils—for instance, in Greater London and six metropolitan county areas—and often shifted the residual powers to central departments or appointive boards rather than to other elective local jurisdictions.

To add to this litany, the Conservatives have now moved to abolish property taxes entirely and replace these with a "community charge." Known to its opponents as a poll tax, the latter is a per-head levy against all voting-age residents of a locale. It is a highly regressive measure: It will place a much greater burden on the poor than does a property tax. The Conservatives have embraced this approach, however, as a means to har-

---

The story of the years since 1979 is of increasing centralization. Local authorities feel that their autonomy and discretion have been diminished. . . . The new feature of Mrs. Thatcher's government is that it has jettisoned previous conservative beliefs in a balanced or mixed constitution, based on a sharing of powers between a number of institutions, in favor of a more continental, or even Marxist, notion of state as a single unified entity, whose only alternative is the market. Ideology has driven this government to an extent never seen in British Conservative government before. Its ideology of fundamental change has led to challenge the very foundations of local government.

SOURCE: George W. Jones, *Governance*, p. 176.

---

ness Labour-dominated local authorities. As the theory goes, councils that spend generously on social programs will run the risk of antagonizing the very voters whom they seek to help—the poor.

One bromide that appears in the U.S. press asserts that Mrs. Thatcher has introduced an age of "popular capitalism" in the United Kingdom. We might infer from this nomenclature that the privatization of former public corporations has increased the involvement of the average citizen in the ownership of shares in British business. In turn, giving people "a piece of the rock" conceivably would enhance their self-reliance and sense of political efficacy.

Some of the hard data run against this inference, notwithstanding its intuitive appeal. As we saw in Chapter 3, the Thatcher years have actually heralded an abrupt halt to the wider distribution of wealth down to lower strata in society. Further, the sale of shares to rank-and-file citizens does not mean that they will retain them.[12] This has been the case with several of Mrs. Thatcher's major share sales over the past several years. Within a few months, the original number of shareholders tends to collapse to a much more modest figure: for British Aerospace, from some 158,000 to 27,000; Amersham International, from 62,000 to 10,000; Jaguar, 125,000 to 49,000; British Telecom, 2.2 to 1.6 million; British Airways, 1.2 million to 420,000.

It becomes obvious that many small shareholders quickly sell their stocks to larger shareholders. They choose, in other words, to pocket quickly the difference between the low price set by the government to make the shares attractive and the actual return that they can command on the open market. Institutional investors—large pension funds, in-

[12] Roger Buckland, "The Costs and Returns of Privatization of Nationalized Industries," *Public Administration*, 65 (1987):241–58.

surance companies and trusts—quickly vacuum up the discarded shares. For instance,
while the ratio of equities in institutional versus private hands reached 1.8 in 1985, it
stood at 1.2 in 1970. Thus Mrs. Thatcher
must go a long way before returning "popular capitalism" to its 1970 level.

Indeed, one major share sale pointed up the
degree to which institutional buying can actually pose threats to national security. One
week after the October 1987 stock market
crash, Mrs. Thatcher persisted in selling the
32 percent that the U.K. government held in
British Petroleum (BP). The uncertainities
brought on by the crash, however, had scared
off most individual investors. Institutional
buyers moved in at bargain-basement rates.
Leading the pack was the Kuwait government, which ended up with over 20 percent
ownership of BP. A year later, the U.K. Department of Trade and Industry, citing the
obvious national security issue, ordered Kuwait to divest itself of over half its shares.

In assessing popular capitalism, we should
also keep in mind the fact that Mrs. Thatcher's stress of the service sector over manufacturing propelled a 24 percent decrease in
union membership during her first two terms.
The United Kingdom would require a great
deal more individual ownership of stocks
than actually presented itself from share sales
to offset the losses of leverage suffered by
workers through the precipitous decline of
the unions.

Limits to the Public Right to Know

As we saw in Chapter 3, Britain has no bill
of rights. Of course, this does not mean that
Britons entirely lack freedoms comparable to
those enjoyed by Americans. They simply
cannot call upon an established guarantee of
their rights. This constitutional condition
bears clear implications for political participation; in no small measure, democracy runs

on the public's knowledge about how the
government operates and how it disposes of
the various matters that it treats.

The strong traditions of freedom of the
press and the public's right to know that prevail in the United States greatly contribute to
the participatory nature of American politics.
However, many influential Britons believe
that such openness is, at best, untidy and
inefficient, at worst, dangerous to the security
of the state. Without a written constitution or
even statutory vehicles such as the freedom
of information legislation available in the
United States, those who become disturbed
over government secrecy find little recourse.
The dominant elite's views regarding how
much the public needs to know determine
almost entirely the contours of what the government will expose to outside scrutiny.

More than anything else, section 2 of the
1911 Official Secrets Act stands in the way of
freer access to government information. This
act strictly proscribes civil servants from providing information of any kind to those outside government unless specifically authorized to do so by their superiors. As a result,
interactions between Whitehall bureaucrats
and journalists technically operate within the
confines of official briefings by a department's information staff, and severely limited
sessions with line civil servants. Similar strictures apply to officials' interactions with interest groups and members of Parliament.

There are ways of getting around this system. Top journalists frequently enjoy informal ties with the Whitehall elite that permit
them to take top officials to lunch and extract
information on an off-the-record basis.
Many relationships become strong enough
that the officials will take phone calls from
journalists or send them government documents through the mail in plain brown enve-
lopes. The upper echelons of Whitehall turn a
blind eye to many of these activities. In fact,
many at the upper reaches will participate in

the unauthorized sharing of information—often for reasons that relate to intramural conflicts with other top mandarins or severe differences with the political leadership. However, such "tactical leaking" can severely damage officials' credibility and careers if they become indiscreet.

Recent events have placed the conventions surrounding this cat-and-mouse game under severe strain. First, the Ponting case arose in 1984, involving Mr. Clive Ponting, a rapidly rising assistant secretary in the Ministry of Defense who had received kudos and an honor—Officer in the Order of the British Empire—from Mrs. Thatcher for his work in an earlier efficiency exercise in his department. Ponting had moved to a unit responsible for determining, among other things, what type of information should be made available to Parliament.

Part of Ponting's work involved advising ministers on how much they should disclose to the House of Commons Foreign Affairs Committee, which was conducting an inquiry into Britain's war with Argentina over the Falkland Islands in 1982. In the course of this activity, Ponting became convinced that ministers would have to reveal an embarrassing fact: The Argentinean cruiser, General Belgrano, had actually turned away from the British exclusionary zone surrounding the Falklands before it was attacked and sunk. When it became clear that the government would not divulge this information—indeed, that it would continue to tell Parliament the opposite—Ponting took matters into his own hands and sent copies of the relevant documents to a Labour MP.

The government readily traced the leak to Ponting and chose to prosecute him. The justice who presided at the trial gave strict instructions to the jury. He even impugned Ponting's defense that he had only the interest of the state in mind, by telling the jurors that there was no distinction between the interests of the government of the day and the state. Unswayed, the jury acquitted Ponting. In the process, they raised fresh questions about the future viability of section 2 of the Official Secrets Act.

We discussed in Chapter 3 the successor to this case. It involved Peter Wright's revelations in the book *Spycatcher* of the inner operations of MI5, Britain's highly secret domestic security agency. After tortuous legal proceedings that had the crown arguing its case in Australia, Hong Kong, and New Zealand as well as in England, the juridical standing of official secrecy has eroded further. Now, even a crown prosecution that invoked an alleged "lifelong duty of confidentiality" rather than the Official Secrets Act has failed. The British tradition of uneven enforcement of secrecy had not helped the crown's case; during proceedings in Australia, Wright's attorney revealed that the government had chosen not to halt the publication of a book appearing in 1981 that contained the essence of his client's revelations about MI5.

Signs of strain have developed elsewhere in the U.K. tradition of selective transmission of information. In fall 1986, two quality newspapers, *The Guardian* and the newly formed *Independent,* decided to take on one of the most venerable institutions in the British system of secret government: the daily briefing given to select members of the press—called the "lobby correspondents"—given by the prime minister's press secretary. The two papers claimed that such sessions often involve government manipulation of the news—even "disinformation" that deliberately misleads the public. They have chosen to boycott these briefings until they can at least attribute the source of the material they receive from the press secretary. Currently, lobby correspondents must employ euphemisms such as "a Whitehall source" so as to obscure the fact that they have been spoon-fed by No. 10.

More alarming, very serious differences

Tale of two cities

Cartoon from *The Guardian*, December 3, 1986, contrasts Ronald Reagan's response to the appearance of administration wrongdoing in connection with the Iran-Contra Affair with Margaret Thatcher's refusal to launch an inquiry into Peter Wright's allegations concerning MI5.

have arisen between the Thatcher government and the British Broadcasting Corporation (BBC). As a state-owned broadcasting system, the BBC has earned a worldwide reputation for even-handed coverage of public affairs. The maintenance of this record requires, presumably, that the network render critical assessments of those government positions and actions that do not stand up well under analysis. Normally, British governments grouse when they believe that BBC has slipped into excessively negative coverage. Yet they generally eschew specific actions that might cross the line between displeasure and interference.

The Thatcher government has changed the atmosphere very substantially by in fact making it increasingly difficult for the BBC to do its job. Here, the winter of 1986–87 marked a low point for BBC. In October 1986, Norman Tebbitt—then a cabinet minister and chairman of the Conservative Party—issued a scathing attack of BBC's coverage of the U.S. bombing raid on Libya that had taken place earlier that year. Several other interventions followed this one.

In the first rounds, Alasdair Milne, the BBC director general, seemed to have effectively held off Mr. Tebbit. But the government moved with full force in January 1987. In one installment of a six-part series on freedom of information in the United Kingdom called "Secret Society," the BBC planned to disclose details of an intelligence program whose existence, if generally known, could embarrass the government acutely. Called "Zircon," the project cost some 500 million pounds, allocated to build a spy satellite for the United Kingdom.

Theoretically, Zircon would make Britain less reliant upon the United States for intelligence. However, two aspects of the program made it highly vulnerable to public criticism. First, the government had kept Zircon under a veil of strict secrecy—even keeping Parliament in the dark. This violated a concordat it had struck with Parliament. Specifically, it had agreed to notify in confidence the chairman of the House of Commons Public Accounts Committee whenever it embarked on a secret project totaling over 250 million pounds during its life. Second, the satellite itself was judged as nearly technologically obsolete. (Indeed, the government abandoned Zircon entirely in summer 1987.)

When the government found that BBC's "Secret Society" series would reveal the existence of Zircon, it put pressure on director general Milne to ban the film. However, a reporter who had worked on the series chose to publish the essence of the Zircon story in his magazine, *The New Statesman*. In what appeared as a vindictive step, the government then raided the BBC offices in Glasgow where the series was produced and confiscated all of the tapes of the programs and the film from which they were derived. Only a few days before, Milne had resigned as director general in response to an invitation from chairman of the BBC board—a Thatcher appointee who had only recently assumed his position—to leave quietly.

CONCLUSION

This chapter has probed the important area of governance that relates to political culture. It observed at the outset that democratic systems must seek a delicate balance between the authority of the state and its responsiveness to the public will. It also noted that Britain has erred traditionally in favor of the former. In fact, scholars have characterized it as a deferential political culture in which citizens, although reasonably well oriented to political participation, tend to give the benefit of the doubt to political authorities.

The turmoil of the 1970s and 1980s does not seem to have altered this situation tremendously. With respect to political socialization, immense class differences persist. However, these do not translate well into class consciousness. Only region and race loom as threats to the politics of deference—the former because of the degree to which the North has lagged behind the South in economic recovery, and the latter because

Britain only gradually has come to terms with the fact that it is now a multiracial society.

With respect to participation, Britons remain more strongly oriented to support of the regime than to participation in the political process. Indeed, a number of areas present themselves in which the citizenry seems to have lost ground in the past decade. Despite their strong national feelings, the Scots and the Welsh have abandoned hope of devolution. The Catholics in Northern Ireland continue to bottle up their aspirations in face of the impasse between the Protestant majority and the U.K. government. Mrs. Thatcher has beaten down assertive local authorities and substantially altered their constitutional position. Economic forces and public impatience with labor strife have led to a dramatic decline in union membership.

Some find cause for celebration in Mrs. Thatcher's selling off of state-owned enterprises. However, the data suggest that privatization has failed to usher in the era of "popular capitalism." More alarming, the Ponting, Wright, lobby correspondent, and BBC cases suggest that recognition of the public's need to know runs up against intransigent opposition from the Conservatives and Whitehall.

References and Suggested Readings

ALMOND, GABRIEL A., and SIDNEY VERBA. *The Civic Culture: Political Attitudes and Democracy in Five Nations*. Princeton: Princeton University Press, 1963.

BUCKLAND, ROGER. "The Costs and Returns of Privatization of Nationalized Industries." *Public Administration* 65 (1987): 241–58.

BUDGE, IAN, and DAVID MCKAY et al. *The Changing British Political System: Into the 1990s*. 2nd ed. London: Longman, 1988.

JONES, GEORGE W. "The Crisis in British Central-Local Government Relationships." *Governance: An International Journal of Policy and Administration* 1 (1988): 162–83.

KAVANAGH, DENNIS. "Political Culture in Great Britain: The Decline of the Civil Culture." In *Civic Culture Revisited,* eds. Gabriel A. Almond and Sidney Verba. Boston: Little, Brown, 1979.

———. *British Politics: Continuities and Change.* Oxford: Oxford University Press, 1985.

MARSH, ALAN C. *Protest and Political Consciousness.* London: Sage, 1978.

NORTON, PHILIP. *The British Polity.* London: Longman, 1984.

PONTING, CLIVE. *The Right to Know: The Inside Story of the Belgrano Affair.* London: Sphere, 1985.

ROSE, RICHARD. "Ordinary People in Extraordinary Economic Circumstances." In *Challenge to Government.* London: Sage, 1978.

———. *Politics in England: Persistence and Change.* Boston: Little, Brown, 1986.

MILLER, W. L. "Social Class and Party Choice in England: A New Analysis." *British Journal of Political Science* 8 (1978): 257–84.

WRIGHT, PETER. *Spycatcher: The Candid Autobiography of a Senior Intelligence Officer.* New York: Viking, 1987.

5

Parties and Elections

In the United States, pursuit of the presidency has reached such proportions that campaigns for party nominations and the election appear to drag on interminably. The paramountcy of the presidential race over congressional elections reflects the U.S. voters' greater interest in persons than in competing political parties. With the separation of powers, a party can fail to gain control of even one house of Congress—as the Republicans have in the majority of elections since World War II—and still determine the national agenda through possession of the presidency.

The visitor to Britain would be astounded during the first few weeks after an election. Discussions turn immediately to party matters. They concentrate on how the winners as a team are gearing up to seize control of and redirect the ship of state, or in the case of a reelected government, retooling to ensure the maximum possible thrust from their renewed mandate. There is also a surprising amount of discussion of the losers. Newspapers devote pages of space, and TV and radio networks dedicate hours of time, to analyses of the efforts of the vanquished to regroup and launch upon the arduous task of altering their organization and appeal so as to better prepare themselves for the next election.

Of course, the victorious party—provided it has an absolute majority of seats—need not face the voters until the expiration of the five-year life of a parliament. Thus, the public fascination with intramural party politics even in the wake of an election tells us something. An assessment of electoral politics in Britain must go beyond the party system and voting behavior. It must also examine several issues associated with the internal operation of political parties. These include the patterns of membership, relations between the leadership and the rank and file, and the effects of intramural dynamics on the process whereby a party adapts its appeal in response to changes in the electoral environment.

In this chapter we will take on two tasks. First, we will examine the various issues surrounding party organization—especially those that have assumed special importance for the Conservatives, Labour, the Liberals and the Social Democrats in the Thatcher era. We will also look at the very substantial differences in party platforms, especially between the Conservatives and Labour. Second, we will outline key elements of the operation of the electoral system in Britain—in particular, insofar as these amplify trends in voting behavior. To this end, we will take a close look at the 1987 election in an effort to ascertain the condition and direction of party politics in Britain.

PARTIES

Origins

There are now three main parties in Britain. These are the Conservatives, who currently form the government, Labour, the largest party in the opposition, and the Social and Liberal Democrats, a new party formed in 1988 through the amalgamation of the Liberal Party and the Social Democratic Party. A fourth party, commonly referred to as the "Owenites," consists of former members of the Social Democratic Party who refused to join with the Liberals.

Both the Conservative and Liberal parties emerged in the nineteenth century. Their development coincided with the expansion of the voting franchise. It also marked prime ministers' heightened awareness of the need to base their governments on a relatively reliable corps of MPs. A centralized party machinery assisted MPs in competing for the votes of the ever-expanding electorate. In exchange, the MPs committed their support to whoever carried their party banner in the House of Commons.

The Conservatives formalized their party in the 1830s, before the Liberals. Those who embraced the Conservative Party tended to uphold the traditions of the aristocracy. Most members of the party's leadership belonged to the nobility or were large landholders. For this reason, the party inherited the label

"Tories" from their eighteenth-century antecedents. It stressed the values of agricultural interests, the Church of England and the constitutional status quo that the Tories had championed. However, the Conservative Party differed from the Tories in the degree to which it tempered its stances in order to attract the support of newly enfranchised segments of society.

The party experienced a period of decline with the defeat of agricultural interests upon passage of the Corn Laws in 1846. However, it eventually recovered and learned along the way how to package its traditional values in ways that would appeal to the continually broadening electorate. The party consistently resisted political and social reforms, but it always seemed to know when it should make accommodations. After World War II it embraced views of welfare programs and the role of state ownership of various industrial sectors which did not differ that radically from the stances taken by the other parties.

The Liberal Party also developed only gradually into a formal organization. After the 1868 election—the first following the 1867 expansion of the franchise—the party took full shape. It consisted of members from three separate political traditions.

First, the "Whigs" represented those who enjoyed the franchise before the reforms beginning in 1832. While the Whigs had constantly struggled with the Tories over parliamentary reform, many of their policies derived from the peculiar preoccupations of wealthy merchants and industrialists. Second, "Liberals" became a force in the great movements of the mid-1800s. They fought for the expansion of the franchise and the abolition of the Corn Laws. They rallied around the belief that individual—as opposed to group—concerns should govern politics. They decried the tendency for groups based on special interests, such as the landholders and those involved in commerce, to dominate elections and Parliament. Third, "Radicals" took the Liberal suspicion of politics based on special interests one step further. They believed that ultimately individual interests—rather than those of groups within society—should determine the great issues of state. This required a process of mobilizing mass involvement in politics and revamping parliamentary government to assure that legislation actually reflected the will of the majority.

Encompassing these three disparate traditions meant that the Liberal Party lacked the natural constituency that the Conservatives enjoyed. After taking formalized shape in 1868, it did establish itself as the first modern political machine in Britain, organizing itself on a representational basis throughout the country, and holding a large annual conference that actually adopted policies the leadership took seriously. Further, its members in the House of Commons displayed an unprecedented degree of discipline.

In many respects, the Liberal Party became a victim of its own success. Among its many accomplishments, it established the doctrine of *free trade* (which assured that the working class would enjoy growing supplies of relatively affordable food), worked to extend the franchise to all males, laid the groundwork for the welfare state, and imparted legal recognition to the trade union movement. Taken together, these policies both strengthened the place of the working class in British society and legitimized its efforts toward collective action. After World War I, the Liberal Party began to yield to Labour. The latter had become the natural party of those who had benefited the most from the former's policies.

The Labour Party started in 1900 as a political movement called the Labour Representation Committee. This organization consisted originally of trade union officials and socialists working to complete the expansion of the franchise. It also sought to promote working-class candidates for Parliament.

The Labour Representation Committee became the Labour Party in 1906. In the same year, 29 Labour candidates won seats in the House of Commons. The party drew 22 percent of the votes—against 12 percent for the Liberals—in the first election (1918) in which the franchise extended to all adult males. In several subsequent elections it enjoyed a somewhat smaller edge over the Liberals. However, it pulled ahead decisively in 1935, with 38 versus 6 percent of the vote. From 1918 through to 1935, the non-Conservative vote split so that the Conservatives—either by themselves or in coalition—managed to stay in power. Labour, however, won a landslide victory in 1945 and formed its first government. It subsequently formed governments after the elections of 1964, 1966, and February and October of 1974.

The Labour Party has struggled with ideological baggage that has limited its ability to attract voters in the middle of the political spectrum. Through the 1950s, its commitment to further nationalization of industries and expansion of the welfare state stood at variance with the mood of the country. Harold Wilson's ability in steering the party to more pragmatic approaches to its long-range agenda contributed greatly to the recovery in its political fortunes in the 1960s. However, the party never fully shed the literalism of its commitment to socialism. For instance, it has never rescinded Clause IV of its 1929 constitution calling for "common ownership of the means of production, distribution, and exchange, and . . . popular administration and control of each industry and service."

Since the 1960s, the party has also promoted several causes which, however worthy, have tended to arouse fears among voters in the center. Among these are its advocation of Britain's renouncing nuclear weapons and barring them from the United Kingdom. The party also has gone to lengths in promoting the rights of women, ethnic and racial minorities, and gays. In the United States, the Democratic Party's commitment to the protection of similar groups has earned them the accusation that they have succumbed to special-interest politics. In the United Kingdom, a blunter term—Loony Left—points up the degree to which average Britons remain somewhat less sensitized to the extent of discrimination than Americans.

The efforts to establish the Social Democratic Party (SDP) emerged after Labour lost power in 1979. Disillusionment among moderate Labour MPs and activists with the prospects of a Labour Party that was increasingly under the sway of the left spawned the move. The SDP did not formally organize itself as a separate party until 1981. Before the election of 1983, it had acquired 28 MPs, all but one of whom had defected from Labour. After two relatively weak performances in the elections of 1983 and 1987, it combined with the Liberal Party in 1988.

Organization

Any American observer of British party politics will soon note one phenomenon: The Conservative and Labour parties have taken increasingly radical positions since the 1970s. This owes in no small part to their different ways of operating. In the 1960s and 1970s, Labour's membership pushed hard for a democratization of their party's internal procedures. By the early 1980s the party had become more responsive to rank-and-file participation; but this had the negative effect of frightening many traditional party supporters. Meanwhile, the Conservative Party made virtually no advances toward democratization.

The heightened accommodation within the Labour Party to strident voices opened it to the accusation that it had sold out to the "loony" segments of society. Through a relentless process of attrition, moderate Labourites have felt increasingly isolated in their own party. This takes us far in explaining why the Social Democratic Party emerged in 1981. It also accounts for the degree to which the Conservative Party under Mrs. Thatcher has departed from centrist positions. The only other party realistically capable of forming a government appears to have slipped into doctrinal disarray.

The Conservatives functioned in a more hierarchical manner than did the Labour Party—even in times when the latter kept its house in relatively strict order. The Conservatives' disciplined style has combined in an especially potent way with the slippage in Labour's appeal to the center. It has allowed radical Conservatives to weigh in heavily in their party and swing the balance further to the right.

Within parties, *wards* are the building blocks of the organizations. Ward boundaries roughly correspond to the electoral divisions of local governments. Parliamentary constituency organizations thus brigade together several wards. At both levels, parties hold general meetings, elect executive committees, chairpersons and secretaries and, in many cases, retain a paid agent.

At the national level, each party holds an annual conference in the early fall. Each constituency sends one or more delegates, depending on its size, to this meeting. The conference also includes the representatives of affiliated groups such as women, youth and trade union members. Here rests one of the acute difficulties of the Labour Party: The block of delegates either directly representing or controlled by unions makes up approximately five-sixths of the annual conference. This fact, and its concomitant effect on the tone and actions of conferences, contributes greatly to Labour's difficulties in appealing to the center. The decline in union membership over the past decade along with the militant stances of organized labor have made the average voter skeptical about the legitimacy of Labour's system of representation. Union-dominated annual conferences tend to make them downright skittish.

Each of the parties maintains central bureaucracies in London. Between elections, these attend to various functions necessary for keeping the party fit for the next contest. The central offices can hold considerable sway over constituency associations—especially if the party has launched a program of reforms to improve its performance. In this regard, local party agents work at least as much to the agenda set in London as to constituency needs. The central bureaucracies also include research capabilities.

Here the Conservative Party has enjoyed an edge. It operates two policy staffs. The oldest—the Conservative Research Department—provides some 12 to 15 professionals. These advise ministers on policy within their portfolios. In the period between 1974 to 1979 during which the party was in opposition, the research department played an important role in supporting shadow ministers. Indeed, it helped ministers devise detailed plans that quickly came to the fore once Mrs. Thatcher became prime minister. Meanwhile, the Center for Policy Studies—created in 1974 with the enthusiastic support of Mrs. Thatcher—issued a plethora of papers that contributed greatly to the ideological reorientation of the party. None of the other parties' research facilities have attained the level of funding, the clarity of mission or the effectiveness of these two units.

This brings us to the nub of the organizational issue as it affects the coherence of the three main parties. The leaders—who assume the prime ministership if their party forms the government—differ as to the sway that they hold over their organizations. The Conservative leader—currently Mrs. Thatcher—appoints the party chairperson. This person, in turn, presides at party conventions and directs the *Central Office* in London. Party conventions do not select the leader of the party. Instead, a meeting of the parliamentary party—all Conservative MPs—elects the leader. In addition, the chairperson of the party tightly stage-manages annual conferences so that only resolutions conforming to the acceptable line reach the floor.

Theoretically, the Central Office, whose staff retain their positions at the pleasure of the chairperson and the leader, shares power with the *National Union,* an umbrella organization of constituency associations. However, the Central Office has over the past several years largely eclipsed the authority of the National Union. In fact, a 1987 rule change provides that Central Office guidelines for constituency operations—termed "model rules"—take precedence over all other procedural norms.

Nothwithstanding the strength of her control over the Conservative Party through the Central Office, Mrs. Thatcher did come in for a surprise in fall 1987. Norman Tebbit—the minister we met in Chapter 4 who had fired several shots across the British Broadcasting Corporation's bow during the buildup to the election—relinquished his cabinet membership after the 1987 election. He also revealed that he wanted to resign as chairman of the party. Mrs. Thatcher hoped to maneuver Lord Young into the post.

Young—though also a minister—had never run for election. He could not even serve in the cabinet had Mrs. Thatcher not appointed him to the House of Lords in 1984. Mrs. Thatcher had increasingly relied upon him for alternate advice. At various times during the 1987 campaign he even began to vie with Tebbit for the limelight as the prime minister's principal political adviser. However, a revolt within her cabinet scotched the Young appointment. Young had just received a major cabinet promotion when Mrs. Thatcher moved him from the Department of Employment to the Department of Trade and Industry. Ministers believed that entirely too much power would be concentrated in his hands. They forced Mrs. Thatcher to appoint another minister to the post.

Even though the Labour Party has always given obeisance to the rhetoric of a mass party, it managed itself along hierarchical lines until the early 1980s. Ironically, the changes adopted at that time constituted a delayed reaction to the pressures for democratization that had built up beginning in the late 1960s. However, these reforms took so long to be realized that the public mood had changed by the time they received assent—often grudging—from the party leadership. This turn of events has put the party in an awkward situation. On the one hand, it continues to grapple with the manifest untidiness of implementing broader participation. On

Not even Mrs. Thatcher could get away with giving a cabinet minister a major portfolio *and* chairmanship of the party. *The Guardian* depicts the Lord Young episode (October 30, 1987).

the other, democratization no longer engages the attention of the public to the degree that it did during the late 1960s and most of the 1970s. Labour has found itself in that least enviable of situations: following an agenda that has become passé—or worse, unpopular.

Until the changes in rules, the parliamentary party elected the leader—as remains the case with the Conservatives. The National Conference theoretically established party policy. In reality, the parliamentary party determined the timing and the substance of Labour's efforts to press these objectives. On the other hand, the Labour leader has not usually enjoyed the control over the party headquarters that the Conservative leader has over the Central Office. Instead, the National Executive Committee (NEC) maintains a strong influence over the party headquarters.

The annual conference elects the members of NEC, which includes backbench MPs, union leaders and other party activists in addition to members of the parliamentary party leadership. The two main officers of NEC—the chairman, who normally holds the post for only one year, and the general secretary—both serve at its pleasure. Thus, even before democratization, these arrangements limited the usefulness of party headquarters to the leadership, even during elections.

Substantial reforms in the early 1980s followed three general lines. First, local constituency selection committees received enhanced powers with respect to the choosing and reviewing of candidates for the House of Commons. Since 1981, all approved candidates, even sitting MPs, must face mandatory reselection proceedings before receiving the *nihil obstat* of their constituency association. Second, NEC has increasingly taken to itself the writing of the party program and manifesto. Third, according to a procedure adopted in 1981, an electoral college, rather

. . . In the final week of the [1974] campaign . . . a number of operations handled by the Labour party organisation, then located in Transport House in Smith Square, went sadly, if hilariously, wrong. The arrangements for the party leader's meetings and of media coverage were often appalling. In the middle of the campaign Transport House completely ran out of paper and was therefore unable to print and issue enough press handouts (officials had failed to foresee that an election campaign would require extra paper). One of the better senior officials frequently broke down and wept. An early sign of his feeling stress was when he agitatedly took off his shoes in the middle of a committee or conference; a final sign was when he stormed out of the meeting in his socks. On the Friday after the election Mr. Wilson flew back from his Liverpool constituency with his team while the final results were still being declared and the outcome was as yet unclear. On landing at Heathrow Airport he telephoned Transport House to discover whether the final results would confirm that there would be a Labour Government; however, nobody at party headquarters appeared to be following the results, in which they might have been presumed to have had an interest. Sadly . . . much of the energy as existed in the then upper levels of Transport House was devoted to petty jealousies and internal squabbling, with little apparent concern for the need to unite in order to defeat the Conservatives.

SOURCE: Bernard Donoughue—former adviser to Harold Wilson and James Callaghan in *Prime Minister*, 1987, p. 43.

than the parliamentary party, selects and annually reviews the leader and deputy leader of the party. Within the college, affiliated trade unions claim 40 percent of the members, while the parliamentary party and constituency organizations each have 30 percent of the electors.

Of all the reforms, those centering on the choice and reselection of parliamentary candidates have caused the greatest embarrass-

ment to Labour since their implementation. This became painfully apparent to the party leadership during the buildup to the 1987 election, when selection committees held captive by the far left produced candidates whose very nominations raised grave concerns about the direction of Labour. The situation stemmed largely from the practice whereby branches of the local organization appointed delegates to selection committees. This practice severely limited individual party members' access to the process.

Neil Kinnock achieved an important reform that should mitigate the degree to which radical branches of the party can gain control of the selection process. In fall 1987, he won

But it was Ms. Mary Duffy from Stockton, who gave a vivid description of life in a constituency Labour Party, who roused the conference. "I don't know what kind of delegates you have on your [own local] GMC [General Management Committee] but some of mine are good, some are bad and some are plain stupid," she said.

Her last GMC had been inquorate, the activists, those she described as the "politicals," had turned up but those who had joined the party to be a councilor and the peak of whose ambition was to become Mayor and meet the Queen were more typical. "That's the kind of people we have as delegates. Yours might be totally intellectual, ours are not," she said to laughter. "So when the GMC meets we have very little political debating."

To those that argued that the decision should be left in the hands of the GMC delegates she said: "That is the biggest laugh. We don't debate anything except drainage and repairs. So the idea that it is so democratic for these delegates to come and give their wisdom over the heads of ordinary members is ridiculous." She earned the biggest ovation of the day.

SOURCE: *The Guardian*, September 29, 1987, reporting the remarks of Mrs. Mary Duffy—a delegate to the Labour conference—in support of party reforms.

the party conference over to greater accommodation of the principle of one person, one vote. From now on, any party member will be able to attend a selection meeting. Labour did not entirely abandon special recognition of those affiliated with branches of the party. Nonattached voters will have their ballots weighted so that their aggregate value will not exceed the proportion of nonaffiliated delegates under the old system. For instance, if nonaffiliated delegates constituted three-quarters of the voters under the old system, their votes would only make up for 75 percent of the weighted ballots under the new procedure.

The two smaller parties, the Liberals and the Social Democrats, have only recently merged. Thus, we must wait and see what the contours of the new organization will be. From past performance, however, we can predict that the new framework and its operation will follow relatively democratic contours.

The Liberal Party embraced a participatory approach during the period in which the pressures for democratization were the most intense. The Liberal Party Assembly, as the annual conference was called, played an important role in the discussion and formulation of key policies. However, the party leader and his principal colleagues in Parliament ultimately decided the exact lines of the Liberal agenda. This became clear in the build-up to the 1987 election. The assembly took an abolitionist stance regarding nuclear weapons in fall 1986. Nonetheless, David Steel, the leader, worked out a compromise with David Owen, his Social Democratic Party opposite number. Here the Alliance platform adopted by both parties allowed for retention of a British nuclear capability.

The assembly consisted of an amalgam of constituency, parliamentary party and national organization delegates. A special convention elected the leader. This included constituency representatives chosen by mail ballots of rank-and-file members. Because of the lack of prominence of the parliamentary party in the House of Commons, the central party organization held relatively little sway over constituency associations.

The Social Democratic Party followed a similarly participatory line of governance. A postal ballot to the entire membership selected the chairperson, who presided over the Council for Social Democracy, an executive body that debated the major issues associated with policy and organization. On the other hand, representatives of constituencies selected the leader. As with the Liberals, the leader could take stances on the substance and timing of policy objectives that ran counter to the council.

Platforms

As we have seen, the British vest considerable importance in the process whereby parties arrive at their policy platforms. Annual conferences ratify the central elements of a party's policy agenda. In the case of the Conservatives, the leadership holds very tight rein on proceedings; thus, substantial divisions between the stated policy objectives of the leadership and those of the conference rarely occur. In the other parties, democratization has greatly increased the likelihood of major differences between the two levels.

The higher democratization of the Labour and Liberal and Social Democratic parties in comparison to the Conservative Party comes at a cost of electoral appeal. This owes largely to the fact that the very menu of issues that receives attention in Conservative platforms tends to reflect more faithfully the concerns that might serve as focuses of public debate. In short, the Conservatives have occupied the natural center in the United Kingdom. The other parties must work harder to demonstrate to the electorate that they too can lay claim to the moderate middle between extremes. The process of democratization has made this task increasingly difficult.

British political scientists have found that the bulk of voters tend to focus on family-centered issues.[1] In this respect, economic issues such as the cost of living, prices, and employment always loom large. Politics starts with bread-and-butter issues. Even those other matters that might become important in the wider community, like housing, crime, and immigration, take a back seat to whether the family lacks adequate take-home pay or finds its future economic security threatened.

Within the complex array of issues contending for attention from individual parties, thematic emphases emerge over the years. For instance, a study of party manifestoes between 1924 and 1983 revealed that the Conservatives consistently played up the Commonwealth, regional priorities, individual enterprise and efficient administration. Labour, on the other hand, stressed control of the economy, social justice and support of international cooperation.

Another study examined to what degree the two parties' platforms resonated with the public preoccupations of the day during elections between 1950 and 1979. It found that the Conservatives adopted positions that corresponded to the public mood more often than did Labour. However, two issues, if looming large in a given election, could lessen the Conservatives' natural advantage: redistribution of wealth and social welfare.

The reemergence of the Liberal Party as a significant political force and the launching of the Social Democratic Party changed this bipolar competition for the center very substantially. As we will see in the section following, these two parties—separately in 1983 and together under the Alliance in 1987—began to appeal to a sizable proportion of middle-of-the-road voters. Their presence on the electoral scene obviously began to crowd both of the main parties out of the center. To date, however, Labour has had the greatest difficulty by far retaining at least some of its presence there.

A comparative look at the 1987 platforms of the three parties (Conservative, Labour and Alliance) underscores this point. Several matters addressed in the platforms hardly rated as burning issues to the bulk of the electorate. Thus, the Conservatives chose in many instances to eschew bold promises of any kind. The government party piously ruminated about its intention to maintain the level of public support of the arts and to encourage contributions from the private sector. Both Labour and Alliance felt compelled to call for major reforms—including creation of a Ministry for Arts. Did they ask themselves how many rank-and-file voters worry about the arts? Did they also anticipate the electorate's view of proposals for another department? Has not much of Mrs. Thatcher's success stemmed from stroking the general public by earnestly agreeing that government needs to shrink?

Other fields suggest themselves in which the two opposition parties came across as overly innovative in areas where most of the electorate seemed decidedly complacent. The Conservatives have taken a number of actions against local governments and the media that infringe upon the principle of local responsiveness and freedom of the press, yet the public has paid scant attention. Nonetheless, both opposition parties argued vigorously for sweeping reforms favoring regional authority and freedom of information. The Conservatives condemned, in general terms, racial discrimination. The two opposition parties introduced legislative proposals de-

[1] Ian Budge and David McKay et al., *The New British Political System: Government and Society in the 1980s* (New York: Longman, 1985), p. 90.

Table 5.1   How the Party Manifestoes Compare

	Conservative	*Labour*	*Alliance*
Industry and employment	More privatization—water and electricity Continued measures to increase competition Legal protection for consumers Encourage self-employment and small businesses Improve community employment programs and training services Under 18s not eligible for benefits if they choose unemployment Regional assistance	Capital repatriation scheme Set up British industrial investment bank Regional development agencies Set up British enterprise to take public stake in firms Encourage cooperatives New Ministry of Science and Technology National economic summit to examine unemployment followed by national economic assessment Reduce jobless by one million in two years 500,000 jobs in infrastructure renewal Early retirement for over 60s Reduce employers' national insurance contributions in target areas 360,000 new jobs and training places 300,000 new jobs in health, education, and caring services	Industrial investment bonds Cabinet industrial policy committee More research funding Reduce unemployment 1 million in three years Capital spending 1.5 billion on schools, hospitals, etc. Incomes strategy backed by counter-inflation tax Cut employers' national insurance contribution 25 percent 200,000 jobs in building and investment Recruitment incentives to encourage companies to take on 270,000 200,000 education and training places Retirement at 62 60,000 jobs in health and social services

signed to address the grievances of specific groups.

In all of this, it appears that the opposition forgot a bitter reality of politics: If the electorate has come to the conclusion that there has been too much change on too many fronts, then the maintenance of the status quo will become the center position. This immediately forces calls for elaborate remedial action out of the mainstream. Thus, the 1987 campaign saw many issues in which both Labour and the Alliance found themselves splitting hairs over reform proposals that proved less than compelling to most voters.

To be sure, several issue areas commanded enough attention that the Conservatives had to put forth specific plans of action. Table 5.1 summarizes the positions staked out by the Conservative and opposition party manifestoes in three policy fields: industry and employment, education, and local government. In each case, the Conservatives, banking on the fact that the public has broadly supported the thrust of their policies, simply advocated more of the same. In the fields of industry and employment, they promised further moves toward reducing government's direct ownership or regulation of economic sectors.

Table 5.1 How the Party Manifestoes Compare (*Continued*)

	Conservative	Labour	Alliance
Education	State school rights to opt out of Local Education Authority control Inner London borough rights to leave the Inner London Education Authority School budgets controlled by heads and governors National core curriculum with testing at 7, 11, and 14 Expand assisted places scheme for fee-paying schools Reform of student grants	Nursery education for all 3 and 4 year olds More investment in schoolbooks, equipment and buildings More access for adults to higher education Abolish assisted places scheme for fee-paying schools Abolish public subsidies to private schools National core curriculum	One-year's preschool education for all Schools to have full charge of their own budgets Unified Ministry of Education, Training and Science Higher education places up 20 percent in five years
Local government	Reduce role of local authorities Poll tax to replace property taxes Standard national business property tax Planning powers transferred to urban development corporations Privatize local services Widdicombe Report implemented	Elected strategic authority for London Consultations on regional devolution for England Maintain existing property tax system Repeal Scottish community charge Annual local elections Local government "Quality Commission"	Transfer of powers from national to local government Elected regional assemblies for England, including London Local income tax instead of property tax

SOURCE: *The Guardian,* May 22, 1987.

They also outlined further efforts to treat chronic unemployment with retraining rather than payment of benefits. The proposals touching upon education and local authorities both built on the Conservative commitment to less latitude in which local authorities might pursue and fund their own policies, and greater reliance on the private sector in provision of services—including schools.

The Conservatives had positioned themselves as custodians of the perspective on the role of the state that had dominated the 1980s—the view that much of what government does should be left to the free market.

This strategy gave the opposition parties two choices. First, they could try to convince the public that they could pursue a better blend of government intervention and encouragement of the free market than could the Conservatives. Second, they could refute the Conservative stance and recommend further efforts on the part of government to direct the operation of the economy.

For the most part, the Labour and Alliance manifestoes leaned toward the second approach. As Table 5.1 suggests, the Labour party in particular put forward a wish list of programs and expenditure proposals. These harked back to Keynesian views of management of the economy, and revealed little effort to accommodate the shift in the public mood toward market-oriented solutions.

The Alliance followed much the same approach. However, their proposals came out in nearly every instance as cheaper—in terms of expenditure—than Labour's. This left the impression that they had simply split the difference between the Conservatives, who made few proposals entailing additional spending, and Labour. Both parties had tried to shift the public's focus back to economic intervention and the social agenda. However, they faced an intractable difficulty: Most Britons, even many who had yet to partake in the good times, believed that Mrs. Thatcher's policies had restored prosperity.

As if this were not enough, the issue of defense represented another area in which the opposition parties faced almost overwhelming odds. It also provides us a clear illustration of the consequences of party democratization. In fall 1986, Labour along with the constituent parties of the Alliance—

the Liberals and the Social Democrats—placed national defense in the center stage as a concession to pressures from their annual conventions. These had all urged strong stances against Britain continuing to maintain its own nuclear force or allowing the United States to base nuclear weapons in the United Kingdom.

Table 5.2 points up the degree to which the Conservatives, Labour, and the Alliance differed on key defense issues. Conservatives appealed to nationalism by insisting that the United Kingdom possess its own deterrent. It also played into the public perception that Britain has more leverage in the world political arena when it aligns itself clearly with the United States than when it does not. Labour tried to pursue the opposite tack—a strategy that would have required a massive reeducation system to succeed.

The Alliance, as was its wont, tried to ply a middle course. It argued for the cancellation of Britain's purchase of Trident—the next generation of submarine-based nuclear weapons—and the modernization of the Po-

Ronald Reagan looks on with bemusement as the Labour Party Conference in Blackpool throws nuclear armaments overboard from the *UK Defence*. A tortured Mrs. Thatcher is on the bow. *The Guardian,* October 3, 1986.

The Blackpool Tea Party

Table 5.2 Comparing the Three Parties' Defence Manifestoes in 1986

	POLARIS	TRIDENT	CRUISE	US BASES	NATO	ARMS CONTROL
ALLIANCE	Still in two minds	Cancel	Limit deployment under "dual key"	Maintain under closer control	Strengthen the European pillar	Promote test moratorium and weapons-free zone
CONSERVATIVE	Phase out for Trident	Continue to deployment	Continue Nato deployment plan	Maintain under present rules	Support status quo	Seek multilateral cuts while continuing tests
LABOUR	Decommission unconditionally	Cancel	Remove from UK	Maintain without nuclear weapons	Promote new non-nuclear strategy	Stop testing and work for European weapons-free zone

SOURCE: *The Guardian*, October 29, 1986.

laris system. It also would have permitted U.S. cruise missiles to remain in the United Kingdom. However, it would insist that Britain share, under a "dual key" agreement, authority over actual use of these missiles.

The Alliance strategy came apart. On the one hand, the Liberal party conference in September 1986 had voted for complete abolition of Britain's nuclear capability. On the other, David Owen, the Social Democratic Party leader, waffled right through to the June 1987 election over whether the United Kingdom should actually scrap its commitment to Trident. The spectacle of a party under dual leadership—David Owen and the Liberal's David Steel—and of two minds on the meaning of a common policy did not foster electoral confidence in the Alliance's aptitude for governing.

ELECTIONS

The Rules of the Game

Unlike the United States, Britain has no fixed schedule for national elections. How-ever, each Parliament comes to an end five years after the most recent general election. Prime ministers can ask the monarch to dissolve Parliament at any time during this five-year interval. Dissolution automatically starts the wheels in motion for an election, which must take palce within 17 days (not including Sundays and holidays). Normally, prime ministers wait until a Parliament approaches its fourth year before seriously considering whether they should ask for dissolution. In case of a minority government—that is, one formed by a party that does not have a majority of seats in the House of Commons, the opposition parties might force the prime minister to ask for dissolution.

One of the most contentious issues surrounding the British electoral system concerns the practice whereby a candidate for the House of Commons need only obtain more votes than any opponent to win a seat. This rule which is identical to that which applies in U.S. congressional elections is known as the "first-by-the-post" system. Its opponents include Fred Ridley, a Professor of Politics at

Two meetings of the two Davids.
SOURCE: Peter Jenkins, *Mrs. Thatcher's Revolution* (London: Pan Books, 1989).

Liverpool University. After the 1987 election Ridley published a newspaper article in *The Guardian* asserting that Britain now had the least democratic society in Europe (see Table 5.3). He used, as his definition of democracy, "government by the whole people of the country, especially through representatives whom they elect." His article simply underscores the fact that the first-by-the-post system in Britain distorts the will of the electorate. With multiple parties, it all too often awards seats to those who drew less than 50 percent of the vote.

Many other European systems make at least some accommodation for the votes given to parties that do not win pluralities. For instance, Germans select members of their lower house half on the basis of single-member districts and half on the basis of the proportion of voters supporting a party list

Table 5.3 Britain ranks the lowest among European democracies with repect to the proportion of voters who supported the party/parties that formed the government after the most recent election as of August 1987.

Switzerland	77.5%
Luxembourg	68.4%
Italy	57.4%
Germany	55.8%
Austria	52.9%
Netherlands	52.0%
Denmark	52.0%
Belgium	50.2%
Sweden	50.0%
Norway	49.0%
Finland	48.9%
Ireland	47.3%
Greece	45.8%
France	44.9%
Spain	44.1%
Portugal	44.0%
United Kingdom	42.3%

SOURCE: Fred Ridley. At the Bottom of The Democracy League. *The Guardian*, August 10, 1987.

devised at the Land (state) level. The latter element of the German system is called *proportional representation* (see Chapter 22).

A further feature of the British system deepens the unrepresentativeness of British governments. The distribution of votes throughout the country makes it too easy for a party to win an absolute majority of seats in the House of Commons without obtaining the same level of support in the electorate. In many other European systems, the strongest parties rarely obtain an absolute majority of seats in the lower house. Therefore, they form coalitions with other parties to secure majority assent to their legislative program. Such alliances broaden the support base in the electorate for the government of the day.

Table 5.4 indicates some distortions that come from the current electoral system. In the five elections since 1974, no party has formed a government with more than 44 percent of the votes. In fact, Labour "won" the February 1974 election with only 37 percent of the national vote—a figure that translated into 47 percent of the seats. In elections of February and October 1974 and May 1979, the Liberals garnered, respectively, 19, 18 and 14 percent of the vote. This support, however, yielded only 2 percent of the seats in each instance.

The participation of the Social Democratic Party (SDP) in the elections of 1983 and 1987 produced a combined drawing power for the Liberals and SDP under the Alliance banner of, respectively, 26 and 23 percent, yet the Alliance gained only 4 and 3 percent of the seats in the respective elections. At the same time, the Alliance "factor" disturbed the balance in the relative yields of Conservative and Labour votes. The 1983 election saw the Conservatives gain 57 percent of seats with 42 percent of the vote. The comparable Labour figures were 28 and 32 percent. A similar pattern emerged in 1987, with the Conservatives getting 58 percent of the seats

Table 5.4   Percentage of Votes and Seats Obtained since 1974

Party	1974 (Feb. 28)		1974 (Oct. 10)		1979 (May 3)		1983 (June 9)		1987 (June 11)	
	Votes	Seats	Votes	Seats	Votes	Seats	Votes	Seats	Votes	Seats
Conservative	38%	47%	36%	44%	44%	53%	42%	57%	43%	58%
Liberal	19%	2%	18%	2%	14%	2%	14%	3%		
Social										
Democratic	*	*	*	*	*	*	12%	1%		
(Alliance)	*	*	*	*	*	*	(26%)	(4%)	23%	3%
Labour	37%	47%	39%	50%	37%	42%	28%	32%	32%	35%
Other	6%	4%	7%	4%	5%	3%	4%	7%	2%	4%

* Did not exist in this election.

for 43 percent of the vote, and Labour realizing 35 percent for 32 percent.

Both Alliance parties had grasped the nettle and proposed replacement of the first-by-the-post system. In view of the "lost" votes of the Liberals and the SDP in the last two elections, we can certainly understand their position. However, the Alliance—now the Social and Liberal Democrats—will not readily win over the Conservatives and Labour to their view. Even though Labour's recent gains have been slight, it still benefits from the current arrangement. Notwithstanding its poor showing in 1983 and 1987, it continues to style itself as a contender for the windfalls that have frequently enough bestowed the party with working—even large (1945 and 1966)—majorities from electoral pluralities. Proportional representation appears to be, as the British say, a "nonstarter."

The Legacy of Mrs. Thatcher's First Term

For Labour and the Alliance parties, many dire predictions have emanated from Mrs. Thatcher's resounding victory in 1987. Some commentators view it as a total realignment heralding a period of Conservative domination of British politics all the way into the next century. Before assessing the signifi-

cance of the election and how the opposition parties have responded to the grim scenarios, we should look back into the Thatcher years to discover the origins of this resounding success.

We begin our account before the 1983 election. Mrs. Thatcher emerged from the 1979 election with 339 seats—22 more than she required to control the House of Commons. Considering the radical nature of her policies, this majority provided less than an optimal cushioning. In fact, Mrs. Thatcher had to reverse herself on some stances in order to avoid embarrassing revolts on the part of her own backbenchers.

Economic policy proved to be one area in which Mrs. Thatcher refused to flinch. We have already noted in Chapter 3 the degree to which Thatcher's increase in the value-added tax, deep cuts in public expenditure and exceedingly tight control of the money supply combined to depress the economy. These seemingly draconian policies stemmed from the view of her most trusted advisers that only shock treatment would jolt British industry out of its lethargy.[2]

The shock produced some severe side ef-

[2] William Keegan, *Mrs. Thatcher's Economic Experiment* (Harmondsworth: Penguin, 1984), pp. 119, 158.

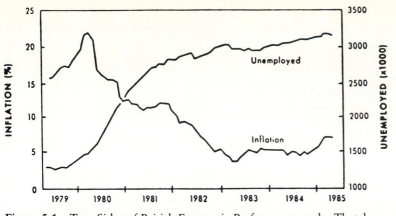

Figure 5.1 Two Sides of British Economic Performance under Thatcher
SOURCE: Helmut Norpoth, "Guns and Butter and Government Popularity in Britain," *American Political Science Review* 81 (1987):951.

fects. At the outset, inflation rose to over 20 percent (Figure 5.1). However, by early 1980 it began a gradual decline to only slightly above 10 percent by the end of the year. On the other hand, unemployment started a sharp upward trajectory early in 1980, rising from under 1.5 million to nearly 2.5 million by the end of the year. Both trends continued through 1981—with unemployment approaching 3 million and inflation dipping close to 10 percent by the end of that year.

During the first two full years of Mrs.

Thatcher's government, the public seemed to repudiate the Thatcher program. By the end of 1981, their approval of her performance had plummeted to 25 percent (Figure 5.2). Analysts believe that voters' disenchantment came from the unprecedented rise in unemployment. They chose not to give credit to Thatcher for reducing inflation.[3] Some ob-

[3] Helmut Norpoth, "Guns and Butter and Government Popularity in Britain," *American Political Science Review*, 81 (1987): 954.

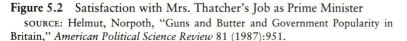

Figure 5.2 Satisfaction with Mrs. Thatcher's Job as Prime Minister
SOURCE: Helmut, Norpoth, "Guns and Butter and Government Popularity in Britain," *American Political Science Review* 81 (1987):951.

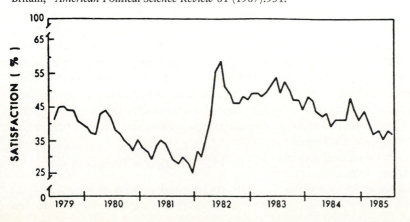

Police keep watch on demonstrators opposed to Prime Minister Margaret Thatcher during a campaign visit by Mrs. Thatcher to the Midlands, previous to the June 1983 general election.
SOURCE: Reuters/Bettmann Newsphotos.

servers believe that this state of affairs was turning around by early 1982—that people were beginning to give Mrs. Thatcher credit for bringing down inflation. And a slight improvement in Mrs. Thatcher's support did reveal itself early in 1982.

At this point, we must account for an event that turned the public mood around completely. On April 2, 1982, Argentina occupied two British possessions: the Falkland Islands and South Georgia Island. Over the next two months, Mrs. Thatcher led the country through the arduous process of regaining the islands through military means. In the process, her public support rocketed to just shy of 60 percent. This political ascent was as sharp a restoration of public confidence as a leader in any democracy ever experienced.

Mrs. Thatcher's handling of the crisis did more than simply rehabilitate her standing as a decisive and effective leader. It also enshrined her credibility. Over the next 12 months ending with the election of June 9, 1983, not even continued concern over relentless unemployment—by then hovering around 3 million—could erode the immense Falklands factor. Of course, Michael Foot, the leader of the Labour Party through the 1983 election, contributed greatly to a Conservative appeal based on leadership ability. He seemed increasingly to embody the antithesis to decisiveness and effectiveness.

The 1987 Election in Perspective

The rocky road to Mrs. Thatcher's third election victory was incongruous with her resounding success. However, her eventual triumph was predictable when we recall the depth of Labour's defeat in the 1983 election. Its 28 percent of the 1983 vote was 14 percent below the Conservatives and only 2 percent above the Alliance parties. Eyes began to focus on whether the Alliance would overtake Labour as the second great party. Many observers began to speculate about the emergence of a three-way struggle in which the Conservatives, Labour and the Alliance would ultimately draw roughly the same proportion of voters.

The Conservatives did not maintain a consistently high level of support throughout the second Thatcher term. The county election results in May 1985, for instance, pointed up the potential appeal of the Alliance (these results excluded Scotland, London and the metropolitan boroughs, none of which went to the polls that spring). The proportion of seats held by the Conservatives in the shires holding elections slipped from 48 to 44 percent. Labour experienced a decline from 35 to 32 percent. The Alliance, on the other hand, doubled its share of seats from 10 to 20 percent. Did this mean that it would finally be able to translate its national support into seats in the House of Commons come the next general election?

Later in 1985, the MORI poll began to track a period of doldrums for the Conservatives. In the early fall, for instance, their support dipped almost to 30 percent—below Labour's and almost equal to the Alliance's. Summer 1986 saw a particularly fickle mood in the electorate. An early July poll put the Conservatives 5 percent behind Labour. In the midst of a July 18–22 poll, Buckingham Palace had made it plain that the Queen ob-

Victory for the Conservatives in the British elections of 1987.
SOURCE: Derek Hudson/Sygma.

jected to Mrs. Thatcher's refusal to entertain proposals to stiffen sanctions against South Africa for its apartheid policies.

The issue loomed so large because the government's stance was driving a wedge between Britain and the rest of the Commonwealth. The interviews taken by MORI before the "Palace row" indicated that the Conservatives had switched positions with Labour and enjoyed a modest lead. Those conducted after the row revealed that Labour regained all of its losses. A subsequent poll, taken on July 30–31, put Labour nine points ahead of the Conservatives at 41 percent. And, the Alliance had enjoyed a shorter spurt placing it at 25 percent.

As we have seen before, the October party conferences radically altered Labour's and the Alliance's prospects. Initially, the effects showed themselves in a dramatic decline in the appeal of the Alliance. This was bad news for Labour as well. Labour, more a party of resort than the natural government party, actually stood the best chance of winning if the Alliance captured just enough moderate constituencies to make the Conservatives vulnerable to a Labour surge.

Analysts can actually work out the probable outcomes in seats for various combinations of support for the three main parties. They project the likely results in each seat based on previous voting behavior in the constituency and the likely effects of national swings toward and away from the parties. For instance, two British authors, writing in the leading assessment of the 1983 election, noted that the Conservatives enjoyed on average a 16-seat edge in the various percentage shares of support that they held in relation to Labour.[4] This bias in favor of the Conservatives owes largely to the fact that they win their seats with smaller margins—thus, more efficiently—than does Labour.

An elaborate array of such projections appeared in *The Guardian* newspaper in May before the 1987 election. It demonstrated the degree to which Labour had to catch up with the Conservatives. It also underscored the fact that Labour would have to benefit from an exceptional Alliance performance.

The Guardian predicted that the worst case for Conservatives, while still winning an absolute majority of seats, would be 38 percent of the popular vote. In this situation, they would survive a 26 to 33 percent vote for Labour and a 27 to 34 percent vote for the Alliance and still form majority governments of 326 to 334 seats. On the other hand, Labour could form a majority government of 326 to 331 seats with only 37 percent of the vote. However, the electorate would have to keep a tight harness on the Conservatives—between 27 and 30 percent of all votes—while giving between 31 and 35 percent to the Alliance—an unlikely prospect.

Where To Now?

The actual 1987 election results—43 percent of the vote and 375 seats for the Conservatives, 32 and 229 for Labour and 23 and 22 for the Alliance—suggests two things pertaining to the length of Mrs. Thatcher's hegemony. First, Labour regained some of the ground it lost when routed by the Conservatives in 1983, while still falling short of the votes that would give it even a bare majority. In fact, some revised projections incorporating the 1987 results suggest that Labour would have to take 8 percent from the Conservatives in order to emerge from the next election with a majority of one. Second, the inroads made by the Alliance were inadequate to weaken the Conservatives or make them vulnerable to Labour gains.

---

[4] John Curtice and Michael Steed, "Appendix 2: An Analysis of the Voting," in David Butler and Dennis Kavanaugh, *The British General Election of 1983* (London: Macmillan, 1984), p. 361.

The question arises as to whether 1987 has set in stone Conservative rule on into the next century. To be sure, the distribution of seats —apart from deaths and resignations— remains fixed through the life of a Parliament. But times might change. Thus, reports of the demise of Labour as a viable pretender to power might be premature.

Some data from the Gallup election survey (June 10 and 11, 1987) present some clues to what must happen before Labour will stand a chance of forming a government. When respondents were asked to name two main issues, the four concerns receiving the most mention were unemployment (49 percent), defense (35), the National Health Service (33), and education (19). In the case of the three "social" issues, respondents actually believed that Labour would do a better job than the Conservatives. The party held 34, 49 and 15 percent edges among those citing unemployment, the National Health Service and education, respectively, as important. However, when defense was a key issue, the Conservatives won by a margin of 63 percent over Labour. The softening of Labour's stance on nuclear disarmament in Fall 1989 should make it more competitive in this regard.

A study of the tremendous success of Ronald Reagan in the election of 1984 has highlighted the degree to which fate dealt the president a lucky hand.[5] That is, the public mood about economic performance reached an apogee at the optimal time for a landslide victory. The 1987 Gallup election poll suggests a similar effect in Mrs. Thatcher's victory.

Notwithstanding unemployment that re-

mains over 3 million, Britons had taken a bullish turn on their futures. In fact, Gallup had recorded a dramatic swing in the voters' view of the economy and their own prosperity. In September 1986, 32 percent more people thought the economy was getting worse than believed it was getting better or staying the same. By election day, the balance had swung to +15 percent on the side of those who saw light at the end of the tunnel. With respect to respondents' views of the finances of their household, a 12 percent skew in the direction of pessimism had become a slight— 2 percent—bias toward optimism.

Observers who project a Conservative dynasty from the 1987 election results engage in a risky speculative enterprise. Several factors must continue to carry weight. First, Mrs. Thatcher must sustain a nearly flawless performance and continue to come across as a decisive and effective leader. If the current government ran the entire life of the present Parliament—till 1992—Mrs. Thatcher will have almost turned 67 and have served as prime minister for over 13 years.

Pierre Elliott Trudeau, the immensely adroit and popular Canadian prime minister, recognized as he approached 65 and had served for over 15 years, that it was time to step down. Clearly the Canadian electorate and the Liberal party notables alike had tired of the prime minister. Grapes ripen more slowly than strawberries, but if left on the vine too long, they shrivel. The departure of Mrs. Thatcher from the prime ministership or her refusal to withdraw at the appropriate time could result in a leader without followers.

Second, we cannot assume that voters' views of the economy and their stake in it will remain static. Like Ronald Reagan in 1984, Mrs. Thatcher faced the electorate at a time of relative optimism. British prime ministers enjoy the benefit of greater maneuverability in this respect. Like presidents, they can pur-

[5] D. Roderick Kiewet and Douglas Rivers, "The Economic Basis of Reagan's Appeal," in *The New Direction in American Politics*, ed. by John E. Chubb and Paul E. Peterson (Washington, D.C.: Brookings, 1985), pp. 71–72.

"Not so fast, children! We're ahead of schedule so we'll wait for an emptier one!"

The leaders of the opposition wait on a near-empty underground train as Mrs. Thatcher makes it clear to her party that she will determine when the time (for the election) is auspicious (*The Guardian*, April 8, 1987).

sue policies that will work toward desirable economic conditions at election time. However, they also enjoy the luxury of choosing the date for the next election. Still, prime ministers can get the economy, the timing for the election or both wrong. Can we assume that Mrs. Thatcher is invariably charmed?

One key consideration about individuals' feelings about the future and the Conservative's performance in 1987 relates to the issue of privatization. The Conservatives pursued this policy—discussed in greater detail in chapter 4—with a vengeance in the buildup to the election. It involved selling off shares in state enterprises well below market rates. This allowed average citizens to realize windfall returns when they resold these shares. Historically, Keynesian governments have greased the palms of voters with increased spending in social programs just before elections. The Conservatives used the stock market to accomplish the same end.

The question arises whether there are limits to the pursuit of this strategy. In time, the government will run out of state enterprises suitable for delivery to the public sector. For instance, two current candidates for privatization are water and electricity. Yet, selloffs in both these cases might produce a backlash from people who support privatization but still believe that the government must maintain control over core service industries. On this subject, some analysts have probed election survey data to assess whether the Thatcher years have seen an erosion of voters' perceptions of the baseline role of government.[6] They have failed to confirm any such slippage.

Events immediately following the stock

[6] Harold D. Clarke, Marianne C. Stewart, and Gary Zuk, "Not for Turning: Beliefs about the Role of Government in Contemporary Britain," *Governance: An International Journal of Policy and Administration*, 1 (1988): 271–88.

market crash in October 19, 1987 also give pause. As it turned out, the Conservatives had scheduled a major sale of British Petroleum shares for the week after the crash. They doggedly refused to call off the sale, averting a disaster by propping up the offer with staggered payments and Bank of England guarantees so that the sale did not deepen the crash itself.

The whole experience proved a failure as "popular capitalism." The purchases by private citizens fell far short of anticipated levels, and merchant bankers had to come to the rescue. The episode underscored two obvious facts that had apparently escaped the promoters of privatization. First, every market has a saturation point. Second, the attractiveness of shares expands or contracts in relation to whether the stock market is bullish or bearish. Investors reminded us that Mrs. Thatcher might not be able to use privatization in future elections to the degree that she did in the buildup to 1987.

Finally, it remains to be seen what appeal the Alliance parties will enjoy now that they have merged completely under the banner "Social and Liberal Democrats." The 1987 electoral verdict drove home the fact that the Alliance could not survive as a loose federation of the Liberal and Social Democratic parties under two heads. Even if the unitary party projects less ambiguity, its actual operation might prove as cumbersome as its name.

The merging of the two parties in the Alliance might prove more difficult than anticipated. To start with, David Owen, the former leader of the Social Democratic Party (SDP), has refused to join the merged party; a remnant, dubbed the "Owenites," has clung to him under the SDP label. The conferences in which the respective parties decided upon union *without* Owen were still not so smooth. In particular, the SDP had to make a number of embarrassing policy concessions in order to adopt the Social and Liberal Democratic manifesto. The new party's rocky merger process contributed in February 1988 to Labour's attaining 42 percent in a Marplan poll—the highest level of support that it had attracted in six years. It remains to be seen whether the Social and Liberal Democrats' problems will continue to give such a boost to Labour.

CONCLUSION

This chapter has examined party organization and the electoral process in the United Kingdom. It has assessed the effects of democratization in the Labour and Liberal parties on their electoral viability. It has also traced the development of the Social and Liberal Democratic Party from the emergence of the Social Democrats and through the Alliance period. Focusing on the Thatcher years, it then examined how the electoral system functions, while discussing the significance of the last two elections.

It appears that interest in democratization has ebbed due to less demand from the general public. Labour, the Liberals and SDP have had to learn lessons about the costs incurred when participatory reforms take place too quickly or in ways that alarm relatively nonattentive voters.

Labour and the Social and Liberal Democratic Party stand a better chance of appearing as coherent and disciplined over the next several years. We might also expect Mrs. Thatcher and her brand of Conservatism to lose some appeal with aging—both of the prime minister and of her coterie. In addition, as our discussion has suggested, Mrs. Thatcher enjoyed tremendous luck in the timing of and circumstances surrounding both the 1983 and 1987 elections. Will this hold in the next outing?

References and Suggested Readings

ALT, J. E. "Dealignment and the Dynamics of Partisanship in Britain." In *Electoral Change in Advanced Industrial Societies*, eds. R. J. Dalton, S. C. Flanagan, and P. A. Beck. Princeton: Princeton University Press, 1984.

BEER, S. J. *Britain Against Itself: The Political Contradictions of Collectivism*. New York: Norton, 1967.

BEER, S. J. *Modern British Politics: Parties and Pressure Groups in the Collectivist Age*. London: Faber and Faber, 1982.

BELOFF, MAX, and GILLIAN PEELE. *The Government of the United Kingdom: Political Authority in a Changing Society*. London: Weidenfeld and Nicolson, 1985.

BUTLER, DAVID, and DENNIS KAVANAGH. *The British General Election of 1987*. London: Macmillan, 1988.

CLARKE, HAROLD D., MARIANNE C. STEWART, and GARY ZUK. "Not For Turning: Beliefs about the Role of Government in Contemporary Britain." *Governance: An International Journal of Policy and Administration* 1 (1988): 271–88.

CREW, I., B. SARLVIK, and J. ALT. "How to Win a Landslide Without Really Trying: Why the Conservatives Won in 1983." In *Britain at the Polls, 1983,* ed. A. Ranney. Durham, NC: American Enterprise Institute and Duke University Press, 1985.

CURTICE, JOHN, and MICHAEL STEED. Appendix 2: An Analysis of the Voting. In Butler and Kavanagh, 1984.

FORMAN, F. N. *Mastering British Politics*. London: Macmillan, 1985.

FRANKLIN, MARK. *The Decline of Class Voting in Britain*. Oxford: Clarendon Press, 1985.

KAVANAGH, D. *Thatcherism and British Politics: The End of Consensus*. Oxford: Oxford University Press, 1987.

KEEGAN, WILLIAM. *Mrs. Thatcher's Economic Experiment*. Harmondsworth: Penguin, 1984.

KIEWIET, D. RODERICK, and DOUGLAS RIVERS. "The Economic Basis of Reagan's Appeal." In *The New Direction in American Politics,* eds. John E. Chubb and Paul E. Peterson. Washington, D.C.: Brookings, 1985.

NORPOTH, HELMUT. "Guns and Butter and Government Popularity in Britain." *American Political Science Review* 81 (1987): 949–59.

6

The Prime Minister, Cabinet, and Whitehall

London is a very different town from Washington. It more nearly resembles New York and Washington rolled into one. London thus serves as the hub for virtually every type of activity in England. In fact, London knows few rivals as a world-class center. In some respects, it remains a more important city for finance, the performing arts and the media than it does for politics. Britain has lost a great deal of standing in the sphere of international affairs. Yet, London remains among the most powerful and influential cities in many fields of human endeavor.

Unlike Washington, the political side of London comes across as subdued. Buckingham Palace provides a clear enough landmark for tourists. However, most visitors recognize that the building, the people who occupy it and the soldiers who guard it are all busy with ceremonial functions. Except in rare and isolated instances, the monarchy plays no substantive role in British politics. For the most part, only relatively modest statues that crop up randomly in squares and circles commemorate the great political leaders—including prime ministers. Wash-ington remembers presidents in the same idiom that Rome used to give homage to gods and former emperors. Britain does not even honor its greatest monarchs this way.

Of course, Westminster Palace occupies a

No one can approach to an understanding of the English institutions, or of others, which, being the growth of many centuries, exercise a wide sway over mixed populations, unless he divide them into two classes. In such constitutions there are two parts (not indeed separable with microscopic accuracy, for the genius of great affairs abhors nicety of division): first, those which excite and preserve the reverence of the population—the *dignified* parts, if I may so call them; and next, the *efficient* parts—those by which it, in fact, works and rules. There are two great objects which every constitution must attain to be successful, which every old and celebrated one must have wonderfully achieved: every constitution must first *gain* authority, and then *use* authority; it must first win the loyalty and confidence of mankind, and then employ that homage in the work of government.

SOURCE: Walter Bagehot, *The English Constitution,* 1867.

special place in the minds of Americans. This august building on the banks of the Thames contains both the House of Commons and the House of Lords. Its famous tower stands as a worldwide symbol for parliamentary democracy. Yet the structure and its precincts do not leave the impression given on Capitol Hill in Washington of a mighty and energetic legislative branch. Lords in Britain have no private offices and staff. MPs, who usually share their offices with at least one colleague, occupy various nooks and crannies that they have found in several buildings close to Parliament. None of these facilities were designed for their current function. And no uninitiated passerby could imagine that the buildings count for anything in the great scheme of governance.

Westminster Palace is located in a large square. With our backs to the palace, Parliament Street begins at our right and becomes Whitehall one block to the north. In Washington, the main government departments line broad boulevards. Whitehall, on the other hand, is a narrow canyon. For a few blocks to the north, most of the buildings on the right are nondescript commercial structures. On the left, we find in huge edifices, mostly of Victorian vintage, Her Majesty's Treasury, the Foreign and Commonwealth Office, and the Cabinet Office. About halfway up, the Ministry of Defence and the Ministry of Agriculture, and Fisheries and Food (MAFF) rise to the right.

All these structures bespeak bureaucratic power. Two of the departments along this

---

The Queen is only at the head of the dignified part of the Constitution. The Prime Minister is at the head of the efficient part. The Crown is, according to the saying, the "fountain of honour"; but the Treasury is the spring of business.

SOURCE: Walter Bagehot, *The English Constitution,* 1867.

---

corridor—the Treasury and the Cabinet Office—function as nerve centers for the entire state apparatus. But only a small fraction of "Whitehall"—a term applied to the entire standing bureaucracy and to all departments —lays claim to this cherished address. The rest of Whitehall brigades itself in buildings spread throughout London. Except for Inland Revenue, which occupies a former palace several blocks down the Thames along the Strand, other departments have found utterly functional accommodation, often in modern office towers that could just as easily pass as the headquarters of financial or commercial concerns.

One final address deserves mention. In the midst of Whitehall, one finds a narrow alleyway guarded by barriers and a few police constables. It bears the name "Downing Street." Peering in, one can see a row of Georgian townhouses. One of these—No. 10— serves as both office and residence of the prime minister.

Less than ten years ago, visitors could move freely through this passageway. To get into No. 10, you simply presented yourself to the bobby standing at the door. He either would already expect you or duck his head in the door to see if you had an appointment. Even with the barrier and the police pickets barring free access to Downing Street, No. 10 stands in stark contrast to the White House. How like the British. They enshrine the ceremonial head of state in Buckingham Palace behind massive fences secured by crack troops. The person who actually wields the executive authority over the government works and resides in a lightly guarded townhouse.

This chapter will examine what actually happens in No. 10 Downing Street and Whitehall—in the inclusive sense of the term. Chapter 7 will look at Westminster. In addition, Chapter 7 will consider the degree to which all three centers of power and political activity—No. 10, Whitehall and Westminster—must take into consideration other factors that impinge on British governance. We will look at the role of the judiciary insofar as it touches on policy. We will also examine relations between Whitehall and local governments. Finally, we will assess the significance of the European Economic Community as an international body whose functions and legitimacy increasingly provide an overarching context for British domestic and foreign policies.

THE CABINET SYSTEM OF GOVERNMENT

In recent years, American presidents have asserted that they wish to achieve a higher degree of "cabinet government" in the executive branch. Presidents Ford, Carter and Reagan all took up this theme. They argued, essentially, that the president could not run the U.S. government alone, but required some devolution of decision-making. This could take two forms. Presidents could make it clear to individual cabinet secretaries that they should use greater discretion and refer fewer issues to the White House. They also could foster the development of cabinet-level bodies in which department heads work out as many matters of detail as possible before bringing policy proposals to the president.

The Iran-Contra affair is an instance of the inadequacy of U.S. cabinet government. Collective consultation failed. The administration surreptitiously pursued a policy that was bitterly opposed by two cabinet officials with an inherent stake in the issue—the secretaries of state and defense. Further, individual discretion and integrity simply disappeared. National security adviser John Poindexter felt justified in embarking on highly questionable activities without direct presidential approval. Poindexter argued that the president

So, although I was convinced that we could properly do it [divert profits from arms sales to Iran to aid the Contras], and that the president would approve, if asked, I made a very deliberate decision not to ask the president so that I could insulate him from the decision and provide some future deniability for the president if it ever leaked out.

SOURCE: Rear Admiral John Poindexter in testimony to the U.S. Senate and House of Representative hearings on the Iran-Contra affair, 1987.

would want the actions carried out but would not want to know about them.

Keeping in mind the timeliness of this issue to American politics, we examine closely what is meant by cabinet government in the United Kingdom. In many respects, the British system serves as an archetype of collective cabinet government. Under constitutional convention, all British executive power resides in cabinet. This body, while acting in the name of the monarch, in fact exercises all of the monarch's authority.

The prime minister presides in cabinet as first among equals: making the final judgment in preparation of its agenda, chairing its deliberations, ultimately discerning what the consensus is, and taking the lead in assuring that departments actually follow through on cabinet decisions. Yet, cabinet, the tradition goes, determines collectively all major policy positions of the government. The conventional view of the British system also assumes unwavering loyalty among the members of the government party in the House of Commons. In theory, this assures that cabinets can attain parliamentary approval of their legislative programs with relative ease.

Changes in the Conditions for Cabinet Government

Of course, no system—even a model for the rest of the world—would operate so smoothly in practice. And developments over the past two decades have not spared British cabinet government. First, despite victory at the polls, a winning party may fall short of an absolute majority in the House of Commons. In fact, winning parties have done just this in six of 24 elections between 1900 and 1987.

The emergence of the Social Democratic Party and its alliance and ultimate merger with the Liberals has presented the specter of a "hung" Parliament. Such a Parliament would emerge from an election result in which no party clearly obtained even a viable plurality of seats. No one party would be able to form a government on the basis of an informal understanding whereby another party would agree to support its legislative program. A "hung" outcome would force a series of negotiations whereby two parties would ultimately have to come together in a coalition. This arrangement would necessitate the assignment of cabinet posts to MPs

from each party on some agreed-to provision for the division of posts.

The public opinion polls that pointed to a very close election through much of 1985 and 1986 engendered a great deal of debate about how readily this process of coalition building would work in a country that is used to relatively clear verdicts from the electorate. In turn, Britons would take time getting acclimatized to coalition government. For instance, cabinets would not be able to maintain anywhere near their accustomed discipline if they included MPs from more than one party. We have already noted in Chapter 3 that party discipline has weakened in the British House of Commons even under majority governments. This has increased the frequency with which prime ministers must retreat from public stances because their cabinet colleagues urged caution in the face of resistance from disgruntled backbench MPs.

The solidarity that we associate with cabi-

A 1985 meeting of Misc. 95, a Cabinet Committee chaired by Mrs. Thatcher, in the Cabinet Room at 10 Downing Street. On Mrs. Thatcher's right sits Cabinet Secretary Sir Robert Armstrong.
SOURCE: BBC Enterprises.

net government thus does not come as naturally to the British as many American observers have thought. Increasingly, prime ministers find themselves absorbed with the task of teasing consent from their colleagues. In the meantime, running Britain has not gotten any easier. When Mrs. Thatcher formed her new cabinet after the election of 1987, it took in fully 21 cabinet members. In addition, 29 ministers assumed day-to-day responsibility for chunks of departments but did not belong to the cabinet. There were 23 departments of state in Whitehall.

All this adds up to an immense coordinative task. It requires that the prime minister spend a very large part of her time making sure that the various goals of her administration mesh. She must also see to it that the programs that implement these policies function effectively and efficiently. In other words, some issues require that the prime minister take the lead in coordination and not simply defer to her cabinet colleagues' perceptions of when and how they should resolve the matter. The prime minister shoulders ultimate responsibility for assuring that Whitehall adopts and adheres to sound management principles.

In response to the demands of the position, recent prime ministers have assumed increasingly high profiles and accumulated more and more staff resources. These trends have occasioned complaints that prime ministers have gradually transformed cabinet government into a variant of presidentialism—dubbed "priministerialism"—with prime ministers usurping the authority of cabinet. Allegedly, they can so manipulate cabinet deliberations and the machinery of government that they can operate as if all executive power centered on themselves. This being the case, the critics say, prime ministers effectively enjoy the same latitude as presidents in deciding the central positions of their administrations.

Within the debate about the current nature

[The prime minister] is now the apex not only of a highly centralised political machine, but also of an equally centralised and vastly more powerful administrative machine. In both these machines, loyalty has become the supreme virtue, and independence of thought a dangerous adventure. . . . The post-war epoch has seen the final transformation of Cabinet Government into Prime Ministerial Government. Under this system the "hyphen which joins, the buckle which fastens, the legislative part of the state to the executive part" becomes one single man.

SOURCE: R. H. S. Crossman, "Introduction" to Walter Bagehot, *The English Constitution*, 1867 (1963 edition).

of the British system rests an irony: It appears that Britons and Americans do not understand one another's systems very well. Presidents hardly enjoy the immense power to act on their own attributed to them by British critics of the modern prime ministership. This fact becomes apparent when we look at the degree to which presidents fail to work their will with Congress. It also comes to the fore in the innumerable circumstances in which presidents cannot win agreement on major issues from their cabinet secretaries and the bureaucracies that they are supposed to direct. Further, on this side of the Atlantic, Americans continue to romanticize the collective nature of cabinet government in Britain. Many even think that British cabinets take votes and the majority inevitably wins the day—impressions that have rarely reflected reality.

We can engage in much more productive inquiry if we remember that the systems differ in very substantial ways. Often it helps to remember that both the presidency and the prime ministership have changed in response to the complexities of executive leadership in our current era. Britons perhaps would correctly note that the American presidency has adapted to the requirements of modern executive leadership more quickly than has their own prime ministership. They probably should refrain, however, from labeling British developments toward modernization of the prime ministership as "presidentialization."

The British Cabinet in Perspective

Americans and Britons alike should take greater care to place their respective executive systems into a wider context. We style presidents "chief executives." Of course, presidents also serve as the head of state—a largely ceremonial function that the queen assumes in the United Kingdom. We construe prime ministers as "first among equals." In the cases of both presidents and prime ministers, we are talking about the principal executive authority of the land: the effective head of government. Both individuals have to appoint colleagues who will advise them and run parts of the state apparatus.

On the one hand, prime ministers and presidents want to give these political authorities a voice in matters that do not fit neatly into a single "portfolio" and require wider consultation. On the other, both presidents and prime ministers want to maintain the ability to decide things on their own when chronic impasses and severe emergencies justify such interventions. The British have tended to stress the necessity of wide consultation and the Americans, to favor the prerogatives of the chief executive. Britons have not always placed themselves in the same spot on the continuum between collective and concentrated executive authority. This becomes clear when we examine the ebbs and flows of cabinet government in history.

Cabinets first emerged in Britain as informal instruments of monarchical rule, developing under a system in which the exercise of executive authority was—as is the case

today in the U.S. government—concentrated in one person. This individual was the sovereign. The term "cabinet" did not gain currency until the early 1600s. Indeed, constitutional writings did not fully acknowledge the cabinet's legitimacy and functions until the mid-1800s.

The first cabinets operated essentially as executive committees of the Privy Council. The latter body had only emerged in the fifteenth century as the recognized coterie of the monarch's most trusted advisers and government officers. Cabinets began to develop when the Privy Council became too large and unwieldy, allowing monarchs to consult in relative secrecy with the most trusted and powerful privy councilors. Cabinet focused only on the most sensitive and nettlesome problems faced by the monarch. Members of this body obtained and retained their positions at the pleasure of the monarch; thus, they enjoyed their authority only when the ruler chose to share regal prerogatives. Apart from the obvious fact that they were not elected, British monarchs related to their cabinets more as presidents than as prime ministers.

British monarchs' use of cabinets did not always follow the same lines.[1] James II (1685–88) convened his cabinet every Sunday and even assigned a clerk to arrange its business. George I (1714–27) ushered in a period in which the regularity both of cabinet meetings and the king's attendance fell off. Thus, even as coordinative tools that worked at the pleasure of the monarch, cabinets played significant roles only for sovereigns capable of giving coherent direction to the myriad affairs of state.

During the nineteenth century, the monarchy declined considerably. Concomitantly, Parliament's power rose at the expense of the

[1] John P. Mackintosh, *The British Cabinet* (London: Stevens, 1977).

. . . For practial purposes after 1717 the Cabinet ceased to be a body meeting with the King.

The reasons for this change have not been pinpointed but a number of motives are fairly evident. The old explanation that George's [I, (1714–27)] inability to speak English led to the withdrawal has been abandoned since the problem of communication had evidently been overcome for the best part of three years after George's accession. The chief reason was that George's personality altered the situation. He was both ignorant of English affairs and stupid and could never be at ease presiding over a wide-ranging discussion among ten or twelve Cabinet ministers. Like many stupid men he was suspicious and preferred to lean on his German advisers and mistresses and perhaps one or two Englishmen. The politicians, for their part, sensing this situation, preferred to consult with the King in private and not at the Cabinet where misunderstandings and animosities could so rapidly arise and flourish.

SOURCE: John P. Mackintosh, *The British Cabinet*, 1977.

executive. Initially, these developments resulted in the enhancement of the most prestigious ministerial domains to the point where some departments became virtual baronies.

One area where this was clearly the case was foreign policy and defense. The foreign secretary, the chancellor of the exchequer, and the ministers of the two military services —the Army and the Navy—worked out many matters either within their own departments or between themselves, with little or no reference to cabinet or the prime minister. During the last half of the nineteenth century, various military crises and disasters sparked efforts to institutionalize consultation regarding foreign policy and defense. However, the principals of the key departments continued to frustrate such efforts by refusing to coordinate their activities beyond technical matters.

The baronial pattern persisted through to

War in the twentieth century has raised the problem of co-ordination in an acute form by bringing about sudden increases in the scope of government action. At the highest level, the need to impose coherent policy without undue recourse to the interdepartmental bargaining typical of peacetime Cabinets has led in both wars to the creation of small bodies with supreme authority to direct the war.

SOURCE: John Turner, *Lloyd George's Secretariat*, 1980.

1916, when David Lloyd George became prime minister. He broke the logjam over the coordination of Britain's war effort by ignoring cabinet and creating a new body, the War Cabinet, which assumed the coordinative tasks the prime minister could not fulfill on his own. Only one member of this new body administered a department as well. Of course, the urgent circumstances of a brutal and seemingly intractable war greatly aided Lloyd George's imposition of coherence.

Significantly, Lloyd George's approach to the prime ministership simply quickened a process that had already begun. Since the late 1800s the degree to which the electorate identified parties with their leaders had already begun to undermine the baronial positions of ministers. Prime ministers were exercising both more discretion in the selection of cabinet members, and more personal authority within the executive. After the war, they increasingly mandated ad hoc groups of ministers to prepare the especially sensitive elements of policy initiatives for presentation to the entire cabinet.

The use of such bodies can spark resentments in cabinet. Ministers consistently not included in key ad hoc groups that touch on their domains can become obstructionistic— even obstreperous—in meetings of full cabinet. In recognition of this fact, prime ministers eventually moved toward the institutionalization of cabinet committees. In this regard, Lloyd George also proved himself a man ahead of his time. Close to the end of the war, he created standing committees for economic defense and development, home affairs, and postwar priorities. The period between the world wars saw only sporadic adherence to this level of regularization.

Since World War II, all prime ministers have adhered more or less to a system of routinized cabinet consultation through a network of standing cabinet committees—although the longer Mrs. Thatcher stays in power the less she works through formalized groups. The canons of secrecy that enshroud the operation of the British executive keep us from obtaining exact knowledge of every part of the system. However, some prime ministers have indulged themselves in committees of all sorts.[2] Clement Attlee (1945–51) had 148 standing and 313 ad hoc committees operating at various stages of his administration. Harold Wilson's first government (1964–70) saw more than 230 ad hoc groups by early 1969. Mrs. Thatcher, on the other hand, has shown relative parsimony.

The method adopted by Ministers for discussion among themselves of questions of policy is essentially a domestic matter, and is no concern of Parliament or the public. The doctrine of collective responsibility of Ministers depends, in practice, upon the existence of opportunities for free and frank discussion between them, and such discussion is hampered if the processes by which it is carried on are laid bare. For these reasons it is also the general practice to avoid, so far as possible, disclosing the composition and terms of reference of Cabinet Committees and, in particular, the identity of their Chairmen.

SOURCE: Winston Churchill in a 1952 confidential directive to Cabinet.

[2] Peter Hennessy, *Cabinet* (Oxford: Blackwell, 1986), pp. 100–1.

By 1986, she had only used between 30 and 35 standing committees and some 120 ad hoc groups.

Whatever the preferences of individual prime ministers, we can expect that any government will operate standing committees in some specific areas that always require careful coordination. These include planning for legislative sessions and management of parliamentary affairs, economic strategy, overseas and defense policy, relations with the European Economic Community, home and social affairs, and security and intelligence. And we can assume that networks of regularized subcommittees function under each of these umbrellas.

THE PRIME MINISTER AND THE RESOURCES AT THE CENTER OF GOVERNMENT

Britons do not normally employ the term "chief executive" when referring to prime ministers. Conventions integral to the British unwritten constitutional system require that prime ministers—unlike presidents—exercise their authority only after consultation with the cabinet colleagues. In their capacity as head of government, however, prime ministers fulfill a host of functions which, taken together, make observers wonder whether in practice they operate as chief executives. We can best examine the multiplicity of the prime minister's roles by looking at what those working for her do. The prime minister draws upon two resources; her personal staff in No. 10 Downing Street, and the various secretariats operating out of the Cabinet Office.

No. 10 Downing Street

The closer we get to power, the more crowded the office facilities. This certainly applies in Washington. Deputy assistants to the U.S. president ensconce themselves in huge accommodations in the Old Executive Office of the President across an alley from the White House. Their bosses—assistants to the president and above—trade opulence for proximity. They vie, thus, for relatively cramped offices in the West Wing annex to the White House. The same pattern holds in Whitehall. To be under the same roof as the prime minister, some 70 people tolerate conditions that otherwise would border on insufferable.

Prime ministers pretty much determine the specific contours of their No. 10 staff on their own. However, some positions appear to be permanent features of the organizational chart. These include the private secretaries, a foreign affairs adviser, a political adviser, a policy adviser, a press secretary, a secretary for governmental appointments and a member of the House of Commons who serves as parliamentary private secretary.

The private secretaries—five officials all

Few people in England would know this man. However, as Secretary of the Cabinet from 1973 to 1979 he was the power behind the throne for four prime ministers—Heath, Wilson, Callaghan, and Thatcher.

SOURCE: Peter Hennessy, *Whitehall* (London: Secker & Warburg, 1989).

tolled—cram themselves into two small rooms immediately adjacent to the prime minister's office. These assistants are all permanent civil servants on loan from various Whitehall departments. In the White House, such career officials would never be trusted to work so directly for the president. In No. 10, the private secretaries essentially run the switchboard for the prime minister's communication with cabinet secretaries and various parts of Whitehall. They make abundant use of their highly developed networks of contacts in departments. They also can gain entry to virtually any Whitehall meeting of cabinet secretaries or officials in which the prime minister has an interest.

Through these means, private secretaries gather an immense amount of intelligence on what is happening with various policy proposals, and what has gone wrong with controversial programs and why. They brief the prime minister directly, and do not hesitate to suggest the major issues at hand and how the prime minister might resolve them. Even when the prime minister communicates wishes directly to a cabinet secretary, private secretaries, as often as not, explain the prime minister's mind when departments come back to No. 10 for further clarification.

Now someone has to tell the prime minister that this is what you have got, and suggest to her the sequence in which she should read these in order to make sense of them, to draw together the salient points that they are making—hopefully they are all moving in some kind of direction—bring out the points of conflict and so lead the prime minister to the point where she is able, without having herself to write an essay, to give specific directions as to what she wants done on the issues that are now before her.

SOURCE: A member of the prime minister's private office as quoted in Colin Campbell, *Governments Under Stress*, 1983.

Although not a private secretary, the *foreign affairs adviser* warrants mention here. The position emerged in the wake of the Falklands crisis, in acknowledgement of the fact that the prime minister required someone very eminent within the foreign affairs field in No. 10. The presence of such an adviser there would give permanent officials in Whitehall a highly credible point of contact when and if threatening developments had failed to get sufficient attention from their ministers. The incumbents to this position have all been retired senior officials from the Foreign and Commonwealth Office.

Two other career officials who are fixtures in No. 10 are the *secretary for appointments* and the *press secretary.* The former person manages the process whereby the prime minister exercises a key prerogative: recommending to the monarch the names of recipients of government appointments and honors. Such awards, of course, constitute a major source of patronage to party faithful. However, many jobs and honors in fact go to individuals more on the basis of their being among "the great and the good"—people with distinguished careers in one or another walk of life. As a deferential society, Britain takes special pains to formalize membership in the establishment with board memberships and honorific titles.

The role of the press secretary as a career official simply on loan from Whitehall has come in question of late. The two most recent occupants of this position—Tom McCaffrey under James Callaghan and Bernard Ingham under Margaret Thatcher—both became so attached to their prime minister that their nonpartisanship came in question. McCaffrey in fact went with Callaghan to head his office when he lost the election in 1979 and became the leader of the opposition. Ingham has served Mrs. Thatcher since 1979.

The press secretary plays a vital role. The emphasis on secrecy in Whitehall contributes to this; through it, the press secretary can—much more effectively than the opposite number in the White House—control the timing and substance of most statements and information flowing from ministers and government departments. Secrecy also allows the press secretary to make maximum use of the briefings of lobby correspondents (see Chapter 4) to put the prime minister's "spin" on media coverage of conflicts within cabinet and between departments.

All of the remaining assistants in No. 10 are "party-political" advisers. This means that they gain and hold their positions at the pleasure of the prime minister on the basis of their political loyalty. Two of these officials pretty much center their work on mending fences in the party. The *parliamentary private secretary,* a member of the House of Commons, maintains liaison between the prime minister and backbench MPs. The *political secretary* monitors the prime minister's party-political affairs, including relations with the party organization and the assessment of the electoral benefits to or fallout from prime ministerial actions. These might range from high-order policy decisions to seemingly trivial though potentially sensitive issues such as whether No. 10 should receive a delegation of party members or voters.

A third official—*policy adviser*—heads a unit—usually ranging in size between five and ten officials—that has taken one or another form in the No. 10 organization chart since 1970. Bernard Donoughue, who headed the policy unit from 1974 to 1979, earned a reputation as a policy professional who, though a party-political appointee, developed strong links with the major figures of the permanent bureaucracy. The heads of the policy unit under Mrs. Thatcher have become a hidden hand to make sure that policy commitments of great importance to the prime minister are resolved in a satisfactory and timely way.

Under both parties, the policy unit's effectiveness depends a great deal on the resourcefulness of its members. These advisers must learn how to obtain access to key committee meetings and tap into the private office for a steady flow of essential documents. They do not always achieve this degree of maneuverability. However, they can exert considerable leverage when they do.

The Cabinet Office

Next door to No. 10, we find the *Cabinet Office*, with its entrance facing Whitehall. This organization represents a resource unlike anything American presidents can tap. To be sure, it incorporates some organizations that do not play vital roles in policy formulation. However, if we isolate attention on the secretariats that support the cabinet committee system, we find that its staffing vastly exceeds comparable resources in the U.S. executive branch.

The National Security Council staff and the parallel domestic office—the Domestic Policy Staff under Carter and the Office of Policy Development under Reagan—perform the same functions in the United States as the Cabinet Office does in the United Kingdom. In a 1981–82 comparison, however, the two U.S. agencies claimed only 110 staff members and spent around seven million dollars,[3] while the Cabinet Office policy secretariats employed 331 staff members and spent over 10 million pounds. These figures highlight the substantially greater emphasis placed by the British executive branch on the task of supporting collective decision-making. The contrast becomes even more stark when we consider that all of the officials working in the Cabinet Office are permanent civil servants on loan from Whitehall departments. The U.S. offices responsible for coordination, on the other hand, consist largely of political appointees many of whom have accumulated relatively little experience in government.

In principle, the Cabinet Office works first for the cabinet. In this respect it has several central roles in the process whereby cabinet governs over policy issues:

1. It advises officials from elsewhere in Whitehall on how to prepare issues for interdepartmental and cabinet consideration.
2. It monitors this preparation process to assure that departments have adequately consulted with other interested agencies—especially the Treasury, which controls the purse strings.
3. It advises on when an issue is ready for consideration by a cabinet committee.
4. It transmits committee recommendations to the prime minister and to the entire cabinet.
5. It drafts cabinet minutes and communicates decisions to all concerned parties.
6. It takes the lead in ensuring that decisions are actually implemented.

In this country . . . we haven't got a prime minister's department. In theory, the Cabinet Office serves all ministers; in practice, it serves the prime minister a good deal more than anyone else. But he hasn't got a department to serve him. He has, at No. 10, very efficient private secretaries who can deal with his daily life and his mail and that sort of thing. But, they, when they want advice, almost always look here. I mean I don't want to pretend we are a prime minister's department under another name, because we're not. We haven't got that position yet, and the prime minister isn't the chief executive. He can't overrule his colleagues just like that. He's got to get his consensus in cabinet. But we are the department that services him.

[3] Colin Campbell, *Managing the Presidency: Carter, Reagan and the Search for Executive Harmony* (Pittsburgh: University of Pittsburgh Press, 1986), p. 19.

SOURCE: A member of the Cabinet Office as quoted in Campbell, *Governments under Stress*, 1983.

The reader has probably already noticed that these functions relate as much to the prime minister's role as the head of government as to cabinet's standing as the ultimate locus of executive authority. Fulfillment of the last three functions in particular requires that members of the Cabinet Office work very closely for the prime minister.

We saw above that a great deal of controversy surrounds the issue of whether prime ministers have reached the point where they in effect operate as chief executives. Astute use of the Cabinet Office certainly places any prime minister at a clear advantage in those situations where personal leverage and institutional resources count the most. However, no Cabinet Office would retain effectiveness and legitimacy if it became totally captive of the prime minister. It does have a special relationship to the prime minister, but it also must remain responsive to requirements of cabinet for secretariats able to facilitate its decision-making processes in a relatively detached way. The Cabinet Office that loses its capacity for neutral brokerage will decline in legitimacy.

Whitehall Departments

Whitehall departments function under the direction of individual cabinet secretaries—*not* the prime minister. All of the major departments have ministers of state and under-secretaries of state who assists their cabinet secretary in overseeing policy development and the operation of programs. For instance, the Department of Health and Social Security—before it was split into two departments in summer 1988—had separate ministers for health and social security plus three under-secretaries of state. All such officials belong to either the House of Commons or the House of Lords and owe their appointments to the prime minister.

The prime minister's influence over departments does not end with the power to appoint, shuffle and dismiss cabinet secretaries and ministers. The prime minister has general responsibility for the management of Whitehall, maintaining authority over the development of the civil service, thus ultimately determining personnel policies that concern major changes in the duties, privileges and compensation of permanent officials. The of-

Robin Butler's career reflects the "neutrality" of Whitehall mandarins. Butler, the handsome young man behind Prime Minister Harold Wilson, served as a private secretary to both Edward Heath and Wilson, as principal private secretary to Margaret Thatcher, and presently as secretary of the cabinet and head of the civil service.

SOURCE: Bernard Donoughue, *Prime Minister* (London: Jonathan Cape Ltd., 1987).

One of the reasons why no rigorous reconsideration seems to have been given to the qualities needed by senior officials or to the grading system may be the need felt by senior officials to select "leaders." . . . Leadership has the quality of a "hurrah" word among certain sections in British society, particularly the middle and upper classes which have provided the core of officers in the armed forces and senior officials in the higher civil service.

SOURCE: Richard A. Chapman, *Leadership in the British Civil Service*, 1984.

ficial responsible for the Cabinet Office—the *cabinet secretary*—serves, in the formal capacity as head of the civil service, as the prime minister's principal adviser on these matters.

Prime ministers tend to focus their involvement with Whitehall personnel issues on those pertaining to the uppermost groups. For instance, prime ministers must personally approve all promotions to the top two rungs: *permanent secretaries* and *deputy secretaries*. The former stand at the very top of Whitehall departments.

In many respects, *permanent secretaries* rival ministers in their power over departments. They normally bring a wealth of experience in the department to their work. They also control the careers of the permanent officials whose cooperation cabinet secretaries must have if they are to achieve their goals. As for *deputy secretaries*, they enjoy considerably greater leverage than do ministers of state or under-secretaries of state. The former shoulder hierarchical responsibility for major clusters of departmental activities; the latter simply receive delegated responsibility from cabinet secretaries to monitor the development of policies and the operation of programs within the department.

In comparison to the U.S. president, the prime minister can reorganize Whitehall with relative ease. Strictly speaking, Mrs. Thatcher can redistribute responsibilities to and between departments without any more than perfunctory consultation of cabinet. Realistically, she would have to ensure that key colleagues agreed with her major initiatives. Yet, no prime minister would face the inherent intractability that a president wishing to reorganize the U.S. executive branch does. Besides, Parliament invariably passes any required enabling legislation with barely a comment.

It would take an entire chapter to begin to describe the bureaucratic cultures operating within various Whitehall departments. By any standards, the world of the British civil servant is exceedingly closed and stratified. The strong secrecy norm limits the degree to which officials can speak with outsiders interested in the policies and programs for which they are responsible. Consultation with interest groups normally takes the form of structured sessions, often in the presence of a cabinet secretary or a minister. One finds virtually no informal, day-to-day interaction with backbench MPs and Lords. However, parliamentary committees increasingly call upon officials to give testimony.

The stratification of the British civil service owes largely to the sharp distinction between the *administration group* and the rest of the nonclerical or non-blue collar government employees. The former work within a separate corps of officials who, even if they have not achieved sufficient rank, have been selected and trained on the basis that they will assume substantial roles in policy-oriented

You have to have a view of what the British economy can stand. Ministers left to themselves would do things which would not be consistent with the proper management of the economy.

SOURCE: A Treasury official as quoted by Colin Campbell, *Governments under Stress*, 1983.

positions. The others—executive officers, specialists, scientists and senior technicians—only by rare exception take on major policy positions.

The administration group has received a great deal of critical comment over the years. Many view it as an anachronistic holdover from Victorian times. The selection of these officials certainly raises serious questions. For most, it takes place in their final year of university or soon after. It involves a series of exams and interviews which, it is thought, give an edge to candidates from Oxford and Cambridge. Critics believe, thus, that it encourages those with an air of intellectual and social superiority. When we consider the fact that most members of the administration group are generalists without graduate or professional education, we can see how their special status grates against the sensitivities of civil service groups with advanced credentials. Ministers also often resent these mandarins' tendency to behave as if only they could discern the longterm interests of Britain.

MRS. THATCHER AS PRIME MINISTER

Mrs. Thatcher shares with former U.S. president Ronald Reagan the reputation for having reversed the tide of the welfare state and entrenching a host of market-oriented policies. Some assessments of President Reagan attribute his success in enshrining his central policies—reduced taxes and domestic spending, and increased defense spending—to the speed with which he essentially overrode the permanent state apparatus.[4]

These analyses urge that future presidents must focus much more on their "responsive competence." They should, if necessary, forget about trying to make certain that their decisions are made on the basis of the most rigorous analysis available, or that the public service operates with optimal efficiency and effectiveness. The point is to centralize decision-making as much as possible in the White House and allow only those who pass severe loyalty tests to assume appointive positions in the agencies.

Other students of the presidency adopted what had, before the Iran-Contra affair, become the minority view. Rockman argues, for instance, that executive leaders must blend public standing, intra-elite relations, organizational and management ability, and policy knowledge and analysis.[5] Through this they achieve both political responsiveness *and* creative engagement of the state apparatus, or "policy competence." Reagan's lack of interest in detail and engagement in the day-to-day affairs of state simply exacerbated the negative consequences of overriding the standing bureaucracy.[6] He occupied the office "president" without fully understanding, let alone utilizing, the institutional resources of the presidency.

Margaret Thatcher has demonstrated the same attributes. Yet apart from the Falklands crisis, which she pulled out of the fire, Mrs. Thatcher's approach has failed to produce a debacle. She has proved most successful at responsive competence. In some respects, it borders on rule by fiat.[7] She has established a cabinet system in which conviction has become nine-tenths of the law. She regularly

[4] Terry M. Moe, "The Politicized Presidency," in *The New Direction in American Politics,* ed. by John E. Chubb and Paul E. Peterson (Washington, D.C.: Brookings, 1985).

[5] Bert A. Rockman, *The Leadership Question: The Presidency and the American Political System* (New York: Praeger, 1984); and Colin Campbell, *Managing the President: Carter, Reagan and the Serach for Executive Harmony.* (Pittsburgh: University of Pittsburgh Press, 1986).

[6] Campbell, *Managing the Presidency,* pp. 5–6, 20–22.

[7] Hennessy, chapter 3.

browbeats ministers when they disagree with her. Cabinet meets less regularly and considers fewer submissions.

Charmed circles of ministers in especially good grace with the prime minister often resolve issues which then receive only pro forma discussion in standing committees or the entire cabinet. The prime minister has taken exceptional liberties with Whitehall by introducing personalized criteria into the selection and advancement of senior permanent officials; she has advanced officials who adopt a "can do" approach to her agenda and priorities over more traditional civil servants who might stress the obstacles and pitfalls to her policies. She also has brought about sweeping reorganizations with little or no consultation of her cabinet colleagues and virtually no regard for civil service morale.

It remains to be seen how long the system will withstand the immense strains placed on it by the force of Mrs. Thatcher's personality. In late 1985, an uproar arose over the prime minister's handling of a dispute between her defense minister, Michael Heseltine, and her trade and industry minister, Leon Brittan, over the future of the Westland helicopter manufacturers. Heseltine ultimately resigned in protest over Thatcher's highly manipulative approach. Her tactics, according to Heseltine, involved alternating between ad

---

Ministers increasingly voice concern . . . about the way key decisions are being taken by Mrs. Thatcher and small groups of ministers without reference to the full Cabinet—a practice which they say has contributed to failings in the presentation of policies. One minister said privately last week that Mrs. Thatcher probably has used Cabinet less than any prime minister since the war. Some MPs are calling for a return to genuine *Cabinet Government*.

SOURCE: *The Times*, March 5, 1984.

---

hoc groups and the appropriate standing committee in search of the right mix of ministers, conveying to the press distorted accounts of ministers' preferences, and expunging from cabinet minutes any record of dissent.

Only the release of the salient cabinet documents—30 years or more from now—will help us establish whether Heseltine rendered an accurate account of his treatment by the prime minister. We do know, however, that the secretary of trade and industry resigned his post in late January 1986. He had been caught red-handed having his information officer select highly prejudicial excerpts of a letter from the solicitor-general to Heseltine and leak them to the press. The entire episode contributed significantly to the government's slide in the polls through the next six months. But questionable competence of the opposition contenders and hype over the performance of the British economy eventually obscured memories of the incident. Nothing succeeds like success. And notwithstanding her imperious style, Mrs. Thatcher has maintained her credibility as the leader for the times. Her imperious style has re-emerged as an issue midway through her third term. In October 1989, it led to the resignation of the chancellor of the exchequer over whether Britain would enter the European Monetary System. This episode helped Mrs. Thatcher's popularity to decline to the lowest point of any prime minister since polling began 50 years ago.

CONCLUSION

This assessment of the role of the prime minister, cabinet and Whitehall has attempted to put our understanding of the British executive branch in a sharper perspective. Looking from across the Atlantic, we might tend to romanticize how exactly the British system functions. In particular, we might give excessive credence to the U.K. constitutional conventions whereby executive authority is supposed to be exerted collectively by cabinet.

The case of Mrs. Thatcher perhaps overdemonstrates the point. Today there can be little question that a "conviction" prime minister can operate as monocratically as the most powerful president. However, we have to recognize that personalities rarely introduce such huge distortions into the operation of cabinet government. Most prime ministers stay within the conventional parameters of their prerogatives. We can say this while still acknowledging that recent prime ministers have found themselves much more capable of providing central direction to their administrations than did their predecessors.

References and Suggested Readings

ABERBACH, JOEL D., ROBERT D. PUTNAM, AND BERT A. ROCKMAN. *Bureaucrats and Politicians in Western Democracies.* Cambridge: Harvard University Press, 1981.

BAGEHOT, WALTER. *The English Constitution.* First published 1867. 1963 edition by R. H. S. Crossman. London: Fontana.

CAMPBELL, COLIN. *Governments under Stress: Political Executives and Key Bureaucrats in Washington, London and Ottawa.* Toronto: University of Toronto Press, 1983.

———. *Managing the Presidency: Carter, Reagan and the Search for Executive Harmony.* Pittsburgh: University of Pittsburgh Press, 1986.

CHAPMAN, RICHARD A. *Leadership in the British Civil Service.* London: Croom Helm, 1984.

HECLO, HUGH, AND AARON WILDAVSKY. *The Private Government of Public Money: Community and Policy Inside British Politics.* Berkeley: University of California Press, 1974.

HENNESSY, PETER. *Cabinet.* Oxford: Blackwell, 1986.

HOGWOOD, BRIAN W., AND THOMAS T. MACKIE. "The United Kingdom: Decision Setting in a Secret Garden." In *Unlocking the Cabinet: Cabinet Structures in Comparative Perspective,* eds. authors. London: Sage, 1985.

JONES, G. W. "The United Kingdom." In *Advising the Rulers,* ed. William Plowden. Oxford: Blackwell, 1987.

MACKINTOSH, JOHN P. *The British Cabinet.* London: Stevens, 1977.

MOE, TERRY M. "The Politicized Presidency." In *The New Direction in American Politics,* eds. John E. Chubb and Paul E. Peterson. Washington, D.C.: Brookings, 1985.

PLOWDEN, WILLIAM. "The Higher Civil Service in Britain." In *The Higher Civil Service in Europe and Canada: Lessons for the United States,* ed. Bruce L. R. Smith. Washington, D.C.: Brookings, 1984.

ROCKMAN, BERT A. *The Leadership Question: The Presidency and the American Political System.* New York: Praeger, 1984.

ROSE, RICHARD. "British Government: The Job at the Top." In *Presidents and Prime Ministers,* eds. author and Ezra N. Suleiman. Washington, D.C.: American Enterprise Institute, 1980.

———. "The Political Status of Higher Civil Servants in Britain." In *Bureaucrats and Policy Making: A Comparative Overview,* ed. Ezra N. Suleiman. London: Holmes & Meier, 1984.

TURNER, JOHN. *Lloyd George's Secretariat.* Cambridge: Cambridge University Press, 1980.

7

An Increasingly Crowded Field: Players Beyond the Executive

We now step out of the vortex of power in the United Kingdom. In this chapter we will examine the roles of Parliament, the judiciary and local governments. We will also assess how Britain's membership in the European Economic Community affects the exercise of sovereign authority over the various affairs of state. Finally, we will look at the role of interest groups in the process by which government policies take shape.

Obviously, we have touched on many of the constitutional issues connected with the legitimacy and power of these various elements of the governmental and political processes in earlier chapters. Some points, however, bear repeating. These matters effectively overarch the entire operation of the interrelationships between executive power, parliamentary authority, jurisprudence, local autonomy and European unity.

In Chapter 3, we saw how the elements of central government derive their legitimacy and authority from interlocking channels. The genius of Britain's cabinet system of government rests on the cooperation among those who control Parliament, those who assume executive authority in the principal posts of the land, and those who administer justice.

Among parliamentary legislatures, Westminster enjoys almost paragon status. This owes in no small part to the eloquence and dispatch with which it considers and treats the great affairs of state. This "efficiency," of course, means that backbench MPs within the governing party must frequently bite their tongues. The judiciary, until very recently, has maintained an external posture of obeisance to the letter and the intent of Parliament. It eschews interpretation based on broader principles such as fundamental civil liberties. We have seen in Chapter 3 that cracks have developed in communality of authority in the central government. This chapter will probe the dimensions of these fissures.

In Chapter 4, we briefly examined efforts to accommodate the distinctive character of Scotland, Wales and Northern Ireland, with respect to the devolution of some of the administrative apparatus of the central government to the provinces. We touched, as well, on the changing status of local governments that has stemmed largely from Margaret Thatcher's efforts to circumscribe their ability to extract their own revenues. We will in this chapter focus more closely on the characteristics of provincial and local governance.

Finally, as we found in Chapter 3, Europe plays an enhanced role in the United Kingdom—especially with respect to civil liberties and economic policy. Here, as well, we will inquire more deeply into the dynamics whereby British political leaders and institutions must now take much greater cognizance of Europe while developing and administering policies and programs.

WESTMINSTER IN TRANSITION?

The British Parliament divides into two chambers: the House of Lords and the House of Commons. The former body consists of some 1,200 members. The number is not fixed, because the institution includes four groups that vary in size: hereditary lords, peers appointed for life, the law lords—senior members of the judiciary, and archbishops and bishops representing the Church of England—the established religion of the United Kingdom. Except for hereditary lords, all members of the House of Lords receive their appointments from the monarch on the advice of the prime minister. With respect to life peers, accession to the upper house often serves as a reward for political service either within the House of Commons or through contributions to and work for the party. The practice of appointing life peers began in 1958. Even the relatively conservative constitutional authority, Walter Bagehot, had advocated life peerages in the latter part of the nineteenth century.

An assembly in which the mass of the members have nothing to lose, where most have nothing to gain, where every one has a social position firmly fixed, where no one has a constituency, where hardly any one cares for the minister of the day, is the very assembly in which to look for, from which to expect, independent criticism. And in matter of fact we find it. . . . But such criticism, to have its full value, should be many-sided. Every man of great ability puts his own mark on his own criticism; it will be full of thought and feeling, but then it is of idiosyncratic thought and feeling. . . . There ought to be many life peers in our secondary chamber capable of giving us this higher criticism. I am afraid we shall not soon see them, but as a first step we should learn to wish for them.

SOURCE: Walter Bagehot, *The English Constitution,* 1867.

The House of Lords is an anachronism in a democratic era. It harks back to oligarchical times. With the gradual rise of the House of Commons during the nineteenth century, those wishing to preserve the upper house sought a restraint against the unbridled popular will as expressed by the majority in the lower house. At the time, only members of the nobility belonged to the chamber. The current House of Lords boasts a more eclectic complement—thanks to the institution of life peerages. And it no longer views itself as a bulwark against excessive democracy. However, the existence of the institution still provides the British establishment leverage in the political process that other segments of society lack.

Efforts to reform the House of Lords have come slowly. Despite deadlocks between the upper and lower houses throughout the nineteenth century, Parliament did not limit the legislative powers of the former until 1911. From that year, "money" bills—those concerning taxation and expenditure—automatically received royal assent one month after reaching the House of Lords. According to the 1949 Parliament Act, the upper house cannot delay other public bills passed by the House of Commons for more than two successive sessions (with the exception of cases in which less than one year has elapsed between second reading of the bill in the first session and its third reading in the next session).

The House of Lords can produce some embarrassing reversals for the government party, although few of these touch at the very heart of bills. Mrs. Thatcher's government in particular has tended to rankle lords. As a result, bipartisan movements within the upper house have forced amendments in a great deal of government legislation. A 1986 count put such changes at 100 since Mrs. Thatcher first formed her government in 1979 (*The Guardian*, October 16). This relatively intense activity has tended to center on legislation covering schools and local government.

The House of Commons takes in 650 elected members of Parliament all of whom represent single-member constituencies. Most of the government's legislation passes through the House of Commons before proceeding to the House of Lords. The executive introduces the overwhelming majority of bills that ultimately gain royal assent. Only the executive can originate bills that involve taxation or spending. This stands in stark contrast with Congress, where individual senators or representatives put forth a large proportion of legislative initiatives, which then appear under their names. The House of Commons does make very modest provision in its schedule for "private-member" bills. However, precious few of these ultimately become law.

As with any legislature, bills must pass through several stages. *First reading* involves formal introduction of the measure, and does not entail debate. *Second reading* allows for a lengthy debate on the policy and programmatic merits of the proposed legislation. After second reading, the bill goes to *standing committees* consisting of 16 to 50 members. These bodies examine bills clause by clause. However, they really do not deserve the title "standing." Rather, they come into being on an *ad hoc* basis in response to specific initiatives. The leadership of the various parties will exert considerable control over the membership of these bodies. The government party in particular will want to avoid embarrassing criticism from one of their MPs.

Standing committees can introduce amendments to legislation. However, these must concern technical matters associated with the implementation of policy and not the principles behind it. Governments themselves introduce many amendments at this stage, virtually all of which will receive endorsement from the respective standing committees. Only a minuscule proportion of amendments proposed by individual MPs without explicit government backing gain the support of standing committees. If the bill has been changed, it must proceed through the *report* stage in the House of Commons before the amendments are accepted. Whether revised or not, the bill must pass through *third reading*. However, it will receive additional consideration in debate only if six MPs have submitted a motion beforehand calling for further discussion.

Formal divisions—occasions in which members file out of the house to register their votes for or against a bill or an amendment—occur relatively frequently. In the six parliamentary sessions between 1974 and 1980, the total number of sitting days ranged between 86 and 244; meanwhile, between 110 and 500 divisions took place.[1] In all but

---

[1] Philip Norton, *The British Polity* (London: Longman, 1984), p. 267.

two sessions, the ratio of divisions to sitting days was at least two to one. It is not unusual for MPs to congregate in the house at 1:00 or 2:00 in the morning in response to the division bells.

The number of the votes that see Conservative or Labour MPs taking stands at variance with their party has increased dramatically in the past two decades. There were seven parliaments from 1945 to 1970. Only under the 1959-to-1964 parliament did MPs cast dissenting votes in more than 10 percent of divisions.[2] In fact, three parliaments witnessed three percent or fewer such divisions. The three parliaments between 1970 and 1979 produced dramatically different figures: The divisions with dissenting votes rose to 20, 23, and 24 percent in the 1970–74, 1974, and 1974–79 parliaments, respectively.

This trend has not spared Mrs. Thatcher, despite her forceful leadership and her large majorities in the House of Commons. For instance, the first session of the 1983–87 parliament produced divisions with dissenting votes that came to 25 percent of the total. Of the 115 divisions that produced defections, 62 included Conservative MPs. Philip Norton has examined 18 of the more significant divisions in the 1979–83 parliament.[3] In these cases, the number of Conservative dissenters ranged between six and 51. Seven of the revolts resulted in no effects on the bill; three led to withdrawal of the offending provision; four ended with the government accepting an amendment; and four led to a government commitment to review its policy—in three cases the review accommodated the dissenters' concerns. We can see,

thus, that recalcitrance among a substantial number of government MPs can lead to concessions even from the likes of Mrs. Thatcher.

According to parliamentary procedure that prevailed until the 1970s, the loss of a vote in a major division would spell the end of the government. That is, it would constitute a *prima facie* evidence that the prime minister and cabinet could no longer rely on the support of the House of Commons. However, Edward Heath suffered five such losses between 1970 and 1974, and the succeeding Labour government absorbed defeats on expenditure, tax, Scottish devolution and wage restraint measures.[4] Indeed, in 1978 James Callaghan lost a major pay guideline provision that—notwithstanding its status as a centerpiece of his economic policy—failed to win the support of the house. In today's practice a government must declare a vote as a matter of "confidence" and lose it before there is pressure to ask the monarch to dissolve Parliament.[5] Or the opposition can force the government's hand with a motion of "no confidence."

In American minds, perhaps *question time* stands out most vividly as the opportunity for holding the government accountable for its actions. From Monday to Thursday each week, MPs address questions directly to ministers in an effort to force the government to explain its policies and administration. The approach especially appeals to American observers during occasions such as the Watergate and Iran-Contra scandals. It seems to allow MPs to get to the bottom of executive-branch wrongdoing much more directly than is possible through the avenues open to Congress.

[2] Philip Norton, "Behavioural Changes: Backbench Independence in the 1980s," in *Parliament in the 1980s,* ed. author (Oxford: Blackwell, 1985), p. 24.

[3] Norton, "Behavioural Changes: Backbench Independence in the 1890s," p. 30.

[4] Leon D. Epstein, "What Happened to the British Party Model," *American Political Science Review,* 74 (1980):19.

[5] H. Harvey and L. Bather, *The British Constitution and Politics* (London: Macmillan, 1982).

The significance of question time falls somewhat short of the myth built up on this side of the Atlantic. For one thing, the entire practice follows highly routinized channels. It takes place only between 2:30 and 3:30. The prime minister will take questions for only 15 minutes on Tuesdays and Thursdays. By the same token, other ministers know precisely which days they may be called upon. MPs must give advance notice in writing of their interventions, which they may follow up with oral supplementary questions. Frequently, ministers appear armed with thick briefing notes from which they read canned answers. If they become flustered, they can receive support from the officials in their department, who can slip a note from the official box in the corner of the house to the right of the speaker's chair. Ministers, of course, must uphold the policies of the government no matter how reasonable the opposition criticism. In fact, they often offer themselves

freely as lightning rods or human shields to protect the prime minister from admitting to some embarrassing stance or incident.

These procedures contrast sharply even with practices in other parliamentary systems that follow the Westminster model. For instance, Canadian ministers—including the prime minister—must accept questions whenever they appear during question period, and they enjoy no right of prior notice. And the substantially less decorous Canadian house would not suffer gladly anything but ad lib responses that display clearly the ability of the ministers to think on their feet about the issues for which they hold executive and administrative responsibility. They have no ready recourse to their officials while fielding questions.

Notwithstanding its defects, question time in the British House of Commons still plays an instrumental role in the parliamentary process. In an adversarial system, much of the

Sir Michael Havers, the Attorney General, was forced to take a leave from office after a succession of attacks on his handling of the Thatcher government's legal affairs. Cartoon from *The Guardian*, February 6, 1987.

power of the opposition hinges on its ability to undermine trust in the government party. Also, no opposition party will attract sufficient popular support to loom as a contender for the government mantle unless it appears to be a viable alternative. Question hour is the main occasion for the opposition to drive home the points necessary to swing the electorate toward its policies. Nevertheless, the use of question hour to force the government to account for its actions falls short of the cleansing power ascribed to it by some American observers.

One difference between the House of Commons and Congress in their pursuit of accountability is the failure of the question hour in Commons to attain its presumed objective. Too often, the opposition parties pry open a can of worms only to find that the government can frustrate their efforts to go further. Thus, they can expose ineptitude or venality, but they can't actually bring those implicated in wrongdoing to account for their actions.

This situation has owed largely to the weakness of parliamentary committees. The opposition can harp on government misdeeds as long as it wants. Yet the government itself must support any effort to launch a formal committee inquiry before any serious investigation can take place. Even if a committee examines a question exhaustively, the government ultimately determines whether the House of Commons will debate its report and act upon its recommendations.

Developments since 1979 have made it easier for MPs to press for inquiries into the actions of ministers and officials. In that year, the newly elected Conservative government completely revamped the committee system. In the process, it created 14 *select committees*. Each of these covered a major policy field that paralleled the departmental structure in Whitehall. These included Agriculture, Defence, Education, Science and Arts, Employment, Energy, Environment, Foreign Affairs, Home Affairs, Industry and Trade, Social Services, Transport, Scottish Affairs, Welsh Affairs, and Treasury and Civil Service. Working from these specialized committees with specific responsibilities for shadowing various departments, MPs can more readily convince the government that they should hold formal inquiries into clear instances of negligence or wrongdoing. However, committee positions go to parties in proportion to their representation in the House of Commons. Thus, the government can still influence the depth of inquiries and the tone of the resulting committee report.

The new arrangement completely revamped the leverage of committees in the House. All but the Scottish Affairs Committee have only 11 MPs. This imparts great status to committee membership. While party whips play a role in allotting positions, they can only with difficulty remove MPs from their assignments during a parliamentary session. Select committees, unlike standing committees, can operate when Parliament is not in session. This greatly reduces the pressure for MPs to bring special inquiries to a quick conclusion just because Parliament has adjourned. Each committee retains the assistance of a senior member of the parliamentary staff and is funded for the use of expert advise.

Committees have not turned the House of Commons into a Congress-style legislature. Discipline still prevents unbridled criticism from MPs who belong to the government party. Parliament still lacks the powers vis-à-vis the executive to subpoena cabinet secretaries or senior officials as legislative committees do in the United States. MPs must also play an endless game of cat-and-mouse with Whitehall bureaucrats who do testify. In observance of the secrecy conventions of the British system, such permanent civil servants pretty much confine themselves to elaboration of technical details. They will not delve into issues associated with the conduct of ministers and Whitehall colleagues.

Notwithstanding the emergent nature of committees in the House of Commons, they have made their impact felt. Senior Whitehall officials increasingly find themselves testifying before these bodies. In fact, some 1,300 civil servants made a total of nearly 1,800 appearances before select committees in the 1979–83 Parliament.[6] This constitutes no small development, in view of the fact that most of these individuals would have experienced virtually no such exposure to the House of Commons throughout their career had the system not changed.

Indeed, some investigations have dug deeply into executive affairs. These include the Defence Committee inquiry into the events surrounding the resignations of the secretaries of defence and trade and industry over the Westland Affair, the Foreign Affairs Committee investigation of the sinking of the Argentinean cruiser *General Belgrano* during the Falklands War, and the Industry and Trade Committee examination of the cause of the 1985 collapse of an international tin cartel that the U.K. government had helped to maintain. In all three cases, the respective committees ran into numerous roadblocks in their efforts to uncover all of the pertinent facts. In each instance, however, the committee hearings helped to establish the legitimacy of such studies even within the constraints of the parliamentary system.

THE JUDICIARY

We have noted that courts play a different role in the United Kingdom from that of their counterparts in the United States. Britain has not enshrined the fundamentals of its constitutional system in a single written document. Nor has it enumerated the rights of citizens in a formal charter. Thus, the will of Parliament as embodied in statutes serves as the most authoritative source of the law of the land. Traditionally, this fact has sharply constrained judicial interpretation. Judges lack such higher references as a Constitution or a Bill of Rights with which to pass judgment on the legal standing of statutes. In case of ambiguity, they focus their deliberations on discernment of what Parliament intended. There are no "founding fathers" whose original intention judges could attempt to divine.

We cannot conclude from this that the judiciary does little that affects the contours of policy and administration in the United Kingdom. The activity of courts permeates British society. Further, they deliberate on a host of issues that do not involve conflicts in meaning of acts of Parliament but still require interpretation. These include the enactments of local authorities, the standing of government regulations insofar as they draw upon ministers' discretionary powers imbedded in acts of Parliament, ruling on the validity of specific applications of statutes in individual cases, and treating the huge load of cases relying upon *common law,* rather than specific statutes, for resolution.[7] Common law reflects the accumulated customs for the administration of justice, including many matters which relate to fundamental rights, that date back to Anglo-Saxon times.

The judicial system operates at five levels. On the lowest tier, we find *magistrates' courts*. Here local justices of the peace—appointees who are not lawyers—try minor criminal cases. They also preside at the remand hearings in which all criminal pros-

[6] Stephen J. Downs, "Structural Changes, Select Committees: Experimentation and Establishment," in Norton, p. 62.

[7] Ian Budge and David McKay *et al., The New British Political System: Government and Society in the 1980s* (London: Longman, 1985), pp. 164–65.

High Court, London.

SOURCE: Printed with permission of Peter Hunter, Amsterdam.

ecutions, regardless of the gravity of the offense, receive preliminary examination. On the next rung, two different courts handle separate branches of law. *County courts* hear the vast majority of civil cases; *crown courts* handle all criminal offenses that are too large for magistrates to try on their own. Professional judges staff both courts. An overlap exists between crown courts and the next level, known as *High Court,* where the major criminal cases are heard.

The next three levels take us to the elite of the British judiciary. First, the High Court, which is based in London, includes some 100 judges and divides into three units. The *Chancery Division* rules on matters concerning trusts, inheritance, property, corporate law and taxes. The *Family Division* judges the more difficult contested divorce cases. The *Queen's Bench*—the largest division by far—handles three types of cases: the most important criminal trials; civil disputes that involve statutory law as opposed to common law; and administrative matters touching upon the behavior of officials of state toward individuals.

On the next tier up, we find the *Court of Appeal.* This body, presided over by the *master of the rolls,* functions in two divisions; criminal and civil. Consisting of around 30 members, the court considers cases in three-judge panels some of which, in criminal cases, would include one or more members of the Queen's Bench. Civil cases may be taken beyond the Court of Appeal to the House of Lords *Judicial Committee.* Here some 12 *lords of appeal*—members of the upper house especially appointed for their judicial experience—break into panels of five to share a workload in the neighborhood of 50 cases per year.

We should not lose sight of the limits of judicial interpretation in the United Kingdom, fixed as it is on divining the intent of acts of Parliament. However, judicial review has become an area of significant growth. The tortuous route of the Peter Wright case— discussed briefly in Chapter 3—demonstrates the degree to which some cases engage the judiciary profoundly. The various opinions rendered by judges along the way also point up the extent to which courts increasingly venture judgments about the prerogatives of the executive branch; they will assert themselves in those cases where they find that ministers and officials have taken actions against individuals that overstep statutory authority or their attached discretionary powers.

As we saw in Chapter 3, the Wright case involved a retired member of the British security and intelligence agency. This individual sought in 1986 to publish a book, *Spycatcher,* that would disclose serious wrongdoing and security lapses in that agency. Since Mr. Wright resides in Australia and has been able to publish the offending book in that and other countries, the British case has focused on the right of newspapers to report on his book.

In June 1986, a High Court judge granted the government an injunction against publication of either the book or newspaper accounts of its contents. However, a series of subsequent rulings began to whittle away this very sweeping order. These were handed down by the High Court and the Appeal Court in July 1986, and by the latter in July 1987. All three judgments quarreled in particular with the government's efforts to restrict newspaper coverage of judicial proceedings in the United Kingdom and in Australia.

On July 30, 1987, a five-member panel of law lords—lords of appeal—upheld the original court injunction against the newspapers in a 3-to-2 decision. In fact, they added a further constraint by prohibiting newspapers from reporting allegations made by Mr. Wright in Australian courts. One minority opinion, however, involved a momentous change of heart from no less than the senior law lord. This judge, Lord Bridge of Harwich, had previously earned a reputation for deference to the executive. In fact, he had, while chairman of the Security Commission, taken only three days to examine over 6,000 phone tap warrants and rule that they all had been properly authorized. This feat had drawn the bitter complaint that he was the "poodle of the executive" from Roy Jenkins, a former Labour cabinet minister and a co-founder of the Social Democratic Party.

Freedom of speech is always the first casualty under a totalitarian regime. Such a regime cannot afford to allow the free circulation of information and ideas among its citizens. Censorship is the indispensable tool to regulate what the public may and what they may not know. The present attempt to insulate the public in this country from information which is freely available elsewhere is a significant step down that very dangerous road. The maintenance of the ban, as more and more copies of the book *Spycatcher* enter this country and circulate here, will seem more and more ridiculous. If the Government are determined to fight to maintain the ban to the end, they will face inevitable condemnation and humiliation by the European Court of Human Rights in Strasbourg. Long before that they will have been condemned at the bar of public opinion in the free world.

SOURCE: Lord Bridge of Harwich, 1987.

In his judgment on *Spycatcher,* Lord Bridge poignantly raised serious second thoughts about his view of the British constitution. He noted the fact that Britain, while a signatory of the European Convention of Human Rights, still has not adopted this code formally as part of British law. For himself, he had taken the view that such charters place rights such as the freedom at issue—speech—on "too lofty a pedestal." He also trusted "in the capacity of the common law to safeguard the fundamental freedoms essential to a free society." In the strongest possible terms, he then offered the caveat that totalitarian regimes strike first at freedom of speech when they begin to establish themselves. He noted too that the government's decision could not survive either "the bar of public opinion in the free world" or the inevitable condemnation of the European Court of Human Rights.

Three newspapers, *The Guardian, The Observer,* and *The Sunday Times,* all defied the government injunction by proceeding with detailed accounts of *Spycatcher.* Smuggled copies of the book were freely available throughout the United Kingdom. The government continued its prosecution in the High Court. However, it lost its case there in December 1987. In February, it then faced a resounding rejection of its arguments in a unanimous ruling by a three-judge panel of the Court of Appeal that included the master of the rolls.

All of the opinions gave weight to the view that the executive cannot completely suppress allegations of "iniquity" in the very services that avowedly dedicate themselves to

---

The freedom of the press is not an optional extra. It is a right to be recognised unless compelling reasons for restraint are shown. Here they were not.

SOURCE: Lord Justice Bingham, 1988.

A candid shot of Sir Robert Armstrong, the secretary of the cabinet who pressed the case against Peter Wright. When caught giving misleading testimony to an Australian court, Sir Robert pleaded that he had simply been "economical with the truth."

SOURCE: Peter Hennessy, *Whitehall* (London: Secker & Marburg, 1989).

national security. One of these even recommended a proper sequence for legitimate disclosure of misdeeds. If the executive clearly refuses to deal with these, then those concerned may seek remedies in Parliament and—failing these—resort to publication in the press.

On October 13, 1988, the government lost its final appeal. A panel of five law lords ruled that the papers could proceed with publication of the allegations contained in *Spycatcher.* On behalf of his colleagues, Lord Keith of Kenkel explained that all possible damage to national security had already occurred through the publicity that Mr. Wright's allegations had thus far received. Thus, a continuation of the injunction would not make sense. The law lords made it clear that they did not base their ruling on broader issues such as balancing the various interpretations of public interest or the nature of freedom of the press.

The last word on the *Spycatcher* serves to illustrate that notwithstanding ferment within the judiciary over the proper role of the executive and the protection of democratic freedoms, the most senior judges in the land will dodge these issues when the opportunity presents itself.

GOVERNMENT AT THE PROVINCIAL AND LOCAL LEVEL

We discussed the operation of government beyond the central apparatus in Chapter 4. We noted that the U.K. government administers many programs through the Scottish Office, the Welsh Office and the Northern Ireland Office rather than through Whitehall. We also observed that nationalists seeking devolution of legislative powers to these provinces have faced decisive setbacks. Devolution referenda for Scotland and Wales failed in 1979, and civil unrest in Northern Ireland led to the suspension of that province's separate legislature, Stormont, in 1972. Chapter 4 also pointed up the degree to which Mrs. Thatcher has curtailed the powers and authority of local governments throughout Britain.

The Provinces

Notwithstanding the lack of autonomous legislative powers, considerably different administrative structures manage the affairs of the three provinces from those functioning directly out of Whitehall. In the case of Northern Ireland, a distinct civil service operates numerous departments. These include six major agencies—Agriculture, Economic Development, Education, Environment, Finance and Personnel, and Health and Social Services—each of whose functions parallel those of Whitehall departments. A Whitehall-based department, the Northern Ireland Office, supports the secretary of state for Northern Ireland in developing and overseeing the policies administered by Northern Ireland Civil Service. It also maintains special responsibility toward law and order in the province.

Neither the Scottish Office nor the Welsh Office maintains a large establishment in London. The former enjoys a sounder base than does the latter. The secretary of state for Scotland draws, in fact, on separate statutory authority in several policy areas, administering laws passed by the British Parliament but which apply specifically to Scotland. The counterpart for Wales overwhelmingly executes statutes which pertain both in England and Wales.

We might ask whether these various structural features mean anything to the average citizen in the provinces. For the most part, they simply provide a context in which civil servants can gear the administration of policies to the peculiar requirements of a national region. Yet, even this must be done with limited parameters. For instance, none of the offices exerts a great deal of discretion over budgeting; the expenditure of an office in specific areas must, with few exceptions, follow broadly the contours of that in England. For example, the Scottish Office cannot decide unilaterally to reduce sharply expenditures on new bridges so as to pour additional funds into its health services.

In the case of Scotland, the separate statutory authority for many governmental areas does improve the chances that programs will be administered differently. The organization of the legal system, schools, universities and local government, to name the most obvious areas, has followed a substantially different path in Scotland than in the rest of the United Kingdom. Thus, one derives a more palpable sense of administration discretion in the Scottish Office than one discerns in the Welsh Office. A similar pattern might have prevailed in Northern Ireland had not the deep divisions between Protestants and Catholics coupled with the imposition of direct rule militated against quasi-autonomous provincial governance even in matters of administrative practice.

Local Government

The British refer to their local governments as "local authorities." These entities have suffered a huge bloodletting of power under Mrs. Thatcher. As we noted in Chapter 4, this dramatic turn of events has resulted from five Conservative policies: (1) relying more on cabinet authority and less on Parliament in instigating change; (2) limiting local authorities' discretion in implementing statutes; (3) sharply constraining their spending powers; (4) curtailing their ability to raise revenues; and (5) abolishing the Greater London Council and six metropolitan counties.

There are some 500 main local authorities in England and Wales.[8] These include the governing bodies of metropolitan districts, county councils and county districts. Within this very complex system, the larger authorities assume responsibility for local administration of much of education, social welfare, police, and regional and town planning. In many areas, the central government might operate alongside local authorities. In the postsecondary education field, for instance, polytechnic institutes come under the juris-

diction of local authorities, while universities come under the sway of Whitehall.

With the exception of the provision of housing, smaller local authorities look after the less significant activities that metropolitan districts and county councils choose not to take under their umbrellas. The Scottish system operates more hierarchically than does that in England and Wales.[9] The province divides into nine regions with clear overarching responsibility for the districts below them. The regions also assume functions associated with water and sewage that do not fall within the compass of local authorities in England and Wales. Due to the unrest, in Northern Ireland the more significant operations of local government have become almost totally absorbed by the central government administrative apparatus.

By the late 1980s, local governments were spending approximately 40 billion pounds a year—about one quarter of public expenditure. A 1980 study reports that local authority employees accounted for close to 40 percent of those working in the public sector in 1977.[10] Obviously, any government in London, especially a market-oriented Conservative one like Mrs. Thatcher's, would take on the task of limiting local spending authority and the size of its labor force.

Local governments have relied upon three main sources of revenue: (1) *rates*—the tax levied upon property, (2) charges for specific services, and (3) various grants from the central government. The latter include aid based on entitlement to support for specific programs, funds for housing, and the Rate Support Grant (RSG). In addition to providing a baseline for the infusion of funds from the central government, the RSG seeks to main-

[8] George W. Jones, "The Crisis in British Central-Local Government Relationships," *Governance: An International Journal of Policy and Administration,* 1 (1988):167.

[9] Budge and McKay, p. 118.

[10] Richard Parry, "The Territorial Dimension in United Kingdom Public Employment," *Studies in Public Policy,* 65 (1980), as cited by Budge and McKay, p. 112.

tain relative parity in the resources available to local authorities. It entails an elaborate process for negotiations between the Department of the Environment in Whitehall and the various local governments.

The intricate RSG consultations took especially formal shape with the institution in 1975 of the Consultative Council on Local Government Finance. The negotiation process became important to Whitehall's macroeconomic policies. The consultations yielded a series of fiscal years in which aggregate local authority spending came very close to target.[11] In fact, local authorities' spending more frequently fell short of the agreed figures than it exceeded them.

The Thatcher government has truncated the RSG consultative regime by imposing mandatory ceilings on local authority spending. This has closed out many options for councils to decide on their own what level of service to maintain in their area. In fact, local authorities have lost some of the Rate Support Grant if their expenditures have exceeded the limits imposed by the central government.

As we saw in Chapter 4, local authorities will soon lose their right to charge taxes based on property values. Instead, they will have to resort to a per-head "community charge" that will prove especially onerous to the poor. Local authorities will find themselves even more sharply constrained under these circumstances. We might reasonably ask whether local governments will retain any significant capacity to discern and respond to the needs of their communities under the strictures imposed by the Thatcher government.

ON BEING EUROPEAN

Many Americans view England as the gateway to Europe. Certainly, a large proportion

of them pass through London even if business or pleasure takes them to the continent. Yet, U.S. visitors will find that Britons do not automatically consider themselves European. As an island people, they still feel somewhat remote from the mainland. Until the tunnel under the English Channel is completed in the next few years, they still must fly or take a ferry to reach their closest mainland neighbor, France.

In addition to this physical barrier, Britons have not advanced greatly in overcoming a psychological block about foreigners and different languages. Precious few Britons—even leaders in politics, business and the scholarly world—are fluent in a second language. This contrasts with the French political, economic and educational elite, many of whom can at least struggle through a conversation in English. Of course, the Dutch, Germans, and Scandinavians count a large proportion among their leadership who speak English fluently.

Britain did not jump at the chance to integrate itself more fully into Europe as the movement for greater unity built up steam on the continent. The United Kingdom joined the Council of Europe, an organization for advancing European unity that is distinct from the European Economic Community (EEC), as a founding member in 1949. However, the leaders of both the Conservative and Labour parties encountered domestic resistance in marshaling support for British entry into the EEC after its creation in 1957. Not all of the blame rests on Britons' dithering about joining the EEC. In 1963, the French President, General Charles de Gaulle, brought entry negotiations to an abrupt end by vetoing British admittance. De Gaulle thwarted Britain once again in 1967.

De Gaulle's resignation as president cleared the way for renewed negotiations, which began in 1970. The Conservative government of Edward Heath (1970–74) man-

[11] Jones, p. 172.

Paris, March, 1984: Breakfast and a discussion by Prime Minister
Thatcher and President Mitterrand of the budget of the European
Economic Community.

SOURCE: Laurent Maous/Gamma.

aged to win a House of Commons endorsement of entry by 356 votes to 244 in October
1971. It obtained this large victory—notwithstanding 39 defections—due to the support or abstention of nearly 90 Labour MPs.
The issue did not stop there. The Labour government under Harold Wilson sought a rene-
gotiation of the terms of Britain's entry in
1974. Ultimately, it put the revised terms to a
national referendum in June 1975. This carried with a 67 percent "Yes" vote. However,
doubts have reemerged occasionally in both
parties, especially Labour. For instance, its
National Conference overwhelmingly supported a withdraw-from-Europe proposition
in 1980. EEC membership did not rank as a
top issue in the 1983 and 1987 general elections.

The EEC has become a formidable executive, bureaucratic, legislative and judicial

complex in its own right, and Britons have played an active role in all four arenas. Mrs. Thatcher has gained almost unrivaled standing among EEC political leaders, much as she has established herself as one of the more dominant statesmen in world affairs. The British secretary of state for foreign and commonwealth affairs belongs, along with counterparts from other member states, to the *Council of Ministers,* which serves as the continuing executive council of the EEC. Various "technical councils," whose makeup includes ministers from member countries responsible for specialized policy areas such as agriculture, hammer out policy and programmatic details. In this respect, they function very much as ministerial committees in the United Kingdom operate in relation to the cabinet.

The *European Commission* serves as the locus of the bureaucratic side to the EEC. It consists of two senior officials from each of the big-four countries—Britain, France, Italy, and West Germany—and one official from each of the other members. It essentially serves as a steering committee for the EEC bureaucracy located in Brussels. Thus, its mandate extends beyond the type of secretariat function that, as we saw in Chapter 6, the British Cabinet Office performs. The Treaty of Rome imparted to the commission responsibility for developing its own policy proposals and presenting these initiatives to the Council of Ministers.

The *European Parliament* functions as the legislative branch of the EEC, while the *Court of Justice of the European Communities* operates as the judiciary. The former institution emerged in 1979 and incorporates elected representatives from all EEC nations. U.K. voters send 78 members to this body, which meets in Strasbourg, France, and holds many of its committee hearings in Brussels, Belgium. The parliament effectively enjoys only investigative powers. It can dismiss the com-

mission and reject the EEC budget. However, either action would require a two-thirds majority. The Court of Justice of the European Communities—not to be confused with European Court of Human Rights—hears cases in which the legislation of member states conflicts with the provisions of the Treaty of Rome.

The EEC has carved out three broad goals for itself: establishing a customs union; forming a common market; and harmonizing social and economic policies.[12] The EEC has accomplished the first of these objectives. That is, each member state has yielded direct authority over fixing trade quotas, taxes and subsidies to the EEC. Indeed, the EEC functions on behalf of its member states in General Agreement on Tariffs and Trade (GATT) negotiations.

With respect to establishing free exchange of labor, capital and goods between members—a true common market, agriculture has served as the only field in which a union of this nature has pertained. However, 1992 will mark the eradication of most of the remaining barriers to establishment of a common market. And toward the end of harmonizing social and economic policies, the EEC has appropriated significant resources for a European Regional Development Fund. The assistance has gone to areas within member countries that have deindustrialized or still require infrastructure.

The *Value-Added Tax* (VAT)—a financial instrument whereby governments exact a tariff each time goods pass through a stage in the productive or commercial processes—has been adopted by every EEC nation. This has assisted the consistency of revenue extraction in relation to industry and consumption throughout the EEC. The *European Monetary System* (EMS) should also receive mention here. While it is not a mandatory EEC

---

[12] Budge and McKay, p. 141.

policy, it depends on the formal or tacit participation of most of the community. It consists of a mutually agreed-upon formula whereby no member will permit the value of its currency to drift above or below specified parameters. Members of the EMS have a collective capacity to intervene in the currency markets in instances where a country finds it impossible to stay within the designated limits.

Britain has not proven to be an exemplary member of the EEC. Part of the difficulty stems from the fact that the country gains little if anything from the Common Agricultural Policy (CAP). It simply lacks sufficient numbers of the small and relatively inefficient farms that benefit so much from CAP elsewhere in Europe. Britain also has withheld itself from the European Monetary System (EMS) since its inception in 1978. Even under Labour, the British Treasury worried about pressures on the pound—upward from the U.S. or downward from Germany—that would make it extremely difficult to keep the currency within the set limits.

The British drive a hard bargain with their European partners. Mrs. Thatcher has consistently forced her counterparts into major concessions on the EEC budget. Her strongly monetarist inclinations have kept her from committing Britain to the EMS. Just the same, the Treasury has come around to the wisdom of full membership. In fact, it kept the pound within limits compatible with full participation through much of the mid-1980s. This tacit policy led ultimately to the dispute in October 1989 between Mrs. Thatcher and Nigel Lawson—the chancellor—which ended with the latter resigning from the government.

On other fronts, Britain appears to be odd man out in more than its share of EEC disputes. For instance, it isolated itself in two key discussions in 1987: development of a joint policy on technological change, and the

A booklet, *Guidance on the Exercise of the Presidency,* was circulated last May to those British officials who were chairing EEC committees in Brussels during the second half of 1986.
. . . Paragraph 10 of the chapter on "tactics" explains how to block progress if agreement would be counter to British interests.

"The UK's objective may be to delay a decision (e.g., until after the UK Presidency). As long as the UK is not isolated, the simplest device will be for the chairman to let delegations ramble on.

"Provided that agreement is not actually staring him in the face, he may be able to conclude that a number of new issues have been raised which require consideration in capitals and reflection by the Commission."

When the day comes to resume the discussion "meetings can then be cancelled because another group needs the meeting room . . . and so on."

The guide concedes that it is the chairman's duty to be "even-handed in his dealings with all delegations" and that the "task of promoting the UK's objectives" falls, in theory, to another official occupying the UK chair.

But it goes on to suggest the possibility of discreet collusion. "It is not uncommon for the national delegation to take an extreme position at one end of the spectrum, leaving the Presidency scope for an apparently even-handed compromise which is actually highly acceptable to the national delegation."

SOURCE: *The Independent,* February 6, 1987.

EEC contribution to an international effort to address the crisis over the earth's ozone layer. To those who chalk up these obstructionist reflexes to coincidence, a document leaked to the press in 1987 gives pause for thought. The chairmanship of EEC bodies rotates in six-month terms. Britain assumed the chair for the second half of 1986. A confidential British directive issued in anticipation of the chair revealed that Whitehall even coaches its officials in obstruction.

WHITEHALL, PARLIAMENT, AND INTEREST GROUPS

Just before he left office, President Ronald Reagan spoke of "iron triangles" that dominate politics in Washington. These are coalitions of key players that can prevent the government from responding in a timely way to the most urgent problems faced by the nation. He noted that these iron triangles consisted of interest groups, Congress, and the media.

In fact, Mr. Reagan took liberties with a tried-and-true political science concept in the United States: that subgovernments develop within specific policy sectors through which those with the highest stakes work out deals with one another that protect the status quo. Frequently, innovators (including presidents) find it virtually impossible to dislodge these iron triangles. Mr. Reagan departed from the usual understanding of which three sectors form subgovernments by including the press and excluding government departments. The classic statement of the theory holds that the myriad specialized offices and bureaus of departments and agencies form cozy relations with both their clients—that is, interest groups, and their patrons—congressional committees and subcommittees. Held together by mutual political advantage, these subgovernments cohere in such a way that they can thwart most efforts on the part of a president to change policies or to withdraw resources.

We find little evidence of iron triangles in Britain. A look at the relations between interest groups, Parliament and the bureaucracy in the United Kingdom suggests that one of the elements—Parliament—simply does not play a substantial enough role in the policy process. This owes largely to the weakness of committees in the House of Commons and the House of Lords. Above all else, iron triangles run on monopolies of information. With only a nascent tradition of specialized committees, Parliament finds itself greatly hampered in finding out enough about the issues it considers to gain leverage with the other players. In addition, the House of Commons performs little detailed review of the resources that the government has earmarked for various programs. Thus, neither British interest groups nor departments spend anywhere near the amount of time explaining themselves to legislative committees as their counterparts in the United States do.

Interestingly, British MPs indulge in one practice most Americans would view as fraught with conflict of interest: Over 100 MPs receive retainers from corporations and interests groups. MPs must report these arrangements in a public register. They must also note any such relationships whenever they speak on issues of concern to those from whom they receive retainers. Normally MPs who take retainers also assume a title in the firm or organization that they represent. That is, they usually become "directors" or "consultants."

According to a 1987 agreement, MPs' salaries must stay within the range of those for principals in the career civil service—officials who work as far as seven levels down in departmental hierarchies. In 1987, the salary assigned to MPs came to 18,500 pounds. In dollar terms, this figure would come to less than half of what members of the House of Representatives make. We can see, thus, that retainers can make the difference between a strapped and a comfortable standard of living for MPs who have not based their careers on private wealth.

Retainers do more than simply allow MPs to augment their relatively meager salaries. The House of Commons supplies MPs with neither adequate funds for staffs nor suitable offices. An affiliation with a company or interest group thus can provide an MP with the amenities necessary to function effectively.

Taken together, the retainers and amenities make many MPs somewhat beholden to their clients. One must ask, then, whether the disclosure rule alone acts as an adequate check on conflict of interest in the House of Commons. Some MPs have become so dependent upon directorships and consultancies that one can hardly conceive that they enjoy much latitude for independent judgment. Conservative MPs tend to enter into retainer arrangements more than do the members of the other parties. Thus, the practice works a subtle effect toward reinforcing the pro-business bias of the Conservatives.

On the other side of the House of Commons, a longstanding Labour practice helps maintain the special relationship between the party and trade unions. We saw in Chapter 5 that the Labour Party started in 1900 as a committee working to encourage members of the working class to run for election to the House of Commons. Currently, unions sponsor the candidacies of around 50 percent of Labour MPs. This does not mean, however, that half of all Labour MPs are working class. For the most part, Labour MPs have graduated from university or worked in white-collar jobs before running for the House of Commons. Still, those wishing to obtain nomination in heavily working-class constituencies must come to terms with local trade union organizations. And this fact—along with the formal links between the party and trade unions—tends to galvanize the attentiveness of individual Labour MPs to the claims of the unionized worker.

As indicated above, individual backbench MPs do not play a very significant role in determining the actual contours of government policies and budgets. Even if some MPs have established very close links to outside groups and interests, we cannot inflate these to iron-triangle status. Here we come to an ancillary reason for the relatively low salience of most MPs in the policy-making process.

Generally, permanent civil servants in Whitehall departments avoid any direct contacts with MPs, except when providing testimony or accompanying their minister to parliamentary committees. More than just the links between MPs and the outside lack strength, regularity and durability. Thus, the ties between MPs and Whitehall officials fall considerably short of what "iron" connotes.

When we search for where outside groups and interests go when they want to influence government, we have to focus our attention on the process whereby Whitehall gathers advice and information. To be sure, the prime minister and cabinet secretaries fashion policy agendas which they busy themselves trying to fulfill during their term of office. And along the way, backbench MPs can weigh in from time to time either to support the government's plans or to caution it about how best to proceed. However, ministers overwhelmingly rely on permanent civil servants to examine the likely consequences of various policy proposals, to advise on the timing and approach of new initiatives, to recommend how resources might be allocated so as to reflect the government's priorities, and to implement resulting programs.

Within this framework, it becomes crucial that outside groups and interests try to influence the advice that permanent civil servants give to ministers. It becomes equally critical that they engage in discussions with officials on ways in which the latter will exercise the discretion that they receive to judge on their own many of the fine points of implementation. Whitehall departments have proven over the past two decades to be increasingly receptive to establishing ongoing consultative ties with individuals and groups that take a keen interest in their activities. Obviously, these ties vary according to the status of the outside clients and the extent to which high-level civil servants perceive that they require the groups' cooperation in order to develop and administer policies and programs. The point is that a significant cultural change has taken hold in Whitehall. Twenty years ago officials would confine their direct encounters with outside groups and interests to formal meetings, usually presided over by a minister, or social engagements. Now many senior officials in Whitehall maintain relatively well-developed networks of contacts whom they consult on a regular basis.

Some interest groups enjoy easier access to Whitehall than others. Two factors influence access more than any others. First, it helps immensely if a group "has a letter box," meaning that a significant bureaucratic organization concentrates its activities in an area that corresponds to that of the outside group. For instance, business organizations can develop relations with the Department of Trade and Industry, oil producers with the Department of Energy, farmers and fishermen with the Ministry of Agriculture, Fisheries and Food, and physicians with the Department of Health.

Other obligations might limit a department's level of commitment to the positive agenda of specific groups. Environmentalists will find that the Department of Environment shoulders responsibility for a host of government programs that might conflict with their goals. The Ministry of Defence does not refuse to speak with representatives of the Campaign for Nuclear Disarmament; however, we could hardly expect its officials to embrace the group's objectives.

The second factor is how much leverage the group enjoys when it presses its appeals. Some groups speak for virtually all the people within their area. For instance, the British Medical Association, the National Farmers' Union and the National Union of Mineworkers brigade over 90 percent of potential members within their organizations. Others, such as environmentalists and comsumer groups, incorporate as paid members a relatively small proportion of the people who identify with their causes.

Britons tend less than Americans to involve themselves in movements not directly associated with their livelihood. This makes mobilization of support more difficult for groups dedicated to a cause that cuts across occupational interests. Relatedly, groups attain different levels of legitimacy in the eyes of officials. Some organizations that engage in demonstrations and strikes might offend the codes of propriety prevailing in Whitehall. Others might simply press viewpoints that officials know articulate positions held only by those on the fringes of society.

Some sectors of interest group activity become so complex that overarching organizations form. These institutions try to give greater coherence to the process of influencing government from the standpoint of a major segment of society. For the business community, the Confederation of British Industry (CBI) tries to hammer out and communicate to the government common positions on issues affecting the economy. CBI consists of some 12,000 corporate members—many of which have fewer than 50 employees. For workers, the Trade Union Congress (TCU) serves as ringmaster for nearly 150 unions' collective efforts to influence government.

During the 1960s and the 1970s, governments around the world tried to develop ways of bringing business and union leaders more regularly into consultations on the management of the economy. In this period, both the Labour and Conservative governments tried to devise mechanisms whereby Britain could follow this approach. They believed that they could improve the performance of the British economy through a direct transaction. By teasing out of business and union leaders concessions on prices, production, wages and trade practices, the government would gain a more stable environment in which to plan the economy. For their part, the business and union leaders would benefit from having a direct say in the contours of government policies.

The various consultative processes arising from this approach produced less than satisfactory results. It became clear that neither the CBI nor TUC could actually deliver their memberships' support of the policies that emerged from consultations with the government. This owed substantially to the fact that neither organization could exert a tight control on the actions of its members. TUC came off especially poorly in its efforts to get unions to adhere to its agreements with governments on pay. The resulting disillusionment and—by 1979—chaos contributed to Mrs. Thatcher's resolve not to attempt to manage the economy through consultative mechanisms.

CONCLUSION

This chapter has followed upon the previous chapter's treatment of the role of the prime minister, cabinet and Whitehall that perhaps left readers wondering whether any other elements of the policy process matter. On closer inspection, we can say that improvements in the leverage of Parliament and the judiciary as well as the exigencies of belonging to the EEC have all complicated the lives of political executives and bureaucrats. Domestically, the executive branch—especially under Mrs. Thatcher—still can get its way most of the time. It simply has to explain itself a great deal more to both Parliament and the courts. Meanwhile, officials interact more frequently with individual interest groups—notwithstanding the fact that formal consultative processes involving the CBI and TUC have played a greatly reduced role. When Britain entered the EEC, the nature of such an alliance immediately imposed constraints on the British executive, thus slowing dramatically the process of developing and implementing policies. Finally, local authorities have—of course—faced a sharp diminution of power the extent of which still remains to be fully revealed.

References and Suggested Readings

ARTHUR, P. *Government and Politics of Northern Ireland.* London: Longman, 1984.

BAGEHOT, WALTER. *The English Constitution,* 1867. 1963 edition by R. H. S. Crossman. London: Fontana.

BIRCH, A. H. *Political Integration and Disintegration in the British Isles.* London: Allen & Unwin, 1977.

BUDGE, IAN, AND DAVID MCKAY et al. *The New British Political System: Government and Society in the 1980s.* London: Longman, 1985.

BURTON, I., AND G. DREWRY. *Legislation and Public Policy.* London: Macmillan, 1981.

DOWNS, STEPHEN J. "Structural Changes, Select Committees: Experimentation and Establishment." In *Parliament in the 1980s,* ed. Philip Norton. Oxford: Blackwell, 1985.

EPSTEIN, LEON D. "What Happened to the British Party Model." *American Political Science Review* 74 (1980):9–22.

GRIFFITH, J. A. G. *The Politics of the English Judiciary.* London: Fontana, 1981.

HARVEY, J., AND L. BATHER. *The British Constitution and Politics.* London: Macmillan, 1982.

JACKSON, R. M. *The Machinery of Justice in England.* Cambridge: Cambridge University Press, 1977.

JONES, GEORGE, W., AND J. STEWART. *The Case for Local Government.* London: Allen & Unwin, 1983.

———. "The Crisis in British Central-Local Government Relationships." *Governance: An International Journal of Policy and Administration* 1 (1988):162–83.

KAVANAGH, DENNIS. "New Bottles for New Wines." *Parliamentary Affairs* 31 (1977):6–21 [a treatment of intergovernmental affairs in European Economic Community].

———. *Dissension in the House of Commons,*

1974–79. Oxford: Oxford University Press, 1980.

_____. *The British Polity*. London: Longman, 1984.

_____. Behavioural Changes: "Backbench Independence in the 1980s." In *Parliament in the 1980s,* ed. author. Oxford: Blackwell, 1985.

PARRY, RICHARD. "The Territorial Dimension in United Kingdom Public Employment." *Studies in Public Policy* 65, 1980.

RADICE, LISANNE, ELIZABETH VALLANCE, AND VIRGINIA WILLIS. *Member of Parliament: The Job of a Backbencher*. London: Macmillan, 1987.

ROSE, RICHARD. *The Territorial Dimension in Government: Understanding the United Kingdom*. Chatham, NJ: Chatham House, 1982.

SCHWARZ, JOHN E. "Exploring a New Role in Policy Making: The British House of Commons in the 1970s." *American Political Science Review* 74 (1980):23–37.

WALLACE, W., H. WALLACE, AND K. WEBB. *Policy-making in the European Community*. Chichester: Wiley, 1977.

8

How Policy Is Made: A Look at Economics and Foreign Affairs

So far, this consideration of British government and politics has attempted to identify and discuss the dimensions crucial to any understanding of the U.K. system. Broadly speaking, we have examined the following issues: (1) the problem of economic, institutional and political decline in Britain; (2) the important themes that emerge with respect to the system's efforts to adapt to adversity; (3) the inherent limitations of the British political culture; (4) parties and elections in a period of realignment; (5) guidance in the heart of the U.K. government—the roles of the prime minister, cabinet and Whitehall; and (6) the significance of elements less central in policy arenas, including Parliament, the judiciary, local governments, the European Economic Community, and interest groups.

Obviously, each of the above issues contains many subtopics that have entered into our discussion. We have also taken special pains in each chapter to relate various structural and behavioral features of the current British system to individual cases. In other words, we have tried to keep in perspective what we have found about the underlying principles of the British polity, putting them in bold relief by examining how what we have asserted about structure and behavior actually manifests itself in specific circumstances.

Following upon this approach, we now move on to an effort to illustrate how the British system works in two policy areas. We have chosen economic and foreign policy. Both of these merit such attention because major decisions in each sector affect the entire political system. A focus on these areas enables us to observe the exertion of power and authority in matters where there is no question about the importance of the stakes. In this respect, they provide us an opportunity to glimpse how the system functions in relation to two dimensions fundamental to its survival and adaptation to new circumstances.

ECONOMIC POLICY: A NATURAL MONOPOLY OF THE TREASURY?

Managing the economy is not an easy task. The difficulties go beyond simply coming out with the right solutions to the various economic problems faced by a country. Often, relatively clear options present themselves. But solutions must work their way through mazes fraught with bureaucratic and political conflict. In the process, even straightforward problems become mindbogglingly complex.

Suppose we were to rank the United Kingdom's economic policy-making process in terms of complexity. We would find that it appears relatively streamlined, particularly if we keep in mind the intricacy of the American system. Even when a U.S. administration is still at the stage of developing its economic forecasts, it must negotiate these through the Department of the Treasury, the Office of Management and Budget, and the Council of Economic Advisers. The same organizations will compete intensely in the process whereby an administration develops its macroeconomic policies. These policies form the broad framework that guides the administration's stances on the use of various economic instruments such as exchange and interest rates, tariffs and other trade restrictions, managing the national debt, spending, taxation and regulation.

When we look at how an administration actually resolves conflicts over the use of these instruments, we find innumerable constellations of countervailing interests. For instance, the early years of the Reagan administration frequently found the Department of Treasury and the Office of Management and Budget at loggerheads over the proper balance between taxation and spending restraint necessary to cut the deficit. The separation of powers also greatly exacerbates the difficulty of achieving coherence in U.S. economic policies. Even if an administration achieves relatively strong consensus over a particular policy, the Congress will almost invariably have another view that will very often prevail to the point where Congress completely obfuscates the policy intentions of the administration.

A Less Complicated World

Unlike the United States, Britain has one department, Her Majesty's Treasury, to control most of the bureaucratic levers affecting the economy. In fact, we find that all the elements key to economic management function under one roof in Britain. That is, the Treasury houses the central operations in the U.K. government responsible for tax policy, financial institutions and markets, monetary policy, overseas finance (including matters involving the European Economic Community), macro- and microeconomic analysis, public expenditure control, and policies pertaining to both private and public enterprises.

Obviously, other departments actually implement many of the policies established by the Treasury. For instance, Inland Revenue and Customs and Excise collect the taxes and duties. Some departments actually can give the Treasury a run for its money in the sway they exert within their own domains. For instance, the Department of Trade and Industry usually plays a very substantial role in any Whitehall discussions about policies that affect commerce and the development of specific industries. However, the Treasury usually dominates the central agency community in the field of economics. *Central agencies* are those government departments that shoulder general responsibility for one or another element of guidance and control functions affecting the whole bureaucracy. In this respect, neither No. 10 Downing Street, which serves the prime minister exclusively, nor the Cabinet Office, which supports the prime minister and cabinet, enjoys the staffing level and the direct access to levers necessary to play consistent roles in the economic policy-making. This does not suggest, however, that they do not have substantial input from time to time.

The British adoption of such a streamlined apparatus for economic policy-making follows upon several efforts in the 1960s and 1970s to break down the Treasury's hegemony. For instance, in 1964 Harold Wilson's first Labour government created a Department of Economic Affairs that was supposed to take the lead in macroeconomic analysis and the development of medium-term economic plans. However, its minister was never able to command the attention from the prime minister that the Treasury's head—the *chancellor of the exchequer*—does. Further, the Treasury maintained control of the "sharp end"—that is, all instruments necessary to actually shape economic policies.

In the United States, the Office of Management and Budget operates entirely separately from the Department of the Treasury; in fact, it reports directly to the president as the lead agency responsible for the administration's policies on government expenditure and management. Whitehall engaged in an experiment, beginning in 1968, whereby a Civil Service Department shouldered responsibility for policies and resources associated with management of the public service. Even this relatively small domain, which accounted for roughly 10 percent of all that government spends, could not escape the Treasury's jealous custodianship. Mrs. Thatcher let the Treasury repossess control over the resource part of the Civil Service Department's responsibilities in 1981, thus relegating the new department, rechristened the Management and Personnel Office, to a management consultancy. The Treasury absorbed even this diminutive function in 1987.

The peculiar nature of the Whitehall culture buttresses the Treasury's hegemony over economic policy. Unlike the U.S. bureaucracy, Whitehall maintains a "village life."[1] A common *esprit de corps* permeates the senior ranks of the British civil service. Thus, officials, whatever their differences, work behind a veil of secrecy in developing the necessary consensus to resolve differences between departments. During the period of policy gestation, this secrecy many times prevents interdepartmental squabbles from attracting any substantial public attention on the details that might have engendered bureaucratic infighting. It is worse than "poor form" to violate the village norm of secrecy. Dissenters who decide to go public expose themselves to prosecution under the Official Secrets Act or, minimally, place their promotion prospects in severe jeopardy.

Cabinet ministers behave within this context in an entirely different way from political appointees in the United States. They will argue their departments' cases vigorously in cabinet and its committees. The press might become aware of an individual minister's reservations about a policy; however, only very rarely will ministers register their concerns publicly. Normally, when cabinet decides a matter, that is it. This is especially the case in the economics policy field. Strictly speaking, the Treasury is the prime minister's department. This is the basis of the special reporting relationship that the chancellor of the exchequer has to the prime minister. Chancellors might strongly disagree with the prime minister. However, a failure on the part of the chancellor to adhere to the policy preferences of the prime minister would constitute *prima*

---

[1] Hugh Heclo and Aaron Wildavsky, *The Private Government of Public Money: Community and Policy Inside British Politics* (Berkeley, CA: University of California Press, 1974).

facie evidence that the latter had lost control of his or her government.

The process whereby a government wins Parliament's approval of key economic policies presents a still starker contrast to that by which a U.S. administration obtains congressional assent to similar initiatives. As we saw in the preceding chapter, backbench MPs on the government side of the House of Commons increasingly brave the threat of reprisals and vote against their party. However, they usually pick social issues, such as the level of welfare benefits or the unpopular poll tax, in which to assert their independence. A backbench revolt on a central element of economic policy would cut too close to a government's viability to attract a substantial numbers of dissenters.

In a less dramatic way, MPs can significantly influence public discussion of economic policy through the *Treasury and Civil Service Committee*. This committee emerged in 1979 at the time that Mrs. Thatcher's new government authorized creation of select committees in the House of Commons to monitor the activities of each of the main Whitehall policy sectors. The Treasury and Civil Service Committee has proven to be one of most active of these new bodies. During the 1979–83 Parliament, it produced 24 reports—more than any other select committee.[2] It also made full use of a provision whereby select committees may contract the services of outside experts, retaining 29 advisers on short-term consultancies.[3] Only the Foreign Affairs Committee exceeded this level of utilization of external advice.

[2] Stephen J. Downs, "Structure Changes, Select Committees: Experiment and Establishment," in *Parliament in the 1980s*, ed. by Philip Norton (Oxford: Blackwell, 1985), p. 62.
[3] Max Beloff and Gillian Peele, *The Government of the UK: Political Authority in a Changing Society* (London: Weidenfeld and Nicholson, 1985), p. 147.

The Treasury and Civil Service Committee does not change the Treasury's mind on many economic issues. However, it does command its attention. It cannot order ministers or officials to testify, nor can it insist upon seeing specific documents. However, Treasury ministers and officials have usually agreed to meet with the committee upon request. Thus, committee hearings have exposed to scrutiny the thinking behind the Treasury's policies and actions to a degree that substantially enhances MPs' ability to enter public debates on economic issues intelligently.

Two Prime Ministers

Since the prime minister and the chancellor of the exchequer hold economic policy so closely to themselves, we should find it instructive to compare briefly the decision process that operated under the two most recent governments. In the case of James Callaghan's government, we will focus on its efforts to limit wage increases; in that of Margaret Thatcher, we will examine the effects of its commitment to monetarism.

James Callaghan. James Callaghan served from 1976 to 1979 as prime minister in the Labour government that Harold Wilson had formed in 1974. During this period, Britain—as most other advanced political systems—struggled with a protracted period of *stagflation*. That is, it encountered simultaneously persistent unemployment and inflation.

Callaghan spent a great deal of his time on economic policy. This emphasis tended to intensify utilization of machinery in the center of government designed to assist coordination of economy policy. In this period, the economics and European secretariats of the Cabinet Office began to assume stronger than usual roles as integrating agents in bringing

I'm not terribly keen personally on setting up de-liberately a countervailing force. That was part of the idea of the Department of Economic Affairs, creating tension and all that kind of thing. But it tends to waste an awful lot of time. If it's institutionalized, sooner or later perhaps one or the other tends to win.

SOURCE: A Treasury official's reflections upon the advantages of having all the economic levers under one roof. Colin Campbell, *Governments under Stress*, 1983.

about coherent policies. They did this in support of the cabinet committee system within the economics sector, which had become somewhat more active than normal.

To cite one area of especially grave concern in the attempt to control inflation, the government created a cabinet committee that reviewed all wage settlements between employers and unions. This body would often meet twice a week and eventually became hopelessly snarled in the minutiae of pay policy.

In an effort to impose greater discipline on the unwieldy complex of cabinet-level committees, Callaghan, supported by the cabinet secretary, ultimately formed a macroeconomic policy group that became known as "the seminar." This included the chancellor of the exchequer, a trusted adviser to the prime minister who belonged to cabinet but did not have a department, the head of the Cabinet Office "think tank," the top permanent official from the Treasury, and the governor of the Bank of England.

Public knowledge of the seminar might have placed in question the degree to which Callaghan was adhering to the principle of collective decision-making, since its limited membership precluded the direct participation of several ministers in discussions about key elements of the government's economic policies. The committee also gave a few strategically placed civil servants greater access—when compared to that afforded the

The Treasury . . . is more or less the classical Whitehall department where advice is embodied in folklore. That is, the Treasury actually has its own line on different subjects independent of its ministers . . . however, constitutional that might be. . . . Advice, in the first instance at least, will almost 80–90 per cent consist of folklore: "Our line on flexible exchange rates is this and here it is." . . . [Cabinet Office involvement in these cases is] pretty superficial. You mainly have to deal with "The brief has to be up by then, the meetings, the what did they decide for heavens sake."

SOURCE: A member of the Cabinet Office as quoted in Colin Campbell, *Governments under Stress*, 1983.

excluded ministers—to crucial deliberations on the future of the economy. Thus, Callaghan kept the very existence of this body a closely guarded secret.

Notwithstanding the heightened activity in the center, the actual decision process under Callaghan still relied very heavily upon the received wisdom coming forth from the Treasury. During the Callaghan government, wage controls had become a fashionable policy, as advanced economies struggled with efforts to reduce inflation. The approach followed the reconstructed Keynesianism of John Kenneth Galbraith's *Economics and the Public Purpose,* which held that mandatory wage and price controls must make up for the manifest inability of the free market to restrain inflation.

The Treasury had embraced this view enthusiastically, focusing the bulk of its attention on pay controls. Initially, it considered these simply as urgent measures designed to dampen demand. In time, however, it developed the view that a permanent structure for achieving wage restraint would greatly stabilize the economy. Meanwhile, the Labour government's mandate would run out by May 1979. In summer 1978, Callaghan began to come around to the Treasury's

[Direct] incomes policy . . . started as a . . . shock exercise in round one back in '75. Having proved successful with that round, they [Labour] tried it again and then moved into a slightly different idea, not of regarding what had happened as being a once-and-for-all shock exercise but now "Let's try a transition gently into something freer." The present operation is not only a further step in that transition, tightening the thing down further, but—as we made absolutely clear in our white paper—really this government is now persuaded that some permanent framework of a direct attempt to influence the way that leg of the economy goes is part of the scheme of things.

SOURCE: A Treasury official as quoted in Colin Campbell, *Governments under Stress,* 1983.

view that the government should extend the pay policy to another phase.

Inflation had declined to the point where unions began to chafe at the bit in anticipation of a return to free collective bargaining. To the Treasury, however, controlling inflation involved political and psychological warfare as much as economics. A five percent pay limit would provide a smoother transition to a "freer" wage policy. That is, it would send the signal to the unions that there would not be an immediate return to unrestricted collective bargaining.

By his nature Callaghan tended to take the longer view of policy issues. He could thus readily grasp the Treasury point that an extended restraint program would deepen the process of reeducation whereby the unions might ultimately accept a permanent regimen for wage negotiations. More important, the specter of a Labour prime minister extending the pay limits despite the decline of inflation and the protests of unions might send just the right message to middle-class voters. Callaghan saw in continued restraint an opportunity to broaden his electoral appeal.

The entire strategy anticipated a fall 1978

election. However, the polls took a dramatic turn for the worse in September. Callaghan, who only a few months before had sold reluctant ministers on the Treasury's plan as an election ploy, sprung on his cabinet the news that a fall vote was off. The Labour government now faced what would become known as the Winter of Discontent.

Unions militantly resisted the further imposition of wage restraint, and an endless succession of strikes ensued. Further, in December Parliament—in which Labour held less than an absolute majority of seats—refused to continue sanctions against private sector firms that reached wage settlements violating the five percent limit. By January, strikes had just about brought the country to a standstill. To make matters worse, Britons faced winter weather as bitter as they had ever experienced. Callaghan, abetted by the Treasury, had proved too clever by half. Had he listened to his cabinet rather than to the Treasury in summer 1978, Britain might never have had a Thatcher government. Even if Labour had lost a fall 1978 election, Mrs. Thatcher would have lacked a Winter of Discontent to run against in 1983 and 1987!

Margaret Thatcher. If James Callaghan displayed a penchant for pay policy, Mrs.

Mrs. Thatcher with her political mentor, Sir Keith Joseph.
SOURCE: Hugo Young, *One of Us* (London: Macmillan, 1989).

Thatcher developed an ardor for *monetarism*. As we noted in Chapter 3, this came from her close attachment to Sir Keith Joseph, who had converted to monetarism after the debacle of the Heath government. Sir Keith believed that imposition of tight restraint on the money supply offered the only means to control inflation and get British industry back into the competitive position.

Mrs. Thatcher imposed immense discipline over the economic policy apparatus. She began with herself. From the outset she eschewed personal involvement in microeconomic issues. She preferred, instead, to focus

Mrs. Thatcher reciting St. Francis of Assisi's prayer for peace on her first day at No. 10 Downing Street.

SOURCE: Hugo Young, *One of Us* (London: Macmillan, 1989).

One Cabinet minister, a member of the Economic Strategy Committee but not of this most secret inner group, which was meeting straight afterwards, was a bit slow to gather his papers. As he was about to leave, Sir Geoffrey Howe, then Chancellor of the Exchequer, launched into his paper on the plan to abolish exchange controls. "Oh," says the laggardly minister, "are we going to do that? How very interesting." Embarrassed silence. Then Sir Geoffrey says, "X, I'm afraid you should not be here." X departs Cabinet door left.

SOURCE: Peter Hennessy, *Cabinet*, 1986.

on the fundamental tenets of the monetarist view. If she got her macroeconomic policies right, her assumption went, the rest would fall into place. In some respects, this constituted a self-fulfilling prophecy. Tight monetary policy would greatly limit the degree to which ministers could press claims for tax exemptions or additional spending for their clients and pet programs.

Mrs. Thatcher lacked total consensus on the monetarist approach. However, she adroitly employed the devices at her disposal for rigging the Whitehall machine so that it would follow her leadership. She packed the key economy strategy committee with monetarist ministers. Indeed, she took a leaf from the Callaghan administration and formed a still more elite group through which she worked when she anticipated or encountered difficulties in the larger committee. She also used her appointive powers most imagina-

We . . . had a framework for the economy basically neo-Keynesian. We set the questions which we asked ministers to decide arising out of that framework, so to that extent we had great power . . . .

SOURCE: Sir William Armstrong (former permanent secretary of the Treasury) as cited by Richard Chapman, *Leadership in the British Government*, 1984.

tively. For instance, she retained dedicated monetarist advisers in No. 10. She also allowed the chancellor of the exchequer to develop a small team of party-political economic advisers in the Treasury. Finally, she took the unprecedented step of appointing an outsider and committed monetarist as chief economic adviser in the Treasury and head of the economic service for the entire permanent bureaucracy.

In this regard, we encounter a truly remarkable feature of the Whitehall system. The Treasury has long recognized that it must adapt its view of how the economy runs to the times. In the 1960s, it preserved its hegemony in Whitehall because it marshalled its resources behind setting the policy agenda in ways that comported with prevailing neo-Keynesian notions. During the late 1970s, it went through an extremely painful process of responding to the growing attractiveness monetarism held for the world's ranking economists and politicians. As early as 1977, the monetarist sympathizers within the Treasury

began to prevail in some crucial battles. At the advent of the Thatcher government, they had positioned themselves to take over the leadership of the department. In classic Treasury form, time healed the wounds and many neo-Keynesians even converted to the monetarist faith.

Notwithstanding Mrs. Thatcher's very capable maneuvers and the Treasury's adjustment to monetarism, the government did not always find it easy to adhere to its macroeconomic policies. Under the rubric of monetarism, it focused its efforts on working through the Bank of England to manipulate the *Minimum Lending Rate* (MLR—the rate of interest at which the Bank of England lends money to "discount houses" in which banks borrow and lend on the short term). A high MLR will decrease the supply of money; a low MLR will increase it.

Although the government did set its sights on targets for the money supply and kept them there, it encountered greater difficulty deciding what other levers to pull in managing the economy. When she came into power, Mrs. Thatcher granted a substantial tax cut. A persuasive segment of cabinet talked her into balancing this move with an increase in the consumer tax—VAT. They argued that, otherwise, people would simply spend the added disposable income accruing from the tax cut, rather than investing it. In fact, the public went on a spending spree anyway. The combined effects of the tax cut and the increase of VAT soon pushed inflation beyond 20 percent.

Presented with an economy awash with money, the Treasury kept increasing interest rates. In due course, this strategy priced British goods out of the international trade market. Whenever interest rates in one economy attain a level dramatically higher than those in other nations, foreign investors will seek the most opportune rates and flood that country with money. If this trend persists, it

---

We have still got undercurrents of this Keynesian-Friedmanite dilemma. Those are the extremes. . . . On some of these things it becomes difficult to talk because really quite basic gut feelings about the way the economy works are not consistently shared. . . . It came perhaps most forcefully to the top a year ago [1977] when it just happened to focus on the question of whether the exchange rate should be let go in the interest of stopping an inflow of funds . . . . It was resolved not by agreement but by one of those kinds of drifts of opinions where you suddenly found that a minority had become a majority and so a decision was taken that way. [The pound was allowed to float up in an effort to keep the British money supply down.] This left a certain amount of unhappiness behind among people who felt it was the wrong decision.

SOURCE: A Treasury official as quoted in Colin Campbell, *Governments under Stress*, 1983.

can trigger a vicious circle in which the policy makers in the deviant country continually raise interest rates to reduce the money supply. In fact, such responses simply attract more foreign money.

Eventually, the country's currency will break through a threshold whereby potential importers of goods and services will no longer be able to tolerate the adverse rates of exchange. This is precisely what happened to the British economy in the immediate aftermath of Mrs. Thatcher's policies. With seriously dampened demand for British goods, manufacturing industries—as we saw in Chapter 3—suffered a precipitous decline, and unemployment began to increase exponentially. Whether or not the government would flinch—that is, modify its monetarist approach—began to loom as the dominant question of the day.

As we noted in Chapter 3, in 1981 the government began to ease its policies. However, it resisted taking any action that would amount to a U-turn—a clear departure from monetarism. And the eventual decline of inflation below double-digit figures allowed for considerable reductions in the Minimum Lending Rate.

Interestingly, conflicts over the degree of monetarist observance have again arisen in Mrs. Thatcher's third term. In this respect, it is important to recall that the government created a miniboom in the economy in 1986. It did this by allowing interest rates to fall to a point where the declining value of the pound began to place British goods in a relatively competitive position.

In Chapter 7 we discussed the perennial controversy over whether Britain should enter the European Monetary System (EMS). The EMS limits the reflation or deflation of the currencies of individual nations according to agreed parameters established by the value of a "basket" of European currencies. By 1986, the Treasury had brought the prime

. . . There was quite a lot of resistance to ideas of the new government in the early stages, there was certainly a very strong feeling among the skeptics that . . . there would have to be U-turns. . . . around November, December [1979], when things began to look very dirty and they were having great pain and grief over public expenditure discussions and the skeptics would say "Oh, we've seen this before, which way will the U-turn go and hadn't we better start some contingency planning for the things that we ought to be doing." . . . That died away because they did indeed soldier on. . . . The MLR [Minimum Lending Rate] went up from 12 to 14 percent and that of course has an effect on mortgage rates and mortgage rates are a well-known political Pavlovian problem and we all read the prime minister in the newspaper as saying she didn't like this at all, we were losing control and she didn't want mortgage rates going up and so forth. In November we put the MLR up from 14 to 17 percent and those who had not been close to the situation were fearful of a tremendous lambasting from the prime minister for letting interest rates go up so high, though of course what was proposed certainly accorded with the views of the hawks on monetary policy and it was a confirmation to some and a salutory surprise for others that the prime minister didn't make any fuss about it. She accepted it. She said, "You've got it wrong but since we are where we are, you'd better change it."

SOURCE: A Treasury official in interview with Colin Campbell, 1980.

minister far enough along that she agreed to allow the pound to participate *de facto* in the EMS by staying within specified values in relation to the other currencies. Mrs. Thatcher refused, however, to agree to formal membership in the EMS.

This amicable arrangement suited the Treasury until 1988. As a result of the October 19, 1987 crash, investors began to lose confidence in the U.S. dollar and to cut back on their financial holdings in the States. Under these circumstances, the pound began to reflate to the point where only limits on interest rates—along with interventions from the Bank of England—could keep it within the informally adopted EMS parameters. Ultimately, the prime minister and the chancellor of the exchequer could no longer conceal the fact that they disagreed on membership in the EMS. Further, it became clear that the prime minister had again poised herself to fight any pending inflationary pressures with high interest rates.

Meanwhile, the chancellor worried more about good citizenship within the European community and the danger of dampening the British economic recovery with excessive monetary controls. He found support in sympathetic statements by the secretary of state for foreign and commonwealth affairs. It appeared as if a damaging cabinet storm was brewing. By May 1988, however, Mrs. Thatcher yielded to the counsel of the Treasury and the chancellor, and the urging of the foreign secretary. She allowed that even if the pound had exceeded its EMS limits it would

not, contrary to her previous assertions, rise to the level determined by the monetary markets. However, the issue reemerged in spring 1989 when Mrs. Thatcher came under pressure from her cabinet and other European leaders to commit herself to eventually joining the EMS. After making a vague agreement, she turned around and demoted her foreign secretary in her summer cabinet shuffle. Further efforts to renege on her undertaking with other EEC leaders led in October 1989 to the resignation of her chancellor—Nigel Lawson—from the cabinet.

Parliament—especially the Treasury and Civil Service Committee—has continued to debate the issues surrounding the monetarist approach. However, it has not effectively intervened at any of the major turning points in the process whereby the Thatcher government has made macroeconomic policy. The most substantial interventions have occurred, thus, around the fringes of these policies. Parliament has been able to win the government over to ameliorative amendments in cases

Mrs. Thatcher yielded to pressure for Nigel Lawson—the chancellor—and Sir Geoffrey Howe—the foreign secretary—to control the rise of the pound through Spring 1988. *The Independent,* May 18, 1988.

where tax or spending policies derived from monetarism might place seemingly unjust burdens on particular segments of the population or sectors of the economy.

FOREIGN POLICY

The Iran-Contra affair reminded Americans about the need to adequately coordinate decisions concerning foreign policy. There are at least four important players in any major presidential decision on foreign policy: the secretaries of state and defense, the assistant to the president for national security affairs, and the director of the Central Intelligence Agency. Issues with major budgetary implications will almost inevitably involve the director of the Office of Management and Budget. Those touching on substantial economic and commercial interests will draw in the treasury secretary and perhaps even the commerce secretary and the U.S. trade representative. Especially strong relationships between the president and individual cabinet members can enter into national security deliberations even in cases where the departments headed by those cabinet members would not normally concern themselves with foreign affairs. For instance, John F. Kennedy relied very heavily upon his brother Robert, the attorney general, during the 1962 Cuban missile crisis. Ronald Reagan allowed Edwin Meese, his counselor (1981–85) and attorney general (1985–88), to attend meetings of the National Security Council on a regular basis.

Some might wonder why so many cabinet secretaries—each of whom might press an array of departmental concerns that might simply complicate the decision process—find such ready access to national security affairs. After all, the departments of state and defense control the two instruments—diplomacy and military force—by which the nation pursues

its foreign policy. Yet, we certainly know that most problems do not fit completely into one or both of these departments. Besides, the president often will side with one or other secretary, or stake out a position at variance with both. Thus even in the U.S. system, in which executive authority ultimately rests with the president, situations arise that remind us once again that coordination does not just happen, but requires some regularization of the process of consultation by which the president reaches decisions.

Interestingly, those who advocated creation of the statutory body that bears responsibility for coordination of foreign policy decisions in the United States—the National Security Council (1947)—used as their pattern Winston Churchill's War Cabinet.[4] Of course, the U.S. Constitution does not compel the president to consult widely before making foreign policy. However, those who had observed the British cabinet's handling of World War II discerned instrumental advantages to some sort of regularized machinery for decision-making in the national security field.

The result was the creation of the NSC by an act of Congress in 1947. The burden of the assessments of what brought about the Iran-Contra affair suggests that the United States must relearn the lesson brought back from the United Kingdom in 1945. For this reason it is instructive for us to examine more closely how the collective decision-making apparatus for national security actually operates in Britain. We will examine and contrast James Callaghan's and Margaret Thatcher's handling of the Falklands crises in, respectively,

---

[4] Anna Kasten Nelson, "National Security I: Inventing a Process (1945–1960)," in *The Illusion of Presidential Government,* ed. by Hugh Heclo and Lester M. Salamon (Boulder, Colorado: Westview Press, 1981), p. 231.

1977 and 1982. First, however, we should study the structural features of the British national security policy process.

The Apparatus

Strictly speaking, the cabinet must decide major foreign policy issues. The prime minister, who enjoys neither the status of a chief executive nor the title "commander in chief," must give due deference to the convention of cabinet consultation. In the practical order, prime ministers have departed from literal adherence to this principle. We noted in Chapter 6 that David Lloyd George, who became prime minister in the midst of World War I, formed a "War Cabinet" consisting of only five ministers.[5] Interestingly, only one of these actually had direct responsibility for a department. The rest essentially functioned as prime ministerial overseers of key elements of the war effort. Even though peace came in November 1918, Lloyd George did not reconstitute a traditional cabinet until October 1919.

During World War II, Winston Churchill also adopted the War Cabinet format. However, his was a more inclusive body than was Lloyd George's—it ranged in size between 8 and 11 members.[6] Further, most of these ministers maintained specific departmental responsibilities. And Churchill held a weekly "cabinet parade" that included ministers who did not belong to the War Cabinet. These meetings attempted to apprise the entire ministry of major developments in the war effort.

The institution of war cabinets during the two world wars built upon a practice that emerged in the late nineteenth century. Al-though it operated under different titles, some sort of "defense" committee had functioned through most of the past 100 years; the current body is known as the Oversea and Defence Committee (OD). Unlike the National Security Council, OD enjoys no statutory base. It owes its existence entirely to conventional practice. In addition, its exact membership remains an official secret. However, the committee claims the distinction of being the first such body whose existence the government admitted—an action taken in the early 1920s because the media tended to fan speculation over impending military engagements every time they saw the chief of staff enter No. 10 for a meeting. It became necessary to assuage public anxieties by revealing why the chief of staff was visiting No. 10 so much!

The 1983 Franks inquiry into the Falklands War did reveal that the prime minister chairs OD and that its membership "includes" the secretaries of state for foreign and commonwealth affairs and for defense, and the chancellor of the exchequer (the minister in charge of the Treasury).[7] Currently, only the chief of defense staff regularly attends OD. However, the committee will request the presence of the chiefs of staff of individual services whenever this seems necessary.

Other sources indicate that additional ministers often attend—simply because issues requiring their involvement arise with considerable regularity.[8] We would certainly count among the most regular of these *ad hoc* participants the lord president of the council, by virtue of his role as leader of the govern-

---

[5] John P. Mackintosh, *The British Cabinet* (London: Stevens, 1977), pp. 371, 382.

[6] Mackintosh, pp. 492–93.

[7] "Great Britain, Committee of Privy Councillors, Franks Report," *Falkland Islands Review* (London: Her Majesty's Stationery Office, 1983), p. 93.

[8] Richard Crossman, *The Diaries of a Cabinet Minister*, vol. 3 (London: Hamish Hamilton and Jonathan Cape, 1977); and Peter Hennessy, *Cabinet* (Oxford: Blackwell, 1986).

ment party in the House of Commons; the secretary of state for home affairs, especially due to his responsibility for MI5, the domestic intelligence agency; the secretary of state for Northern Ireland, because of the instability of that province; the secretary of state for trade and industry, since diplomacy often entails trade issues, and the development of the defense system relies heavily upon British industries; and chief secretary of the Treasury, as many foreign affairs and defense issues will require the allocation of new funds. We might assume that ministers who do not formally belong to OD will press the case that they should attend on an *ad hoc* basis when committee discussions touch upon concerns central to their departments' mandates.

The reader has probably already concluded that OD, whatever its formal membership, does not prove to be any better "bounded" than the National Security Council in the United States. Both presidents and prime ministers find it difficult to exclude interested cabinet secretaries from official and widely known deliberations having widespread repercussions. Pressures toward inclusion in formal bodies weigh almost as heavily on prime ministers as they do on presidents. Almost inevitably, such pressures force them to treat the most sensitive and potentially intractable foreign policy decisions in exclusive groups that might even operate without the knowledge and consent of other interested cabinet secretaries.

Although we should not inflate its role, Parliament can influence the course of foreign affairs decisions in some cases. We have already noted in other chapters instances in which this has happened. In May 1980, Mrs. Thatcher succumbed to backbench pressure and withdrew a provision that would have imposed retroactive trade sanctions against Iran. Before the Argentinean invasion of the Falkland Islands, British governments had moved very cautiously in negotiations partly because they feared that ultra-nationalists among Conservative MPs would label any type of disengagement "capitulation." When it became clear that the Thatcher government had not adequately anticipated the possibility of the 1982 Argentinean invasion, howls of protest in the House of Commons forced the resignations of three ministers. These included the secretary of state for foreign and commonwealth Affairs, Lord Carrington.

After the Falklands War, MPs from both sides of the House of Commons raised enough questions about the way in which the crisis occurred and how it was handled to prompt the government to create the Franks Committee. Subsequently, the House Select Committee on Foreign Affairs brought to light many embarrassing circumstances surrounding the war. Similarly, deep skepticism of government actions surrounding the Westland affair, which concerned the rescue of Britain's only military helicopter manufacturer, led to two ministerial resignations and a prolonged inquiry by the Select Committee on Defence.

Two Approaches to Similar Crises

The Falklands War lasted from the time of Argentina's invasion of the islands on April 2, 1982 until their recapture by the British on June 14, 1982. This marked the 150th year of continuous British occupation of the islands—against Argentina's protests. While the Falklands issue had simmered throughout this period, the two parties had engaged themselves in especially serious negotiations since 1965. Britain appeared to be inching toward acceptance of Argentinean sovereignty over the islands. However, Conservative and Labour governments alike feared the appearance that the residents of the islands, who are overwhelmingly Britons, had been forsaken by a negotiated settlement. If not handled very delicately, any arrangement that would cede sovereignty would outrage Parliament. The view developed that a middle ground would be to transfer sovereignty to Argentina and then lease back the islands so that the colony might remain British.

James Callaghan. To begin our examination of Callaghan's handling of the 1977 Falklands crisis, we should first outline how the OD process normally would work in response to new developments in the Falklands.[9] Each Monday committees called "current intelligence groups" meet in the Cabinet Office. These bodies focus on various sectors of the world and include representatives from the intelligence-gathering agencies and the departments with especially strong interests in the area involved. For the Falklands, the relevant committee was the Latin American Current Intelligence Group.

A Joint Intelligence Committee of officials meets Wednesdays to assess the material gathered by the current intelligence groups and compile a "Red Book" summarizing their findings. The Red Book circulates to ministers on OD on a "need-to-know" basis. When the system functions properly, the evidence of impending military action that would endanger the Falklands would prompt one or more ministers to call for a meeting of OD.

Throughout the period of negotiations that began in 1965, British governments kept a weather eye for any indications that Argentina might attempt to invade the islands. In fall 1977, the military regime in Argentina had made several threatening moves indicating that they might take military action. Notwithstanding resistance from the Ministry of Defence, which argued that it could not spare the required vessels, the foreign secretary under the Labour government, David Owen, eventually convinced the prime minister, James Callaghan, that circumstances called

for a "trip wire" against a possible invasion.[10] Eventually, Callaghan called a meeting of the Oversea and Defence Committee that authorized the deployment of a nuclear submarine and two frigates in the Falklands area.

The government kept this mission a secret, and analysts cannot demonstrate with certainty that the Argentineans knew about the force, much less that they cancelled an impending invasion on the basis of its proximity to the islands.[11] Such a force probably would not have thwarted a determined invasion attempt. However, it would have proscribed smaller actions and even given pause for thought over a full-scale military initiative. In this respect, the Oversea and Defence system worked. It had brought early warnings of possible aggression to the attention of the appropriate parties. Further, it had facilitated a commitment of resources in a timely fashion.

Two factors explain why the Callaghan government acted so decisively in 1977. The first relates to prime ministerial focus. Callaghan had served in the British Navy during World War II. While prime minister, he took a passionate interest in the fleet—right down to maintaining his own records on the positions of various vessels.

The second factor behind the government's performance stems from process. We already have noted the degree to which Callaghan relied upon cabinet consultations. In the buildup to the 1977 crisis, the OD process engaged itself much more vigorously than it would in 1982 under Mrs. Thatcher.[12] In a February 1976 meeting of the OD Committee, Callaghan had requested a full assessment from the defense secretary of the mili-

---

[9] Hennessy, pp. 114–15.

[10] Simon Jenkins, "Britain's Pearl Harbour," *The Sunday Times,* March 29, 1987, p. 29.
[11] Franks Report, pp. 18–19.
[12] Franks Report, pp. 14–18.

But I have no doubt in my mind from my own experience over many years on this subject that that was a war that could have been avoided if we had taken the proper and prudent precautions at the time when the signs became evident, and it was the neglect of Ministers which led to the Falklands war. . . . Matters of this sort should be put on the Cabinet agenda, if they seem to be of that importance. . . . Because of my background, I asked the Admiralty every week to send me a map of the world, about the size of this blotter in front of us here, which set out the position and disposition of every ship in the British Navy, including all the auxiliaries, so that I could know exactly what we could do and how long it would take us to get to the Falklands and where we needed to be. That is the kind of thing that I think a Prime Minister must do. There are small things he must do, and large things. That's one of the small things he must do that can save a very large catastrophe.

SOURCE: James Callaghan in a 1986 interview with Peter Hennessy, Brook Productions, Channel 4, "All the Prime Minister's Men," May 1986.

tary options should Argentina take direct action in the Falklands. In March he then called for a full OD review of British policies toward Argentina. This study engendered a revamped stance toward negotiations that received full discussion in subsequent meetings of OD.

Notwithstanding the renewed overtures, the situation began to deteriorate rapidly in fall 1976. It was during this period that the foreign secretary requested the paper on the military options from the defense secretary that formed the basis for the former's request of a "trip wire." Further, this account only covers the activities of OD. Through 1976 and 1977, the Joint Intelligence Committee frequently updated the interdepartmental assessment of the Falklands situation.

Margaret Thatcher. In contrast to the Callaghan administration, Mrs. Thatcher's government's handling of similar signs of a brewing crisis provides a textbook case of failure on the part of the OD system. Mrs. Thatcher found OD's highly routinized processes a bit tedious. Thus, she was loath to have set times for OD meetings. She much preferred engaging herself when specific crises emerged. Besides, Lord Carrington, the foreign secretary, disliked ministerial meetings. Rather than pressing for OD sessions, he normally would try to transact his business through correspondence with his cabinet colleagues. Further, the government had imposed a series of cuts of the defense program that had absorbed much of the OD community's time during the first three months of 1982. This process—along with the usual menu of major issues which present themselves—pretty much preordained that the Falklands would remain on the backburner.

In early 1982, the United Kingdom found itself in a similar position regarding the Falklands to that which had emerged in 1977. The Argentineans were trying to speed up the pace of negotiations, yet it was clear that the Thatcher government would encounter extreme difficulty in selling a settlement to the islanders and their advocates in the House of Commons. Talks between the two nations in New York in late February had made little progress. A hard liner, General Leopoldo Galtieri, had assumed the presidency on December 1981. Further, the regime began to play up the Falklands issue—perhaps as a diversion of public attention from human rights concerns and rising alarm over the poor performance of the economy.

The Franks report chronicles just how little the OD system had taken note of developments in the Falklands. The Joint Intelligence Committee had conducted a full assessment of the Falklands situation in July 1981. It concluded that only severe provocation by Britain or an abandonment of trust in the negotiation process would induce Argentina

A triumphant Mrs. Thatcher visits troops in the Falkland Islands.

SOURCE: Hugo Young, *One of Us* (London: Macmillan, 1989).

Mr. James Callaghan

. . . is the Prime Minister aware that the Government's decision to withdraw and pay off HMS "Endurance" . . . is an error that could have serious consequences?

The Prime Minister

I recognize that this is a very difficult decision for my right honourable Friend the Secretary of State for Defence. . . . There are many competing claims of the defence budget, even though we are increasing it substantially . . . the defence capability of that ship is extremely limited. My right honourable Friend therefore felt that other claims on the defence budget should have greater priority.

SOURCE: Parliamentary questions on the withdrawal of the Endurance, February 9, 1982.

to invade the Falklands.[13] The Latin American Current Intelligence Group had failed even to discuss the Falklands in its 18 meetings between July 1981 and March 1982.[14] Notwithstanding developments during the three months leading to the invasion, neither the OD Committee nor the cabinet focused on the Falklands until Argentina took concrete military actions. That is, the cabinet did not discuss the situation until March 23, when Argentinean forces occupied South Georgia Island, and OD did not examine the issue until April 1, the day before the invasion of the Falkland Islands.[15]

If the Argentineans were determined to invade the Falklands, we cannot say that any British move, short of timely deployment of a full naval task force, would have prevented such an action. However, the Thatcher government made a number of errors in its handling of the Falklands. Some of these badly miscued the Argentineans about Britain's resolve to protect the Falklands. Others involved failure to take the military precautions

necessary to prevent an actual invasion. Two examples point up the magnitude of some of these errors.

The first of these concerns Britain's resolve. For years, the ice-patrol ship HMS *Endurance* had provided a token but symbolically important naval presence in the waters surrounding the Falklands. However, the 1981 Defence Review had judged that the vessel was not cost effective.[16] In June 1981 the government announced that the *Endurance's* 1981–82 voyage would be her last. The foreign secretary had protested this decision on several occasions. However, the defense secretary would not reverse himself. The Foreign Office had become particularly distressed that the Argentinean press had trumpeted the move as abandonment of the Falklands. However, the foreign secretary's protests fell short of actually bringing the matter to the OD Committee—although he did suggest that he might do this in a letter to the defense secretary dated February 17, 1982. We can

[13] Franks Report, pp. 26–27.
[14] Franks Report, p. 83.
[15] Franks Report, p. 79.

[16] Franks Report, pp. 33–34.

safely conclude that Lord Carrington was not particularly enthused about fighting the Ministry of Defence on the issue—especially since the stringency-minded prime minister would probably side with the plans to withdraw the *Endurance*.

The second error of judgment consisted of a failure to take advantage of an opportunity to improve Britain's preparedness in response to clear indications of a possible invasion.[17] After a disappointing round of negotiations in New York on February 26 and 27, the Argentinean regime began to signal the fact that it planned to take military action if the impasse continued. It did this first in a terse unilateral communiqué at the end of the New York meeting. Following upon this, seemingly informed Argentinean press comment reported that unnamed official sources in Buenos Aires had spoken explicitly of plans for direct military intervention.

On March 3, the British ambassador to Argentina cabled London about the press commentary on the significance of the unilateral communiqué. The prime minister wrote on her copy of the telegram, "We must make contingency plans." However, her private secretary did not get around to conveying the prime minister's comments to the Foreign and Commonwealth Office—with copies to the Ministry of Defence and the Cabinet Office—until March 8. On the same date, the prime minister asked the defense secretary how quickly the Royal Navy could deploy ships to the Falklands. According to the Franks report, the window of opportunity had already shut.[18]

Even if the government had made a small deployment—similar to Callaghan's—it would have had to act by March 5 in order to play any role in deterring the invasion of April 2. Ironically, on precisely that date Mr.

I think it is reasonable to observe that the major issues of the Falklands War were more or less written in the stars. There wasn't actually a great sense of option or choice. It was clear the task force had to go. Having gone, it was clear that, if it reached there before any kind of serious and sensible peace proposal could be offered, . . . the task force then had to do something. It was clear that . . . fudge proposals from the Argentinians which amounted to saying "We've done what we've done now let's negotiate from here" were quite unacceptable and it was clear that the task force had to land and do its bit. So I think, of course, it was right and proper that these things came to Cabinet. But I think it would be glorifying things a bit to say that re-created Cabinet government in its full glory.

SOURCE: David Howell, secretary of state for transport at the time of the Falklands War, as quoted by Peter Hennessy in *Cabinet*, 1986.

J. B. Ure, a senior career official in the Foreign and Commonwealth Office, asked the permanent head of the foreign service for permission to depart from Whitehall practice.[19] Normally, career officials do not disclose to ministers the secret actions of their predecessors. Mr. Ure requested and obtained clearance to tell Lord Carrington about Mr. Callaghan's deployment of the nuclear submarine and two frigates to the Falklands area in 1977. Lord Carrington did not register much interest in this option. Indeed, the government dithered and only vaguely anticipated an OD Committee meeting in which it would fashion an appropriate response to Mrs. Thatcher's request for military contingency plans.

Of course, Mrs. Thatcher acted decisively once the invasion took place. In fact, she chaired a "War Cabinet" that met almost daily to coordinate the war effort. This included the home secretary, the new Foreign Secretary Francis Pym, the defense secretary,

---

[17] Franks Report, pp. 40–45.
[18] Franks Report, p. 82.

[19] Franks Report, p. 43.

and the paymaster general who, more importantly, served as the chairman of the Conservative Party. The committee, thus constituted, viewed its coordinative task as harmonizing the various diplomatic and military moves *and* garnering and maintaining the support of cabinet, Parliament and the public.

Mrs. Thatcher, already under harsh scrutiny over her economic policies, had just fumbled the ball badly. She had done so by failing to pay due attention to a volatile situation. She had also allowed the apparatus designed to compensate for limits to prime ministerial attention span to run down. Ministers simply had not come together at a timely moment to exchange views on the brewing crisis. Perhaps the Falklands did not mean much to the United Kingdom. However, their loss to the Argentineans due to an invasion that the government had failed to anticipate would be a devastating blow to the prime minister's fortunes. Mrs. Thatcher's political future and the recapture of the Falklands became inextricably linked. There would be no room for a negotiated end to hostilities. The ultimate British victory over the Argentineans covered a multitude of sins of omission. It also handed Mrs. Thatcher proof positive that she provided just the type of tough leadership many Britons believed their country required.

CONCLUSION

This chapter has attempted to flesh out what we learned in chapters 6 and 7 about the roles of various institutions within the policy process. We focused our attention on how economic and foreign policy are made. We also contrasted the approaches taken under James Callaghan and Margaret Thatcher.

We saw, of course, that the personalities and interests of prime ministers influence the way in which the policy process operates. For instance, Mr. Callaghan's reliance upon collective decision-making helped bog down his government in seemingly interminable deliberations over pay policy. However, his consultative approach paid dividends in his handling of the Falklands crisis in 1977. Mrs. Thatcher's tendency to tire of cabinet government got her into perilous straits in the 1982 Falklands crisis. However, her assertive leadership style helped her act decisively once confronted with an actual invasion. This character trait has also enabled her to adhere to popular policies such as monetarism and privatization, even when she encounters resistance because they depart from the received wisdom in the political and bureaucratic establishments.

We have seen that not all the institutions involved in the policy arena enjoy the same leverage in various decision processes. The more urgent and sensitive the matter, the greater the likelihood that *ad hoc* groups will form in cabinet to seek a solution that can then be presented as a *fait accompli* to the rest of the government. Some departments are more equal than others. Even in Mrs. Thatcher's struggle with the Falklands, we found that the Foreign and Commonwealth Office was deferring to the Ministry of Defence over whether HMS *Endurance* should be withdrawn and whether further vessels should be sent to the Falklands. In turn, the Ministry of Defence found that economy measures imposed by the 1981 Defence Review sharply constrained its ability to provide a presence in the area. Of course, the Treasury had imposed the fiscal constraints operating behind the Defence Review.

We did not discuss extensively the role of Parliament in the policy process. We examined the ways in which debates in the House of Commons and specific committee inquiries can influence decision-making around the fringes. To date, Parliament has not developed to the point where it goes beyond that. However, the loosening of party discipline and the strengthening of the committee system have worked to improve appreciably Parliament's role.

References and Suggested Readings

ALT, JAMES. *The Politics of Economic Decline: Economic Management and Political Behavior in Britain since 1964.* Cambridge: Cambridge University Press, 1979.

BELOFF, MAX, AND GILLIAN PEELE. *The Government of the UK: Political Authority in a Changing Society.* London: Weidenfeld and Nicholson, 1985.

CAMPBELL, COLIN. *Governments under Stress: Political Executives and Key Bureaucrats in Washington, London and Ottawa.* Toronto: University of Toronto Press, 1983.

CHAPMAN, RICHARD A. *Leadership in the British Civil Service.* London: Croom Helm, 1984.

CROSSMAN, RICHARD. *The Diaries of a Cabinet Minister,* vol. 3. London: Hamish Hamilton and Jonathan Cape, 1977.

DAHRENDORF, RALF. *On Britain.* London: BBC, 1982.

DONOUGHUE, BERNARD. *Prime Minister: The Conduct of Policy Under Harold Wilson and James Callaghan.* London: Jonathan Cape, 1987.

DOWNS, STEPHEN J. "Structural Changes, Select Committees; Experiment and Establishment." In *Parliament in the 1980s,* ed. Philip Norton. Oxford: Blackwell, 1985.

ELLES, DIANA. "The Foreign Policy of the Thatcher Government." In *Thatcherism: Personality and Politics,* eds. Kenneth Minogue and Michael Biddiss. London: Macmillan, 1987.

[FRANKS REPORT] COMMITTEE OF PRIVY COUNCILLORS. *Falkland Islands Review.* London: Her Majesty's Stationery Office, 1983.

HECLO, HUGH, AND AARON WILDAVSKY. *The Private Government of Public Money: Community and Policy Inside British Politics.* Berkeley, CA: University of California Press, 1974.

HENNESSY, PETER. *Cabinet.* Oxford: Blackwell, 1986.

HOLMES, M. *The First Thatcher Government, 1979–1983: Contemporary Conservatism and Economic Change.* Brighton: Wheatsheaf, 1985.

JENKINS, SIMON. "Britain's Pearl Harbour." *The Sunday Times* March 29, 1987.

OLSON, MANCUR. *The Rise and Decline of Nations.* New Haven: Yale University Press, 1982.

RIDDEL, PETER. *The Thatcher Government.* Oxford: Blackwell, 1985.

YOUNG, HUGO, AND ANNE SLOMAN. *The Thatcher Phenomenon.* London: BBC, 1986.

II

FRANCE

9

> For twenty years after the War, I used to say our situation was like the man falling from a skyscraper. As he passed the fourteenth floor he called out, "It's not too bad so far!"
> — JOAN ROBINSON

> Two roads diverged in a wood.
> — ROBERT FROST

At the Crossroads

Like the other countries of the industrial world, France has been troubled by the major changes in the world economy that have occurred since World War II and especially since the oil crisis of 1973–74. The persistent stagnation that all economies have known since the crisis has made traditional approaches to economic problems obsolete. After twenty-three years of postwar conservative rule, France elected François Mitterrand and a Socialist team to reduce increasing unemployment and to rejuvenate a decaying industrial base. Five years later voters elected a conservative majority in Parliament, not only rebuffing the Mitterand experiment, but creating conditions that would severely test the political institutions of the Fifth Republic. As these institutions had given France the longest period of stability it had known in the modern era, the stakes were high.

BACKGROUND

France is a country where ways of doing business and government's relation to the economy have been long established. Above all, it is a country where government has traditionally had the responsibility of assuring the well-being and growth of the French economy. The various institutions that constitute the French government, that is to say, the state, have long had a special place in directing the progress of the French society.

It was the French state that pushed the country from an agricultural backwater to a dynamic industrial nation. This was es-

---

The essential French view, which goes back to well before the Revolution of 1789, is that the effective conduct of a nation's economic life must depend on the concentration of power in the hands of a small number of exceptionally able people, exercising foresight and judgment of a kind not possessed by the average man of business. The long view and the wide experience, systematically analyzed by persons of authority, are the intellectual foundations of the system.

SOURCE: Andrew Shonfield, *Modern Capitalism* (New York: Oxford University Press, 1969), pp. 71–72.

pecially true after World War II, when seemingly tireless government officials worked long hours to overcome various bottlenecks, scarce resources and production obstacles to bring France, sometimes kicking and screaming, into the twentieth century. By the 1960s France was a full and contributing member of the world economy.

Of course, the French growth experience had much in common with that of other industrial countries. Like the other countries of western Europe, France was a recipient of U.S. aid under the Marshall Plan immediately after World War II. Indeed, West Germany, Italy, France, and even Britain all experienced "economic miracles" as they rebuilt their economies from the devastation wrought by the war. The injection of capital from America was put to good use in Europe, as its highly educated workforce turned investment into a sixfold increase in productive capacity. The universal acceptance of Keynesian policy techniques led to a smoothing out of each nation's business cycle, making recessions more tolerable and quickening the return to prosperity. In fact, recessions were so inconsequential during the first two postwar decades that E. J. Hobsbawm, the dean of British economic historians, referred to the period as "the Long Boom."[1]

A host of international factors all contributed to the tremendous European resurgence, not the least of which was the liberal economic order established with the enthusiastic support of the United States. In 1944, at Bretton Woods, New Hampshire, the victorious allies laid plans for a set of international institutions that would lower trade barriers and facilitate exchange between countries. Among these, the International Bank for Reconstruction and Development performed just as its title suggested: it helped to finance

European reconstruction. The International Monetary Fund financed the short-term needs of its member countries. Eventually, an international set of rules regulating trade, the GATT (General Agreement on Tariffs and Trade), was developed, enhancing trade between all developed non-communist countries.

At the European level, the Office of European Economic Cooperation, the European Payments Union and the European Economic Community all facilitated intra-European exchange and mutual economic growth. France, like its neighbors, grew robust in a favorable international climate. Like its neighbors as well, its growth figures were stupendous after World War II. But unlike the other countries of Europe, there were peculiarly French reasons for the country's economic success.

One of the most important French mechanisms for promoting growth was national economic planning, performed by the *Commissariat au plan*. Well within the "statist" tradition (that is, the traditional role of the French government to intervene in markets), economic planning was a procedure whereby government officials met periodically with private sector representatives to compare notes, avoid production bottlenecks and jointly develop market projections for the entire French economy.[2] The idea was to maximize the opportunities for French firms, to facilitate their growth and to increase the employment possibilities for all French citizens. This partnership of government and private industry has been largely credited for the success of the French economy after World War II. It was, however, a partnership that would become increasingly troubled.

[1] E. J. Hobsbawm, *Industry and Empire* (Baltimore: Penguin Books, 1966).

[2] See especially Andrew Shonfield, *Modern Capitalism* (New York: Oxford University Press), chap. 5; and Stephen S. Cohen, *Modern Capitalist Planning: The French Model* (Berkeley and Los Angeles: University of California Press, 1977).

Part of the reason for the troubled partnership is that large numbers of people were excluded from the policy process. France's democracy was not rebuilt as quickly as its economy. Not only was policy made by an extremely small number of public and private elite, but the interests of labor were almost entirely excluded from meaningful representation in policy circles.[3] This meant that

[3] On the collaboration of public and private elite, see Ezra N. Suleiman, "Industrial Policy Formulation in France," in Ezra N. Suleiman and Stephen J. Warnecke, eds., *Industrial Policies in Western Europe* (New York: Praeger, 1975); on the exclusion of labor from macroeconomic planning, see Mikkal Herberg, "Planning, Politics and Capitalism: National Economic Planning in Britain and France," *Political Studies,* 29 (December 1981). While on the whole labor was a junior partner in French economic growth, workers in industrial sectors did not do as poorly as those in agriculture or services. I am grateful to Michael Loriaux for pointing this out.

France's tremendous economic growth was partially financed by keeping wages artificially low. This kept the costs of French products down, and made profit margins correspondingly attractive to investors. But there was a political price to be paid. French workers could look across the border at Germany and see that their salaries had not kept pace. Their disgruntlement with the political system dominated by conservative elites made them ripe for change.

Thus in 1968, when students demonstrated for reform of the French educational system, workers also took to the streets in another kind of partnership: an alliance with the students. A proliferation of workers' strikes and student demonstrations spread throughout the country. France in May 1968 was closer to a genuine social revolution than at any time since the Great Revolution of

Paris 1968: Students and workers march to support the call for a "socialist society."
SOURCE: (c) Henri Cartier-Bresson. Archives Magnum/Magnum Library.

1789. General De Gaulle called new elections in the face of the upheavals. Middle-class and small-town French voters were frightened by the specter of a left-wing revolution, and supported the conservatives *en masse*. But the newly elected conservative economic managers had learned a valuable lesson. Wages were permitted to rise, and this presented the country with a new set of problems.

THE ROAD TO DECLINE

For a short period (1969–73) France reconstituted its productive forces and groped back toward its postwar habits. The world, however, had changed. The very openness and freedom of exchange that had promoted economic growth for so long began to backfire. Japan began to dominate world markets with cheap, high quality goods. Newly industrializing countries, such as South Korea and Brazil, penetrated many of Europe's markets for traditional manufactures. It was hard for countries whose workers had gained higher living standards to compete with the new, low-wage producers.

The *coup de grace* was the oil crisis of 1973–74. While the increased competition and saturation of world markets had occurred gradually, the sudden disruption of oil supplies and accompanying meteoric price increases dealt a final blow to the postwar system.[4] The huge increase in the price of oil sent all industrial prices skyrocketing. The tremendous price rises (i.e., inflation) proved highly resistant to traditional Keynesian management techniques. Immediate reactions to increased prices led to a precipitous decline in world demand for goods and services. The world economic pie ceased expanding, and competition grew even more intense for that which remained. The stagnant growth exaggerated conflicts of interest between social groups within countries as well as intensifying the basis for conflict among the industrial countries.[5] In short, the halcyon days of seemingly limitless expansion, where all seemed possible and a better tomorrow seemed inevitable, were gone forever. The industrial world, Europe especially, and France inevitably, appeared doomed to decline.

The industrial stagnation of the 1970s and 1980s resisted the cures that had worked so well in the postwar years. Government spending created inflation without creating jobs. Inflation became so entrenched that it could only be controlled by draconian measures that reduced employment to levels reminiscent of the Great Depression of the 1930s.

France, of course, was not alone. These problems occurred throughout the noncommunist industrialized world. They were perhaps felt most intensely in Europe. And nowhere were such economic issues more politicized than in France. As in other countries, discussions about what to do about the crisis were motivated by partisan conflict. But the peculiar nature of the economic crisis left France especially vulnerable to collapsing social consensus and a widening gap in the policy alternatives offered to voters.

ECONOMIC DECLINE AND POLITICAL VOLATILITY

Economic theories are, in a sense, road maps for policymakers. The conditions of the 1980s did not fit the theories that had guided

---

[4] The argument that industrial decline in Europe and America is due to the saturation of mass production markets is made most forcefully in Michael Piore and Charles Sabel, *The Second Industrial Divide* (New York: Basic Books, 1984).

[5] On the intensity of interest group conflict and its effects on public policy, see Lester Thurow, *The Zero Sum Society* (Baltimore: Penguin Books, 1978).

the postwar resurgence. Politicians of many colors were left without a reliable guide to good policy. In such circumstances it was easy for political reflexes to take over. Conservatives, never happy with the welfare state or infringements on the market associated with government intervention, saw these issues as the source of the new economic difficulties. Socialists, always mistrustful of unfettered markets, saw increased government intervention as the cure. Most importantly, those out of power saw the policies of those *in* power as the source of the country's economic hard times.

To the extent that politics in most industrial countries before the 1970s were consensual, at least in the sense that all of them shunned political extremes, the consensus broke down after the crisis. Ideological divisions reappeared with a vengeance. The elections of Ronald Reagan and Margaret Thatcher represented major breaks with the *status quo* in the United States and Britain. In 1983 West Germany experienced its first successful vote of "no confidence" since the Weimar Republic.

In France, where ideology has always been important and mistrust of the political opposition endemic, the tendency toward extreme alternatives was especially pronounced. After almost two-and-a-half decades of conservative political hegemony, voters turned to François Mitterrand and elected with him a crushing majority of Socialists in the National Assembly. From 1981 to 1986 the Socialist government nationalized industries and created the largest public sector of any capitalist country, yet economic stagnation continued. In 1986 a conservative coalition recaptured the Parliament and promptly rolled back most of the Socialist reforms. The 1980s proved to be a decade of ideologically motivated experimentation.

It is important, however, to qualify the extent to which the chasm in French politics was really widening. The experience of power had a moderating influence on the Socialists. After 1982, when the initial results of their program became clear, they retracted many of their reforms. By 1986 the differences between the Socialists and their conservative opponents was more rhetorical than real.

THE RECENT PAST: ROLLING BACK THE STATE

The break with *étatisme* ("statism") actually occurred with the election of Valéry Giscard d'Estaing to the presidency in 1974.[6] While previous presidents had been conservatives, their Gaullist ideology was sympathetic to a powerful state, where public interest and national unity stood in stark contrast to an image of competing selfish interests that would leave France rudderless and vulnerable. Giscard, on the other hand, was trained in economics and subscribed totally to the doctrines of that profession. The state, in Giscard's view, was lumbering and inefficient as an economic actor, and he perceived his election as a mandate to limit its role.[7]

The French term for reducing the interventionist role of the state is *libéralisme*. Unlike its English cognate, this philosophy approximates what Americans term "conservatism," at least insofar as it advocates opening the economy to market forces and reducing government intervention in the economy.[8] Despite Giscard's immense power, in-

[6] For an analysis of Giscard's policies as well as those of his prime ministers, Jacques Chirac and Raymond Barre, see Volkmar Lauber, *The Politics of Economic Policy: 1974–1982* (New York: Praeger, 1983).

[7] For a statement of Giscard's ideology, see his *French Democracy* (Garden City, NY: Doubleday, 1977), trans. Vincent Cronin.

[8] Both "liberals" and "conservatives" in the United States derive their philosophies from nineteenth century

herent in a French presidency with a (theoretically) friendly majority in the National Assembly, he found it difficult to impose his tastes in economic theory. Neither the fundamentally Gaullist bureaucracy nor Giscard's coalition partners were especially attracted to rolling back the state apparatus that they, in fact, controlled. Not surprisingly, both interest groups and administrators favored retaining policies and programs set up for their protection.[9]

For a variety of reasons, including the failure of his economic program, Giscard d'Estaing was turned out of office in 1981 and the Socialists took command for the first time since the founding of the Fifth Republic in 1958. Far from rolling back the state, the Socialists gave statism a shot in the arm. They nationalized five industrial corporations and almost the entire financial sector.[10] During the first year in office, the Socialist government also pursued a policy of deficit spending to increase the demand for goods and for people to produce them. But the French used their extra income to buy imported goods, so the results were a foreign exchange crisis that ultimately forced retrenchment and austerity.

While the nationalizations had very little to do with the hard times to follow—indeed, most of the nationalized corporations had been brought back to profitability under Socialist management[11]—they formed a convenient focus for attacks by the conservative opposition.

Oddly enough, the Socialists were the ones who made significant moves to roll back the state. While nationalization was part of an overall statist program, the experience of power forced modifications. The failure of the 1981 program to stimulate the French economy discredited the left wing of the party and opened opportunities for the centrists. Led by finance minister Jacques Delors and later by prime minister Laurent Fabius, the moderates urged a sharp revision of the government's economic policies. Not only did they urge considerable budget cutting (the French deficit slightly exceeded 3 percent of GNP, modest by U.S. standards), but they acted to dismantle much of the French regulatory apparatus, including price and credit controls, and regulations of French capital markets.[12]

Dramatic unemployment rates, which had actually risen as the Socialists allowed troubled industries to shed personnel, made the economy an attractive issue for conservatives. The problem for them was one of "product differentiation": making their policies appear different from the Socialists. How could the center-right parties distinguish themselves from the (now) very moderate Socialists who had beaten them to the punch on

---

liberalism as represented by such authors as John Stuart Mill. The latter preached a reduced role for the government (or "state") both in the marketplace and in regulating public morals. American liberals prefer a lack of government on moral issues, while French liberals and American conservatives are primarily concerned with containing state intervention in the marketplace.

[9] For a case study of the oil industry's rebellion against Giscard's "liberal" reforms, see Harvey B. Feigenbaum, *The Politics of Public Enterprise: Oil and the French State* (Princeton: Princeton University Press, 1985), chap. 4. For another case study of clientelism in France see Ezra Suleiman, *Les Notaires* (Paris: Senil, 1987).

[10] For an excellent assessment of economic policy under the Socialists, see Peter A. Hall. "Socialism in One Country: Mitterrand and the Struggle to Define a New Economic Policy for France," in Philip B. Cerny and Martin A. Schain, eds., *Socialism, the State and Public Policy in France* (New York: Methuen, 1985).

[11] Harvey B. Feigenbaum, "Democracy at the Margins: The International System and Policy Change in France," in Richard E. Foglesong and Joel D. Wolfe, eds., *The Politics of Economic Adjustment* (New York: Greenwood Press, 1989). See also *The Wall Street Journal,* April 18, 1985.

[12] For the importance of the latter, see John Zysman, *Governments, Markets and Growth* (Ithaca: Cornell University Press, 1983).

issues of political decentralization, deregulation and modernization of industry? In essence, the post-1982 policies of the Socialists deprived the conservatives of offering voters a real alternative, save in one area: the nationalized industries.

POLICIES OF THE CONSERVATIVES AFTER 1986

In some ways one can interpret the conservative adoption of privatization—i.e., the sale of nationalized companies to private investors—as part of a process of policy diffusion.[13] There is no question that the conservatives were influenced by British experience as well as by the political success of Ronald Reagan. However, it seems quite clear that the Gaullists and Giscardians (followers of Giscard d'Estaing) were more attracted to denationalization as an electoral strategy than as a purely economic policy. Not only were the public enterprises (for the most part) profitable and efficiently run, but a key conservative policy advisor admitted in public that there was no theoretical reason that the nature of ownership should affect the firms' management.[14]

The coalition of Gaullist and Giscardian parties (the RPR and UDF, respectively) came

to power with a two-seat majority on March 16, 1986. After some stalling, legal wrangles, and assorted inter- and intra-party bickering, the National Assembly passed Law 86-793 on July 2, 1986, authorizing the denationalization of some sixty-six firms.[15] The conservative hit list not only included the five industrial groups and myriad banks nationalized by the Socialists, but also aimed at privatizing older public firms. Nationalized insurance companies, advertising agencies, oil companies, glass factories, television networks, and steel mills all were to go on the block, albeit to different degrees,[16] and at different times, with the entire project to be completed by 1991, the end of the parliamentary term. Essentially, the aim was to privatize all public sector firms where there existed the possibility for competitive markets.[17]

JUSTIFICATIONS FOR DENATIONALIZATION

The justifications for denationalization were familiar. Public management was assumed to be inherently inefficient, although evidence for such assumptions, excepting, perhaps, for overemployment in the railway, steel and banking sectors, was scarce. Yet, the most frequently cited reason for the privatization effort was the expected fiscal windfall from the sale of public assets.[18] Over 200 billion

---

[13] Cf. David Collier and Richard E. Messick, "Prerequisites versus Diffusion: Testing Alternative Explanations of Social Security Adoption," *American Political Science Review*, 69 (December 1975). For an overview of privatization policies, see "Privatization: Everybody's Doing It, Differently," *The Economist*, December 21, 1985.

[14] Jean-Claude Casanova's remark at the conference on "Change and Continuity in Mitterrand's France," Harvard University, Cambridge, Massachusetts, December 17, 1985. Along with Renault, the least efficient nationalized firms were the banks, but it was not obvious that their inefficiencies, largely due to over-hiring, were related to the legalities of ownership: *The Financial Times*, July 22, 1986.

[15] *Journal Officiel*, July 3, 1986. A final law was passed on August 6, 1986.

[16] The conservatives left open the percentage of ownership that would be privatized for each company. See David R. Cameron, "The Nationalized Industries after March 16," *French Politics and Society*, 14 1986): 20.

[17] *Ibid.*, p. 20. The project was never completed because the conservatives lost the 1988 elections.

[18] See, for example, Dominique de la Martinière, "Privatisations," *Revue des Deux Mondes*, October 1986, p. 115.

francs were estimated to accrue to the treasury from privatizing the nationalized firms. This, in turn, would allow the government to cut taxes, improving profit margins and, therefore, encouraging investment.[19] Under a policy of privatization, the conservatives argued, the French economy would take off.

Privatization, however, was meant to solve more than the government's problems with cash flow. As in Britain, the espoused purpose was to encourage small shareholders, creating a "people's capitalism."[20] Small investors have a reputation for conservatism and reluctance to buy stocks.[21] Thus, small investors were given especially low stock prices to entice them to buy. The idea was to provide average French citizens (and voters!) a material interest in rejecting Socialism.[22]

The question was: Was there enough money in France to buy back the firms? Conservatives were especially vulnerable to the charge that the privatized firms would be

[19] Jean-Maxim Leveque, "Réussir les Dénationalisations," *Le Monde,* June 25, 1985.
[20] de la Martiniere, p. 117.

[21] For a portrait of the French small investor, see *The Wall Street Journal,* November 5, 1986.
[22] Harvey B. Feigenbaum, "Public Enterprise in Comparative Perspective," *Comparative Politics,* 15 (1982).

François Mitterrand addresses a meeting in Strasbourg, May 1988.
SOURCE: Bisson/Habans/Sygma.

bought by foreigners. Eventually the problem was solved by selling large blocks of stock to selected French businesses, but the result of this tactic was to have the Conservatives open to charges of favoritism.

The spring of 1988 saw François Mitterrand's reelection and brought the Socialists back into power. It is perhaps most revealing that economic issues were not greatly discussed during the campaign. Once back in power, the Socialists did not re-nationalize the privatized firms, nor did they take any other steps that were dramatically different from either the Conservatives' or their own policy of austerity, which had become the common, although *ad hoc,* economic answer to the problems of industrial stagnation.

CONCLUSION

Nationalization and privatization were at once polar opposites and two sides of the same coin. Both were intended to stimulate new investment and create jobs. Advocates of nationalization assumed that the state was best able to guide investment to its most important uses. Privatization aimed at channeling funds to industry by allowing the government to reduce taxes and by attracting new investors into the French economy. Advocates of both policies claimed that they were promoting the extension of democracy.

As the decade of the 1980s drew to a close France was once again at a crossroads. Two roads seemed to diverge: rolling back the state or increasing its role in the economy. Like the other countries of the industrial world, there was no consensus upon which to draw for policy guidance or support. While there was no dearth of politicians eager to take charge, most were aware that the route was uncharted. Not unlike its neighbors, France, if it were to solve the problems of the late twentieth century, would depend on luck, imagination—and politics.

References and Suggested Readings

CERNY, PHILIP G., AND MARTIN A. SCHAIN, EDS. *Socialism, the State and Public Policy.* New York: Methuen, 1985.

COHEN, STEPHEN S., AND PETER A. GOUREVITCH. *France in the Troubled World Economy.* London: Butterworths, 1982.

FOGLESONG, RICHARD, AND JOEL WOLFE, EDS. *The Politics of Economic Adjustment.* New York: Greenwood, 1989.

GOUREVITCH, PETER A. *Politics in Hard Times.* Ithaca, NY: Cornell University Press, 1986.

KATZENSTEIN, PETER J., ED. *Between Power and Plenty.* Madison: University of Wisconsin Press, 1978.

LAUBER, VOLKMAR. *The Politics of Economic Policy: France 1974–1982.* New York: Praeger, 1983.

PIORE, MICHAEL J., AND CHARLES F. SABEL. *The Second Industrial Divide.* New York: Basic Books, 1984.

SHONFIELD, ANDREW. *Modern Capitalism.* New York: Oxford University Press, 1969.

Every time I fill an office, I create a hundred
malcontents and one ingrate.
— LOUIS XIV

10

A Legacy of Instability

In the period immediately after World War II
and the two decades that followed, American
political scientists were especially concerned
with the issue of democratic stability. Having
recently emerged from a period in which
much of continental Europe had succumbed
to fascist dictatorship and threats from the
political extremes were very real, it is easy to
understand this preoccupation. In this context, the situation of France was viewed as
especially precarious. Not only did France
emerge from the war with a fragile political
system where left and right extremes were
generously represented, but there was little in
French history that allowed one to predict
with any confidence that democracy would
survive. Indeed, between the French Revolution of 1789 and the oil crisis of 1974, France
had known five republics, two monarchies,
two empires, and a fascist dictatorship. This
was not a track record to inspire confidence.
In this and the next chapter, we shall examine
competing explanations for such a shaky
history.

POLITICAL RESPONSES TO
SOCIAL CONFLICT

In fact, while turbulence was frequently the
norm, it would be a distortion to view the
history of French political institutions simply
as spontaneous responses to intermittent
chaos. If there is any thread tenuously uniting
the series of political regimes, it is that the
very deep divisions in French society led to
responses on the part of political elites that
both reinforced and undermined the power
of central political institutions.

All political institutions are, in a very basic
sense, the result of preceding political conflict.[1] They are efforts aimed at routinizing
patterns of behavior in response to previous
conflicts so as to resolve (or suppress) those
conflicts. Political institutions are mechanisms aimed at facilitating specific kinds of

[1] See, for instance, John Zysman, *Governments, Markets and Growth* (Ithaca, NY: Cornell University Press,
1983).

168

social behavior. Thus, the development of the absolutist kings at the end of the sixteenth century was a response to the conflicts engendered by a decaying feudal order, an attempt to shore up an agricultural system of manors and estates ruled by an aristocracy, benefiting from traditional privileges. The Revolution of 1789 was a response to the inequities of absolutism. And so on down the line.

These statements, of course, could easily be rejected by historians as glib and simplistic, an injustice to French history. Certainly, they paint complex events with a very broad brush. But it may be useful to view those events as intricately interwoven in a way that suggests a pattern, a pattern that makes present political institutions more comprehensible.

Louis XIV of France, the Sun King.
SOURCE: Culver Pictures, Inc.

THE DECAY OF FEUDALISM AND THE ORIGINS OF MODERN FRANCE

The borders of modern France were principally achieved by the eighteenth century and are perhaps the most enduring achievement of the absolutist kings. By "absolutist" one means that these kings were able to rule without sharing power. During the feudal period, administrative and political authority was shared among kings and *vassals* (i.e., aristocrats) so that each had reciprocal rights and obligations. Kings were frequently dependent on the aristocrats for financial and military support, and the constellation of power and authority was decentralized at best and fragmented at worst. Sovereignty was parcelled among competing power centers. Indeed, kings often had more to fear from potential rivals among their own aristocracy than they did from foreign powers. The French kings were quite aware of this, and the history of France during the feudal period was one not only of extending the

borders of control of the royal house outward from Paris, but also of increasing the subjugation of aristocratic vassals. It should be noted that even in the heyday of absolutism Louis XIV was less powerful than Napoleon would be. This was because the king never completely dominated the aristocracy.

The development of absolutism was both the product of a long period of consolidation and the immediate result of the crisis of feudalism in the seventeenth century.[2] The deep structural challenge to feudalism throughout Europe was the extension of the market system. This allowed new groups to grow wealthy and to command the resources necessary to challenge aristocratic power.

The Achilles' heel of absolutism was, para-

[2] This argument draws heavily on Perry Anderson's *Lineages of the Absolutist State* (London: Verso, 1974), chaps. 1, 2, and 4. In the strictest sense, feudalism had seriously decayed by the fourteenth century. I am grateful to Michael Loriaux for making many helpful suggestions to improve this chapter.

The immediate causes of feudal erosion in France were military and political: . . . the history of the construction of French Absolutism was to be that of a "convulsive" progression towards a centralized monarchical State, repeatedly interrupted by relapses into provincial disintegration and anarchy, followed by an intensified reaction towards concentration of royal power, until finally an extremely hard and stable structure was achieved. The three great breakdowns of political order were, of course, the Hundred Years War in the 15th century, the Religious Wars in the 16th century, and the Fronde in the 17th century. The transition from the medieval to the Absolute monarchy was each time first arrested, and then accelerated by these crises, whose ultimate outcome was to create a cult of royal authority in the epoch of Louis XIV with no equal anywhere in Western Europe.

SOURCE: Perry Anderson, *Lineages of the Absolutist State*, p. 86.

doxically, the feudal order it was meant to preserve. Louis XIV and his successors conceived of their role in the terms of their feudal precursors. The traditional way for monarchs to increase their power was territorial aggrandizement. Attempts at military expansion against England, Spain, and Holland greatly burdened the financial resources of the country. The king's attempt to pay for his military program with higher taxes alienated

The *Bourgeoisie*

The origins of the term *bourgeoisie* are found in the French word *bourg* or town, which in turn derives from the German *Burg* ("fort"). Towns in the Middle Ages were fortified, and it was there that goods could be safely bought and sold. Townspeople, then, derived their living from commerce, hence, the later association of "bourgeoisie" with the founders of capitalism. They were a "middle" class in that they were weaker than the aristocrats but stronger than the peasants.

important groups, especially the middle classes or *bourgeoisie,* and undermined his overall domestic support. An attempt to tax the aristocrats led to the convening of the *Estates General*. The ultimate result would be the world's most democratic revolution. But first, some background is necessary.

CIRCUMSTANCES LEADING TO THE FRENCH REVOLUTION

The French Revolution, even more than its American predecessor, was the seismic event of the eighteenth century. It was the cataclysm that shattered European feudalism and marked the genuine beginning of modern politics. The reasons for that revolution can hardly be reduced to a few factors, or *variables,* as we call them in social science. Nevertheless, tracing the impact of a few important influences on political events is a useful and illuminating exercise.

An important study completed in the 1960s by Barrington Moore, Jr., sheds much light on French history.[3] Moore's study focussed on the transition from feudalism to modern political regimes in England, France, America, India, Japan, and China. It was his contention that the political institutions that eventually developed were especially shaped by the development of agricultural markets. Commercialization of different agriculture products generated different economic incentives, and these incentives had political ramifications.

An important contrast here was found between England and France. In England, aristocrats developed an interest in the commercial benefits of raising sheep. Aristocrats influenced friends and relatives in Parliament

[3] *Social Origins of Dictatorship and Democracy* (Boston: Beacon Press, 1966), chap. 2.

to pass enclosure laws abrogating the traditional rights of peasants to common pastures so that lords could use the land exclusively for sheep. The resulting wool was marketed by the urban commercial classes (the bourgeoisie) and, thus, a mutuality of interest developed between the aristocrats and their allies in the towns. By depriving peasants and small farmers of their livelihood, the enclosures disrupted the countryside, and the growing wealth of the aristocrats disturbed the king. The king found himself in opposition to the powerful allied interests of the bourgeoisie and aristocracy. The victory of this alliance restricted the growth of the monarchy. In legal terms, the confrontation resulted in supremacy of Parliament (an aristocrat-dominated institution) over the Crown. By the time of the Glorious Revolution of 1688, the principle of constitutional monarchy was established.

In Britain, successive economic conflicts were also solved politically, usually by giving new groups the vote. Thus, the bourgeoisie were given a stake in the political system by the Great Reform of 1832, and the skilled workers gained entrance into the system after the Great Reform of 1867. Critically, political conflicts were solved at each major crisis by extensions of British democracy.[4]

The French responses to the commercialization of agriculture was entirely different, and with its own dramatic consequences. Whereas the product that launched British democracy was wool, France, Moore tells us, would suffer the consequences of an economy based on wine. French markets for wine were smaller than those for wool in Britain, and the incentives generated by its production and sale would lead the country down a very different path to political democracy. Broadly, the development of the wine trade would fuse the interests of the aristocracy and

the king and would solidify the forces hostile to democracy.

First, it is important to note that commercial agriculture was much slower to develop in France than in England. To the extent that wine was produced for markets at all, most was destined for local consumption. This meant that concern about the king's regulations or any other aspect of economic policy would not engender much interest on the part of the French, especially the aristocrats and bourgeoisie.[5] Most importantly, wine production had economic characteristics that had very different political ramifications than the production of wool. Unlike wool, wine production did not force peasants off their traditional lands. There are no significant *economies of scale* in the making of wine. This means that there was no incentive to amalgamate the small holdings of peasants into large estates for reasons of efficiency. There was, therefore, no reason to depopulate the countryside.

Furthermore, wine production did not have what economists call "spread effects." Wool production generated the possibility for related industries, such as weaving, textile industries and, eventually, steam engines. Aside from bottles and corks (the latter were produced in Portugal), and a modest distribution system, wine could not fuel an industrial revolution. Profits were relatively small, aside from the prestige wines we know today, and implementation of new wine technologies as generators of greater profits were rare—read, negligible.

What this means from the point of view of a contrast with England is that French

---

[4] Moore, chap. 1.

[5] However, Alexis de Tocqueville pointed out that by the late eighteenth century there was considerable concern about the regulation of guilds and industry, especially in Paris. See his *The Old Regime and the French Revolution* (New York: Doubleday, 1956; originally published in 1856).

aristocrats continued to live from peasant dues. As the economic possibilities for improving the peasants' lot were relatively meager, this meant that any improvement in the aristocrats' income would come at the expense of the peasants. This was further aggravated in periods of bad harvests or during occasional periods of inflation, when the bite of the lord of the manor was especially painful. Moreover, feudal traditions limited the possibilities for enrichment of even the prosperous peasants. All of these conditions provided the foundation for peasant hostility to the feudal order. That order was enforced at the top by the king of France.

The fate of the French aristocrats, unlike those in England, was closely tied to the fate of the king. Importantly, the bourgeoisie also had an economic interest in maintaining royalty. The French bourgeoisie was smaller than that of England and had a very different commercial outlook. This was because much of this class depended for their livelihoods on the sale of luxury goods and weapons. As their principal clients were royal and aristocratic families, they had a clear stake in the absolutist system. As France entered the eighteenth century, the forces behind absolutism seemed insurmountable.

The power of the king was reinforced by the way in which the state was financed. Feudal traditions generally limited the ability of the king to tax the aristocracy. Thus, the king tended to finance governmental activities by taxing other classes and by selling positions in the bureaucracy to affluent members of the middle classes. This "venality of offices" had a number of effects. It reduced the efficiency of the royal administration, created a quasi-nobility out of the upper reaches of the French bourgeoisie as office holders passed their bureaucratic titles and rents to their children, and reinforced the loyalty of that class to the royal establishment.

The constant wars of the absolutist kings continued to put a strain on royal finances. With aristocrats unwilling to shoulder more of the burden, offices and taxes proliferated. Ultimately, the overtaxed segments of the bourgeoisie became alienated from the system, and many began to favor radical change. Here they found allies in the disaffected peasants and the urban poor. By the time Louis XVI called a meeting of the Estates General, the traditional feudal assembly necessary to legitimize new levies, the country was ripe for change. In 1789 France exploded.

For the next ten years the country experienced unprecedented instability as different sectors of French society grappled for power. At first (1789–92) the revolution was dominated by the bourgeoisie in alliance with liberal aristocrats and clergy, institutionalized as the *Constituent Assembly,* a constitutional but still monarchical regime. Urban dissatisfaction and mass uprisings pushed the revolution to form the first republic, the *Convention* (1792–95), that voted the execution of Louis XVI. The Convention, dominated by a left-wing faction of the bourgeoisie, the *Jacobins,* and especially by a group of Jacobins called the *Girondins,* led France into war with the surrounding aristocratic regimes. The latter were, in fact, poised to attack anyway under the leadership of Prussia and Austria. This led to the formation of a war cabinet, the Committee of Public Safety, under the leadership of Maximilien Robespierre. The Committee of Public Safety, though much maligned later for its abuses, was clearly sympathetic to the demands of the urban poor as well as reasonably competent in running the war effort. Their abuses were considerable, however, as Robespierre (originally the author of a bill abolishing capital punishment) and his allies used the genuine internal and external threats to the revolution as an excuse to wipe out their enemies: Over 40,000 went to the guillotine during the Reign of Terror. This ultimately led to the

The Fall of the Bastille, July 14, 1789.
SOURCE: Culver Pictures, Inc.

revolt of the Convention against its own executive and the establishment of a new constitutional republic, the *Directory*.

NINETEENTH-CENTURY FRANCE: IMPERIAL AND REPUBLICAN EXPERIMENTS

The Directory oversaw the first genuinely free elections under republican auspices in France. However, after years of violent left-wing rule, peasant sympathies turned conservative and a pro-royalist assembly was elected. This prompted one of the country's most able generals, supported by many republicans, to initiate a *coup d'état*.

On the Eighteenth Brumaire, Year VIII (November 9, 1799; see below, "The Revolu-

The Revolutionary Calendar

The revolutionaries were so committed to break with the past that they renamed the calendar. Dating the calendar from the founding of the First Republic (September 22, 1792), the months were: Vendémaire, Brumaire, Frimaire, Nivôse, Pluviôse, Ventôse, Germinal, Floréal, Prairial, Messidor, Thermidor, and Fructidor. They were especially concerned with breaking the power of the church by eliminating the daily reminder of the Christian calendar.

SOURCE: R. R. Colton and Joel Palmer, *A History of the Modern World to 1815*, 5th ed. (New York: Alfred A. Knopf, 1978), pp. 341–82.

tion Calendar"), the general, Napoleon Bonaparte, took control of the government and launched France on the road to modernity.

Bonaparte initially organized his dictatorship as a reorganization of the First Republic, calling it "The Consulate," with himself as First Consul. Later, with victories abroad and confidence at home, the First Consul transformed himself into Napoleon I, Emperor of the French (1804).[6]

NAPOLEONIC FRANCE

Alexis de Tocqueville, in a famous study, noted that the preceding efforts of the French kings to centralize power in the capital facilitated the work of the revolutionaries.[7] By seizing Paris, the rebels were able to seize the entire country, and that is exactly what they did. The class content of power changed in 1789, but the organization of administration remained intact. Even under the revolutionaries, France remained highly centralized, and that centralization would greatly affect the stability of French politics down to the present day.

It was Napoleon, however, who is credited with giving France its modern centralized form. Under the Constituent Assembly and the Convention, the revolutionaries returned power to local elected authorities, after first abolishing the old aristocrat-dominated provinces and redrawing constituencies into 96 roughly equal *départements*. Under Napoleon, the departments lost their independence and fell under the tutelage of prefects appointed by Paris. The system very much re-

---

[6] This was with some ambivalence, however, and in deference to his original Jacobin sympathies, the original coinage bore the inscription: "French Republic; Napoleon, Emperor."

[7] *The Old Regime and the French Revolution.*

The Centralization of France

Writing in 1855, Tocqueville described the Napoleonic system as an iteration of the Old Regime: "We find a single central power located at the heart of the kingdom and controlling public administration throughout the country; a single Minister of State in charge of almost all the internal affairs of the country; in each province a single representative of government supervising every detail of the administration. . . . Is not this exactly the highly centralized administration with which we are familiar in present-day France?"

SOURCE: *The Old Regime and the French Revolution*, p. 57.

sembled that of the Old Regime, where the king's *intendents* performed the same role.

Yet Napoleon's innovations went much further. He established France's first *meritocracy*, where government positions were filled by virtue of talent and intelligence rather than aristocratic origin or venality. The heart of the government was the Council of State, which advised the emperor and exists to this day as the country's highest administrative court. To train such talent for public work, the university system was reorganized, and specialized "great schools" were established, such as the Ecole Polytechnique, France's top engineering school. Under the emporor's guidance, the Council of State overhauled the nation's legal system, giving France a systematic and egalitarian set of laws, known collectively as the *Code Napoléon*, that were the most progressive of their day.

The regime was, of course, still a dictatorship. The quasi-elective legislative body that replaced the Constituent Assembly and the Convention had no powers of deliberation and served largely to legitimize Napoleon's rule. The Tribunate, a kind of senate, had no power to enact legislation, although it could openly discuss proposed legislation.

Ultimately, the regime was undermined

not by its exclusion of popular will, but by the emperor's external expansion. Napoleon's attempt to extend the French empire to the limits of Europe menaced all aristocratic regimes, and they fought back. Led by Britain, Prussia, and Austria, the aristocratic alliance finally defeated Bonaparte in 1815 and restored the Bourbons to the French throne.

THE RESTORATION AND THE JULY MONARCHY

The victorious aristocratic powers successfully replaced Napoleon with the brother of Louis XVI, Louis XVIII, the son of the old king having died in prison. Yet the restoration did not mean a reestablishment of feudalism. The French bourgeoisie had grown stronger in the period from 1789 to 1815. Lands that had belonged to the aristocracy and the church were purchased by many bourgeois and well-to-do peasants. This made them a significant obstacle to the reestablishment of the Old Regime. Louis XVIII had to settle for a constitutional monarchy guaranteeing freedom of speech and property. Wealthy nonaristocrats were allowed to vote and serve in the legislature. Thus, while the French system was somewhat less democratic than even the unreformed British Parliament of the same period, formal aristocratic privileges were not restored.

The kings took an active role in government during the restoration. Both Louis XVIII and his successor, Charles X, became closely identified with specific policies. The latter's close association with ultra-royalist prime minister Polignac proved to be his undoing. The king's refusal to appoint a different head of government after the 1830 elections, which overwhelmingly repudiated the Ultras, alienated the bourgeoisie and parts of the aristocracy. When riots in the streets of

Paris broke out as a reflection of economic crisis, the bourgeoisie and liberal aristocrats threw their support to the Duke of Orleans, a descendant of Louis XIII. Charles X abdicated, and the July Monarchy was established under Louis-Philippe of Orleans. Because of its economic base of support, the regime also became known as the Bourgeois Monarchy.

THE BOURGEOIS MONARCHY: 1830–48

The character of the new regime was perhaps best summed up by the British historian, Alfred Cobban:

> The so-called "bourgeois monarchy" was in fact an oligarchy of landowners. In the absence of a more detailed analysis of Orleanist society, we must not read too much into this statement; but at least it suggests that the landed wealth of the country was no longer mainly in the hands of old legitimist [pro-Bourbon] families, but partly in those of a class of new men, who had doubtless made their wealth in many ways in the course of the *ancien regime* and the Revolution. Their figures, like that of Pere Grandet, dominate the novels of Balzac. Their new wealth had largely been invested in land, and they were now a well-established propertied class, with a sufficiently strong sense of its own interests to use the revolution of 1830 to oust the legitimist-clerical regime of the restored Bourbons, and at the same time prevent the republicans from acceding to power.[8]

Befitting its title, the bourgeois monarchy's main successes and ultimate failure were to be found in the French economy. While the king mainly concerned himself with foreign

[8] Alfred Cobban, *A History of Modern France. Volume Two: From the First Empire to the Second Empire. 1799–1871* (Harmondsworth: Penguin, 1965), p. 98.

policy, the government presided over the beginnings of industrialization. Most notably, the beginnings of modern industrial infrastructure were promoted by the regime. Canals and roads were improved. Railways began to make an appearance. Importantly, state-sponsored schools overtook the older parochial (church-run) schools as the vehicle for mass education.

As France slowly became industrial, a new class of urban workers gradually assumed political importance, especially in the city of Paris. A bad harvest in 1846 and a deepening economic crisis created hardship, particularly for these workers. The regime of Louis-Philippe, based on the support of landed wealth, was not especially sensitive to the workers' needs, nor to the needs of those whose livelihood depended on commerce. Parisians took to the streets again in 1848, and this time the result was the Second Republic.

THE SECOND REPUBLIC AND THE SECOND EMPIRE

The street riots of 1848 coincided with the increased audacity of the republican opposition to Louis-Philippe. With the sympathy of the National Guard supporting them, the republicans formed a provisional government in Paris. Men of democratic ideals, their actions would ultimately undermine democracy in France. The republicans instituted universal suffrage. This shifted formal power to the largely illiterate peasants, especially amenable to the leadership of local notables and a conservative clergy. Peasant votes assured the creation of a conservative constituent assembly.

The assembly wrote the constitution of the Second Republic, which allowed for a powerful, popularly elected president. Knowing

that this would mean the election of a conservative to the post, given the proclivities of peasant voters, the Left fulminated and Parisian workers once again rioted. This frightened the bourgeoisie, no less than it did the peasantry who recalled the Red Terror of Robespierre, and feared confiscation of their property. This time the army, composed mainly of peasants, stepped into quell any possibility of a socialist revolution. In the succeeding election, a conservative was indeed elected to the presidency. His name was Louis Napoleon Bonaparte.

Louis Bonaparte was Napoleon I's nephew. He had grown up mostly in exile and was rather more of an adventurer than a politician. In his youth he had been active in Italian revolutionary politics, and he spoke French with something of a German accent. He was, however, more interested in power than in principle. At the time of his election he had already served time in a French jail for having led an abortive coup attempt. His talents, in fact, lay more in public relations than in intellect. His speeches were especially seductive to the peasantry, while the French elite, as well as other Europeans, were more circumspect (Otto von Bismarck, the "Iron Chancellor" of Germany, would later call him "the greatest mediocrity in Europe").

While Louis Bonaparte owed his election to the French peasantry, his eventual power would be exercised as a result of divisions in the French bourgeoisie. The conflicting interests of agriculture and industry, land and capital, were not easily reconciled in the parliament of the Second Republic.[9] Bonaparte was able to take advantage of these conflicts in a period of economic recession and crisis;

[9] The most famous version of this argument was articulated by Karl Marx in his essay, *The Eighteenth Brumaire of Louis Bonaparte,* originally published in 1852. Marx wrote his analysis as a series of newspaper articles for a German language weekly published in New York.

when, once again, the streets of Paris promised to erupt, he led a *coup d'état* against the Republic and declared himself emperor. Thus began the Second Empire, with Louis Bonaparte dubbing himself Napoleon III.

FRANCE INDUSTRIALIZES

The fact that the peasants were on the winning side of the French Revolution and the subsequent acquisition of large amounts of land by the French bourgeoisie were significant factors retarding the spread of industry. The political clout of the peasants during periods of universal suffrage and the bias toward landed interests during the Bourbon and Orleanist monarchies greatly inhibited industrialization along the lines of the British model. Napoleon III, however, broke with these trends, and his regime established the political conditions necessary for economic change. Influenced by the writings of Saint-Simon, who saw French backwardness as a product of a lack of credit, Napoleon III adopted policies favorable to credit expansion, which, not coincidentally, were also favorable to his friends in banking circles.[10]

More importantly, the state took an active role in promoting industrial expansion. New financial institutions were established to promote industrial investment. The state guaranteed a 4 percent return on railroad investment, which, in turn, created a demand for the products of heavy industry such as steel and coal. Tariffs were lowered to stimulate competition. By the end of the 1860s France was the European continent's largest industrial power.[11]

Industrialization reinforced the central role of Paris. Paris was the natural hub of the railroads. Investment tended to flow to Paris, where the largest consumer market existed, and where an educated workforce could most easily be found.

With some important exceptions, firm size tended to remain small, however. Companies were family-owned, and those that employed more than a handful of workers were relatively rare. This not only limited economies of scale and thus restrained French firms from being internationally competitive, but also made them more difficult to unionize. French society, therefore, remained alienating for the urban workers. While Napoleon III was not wholly unsympathetic to the plight of the worker, he had other priorities. Moreover, the emperor could count on the support of both the peasantry and the bourgeoisie. He could afford to let the workers go. It was not unnatural, therefore, that French workers should gravitate toward socialism at a very early stage in the country's industrial development. This phenomenon would come back to haunt future regimes.

Ultimately, Napoleon III's undoing, like that of his uncle, came from outside French borders. Rising competition from Prussia and the expansionist ambitions of Bismarck and his supporters eventually came into conflict with France. After a demoralizing defeat at Sedan, with Napoleon III leading troops in the field, the Franco-Prussian War came to a close when the emperor of France surrendered.

Although the emperor had surrendered, the war continued for a few months under the auspices of a provisional government. A lengthy siege of Paris and a failed counteroffensive led to a final and ignominious end to the war. Conditions were ripe for another attempt at republican government. This time the attempt would succeed.

---

[10] Most notably, the Péreire brothers.

[11] For a highly readable acount of French economic history during these years, see Tom Kemp, *Industrialization in Nineteenth Century Europe* (London: Longman, 1969), chap. 3.

THE THIRD REPUBLIC

The Third Republic would ultimately prove France's most successful attempt at parliamentary government. It started, however, inauspiciously. Not only was the new assembly faced with the immediate task of suing for peace, but initial elections, dominated once again by the peasant vote, brought to power a very conservative assembly, mostly of monarchists. The new government attempted to disarm the left-wing city guard and passed new laws requiring workers and lower-middle-class people to pay tremendously inflated rents. This led Parisians once again into an uproar. The national government simply abandoned the capital for nearby Versailles, with Parisians left to their own devices, much as had been the case during the Prussian siege. Resentful Parisians, mostly lower and middle classes, formed an independent municipal government, which they dubbed the *Commune* (March 28, 1871) after the radical experiment in city government of 1792. The Commune of 1871 actually did very little that was radical except resist the authority of the national government in Versailles. This was enough. Under the leadership of the conservative prime minister Thiers, the *Versaillais* ruthlessly and barbarously repressed the *Communards*. Paris was defeated, but the Commune entered permanently into the mythology of the French left.

The monarchist assembly, though divided among Legitimists, Orleanists, and Bonapartists, managed to elect a conservative general, MacMahon, to the presidency in 1871. By 1875, the mood of the country had changed considerably, and a majority of republicans were elected to the new *Chamber of Deputies,* the principal house of the French parliament. MacMahon immediately dismissed the assembly and attempted to rig new elections to return a royalist majority.

However, the republican tide was too strong for even a corrupt electoral system. The republican majority was renewed and the presidency fell into disrepute. From then on, until 1958, the legislature would dominate French democratic regimes.

The period from 1871 to 1914 is generally considered the high point of French parliamentary government. Though dominated by conservatives, the Third Republic even recognized organized labor by 1884, although workers were far from integrated into the political system.[12] While politics remained highly polarized between right and left, most the country's problems were handled reasonably effectively by democratic solutions worked out in the context of a representative assembly. Not without interludes of crisis, such as the Dreyfus Affair (see boxed insert, chapter 11), by and large the Third Republic was successful until World War I. After that watershed, France's problems became more difficult and the ability of the country's political institutions to solve them became more questionable.

The beginning of the end came in 1929, and once again the source of France's problems was external to the country's borders. The source was, of course, the world economic collapse announced by the New York stock market crash. Because protectionist measures had kept France isolated from the world market during most of the life of the Third Republic, the Great Depression did not begin to affect most of the French until 1931. Then it struck with a vengeance. Unemployment climbed to over 3 million and was probably much worse than it appeared, as

[12] On this point see Gregory M. Luebbert, "Social Foundations of Political Order in Interwar Europe," *World Politics,* 39 (1987):452–56. Luebbert relies for much of his information on Val Lorwin, *The French Labor Movement* (Cambridge: Harvard University Press, 1954).

underemployment was greatly disguised by the large numbers of people still living (wretchedly) in the countryside. Government policies only made things worse, as orthodox economic solutions prescribed reduced government expenditure and reductions in real wages.[13]

Government ineptitude as well as popular perception of official corruption led to increasing discontent, which once again spilled into the streets. The ranks of both left- and right-wing organizations were swelled by the misery of the Depression and its intractability in the hands of centrist politicians. Tension reached a high point when fascist leagues, such as the *Croix de Feu,* marched on the Chamber of Deputies on February 6, 1934. The attempted coup d'état was foiled by loyal companies of police, but the situation appeared touch-and-go during the six hours of street fighting.[14]

THE POPULAR FRONT

The near catastrophe of February 6, 1934, traumatized the various factions of the French Left enough to patch up their differences to form an alliance for the coming elections. On the other hand, the failure of the coup disoriented the forces on the Right. The result was a victory for the left-wing parties in the elections of 1936. A cabinet of Radicals (who were actually centrists, despite their name) and Socialists, supported by the Communists, was formed under the leadership of Leon Blum, a moderate socialist. The coalition took the name "Popular Front."

[13] For an examination of the influence of economic orthodoxy and its comparative impact on different countries during the Great Depression, as well as during other crises, see Peter A. Gourevitch, *Politics in Hard Times* (Ithaca: Cornell University Press, 1986).

[14] On this, see Cobban, volume 3, pp. 137 ff.

In the desperate conditions of the Depression, factory workers interpreted the left's electoral victory as the first step in a social revolution. Some began occupying factories, while others took the occasion to strike. The highly charged atmosphere frightened the industrialists, who also thought a social revolution was at hand. Representatives of both sides of the class divide met at the Hôtel Matignon, the prime minister's official residence, and hammered out an agreement that gave significant concessions to the French working class. Not only were wages raised, unions recognized and the forty-hour week conceded, but for the first time, workers received paid vacation. That summer many workers saw the ocean (only three hours from Paris by train) for the first time in their lives.

The Matignon Agreements were a milestone for blue-collar workers, but the millstone of the Depression was too heavy to be buoyed by such measures. Revolution was averted, but the Popular Front was unsuccessful in bringing France out of the Depression. Attacked on both left and right, the Blum government resigned thirteen months after its electoral victory.

WORLD WAR II AND VICHY

If the deep causes of the collapse of the Third Republic were rooted in the world depression, the *causa proxima* of its demise was World War II. France declared war on Germany after the latter attacked Poland, a French ally, in September of 1939. Organized by the general staff to fight a trench war, France was poorly equipped to repel the highly mobile and mechanized German war machine. It was only a matter of time before the French were defeated on humiliating terms. The end came on June 22, 1940, with the signing of an armistice.

The defeat gave the French right, many of

them fascist sympathizers, the opportunity they had been denied on February 6, 1934. After the armistice, the north of France was occupied by German troops. At the same time, a fascist state was set up in the south; fearful of an urban proletariat, its leaders chose the sleepy resort of Vichy as the new capital and inaugurated a dictatorship under the personalistic rule of Marshal Pétain. Pétain had been a hero of the battle of Verdun during World War I and had been a figure with considerable right-wing support during the 1930s. The conservative last parliament of the Third Republic had turned to him to negotiate the armistice and he, in turn, had no clear ideas about the kind of conservative regime he would head. The building of a fascist state owed more to his underlings than to Pétain himself. Much of its construction would rely on the efforts of Pierre Laval, a right-wing politician during the 1930s, and on Admiral Darlan, commander of the Navy during the war.

While the high echelons of government were subject to considerable intrigues by various politicians of the right, the fascist government was, in fact, managed by the French bureaucracy. The French bureaucracy had been a traditional source of employment for the bourgeoisie, and most of the higher officials were not only from upper-middle class or even aristocratic origins, but frequently sympathetic to the far right. They were all too willing to suppress labor, enforce racist legislation and implement a quasi-nazi regime. Indeed, partially due to these activities, the upper administration would be a target for reform immediately and continually after the liberation of France.

THE RESISTANCE AND THE LIBERATION

The advent of the Vichy government was a new phenomenon for France. Fascism, as an

The Rationale of the Resistance

In the Second World War republican France passed from the humiliation of total collapse to the moral ambiguity of divided allegiance. Sabotage and rebellion were the needs of patriots, loyalty and obedience the virtues of defeatists and collaborators, murder and torture part of the normal machinery of government and assassination the method of "opposition."

SOURCE: Cobban, vol. 3, pp. 199–200.

ideology that attempts to popularize an oppressive form of capitalism by playing on nationalist feelings, found fertile ground in much of the country.[15] Indeed, opposing fascism, which, as in Germany, had come to power legally, took a good deal of courage. Vichy turned traditional patriotism on its head.

Two main groups resisted Vichy: the Communist Party and the followers of General de Gaulle. De Gaulle had been undersecretary for war briefly before the armistice, and fled to England when defeat was apparent. From the very beginning he urged the French to resist Vichy and set up an exile government in London. He also organized a nationalist Resistance to sabotage the German war effort from within France. The Communists formed the other major group after the invasion of the Soviet Union in 1941.

While the Gaullists and Communists cooperated in the face of the common enemy, in fact they competed, each wanting to impose a specific vision of postwar France. It has, in fact, been argued that defeating the Communists was de Gaulle's principal goal, which he

[15] See especially Robert O. Paxton, *Vichy France* (New York: Alfred Knopf, 1973). This point is also brought out dramatically in Marcel Ophels's classic documentary, *The Sorrow and the Pity*. For an analysis of fascism as a general category of political development, see Moore, chap. 8.

subtly pursued by closely cooperating with them.[16]

While the Resistance movement was actually quite small and its military achievements debatable, its political importance was supreme. The organization was sufficiently large and active to make it impossible for the Allies to ignore. De Gaulle used the organization to replace local governments as different regions were liberated and, thus, the Resistance formed the natural nucleus of the postwar government. In 1944, a provisional government began the task of restoring re-

publican and democratic government to France. A new constituent assembly was elected, and the wheels of the Fourth Republic were set in motion.

THE FOURTH REPUBLIC

For all practical purposes, the Fourth Republic was simply a continuation of the Third. This was not the original intention of either its founders or the French people. A referendum held after the liberation rejected resuming the Third Republic and mandated a new constitutional convention. The first draft of the new constitution, which included a change to a unicameral legislature, was re-

---

[16] Cobban, volume 3, p. 201. This was a strategy that would be proven useful, three decades later, by François Mitterrand (see pp. 477–79).

June 1945: The liberation of France. On French soil for the first time since the German occupation, General de Gaulle walks through the streets of Bayeux accompanied by enthusiastic crowds of his fellow countrymen.

SOURCE: Culver Pictures, Inc.

jected by French voters, and the second draft restored most of the institutions of the Third Republic. The new regime was still a parliamentary republic, with executive power in the hands of a prime minister and cabinet responsible to the lower house. With France still divided into many political parties, none large enough to dominate, coalitions remained fragile and cabinet stability was difficult to achieve. De Gaulle, refusing to participate in an enterprise dominated by parties, withdrew from the government and, gradually, from politics as well.

The principal achievement of the Fourth Republic was economic reconstruction. The discrediting of the right because of its collaboration with the Nazis left French government in the hands of socialists, socially oriented Catholics, and communists. While these three groups would eventually come to loggerheads, they agreed in the early years on a high level of government intervention to rebuilt the economy (see Chapter 9). The results, supported by U.S. economic aid, were stunningly successful. By the end of the 1950s the economy had totally recovered.

Important Dates in French History

58–5 B.C.	Julius Caesar conquers Gaul
486 A.D.	Clovis, King of the Franks, defeats Roman governor of Gaul
800	Charlemagne becomes Emperor
987	beginning of the Capetian dynasty in France
1302	Philip IV calls the first Estates-General
1337–1453	France defeats England in the Hundred Years' War
1789–99	the French Revolution
1792	establishment of the First Republic
1799	Napoleon's coup d'etat
1804	establishment of the First Empire
1815	defeat of Napoleon at Waterloo and Restoration of the Bourbon dynasty
1830	establishment of the July (Bourgeois) Monarchy
1848	establishment of the Second Republic
1852	Napoleon III's coup d'etat and establishment of the Second Empire
1870–71	Franco-Prussian War
1871	establishment of the Third Republic
1899	retrial of Dreyfus
1914–18	World War I
1936	Popular Front forms government
1940	defeat of France in World War II
1940–44	Vichy regime in south of France, Germany occupies north, then entire country
1944–46	De Gaulle head of Provisional Government
1946	Fourth Republic established
1946–54	French Indo-Chinese War
1954–62	Algerian War
1957	Treaty of Rome signed, establishing the Common Market
1958	establishment of the Fifth Republic
1981	Mitterrand elected, first Socialist government of the Fifth Republic
1986–88	"Cohabitation" of conservative prime minister and Socialist president
1988	reelection of Mitterrand, first president to be reelected in the Fifth Republic

It was, however, the crumbling French Empire that would instigate the demise of the Fourth Republic. The communists broke with their partners over voting war credits to quash the revolt in French Indochina (Laos, Cambodia, and Vietnam). It was the revolt in Algeria, though, that provided the coup de grace.

French colonization of Algeria dated from 1830. The large territory had been divided into three *départments* with ostensibly the same political status as any departments in metropolitan France. In fact, the Arab natives, by far the numerical majority, were vastly underrepresented and given the inferior status of French "subjects" rather than citizens.[17] In 1954 a bloody revolt began, using terrorist methods, which invited ruthless repression from Paris. In 1958 the ignominious battle, with torture used by both sides, greatly divided the sympathies of metropolitan France. Political leadership in the French parliament was weak, as governments were paralyzed over how to conduct the war. Fearing that a left-of-center government would grant Algeria its independence, French army garrisons in Algiers revolted on May 13, 1958. The army revolt soon spread to Corsica, and French politicians began to fear the possibility of a right-wing coup d'état in Paris. There seemed only one way out: Charles de Gaulle.

The French habit of looking to a single man to save the country from trying times had a long set of precedents: the two Bonapartes, Pétain, and de Gaulle during World War II. A military man and a traditionalist, de Gaulle was expected to have the confidence of the army and the Right. His credentials from the Resistance made him acceptable, albeit reluctantly, to the Left.

De Gaulle's participation carried a price. Long convinced that a parliamentary system could never provide the stability that France needed, de Gaulle demanded that the institutions of republican government be changed if he were to again enter politics. The desperate politicians of the Fourth Republic reluctantly agreed. Working in close cooperation with Michel Debré, a close colleague from the Resistance, de Gaulle created a set of institutions that allowed for a strong presidency and a submissive parliament. A new Republic was being born, a Fifth Republic. Political life under these new institutions will form the subject of the coming chapters.

References and Suggested Readings

ANDERSON, PERRY. *Lineages of the Absolutist State.* London: Verso, 1979.

BLOC, MARC. *Strange Defeat,* trans. Gerard Hopkins. New York: W. W. Norton, 1968.

COBBAN, ALFRED. *A History of Modern France.* Harmondsworth: Penguin, 1965.

KEOHANE, NANERL O. *Philosophy and the State in Modern France.* Princeton: Princeton University Press, 1980.

LACOUTURE, JEAN. *De Gaulle,* trans. Francis K. Price. New York: Avon, 1968.

MOORE, BARRINGTON, JR. *Social Origins of Dictatorship and Democracy.* Boston: Beacon Press, 1966.

PAXTON, ROBERT O. *Vichy France.* New York: Alfred A. Knopf, 1973.

[17] Alfred Grosser, *La IVᵉ République et la Politique Extériure* (Paris: Armand Colin, 1961).

11

I denounce a *sickness* that gnaws us in every limb. . . . Profligate anarchy or reaction, it's all the same, since the sickness comes from the country itself, which has been incapable of organizing itself under any of the different forms of government it has successively tried in the past century.

— GEORGES CLEMENCEAU

A man thinks differently in a palace than in a hut.

— LUDWIG FEUERBACH

A Fragmented Political Culture

The frequent failures of political institutions in France, especially when compared with the relative stability of structures in Britain and elsewhere in the English-speaking world, have intrigued political scientists. This chronic instability as well as the interwar fascist experiences in Latin and Germanic Europe led many political scientists to wonder if Anglo-Saxon culture were especially favorable to the growth and stability of democracy.

By most accounts, French society was deeply divided. Levels of trust between left and right and between religious and antireligious groups were extremely low. People were ambivalent about the role of democratic (or any) government and had mixed feelings about public officials and elected representatives. Such attitudes might explain why democratic governance had such a fragile hold on French society.

Is There a "Civic Culture"?

If the democratic model of the participatory state is to develop . . . it will require more than formal institutions of democracy—universal suffrage, the political party, the elective legislature. These in fact are also part of the totalitarian participation pattern, in a formal, if not functional, sense. A democratic form of participatory political system requires as well a political culture consistent with it.

SOURCE: Gabriel Almond and Sidney Verba, *The Civic Culture* (Boston: Little Brown and Company, 1963), p. 3.

POLITICAL CULTURE AS A CONCEPT

The concept of "political culture" posits an important role for the attitudes and orientations that people hold toward authority. It describes a configuration of beliefs, values and symbols common to a nation, or to large groups within a nation, that are directed toward political institutions. Symbols may be concrete, like the flag or the *Arc de Triomphe*. They may be historical figures such as Napoleon or George Washington. They may be ideas that take on a symbolic importance, such as *equality* or *liberty*.[1]

Borrowing from the literature on psychology and anthropology, political culture theory focusses on both the *cognitive* and *affective* orientations toward authority. The examination of cognitive orientations occurs when we ask such questions as: How aware are people of the political system? What is the expected role of government in their eyes? How far does government extend? Do they expect too much from government? What do children know about the political system?

Affective orientations concern the way people feel about their government. Do they like what they see? If people expect too much from government they may be disappointed by it, and that disappointment may easily turn to disaffection. These are important considerations if one is concerned with the problem of political stability.

Countries may often be constituted by people with diverse political orientations and values. The lack of a consensus as to the nature and powers of the political regime may also be a cause of instability. Thus, the process by which political consensus develops about the basic rules of the game and basic agreement on who is to be considered a member of the political community is crucial to understanding the stability of a regime.

THE PROCESS OF NATION-BUILDING

The process by which diverse ethnic groups develop sentiments of solidarity with each other is called "nation building." While we

---

[1] Think, for example, of the word *freedom* as it is used in political discourse in the United States. The nation's highest civilian award is called the "Medal of Freedom." Imagine the political impact of calling it the "Medal of Doing What You Want."

are accustomed to thinking of France as a single nation, a "nation-state," as it were, in fact links of solidarity among the French are of rather recent vintage. By and large, France could be considered a single nation only as of the late nineteenth century.

By almost any measure, France in the early nineteenth century was divided against itself. Regional, cultural and linguistic cleavages, harking back to before the Middle Ages in some cases, divided France into many separate communities. Perhaps most important was the language cleavage.

Nations are people "shaped to a common mold by many generations of shared historical experience."[2] They have frequently been defined by the language they speak as well as the symbols they share. The German nationalist philosopher J. G. Fichte remarked that language ". . . developed continuously out of the actual common life of . . . people."[3] By this measure, France was hardly a nation in the early or even mid-nineteenth century.

Until the nineteenth century, France was really a collection of nations rather than a single entity (Figure 11.1). More often than not people spoke a regional dialect derisively called a *patois* by Parisians. In some cases people spoke entirely different languages. In

---

[2] Rupert Emerson, *From Empire to Nation: the Rise and Self-Assertion of Asian and African Peoples*, quoted in Samuel Beer, *Modern Political Development* in Samuel Beer *et al.*, *Patterns of Government*, 3rd ed. (New York: Random House, 1973), p. 33.

[3] Quoted in Elie Kedourie, *Nationalism* (London: Hutchinson, 1966), p. 66. Kedourie finds the equation of *nation* with *language* as an intellectual foundation of nazism, for it is close to the images of "blood and soil" that fostered xenophobia and anti-Semitism among the German peasantry in the nineteenth and early twentieth century. Also evoking this theme is Alexander Gerschenkron in *Bread and Democracy in Germany* (Berkeley and Los Angeles: University of California Press, 1943). However, for our purposes it is useful to point out the linkages between language and nation-building in the French context.

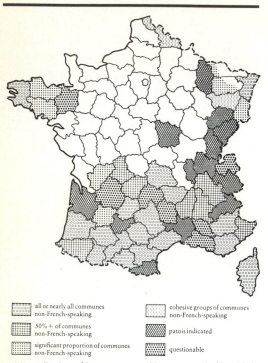

all or nearly all communes
non-French-speaking

50%+ of communes
non-French-speaking

significant proportion of communes
non-French-speaking

cohesive groups of communes
non-French-speaking

patois indicated

questionable

Map 3. Patois-speaking communes, 1863. SOURCE: Archives Nationales, F¹⁷* 3160, Ministère de l'instruction publique, "Statistique: Etats divers."

"In 1863, according to official figures, 8,381 of France's 37,510 communes [local districts] spoke no French: about a quarter of the country's population. The Ministry of Public Instruction found that 448,328 of the 4,018,427 schoolchildren (ages seven to thirteen) spoke no French at all, and that another 1,490,269 spoke or understood it but could not write it, suggesting an indifferent grasp of the tongue. In 24 of the country's 89 departments, more than half the communes did not speak French, and in six others a significant proportion of the communes were in the same position. . . . In short, French was a foreign language for a substantial number of Frenchmen, including almost half the children who would reach adulthood in the last quarter of the century."

SOURCE: Eugen Weber, *Peasants into Frenchmen* (Stanford, CA: Stanford University Press, 1976), p. 67.

the south and southeast people spoke *Occitan* or *Provençal,* Latin-based languages that were as similar to French as to Spanish or Italian. In the northeast they spoke *Alsacien,* a dialect of German. In the northwest *Breton,* a Celtic language, was spoken. Near the Spanish border *Basque* predominated. Originally, only the people of *Île de France* (the region around Paris) and the region north of the Loire river, as well as the aristocracy generally, spoke French.

The French had fierce loyalties to these ethnic regions. Such loyalties were largely tolerated or ignored by the kings of France, so long as such diversity posed no threat to royal administration or power.[4] While there was indeed a France before the Revolution, there was no French nation.

The nationalism that characterized the French Revolution was, in many ways, an idea ahead of its time. The notion of a country populated by citizens united by sentiments of solidarity and loyal to a government that was an expression of their will preceded the political reality. In modern terms, it was Napoleon who set in motion the process that would lead to the final creation of a single French national entity.

Initially, the principal mechanism of national integration was the army, with the nationwide conscription innovated by Napoleon to preserve the fledgling French Republic. Not only did service in the army allow Frenchmen of different regions to meet and depend on each other, increasing levels of trust, but it forced them to speak a common language. Once the military men were demobilized they returned to their homes, taking their acquired language with them.

The returning soldiers not only brought French back to the hinterlands, but brought Napoleonic values with them as well. Such

[4] Eugen Weber, *Peasants into Frenchmen* (Stanford: Stanford University Press, 1976), p. 70.

Figure 11.1   Historical regions of France.
SOURCE: Eugen Weber, *Peasants into Frenchmen,* pp. xv.

Napoleonic ideals as liberty and equality before the law often accompanied the provincials' initiation into the French language. Of course, the principal inculcation of republican values had to await the spread of mass education under the Third Republic.

CENTRALIZATION

Liberty and equality were not the only values given a special impetus by Napoleon. Administrative centralization was equally a part of the Napoleonic heritage. While Tocqueville was quite accurate in remarking that the centralization of political life pre-dated the Revolution (see Chapter 10), it was the administrative apparatus of Napoleon that channelled the development of mass politics.

Napoleon organized the administration of France in such a way as to put certain revolutionary ideas into practice. These ideas reflected the thoughts of the Jacobins (see chapter 10). The Jacobins argued that an egalitarian society required centralization. If different regions of France were free to pass their own laws, citizens of one part of the country would be subject to different requirements than those of another section.[5] Equality required standardization, and standardization required centralization. Thus, Napoleon, for his own reasons as well as because

[5] Consider the situation in the United States as a way of examining the inequities of decentralization: welfare recipients receive much more in California, even taking into account a different cost of living, than they do in Mississippi.

he was the quintessential Jacobin, located all power of decision in Paris. Administration became so thoroughly centralized that it was only a slight exaggeration to say that, for instance, the minister of education could look at his watch at any given moment and know what page of the standard history text every French student in the country was studying.

Napoleonic administration forced a kind of unity on France, but it was a unity that demanded a price. The price was grass-roots democracy. Tocqueville is perhaps the most well-known proponent of decentralization as a guardian of personal liberties. For him, the creation of competing centers of power was the best guarantee against the abuse of authority. Thus, the creation of a federal structure in the United States with powerful state and local governments, as well as a separation of powers at the national level, assured that no one arm of government would get out of hand. The lack of power at the local level in France not only deprived citizens of such safeguards, but also limited the democratic experience of the French population. This has had consequences for both the political elite and the citizenry in general. As Suzanne Berger noted,

> Democratic politics requires that the political system provide experiences of conflict and compromise . . . in sum, a political education, both for political activists and for the interested but less active citizenry. . . . By controlling or eliminating the possibilities for local initiative, the state does limit the risk of having incompetent or corrupt local officials, but at the same time it stunts the growth of responsible local leadership.[6]

Thus, the effect of centralization, itself intended as a correction to the problems of diversity, was to increase the instability of French politics. Lacking experience in compromise, losers in political battles expected, and often received, the worst. Thus, the consequences of defeat in national contests were frequently considered too dire to accept. Potential losers were more than receptive to achieving by *coup d'état* what they were unable to achieve electorally. Such thoughts were all the more likely in view of the various deep cleavages that divided the French.

HISTORICAL DIVISIONS OF THE FRENCH POLITY

One of the longest lasting issues over which the French were divided concerned the role of religion in French politics. While over 80 percent of the population were born into nominally Catholic families, the number of those who viewed religion as an appropriate influence on secular politics were considerably fewer. The hostility or preference for religious intrusion had much to do with French history.

By and large, the church in France has traditionally been associated with conservatism. This harks back to the original association of the Catholic Church with the *ancien regime*. The links of the church with conservative rule were, of course, common in many countries (see Chapter 9 on the role of the church in Italy and Spain, for example), if only because the doctrine of an afterlife tended to encourage temporal passivity *vis-à-vis* the institutions of the time. The doctrine of divine right of kings, which maintained royalty to be the anointed of God, also continued the association of the church with reactionary regimes. Most importantly in France, the high ecclesiastical positions tended to be filled by the aristocracy, and a considerable amount of land was held by the church. All of these links did not endear the church to the opponents

---

[6] Suzanne Berger, *The French Political System* (New York: Random House, 1974), p. 10.

of absolutism.[7] What is interesting about France is the persistence of these associations long after absolutism was overthrown. From the time of the Revolution onward, the church tended to be associated with royalists and the later manifestations of the French right.

What made the church the most enduring opponent of the Republic was the nature of the rest of the anti-Republican opposition. Fragmented as the opposition was among the supporters of different dynasties (Legitimists [pro-Bourbon], Orleanists, Bonapartists, etc.), affection for the church seemed the only commonality. Moreover, the response of the Vatican to the gradual secularization of French society was extremely rigid. Republican deputies to the French parliament were consistently excommunicated until 1892.[8]

Sociological and geographical factors reinforced the antipathy of pro- and anti-church forces. The principal support for the church was located in the countryside. By the mid-nineteenth century the peasantry had lost its revolutionary fervor. Largely uneducated and fearful of that which they did not understand, French peasants were often dependent upon priests for temporal as well as spiritual guidance. It was not unusual for them to take their cues from the village *curé* (priest) when it came to politics.[9] Conversely, anticlerical sympathies were to be found primarily in the cities, especially Paris. Thus, given the degree of centralization, hostilities that formed around the role of the church in politics tended to coincide geographically with the resentment of the special influence of Paris. Paris viewed from the countryside was secular, industrial, and, until defeat of the Commune, left wing. The peasants, viewed from Paris by the partisans of the Republic, were rubes unwittingly manipulated by the priests and by Rome. Not surprisingly, geographic and secular cleavages became most politicized over the issue of public education.

Education, of course, is the process by which not only information but also values are transmitted from one generation to the next. The issue of who would control the schools was perhaps the most vehemently politicized of the nineteenth century. The Restoration and Second Empire, based on conservative support, left the church an influential role in the education of French youth. It was the Third Republic that really took the lead in secularizing public education. That secularization not only educated but often alienated the agricultural population in the provinces. But it was the full-scale effort to establish mass education by the Third Republic that not only finally unified France linguistically, but inculcated democratic values at the same time.[10]

REGIONAL AND ECONOMIC CLEAVAGES

The centralization and economic integration of the country also had a divisive effect on the French political culture. Economic unification of the country actually occurred under the absolutist kings, especially under the

---

[7] To be fair, the absolutist kings had their differences with Rome. The former wished to control clerical appointments within France. Louis XV expelled the Jesuits from France, and many sectors of the clergy allied themselves with the Third Estate and against the king at the time of the Revolution.

[8] See Berger, pp. 21 ff.

[9] This was especially true in the underdeveloped west of France. Such pro-clerical attitudes were weakest among the peasantry of the Midi (south), many of whom had a strong anti-clerical tradition.

[10] Weber, pp. 330–38. Regrettably, this inculcation also laid the foundation for a rampant and rabid nationalism that would have horrid consequences in World War I and even later in the government of Vichy.

guidance of Louis XIV's minister Jean Baptiste Colbert. Colbert took the lead in encouraging the construction of infrastructures such as canals and roads. By the mid-nineteenth century the railroads not only completed the unification of the French market, but also stimulated the demand for industrial goods, putting France on the road to a modern economy.

It might, however, be argued that France became a single economic unit too early for its own good. It is a natural tendency for businessmen to invest near pre-existing infrastructures, as well as near markets and suppliers. Just as in the case of the unification of the Italian *Mezzogiorno* (southern Italy) with the more prosperous north, the integration of some of the poorer French departments with the rest of the country distorted economic growth.[11] The major French cities, and especially Paris, grew richer, while less developed regions stagnated. Had the latter areas not been politically integrated into France, they might have been able to erect tariff barriers to protect infant industries. As it was, resources flowed to the center.

The political result of this economic distortion was resentment. Previous regional tensions were compounded by the effects of poverty. It was not an accident that persistent separatist sentiment ran highest in the economic backwaters of Brittany and Corsica.

Even where conditions were less extreme, resentment of Paris ran high. Partially, this was a heritage of the religious split between the anticlerical workers and intellectuals in Paris and the religious peasants in the countryside. However, even as religious differences faded, the monumental differences in cultural and economic opportunities between the capital and the provinces did not. The situation was accurately described as "Paris and the French Desert."[12] We shall return to this problem in Chapter 15.

Figure 11.2   Poorest departments by tax revenues, 1857.

SOURCE: Eugen Weber, *Peasants into Frenchmen*, p. 181.

□□□ under 20 francs

▤ under 25 francs

CLASS CLEAVAGE IN FRANCE

Economic differences between haves and have-nots are certainly not greater in Europe than in the United States. However, cleavages between socioeconomic classes have traditionally been more politicized on the eastern shores of the Atlantic. Nowhere, with the possible exception of Great Britain, have economic distinctions served more to rally citizens to political purposes than in France. If

[11] See Figure 11.2. Cf. Uwe Kitzinger's argument, cited in Jack Hayward, "The Prospects for British Regional Policy," *Journal of Common Market Studies*, 11 (1973):287.

[12] Jean-François Gravier, *Paris et le Desert Français* (Paris: Flammarian, 1972).

France is a country of two political cultures, one of the left and one of the right, then that distinction owes much to the division of social classes.

The greater hostility that social classes hold for each other is at least partially due to the conditions under which France industrialized. These, in turn, were affected by the political role of the French peasantry. The French Revolution could not have taken place without the active support and participation of the peasantry. All successive regimes were obliged to take into consideration the needs and demands of this most numerous social class. The result was almost a century and a half of protectionist legislation aimed at sheltering the peasants from economic competition, allowing generations to remain on small, inefficient farms.

Unlike England, where common pastures were enclosed and forbidden to peasants, France gave few incentives to leave the land. Consequently, there were fewer people available for work in factories, and industrialization proceeded slowly. Those manufacturing firms that did arise tended to be small, inefficient, and conservative. The high costs of production and the slow growth made the bourgeoisie's hostility to wage demands especially rigid. As a working class gradually emerged with a concomitant rise in industry, it found itself surrounded by hostile forces. As factory owners, the bourgeoisie, of course, had interests that directly conflicted with those of their workers. Moreover, at the political level, the bourgeoisie found ready allies in the peasantry. Both groups were committed to the defense of property and hostile to the socialist sympathies of the workers. Numerically, this conservative coalition could control the state, making radical, antigovernment ideologies all the more appealing among the workers.

Tragically, the economic lines that divided the French coincided with religious sympathies. Workers perceived the church as the icon of the peasantry and the ally of the bourgeoisie. Workers were by and large secular, while the faithful were essentially drawn from the ranks of the peasants and bourgeois. The impact of this lack of "cross-cutting cleavages" was to reduce levels of trust among the social classes. By contrast, the United States, with high levels of religiosity among all social strata,[13] benefited from "overlapping memberships." Workers and management might be divided on economic issues, but on the same side of the fence on religious issues. They might disagree on the shop floor, but meet socially at church events. Thus, disagreement on some issues is mitigated by agreement on others.

In France, social classes were polarized on religious as well as economic beliefs. Where in the United States mobilized groups would change depending on the specific issue, in France the opponents were always the same. The result was a very low level of trust between right and left, and a genuine fear on each side that if the other were elected to office it would not willingly give up power. Such conditions made support of a *coup d'état* and other kinds of extra-constitutional action appealing to "out" groups. This was a formula for political instability, and many social scientists attribute the volatility of French politics to this factor.

POLITICAL CULTURE AND THE ROLE OF THE STATE

Not only do political scientists look to French political culture for an explanation of recur-

[13] Voting behavior studies show the United States to be much less secular than Europe or Japan. See, for example, Walter Dean Burnham, "The 1980 Earthquake. Appendix A. Social Stress and Political Response: Religion and the 1980 Election," in *The Hidden Election*, eds. Thomas Ferguson and Joel Rogers (New York: Pantheon Books, 1981), pp. 132–40.

The Dreyfus Affair

Political culture is fraught with symbolism. Perhaps the most dramatic symbol of France divided into Left and Right is the "Dreyfus affair."

Alfred Dreyfus (1859–1935), a French army officer of Jewish extraction, was arrested on October 15, 1894, on charges of spying for Germany. He was convicted the following December and sentenced to life imprisonment on Devil's Island. In 1896 a member of the French general staff, Georges Picquart, found evidence that Dreyfus was innocent, but the army maintained a cover-up.

Many on the French Left urged a retrial, including the author Emile Zola, who spelled out the case in his famous article, "J'accuse!" ("I accuse!"). The eventual retrial in 1899 had all the characteristics of a kangaroo court and Dreyfus was again found guilty, but he was pardoned by President Emile Loubet a few days after the verdict. Finally, the case was reviewed in 1906 by France's highest court of appeal, and Dreyfus was found innocent.

The importance of the case had less to do with the turpitude of the army than with the political battle outside the courtroom. Divisions of left and right crystallized around the affair. Socialists and republicans favored Dreyfus, while the right argued that to question the army was unpatriotic and villainous. As historian Barbara Tuchman put it, "Rent by a moral passion that reopened past

SOURCE: Culver Pictures, Inc.

wounds, broke apart a society and consumed thought, energy and honor, France plunged into one of the great commotions of history."

SOURCE: Barbara Tuchman, *The Proud Tower* (New York: Bantam Books, 1966), p. 196.

rent constitutional (and extra-constitutional) changes, but they also see the culture as explaining the persistently large role citizens have accorded the state. That is, the French state performs many tasks that in other countries are left to the private sector. Part of the reason for this is that French people are said to dislike dealing with each other in a face-to-face manner and thus require intermediaries to a greater extent than other cultures. So, for example, where labor-management bargaining is a private matter in

the United States or Britain, in France both sides look to the state to solve disputes.[14] It was in this long tradition that the Socialists legislated a fifth week of vacation for all French workers when they achieved power in 1981. (Vacations are a matter of private con-

[14] See especially, Michel Crozier, *The Bureaucratic Phenomenon* (Chicago: University of Chicago Press, 1964), pp. 213–37; and Stanley Hoffmann, "The Paradoxes of the French Political Community," in *In Search of France*, eds. Hoffman et al. (New York: Harper and Row, 1962).

tract in the United States and Britain.) Similar actions had been taken by the Popular Front government in the Matignon Accords of 1936 and by the Gaullist government in the Grennelle Agreement of 1968. A law limiting layoffs was passed by the conservative Giscard d'Estaing government in 1975 (and repealed by the Conservative government of 1986).

These, of course, are examples of state intervention in only one area of human activity. More important for the purposes of this book is a consideration of the cultural foundations underlying the activities of the state in all areas, but especially the economy. Much of the state's influence has to do with the high prestige accorded to it by most of the French. Moreover, the state frequently became interventionist because of the lack of French people adventurous enough to start new firms.

French culture, then, produced few real en-

The concept of free enterprise, as developed in the England of the nineteenth century and transplanted to the United States, with its postulate of a competitive struggle for markets and drastic penalties for failure and with its emphasis on earning more and more for producing more and more for less and less, has never really been accepted in France. Instead, France [until the latter part of the Fourth Republic] . . . continued to cherish the guild organization of the pre-Revolutionary period. This ideology may be summed up briefly as follows: every man has his place in society, should produce enough goods and services of quality to maintain his place, and has a right to the living earned in this manner. In other words, the justification of survival lies not in the ability to make a profit, but in the correct performance of a social function.

SOURCE: David Landes, "French Business and the Business: A Social and Cultural Analysis," *Modern France: Problems of the Third and Fourth Republics,* ed. Earl Meade (New York: Russell and Russell, 1964), p. 348.

trepreneurs. It was therefore left to the state to proceed where businessmen feared to go. Thus, the culture of French businessmen reinforced the impact of interpersonal behavior in France: both encouraged a greater role for the state.

Traditional French political theory also legitimized the role of the state. Jean-Jacques Rousseau, in his famous *Social Contract,* saw the importance of an all powerful "elector" who alone could stand above the fray of personal interests to represent the general interest. This theme was also picked up in the Napoleonic state, the supremacy of which was justified because it was representative and, therefore, deemed democratic.[15] Moreover, a powerful state was acceptable to both left- and right-wing political traditions. Jacobinism saw the state as the great equalizer, while the right saw the state as the national interest incarnate. No less a conservative than Michel Debré, a noted Gaullist and principal author of the Constitution of 1958, could write: "The State represents the national collectivity. The services under its charge are tasks it performs on behalf of the general interest."[16]

RECENT TRENDS

French culture seems to be at the root of the power of the state, yet, as we noted in Chapter 9, the extensive role of the French state in the nation's economy has recently come into question. Even before the Conservatives came to power in 1986, the enthusiasm that greeted the Socialists' introduction of political decentralization in 1982 suggested that

[15] Ezra N. Suleiman, *Power, Politics and Bureaucracy* (Princeton: Princeton University Press, 1974), p. 22.
[16] Michel Debré, *Au Service de la Nation* (Paris: Edition Stock, 1963), p. 11, quoted in Suleiman, p. 21. See also Berger, p. 9.

the cultural foundations of the Napoleonic state had considerably weakened (see Chapter 15).

The popularity of neoclassical economic solutions advocated by Giscard d'Estaing, Raymond Barré and other politicians of the right among a growing segment of the French electorate also suggested that the assumptions of many French had changed. Certainly, the election of the conservative parliament of 1986, after a campaign emphasizing denationalizations, indicated that the role of the state could now be safely questioned, although the Conservative election victory of that year was more likely due to conjunctural elements than fundamental ideological changes among voters. Nevertheless, conservative writers such as Guy Sorman found a ready audience for his adulatory *La Revolution Reagan,* and Alain Cohen-Tanugi could advocate the increased use of private lawyers in a self-regulating *societé contractuelle* to replace many state functions without incurring the laughter that might have been reserved for such ideas a few years earlier.[17] Looking beyond the theorists, the increase in French venture capitalists, responding to changes in the tax laws made by the Socialists, strongly suggested that entrepreneurial lethargy could no longer be cited as an easy justification for state intervention.

While it has now become commonplace to discount the importance of the religious cleavage in French society, at least since the middle of the twentieth century, accounts of its demise may have been exaggerated. Certainly, like all modern societies, France has

[17] Cohen-Tanugi, *Le Droit sans L'Etat* (Paris: P.U.F., 1986).

"I'll warn you that we have a slight political disagreement.
SOURCE: *Le Monde,* April 3–4, 1988, p. 6.

become more secular. Moreover, since the papacy of John XXIII (and even before), the church has become a less predictable political force, with many priests being as frequently associated with the Left as with the Right. Recent polls have shown that religious Catholics can no longer be expected to vote as a bloc for the parties of the Right. During the legislative election of 1978, 14 percent of practicing Catholics voted for parties of the left. By the time of the 1988 presidential election, more than one in five expressed a preference for the Socialist candidate, François Mitterrand.[18]

However, the majority of practicing Catholics still vote to the right, and conservative religious sentiment can still be mobilized on some issues. This was especially true with the attempted educational reform of 1983. The Socialists, looking to rejuvenate the enthusiasm of the rank and file after losing considerable public support for their economic policies, introduced legislation aimed at bringing church-run schools under more direct control of the state. This provided an excellent opportunity for the conservatives to mobilize their supporters in massive street demonstrations to protest infringements on *l'école libre* (the euphemism for private, *viz.* Catholic, schools). Reaction against this proposed state intrusion on the religious prerogatives of the bourgeoisie was severe enough to force the withdrawal of the education reform bill.[19]

CONCLUSION

This chapter has examined the role of French political culture as an explanation for many of the phenomena noted in Chapters 9 and 10. Certainly, the fragility of French political institutions followed logically from an examination of the values and orientations of the citizenry. It was especially the lack of political consensus that made questionable the viability of any of the country's historical constitutional arrangements. Not only was France deeply divided along linguistic, religious and economic lines, but these cleavages were politically reinforcing. Many of these divisions lasted well into the twentieth century.

Paradoxically, while some cultural characteristics weakened political institutions, others strengthened the role of the state. This was especially true of standards of interpersonal behavior as well as the habits of the French business class, who shied from risk and found shelter in the policies of the state.

More recently, government policies have suggested that some attitudes have changed, at least in terms of the economic demands voiced by some of France's traditionally conservative strata. On the other hand, the persistence of many old schisms, such as those of class and religion, suggest that announcing the death of France's fragmented political culture may yet be premature.

References and Suggested Reading

ALMOND, GABRIEL, AND SIDNEY VERBA. *The Civic Culture.* Boston: Little Brown, 1961.

BERGER, SUZANNE. *The French Political System.* New York: Random House, 1974.

HOFFMANN, STANLEY, et al. *In Search of France.* New York: Harper Colophon, 1962.

PEYREFITTE, ALAIN. *The Trouble with France,* trans. William R. Byron. New York: New York University Press, 1986.

TOCQUEVILLE, ALEXIS DE. *The Old Regime and the French Revolution,* trans. Stuart Gilbert. Garden City, NY: Doubleday, 1955.

WEBER, EUGEN. *Peasants into Frenchmen.* Stanford: Stanford University Press, 1976.

[18] Henri Tincq, "La Decouverte d'Une Nouvelle Laicité," *La Monde,* April 3–4, 1988, pp. 1, 6.

[19] On the overall politics of this educational reform, see John Ambler, "Constraints on Policy Innovation: Thatcher's Britain and Mitterrand's France," *Comparative Politics,* 20 (1987): 85–107.

12

The administration must be able to resist all pressures. But the administrators must know how to distinguish between groups that are *sérieux* and those are not.[1]

— FRENCH HIGHER CIVIL SERVANT

Decline, Alienation, and the Organization of Interest

While social harmony has always been in short supply in France, the economic stagnation of the 1970s and 1980s served to intensify conflict at many levels. Moreover, many of the traditional mechanisms for expressing organizational interest have lost their effectiveness. In this sense France is not very different from other advanced industrial countries. As in Britain and Germany, small business has declined. Napoleon's derisive description of Britain as a "nation of shopkeepers" not only misses its original target, but misses the mark in France and Germany as well. Labor unions have lost power almost everywhere. Most distressing of all, racism has waxed significantly in all three countries.

INTEREST GROUPS

Alexis de Tocqueville noted in his famous study of *Democracy in America* that one of the principal differences between the United States and France was the relative abundance of interest groups in the former and their relative scarcity in the latter. Interest groups (or "secondary associations," in modern political science parlance), Tocqueville reasoned, were not only useful for articulating demands to government; they were also an important deterrent to possible abuse by the state. These watchful and politically sophisticated amalgams had their members' interests at heart and reduced the potential for demagogues to dupe the unwary. Such groups became a kind of buffer between citizen and state in America, while France remained relatively unprotected.[2]

France's aversion to intermediaries between citizen and state had some logical historical grounding. During the era of Absolutism, the only semi-independent organiza-

[1] Quoted in Ezra N. Suleiman, *Politics, Power and Bureaucracy in France* (Princeton: Princeton University Press, 1974), p. 316.

[2] Cf. William Kornhauser, *The Politics of Mass Society* (New York: Free Press, 1958).

196

tions in public life were the *parlements* (actually local courts run by aristocrats) that were notoriously corrupt and associated with entrenched privilege. When Louis XV finally abolished them, there were no regrets among the citizenry. In this context the comments of so enlightened a figure as Voltaire could be understood: "I consider it better to serve under a well-born Lion . . . than under two hundred rats of my own kind."[3] Rousseau concurred: "It is essential, if the general will is to be able to express itself, that there should be no partial society within the State and that each citizen should think only his own thoughts."[4] This sentiment endured well after the Revolution. Thus, part of the reason for France's occasional lapses into the caesarism of the Bonapartes, Pétain and others

[3] Quoted in Pierre Avril, *Politics in France*, trans. John Ross (Baltimore: Penguin Books, 1969), p. 131.

[4] Quoted in Suleiman, *Politics, Power and Bureaucracy in France*, p. 319.

has been attributed to this atomization of French society.[5]

To the extent that France has had interests groups, often they have been limited to those created, or at least officially recognized by, the French government. This kind of group organization reached its apogee during the Vichy period (1940–44) and is often described as "corporatism."[6] Under the fascist

[5] Marx's description of the French peasantry as a "sack of potatoes" in *The Eighteenth Brumaire of Louis Bonaparte* implicitly offered a similar kind of reasoning.

[6] Philippe Schmitter calls this "state corporatism" to distinguish it from the more benign kind of interest group organization found in countries like Austria or Switzerland, where officially recognized groups are nevertheless democratic and independent of government control. This latter kind of organization Schmitter calls "societal corporatism." State corporatism is normally associated with fascism. See Schmitter's "Still the Century of Corporatism?" in *Review of Politics*, January 1975. On democratic corporatism, see Peter J. Katzenstein, *Small States in World Markets* (Ithaca, NY: Cornell University Press, 1984).

Figure 12.1   Corporatism. Under corporatist arrangements, such as the Vichy regime, all interest groups are organized into exhaustive "peak associations," which, in turn control membership through local associations. Under fascist regimes the state controls the leadership of the peak associations and corporatism becomes a mechanism of social control. Under democratic regimes like those in Austria or Sweden the leadership is elected by their respective members and corporatism becomes a mechanism for democratic bargaining with the state. Corporatism facilitates the implementation of bargains made between interest groups and the state.

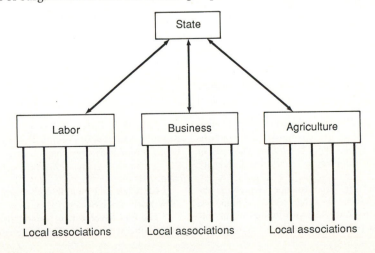

regime established by the Vichy government, French society was officially organized by economic sector into "corporations" that, while nominally self-regulating, were controlled by pro-government officials at the top of each organization.

Even after Vichy, French governments sought to identify specific groups and offer them special access to policy-making in exchange for some measure of social control. This was especially true in agriculture, where Gaullist governments developed a special relationship with the *Fédération nationale des syndicats d'exploitants agricoles.*[7] Indeed, the French governments of the Fifth Republic have always played favorites, although this is nothing new. During the Third and Fourth Republics preference was usually given to the needs of agriculture and small business, both notoriously inefficient, while labor and consumers were slighted. The Fifth Republic favored large enterprise. Labor was favored under the Socialists.

The weakening of parliamentary powers under the Fifth Republic did change the venue of interest group–government relations, however. To some extent this change actually occurred before the change in constitutions, but the biases of *hauts fonctionnaires* (higher civil servants) made themselves fully felt after 1958. Before that date lobbies were oriented to the specialized parliamentary committees in relations that were not unlike the "iron triangles" of American policy-making.[8] Victories of the alcohol or private school lobbies were often spectacular when the influence of parochial deputies could be counted on.[9] After 1958, the bureaucracy became preponderant. The preferences of the Gaullist bureaucracy were simple: Lobbies representing large enterprises were "*sérieux*" ("serious"); the others were not.[10]

Predictably, this situation changed somewhat under the Socialists, when organized labor joined the ranks of the "sérieux." Business groups considered themselves adversaries of the government at this point, but, in fact, were treated in the same privileged fashion as under the conservatives. Indeed, this was of necessity, for even though the Mitterrand government had significantly expanded the public sector, over 80 percent of the economy, and therefore the vast majority of jobs, remained in private hands.[11] After the Conservative victory of 1986, the situation returned to the pro-business norms of the Fifth Republic.

INDUSTRIAL DECLINE: THE *PATRONAT* AND THE CRISIS OF ORGANIZED LABOR

Unlike Germany or, to some extent, Britain, employers' associations were rather slow to form in France. This was primarily because the weakness of organized labor and the conservative policies of French government made such associations unnecessary.[12] Aside from government-sanctioned cartels to restrict competition in various sectors, industry

---

[7] John T. S. Keeler, "Corporatism and Official Union Hegemony: The Case of French Agricultural Syndicalism," in Suzanne Berger, ed., *Organizing Interests in Western Europe,* (Cambridge: Cambridge University Press, 1981).

[8] The notion of the "iron triangle" represents the mutual interdependence of congressional committees, relevant bureaucrats and concerned lobbies in the formulation of public policy.

[9] Bernard E. Brown, "Pressure Politics in the Fifth Republic," *Journal of Politics,* 24 (1963); Susan Berger, *French Political System,* chap. 4.

[10] Suleiman, *Power, Politics and Bureaucracy,* chap. XII.

[11] Cf. Charles E. Lindblom, *Politics and Markets* (New York: Basic Books, 1977), chap. 13.

[12] The *Le Chapelier Law* inspired by early nineteenth century liberal economics even made associations illegal.

associations as lobbies were rare, and were traditionally weak compared to the state.

The principal national employers' association in France is the *Conseil national du patronat français*, known usually as the *Patronat*. The organization was originally formed in response to the generalized labor unrest in 1936 as the Confédération générale de la Production Française (CGPE).[13] However, as a centralized organization representing the united interests of French capital, the *Patronat* has never played the kind of role that similar federations have in central and northern Europe. Bargaining and lobbying have traditionally been at the level of the trade association. The role of the CNPF has been more one of loose coordination and general public relations. One author has refused to mince words and simply labelled the organization as "impotent."[14] Henry Ehrmann put it another way: "One cannot help asking if the CNPF did not exist, would anybody invent it?"[15]

Part of the reason for the weakness of the *Patronat* is that capital itself is divided. Business groups are divided into buyers and sellers, competitive and noncompetitive enterprises. They rarely have the same policy interests, except on such general issues as lower taxes, reduced labor costs and the like. Even here, consumer industries wish their consumer-customers to be well paid, which means some other industries must accept higher wages, while export-oriented industries, who sell to the consumers of other countries, merely want low wages to reduce their costs.

Small businesses have traditionally been fearful of large enterprises, the latter having higher volume and lower costs, and they have formed their own organization of small and medium-sized firms, the *Confédération générale des petites et moyennes entreprises*. They have occasionally been successful in influencing legislation aimed at preserving small retailers.

The lower ranks of management have often seen their interests better defended by white-collar trade unions than by professional associations, and have been drawn to the *Confédération générale des cadres* (general confederation of executives).

If, however, the historic position of employers' organizations has been weak in France, organized labor has hardly been strong. France has five major trade union confederations that are ideologically divided. The largest is the *Confédération générale de travail* (general confederation of labor), which is closely associated with the Communist party. The second largest confederation is the *Confédération française et democratique de travail* (French and democratic confederation of labor), which was originally associated with the Catholic union movement and now is closer to the Socialist Party. The *Confédération française des travailleurs chrétiens* (French confederation of Christian workers) represents the remainder of church associated unions. *Force ouvrière* (workers' force) is a traditionally conservative union organization focussing on narrow work-related issues similar to the American AFL-CIO (indeed, the AFL-CIO helped to create the F.O.) and has been the fastest growing of the French labor organizations. The *Confédération générale des cadres* (see above) represents white collar workers.

While the prinicpal divisions between the unions are ideological, the absence of laws permitting union shops (enterprises where a single union is allowed to monopolize recruitment after an employee vote) has rein-

[13] The classic examination of the French employers' association is Henry W. Ehrmann, *Organized Business in France* (Princeton: Princeton University Press, 1957).

[14] Henri Weber, *Le Parti des Patrons: Le CNPF (1946–1986)* (Paris: Seuil, 1986).

[15] Ehrmann, review of Weber, *Le Parti*, in *French Politics and Society*, 5, 3 (June 1987):46.

forced these divisions. For whatever reason, however, the fact of division has consistently meant that labor in general has been in a weak position *vis-à-vis* management. These divisions, added to the sobering statistic that less than one-fifth of the work force belongs to any union at all, have compounded the present crisis of French unionism. Moreover, the decline in the effectiveness of Keynesian policies and the popularity of neoconservative calls to "roll back the state," in this case the unions' traditional ally when the left comes to power, have made labor especially vulnerable (see Figure 12.2).

French unions have historically been weak, partially as a consequence of late industrialization. Retarded industrialization meant that French firms were usually smaller than those in more advanced countries and were frequently family-run. Smaller firms meant that unions had to organize more enterprises to reach the same percentage of the work force as in other countries, and family-run firms often meant greater management resistance to union demands. This was especially true if demands were viewed as encroaching on management prerogatives (almost always the case), but occasionally family-run firms did have a tendency to improve working conditions in a kind of paternalistic way, providing recreation facilities and child care, for example. The Michelin tire company, to name one such family-run company, though hardly small any more, fit this description.

The stagnation that affected Europe starting in the 1970s was especially problematic for organized labor. Traditional industries, such as steel, coal and textiles, that had the highest levels of union membership were especially affected. Stagnating demand and increasing competition from the newly industrialized countries, as well as from Japan, created pressure for layoffs, wage reductions and other give-backs. While jobs were being lost in old industries, some were being created in service industries, but these were notoriously poorly paid and sufficiently dispersed so as to inhibit unionization. This situation was of course not unique to France, but the strategies of French unions compounded their problems. Union leadership was slow to adapt to the new situation and often tried to apply leverage more appropriate to an expanding economy.[16]

The position of labor in general and unions in particular improved briefly under the Socialist administration of 1981–86. However,

Figure 12.2 Comparison of unionized with salaried employees in a variety of countries.
SOURCE: *Le Monde*, May 31, 1988.

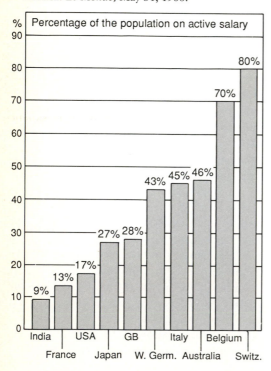

[16] George Ross, "French Labor and Economic Change," in Gourevitch and Cohen, eds., *France in the Troubled World Economy* (London: Butterworths Scientific, 1982).

the right to strike under certain conditions strikes become illegal under all other conditions.[17] Bargaining shifted from sector-wide negotiations to enterprise-level negotiations, shifting worker identification to the prospects of the company rather than reinforcing class solidarities. Also as a consequence of the *loi Auroux*, the role of the state as an intermediary between labor and management was reduced. In short, industrial relations in France have become much more collaborative and much more like those in conservative countries like the United States (and even Japan).[18]

VOTING BEHAVIOR AND THE MARGINALIZATION OF FRENCH COMMUNISM

The economic stagnation of the 1970s and 1980s profoundly affected the behavior of voters as well as the interaction of interest groups. Voting turnout in France has always been higher than in the United States for a number of reasons. The high turnouts have in part been reflections of the lack of opportunity for other forms of legitimate political expression. Since power was concentrated in Paris, local elections were of little salience and, therefore, of little interest to voters. Low levels of collective bargaining and the crucial interventions of the state in industrial relations also underlined the importance of national elections. This was equally true for agriculture, given farmers' dependence on state

Coal miners of the French leftist union CGT ask the French government to respect its promises. In March 1984 an estimated 10,000 miners protested the government's plans, marching to the coal board's headquarters in Paris.

SOURCE: UPI/Bettmann Newsphotos.

even some of the Socialist reforms actually reduced the bargaining effectiveness of organized labor. The *loi Auroux* of 1982 was intended to give workers more control over their working conditions and in many ways was similar to the Wagner Act in the United States, requiring employers to participate in collective bargaining and guaranteeing workers' rights. But the new law also guaranteed employers' rights and often had consequences unintended by its Socialist authors. As Mark Kesselman put it, "By guaranteeing

[17] Mark Kesselman, "Conclusion" in Kesselman and Groux, eds., *The French Workers' Movement* (London: Allen and Unwin, 1984), p. 316.

[18] Guy Groux, "Organized Labor and Industrial Relations," paper presented to the panel "Changing Patterns of French Political Economy: an End to French Exceptionalism?," Sixth International Conference of Europeanists, October 30–November 1, 1987.

subsidies and the traditional role of parliamentary deputies as ombudsmen for farmers' interests.

The transformation of the French economy after the Second World War from an agricultural to an industrial society affected the interests and voting patterns of French citizens. A second, more gradual transformation toward a service-oriented economy also made its mark on French politics.

The majority of French voters supported conservatives during much of the time after the war, although for the first few years the sorry record of the pro-nazi collaborators and the association of the Resistance with the political left tarnished the reputation of the right. The charisma of de Gaulle and the special circumstances of the Algerian war did much to restore the power of the Right, but deeper causes were also at work. The conservatives returned to popularity for two main reasons. First, late industrialization meant that much of the electorate earned its livelihood from agriculture or small business. These groups were threatened by the modernization of the economy and were attracted to candidates that announced fidelity to the status quo and who preached loyalty to traditional values with nationalist appeals. Moreover, these groups were terrified by the proclamations of working class leaders and suspicious of the intellectuals associated with the Left. Canny politicians, especially de Gaulle, were able to parlay these sentiments into extended tenure of office. When the student and worker uprisings occurred in 1968 (see chapter 9) de Gaulle was able to capitalize on the average French voter's fear of radicals, and especially the image of the Communist Party, to turn the subsequent elections into a landslide for the right. Indeed, the left could only come to power when the fears of a Communist-dominated government were allayed.

THE DECLINE OF THE COMMUNISTS

The decline of the Communist electorate had three broad causes: the transformation of the economy, errors in the political strategy of the Communists themselves, and an effective strategy by their rivals, the Socialists. The first explanation is sociological. The gradual decline of traditional industries and the increasing orientation of the French economy toward the service sector eroded the historic base of the Communist electorate. The high point of Communist sympathies was, of course, immediately after the war. Not only were the Communists among the bravest and most tenacious fighters in the Resistance, but the need to rebuild the economy from the postwar ruins lent credence to the productivist assumptions of the Communist economic strategy.[19] The base of Communist support has always been blue collar workers. Thus, the modernization of the French economy after the war guaranteed a significant source of support for the party, at least at the polls, if not on membership rosters. However, as blue collar jobs were eliminated by both competition from abroad and the shift into services, the constituency of people who could most readily see the appeal of the Communist vision began to disappear.

As the base disappeared, the leadership of the party failed to see the need to find

---

[19] These assumptions were broadly shared and contributed to the consensus necessary to make French economic planning a success. Cf. Peter Hall, *Governing the Economy*, chap. 6; and Stephen Cohen, *Modern Capitalist Planning: The French Model* (Berkeley and Los Angeles, 1977). This contrasts with the anti-productivist prejudices of the late 1970s represented by the "Green" movements across Europe. See Volkmar Lauber, "From Growth Consensus to Fragmentation in Western Europe: Political Polarization over Redistribution and Ecology," *Comparative Politics*, 15 (1983).

replacements. Partially, this was because unlike the Italian Communist Party, the leadership in France was more concerned with the demands of its present blue collar membership than with the potential for victory at the polls by an appeal to other strata. Had they identified common interests with such groups as the newly emerging waves of white collar workers, decline might have been forestalled, but the party would have been transformed.[20]

Another source of Communist support, totaling consistently about 25 percent (including members' votes) of the electorate until the 1970s, was the protest vote. This was the expression of voters alienated from the capitalist system as it operated in France or disaffected with the government of the day and its non-communist opposition. Such voters did not vote for the Socialists because of the pivotal role they played in the Fourth Republic and the Algerian War, or because that party was not viewed as sufficiently radical.

It was the electoral strategy of François Mitterrand that eroded the protest vote destined for the Communists. Mitterrand almost single-handedly built a new Socialist Party from scratch (see Chapter 13). Not only did the new Socialist Party reject association with the old party of the Third and Fourth Republics, but Mitterrand resolutely pushed the orientation of the party leftward so as to capture much of the Communists' former constituency. This was done by signing a common platform with the Communists in 1972, which called for most of the nationalizations that eventually took place ten years later. When the two parties broke the pact in 1978 because the Socialists refused to accede to additional Communist demands, the Socialists surpassed the Communist vote in the legislative elections of that year. This seemed to guarantee that not only would the Socialists not cave in to the Communists for the sake of an election, but that in any future Leftist government the Communists could never be more than junior partners.

DE-ALIGNMENT

Most of the recent research on voting behavior in France suggests that a process of de-alignment is taking place.[21] While party identification has never had quite the same meaning in France as in the United States, fidelity to at least a general conception of Left or Right has been a consistent trait of the French voter.[22] In the words of one analyst, "The French voter is increasingly up for grabs, unsettled over his or her party loyalties, or indeed over whether to participate in the electoral game at all."[23]

French voters are still more self-consciously ideological than voters in the United States. In one study, only 5 percent of respondents refused to place themselves on a seven point Left-Right scale, where Right correlated with Catholic religious affinity in the traditional manner (see Chapter 11).[24]

Sociologically, the makeup of the French electorate has moved in a direction that

[20] George Ross, "Destroyed by the Dialectic: Politics and the Decline of Marxism, and the New Middle Strata in France," *Theory and Society,* 16, 1 (January 1987); George Ross and Jane Jenson, "The French Left's Triumph and Tragedy: Could It Have Been Otherwise?" (forthcoming).

[21] W. Rand Smith, "Plus ça change . . . ? Elections and Electoral Behavior in France, 1978–86," *French Politics and Society,* 5, 3 (June 1987). Much of the following argument is derived from this article.

[22] Philip E. Converse and Roy Pierce, *Political Representation in France* (Cambridge, MA: Harvard University Press, 1986), chap. 3.

[23] Smith, "Plus ça change . . . ?," p. 40.

[24] Colette Ysmal, *Le Comportement Electorale en France* (Paris: Decouvert, 1986).

should favor the French Left. The country has become more urban, secular and economically modern. Indeed, François Mitterrand averred that in his election of 1981, "The French political majority has just identified itself with its sociological majority."[25]

Political changes happen more slowly, however. Often people whose low income might suggest left-wing voting, voted conservative. Frequently, this was because they had other characteristics, such as inherited property, which suggested an interest identified with the Right. Thirty-one percent of persons with an income of 1,500 francs per month (less than $300 at 1978 exchange rates) voted for the Communists in 1978, but only three percent of people in the same income group, but who had a significant inheritance, voted for them.[26] Indeed, the left-wing landslide of 1981 might well have been a fluke, owing more to divisions in the Right than a shift of voter allegiances to the Left.[27]

RACISM AND THE NATIONAL FRONT

Perhaps one of the most distressing changes in French voting patterns is the recrudescence of overt racism. This is, unfortunately, a common occurrence now in Europe, and is related to the present economic crisis in the industrial world. "Paky-bashing" and football hooliganism have been on the rise in the poorer neighborhoods of Britain for some time, while "Ausländer 'raus!" (Foreigner, go home!) can be seen scrawled on many public places in West Germany. Immigrant groups that were invited into these countries to supply cheap labor in more prosperous times are now seen as competing for scarcer jobs. Culturally distinct groups have become pariahs and the focus of resentment. In France, this has meant, above all, racist attacks on the country's large Islamic community.

Racism is not new in France. The anti-Arab racism is not very different, at least in its clientele, from the anti-Semitism of the early twentieth century and Vichy. People caught in the closing vise of a shrinking economy often look to the simplest explanation for their predicament, and racism is commonly found among groups that are already at the margins of their society: unskilled workers, small businessmen on the precipice of bankruptcy, peasants who understand little of the world outside their immediate surroundings. Disaffection with the incompetence of traditional right-wing elites has also drawn local politicians to the extreme right.[28]

In the past, this segment of the electorate has frequently been vulnerable to the appeals of parties on the far Right. Such groups supported the various fascist extraparliamentary organizations in the 1930s (see Chapter 10). In the 1950s these groups supported the Gaullists (then espousing an anti-parliamentary philosophy) and Pierre Poujade, who led a small shopkeepers' movement in reaction to modernization and European integration. By 1984 supporters of racist and anti-immigrant policies coalesced behind Jean-Marie Le Pen and his National Front. This was essentially a single-issue party demanding "France for the French," but also sharing many economic assumptions of the traditional right in calling for a laissez-faire economy. In the 1984 and 1986 elections some former Communist

[25] Quoted in Smith, p. 43.

[26] Elisabeth Dupoirier and Gerard Grunberg, eds., Mars 1986: la drôle de défaite de la Gauche (Paris: Presses Universitaires de France, 1986); Smith, pp. 42–43.

[27] Alain Lancelot, ed., 1981: Les elections de l'alternance (Paris: Fondation Nationale des Science Politiques, 1986).

[28] James Hollifield, "Immigration, Race and Politics," French Politics and Society, 13 (March 1986):16.

Led by Jean Marie le Pen, members of the National Front protest in Paris in May 1985.
SOURCE: Sygma.

voters turned to the National Front out of protest, but the bulk of supporters had voted for the Gaullists in previous elections. The National Front tends to do best in the south of France, where the French repatriated from Algeria after independence tend to have settled.

The National Front reached its highest level of support in the first round of the 1988 presidential election, with 14.4 percent of the popular vote going to Jean-Marie Le Pen. Some French analysts were unperturbed by this score, noting that traditionally 20–25 percent of the French vote as a protest against the political establishment and that the combined Communist and National Front vote was just over 21 percent. However, others put more emphasis on the sociological con-

text and saw alarming parallels with the rise of fascism during the Great Depression of the 1930s.[29]

On the opposite side of the immigration question, there are now over 800,000 young voters, known as "*les beurs*," who are the sons and daughters of North African immigrants. Not surprisingly, they tend to vote for the Left. Up to this time, however, the "beurs" (butters) had not been intensively studied.

CONCLUSION

This chapter has examined the behavior of interest groups and voters in France. Interest

[29] *Le Monde*, April 26, 1988.

groups, a traditional focus of political scientists, were found to be less numerous in France, with vestiges of corporatism found in those that do exist. The power of organized labor has been especially weak, and the French Communist Party, often touted as powerful, is a mere shadow of its former self. While French voters have become disaffected and are "de-aligning" from traditional parties, partially in response to increased economic uncertainties, these same economic forces have encouraged a recrudescence of racism in the French electorate, especially among groups that have voted for the far Right in the past.

References and Suggested Readings

BERGER, SUZANNE, ED. *Organizing Interests in Western Europe.* Cambridge: Cambridge University Press, 1981.

CONVERSE, PHILIP, AND ROY PIERCE. *Political Representation in France.* Cambridge, MA: Harvard University Press, 1986.

DALTON, RUSSEL J. *Citizen Politics in Western European Democracies.* Chatham: Chatham House, 1988.

EHRMANN, HENRY W. *Organized Business in France.* Princeton: Princeton University Press, 1957.

KESSELMAN, MARK, AND GUY GROUX. *The French Workers' Movement.* London: Allen and Unwin, 1984.

GOUREVITCH, P., A. MARKOVITS, A. MARTIN, AND G. ROSS. *Unions, Change and Crisis.* London: Allen and Unwin, 1984.

APPENDIX

Table 12.A.1   French Presidential Elections During the Fifth Republic (Second Ballot)

(% Votes Cast)		
Mitterrand 44.8	De Gaulle 55.2	1965
Poher 41.79	Pompidou 58.21	1969
Mitterrand 49.19	Giscard D'Estaing 50.81	1974
Mitterrand 51.76	Giscard D'Estaing 48.24	1981
Mitterrand 54.01	Chirac 45.98	1988

SOURCE: Alain Lancelot, *Les Elections Sous La Vᵉ Republique* (Paris: Presses Universitaires de France, 1988), pp. 38, 60, 72, 88; *Le Monde,* Dossiers et Documents, "Le Nouveau Contrat de François Mitterrand," May 1988, p. 75.

Table 12.A.2   Parliamentary Elections During the Fifth Republic (% of those voting*)

PCF	Non-Com Left	Non Gaullist Rt.	Gaullists	Extreme Rt.	
					1st
18.89%	26.34%	31.05%	20.64%	2.57%	Round 1958
					2nd
20.58	21.74	27.39	29.55	.71	Round†
21.87	21.87	19.39	36.03	.76	1st 1962
21.36	23.20	12.84	42.37	.17	2nd
22.51	21.11	17.35	38.45	.20	1st 1967
21.35	25.06	10.65	42.88	.07	2nd
20.2	20.5	12.41	46.44	.08	1st 1968
20.13	21.81	9.41	48.64	—	2nd
21.41	24.43	16.67	36.98	.52	1st 1973
20.61	25.58	7.89	45.92	—	2nd
20.61	29.58	23.89	22.84	.75	1st 1978
18.69	30.94	24.02	26.35	—	2nd
16.13	39.52	21.66	21.24	.29	1st 1981
6.7	50.15	20.47	16.56	—	2nd
9.7	34.3	UDF RPR Coalition		10.1	1986††
		42.1			(only 1 Round)
11.32	23.4	13.74	12.3	6.21	1988
		UDF-RPR Coalition			
3.42	48.6	46.8		1.06	

SOURCES: Alain Lancelot, *Les Elections Sous La Vᵉ Republique* (Paris: PUF, 1988) pp. 19, 20, 32, 34, 44, 49, 50, 65, 66, 76, 78–79, 91, 92–93. *Le Monde,* Dossiers et Documents, "Une Majorité à Inventer", June 1988, pp 30, 42.

* Percentages do not add up to 100% because some minor candidates are excluded.

† Districts where no candidate receives a majority on the first round go to a second round.

†† Single ballot, proportional representation system.

13

It is impossible today to describe seriously
the comparative mechanisms
of political parties; but it is also indispensable to do so.

— MAURICE DUVERGER

The Party System as a Moveable Feast

Party systems are a traditional interest in political science. There are, of course, many va-
rieties of such systems. The two-party system,
characterized by parties ideologically close
together and by a pendulum-like alternation
in power, as in the United States, is a relatively rare phenomenon. The single-party
system such as existed in Communist
countries (until 1989) is more common, and
typically served as an instrument for elite recruitment. Another kind of single-party system, such as is found in Africa, tends to be
used as an instrument to mobilize popular
support. France has a multi-party system, as
do most of the countries of Western Europe.

There are, of course, many different kinds
of party systems even within the broad
"multi-party" category. There are systems
with grossly unequal parties such as in Germany or the United Kingdom or systems with
a number of roughly equal parties (in terms
of membership and votes), as found in central
and northern Europe. Systems may be stable
(i.e., experiencing few changes in government
between elections), as in Germany, or unsta-

ble,[1] as in most of Latin Europe, at least historically. What is intriguing is the question of
why such different categories of party systems come about, and why they change. Historically, France has had relatively unstable
multi-party systems during the Third and
Fourth Republics and a relatively stable
multi-party system during the Fifth Republic.
More recently, there has tended to be a convergence of the parties into two opposing coalitions. Lately, since the 1980s, the ideological divisions between the two camps have
become eroded. The focus of this chapter will
be on explaining this evolution of the French
party system.[2]

---

[1] *Unstable* may be a deceptive term: while governments may change, policies often do not.

[2] Much of my own thinking on the French party system was shaped by Maurice Duverger's course at the
Institut d'Etudes Politiques, which I had the good fortune to take as an undergraduate during the 1969–70
term. In addition, my discussion in this chapter is especially informed by Suzanne Berger's original analysis in
her *French Political System* (New York, Random House,
1974), pp. 59–77.

EXPLAINING PARTY SYSTEMS

The Institutional Approach

Perhaps the most well-known explanation for the variety of party systems in Western democracies is the institutional approach contributed by the French political scientist, Maurice Duverger.[3] Duverger argued that the principal reason for the divergence between two- and multi-party systems was the electoral system. In a nutshell, countries that employed a system of single-ballot, single-member district voting were more likely to tend toward a two-party system, and countries employing proportional representation were more likely to have multi-party systems.

A single-ballot, single-member district is employed in the United States and Britain. There is only one congressman or member of parliament for each district. Only one ballot is held for that seat and the candidate receiving the plurality is awarded the seat. In such an electoral system supporters of small parties will tend to "vote usefully" by abandoning their first choice if the candidate is unlikely to be among the top two and to vote instead for the "lesser of two evils." Thus, small parties tend to disappear and a two-party system emerges.

There are various kinds of proportional representation (PR) mechanisms. The purest, perhaps, are found in the Netherlands and Israel, where each party is accorded seats in the parliament according to the percentage of votes it receives in a single national election. More common is the system used in various countries, and occasionally in France, where each electoral district is presented with opposing slates of candidates (*scrutin de liste*) and the seats of each district (each district has more than one representative, thus is called a "multi-member district") are apportioned to

the parties in accordance with their respective percentages of the vote. Under a system of proportional representation, supporters of small parties have an incentive to remain loyal to their favorites because they are usually assured of at least some representation in the national parliament. Moreover, supporters of small centrist parties have an even greater incentive to remain loyal, because centrist parties are often necessary to the formation of coalition governments. Indeed, this has been the constant role of the Free Democratic Party in Germany and was the historic role of the Radical Party in France during the Third and Fourth Republics. France employed a proportional representation system during most of the Fourth Republic, and again in 1986.

Political parties are well aware of the effect of such voting systems. The Liberal and Social Democratic parties (merged in 1988) in Britain have been extremely vocal in their demands for a PR system that would favor these small, centrist parties. In France, there can be little doubt that the Socialists reintroduced PR in 1986 so as to allow the small, extreme right-wing National Front party to gain seats in the Parliament and gnaw at the expected majority of the traditional conservative parties. Indeed, because of the success of the National Front, which earned about 10 percent of the seats in the National Assembly (the lower house of the French Parliament), proportional representation eroded the traditional conservative representation to a winning margin of only two seats. The National Front lost all but one seat when proportional representation was abandoned in the 1988 legislative elections.[4]

[3] *Les Partis Politiques* (Paris: Armand Colin, 1951).

[4] Indeed, by the first round of the 1988 presidential election, the National Front received 14.4 percent of the vote. Many analysts attributed the growth of the National Front electorate to the legitimacy gained from its representation in the National Assembly; this, in turn, was due to proportional representation.

The normal voting mechanism of the Fifth Republic has been the single-member district, two-ballot system. If no candidate receives an absolute majority, a runoff election is held one or two weeks later where voters must choose again, but where a plurality accords victory. The effect of this system is to encourage coalitions of parties on the second ballot. Frequently, for example, left-wing parties would form agreements to allow withdrawals (*désistements*) of progressive parties in favor of the best placed left-wing candidate, so that they would not be divided on the second ballot. (A lot depended on whether or not the Communist Party wished to play the role of a spoiler.) Parties on the Right have done the same. Thus, it was no surprise to Duverger, who was the first to articulate this phenomenon, that the many parties of France have tended to converge into two broad coalitions of Left and Right since the formation of the Fifth Republic.

Explaining the Party System as a Reflection of Social Cleavages

A second broad category of explanations for party systems relies on an examination of the diverse cleavages in French (or any) society to explain the appearance of the many parties. Political institutions, such as parties, take on their particular shapes because they are, in fact, reflections of deeper social conflict. Thus, the deep fissures in the French social fabric that we examined in Chapter 11 became the basis for divisions in the party system. Differences among social groups over the exclusion of the church from public life led to the formation of pro- and anti-clerical parties, especially during the Third Republic. As France industrialized, the new economic cleavages between peasants, workers and the bourgeoisie also affected the party system.

This explanation does not, of course, exclude the institutional approach. Propor-tional representation made it easier for new parties to appear. The two-ballot elections gave incentives for parties to cooperate, while that cooperation made it possible for the allied parties to survive, rather than fade, as third parties traditionally have in the United States.

While electoral mechanism tells us something about the tendency of the party system to fragment, it is the "social force" approach that informs us about the kinds of demands parties are likely to make. Most importantly, it helps us understand why, in France, new parties have tended to appear on the political left, a process Duverger called "*sinéstrisme*."[5]

Basically, the tendency of parties to appear at the left of the political spectrum is related to France's late industrialization. The rise of the working class made the old party disputes over the role of the church seem irrelevant.[6] But it was the lateness of industrialization that helps explain the intensity of ideological commitment that would characterize French socialism.

The late industrialization retarded the development of the union movement, as we noted in Chapter 12. This meant that a party representing workers' interests would have little financial support in its early years, and this in turn meant that a strong grass-roots organization would have to suffice in the absence of funds. Organization is, of course, the traditional weapon of the Left. Commitment to a chain of command, when short-term material incentives are lacking, requires a common perception of problems and a powerful set of shared goals; in short, an ideology. Marxism proved to be that ideology.

---

[5] France's newest party, the National Front, of course, appeared on the Right, although much of its social base was the same as that supporting the Communists. See pp. 204–05 of this text.

[6] Berger, pp. 67–71.

French socialism was militant from its inception (Marx's daughter, in fact, married one of the country's early socialist leaders, Lasalle). The French Workers' Party (*Parti ouvrier français*) was the first real socialist party to form in 1867, and it gradually evolved into the militant Marxist *Section française de l'internationale ouvrière, SFIO,* the French section of the (First) Workers' International.

By the turn of the century, the political expression of French workers was already facing a fissure as social conditions began to change. A significant improvement in the standard of living of some of the workers, and especially among their intellectual allies, such as teachers and journalists, led to divergences in strategy among the leadership. The Dreyfus affair raised the issue of defense of the "bourgeois republic" from right-wing attack. A current arose professing class collaboration and, eventually, participation in World War I. Others remained militantly anti-capitalist. The issue of militantism versus moderation finally came to a head in 1920 at the Socialist Congress of Tours. There, two-thirds of France's Socialists voted to affiliate with the Third International and became known as the French Communist Party. The minority, under Leon Blum, a school teacher, retained the name SFIO. The party had divided over participation in the First World War and, most importantly, over the issue of support of the Soviet Union, whose recent revolution was a proximate product of that bloodbath. Sociologically, the blue-collar socialists remained radical, while the white-collars became reformist.[7]

The sociological origins of the right-wing parties are more problematic. Partially, this is because as new parties appeared on the Left, the old left-wing parties moved Right. The classic case was the old Radical Socialist Party. In the nineteenth century this party represented the bourgeois Left and was the standard-bearer of secularists. Despite its name, the party advocated a classic liberal philosophy, including a preference for free markets. As the Socialist and Communist parties gradually appeared, the party was pushed to the center, its clientele, as ever, the enlightened middle classes. To its right were parties representing traditional rural interests (*Independents*). In the nineteenth century there were also diverse royalist factions, with occasional Bonapartists and Boulangistes.[8] Some of these became proto-fascist organizations, supporters of which were similar, sociologically, to the present advocates of the National Front (unemployed, lower middle class, and other economically marginal groups; see Chapters 10 and 12).

THE PRESENT PARTY SYSTEM

The present party system, that is, the system that has more or less stabilized since the advent of the Fifth Republic in 1958, has gradually come to resemble the British and American models. The multi-party system has not disappeared, but under the incentive structure of the two-ballot system, and under the economic conditions of advanced industrialism, the parties have tended to coalesce in a bipolar way, with both poles being more moderate then extreme. The Left is less radical and the Right is neither anti-parliamentary nor an advocate of primitive capitalism.

[7] Some further nuances are necessary here. Blue collar workers in the north of France remained loyal to the SFIO, while the Communists acquired the allegiance of many of the disadvantaged in the Midi.

[8] General Boulanger was a late nineteenth century charismatic populist whose ultimate preference for government by *coup d'état* led to his undoing.

The Right: *Rassemblement pour la République*

Perhaps the most stunning transformation of the party system was the development of a majority party under the charismatic spell of General Charles de Gaulle.[9] Unlike all previous republics, the Fifth coasted without the usual coalition governments, and with a powerful executive at its disposal; conservative rule became the norm. The coattail effect of de Gaulle gave the Gaullist party hegemony over French politics for over two decades.

Of course, coattails were not all. Georges Pompidou, de Gaulle's hand-picked successor, worked tirelessly to give the party substance beyond de Gaulle's shadow. Under his stewardship the party became implanted at the local, as well as national, level.

While the party has changed names several times,[10] it has consistently led the other conservative parties. It is now known as the *Rassemblement pour la République (RPR)*, "Rally for the Republic." Philosophically, the party has changed considerably. In the Fourth Republic the party was further to the Right and had resemblances to the rightist movements of an earlier period, being anti-parliamentary (at least anti-Fourth Republic), deeply nationalist and favoring an imperial foreign policy.[11] The attitudes changed during the Algerian war, although the emas-

Prime Minister Jacques Chirac presides over the opening session of the National Assembly, April 1986.

SOURCE: Sygma.

culated parliament of the Fifth Republic is a product of earlier Gaullist suspicions. Unlike conservatives in the United States or Britain, the Gaullists were also committed to substantial government intervention in the economy, when that intervention was thought to be in the national interest. Much like the Jakob Kaiser wing of the German Christian Democrats immediately after World War II, there was also a Left Gaullism with affiliated labor unions, flourishing during the first decade or so of the Fifth Republic.

This has changed. The Gaullists under the leadership of Jacques Chirac have become much more like conservative parties elsewhere in the world, advocating a roll-back of

---

[9] See especially, Ezra Suleiman, *Politics, Power and Bureaucracy* (Princeton: Princeton University Press, 1974), chap. XIII; Berger, pp. 72–77.

[10] The names were, in succession: *Union nationale pour la République (UNR), Union pour la défense de la V^{ieme} République (UDVeR), Union pour la défense de la République (UDR), Rassamblement pour la République (RPR)*. The latest name, "Rally for the Republic," recalls the Gaullist party title under the Fourth Republic, *Rassemblement du Peuple Français (RPF)*, "Rally for the French People."

[11] It would be mistaken, however, to consider the RPF fascist.

the state (with the exception of the police) wherever possible.[12] In fact, the change in philosophy became so pronounced under Chirac that the appellation "neo-Gaullist" became more appropriate.

Union pour la Démocratie Française

The political ally of the RPR is the UDF. The *Union pour la Democratie Française* is actually a coalition of three small parties and two political clubs, united originally to support President Giscard d'Estaing in the legislative elections of 1978. The most important of the three, the *Parti Républicain,* was Giscard's own party. A small party with little articulation at the local level, whose philosophy was and is classically liberal (conservative, or perhaps "libertarian," in the American sense), favoring free markets and small government wherever possible.

The other members of UDF are the tiny vestiges of parties that were important in the Third and Fourth Republics. The *Centre des Démocrates Sociaux*[13] is a remnant of the old *Mouvement Républicain Populaire,* a Christian Democratic party that occupied the center of the political spectrum during the Fourth Republic. The *Parti Radical* is the rump of the old *Parti Radical Socialiste,* the anti-clerical party of the Third Republic. The party split over whether to support the Common Platform of the Left, with the left sympathizers leaving. The other two affiliates of UDF are "political clubs," small groups of elites that have not tried to formally create a mass base of support, and are ideological

centrist. They are the *Club Perspectives et Realities* and the *Mouvement des Démocrates Sociaux.*

Le Front National

The party furthest to the right on the French political spectrum is the National Front. The "party" is in fact more of an interest group in the sense that it really only focuses on one issue: immigration. It does, however, have local as well as national organizations, and it rules in coalition with the traditional conservatives in many local governments—this despite the fact that the latter parties have refused to enter into formal alliance at the national level. (See Chapter 12.)

Led by Jean-Marie Le Pen, a well-known figure on the far Right since the Algerian war, the party has sought to capitalize on the frustrations of working- and lower-middle-class French by advocating expulsion of France's mostly Islamic immigrant population. Other than thinly disguised racism (see Chapter 12), the party has only a vague ideology emphasizing a free market economy linked to pronounced jingoism.

The Left: The *Parti Socialiste*

The *Parti Socialiste* is, after the RPR, the greatest success story in French politics. If the RPR was the first majority party democratic France has ever known, the *Parti Socialiste* is the first majority party that the Left has ever known. It came to that position both through favorable circumstances and through the strategy of its leader and founder, François Mitterrand.

In the 1970s Mitterrand took the remnants of the old SFIO, which had fallen on hard times because of its failures during the Fourth Republic, especially *vis-à-vis* Algeria, and combined it with several left-wing political clubs to produce the new *Parti Socialiste.* As

[12] For an analysis of this recent convergence in terms of policies, see Jeffrey R. Henig, Chris Hamnett and Harvey B. Feigenbaum, "The Politics of Privatization: A Comparative Perspective," *Governance* 1, 4 (October 1988).

[13] The CDS ran a separate slate of candidates for the 1989 elections to the European Parliament. It was then unclear whether or not they would remain a part of UDF.

recounted in the previous chapter, Mitter-rand moved the PS in a leftward direction to capture the protest vote normally accruing to the Communist Party, and was spectacularly successful. Not only did the PS become the largest party on the Left, it became the largest party in the country after 1981.

The victory in 1981 was as much serendip-itous as the product of strategy, however. The Right split over supporting the reelection of President Valery Giscard d'Estaing, the UDF candidate. The Gaullists, led by Jacques Chirac, Giscard's rival, afforded the UDF president only lukewarm support during the second ballot in 1981. Moreover, the poor performance of the French economy since 1974, when Giscard had first been elected, alienated many voters, while fear of a Com-munist-dominated left simply disappeared. Mitterrand won, bringing the Socialist Party on his coattails as the majority party in the National Assembly. Even after the defeat of the Left in 1986, the Socialist Party remained the largest single party in France.

In terms of ideology, the Socialists very much fit Otto Kirchheimer's notion of a "catch-all party."[14] Its left-wing is decidedly Marxist; its middle, the *Mitterrandistes*, is pragmatic; and its right-wing, the *Rocar-diens* (supporters of prime minister Michel Rocard), is social-democratically in favor of a mixed economy. There are small factions as well, linked to specific leaders and based on theoretical differences within the socialist family.

The *Parti Communiste Français*

The Communist Party of France (PCF) was one of the largest in Western Europe, second

only to Italy's, but is now only a shadow of its former self. It may well be argued that it was the size of the Communist Party that kept the conservatives in power for so long. The Red Menace (often pictured on conservative French posters as a grimacing Bolshevik with a knife in his teeth) was adroitly used by de Gaulle and his successors to keep the Left at bay. For much of the postwar period voters needed no reminding: the case of Eastern Eu-rope, and especially that of Czechoslovakia, where the local Communist Party took ad-vantage of its ministries in a coalition govern-ment to take over the state in 1948, loomed large in most French memories. Nor did the French Communist leadership help matters by their continual and slavish endorsements of all Soviet actions.

For a while, during the 1970s, the PCF leadership indulged the party's intellectuals by distancing themselves from the Soviet Union and adopting a "Eurocommunist" in-dependent stance, even dropping the term "dictatorship of the proletariat" from their list of goals. This was a short-lived attempt to expand the electoral base despite reservations from an "un-deStalinized" rank and file. The ultimate failure of this electoral strategy led to a break with the Socialists in 1978, the departure of many intellectuals from the *bu-reau politique* (the ruling committee) of the party, and renewed voter confidence in the Socialists as the latter refused to cede to Com-munist demands for revision of the Common Platform, signed in 1972. If demographics would ultimately lead to the decline of France's Communists (see Chapter 12), the party leadership seemed to make every effort to seal their collective fate, with a Soviet-style comportment repellent to most voters.

The party enjoyed a short revival when, in 1981, Mitterrand asked them to join a united Government of the Left. Mitterrand's rea-sons were not announced, but more than likely, his invitation was intended to assure the

[14] "Catch-all parties" are broadly based parties which incorporate many factions and tendencies. See *Politics, Law, and Social Change*, ed. F. C. Burin and K. L. Shell (New York: Columbia University Press, 1969).

M. Georges Marchais presides over the 20th Congress of the Communist Party, December 1972.

SOURCE: Alain Dejean/Sygma.

cooperation of the Communist-dominated labor confederation, the CGT, and to make sure that the PCF would share the blame for any mistakes the new government might make. Indeed, as unemployment soared under Socialist economic restructuring, the Communists left the coalition to enter into official opposition. They regained some influence after the 1988 legislative elections. The Socialists, forced to form a minority government, required at least tacit Communist acquiescence in order to govern.

Mouvement des Radicaux de Gauche

A few words need to be said about the final member of the Left. The *Mouvement des*

A Communist's Point of View

Being a Communist has brought me many things. It has brought me friends, a way to reflect on both political and personal life. It has permitted me to have confidence in myself and believe in myself. I couldn't think of not being a Communist. It's my life. I don't make an effort to be a Communist. I live it. . . .

I am proud to be a Communist and have always been proud to be a Communist. There were difficult times on the international front, Afghanistan, for example, but I was never embarrassed to call myself a Communist. People did leave the French Communist Party at that time, but many are coming back.

SOURCE: Jean-Pierre Quilgars, Renault factory worker, quoted in the *New York Times*, January 23, 1989, p. A-11.

Radicaux de Gauche is the other half of the old *Parti Radical Socialiste* that broke up over the decision to join the Common Platform of the Left signed in 1972. Indeed, the breakup of the party is perhaps the best indicator that French politics has bifurcated in the last two decades. In a society that divided all issues into right and left, there was no room for a party at the center. Like the old American labor song, the society asks, "Which side are you on?!" Forced to choose, these members of the Radical Party found more in common with the Socialists than with the UDF. While the MRG is small, it has captured a few city halls, bearing testimony to effective local organization as a party, and does not quite fall into the "political club" category. Ideologically, the Left Radicals, despite their misleading name, are closest of the left parties to the center.

RECENT TRENDS

The overall trend of the French party system has been for the various parties to coalesce

SOURCE: Culver Pictures, Inc.

Perhaps the less attractive side of party politics, in France or anywhere else, is the way in which parties finance their operations. In France, there have traditionally been few holds barred, and all parties have tended to abuse their positions when elected. Some examples illustrate the problem.

While left-wing parties have tended to rely on membership dues and union contributions for financing throughout Western Europe, the weakness of the union movement has made French leftist parties more reliant on other sources of finance.

The Socialists and Communists have often had more success at the local level during the Fifth Republic and have used city halls to obtain funds. For example, companies awarded public contracts at the local levels are often expected to pay for "studies" conducted by members of the mayor's party.

On the right, which has more frequently occupied national office, parties have raised money by having intermediaries linked to the party take part of the commissions on national government con-

tracts, recorded as payments to go-betweens. Also, according to the *Canard Enchaine*, the closest thing France has to investigative journalism, conservative parties have used double billing techniques, where businessmen are encouraged to take out advertising in the party journal (at expensive rates) that, in fact, never appears.

The French parliament met in special session in late 1987 to introduce more "transparency" into the system, to make financing a matter of public record and to introduce some spending limits. Copying many of the reforms from U.S. law, a relatively cosmetic law was passed. It should be added that while this, like the bipolarization of the party system and reduced ideological distinctions between the parties, suggests another way in which French politics is becoming Americanized. The funds involved, however, are relatively small compared to those in the United States, mostly because television time is free to all parties. In a way that it perhaps amusing to Americans, French politicians tend to worry about the cost of posters.

SOURCE: *Washington Post,* November 27, 1987; *Le Monde,* November 14, 1987; Jean Claude Masclet and Pierre Mutignon, "Le Financement Publique des Partis et la Reglémentation de leurs Ressources et Dépenses," *Problémes Politiques et Sociaux,* no. 527 (January 10, 1986).

into two broad coalitions of Right and Left, much the way Duverger predicted. However, this coalescing was a long time in coming. While the Fifth Republic was inaugurated in 1958, and was antedated by most of the parties, the Common Platform of the Left was not signed until 1972, and the conservatives' "Liberal" alliance[15] did not formalize until 1986.

Two factors seem to explain the delay. On the Right, the charisma and coattail effect of de Gaulle obviated the necessity for Gaullists to formalize relations with other conservative parties, though the latter were invited into government under Pompidou, and Giscard

served as de Gaulle's finance minister without joining the party. On the left, the pariah status of the Communist Party, coupled to its significant following, hindered the possibilities for any successful electoral alliance to be formed. Logically, the disappearance of de Gaulle and the withering away of the PCF removed these obstacles to coalition politics.

The other major trend in the party system is the convergence of the two coalitions. That is, the policies of left and right have tended to converge in recent years. As the differences between the parties tend to be defined in economic terms, the best explanation for this convergence is the economy.

France has become increasingly locked into the web of interdependencies that have characterized the economies of the advanced industrial countries since the end of World

[15] The RPR and UDF based their alliance on a common preference for low taxes, sale of nationalized industries, de-regulation, and a general "liberation" of private enterprise.

President François Mitterrand campaigns in the first round of voting the French presidential elections, April 24, 1988.
SOURCE: Thierry Orban/Bernard Bisson/Sygma.

War II.[16] This means that the pursuit of an independent economic strategy has become increasingly difficult. As we mentioned in Chapter 9, the Socialists discovered that they could not reflate the French economy when the rest of the world was deflating. Government deficits intended to stimulate demand and, thus, jobs only ended up stimulating imports. That is, French companies did not produce enough goods to absorb the increase in demand generated by government spending. French consumers, who now had more money thanks to government programs, tended to purchase goods from abroad, as there were not enough French goods to meet the demand. The Socialists turned to more market-oriented solutions, such as deregulating capital markets to stimulate investment,[17] and began to look much more like the conservatives. On the other hand, French conservatives were loathe to call for the dismantling of the welfare state.[18] With the stock market crash of October 1987, the privatization program of the conservatives ground to a halt and market solutions lost much of their attraction for French voters. Indeed, the policy disasters of both Left and Right pushed the policy debate to the center—or rather, out of sight: in the presidential debate of 1988 between François Mitterand and Jacques Chirac, a total of two minutes was devoted to the problem of unemployment.

---

[16] On the overall theory of "interdependence," see Robert O. Keohane and Joseph S. Nye, *Power and Interdependence* (Boston: Little Brown, 1977). For the constraints on France, see Stephen S. Cohen and Peter A. Gourevitch, eds., *France in the Troubled World Economy* (London: Butterworth Scientific, 1982).

[17] Old solutions tended not to work because the private sector anticipated government strategies and acted to counter them in advance. See especially, Michael Loriaux, "States and Markets: French Financial Intervention in the Seventies," *Comparative Politics*, 20, 2 (January 1988).

[18] Henig, Hamnett, and Feigenbaum, "Privatization."

CONCLUSION: THE AMERICANIZATION OF FRENCH POLITICS

The bifurcation of the French party system into two opposing coalitions and the convergence of the left and right suggests that French politics is becoming more like that of the United States. Mitterrand's overtures to the UDF after the 1988 election suggest the possibility of politics along the West German model by creating a center-left government similar to Helmut Schmidt's FDP-SPD alliance, but as of this writing the strategy had not born fruit. Not only have announced policies of the parties converged, but the trend toward pragmatic policies and away from solutions dictated by traditional ideologies has made present-day France rather different from the country that was so politically idiosyncratic through much of the modern era.

The principal factors conditioning the change were, of course, first, the advent of the institutions of the Fifth Republic. The electoral system and the institutions themselves have reduced the role for the political center and encouraging right and left coalitions. Moreover, the suppressing of proportional representation is likely to relegate the more radical parties, the PCF and National Front, to the political sidelines, despite persistent social reasons for their existence. This may, however, take some time. Finally, the general crisis of mass production-based economies in the world market has limited the options available to political groups. These conditions that have shaped the current French party system are not likely to disappear quickly.

References and Suggested Readings

BELL, DAVID S. *Contemporary French Political Parties*. New York: Methuen, 1982.

BERGER, SUZANNE. *The French Political System.* New York: Random House, 1974.

DUVERGER, MAURICE. *Political Parties.* New York: Methuen, 1953.

FREARS, J. R. *Political Parties and Elections in the French Fifth Republic.* New York: St. Martins, 1977.

ROSS, GEORGE. *Workers and Communists in France: From Popular Front to Eurocommunism.* Berkeley: University of California Press, 1982.

WILSON, FRANK. *French Political Parties under the Fifth Republic.* New York: Praeger, 1982.

14

The permanence of Parliament is not necessary for the life of the nation. On the other hand, the nation would cease to exist if the services of the administration were stopped.
— HENRI CHARDON

The State Apparatus

The economic uncertainties of recent years have engendered a lively and politically charged debate about whether the state's role in economic management should be increased or diminished. France's long history of state management of the economy has left the country both with a highly articulated apparatus for government intervention and with a convenient target upon which to pin blame for the poor economic performance of recent years. While conservatives blame the state for the problems of the economy, many analysts have attributed France's meteoric postwar growth to a talented and highly trained bureaucracy. It is to that bureaucracy that we now turn.

THE BUREAUCRATIC STATE

All modern states have bureaucracies. Indeed, a well-developed bureaucracy is one of the principal characteristics that distinguish modern polities from those that are termed traditional. Only if power flows from an office rather than a person can one be assured that a political regime will outlast its founders. Moreover, governments develop bureaus and agencies to handle specialized problems.[1] Similarly, routines and standard operating procedures are developed by bureaucracies in the name of efficiency; such procedures arise because certain public problems recur frequently, and routine solutions free officials from having to "reinvent the wheel" each time a problem comes up. Of course, routinized behavior by bureaucracies often inhibits solving new problems if unimaginative office holders refuse to depart from routines.[2]

The French bureaucracy has often been held up as a model of the positive role a state can play.[3] Within the country the bureau-

[1] For the classic literature on bureaucracy, see Max Weber, *The Theory of Social and Economic Organization* ed. Talcott Parsons; (New York: Free Press, 1964); *From Max Weber: Essays in Sociology* ed. by H. H. Gerth and C. Wright Mills (New York: Oxford University Press, 1946), chap. VIII. On the division of labor, see Adam Smith, *Wealth of Nations*.

[2] This fidelity to standard operating procedures was one of the chief sources of criticism in Graham Allison's famous study of the Cuban missile crisis. See his *Essence of Decision* (Boston: Little Brown, 1971).

[3] For example, John Zysman, *Political Strategies for Industrial Order* (Berkeley and Los Angeles: University of California Press, 1977).

cracy enjoys high prestige. Public service has traditionally attracted the best and brightest of French society. Not only was the French bureaucracy the principal instrument of Napoleon, but the chronic instability of republican governments often left the bureaucracy as the main locus of state power, for it was unaffected by continually collapsing coalitions, and often exercised power by default.

THE ROOTS OF STATE POWER

Like almost every other aspect of French political organization, the roots of the bureaucracy's power can be traced to the lateness of industrialization, although some vestiges of that authority derive from earlier historical traditions. Briefly, economic conditions necessitated a strong state if France was to develop, and pre-existing administrative structures facilitated the arrival of such a state.[4]

As noted earlier, even before the Revolution, France had a history of state involvement in the economy. Jean-Baptiste Colbert (1619–83), Louis XIV's minister of finance, did much to initiate the development of infrastructures (roads, ports, canals). The highly centralized administration established by the absolutist kings facilitated the involvement of royal government in shaping the economy. But government involvement in the eighteenth century was common in all European countries. In fact, Adam Smith's famous *Wealth of Nations*, published in 1776, was originally written to persuade public officials and the educated classes of the day to abandon this common practice of mercantilism. Another factor besides a tradition of government economic intervention is necessary to explain the development of a power French bureaucracy.

Lateness of industrialization is one of the most significant factors explaining the power of the French bureaucracy. Briefly, the argument, based on the writings of the economic historian Alexander Gerschenkron, goes like this: By the time France industrialized, Great Britain, its principal competitor, had not only developed an industrial base in textiles, but had proceeded to develop significant, capital-intensive industries such as steel and railroads. If France were to catch up, it would need to amass huge amounts of capital. Given the predominance of agriculture and small-scale business, powerful, centralizing institutions would be necessary to collect highly dispersed savings from a conservative peasantry and middle class. Only the French state could fulfill this function.

Political culture reinforced this tendency. The absence of entrepreneurs meant that there would be little competition for the state as an economic actor. Indeed, most French businessmen feared competition among themselves, as well; and they were all too happy to have the state regulate their respective markets. Moreover, the high prestige of public service facilitated public acceptance of state economic intervention and also served to attract the highest caliber of France's human potential to the state's task.

For all of these reasons, the role of the state grew substantially over the course of the nineteenth and twentieth centuries. However, the timing-of-industrialization argument does not explain why the bureaucracy grew at the expense of other state institutions such as the parliament. Part of the reason is cultural: The cleavages in French society, reflected in the party system, led to highly unstable parliamentary government. Thus, if

---

[4] On lateness of development see Alexander Gerschenkron, "Economic Backwardness in Historical Perspective" in his collection of essays by the same name (New York: Praeger, 1962). On pre-existing structures see Alexis de Tocqueville, *The Old Regime and The French Revolution*. Combining these two analyses, see Peter A. Gourevitch, "The Second Image Reversed," *International Organization*, 32, 4 (Autumn 1978).

the tasks of the state were to be fulfilled, the bureaucracy was in a better position to do the job. Conversely, survival in parliament led deputies to develop very different skills from those necessary to manage an economy. Avoiding decisions and providing services to specific constituencies were more important to the deputy, while the bureaucrat's promotions depended primarily on the efficient performance of assigned tasks. Consequently, to the extent that the economy developed (and many argue that true development did not take off until the mid-twentieth century), it tended to parallel the development of the bureaucracy.

THE RELATION OF STATE TO SOCIETY

The French bureaucracy has also played a robust role in French society because of its capacity to assist social mobility. Different strata of French society have been aided by the employment opportunities offered by the state. In many ways the upper ranks of the public service became the new aristocracy. While service in the military had been a traditional avenue for the gentry, the power of the bureaucracy in France attracted former aristocrats and the upper levels of the bourgeoisie to state service. The French of more modest origins could find employment in the lower ranks of the public sector (as postmen, railroad workers, teachers) and the sons and (eventually) daughters of peasants could rise in status by climbing the ladder of civil service promotions.[5]

While the different divisions of the bureaucracy were, in fact, almost as stratified as the society it reflected, the state preserved its image as a meritocracy, which in turn facilitated its acceptance by all strata. The principal mechanism for maintaining this image was and is the competitive examination. That is, entry to state jobs is determined by performance on competitive examinations that are open to all French citizens. Thus, bureaucrats are presumed to hold their offices on the basis of merit.[6]

In fact, recruitment by competitive examination is so embedded in French culture that it sometimes reaches manic proportions. An advertisement from the *Journal Officiel,* the official journal of the French parliament, illustrates the extent of the phenomenon vividly: "Authorized in three months following publication of the present notice, a competition for the recruitment of two cabinet-makers for the national establishment at Sèvres."[7]

THE CIVIL SERVICE AND THE *GRANDES ECOLES*

The reality of civil service recruitment is of course rather different from the myth, although, to be fair, the caliber of French functionaries is indeed quite high.[8]

Before World War II most senior civil servants were recruited from the *Ecole Libre de Science Politique.* This was a private college

---

[5] On the traditional role of aristocrats, see Stendahl, *Le Rouge et le Noir;* on the bourgeoisie and the bureaucracy, see Ezra N. Suleiman, *Politics, Power and Bureaucracy* (Princeton: Princeton University Press, 1974); on peasants and teachers, see Eugen Weber, *Peasants into Frenchmen* (Stanford: Stanford University Press, 1977).

[6] The reality, of course, is different. Candidates from more privileged backgrounds do better on entrance exams. See page 223 of this text.

[7] Quoted in Pierre Avril, *Politics in France,* trans. John Ross (Baltimore: Penguin Books, 1969), p. 201.

[8] For the best treatment of the French bureaucracy and the role of the *Grandes Ecoles,* see Ezra N. Suleiman, *Politics, Power, and Bureaucracy in France,* and his *Elites in French Society* (Princeton: Princeton University Press, 1978).

in Paris where only those able to pay the tuition, as well as pass the entrance exams, could enter. The school was nationalized after the war, and a new *Ecole Nationale d'Administration* was created with the intent of democratizing recruitment to the civil service as well as improving the training of the state's senior staff.

Students were required to pass rigorous examinations in order to enter *ENA* (successful graduates are called "*Enarques*," while the influence of these graduates on the whole of the public sector has facetiously been dubbed "*Enarchie*," playing on the French word for anarchy). As an additional aid to economically deprived candidates who might otherwise not be able to afford graduate study, students at ENA are paid a salary. In a parallel fashion, the best technically trained civil servants attend the *Ecole Polytechnique*, France's premier engineering school (founded by Napoleon), and are paid a military salary.

The *Ecole Nationale d'Administration* and the *Ecole Polytechnique*, as well as a few other elite graduate schools, are known as *Grandes Ecoles* ("great schools"). The prestige and competitiveness of these schools, if not the actual quality of instruction,[9] are far greater than in the regular university system (e.g., the Sorbonne) and attendance is *de rigueur* if one is to ascend the ranks of the French elite.

The problem is that while the entrance examinations are theoretically open to all French citizens, it is extremely rare for students from poorer economic backgrounds to do well. Partially, this is because ENA demands essay exams, which tend to favor students whose families are well educated, where flowery French is well understood, and

where self-confidence is a subtle product of class origin. Self-confidence is especially important, as prospective ENA students must pass a public oral exam in front of a jury of distinguished senior civil servants. Questioning is meant to prove the candidate's potential to "think on his feet," but, in fact, self-conscious working-class candidates rarely feel sufficiently comfortable to do as well as upper-class candidates. An example illustrates the *panache* needed: A jury member pulls out his pocket-watch and says to the candidate, "Prove to me, sir, that this watch exists." Without losing a beat, the self-confident candidate sweeps up the watch, pockets it, and replies to the startled examiner, "*You* prove to *me* that your watch exists." Those economically less fortunate students who do make it to the *Grandes Ecoles* tend to opt for the scientific track, in universities, where use of language and cultural comportment are less important.

Moreover, the reality of the examination process for both administrators and engineers requires previous attendance at the country's best secondary schools in order to prepare adequately for the ordeal. In the case of ENA, attendance at the country's competitive *Institut d'Etudes Politiques* (the new name for the *Ecole Libre des Science Politiques*), or less preferably, at one of the provincial political science institutes, is also required. Since most of the country's best *lycées* (academic high schools) and its most prestigious political science institute are in Paris, Parisians have an edge.[10] Provincial families that wish to send their children to Parisian schools must be able to afford to do so. This further biases the recruitment process in favor of the economically privileged.

[9] See Suleiman, "The Myth of Technical Expertise," *Comparative Politics*, 10, 1 (October, 1977).

[10] There are, of course, some excellent lycées in the large provincial cities, but even this avenue to social mobility is difficult for the inhabitants of small towns and villages.

DIVISIONS WITHIN THE BUREAUCRATIC STATE

The Grands Corps

The most prestigious of the positions in the French civil service are held by members of the *grands corps*.[11] These are self governing groups of civil servants organized along functional lines. Examples are the Diplomatic Corps, the Financial Inspectorate, Mining Engineers, and Civil Engineers. While there are hundreds of corps, entry into the most prestigious of them is limited to the top graduates of the *Grandes Ecoles*. Social links between corps members are not unlike the "old school ties" in Britain or the United States, but are rather more formalized.

Originally, the corps were established to accomplish specific governmental functions, as their titles suggest. Indeed, corps members do start their careers doing exactly the kind of government service that the title of the corps indicates: administering mines, inspecting finances and the like. However, these elite functionaries rarely do such tasks for very long. Usually, they are "lent" to ministerial cabinets (advisors to government ministers), they move into the directorates of public enterprises, or they leave government service altogether and move to princely salaries in the private sector. The French call this move into private business jobs *pantouflage,* or "putting on the soft slippers." The terminology alone suggests the French image of private sector versus public sector work.

Such interesting and, occasionally, lucra-tive alternatives to the boredom of routine administration not only attract France's best and brightest, but often lead to competition among the corps to capture the best jobs for their members. Different sectors of the French economy have been staked out by diverse corps. The result is that corps members still in the bureaucracy often advocate policies that are good for their respective corps, and the industries they dominate, rather than for the nation as a whole.[12]

Administrative Conflicts

While the existence of the *grands corps* makes the French bureaucracy rather unusual, other aspects of bureaucratic behavior found in France are common in other industrial countries. Conflicts among different departments and agencies over responsibilities and funding are evident in France, just as they are elsewhere.[13]

The most frequent conflicts within the French administration tend to arise over budgets. Each agency has a view of its own role and often requests additional funding to fulfill that role. This may involve creating new projects, hiring new people, raising salaries, or any of myriad ways to spend money. Usually this means coming into conflict with France's most powerful ministry, the Ministry of Finance. In times of contractionary budgets, when departments are expected to reduce expenses, conflicts, of course, become exacerbated.

Clientelism

Battles over policy often involve different agencies championing different alternatives

---

[11] See Suleiman, *Politics, Power and Bureaucracy* and *Elites in French Society;* see also, Jean Claude Thoenig, *Ere des Technocrates: Le Cas des Ponts et Chaussées* (Paris: Editions d'Organisation, 1973); and Feigenbaum, *The Politics of Public Enterprise* (Princeton: Princeton University Press, 1985), chap. IV. Most of the discussion below draws heavily on Suleiman and Feigenbaum.

[12] See especially Feigenbaum, chap. IV.

[13] The classic study of U.S. bureaucratic conflict is Graham Allison's *Essence of Decision* (Boston: Little, Brown, 1971). The evidence for French bureaucratic battles is drawn from Feigenbaum, *The Politics of Public Enterprise.*

to solve a particular problem. Sometimes this may simply be because of genuine differences of opinion about the best way to solve a problem. However, it is frequently the case that bureaucrats have ulterior motives. The most common such motive is protection of a client group in the private sector. The Ministry of Agriculture tends to champion the needs of farmers, the Energy Directorate defends the interests of oil companies, and so on.

The tendency toward clientelism is partially explained by the career patterns of French bureaucrats. Normally, they view their tenure in the bureaucracy as only the first stage in their career. They then hope to find jobs in the private sector, usually in an industry in which they have regulatory experience. Civil servants thus constantly have their ears to the ground waiting for opportunities to move into the industries they are regulating. They are not likely to want to alienate a prospective employer, and so they tend to favor policies that are in the best interest of their "clients."

Such clientelism is not specifically French. Similar situations arise in countries as diverse as America and Japan. In Japan, in fact, *pantouflage* is called *amakudari* or "descent from heaven."[14] Some groups have been especially adept at influencing the public sector. The notaries, a group in France that serves almost no useful function, has managed to survive by adroitly manipulating bureaucrats.[15]

Venality and manipulation, however, are not the only reasons for the close relationship between public and private elites. Bureaucrats also depend on the private sector for information and expertise. While graduates of the *Grandes Ecoles* receive some technical training, schooling is short and bureaucrats are often less technically expert than their counterparts in the private sector. Thus, civil servants tend to rely on businessmen for advice and gradually accept their point of view.[16] Moreover, the French bureaucracy very rarely has sources of statistics and information other than those provided by the industry being regulated. They are thus vulnerable to misinformation and manipulation.

Finally, clientelism is abetted by rivalries among the *Grands Corps.* Civil servants tend to advocate policies on the basis of the needs of an economic sector that a corps has "colonized." For example, through the mechanism of *pantouflage* the corps of mining engineers "colonized" the oil industry. Senior members of the corps now in the private sector subtly pressured junior members still in government service to support policies that would help the oil industry or, at the very least, create jobs for corps members in that sector.[17]

Influence of Political Parties

While various forms of administrative rivalries have divided the bureaucracy for a very long time, direct political influence of the administration has been dramatically transformed since the advent of the Fifth Republic. Specifically, what has changed is the way in which political parties have meshed with the administration.

Like all modern bureaucracies, the French administration is nominally independent of the government of the day. Career civil servants have guaranteed tenure of office, they are allowed to express their political opinions

[14] I am grateful to Dr. Martha Caldwell Harris for pointing this out to me.
[15] Ezra N. Suleiman, *Les Notaires: Les Pouvoirs d'une Corporation,* trans. Martine Meusy (Paris: Editions du Seuil, 1987). The English version of Suleiman's book is *Private Power and Centralization in France* (Princeton: Princeton University Press, 1987).

[16] See Feigenbaum, *The Politics of Public Enterprise,* chap. IV.
[17] Feigenbaum, chap. IV.

freely, although judiciously,[18] and may even run for office without losing their jobs. Under the Third and Fourth Republics, however, the top posts in the bureaucracy were allotted according to political affiliation, a system not unlike that in Italy today. Different parties were accorded specific ministries despite changes in parliamentary coalitions. The Foreign Ministry, for example, was almost always headed by a member of the Christian Democratic Party (MRP), while the Division of Public Health was always left in the hands of the Radicals or Socialists.

All of this changed under the Fifth Republic. The reason was the novel situation of a majority party and the increased power of the executive. The condition of a strong, party-oriented executive made its mark on the bureaucracy, the chief instrument of the executive. De Gaulle and his successors drew heavily on technically trained bureaucrats ("technocrats") to populate their cabinets. Technocrats learned that the key to influence was the proper party connections, and by the 1960s only members of the ruling majority found a ready ear in the bureaucracy.[19]

All of this changed again in 1981 when the Socialists came to power. Mitterrand dismissed over 400 department heads and replaced them with more sympathetic civil servants. Under French law, however, the dismissed bureaucrats could not be fired, and equivalent posts had to be found for them; at the very least, they retained their salaries. The result was an expensive experiment in something resembling the U.S. "spoils system." Ultimately, however, little changed. Dependence on the *Grands Corps* and the social biases in recruitment patterns produced a network of "socialist" bureaucrats that did not differ very much from the previous "conservative" ones.[20]

CONCLUSION

Bureaucracies are necessary to rationalize authority and to depersonalize power. This insures the existence of a regime beyond the lifetimes of those who found it. The French bureaucracy, for reasons of precedent, economic history and political necessity, has been a strong and relatively independent force. While it has been the vehicle for some social mobility, recruitment patterns for the most powerful positions have tended to be biased in favor of those from the privileged segments of French society. Career patterns of bureaucrats also influence the bureaucracy in the direction of those sectors that can offer the most in *pantouflage*. Finally, while the bureaucracy is powerful, it is limited by its own disunity, as divisions arising from administrative, clientelistic and corps rivalries serve as an internal check on the power of the state.

References and Suggested Readings

BOTTOMORE, T. B. *Elites and Society*. Harmondsworth: Penguin, 1964.

CROZIER, MICHEL. *The Bureaucratic Phenomenon*. Chicago: University of Chicago Press, 1964.

FEIGENBAUM, HARVEY B. *The Politics of Public Enterprise*. Princeton: Princeton University Press, 1985.

KEOHANE, NANERL. *Philosophy and the State in France*. Princeton: Princeton University Press, 1980.

SULEIMAN, EZRA N. *Politics, Power, and Bureaucracy*. Princeton: Princeton University Press, 1974.

———. *Elites in French Society*. Princeton: Princeton Unversity Press, 1978.

---

[18] Civil servants are expected to refrain from criticizing policies that they must implement.

[19] See Suleiman, *Politics, Power and Bureaucracy*, chap. XIII.

[20] See Feigenbaum, chap. VI.

15

It is pertinent to point out that we owe our existence to centralization, because our existence did not come about naturally. France is not a natural occurrence; she is the consequence of a political will that never let up in the course of the monarchy, the empires, and the republics.

— ALEXANDRE SANGUINETTI

The Hierarchy of Government

INTRODUCTION

France is, as we have noted, a country of contradictions and paradoxes. Perhaps nowhere is this more true than in the transformation of the country's formal institutions of government. The parade of governments during the parliamentary Fourth Republic led to the transformation of national institutions into a highly stable presidential system. The centralization of the economy under the Socialists also occurred at the same time as the decentralization of the hierarchy of government. Paradoxically as well, the assumption of power by the Gaullist prime minister after 1986 led the Gaullists to undermine the strong presidential authority that their founder had struggled to create.

TRANSFORMATION OF THE NATIONAL GOVERNMENT

Parliament

For most of France's republican history, the chief expression of democracy was the election of deputies to the parliament. While France has oscillated between constitutions favoring a strong executive and those favoring a strong legislature, the *democratic* constitutions favored the legislature until 1958.[1]

Under the legislative constitutions of the Third and Fourth Republics, there was a fusion of executive and legislative authority. That is, the prime minister and his cabinet served as the executive by virtue of their election by the lower house (the *Chamber of Deputies*). They also served at the pleasure of the legislature: if for any reason a majority of the deputies refused to support a policy of the government, a new government would have to be formed. We use the term *government* to mean the prime minister and his cabinet. (In French the cabinet is called the *conseil des ministres,* while under the Third and Fourth Republics the prime minister was also known as the *president du conseil).*[2] Any time a gov-

---

[1] Cf. Berger, *The French Political System,* chap. 2; Pierre Avril, *Politics in France,* chap. 2.

[2] I will occasionally use the term *premier* as synonymous with prime minister. The English word derives from the French *premier ministre.*

227

ernment lost the support of the deputies in a formal vote, it was said to have lost a *vote of confidence*. New elections were not necessary to form a new government unless a new majority could not be established, or unless five years had passed since the last election.

Majorities were difficult to form in both the Third and Fourth Republics for two essential reasons. First, there were a large number of parties in the Chamber of Deputies because of the political divisions in the French electorate (see Chapter 11) and because of the frequent recourse to proportional representation as the chief voting system. The second essential reason for difficulty in forming majorities was the limited grounds for agreement between the parties—because they represented such diverse sections of the electorate (see Chapter 12).

A subsidiary reason for the instability of governments during the Third and Fourth Republics was the lack of party discipline. Frequently, the collapse of a government meant that new ministers would be drawn from the rank-and-file deputies ("backbenchers," to use British terminology). This gave deputies an incentive to vote against the governments *of which their own parties were members,* knowing that their party leadership had few instruments to punish them, and that committee chairmen especially were likely to become newly appointed ministers. This situation, in turn, was a result of the limited party funds to finance campaigns, leaving backbenchers to rely on their own resources and reducing the impact of any party threat to withdraw support ("withdrawal of the whip" in Britain).[3] Moreover, the refusal of both the Communists (after

1947) and the Gaullists (after 1946) to participate in governments left the potential candidates for ministers to be found among the weakly organized parties of the center.[4]

More often than not, adoption of controversial policies spelled the end of a government. The ever-present possibility that coalition members would defect, even for the most transitory gains, sharply constrained all governments, but especially those of the Fourth Republic. This made it hard to address the increasingly difficult problems facing the country. To some extent this *"immobilisme"* of parliamentary government meant that many of the problems of the country were simply left to the bureaucracy. But as crises arose, incremental bureaucratic solutions became inappropriate, and deputies developed a habit of investing plenipotentiary powers in the prime minister or, eventually, the president. Such was the case of the transitory "dictatorships" of Clemenceau (World War I), Doumergue (the Great Depression), Pétain (Vichy, tragically less "transitory" than originally expected), Pierre Mendes-France (the Indochina War), and de Gaulle (the Algerian War).

It was the last crisis of the Fourth Republic and the parliamentary habit of investing powers in a single "savior" that led to the suicide of the last parliamentary regime. In 1958 France was torn by civil strife over government efforts to quell the Arab rebellion in Algeria, which many of the French considered a part of France. Unable to extricate itself from this part of North Africa, while doubting the loyalty of the army to the Re-

[3] In this sense there were similarities between French and American party systems, both being what Duverger called "bourgeois" or nineteenth-century party systems. See Duverger, *Les Partis Politiques,* chap. 1.

[4] The Communists originally joined the Socialists (SFIO) and Christian Democrats (MRP) in the tripartite governments of 1946–47, but entered quasi-permanent opposition after refusing to vote war credits for the French forces in Indochina. De Gaulle and his followers went into opposition with the adoption of a parliament-centered constitution in 1946.

public should Algeria be granted independence, the leaders of the Fourth Republic turned to de Gaulle. The latter was, at least, a proven democrat whose nationalist credentials were assumed to be attractive to the army. De Gaulle accepted the post as prime minister on condition that the constitution be drastically revised. What resulted was, in fact, a new constitution.

The Fifth Republic

The essential thrust of the Constitution of 1958 was to circumscribe the authority of parliament and to shift power to the executive. The assumption of de Gaulle and his supporters was that parliament was immobilized because of the power of self-interested political parties and the national interest could not, therefore, be served. This was a typical conservative outlook that viewed representation as divisive and assumed that somehow, despite the fact that different segments of French society had conflicting interests (a "zero-sum game," in modern parlance), that a national interest could be found and served, if only political institutions could be placed above the fray. Members of de Gaulle's government therefore reduced the role of parliament, whose very representative nature reflected the conflicts of French society, and attempted to shift authority to the executive. As Michel Debré, a close collaborator of de Gaulle's and principal author of the new constitution, expressed the basic philosophy of the document, "To be sure, the nation is composed of individuals and of groups. But this composition gives birth to an independent and animated body which is, in fact, the nation and, in law, the State."[5]

[5] Michel Debré, *La Mort de l'Etat Republicain* (Paris: Gallimard, 1947), p. 35; quoted in Suleiman, *Politics, Power and Bureaucracy*, p. 24.

Power Under the Constitution of 1958

The Constitution of 1958 created three centers of authority: the Parliament, the government, and the president.

Parliament. As with the Third and Fourth Republics, the new parliament was bicameral: the National Assembly (*Assemblée Nationale*) was the new name for the lower house, with deputies directly elected by districts. The Senate (*Sénat*) was the much less powerful upper house, with senators elected by local electoral colleges.

The powers of the parliament were aimed at providing a democratic check on the government, but with additional clauses aimed at reducing potential instability:

- The government is appointed by the president but can be disavowed by the National Assembly through a "motion of censure."
- A "motion of censure" (i.e., a vote of no confidence) was made difficult to pass: It must be initiated by 10 percent of the deputies, voted in 48 hours, and passed by an absolute majority of all deputies (not just those present); and passage of the motion requires immediate dissolution of the Assembly and new elections.
- Ministers may not be deputies. Deputies must resign their seats if named to the government.
- The legislative powers of the National Assembly are severely constricted: It may legislate only in areas of civil and political rights, crimes, taxes, elections and nationalizations; it may decide only "basic principles" of defense, local government, property, work and welfare; it may not pass detailed "regulatory" laws; only the government may initiate legislation that would increase public expenditure or decrease revenues; the parliament may only sit for six months out of the year, unless called into special session by the president; it votes only on those amendments to legislation that the government accepts; the government can demand package voting (e.g., for the budget).

The National Assembly.
SOURCE: M. Langevin/Sygma.

• The new constitution also reduced the role of committees, which were thought to be vulnerable targets for interest groups.[6] The number of standing committees was reduced from nineteen to six: the subject matter of each committee was intended to be so broad as to inhibit members from developing expertise as leverage against the government (knowledge is power!) and to have so many members as to become unwieldy. Ultimately, though, these reforms could be subverted: Committees still have the power to create smaller, more specialized subcommittees, while special, *ad hoc* committees can also be created. However, the Government's influence over the budget keeps these

[6] Indeed, there is a cozy relationship between lobbies and committees in the United States. Along with relevant bureaucracies, these have been called "iron triangles."

sub- and *ad hoc* committees from being adequately staffed.

The Senate. The Senate, the upper house of the French parliament, is somewhat more powerful than the House of Lords in Britain and considerably less powerful than the U.S. Senate. Like the German and American upper houses, it provides regional representation, with less populous regions being over-represented. This over-representation was intentional. The indirect election of the French Senate (by local elites) and the exaggerated influence of rural areas were intended to make the Senate a conservative check on the National Assembly. To de Gaulle's chagrin, in the first decade of the Fifth Republic the Senate was composed of *anti-Gaullist* conservatives. For this reason he sought to abolish the upper chamber by referendum in April of 1969 only to lose, leading to the General's resignation.

If the government does not intervene, a bill must pass both the National Assembly and the Senate to become law. If the Senate is recalcitrant, the government can give the National Assembly the last word and ignore a negative vote in the Senate. The Socialists met constant opposition to their reforms from the Senate during the 1981–86 session, and, like de Gaulle, were unfettered by this opposition.

The Government. The power and the Achilles' heel of the Gaullist constitution is the government. The government, consisting of the prime minister, ministers of state, ministers, and secretaries of state (junior ministers),[7] is appointed by the president, but can be voted out of power by a motion of censure in the National Assembly. Thus, for the executive to be truly powerful, the president must not have a hostile majority in the lower house of parliament. This situation of a powerful executive with a friendly majority existed from 1958 to 1986.

The constitution of 1958 is unclear as to where ultimate executive power resides, whether in the presidency or in the prime ministry. Largely, the powers of the president and prime minister have been defined by practice, with most of the precedents being set by de Gaulle. De Gaulle took it upon himself to establish the main lines of public policy, and left day-to-day management of the executive to the prime minister. This was a practice of each of his successors and was only modified with the advent of "cohabitation" (see pages 234–35 of this text.)

De Gaulle also established certain "reserved areas" of presidential policy-making:

foreign policy, defense, and constitutional questions. This practice was maintained by his successors, and was extended to economic questions by Valery Giscard d'Estaing, who was trained in economics.

Finally, de Gaulle asserted the president's right to *fire* as well as appoint the prime minister and his cabinet. This right is nowhere in the constitution, but since, parliaments were, until 1986, always friendly to the president, the practice became solidly established.

AN IMPERIAL PRESIDENCY?

For a number of reasons, there has been a worldwide trend of increasing executive power since (at least) the Great Depression of the 1930s. This has partially been a function of the globalization of politics and the increasing importance of foreign policy, a traditional bastion of executive authority. Moreover, the Keynesian economic revolution gave government a primary role in the management of the economy, where, in the interest of coherent policy, the executive has emerged as the principal manager of the nation's economy.

Perhaps nowhere has the shift toward the executive been more pronounced than in France. Certainly, French history has provided both precedents and symbols that have facilitated this shift. Historically, both the kings and Napoleon I have provided heroic symbols and a positive view of executive authority. It is also certain that these historic cues have not been equally received in France, for the Right more than the Left has favored a powerful executive.

While it is essentially true that the constitutions of the Third and Fourth Republics located power in the legislature while the Fifth circumscribed the legislature in favor of the presidency, a look at French history reveals this dichotomy to be less than clear cut.

[7] Ministers of state are most senior. They always attend cabinet meetings. The others attend when invited.

Presidents under legislative regimes had subtle powers, while the vagueness of the Constitution of 1958 leaves the door open for parliamentary assertiveness.

Role of the President under Parliamentary Regimes

The traditional role of the French president has been one of a national symbol, above the sordid fray of normal politics. In legislative regimes the office has been both ceremonial and one of a sort of spare wheel, available should the machinery of government break down.

At the beginning of the Third Republic the office of the president of the Republic was primarily championed by royalists. Despite the debacle of Napoleon III, the republicans were too weak to oppose it, and throughout much of the Third Republic the office was occupied by conservative politicians. This was facilitated by the fact that the president was indirectly elected—a tradition in France until 1962, when de Gaulle urged the popular election of the president to legitimize the powers of the office.

While the prime minister was the constitutional chief executive in both the Third and Fourth Republics, a clever president could wield his ceremonial powers to substantial effects. Jules Grevy, a conservative republican during the nineteenth century, did much to stretch his influence beyond the intentions of those who opposed the Second Empire. The French president, much like the Queen of England, was vested with responsibility for naming a prime minister, subject to the approval of the parliament. Grévy carefully chose weak leaders who, in the absence of strict party discipline, could often find a (transitory) majority to support them as prime minister. As the president's ceremonial function included presiding over cabinet meetings, Grevy then used his powers of persuasion to influence—and occasionally dominate—the cabinet, including its premier.[8]

While the president had no power to overrule the prime minister, frequent votes of no confidence serve the interest of the president. With his seven-year term unaffected, the president remained while premiers came and went. Not only did the president serve as the institutional memory of the executive, but a strong-willed president who had failed to convince the prime minister need only wait a few months and he could try again with the next premier.[9]

Moreover, even though executive power was concentrated in the prime minister's office, it often served the interests of parliament and the cabinet to leave certain powers with the president. This was especially true of foreign affairs, where deputies saw little value to their constituencies in pursuing specific foreign policies and consequently were content to let the president retain power to negotiate treaties and control the armed forces.

THE FIFTH REPUBLIC

The constitution of the Fifth Republic was intended, of course, to be emphatically presidential, although not to the extent of the American Constitution, where a complete separation of powers was defined. The ambiguous role of the government (prime minister and cabinet) made the new French constitution a hybrid of parliamentary and presidential systems. Why de Gaulle and his supporters preferred the hybrid form is not clear, although in 1985, as France was about to venture into "cohabitation" (see page 234), Michel Debré argued that the original

[8] Avril, *Politics in France*, chap. 4; Cobban, *A History of Modern France*, vol. 3, chap. 1.
[9] Avril, *Politics in France*, chap. 4.

intent was that the locus of power would shift between premier and president depending on the nature of the parliamentary majority.[10] This, of course, was self-serving, as Debré backed the Gaullists, who were about to take over the prime ministership while the Socialists retained the presidency.

It may well have been that the Gaullists originally backed the hybrid system both to avoid the appearance of imitating the United States and to avoid the genuine possibility of continual stalemate to which a separation of powers system is always vulnerable.

Formal Powers

The president does have important formal powers. He may dissolve the National Assembly and call new elections, presumably to achieve a friendly majority, but may only do so once a year (to avoid instability).

Perhaps most dramatic to Americans, Article 16 of the 1958 Constitution allows the president to become a kind of temporary dictator if "the institutions of the Republic, national independence, [or] territorial integrity are seriously and immediately threatened and the regular functioning of constitutional public power is disrupted." The only checks on these powers are that the president must consult with the prime minister and speakers of each house and with the Constitutional Council (see pages 235–36 of this text). Parliament must remain in session during the exercise of emergency powers, but cannot legislate.

While Article 16 appears anti-democratic, in fact it was invoked only once, in April 1961, when there was a genuine fear that generals unhappy with de Gaulle's Algerian policy would attempt a *coup d'état*. After the

danger passed, de Gaulle returned to normal constitutional processes.

Also among the formal powers of the president is the power to appoint three of the nine members of the Constitutional Council—the highest court in France on constitutional matters. He may also pardon prisoners, traditionally done at the beginning of the seven-year term—a power Mitterrand used extensively when he first entered office.

Significantly, the president does not have the power to veto laws passed by the parliament.

Informal Powers

Among the president's informal powers is that which is conferred by the prestige of the office. The president is the only official elected by the nation at large, and this gives his demands great legitimacy. If the president is also charismatic, like de Gaulle, or a clever politician, like Mitterrand, he can use this legitimacy to manipulate the other parts of government. In addition, the president has patronage powers, which give him control of the bureaucracy in much the same way that the United States "spoils system" influences the American executive branch.[11]

The president, as in the parliamentary republics, presides over cabinet meetings (the cabinet is still called the *conseil des ministres*). For reasons of efficiency, decision-making rarely occurs in the whole cabinet. Rather, just as in Britain and Germany, decisions are made in cabinet committees (*conseils restreints*), where only those ministers affected by a specific policy issue are admitted to the discussion. This also served to keep the Communist ministers from joining in defense or foreign policy discussions during their par-

[10] Recounted by Nicholas Wahl, Harvard Conference on "Change and Continuity in Mitterrand's France," December 17, 1985.

[11] Except, or course, that unlike America, French bureaucrats are guaranteed a job of equivalent status if they are ousted for political reasons. See Chapter 14.

French troop reinforcements land in Algeria to bolster the large forces already engaged in the battle against nationalist guerrillas seeking total independence for a North African territory of Algeria.
SOURCE: AP/Worldwide Photos.

ticipation in the government of the Left from 1981 to 1984. The president also sets the agenda of cabinet meetings.

"Cohabitation"

As we noted earlier, the hybrid nature of the 1958 Constitution means that the executive shares most of its powers with the parliament. Essentially, this is because of the ambiguous position of the government. In that it is appointed by the president, but can be fired by the National Assembly, the government must be acceptable to both branches. Until 1986 the potential problems of this arrangement remained hypothetical, since presidents had always enjoyed friendly majorities in the parliament. Party discipline assured that the National Assembly would accept whomever the president nominated to the government. In 1986, however, a conservative alliance (RPR and UDF) won a narrow majority in

the National Assembly. As parliamentary and presidential terms do not coincide (they are five years and seven years, respectively), this meant that a conservative National Assembly had to come to terms with a Socialist president.

While the president had the option of calling new elections, the political climate would simply have assured the reelection of the same conservative alliance, a return to a stalemate situation, and a severe loss of prestige (and, therefore, power) for the president.[12] Mitterrand chose to let the election stand.

This situation forced the Socialist president to name a conservative prime minister and

[12] In a similar situation in 1877, the royalist president MacMahon dissolved a republican assembly, only to have the republicans reelected, leaving MacMahon deprived of prestige and influence. See Alfred Cobban, *A History of Modern France* (Harmondsworth: Penguin, 1965), vol. 3, chap.1.

cabinet, for no other would survive a motion of censure in the National Assembly. The problem then became: who would set national policies, the president or the prime minister? The Constitution is not explicit on this point, nor was precedent helpful. The last time a serious divergence between president and prime minister took place was when Jacques Chirac, Giscard's first prime minister (1974–76), tried to eclipse the president. Giscard simply fired him. Though they were from different parties, both were of the conservative coalition, and the conservative deputies simply accepted the president's preeminence. Giscard's UDF accepted the action because the president was head of the party, and the Gaullists accepted the firing of Chirac in deference to the principle of presidential government.[13]

What made the "cohabitation"—as the uneasy Socialist-conservative coexistence was called—work, was the decision by Mitterrand not to oppose the implementation of the conservative program. That program consisted mainly of de-nationalizing the companies taken over by the Socialists in 1982 (see Chapter 9). While Mitterrand announced his decision to accede to the "will of the people," more than likely it was based on a quite accurate calculation that the conservatives would fail to solve France's economic problems and thus would bear the brunt of public dissatisfaction in the 1988 presidential election.

Moreover, there had been a convergence of Socialist and conservative policies since 1981. The Socialists, who had started deregulating the French economy after 1982, began to have their doubts about nationalizations when the overall economy failed to improve with the newly profitable nationalized

companies.[14] The conservatives, for their part, were unwilling to abandon the welfare state (see Chapter 9). There were almost no differences on foreign policy. Thus, "cohabitation" took on an air of American politics when the president and Congress are controlled by different parties: There were differences to be sure, but there were grounds for agreement on fundamentals.[15]

THE CONSTITUTIONAL COUNCIL

A brief word needs to be said about the role of courts at the national level. France, like the rest of continental Europe, has a civil law system based on Roman law. This means that jurists, unlike those in the Anglo-Saxon common law system, see themselves as interpreters rather than makers of law. In most cases there is no concept of judicial review as it exists in the United States. That is, most courts cannot rule on whether or not a law is unconstitutional. Usually, a court can only decide whether a law has been applied properly in a particular case.

The exception to this principle is found in the *Constitutional Council*. The Constitutional Council, an innovation of the Fifth Republic, is composed of three judges appointed by the president of each house of parliament and three appointed by the president of the Republic, totaling nine. Members enjoy nonrenewable terms of nine years. In addition, any living former president of the republic may also sit on the Council. However, unlike the Supreme Court of the United States, there is no illusion in France that the Council

[13] On this episode, see Suleiman, "Presidential Government in France," in Suleiman and Rose, eds., *Presidents and Prime Ministers* (Washington, D.C.: American Enterprise Institute, 1980).

[14] For an explanation of this failure of public enterprise, see Feigenbaum, *The Politics of Public Enterprise*, chap. 6.

[15] Many Socialists, however, did not share this convergence of views and, at least verbally, remained committed to a Marxist vision of social change. This was especially true of the CERES faction of the party.

merely provides an objective interpretation of the Constitution. Rather, recourse to the Council is overtly political.[16]

During the first two decades of the Fifth Republic constitutional challenges were rare. Under Giscard d'Estaing, however, recourse to the Council was made easier (sixty deputies or sixty senators could invoke the Council) and the political opposition (the Left) began to use it to publicize their complaints (the conservative composition of the Council made rulings in the Left's favor next to impossible). Use of the Council became common after the Socialists achieved the majority in the National Assembly. Appeals by the UDF and RPR to the conservative Council were used to block Socialist legislation. For instance, nationalization of major industries was blocked temporarily by objections to the mode of financing the government purchase (nationalizations are legal under the French constitution so long as they are adequately compensated).[17] The Socialists learned from this experience and began filling vacancies with their supporters as they arose.

LOCAL GOVERNMENT

The most significant statement to make about French local government is that until 1982 there was very little of it. As we mentioned in previous chapters, France has been highly centralized since the advent of the absolutist kings. While the kings centralized France to consolidate their power, even progressive reforms took the form of increased centralization. As we mentioned in the last chapter, Louis XVI abolished local courts to curb the corrupt practices of the provincial aristocracy. Napoleon created a highly centralized administration not only to consolidate his own power, but also to create a highly efficient instrument of public service.

Early on, of course, this highly centralized system had its detractors, most often in quarters advocating liberal reforms. Tocqueville, perhaps the best known of these when he wrote in *The Old Regime and the French Revolution,* said that it was the intense centralization of the monarchs that made them especially vulnerable to overthrow, for by seizing Paris one could easily seize the whole country. He was, of course, in favor of extending democracy rather than simply advocating a less vulnerable *status quo.* Most of the critics of centralization have essentially had the same democratic motives, but more recent critics, observing the even more extreme hypercentralization of the Soviet Union, have also argued that the present French system is simply inefficient. Given the growing complaints about French centralization, what is perhaps a more interesting question is why there were no significant reforms until 1982, when the Socialists introduced new local powers in the *loi Deferre.*[18]

One reason for the maintenance of a highly centralized administration was ideological: As we mentioned in Chapters 10 and 11, centralization fit with the Jacobin notion of equality, assuring that citizens were subject to the same laws, no matter where in France they lived. This Jacobin ideology guided the thinking of the French Left, especially the Communists. On the Right, Bonapartists and later Gaullists saw a centralized administra-

---

[16] Increasingly, scholars of the U.S. Supreme Court have recognized the intrinsic political nature of the body. See Martin Shapiro, "The Supreme Court: From Warren to Berger," in Anthony King, ed., *The New American Political System* (Washington, DC: American Enterprise Institute, 1978).

[17] See John T. S. Keeler, "The French Constitutional Council," in Stanley Hoffmann and George Ross, eds., *The Mitterrand Experiment* (New York, 1987).

[18] Cf. Peter A. Gourevitch, *Paris and the Provinces* (Berkeley and Los Angeles: University of California Press, 1980), *viz.* chap. 11.

tion as the best way to marshal the country's resources in the name of the nation and, eventually, as the best way to thwart subnational particularism such as the Breton or Corsican separatist movements. (The Spanish ultimately saw decentralization as a way to achieve the same purpose when they devolved powers on regional assemblies in the Basque and Catalan areas: half a loaf was better than none.)

Moreover, the centralized system functioned reasonably well. This was partly because of the virtues of centralized organization: economies of scale, coherent policy-making, gains from standardization, and so on. Although centralization might, on the face of it, lead to inappropriate policies because Paris ministries were ignorant of local conditions, in fact, there was often a good deal of flexibility. Paris-appointed prefects would work with local officials, even if the latters' formal powers were weak.[19]

Nevertheless, by the 1970s, centralized administration had become quite unpopular.

Elections could be won almost solely by promising more power to the localities. Some reforms did indeed take place, albeit in a piecemeal fashion. Under the *loi Frey* of 1972, metropolitan France was divided into 21 regions with elective regional councils (departments were considered to be too small to be viable economic units) with some taxing and spending powers, while some other new units of government such as *communautés urbaines* or *syndicats à vocation multiple* ("urban communities" and "multipurpose associations") were also created.[20] Yet compared to American, German, or even Spanish local governments, the reform was paltry.

The major reform of France's local government had to wait until the arrival of the Socialists into power. It appears that at least one main reason for the long delay in local government reform was partisan politics. An important analysis argues that any reform of local government during the Fifth Republic would have meant some power-sharing with the political opposition. In this case, the conservatives, during their long period of hegemony, were reluctant to give significant powers to local governments that might be

---

[19] Cf. Jean-Pierre Worms, "Le Préfet et ses notables," *Sociologie du Travail*, July-September, 1966; Mark Kesselman, "Over-Institutionalization and Political Constraint: The Case of France," *Comparative Politics*, 3, 1 (1970).

[20] See Gourevitch, *Paris*, pp. 226 ff.

Mayors: "Interesting! How does it work?"
SOURCE: *Cahiers Français*, no. 220, March/April 1988.

controlled by leftists, especially communists.[21]

Understandably, the Left made decentralization part of their platform, although the Communists, for ideological reasons as well as a perceived weakness in electoral support, were less enthusiastic about the reform.

The reform came in the Deferre Law of 1982, with significant follow-up legislation in 1983 and 1984. The *loi Deferre,* followed by some twenty laws and two hundred decrees, increased the independent authority of the localities. Prior approval of local initiatives by the national government was no

longer necessary, although Paris could disapprove actions *a posteriori*. The reform abolished the old prefect system (Paris-appointed departmental governors) and local executive power was transferred to the presidents of departments and to presidents of regional councils (representing several departments), both offices being elective. Working with local elected officials were local civil servants, independent of the national administration. The 21 regions, each composed of several *départements,* created by the *loi Frey,* were given significantly greater powers (Figure 15.1). However, as of the writing of this book, it was not obvious that local governments would have the financial resources to be truly effective.

[21] *Ibid.,* pp. 228 ff.

Figure 15.1 Administrative Regions of France
SOURCE: *Cahiers Français,* no. 220, April/March 1988 (Supplement).

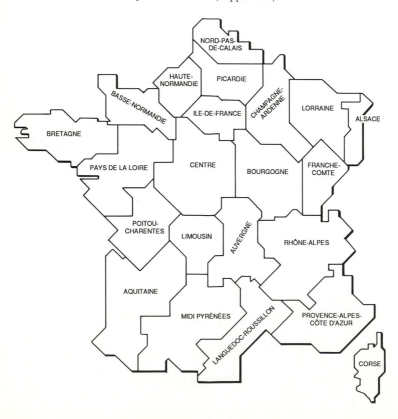

THE EUROPEAN COMMUNITY

The final level of the hierarchy of government is the international level. France was one of the original six members of the European Community (EC), an international organization with significant powers in the area of economic policy.[22] The principal treaty establishing these powers was the Treaty of Rome signed in 1957, creating the European Economic Community (EEC). The EEC was combined with the European Coal and Steel Community and Euratom, the European atomic energy organization, to form a single organization in 1967, now together called the European Community (EC).

The essential idea behind the European Community and especially behind the EEC was that the individual member countries were no longer economically viable or politically powerful because individually they were each too small. Since the Second World War they were dwarfed by the huge continental powers of the United States and Soviet Union. The idea was to gain the economic advantages of a huge single market represented by the American model and to create links of solidarity that would bolster the countries against external threats. Moreover, the millenium of European wars was expected to end with this new solidarity.

By far the most important advances were economic. Under the guidance of the Treaty of Rome, all internal tariffs in the EC were gradually dismantled (this is known as a "customs union") and a common external tariff schedule was agreed upon by all members. The most important effect was the stimulus to trade among the members, which resulted in significant economic benefits. The

new larger markets also served to stimulate the growth of European enterprises and to allow consumers the benefits of increased competition as well as economies of scale. Indeed, trade and GNP of member countries grew so stupendously that almost all the states of western Europe looked either to join the EC or to form some sort of association with it.

More importantly, the EC was more than a simple customs union. It was an attempt to create a supranational body to formulate and implement economic policy. The organization of the EC mimicked national government: The Council of Ministers served as a kind of European cabinet, the European Commission, appointed by the Council of Ministers, served as the head of the bureaucracy, the European Parliament deliberated on broad policy issues, and a European Court adjudicated decisions and complaints relating to EC rules and regulations. However, the real power of the EC government lay with the Council of Ministers, and thus with the Community's member governments, for the Council is composed of ministers of member governments and has the final say in all Community matters. Moreover, all members retain a veto so that in fact the Council does not represent a loss of sovereignty. Recently, however, the European Parliament has evolved in that direction. Originally, the Parliament was composed of delegations from member parliaments and had only an advisory role. Since 1984 members of the Parliament have been elected directly by the voters in each country, and they sit according to political tendency (e.g., French and German Christian Democrats sit together, as do Socialists from all member states), rather than as delegations from each state. The European Parliament can now accept or reject a small portion of the Community budget.

The only genuinely supranational policy that is obligatory for all members (besides the

[22] The original six members were France, West Germany, Italy, Belgium, the Netherlands and Luxembourg. They were joined by Britain, Ireland, Denmark in 1973, by Greece and Spain in 1981, and by Portugal in 1986.

tariff schedule) is the Common Agricultural Policy that is managed by EC institutions. More policies would have become genuinely supranational, that is, policies obligatory despite the objections of a minority of member states, had it not been for the French (and eventually the British, when they joined). De Gaulle refused to consider ceding any national prerogatives (see Chapter 16). The Common Agricultural Policy, under which agriculture is subsidized from a common fund and prices are set by the EC Commission, was approved by France, largely because it was economically beneficial. France paid less into the common fund than was received in subsidies by French farmers, and Germans paid more while receiving less. Thus, the CAP ended up being a device where the Germans subsidized the French. The Germans tolerated this on the basis of promoting the principle of European solidarity, and the French supported it because they gained economically. To date, however, there are no other common policies of the same supranational scope as the CAP, although many potential policies have been discussed. Moreover, since Spain, Portugal and Greece joined the EC, the French have not gained as much from the CAP.

Of course, there are many critics of the European Community. While political centrists normally favored the Common Market, it was criticized by both Right and Left. Originally, the small shopkeepers and other small inefficient businesses lobbied strongly against the Treaty of Rome, fearing cheaper and more efficient high-volume competition from abroad. Most of these were from the far Right of the French political spectrum and were followers of Pierre Poujade (see Chapter 12). Many Gaullists were also suspicious of the EC because of its potential threat to national independence.

On the Left, the Communists criticized the EC as simply a club of capitalists. Clearly,

there was some truth to this criticism. In the new Common Market, capital moved more freely than labor, which was hampered by language and cultural barriers. Investment capital could simply flow to the cheapest labor countries, and businessmen could threaten to move factories to where unions were most cooperative; it was much easier to move industries than for the various national labor unions with different traditions and ideologies to join forces and develop common strategies against multinational corporations.[23] As the Market became a *fait accompli* the left turned its attention to reforming, rather than rejecting, the European Community.

CONCLUSION

Like all countries, France's formal political institutions have been constantly evolving. Most dramatically, France followed the worldwide trend toward strong executives by adopting the Constitution of 1958. Under the auspices of this document the powers of parliament were severely circumscribed. When the president has a friendly majority in the National Assembly, he enjoys constitutional powers greater than any democratic executive. If, however, the majority in the lower house is opposed to the president, the precedent of cohabitation suggests that power will revert to the prime minister.

If the hidden fragmentation in national government has become more apparent in recent years, power has become even more decentralized at the local level. Political forces finally coalesced in 1982 to grant significant powers to localities, yet the national scale of France's economic problems proba-

---

[23] For a more detailed critique of the Common Market from the Left's perspective, see Stuart Holland, *Uncommon Market* (New York: St. Martin's, 1980).

bly meant that serious policy-making options would still remain in Paris.

In fact, the overall direction of problem solving has meant an international approach to macroeconomic policy. In this sense the European Community has offered French citizens a new range of possibilities in raising levels of prosperity, but administratively the EC imposes a supranational level of constraints on the formulation and implementation of public policy.

References and Suggested Readings

ASHFORD, DOUGLAS E. *Policy and Politics in France: Living with Uncertainty*. Philadelphia: Temple University Press, 1982.

GOUREVITCH, PETER A. *Paris and the Provinces*. Berkeley: University of California Press, 1980.

KESSELMAN, MARK. *The Politics of Uncertainty*. New York: Knopf, 1967

ROSE, RICHARD, AND EZRA SULEIMAN, EDS. *Presidents and Prime Ministers*. Washington, DC: American Enterprise Institute, 1980.

TARROW, SIDNEY, PETER KATZENSTEIN, AND LUIGI GRAZIANO, eds. *Territorial Politics in Industrial Nations*. New York: Praeger, 1978.

WILLIAMS, PHILIP M. *The French Parliament*. New York: Praeger, 1968 (reprinted by Greenwood Press in 1977).

16

> "I have always had a certain image of France."
>
> — Charles de Gaulle

> The law of *laissez-faire* [is] . . . the sister of fatality, the ally of wealth, and the accomplice of injustice.
>
> — GEORGES POMPIDOU

Policy: Foreign and Domestic

Perhaps what makes France so interesting are the contrasts it provides with both the United States and the other countries of Western Europe. These contrasts are evident in both foreign and domestic policies. In foreign policy France, more than any other country in Western Europe, has pursued a policy aimed at maximizing independence from the superpowers, while seeking a position of prominence in Europe and the Third World. In domestic economic policy the French state has played an equally distinctive role, a role more pronounced than in any other capitalist country save Japan.

FRENCH FOREIGN POLICY

French foreign policy, especially during the Fifth Republic, has been more consistent than that of most countries, and even the Socialists, who had little else in common with de Gaulle, shared many of his foreign policy concerns.[1] Essentially, these are themes that emphasize French "greatness" and French "exceptionalism."

Influence of Geography and History

The geography of France, unlike that of Germany, provided certain defensible frontiers so that security, while always significant, never quite dominated the domestic politics of the country.[2] It was neither as isolated as Britain nor as vulnerable as Germany. Consequently, the importance of the army was greater than in the former and less than in the latter.

The heritage of the wars of the Middle Ages left France a tradition of rivalry with

[1] Stanley Hoffmann, "Gaullism by Any Other Name," *Foreign Policy*, Winter 1984–85.

[2] Cf. Perry Anderson, *Lineages of the Absolutist State* (London: NLB, 1974), pp. 113–42; pp. 236–78. The notable exception to this description is that the Great Northern Plain, running from Moscow to Paris, created vulnerabilities not unlike those of Germany, and motivated a significant part of French foreign policy.

242

Britain that ultimately translated into a quest for global empire.[3] After the Franco-Prussian War (1870–71) rivalry with Germany dominated French security concerns. Always there would be the crosscurrents of a European or a world vocation. Sometimes oriented toward Europe, sometimes oriented to the world at large, French foreign policy would find its ultimate expression in the vision of Charles de Gaulle.

Gaullist Foreign Policy

The defeat of France in World War II was a shock. Until 1940 France had been considered the greatest military power on the European continent. No one expected the rapid collapse of French defenses in the face of the German onslaught in the spring of 1940.

When the Allies finally won, the position of de Gaulle's government as coequal victor was, in fact, more of a fiction than a reality. However, it became de Gaulle's aim, throughout his period of leadership, to restore France's great power status. To do so required the achievement of three interrelated goals. De Gaulle had to solve the crisis of de-colonization, establish France's independence from the superpowers, and restore the primacy of Europe.

Certainly the most traumatic foreign policy problem at the beginning of the Fifth Republic was that of de-colonization (although some would argue this was a *domestic* problem!). In the latter part of the nineteenth century France established an empire in Africa, for economic reasons as well to capture additional manpower and raw material resources

in the event of another war with Germany.[4] France's rivalry with the other major powers led it to establish colonies (and "protectorates") in the far flung areas of what is now referred to as the "Third World." France's most important colonies were in Indochina (Laos, Cambodia, Vietnam) and Africa (especially Algeria). France also exercised "trusteeships" in the Levant (Syria and Lebanon).

The victory of the democracies in 1945 made it very hard for them to deny democracy to the populations "of color" in the empire. Nevertheless, among the earliest acts of the French government after the war was the reassertion of the French presence on the periphery. Against American wishes de Gaulle moved to reestablish French rule in Indochina, which had been occupied by Japan during World War II, as he headed the Provisional Government preceding the Fourth Republic (1944–46). Almost at the very beginning of the postwar period Vietnamese nationalists fought against the reestablishment of colonial rule as they had fought against the Japanese occupation during the war.

As the cold war intensified, the communist ideology of the Vietnamese nationalists influenced the Americans to underwrite the French effort to reestablish their colony. A

---

[3] Arno Mayer argues that most of Europe was dominated by political relationships rooted in the Middle Ages until the end of the First World War. See his *The Persistence of the Old Regime* (New York: Pantheon Books, 1981).

[4] This was one of the justifications for imperialism in Africa given by Prime Minister Jules Ferry at the dawn of the Third Republic. The importance of economic motives behind the last century's imperialism has been the subject of much debate. The classic work in this regard is V. I. Lenin's *Imperialism: The Highest Stage of Capitalism* (New York: International Publishers, 1939), originally published in 1916. For a critique see Benjamin J. Cohen, *The Question of Imperialism* (New York: Basic Books, 1973). My own preferred explanation is that of E. J. Hobsbawm, *Industry and Empire* (Harmondsworth: Penguin, 1969), although the author focuses primarily on Great Britain. Hobsbawm emphasizes the interconnection of political and economic goals.

series of military defeats culminating in the route of French troops at Dien Bien Phu led the Fourth Republic to give up, and the Chamber of Deputies voted plenipotentiary powers to Prime Minister Pierre Mendes-France to negotiate French withdrawal in 1954.[5]

Almost at the same time as France was quitting Indochina, the Arab population in Algeria began to stir against the inequities of French rule in North Africa. Algeria had formally been divided into three French *départements,* with the French government maintaining that Algeria was as much a part of France as was Provence. While it was true that Algeria, unlike the protectorates of Tunisia and Morocco, had never been an independent country in the European sense, it was equally true that Arabs did not enjoy even legal equality with Algerians of European extraction during French rule. Even under the relatively progressive constitution of the Fourth Republic, Arabs were dubbed French "subjects," while Algerians of European ancestry enjoyed the status of "citizens," a legally superior status.[6] The reality of Algeria was that of a privileged European minority and a deprived Arab majority.

The uprising of Arabs in Algeria grew into a protracted and bloody struggle. The insurgents used terrorist techniques to frighten the Europeans into leaving, while the French army replied with increased repression and, eventually, torture. Not only was the war a drain on French resources, but it also rent the social fabric of the nation. By 1958 the problem seemed intractable to the deputies of the parliament. Political demonstrations grew more frequent and increasingly violent. Division over what to do about Algeria tore at the French polity like nothing since the Commune or perhaps even the revolution.[7] As we have recounted in previous chapters, the ultimate impact was the demise of the Fourth Republic and the return of Charles de Gaulle.

De Gaulle saw the handwriting on the wall. He soothed rioting Europeans in Algeria with an enigmatic "*Je vous ai compris*" ("I have understood you") and promptly set the machinery in motion to extricate France from North Africa. In the resort town of Evian, the new French president granted Algeria independence while assuring France privileged economic relations with the new country.[8] While the Evian accords were signed in 1962, they in fact reaffirmed a set of relationships that France had already established with the majority of its ex-colonies. Morocco and Tunisia had gained their independence in 1956, most of black Africa in 1960, and virtually all, with the exception of Guinea, maintained cordial—and economically privileged—relationships with France. Later, critics would call these relationships, which were quite beneficial to the former mother country "neo-colonialism."

Reestablishing French Independence

If de Gaulle had, once again, extricated France from difficult external circumstances while maintaining fundamentally democratic institutions, he is most remembered by Americans for his conflictual approach to the United States.

De Gaulle's conflicts with the United States

[5] For an excellent account of French foreign policy under the Fourth Republic, see Alfred Grosser, *La Quatrième République et sa Politique Exterieure,* (Paris, Armand Colin, 1961). See also, Guy de Carmoy, *Les Politiques Etrangères de la France, 1944–1966* (Paris: La Table Rond, 1967).

[6] Grosser, chap. 4.

[7] Cf. Miles Kahler, *Decolonization in Britain and France* (Princeton: Princeton University Press, 1984).

[8] These actions nearly cost de Gaulle his life, as disgruntled partisans of a French Algeria formed a secret terrorist organization (*l'Organisation de l'Armée Secrète*) and attempted assassination several times.

went back to the Second World War. First, the United States did not take his London-based government-in-exile very seriously. When the Roosevelt administration did finally distance itself from Vichy, the Americans sought to promote another general as head of the Free French.

It was de Gaulle's return to power in 1958 that created the most friction, however. His vision of France's international role simply did not complement American foreign policy. Most nettlesome for Washington was de Gaulle's decision to withdraw France from the integrated command structure of NATO in 1966. This did not mean that France withdrew from the Alliance, for de Gaulle maintained French commitment to defend its allies; but he refused to put French troops under the command of a foreign, that is, American, general, as the integrated military structure of NATO required.[9]

De Gaulle saw France as occupying the important role of mediator of East-West conflict. He pursued a rapproachment with the Soviet Union, despite his own fierce anticommunism, and directed France to become the first Western country to recognize the People's Republic of China. For de Gaulle, these established French independence, but in an atmosphere emotionally charged with cold-war Manicheeism, Americans saw de Gaulle's conservative *Realpolitik* as immoral neutralism. Ultimately, however, France's independence served American interests, as France provided the diplomatic good offices that allowed the United States to finally withdraw from Vietnam.

Europe

Central to the Gaullist vision of an independent France was the reestablishment of Europe as a focus of world politics. While de Gaulle spoke of Europe "from the Atlantic to the Urals," in fact, the reestablishment of Europe meant the European Community. While de Gaulle had no interest in a supra-national organization of any sort, he saw the Common Market as the first step in the reconstruction of Europe as an independent force in international affairs. The Community would be centered in France and Germany, the continent's two most powerful countries. Moreover, de Gaulle firmly rejected Britain as a member of Europe, not so much because of its historic empire, as because of its special relationship with the United States.[10]

De Gaulle promoted the EC largely because he felt that economic integration would not affect political independence. After 1966 the Treaty of Rome required that the Council of Ministers decide issues on the basis of majority voting, rather than unanimity. For de Gaulle, this compromised France's sovereignty so much that the General simply refused to accept this elimination of French veto power. Majority voting meant France might have to obey an EC decision that it had opposed, and this was unacceptable to the French president (the Treaty of Rome had, of course, been signed under the Fourth Republic). The other members of the Community gave in, and each country retained a veto.

---

[9] Cf. Michael M. Harrison and Mark G. McDonough, "Negotiations on the French Withdrawal from NATO," *FPC Case Studies,* no. 5 (Foreign Policy Institute, School of Advanced International Studies, The Johns Hopkins University, Washington, D.C., February, 1987).

[10] Rebuffed by the United States when de Gaulle wished to share, as did Great Britain, the secret to the atomic bomb, the general gave the go-ahead for French construction of its own bomb. This ultimately led to the development of other areas of technology and indirectly led to France's becoming a major arms maker. It also led France to leadership in the field of civilian nuclear power.

French Foreign Policy after De Gaulle

There are two major reasons why it has been useful to examine foreign policy under de Gaulle. First, it illustrates the importance of the president. Under the constitution of 1958, foreign policy could, indeed, be made by one person. With party discipline in a National Assembly occupied by the president's party (and eventually by a pro-de Gaulle coalition), one need only examine the president's ideas to describe foreign policy. (Of course, it should be added that Gaullism was also favorable to the most powerful interest groups in the society, but we will return to this issue later in the chapter.) Second, it is worth going into Gaullist foreign policy because little has changed since the General left power in 1969.

De Gaulle's two conservative successors took less of an interest in foreign policy. Pompidou, president from 1969 until his death in 1974, was more interested in domestic politics, and devoted his efforts to building up a solid party apparatus and developing links to the local level where Gaullism had been weak. He did manage to continue irking the United States by redeeming U.S. dollars into gold, weakening the American currency and—for this was the point—weakening U.S. hegemony in monetary affairs.

Giscard d'Estaing, president from 1974 to 1981, was the first non-Gaullist president, although he had served as de Gaulle's minister of finance by virtue of his economic expertise. Giscard was more willing to pursue a rapprochement with the United States. Because his term of office coincided with the oil crises of 1974 and 1979, he was faced with tremendous disruptions in the world economy. This put a premium on cooperation with the other industrialized countries, and some agreements were worked out. However, France refused to join the International Energy Agency, an organization of industrialized, oil-consuming countries that was paradoxically based in Paris. The IEA was viewed by Giscard as potentially disruptive of France's warm relations with Arab states, and this refusal was strongly reminiscent of General de Gaulle.

The situation changed somewhat with the accession of François Mitterrand to the presidency. Mitterrand's own fierce anticommunism, as well as his intent to isolate the French Communist Party, brought anti-Sovietism back to a premier place on the foreign policy agenda. This gave France the appearance of being the warmest supporter of the policies of the Reagan administration, a government with which it otherwise shared no common ground. Eventually, this anti-Soviet rhetoric also facilitated cohabitation, for the conservatives in parliament after 1986 had little reason to challenge Mitterrand in the area of foreign policy.

If the Socialists differed at all from their predecessors, it was in their policies toward the Third World. The Socialists were willing to make economic sacrifices to the benefit of less developed countries. Notably, they signed a very generous contract for Algerian natural gas at prices far in excess of the world market price. Socialists frequently supported Third World demands in international meetings for a New International Economic Order. However, as the French economy continued to stagnate, there was little even a socialist France could do for its neighbors to the south.

DOMESTIC POLICY: THE MACROECONOMY

As we discussed in Chapter 9, the dislocations in the world economy that became increasing pronounced after the oil crisis of 1973–74 have profoundly altered traditional practices in the area of economic policy. Demand stimulus policies that formed the bedrock of the conventional wisdom in the postwar era seemed only to stimulate inflation in the 1970s. More importantly, the relatively free trade of that era had served to link the industrial economies so that no country could easily go its own way. France discovered this belatedly, as the stimulative policies the Socialists inaugurated in 1982 increased the demand for imports so that deficit spending in France created more jobs abroad than at home.

The deadened economy of the 1980s seemed a sad end to what had seemed to be one of the world's economic success stories. France had grown stupendously since the war, dwarfing the growth of Britain and making a very good case for the French style of economic policy, a style based on a concept of state-led growth.[11]

French political institutions, as we have seen, were especially well suited to state interventionism in the national economy. Almost all of French history seemed to justify it. The achievement of Jean Baptist Colbert, Louis XIV's minister of finance, and his successors provided reference points for statist arguments. The innovations in banking and state-directed investment in the nineteenth century left France with a base upon which to build. As we noted in Chapter 14, France also devel-

[11] See especially John Zysman, *Governments, Markets and Growth* (Ithaca: Cornell University Press, 1983); Peter A. Hall, *Governing the Economy* (New York: Oxford University Press, 1986).

Inside the Bourse, the stock exchange of Paris.
SOURCE: Alain Keler/Sygma

oped an elite bureaucracy to carry out state development plans, a bureaucracy which for many reasons enjoyed the political clout to get things done. Moreover, after the Fifth Republic was established, the interest group-oriented parliament was too weak to interfere with the projects of the executive and its technocratic bureaucracy.

The two major forces governing French economic policy in the postwar period were the Planning Commission (*Commissariat au Plan*) and the ministerial bureaucracies, especially the ministries of Finance, the Economy, and Industry. All of these were coordinated by the office of the prime minister.

Planning

France's capacity to pursue long-range economic planning has frequently been credited with the country's tremendous growth after World War II.[12] This was not Soviet-style central planning, but rather, "indicative" planning. Indicative planning was a kind of huge market survey done every five years, where major producer groups were invited by the French government to provide information on their market projections for the next five years and to elaborate their needs for inputs. Thus, auto makers would be asked how much steel and other materials they would need, and those material producers would be informed of the expected demand for their products so that they could prepare to produce adequate amounts. The idea was to avoid bottlenecks that might slow down industrial growth or force companies to look to foreign suppliers when jobs might be had by French workers. The French state,

in addition, undertook the commitment to make capital available to key industries that would have spread effects on the rest of the economy, and to provide infrastructure where necessary.[13]

Planning did well during the first two decades of the postwar period. Or at least, the best years of French economic growth occurred when planning was most active. However, as the economy grew, it became more complex. Options supporting one growth strategy would help some industries and hurt others. Consensus crumbled and conflicts became more intense among different segments of French society.[14]

Planning also became a kind of implicit criticism of the government. Establishing five-year targets only highlighted the government's failure when those targets were not achieved.[15] As France became increasingly integrated into the world economy, it became dependent on the outside world for markets and supplies. These were harder to predict and impossible to control. Finally, under Giscard d'Estaing, a president ideologically opposed to state intervention, planning receded to little more than a symbolic role.

The Bureaucracy and the Economy

French bureaucrats are among the most talented and well trained of all developed countries. It was, therefore, reasonable to expect that if state intervention would work well anywhere, it would work well in France. For a while, it did. This was not only because the French planning mechanism allowed the administrative apparatus to accurately target and assist potential areas of industrial

---

[12] See especially Andrew Schonfield, *Modern Capitalism* (New York: Oxford University Press, 1969), chap. V. See also Stephen S. Cohen, *Modern Capitalist Planning: The French Model* (Berkeley and Los Angeles: University of California Press, 1977); and Hall, *Governing the Economy.*

[13] See John Zysman, *Political Strategies for Industrial Order* (Berkeley and Los Angeles: University of California Press, 1977), chap. III.

[14] Hall, chap. 6.

[15] Feigenbaum, *The Politics of Public Enterprise,* pp. 110–13.

growth, but also because the system of elite recruitment facilitated the task. The mechanism of *pantouflage* discussed in Chapter 14 meant that private and public sectors would be populated by executives who knew each other from school, who spoke the same language and who more or less thought the same way. The tendency was to run French economic policy in the interest of big business.[16] This, however, was an improvement over the policies of the Third Republic, which favored the inefficient sectors of small-scale ("Malthusian," in French terminology) agriculture and manufacturing.

The Crisis

The oil crisis of 1973–74 was only the most obvious manifestation of a series of relationships that were affecting the shape of the world economy. The oil crisis was, in fact, a price explosion that forced a transfer of resources to the oil-producing countries and the huge multinational oil companies. It could only have been accomplished by public and private cartels that limited competition and reduced output. This was a situation that was symptomatic of the general trend in the advanced industrial economies.[17]

Some analysts have argued that the stagnation that has become chronic since the oil crisis is, in fact, due to a crisis in a world economy based on mass production.[18]

[16] See Suleiman, *Politics, Power and Bureaucracy,* chap. XII.

[17] This is a controversial analysis supported by the writings of such economists as John Kenneth Galbraith, and was also accepted by the Socialists when they came to power in 1981. Many American economists dispute these contentions and argue that the market, left to its own devices, would become more competitive.

[18] See, for instance, Michael Piore and Charles Sabel, *The Second Industrial Divide* (New York: Basic Books, 1984). For a critical appraisal, see Robert Boyer, "The Eighties: The Search for Alternatives to Fordism," Sixth Annual Conference of Europeanists, Washington, DC, October 30–November 1, 1987.

Briefly, with the rise of the newly industrializing countries such as Brazil, Taiwan, and South Korea, as well as the presence of the already industrialized producers in Japan, Europe, and North America, there are simply more goods being produced than can be consumed in mass markets. In a world of overcapacity, workers are laid off, and the advanced countries have run persistently high levels of unemployment. These, in turn, drive up the expenses of the welfare state and exacerbate the tax burden on those industries that do manage to find markets for their products.

The present industrial crisis is unlike any in the past, and traditional economic theories have not offered very convincing clues as to what should be done. In this atmosphere of uncertainty, partisan politicians have returned to traditional ideologies to comprehend the world around them. Socialists looked to nationalization of major industries as a solution to the crisis, while conservatives argued for a return to "free" markets. The results of both the Socialist and conservative experiments in macroeconomic policy have not been encouraging.

The initial reaction of the Socialists to economic stagnation was nationalization. They reasoned that French industries were losing their competitive edge because French businesses were not investing. Plant and equipment were not being modernized and very little was being invested in research. Since businesses were not investing, the state *had* to do so, so it took over the lethargic private enterprises.

They soon discovered that modernizing meant replacing personnel with machines and closing down factories because demand had been reduced. This meant that unemployment became the principal cost of modernization.

The unprecedented levels of unemployment (unprecedented since the Great Depression) quickly disillusioned Socialist supporters, and the right easily won control of the legislature in 1986.

As we mentioned in Chapter 9, the principal difference between right and left in economic policy was the issue of privatization/nationalization. The right argued that by selling off the nationalized firms the state would make enough money to reduce taxes. With a smaller tax burden, French industries could become more competitive, restore profits and have money left over to reinvest. In two years in office the right sold off more industries than Britain's Margaret Thatcher did in ten. The industries were sold—by and large—for three times more than the Socialists paid for them, indicating, at least, that state ownership had hardly been injurious to the health of the firms.

Certain aspects of the French economy improved during the conservative interregnum from 1986 to 1988. Net capital investment rose and unemployment levelled off. Moreover, the privatizations were successful—in the sense that the conservative government was able to find buyers for the nationalized firms they chose to privatize.

However, it is not clear that the improvements in the French economy had very much to do with the policies undertaken by the conservatives. Many of the improvements were a reaction to changes that had been initiated under the Socialists, especially deregulation and modernization of capital markets and industries. Moreover, the "success" and popularity of the privatization program had more to do with the fact that shares in the previously nationalized firms were sold at bargain prices. After the world stock market crash in October 1987, interest in privatization cooled.

When President Mitterrand was reelected in 1988, he declined to renationalize the privatized firms, or to continue the privatization program. He cited the proximity of new developments in the European common market as reason not to "shake up" the French economy any further. More than likely, he realized that neither nationalization nor privatization had much to do with curing the ills of the French economy.[19]

CONCLUSION

Both in foreign and domestic policies, France provides interesting contrasts. In foreign policy French decision-makers, and especially Charles de Gaulle, have been preoccupied with asserting a special role for their country. France's concern for national independence has proved nettlesome for the United States and occasionally trying for its European allies. Fundamentally, however, France has been a staunch defender of Western values.

Economically, France's statist approach to the development of industry and commerce has earned kudos, while recently attracting criticism from politicians on the right. Conservatives and Socialists agreed on the indicative planning associated with the postwar "miracle," but the changes of the 1970s and 1980s emphasized that the old solutions of both right and left were inadequate to problems that have persisted since the oil crisis of 1973.

References and Suggested Readings

CERNY, PHILIP G., AND MARTIN SCHAIN, eds. *Socialism, the State, and Public Policy in France.* New York: Methuen, 1985.

COHEN, STEPHEN S. *Modern Capitalist Planning.* Berkeley: University of California Press, 1977.

---

[19] In 1992 the members of the European Community were scheduled to implement the Single Market Act, which would eliminate all remaining trade barriers and consequently subject most French industries to very severe competition.

FEIGENBAUM, HARVEY B. *The Politics of Public Enterprise*. Princeton: Princeton University Press, 1985.

HALL, PETER. *Governing the Economy*. New York: Oxford University Press, 1986.

HOFFMANN, STANLEY. *Gulliver's Troubles*. New York: McGraw-Hill, 1968.

KOLODZIEJ, EDWARD A. *French International Policy under De Gaulle and Pompidou*. Ithaca: Cornell University Press, 1974.

ZYSMAN, JOHN. *Governments, Markets, and Growth*. Ithaca: Cornell University Press, 1983.

_____. *Political Strategies for Industrial Order*. Berkeley: University of California Press, 1977.

III

WEST GERMANY

17

The German Situation

In Germany, politics comes with the territory. East Germany, which calls itself a "democratic republic," features a political system not much different from that of the Soviet Union, while West Germany, formally known as the Federal Republic, features one that closely resembles the systems of Britain and France. This is nothing new for Germans. Territorial and political questions have been closely intertwined in their history. The partition of the nation serves as a constant reminder of the past that led to that outcome. It also reminds each half of its respective ties to foreign patron-like powers. While East Germany is only a minimally sovereign country, West Germany is not sovereign to the same degree as is France or Britain either.

Unlike Britain, Germany has not enjoyed the benefit of a moat of oceanic waters. It has not been allowed to thrive, or to wither, in splendid isolation from the outside world. External influences have burned themselves into the face of Germany. Major north-south as well as east-west routes of trade and warfare have run through German territory, bringing in many foreign customs and armies while also luring Germans away from home. Through all of this, Germany has rarely found the time to put its own house in order undisturbed, or to nurture a sense of its own identity that was neither defensive nor aggressive. Geography may not be destiny, but it does not deal its cards randomly.

In the first half of the nineteenth century, when Britain and France already enjoyed the benefits of firmly established nation-states, the area of Germany was largely that: a "geographical expression" devoid of a national government; a patchwork of independent states held together by cultural attachments rather than by political force. Germany was a nation without a state. The attempts to fashion a state for that nation proved a traumatic experience, not only for Germans but also for their neighbors.

Germany, it is often said with a tone of lament, has not had a revolution. Yet few countries have tried as many different regimes. Germany provides a historical laboratory of political experiments. Just consider a German born around the turn of the century. Such a person, provided he or she managed

255

The Berlin Wall, Built in 1961 by East Germany.
SOURCE: UPI/Bettmann Newsphotos.

to survive the perilous political upheavals, witnessed in a single lifetime nearly the full range of regimes that politics has to offer. They were, in the order of appearance: a constitutional monarchy (1871–1918), a pluralistic republic (1919–33), a totalitarian dictatorship (1933–45), and after several years of foreign occupation, a renewed democracy in the Western half (1949—) and a Soviet-style dictatorship in the East (1949—). To put this pace of regime turnover in perspective, note that the United States elected as many presidents between 1912 and 1950 as Germany numbered political regimes.

Every one of those turns of Germany's political road either followed on the heels of dramatic events in world politics or precipitated events of far reaching consequences. As Germans have learned, the outside world intrudes on their domestic politics; and much of the outside world has felt the brunt of Germany in return.

Germany offers a tempting subject for drawing historical lessons and playing what-if games. The dominant school of thought

Figure 17.1   Location of the Federal Republic of Germany in Europe and the World.
SOURCE: *Facts about Germany*, p. 11.

attributes that country's "erratic behavior" largely to the triumph of authoritarian politics over the forces of liberalism that sparked the American and French revolutions, and that gained momentum more gradually in Britain.[1] It was under a "feudal industrial"

[1] In addition to Stern, see Ralf Dahrendorf, *Society and Democracy in Germany*. Garden City, NY: Doubleday, 1967.

. . . In the cataclysms of the twentieth century, she played a decisive role; without the erratic thrusts of German power, neither World War would have occurred; without the two wars, no Bolshevism, no National Socialism, no Cold War, and no divided Germany. This is not to say that Germany was responsible for these events, but that if in the decades of its ascendancy, Germany had pursued a different policy, the configuration of the world would now be profoundly different.

SOURCE: Fritz Stern, *The Failure of Illiberalism* (Chicago: Chicago University Press, 1971), p. xiii.

state that Germany entered the modern age. In a sense, it represents a case of prolonged adolescence under a sometimes benevolent, but at other times malevolent parental regime. The failure to grow up liberal created tensions both at home and in Germany's relationships with the outside world. These tensions ultimately exploded in two world wars and cost both Germany and the world dearly. Only with a great deal of prodding from outside, and under the watchful eyes of its neighbors, has Germany finally, at least in its Western half, settled into a pattern of liberal democracy.

However late the blessings of the modern age may have arrived in Germany, it must be admitted that many triggered rapid developments, be it nation-building, industrialization, the formation of political parties, mass participation or scientific inventions and artistic expressions. No country proceeds smoothly or with one revolutionary stroke from the traditional to the modern age. If anything, Germany is a case of breakneck, rather than retarded, development. Instead of too little and too late, it may be a case of too much and too quickly, of a "restless" country undergoing constant revolution without a respite.[2]

Far from channelling or dominating these "revolutions," the forces of traditional authority in Germany found themselves on the defensive. In the hour of crisis they acted timidly and surrendered quickly. In the twilight of the monarchy in 1918 and of the Weimar Republic in 1933, populist pressure swept aside the forces of authority with ease. So we might ask: Is the lesson of the German experience the mischief of too much authority or of too little? Is it a case of traditional forces misdirecting a nation on its way into the

[2] For this kind of view, see Michael Stürmer, *Das ruhelose Reich: Deutschland 1866–1918* (Berlin: Severin & Siedler, 1983).

modern age, or a case of the forces of modernity exposing their destructive side?

References and Suggested Readings

Facts about Germany: The Federal Republic of Germany, 5th ed. Gütersloh: Bertelsmann, 1985. (Available from the German Information Center, New York.)

German Tribune. (A weekly review of the German press, translated into English; relies heavily on the *Frankfurter Allgemeine,* one of the prestige papers, and *Die Zeit,* a highly respected weekly.)

NOELLE-NEUMANN, ELISABETH. *The Germans: Public Opinion Polls 1967–1980.* Westport: Greenwood, 1981.

SCHWEITZER, CARL-CHRISTOPH et al., eds. *Politics and Government in the Federal Republic of Germany: Basic Documents.* Leamington Spa: Berg, 1984.

18

Unlucky the land that has no heroes.
No, unlucky the land that needs heroes.
— BERTOLT BRECHT (1898–
1956), a dialogue in *Life
of Galileo*

A Restless Nation in the Middle of Europe

As young as the Federal Republic may be, Germany has been in the news for at least 2,000 years. The defeat of Roman legions A.D. 9 in dense forests northeast of the Rhine shocked the Roman Empire, while creating a German folk hero, Arminius, among the victors. The battle called attention to the "Germanic" tribes, whose life and character received an admiring notice later in a book entitled *Germania* by the Roman historian Tacitus.

THE ROMAN EMPIRE IN GERMANY

Indeed, the admiration was mutual. No outside influence has made a more lasting impression on Germany than did the Roman Empire. In time to come Germany's supreme ruler would claim the title Caesar Augustus—*Kaiser* in the vernacular—and his realm would be referred to as the Holy Roman Empire of the German Nation. In other words, Germany took the mantle of Rome, of a Rome to be sure that had con-

verted to Christianity since the days of the original Caesar.

In A.D. 800, an easy date to remember, the Frankish king Charlemagne went to Rome to receive the pope's blessing as emperor of an area that covered large chunks of France, Germany and Italy. In this extension, the empire did not survive its founder, although it remained an ideal; indeed, the European Economic Community formed in 1957 looks remarkably similar to the geographical outline of Charlemagne's realm. Its western part formed the nucleus of modern France, its eastern part that of Germany. There the imperial tradition continued when Otto, leader of the Saxons, was crowned emperor by the pope in A.D. 962.

From then on, as a rule, German kings wore the imperial crown. German history would be irrevocably tied to that supranational symbol. It is well to remember that this was not a "German Empire" but a "Roman Empire." Germans were a part of it, among others, and a German wore the crown, but not by any German right, rather by a sacral blessing provided by the Church. That em-

259

pire lasted almost a thousand years, until 1806, when it was dissolved after the crushing blows of Napoleon's conquest.

The Empire was never a tightly centralized regime. More a confederation, it accommodated a variety of rival states, ranging from free cities along the North Sea coast to archdioceses along the Rhine, to independent counties, duchies, and even kingdoms like those of Bavaria, Saxony, Austria and, later, Prussia. It arguably represented the most diverse confederation assembled under one political roof and sharing a vague sense of belonging to the same nation. How that sense survived at all amidst the relentless territorial splintering boggles the mind. Pluralism, to use a modern term, was an everyday experience within the Empire. The emperor was powerless, for example, to impose a common religion on his subjects when, in the sixteenth century, the Reformation challenged Roman Catholicism. While many territories in the north of Germany went Protestant, many in the south stayed with Roman Catholicism. What each prince managed to do in his territory, what the French king did for France, the English king for England, the emperor could not do for Germany. Religion, it was resolved at the *Reichstag,* the gathering of the 240 or so independent states forming the Empire, was a matter for sub-imperial authorities in Germany to decide.

This privilege exacted a terrible price soon afterwards. Lacking a powerful central authority, the Empire was ravaged by a civil war that turned into a European showdown between the political forces and armies of the Reformation and those of the Roman Catholic Counter-Reformation. With Sweden, Denmark and France joining in, to undermine the Empire as much as to assist their beleaguered religious brethren, the Thirty Years War (1618–48) left Germany scorched and bloodsoaked. Its population was decimated by a war of appalling cruelty, as re-

lated by Grimmelshausen's famous novel, *Simplicissimus.* Already weak at the top, the Empire now suffered from atrophy in its limbs as well. It took over 100 years for Germany to replenish the population losses.

The Westphalian Peace of 1648 sanctioned the sovereignty of the territorial lords of the Empire, including the right to conclude alliances with one another and with foreign powers. By now there were roughly 350 independent territories, and their number would swell rather than shrink in the future. Yet, one should not conclude that the Empire had been read its last rites. After all, the key power within it, the Habsburgs of Austria, wore the crown. The rest of Europe nevertheless grew accustomed to a Germany that posed no threat to anyone. Any significant change in that status quo would not be accepted by them without a fight. That was the message between the lines of the Westphalian treaties.

THE RISE OF PRUSSIA

While Germany as a whole lingered in a political coma, life on its eastern frontier began to stir. Centered in the border region around Berlin, Brandenburg—better known later as Prussia—rose in the eighteenth century to become the major challenger for supremacy within the Empire. No doubt, Prussia was no cradle of parliamentary government or democracy. It was a monarchy in which the king ruled, not just reigned, while others decided policy. "Reason as much as you like, but obey," was the motto.

Authoritarian, Prussia was; a formidable military power, too, to the fear and envy of many of its neighbors. In an age when war was the sport of kings, with or without parliaments, Prussia played the game as well as anyone. The landed nobility, the *Junkers* as they were called, buttressed the king's rule, their key payoff being leading positions in the army and the administration. A "smoking cabinet" at times served as a council for the king to seek advice and consent from the *Junker* class.

Surprisingly, perhaps, Prussia was also a beacon of enlightened and humane government. It fashioned the institution of a modern civil service: professional, free of corruption, and efficient. Prussian courts reached judgments unobstructed by political pressure. Frederick the Great (1740–86) abolished torture as well as censorship of the press. Rule of law became a hallmark of the Prussian state. The Prussian General Law of the Land spelled out limits of police authority and state power.

Indeed, Prussia was a rare voice against religious fanaticism and for religious tolerance. In 1685, when the French king expelled the Protestant Huguenots, Prussia offered them a haven; it did the same for Jews driven from Austria. There was no suppression of the Catholics by the Protestant Church in Prussia. "Let everyone find salvation in his own fashion," Frederick the Great proclaimed. It was in Prussia where Jews, formally emancipated in 1812, felt welcome. True, tolerance paid dividends; the French Protestants and the Jews who settled in Prussia proved a boon to its economy and culture.[1]

Capable of sweeping reforms, the Prussia of the early nineteenth century was a country where servitude had been abolished, where economic feudalism was dismantled, where cities and towns enjoyed a wide measure of local self-government, and where eight years of schooling as well as military service for males were compulsory. In these domains, as well as before the law, equality made large and early strides in Prussia. In the wake of the

1848 revolution, a constitution would be granted providing for a parliament and elections.

A NATION-STATE FOR GERMANY

The revolutions in America (1776) and France (1789) reverberated in Prussia and other parts of Germany. Demands for guarantees of basic rights, a constitution limiting the power of government, and citizen participation through elections began to gather force. At the same time, the invasion of Europe by Napoleon's armies, while exporting some of the revolutionary principles, also stirred up the dormant sense of national identity in German lands. In the "war of liberation" from French occupation, it was not just the Prussian military but the German nation that was roused to duty. Just as Napoleon led a levée en masse, those trying to defeat him also mobilized the masses. The military—especially in Prussia—and the nation would never be the same again.

It was, of course, not just Napoleon's fault (or his credit) that German nationalism stirred. A certain cultural awakening preceded him, with writers like Goethe and philosophers like Kant making German literature and philosophy respectable for the educated in German lands. The Romantic poets revived respect for Germany's cultural heritage. The brothers Grimm went out to collect German folktales from their contemporaries and record them for posterity; few German children have been reared without hearing of those often "grim" tales. Meanwhile, economic development was tugging at the innumerable strings imposed by territorial divisions. The removal of tariffs hindering trade and commerce within Germany was loudly demanded. Industrialization began to turn the wheels of Germany's political unification.

Pressures to create a German nation-state

[1] See Christian Graf von Krockow, *Warnung vor Preussen* (Berlin: Severin & Siedler, 1981).

went hand in hand with demands for constitutional government. The monarchical rule prevailing in most German territories, including Prussia, stood in the way of both at the beginning of the nineteenth century. It is sometimes not clear what those rulers feared more: German nationalism or liberalism. In 1848, a revolution led by middle-class liberals shook that rule and paved the way for a constitutional convention. Meeting in the Paulskirche in Frankfurt, the assembled deputies proposed a constitution for a yet-to-be-united Germany. The proposal, which envisioned a nation-state that would exclude Austria, stipulated a parliamentary monarchy, with the lower house to be chosen by popular elections. The Prussian king was to serve as emperor of the new German nation.

But during the time that it took the deputies to agree on that proposal, the old rulers recovered their strength and quashed the revolution. The Prussian king contemptuously refused the "honor" of the imperial crown, branding it as reeking of the gutter. Even so, the spirit of 1848 did not perish; denied and suppressed, it nonetheless created nearly irresistible pressures for change. The yearning for national unity and the demands for a liberal-parliamentary form of government confronted the old order with an inescapable challenge. Even Prussia bent, conceding a constitution to its citizens barely a year after the king turned down the imperial crown. True, it did not yield on the principle of parliamentary responsibility or mass suffrage, but it granted an elected parliament, which

---

It is not through speeches and majority resolutions that the great questions of our time are decided—that was the big mistake of 1848 . . .—but through blood and iron.

SOURCE: Otto von Bismarck (1815–98), prime minister of Prussia, speech in 1862.

soon would flex its muscle; it also provided for a prime minister. The incumbent of that office would tie Prussia's destiny to that of Germany.

Full of bravado, Otto von Bismarck made his debut as Prussian prime minister in 1862 with his blood-and-iron speech to parliament. It sounded ruthless and menacing, but probably did not miss the historical truth of nation-building by much. Note that just as Bismarck was speaking, the United States was in the midst of a civil war that would make the Union a nation. Neither Britain nor France owed their national unity to speeches or resolutions. Moreover, Bismarck held more cards than brute military force. By deft diplomacy he planned to divide and conquer the opposition to unification. There was also the growing economic prowess of Prussia. The British economist John Maynard Keynes later remarked that it was more a question of "coal and steel" than of "blood and iron." Industrial power would plow under the old agrarian world.

Yet as a nation among others, a German nation-state, it was clear, could only be formed in defiance of the international order that had prevailed since the end of the Thirty Years' War. No doubt the rumbling of the Russian bear, the huffing of the British fleet, and the rattling of Austrian sabers had intimidated the unifiers in 1848. Buying himself the favor of Russia first, and finding a convenient ally in unification-eager Italy, from 1864 to 1871 Bismarck took on, in quick succession, Denmark, Austria and France, leaving England with no chance to intervene.

The war against France in 1870–71 brought in line the reluctant southern German states and swayed an unenthusiastic Prussian king to accept the imperial crown, as it were. So the nation-state came about by a "revolution from above," as opposed to the unsuccessful "revolution from below" in 1848. The princes of the sovereign German

The Emperor of the Newly Unified Germany, Wilhelm I, Returning to Berlin, 1871.
SOURCE: The Bettmann Archive.

states agreed to a confederation, and the constitution never even mentioned the word "nation." To many, this new empire looked suspiciously like a Greater Prussia, what with king, prime minister, and bureaucracy of Prussia in charge of the German empire, not to mention the Prussian army. No matter. The national dream, which briefly came to life in 1848, had been fulfilled; constitutional demands had been met, halfway in some respects, more than expected in others.

THE PRUSSIAN-GERMAN MONARCHY (1871–1918)

The new empire had a national parliament, named after the institution of the previous empire, the *Reichstag*, with legislative and fiscal powers. Its members, moreover, were elected by universal and equal male suffrage, a move that few had demanded and that shocked many. It was Bismarck who pressed for this unprecedented grant of the franchise. Why? To gain the support of the masses for the new Empire and to win their partisan hearts for the Conservatives rather than the Liberals. In that regard Bismarck thought like his Conservative counterpart in Britain, Benjamin Disraeli.

No matter the motive, Prussian authoritarianism would have to contend from now on with a growing mobilization of the masses in the new state. The unintended and, for Bismarck, unwelcome consequence of his generosity was that the partisan voices of those masses soon rang loudly in the Reichstag, and from all corners of the political hexagon. The quickly formed party spectrum comprised just as many parties as did the light spectrum colors: two kinds of Conservatives: one deeply unhappy with the Prussian-German merger, the other agreeable; also two kinds of liberals: the National liberals, the champions of German nationalism, versus the progressives, thwarted by Bismarck in their quest for a more liberal constitution; then, upset and fearful of its minority status, the Center, the political action committee of German Catholicism; and finally, the most radical party, widely suspected of fomenting social unrest and political revolution, the Social Democrats.

This party system took hold of the German electorate almost as swiftly as the Prussian armies conquered Austria and France. Practically overnight, Germany entered national adulthood as well as the modern age of mass politics. Stepping into the twentieth century, the Prussian-German Empire was ensnarled by a web of parties and interest groups. The old authoritarian recipes for governing proved of little use in such a pluralistic system. True, the head of the government, the *Chancellor,* got his job from the *Kaiser,* the emperor. And it was the emperor who could fire him, not the parliament. There was no provision for a parliamentary vote of no-confidence, the essential characteristic of a parliamentary system. Still, it must be recognized that the chancellor could not expect to get much done without or against parliament. Like it or not, the chancellor had to build coalitions, not in any formal sense, but certainly in an *ad hoc* manner, like an American president dealing with Congress. It is fair to say that "the art of government consisted of making deals with the parties and securing majorities in the Reichstag without becoming dependent on them."[2]

While influential, the political parties nevertheless did not govern. They stayed in the waiting room. Much has been made of the missing parliamentary responsibility of the chancellor; that with it, the Empire would have steered in a different, less catastrophic direction. But the truth is that the parties never pressed this demand to the breaking point—and some opposed it in principle. It must also be acknowledged that the parties would have faced a formidable task in forming a government. They were deeply split among themselves, with none near a majority of seats. As it was, the parties in the Reichstag could wield influence without having to shoulder responsibility, a bargain too good to jeopardize for the sake of a constitutional principle.

WORLD WAR I (1914–18)

On the eve of World War I, the Germany that had been the least among equals of the European powers laid claim to the number-one rank. The furious pace of industrialization, technological progress and social mobilization in the half century since 1871 gave Germany a sensation of unprecedented political prowess that was hard to restrain. Gone was the day when a Bismarck could execute cold-blooded but rational *Realpolitik*. Now, accompanied by cheers in the Reichstag, the foreign secretary, and later chancellor (1900–09), Bernhard von Bülow, promised a

The times when the German conceded one of his neighbors the earth [Russia], and to another the sea [England], and reserved for himself the heaven, where the pure doctrine presides—these times are over . . . We do not wish to put anyone in the shadow, but we demand our place in the sun.

SOURCE: Bernhard von Bülow (1849–1929), foreign secretary, speech in 1897.

[2] Michael Stürmer, *Das ruhelose Reich: Deutschland 1866–1918* (Berlin: Severin & Siedler, 1983), p. 107.

more hot-blooded and adventurous course, by claiming a "place in the sun" for Germany.

Impudent and imprudent, as it must look to a neutral observer, Germany discarded the restraints that Bismarck had urged for a nation hemmed in by "envious and distrustful neighbors." A big and boastful buildup of the navy challenged British supremacy on the high seas and sank any hope of an Anglo-German alliance, which would have calmed German fears of encirclement. Their frequent colonial skirmishes notwithstanding, Britain and France agreed to an *entente cordiale,* aimed against Germany. Add to that the alliance between autocratic Russia and democratic France, and a volatile Germany was left with the moribund Austro-Hungarian Empire as its sole friend. Anticipating a two-front war, Germany adopted a military strategy that envisioned a lightning strike against France before England could assist, and before Russia put armies into the field. With timing all so critical, Germany had to strike first in order to have any chance of winning a war that was widely expected all over Europe to come sooner or later.

World War I ended with Germany defeated and in a state of near-revolution. The awesome-seeming monarchy capitulated, more than it was overthrown, and Germany found itself in the doghouse of world politics instead of the sun. At home, the war had sundered a tenuous alliance of domestic forces. The extremes on right and left grew noisier, while the prospects for governing this unruly empire dimmed. The Kaiser abdicated, and political authority fell into the laps of the political parties. The strongest of them was the SPD (Social Democrats), led by a very pragmatic figure, Friedrich Ebert, who abhorred revolution. The SPD quickly joined forces with the army high command to quash a Bolshevik-type revolution as well as uprisings from renegade military units (*Freikorps*).

THE WEIMAR REPUBLIC (1919–33)

As the victorious Allies drafted a peace treaty in Versailles, Germans elected a national assembly to draft a new constitution for what was now a republic. The delegates convened in Weimar, far from the din of the revolutionary fighting still going on in Berlin, and evoked the spirit of Germany's most illustrious poets, Goethe and Schiller. The constitution that they designed was a curious hybrid.

On one hand, it emphasized the parliamentary principle: The chancellor would be responsible to the Reichstag through the vote of no-confidence. On the other hand, the constitution also set up an American-style president, popularly elected and invested with sweeping powers, including the hiring and firing of the chancellor, dissolution of the Reichstag and the emergency powers (Article 48), on which government would heavily rely in times of crisis. Oddly enough, the constitution makers appeared oblivious to the problem of creating majorities in parliament that would make the republic governable. The electoral system mandated "proportional representation" of an extreme kind. It allowed for parliamentary representation of even the tiniest parties. For an already badly splintered party system, more of the disease was prescribed instead of a cure. Far from compressing them, the Weimar party spectrum magnified and multiplied the divisions of German society.

What had been covered up under the monarchy now broke into the open: the inability of the parties in the Reichstag to form authoritative governments. Chancellors in the Weimar Republic lasted less than one single year in office, on the average, compared to nearly a decade in the monarchy until the outbreak of World War I. For the most part, not two, not three, but four parties had to come to terms to give any chancellor majority support in the Reichstag. The old Conservatives, now running under the German National banner, and the newly formed Communist party each cast a spell on the republic. Thus the republic could only be governed if the following parties agreed to lend their support: Social Democrats, Catholic Center, People's Party (formerly the National Liberals), and Democrats (the anti-Bismarck liberals of yesterday). At best, it was government by a bickering middle against an implacable opposition from each side; at worst, it was no government with a parliamentary majority. The extremes could gloatingly outbid each other in exploiting popular dissatisfaction with each patchwork government.

Surprisingly perhaps, right-wing coups of one sort or another did not overthrow the vulnerable Republic, nor did Communist uprisings. The army high command stayed on the sidelines, and the bureaucracy, though mourning the loss of the monarchy, stuck to the republican state when a right-wing putsch threatened it in 1920. Hitler's attempt of a coup in 1923 ended ignominiously. The judiciary, however, let Hitler off with a slap on the wrist. He received an unusually short sentence and was able, in comfortable conditions and aided by trusted assistants, to write *Mein Kampf* while incarcerated.

What saddled the new republic with a crushing mortgage right from the start was the Versailles Treaty, unveiled to a stunned German public in 1919. The treaty stripped Germany of territory in the East, shrank its army to a force suitable for parades but not war, and imposed reparations amounting to more than 100 billion Marks. Instead of rallying public support around an embattled government, that treaty polarized Germany, poisoned public debate, and was grist for the nationalist propaganda mills. "Weimar" and "Versailles" became hated synonyms in wide segments of the German public, two sides of the same coin of national humiliation. The

nationalism that had been aroused before 1914 and was wounded by the defeat of 1918, would attack relentlessly any effort to comply with the provisions of the treaty.

The Depression that began with the crash on Wall Street on 1929 immediately shook the German economy, dependent on American loans to pay off the Versailles bill. As banks failed and companies went bankrupt, unemployment soared to unprecedented levels in Germany: From 6 percent of the workforce in 1928, to 12 percent by September 1930, 30 percent by July 1932, and to 34 percent by early 1933. In eerie tandem with those figures climbed the vote share of a party that had languished at the extremist fringe, the National Socialist German Workers Party (NSDAP) led by Adolf Hitler. From less than 3 percent in 1928, it jumped to 18 percent in 1930 and doubled that share to reach 37 percent in the July 1932 election.

With his party now by far the largest in the Reichstag, Hitler justifiably demanded to be appointed chancellor. With great reluctance and deep disdain for him, President Paul von Hindenburg, a Prussian conservative and World War I hero, finally obliged in January of 1933. There was no love lost between the two, who had just squared off against each other in the presidential election of 1932, with Hitler the loser. By entrusting Hitler with the chancellorship, Hindenburg and his advisers planned to rein in and use the Nazis by offering them a piece of political power. The plan proved futile, as Hitler quickly swept aside his gullible conservative chaperones.

THE APPEALS OF
THE NAZI MOVEMENT

What was it about this party that made it so attractive to so many Germans? There could be little doubt about what the Nazis were

For National Socialism as for fascism, war and the affirmation of war was the essential background, an attempted socialist revolution its immediate genesis, protection by the state and established conservative forces the atmosphere necessary to its growth, and the towering personality of the leader an irreducible element.

SOURCE: Ernst Nolte, *Three Faces of Fascism* (New York: Holt, Rinehart and Winston, 1966), p. 323.

against: Jews, Communists, Socialists, the Weimar system, Versailles, . . . and more. In his speeches Hitler ranted and raved against them with manic energy, blaming Jews and Socialists for Germany's defeat in the war. Speaking more positively, he appealed to dreams of national glory. He extolled a new Germany, powerful and influential in the world, with its "place in the sun" again, although this time with more shade for the rest of the world. Instead of paying the Versailles bill, Germany would tear it up and recover the losses, by war if necessary. By military conquest he would seek more *Lebensraum,* primarily in the East, meaning Russia. There was a promise of great times to come for Germans. Internally, a strong hand would rule, instead of a disputatious parliament and impotent party coalitions.

The name of the party notwithstanding, National Socialism was far more nationalist than socialist. In fact, the Nazis fought their bloodiest battles against Communists, even thought they were not averse to copying their methods.[3] Their deadly hostility toward Marxism of any sort earned the Nazis much sympathy and some overt assistance from established right-wing forces. Financial support from big business, however, did not flow to the party in quantity until it had shown its electoral muscle.[4]

Undeniably there was also Hitler, the man himself, with his talent for galvanizing a devoted following and rousing mass audiences with fiery speeches, a quality that makes one wary of charismatic leaders. Nonetheless, for the first ten years since its founding in 1919, he failed to reach or sway many voters. It seems inconceivable that the Nazi party could have risen from obscurity without a catastrophe like the economic crisis of the 1930s.

The Depression ousted the Republican Party from power in 1932 in the United States, and led to party realignment. In Germany it ousted all republican forces, and led to a realignment of the political system. There the Depression struck a political order that lacked political support among key economic and social elites. In the mass public there were few whose heart beat faster when they thought of "the Republic." Many seemed to be willing to give the parties trying to govern the benefit of the doubt as long as things went reasonably well, but felt no lasting attachments to those parties. When the economy collapsed, they read the collapse as a declaration of political bankruptcy by the government and its parties. However serious and painful the economic misery, those affected by it most sharply, the unemployed themselves, were *not* the shock troop among Nazi voters. As far as can be ascertained today, the proportion of the unemployed that voted Nazi was not higher then the proportion of those with jobs.[5] In other words, many Ger-

---

[3] On this relationship, see the recent book by Ernst Nolte, *Der europäische Bürgerkrieg 1917–1945: Nationalsozialismus und Bolschewismus* (Frankfurt: Ullstein, 1987). The book has aroused a firestorm of controversy. Critics charge that Nolte is offering a moral exculpation of National Socialism. See also discussion of the *Historikerstreit* (historians' dispute) on p. 290.

[4] Henry Ashby Turner, Jr., *German Big Business and the Rise of Hitler* (New York: Oxford University Press, 1985).

[5] See Jürgen Falter, "Unemployment and the Radicalisation of the German Electorate 1928–1933," in *Unemployment and the Great Depression in Weimar Germany,* ed. Peter Stachura (London: Macmillan, 1986).

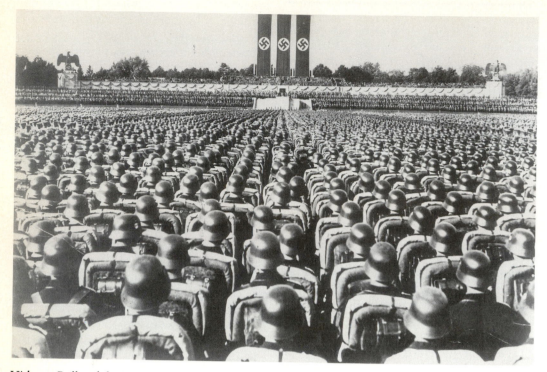

Hitler at Rally of the Nazi Party in Nuremberg, 1936.
SOURCE: The Bettmann Archive.

mans not suffering the worst from the crisis opted for the Nazi party.

In any electoral analysis it is tempting to seek explanations for voter choices in the ideologies of the parties for whom the votes are cast. The assumption is that people vote for a party because they agree with its basic policy premises, its ideology, in other words. This is a most sensible assumption, largely because the opposite—namely that people vote for a party out of disagreement with its ideals—is so patently absurd. In the case of the Nazis, one can argue that this party did not mince words about what it had in mind, that Hitler spelled it out with extreme force in *Mein Kampf* and drummed it into the most illiterate minds. How could anyone fail to grasp the basic thrust of the Nazi ideology? How could anyone not know that in voting for the Nazis they were endorsing a racial doctrine, antiSemitism, the eradication of Bolshevism, the creation of a dictatorial state, and an imperial order in the East?

Among all the prominent figures of the Weimar period, [Hitler] is the only one of whom it can be said unequivocally that he possessed political genius . . . In his person were combined an indomitable will and self-confidence, a superb sense of timing . . . the intuitive ability to sense the anxieties and resentments of the masses, and to put them in words . . . a mastery of the arts of propaganda, great skill in exploiting the weaknesses of rivals and antagonists, and a ruthlessness in the execution of his designs that was swayed neither by scruples of loyalty nor by moral considerations.

SOURCE: Gordon A. Craig, *Germany, 1866–1945* (New York: Oxford University Press, 1978), p. 544.

Sixty years later, it is impossible, of course, to prove what ordinary people knew about the Nazis then. But contemporary research on opinions and voting suggests that it is highly unlikely that they grasped a great deal. The ordinary member of the mass electorate in modern democracies is too ill informed and unsophisticated about politics to comprehend it at a level of ideology or policy.[6]

In all likelihood, the antisemitism, the racial ideology, and promises of a totalitarian political order and a world empire carried little weight for the mass public, important as those sentiments were for the Nazi leadership and activists. If anything, "it seems safe to conclude that the mass base of the Nazi movement represented one of the most unrelievedly ill-informed clienteles that a major political party has assembled in a modern state."[7] No doubt, many Nazi voters in 1932 did not mind a strong leader, a strong Germany, and a revision of Versailles; they would also tolerate restrictions of freedom if that was necessary to get the economy going again. But above all, they voiced dissatisfaction with the parties in office and were willing to give others a chance to govern regardless of the ideological implications. In the battle for the votes of discontent, it was the Nazis who won out, with their populist energy, youthful dynamism, organizational talent, and promises of a better future.

THE NAZI DICTATORSHIP
(1933–45)

With blazing speed, availing himself of emergency powers, Hitler consolidated his grip on power after being named chancellor on January 30, 1933. A totalitarian state took shape within less than a year. Political parties were banned or dissolved except for the NSDAP, which soon controlled every aspect of government and politics. Not having been too adept at using power, the other political parties now proved no more successful in avoiding their own extinction. But the Nazi party did not stop with politics. Through a dense network of organizations, the party undertook to bind each individual German to the new order, young ones in particular through the Hitler Youth. This state did not just give orders, it wanted people to participate, albeit without asking their opinions or tolerating dissent.

Above all, the Nazi state began mobilizing the nation to make Germany a world power. A showdown with the other European nations would be inevitable. From day one Hitler embarked on a gigantic rearmament, in personnel, armaments, navy, air force, and so on. Military spending in 1933 tripled the 1932 amount, rose threefold again by 1936 and once more by 1938. This buildup quickly resulted in a welcome consequence for the German public, however unanticipated: The collapsed German economy revived. Hitler was no economic genius, but it so happened that this drive to restore Germany as a great power also spelled economic recovery for Germany a few years later. In 1936, industrial production surpassed the pre-Depression level of 1928; three of four who were unemployed in early 1933 had jobs again. A Hitler running for reelection in 1936 with the question, "Are you better off now than you were four years ago?" probably would have won a landslide in a free election. The Nazis had succeeded where the Weimar parties had failed miserably.

For most Germans the price was tolerable or yet too remote. No mass executions had taken place. To be sure, political liberty was

---

[6] See the classic study of voting by Angus Campbell, Philip E. Converse, Donald E. Stokes, and Warren E. Miller, *The American Voter* (New York: Wiley, 1960).

[7] Philip E. Converse, "The Nature of Belief Systems in Mass Publics," in *Ideology and Discontent*, ed. David E. Aptes (New York: Free Press, 1964), pp. 253–54.

suspended for all, and discriminatory laws against Jews were adopted. Many citizens with a suspect political past, from the Nazi view, were put in "concentration camps." Although that did not mean certain death in the prewar period, just the sound of that phrase was enough to send a chill down one's spine. The *Gestapo* (secret police) supplemented the regular police to extinguish dissent and opposition before it stirred. No doubt, a not insignificant number of Germans happily endorsed those measures, but the vast majority probably regarded them with indifference; their daily lives were not much different with them or without them.

What did make a palpable difference was

the war that Hitler unleashed. With the attack on Poland in September 1939 Hitler crossed the line between remaking Germany and claiming an unholy empire for the German nation. He also crossed the line between persecution of Jews and their extermination. The "final solution" meant sending Jews to the gas chamber in places like Auschwitz and Treblinka, where millions perished. More than anything else, this gruesome crime has tainted Germany's name and left us with haunting questions. How could it be that a "good-natured people," as Nietzsche put it prophetically, turned out so "vicious"?

Admittedly, the "final solution" was

May 8, 1945: Germany in Ruin.
SOURCE: Turner, *Two Germanies*, Yale University Press.

treated like a state secret in Nazi Germany. This was not a matter of public discussion, nor did the regime boast of it. Responsibility for it was entrusted to a special organization. Few Germans were in a position to know for certain about the death camps and their ghastly business. Even if they heard about the "terrible secret" there was little most individuals would have been able to do without risking their own lives. The only group with any chance of overthrowing Hitler was the German army. In the end, on July 20, 1944, high-ranking officers mounted a well-prepared attempt on Hitler's life but failed. It was the victorious Allies who delivered the world, including the German people, from the Nazi monster in 1945.

A FEDERAL REPUBLIC FOR WEST GERMANY (1949)

Defeat in 1945 placed Germany's destiny into the hands of the United States, Britain, France and the Soviet Union. They had no immediate plans to restore Germany as a self-governing state. But disputes between the Western powers and the Soviet Union soon turned into a cold war, and cooperation among them in occupied Germany froze as well. The United States, Britain and France increasingly joined in their efforts and permitted the creation of common institutions across their zones of occupation. By 1948 those three zones formed a union with a government, for all practical purposes, to handle economic matters, albeit under Western tutelage.

Politics soon followed economics as the cold war threatened to grow hot. In 1948, a week after Stalin imposed a blockade against Berlin the Western powers gave the go-ahead for a constitution to be drafted for a new German state comprising the three Western zones. Delegates from regional parliaments,

which themselves had been elected as early as 1946, met as what was modestly called a "parliamentary council" in Frankfurt, the city of the 1848 national assembly. And just as it had 100 years before, national unity proved an elusive goal.

Afraid that drafting a constitution for the Western part of Germany would jeopardize Germany's national unity—the Eastern zone under Soviet occupation was not a party to the invitation—the parliamentary council issued only a "Basic Law." It was meant for the interim until the Eastern part could join in the deliberation for a new national constitution. On May 8, 1949, exactly four years after Germany's surrender, the delegates approved of the draft for a basic law by a vote of 53 to 12, with most of the opposition coming from Communists and Bavarian representatives. Once accepted by the Allies, the draft was also ratified by all state parliaments except in Bavaria, which objected to what it considered too little authority for the states.

Reading the text of the Basic Law, one gets a sense of the framers trying to put their history lessons to use. Fearful of the threat posed by political parties hostile to freedom and democracy, they expressly permitted the banning of such parties. Reflecting on the fateful role played by President Hindenburg in the closing days of Weimar, they sharply downgraded the authority of the president. He would no longer be chosen by popular election or willed emergency powers; his role in hiring and firing of the chancellor as well as for dissolving parliament would be closely circumscribed.

The new constitution strengthened the authority of the chancellor, who would have less to fear from parliamentary intrigue and party conflict. A "constructive vote of no-confidence" was introduced in an effort to ensure more stability in government. A remarkable innovation, it said in effect that parliament can only bring down a chancellor if it can agree on a successor. The Basic Law also revived and strengthened the role of the *Länder* (states). Judicial review of political laws and acts was vested in a Constitutional Court. Promulgated later, a rather complicated electoral law made it tough for minor parties to obtain seats in the federal parliament. Whatever legal provisions like this one may be worth in actual politics, one must admire the intention of the framers to create a political order that would ease rather than hinder the formation of effective government.

At the same time, more than one good star shone on the fledgling republic in war-ravaged West Germany. Instead of a crushing load of reparations, the country received a generous infusion of aid from its conquerors, especially through the Marshall Plan. Instead of being treated like a pariah, it would soon be invited to join its Western victors as an ally, with an army once again, and as a partner in the coming European Community. For those twists of fortune, Germans had to thank international politics—in particular, the threatening moves of Soviet expansionism and the resolve of the Western powers to contain it. Whatever its own contribution, the Federal Republic in 1949 initiated an age of prosperity that lasted, with slight disturbances, until the mid-1970s. One may wonder how the Republic of 1919 would have fared under similar auspices.

References and Suggested Readings

CRAIG, GORDON. *The Germans*. New York: Putnam, 1983.

HAMILTON, RICHARD F. *Who Voted for Hitler?* Princeton: Princeton University Press, 1982.

JOHANN, ERNST, and JÖRG JUNKER. *German Cultural History*. Munich: Nymphenburger Verlagsbuchhandlung, 1983.

MANN, GOLO. *The History of Germany Since 1789*. New York: Praeger, 1968.

MAYER, ARNO. *Why Did the Heavens Not Darken?* New York: Pantheon, 1989.

MERKL, PETER. *The Origin of the West German Republic*. New York: Oxford University Press, 1963.

STERN, FRITZ. *Gold and Iron: Bismarck, Bleichröder and the Building of the German Empire*. New York: Alfred A. Knopf, 1977.

TURNER, HENRY ASHBY, JR. *The Two Germanies since 1944*. New Haven: Yale University Press, 1987.

19

West German Society Today: Thriving While Shrinking

The Federal Republic is both a small and a big country. In population it leads all European countries other than the Soviet Union, but in area it trails countries like France, Italy and Sweden. To put it in an American perspective, the Federal Republic would fit into the state of Oregon, with the population of California, New York, New Jersey, and Pennsylvania combined. The 61 million West Germans live, for the most part, in densely populated towns and cities. Extensive urban clusters proliferate in the Rhine-Ruhr region, with cities like Düsseldorf and nearby Dortmund and Cologne, or in the Rhine-Main region around Mainz and Frankfurt.

The Federal Republic comprises ten *Länder* (states) and West Berlin (Figure 19.1). West Berlin is a special case. Geographically it is located within East Germany, but politically it belongs to the Federal Republic while remaining under the authority of the victorious allies in World War II. The Länder are sovereign states in the sense that a state in the United States of America is. The Länder have their own elected parliaments, state governments, sources of revenues, spending power, and police. They wield authority over such matters as education and broadcast media. Yet few German states take their statehood as seriously as Bavaria, arguably the oldest of them in its present shape. It was only recently that a petition to provide for a separate Bavarian citizenship lost in court at the highest level.

In the immediate postwar years, West Germany absorbed over 10 million expellees and refugees who lived in the eastern parts of the former German Reich or in Czechoslovakia. Add to them more than two million fleeing from Communist East Germany during the 1950s, and one could easily imagine a festering social problem lasting for decades. That did not happen, as the postwar economic boom facilitated social integration. With the millions of expellees and refugees settled, population mobility slowed down in West Germany. Nowadays one in 25 Germans

273

changes residence in one year,[1] compared to one in five for the United States. Whatever movement crosses state lines favors the southern states of Baden-Württemberg and Bavaria at the expense of Germany's industrial heartland, North-Rhine-Westphalia.

Beginning in the late 1950s West Germany took in workers from abroad in increasing numbers. Called *Gastarbeiter* (guest workers), one in three came from Turkey. All together, including family members, residents from foreign countries presently number four million.[2] Not being German and not even enjoying the status of permanent resident, many of these newcomers live in ghetto-like conditions.[3]

Without this inflow of foreign workers the population of the Federal Republic would have begun shrinking. Its birthrate, as Table 19.1 documents, is far below that of the United States and the other countries covered here. In fact, it is the lowest in the world.

Figure 19.1   The States of the Federal Republic
SOURCE: *Facts about Germany*, p. 25.

[1] Statistisches Bundesamt, *Statistisches Jahrbuch 1986 für die Bundesrepublik Deutschland* (Stuttgart: Kohlhammer Verlag, 1986), p. 80.
[2] *Statistisches Jahrbuch 1986*, p. 31.
[3] See the scathing account by Günter Wallraff, *Ganz Unten* (Köln: Kiepenheuer & Witsch, 1985).

Table 19.1   The Federal Republic by Comparison

	Birth Rate per Thousand	Exports in $Billions	Percent of Workforce Employed in	
			Industry	Services
Federal Republic	9.5	183	41	53
United States	15.7	214	28	68
Great Britain	12.9	101	33	64
France	13.8	98	33	59
Soviet Union	19.6	87	38	42
Italy	10.3	79	34	54
Japan	12.5	176	35	56

SOURCE: Birth Rate and Employment, 1984, *Statistisches Jahrbuch 1986*, pp. 636–39; Exports, 1985, *Der Fischer Weltalmanach '87* (Frankfurt: Fischer Verlag, 1986), p. 910.

Since the early 1970s, more West Germans have died each year than were born: 118,000 more, to be precise, in 1985.[4] A projection by the Federal Office of Statistics foresees the West German population dropping below 30 million by 2030. Already, the modal family in West Germany is one without children; and barely one in six families has two children. This must be perplexing for a country with child allowances and generous maternity leaves. All to little avail, it seems.

Slightly over half of the West German population nowadays has been born since 1945. Germans old enough to have experienced the Nazi regime or to have played an active part in it are fast becoming an extinct species. Already a generation is growing up whose parents were brought up in the Federal Republic. Very soon, the Federal Republic will be older than the average West German.

RELIGION

Nearly 500 years ago, the Reformation originated in Germany. It has left Germany divided along religious lines ever since. In the Federal Republic Protestants and Catholics hold a rough parity, with little over 40 percent for each side. Thus Catholics no longer feel like an embattled minority, as they did in the German Empire.

Each denomination, to be sure, has its regions of strength, with the North favoring the Protestants and the Rhineland and the South the Catholics. This pattern of religious division dates back to the aftermath of the Reformation. With the rule "cuius regio, eius religio" in force, the religious preference of the ruler of a territory at the time dictated the religious preference of the territory's subjects. Already then, we can infer, no central power in Germany could impose one and the same denomination on all Germans.

Few West Germans these days attend church services regularly. Among Catholics, nearly three in ten go to church regularly, and only one in ten among Protestants.[5] Nevertheless, most of the no-shows faithfully pay their contributions to the church of their baptism. That is to say, their contribution is withheld by means of the "church tax." It is one of the arrangements between state and church in West Germany that the state collects an amount approximately equal to 10 percent of one's income tax liability and forwards that to one's church.

In a sense the state recognizes both Protestantism and Catholicism as alternate state religions, each enjoying privileges. In addition to serving as tax collector for them, the state allows each religion to be taught in schools, provides for theology departments in the universities and treats church employees as civil servants. A potentially explosive issue, the linkage between church and state nevertheless stirs little excitement.

ECONOMY

Compared to most other countries or even to Germany in the past, the West German economy is quite unabashedly capitalist. State ownership is rare, largely limited to the traditional domains of postal service, which does include telecommunications in West Germany, rail service, and air transportation. Most of the renowned German firms, like Mercedes, BMW, Krupp, Siemens, Deutsche Bank, and BASF, are privately owned and operated. That is not to deny that government in West Germany, in Bonn or in the state capitals, subsidizes industries here and there. State governments will go to great

---

[4] *Statistisches Jahrbuch 1986*, p. 31.

[5] *Forschungsgruppe Wahlen*, February 1987 survey.

Made in Germany: Assembly of Mercedes-Benz Automobiles in Stuttgart.
SOURCE: Owen Franken, German Information Service.

length to make sure that the flagship company of their state does not move elsewhere.

Moreover, the state in Germany has been quite visible in regulating economic activities. The intervention by the state probably goes far enough in West Germany to dissipate support for sweeping socialism, but not so far as to make "get the state off our backs" a popular rallying cry. The service sector falls under strict regulations. By law, stores must close by 6:30 P.M. on weekdays and by 2:00 P.M. on Saturdays, and stay closed on Sundays. Standards for performance of anything technical are maddeningly stiff, as anyone knows who has tried to get a not-so-new car through the TÜV, the German technical inspection service.

The overall performance of the West German economy, for the most part, is a tale of seemingly endless prosperity.[6] Digging out from the rubble after 1945, West Germany piled on one record year after another, as never before in history. Who in 1945 would have predicted full employment in just ten years, and without inflation? And it was not just a deceptive lull before the inevitable collapse. Apart from the recession in the mid-1960s, the West German economy kept on growing, at full employment and low inflation. It was not until 1974, when OPEC's quadrupling of crude oil prices thrust the West German economy into a recession, that some flaws were exposed.

[6] See Edwin Hartrich, *The Fourth and Richest Reich: How the Germans Conquered the Postwar World* (New York: Macmillan, 1980).

Food trays served on the state-run German rail system come with the following request:

"We hope that you have enjoyed your meal. Now do yourself and the other travelers a favor: Pack the remains of your meal into this plastic bag and close it carefully with the attached tie! Then put it into one of the large trash receptacles near the train doors, thus helping all those who treasure their environment— Many thanks."

To be sure, the sputtering economic performance since then is not all a matter of oil prices. The industrial sector faces hard times on its own account. Since 1945 the composition of the German workforce has undergone a remarkable realignment. Whereas in 1950 still a quarter of the workforce earned a living from agriculture, in 1985 only one in 20 did. From 1950 to 1970, the industrial sector dominated, employing close to one in two. Since then, however, employment in industries has been shrinking. In 1984, 53 percent earned their living from a service-related job, only 41 percent from a job in industry.

During the last ten years, the West German economy has entered the postindustrial age. In a former smokestack city like Essen, where mine elevators used to dot the landscape and where laundry hung out to dry collected black dust before drying, an indoor tennis arena now utilizes the abandoned halls of a coal mine. But the transition to a postindustrial economy has not gone altogether smoothly. The service sector simply has not expanded enough to compensate for the losses of the industrial sector.

In 1981–82 a severe recession hit West Germany. Unemployment topped the 2 million mark for the first time in nearly 30 years. Inflation added insult to injury, and growth became negative. By some counts, the West German economy has extricated itself from the predicament it faced in the early 1980s. The report card for 1986 read: growth at 2.5 percent; prices *down,* actually, by 0.2 percent, for the first time in over 30 years; but unemployment stubbornly staying above 2 million.[7] As long as the economy promises to grow inflation-free at a rate close to 3 percent, West Germans appear to accept, with a sense of resignation, the loss of full employment—an attitude few would have predicted 20 years ago.

However much the industrial sector has shrunk, its relative size still puts West Germany ahead of other Western nations. Manufacturing continues to be a key asset of the West German economy, the mainstay of its exports. Take state-of-the-art high performance cars, for example. More Porsches are sold in the United States than in the country where they are built. Six of every ten cars manufactured in West Germany sell abroad. Mercedes, that symbol of status, craftsmanship, engineering innovation and elegant styling, now ranks as the top company in West Germany, employing over 300,000 people and grossing 3.5 percent of the country's GNP.[8]

Overall, almost one-third of West Germany's gross national product derives from exports and one-quarter goes for imports. Hefty trade surpluses are a regular feature of West Germany's economic performance. France and the United States lead the list of countries buying goods "made in Germany." To keep up its standard of living, the Federal Republic must continue to make high-quality goods and sell them abroad. It needs innovation at home to remain competitive, and a good climate abroad for international trade to flourish, unobstructed by quotas, tariffs, sanctions, threats or other forms of ill will. A country like that cannot afford to play bully

[7] *Week in Germany,* January 16, 1987.

[8] *Economist,* December 6, 1986.

in world politics. It has little choice but to act like the good neighbor towards ideological foes as well as friends.

SOCIAL STRUCTURE

Postwar affluence has done much to blunt the rough edges of class distinctions in West Germany. There is also no upper class of hereditary title and privilege left to set the tone anymore. Blue-collar workers do not feel like second-class citizens. Opportunities for social advancement are far more equal than ever before; family background is not negligible, but education and performance make a crucial difference.

West German society contains a large middle class (Figure 19.2). The self-employed and professionals, the core of the old *Mittelstand* (middle estate), make up roughly one of seven West German households. The new *Mittelstand,* that is people with white-collar jobs of high to medium rank, comprises nearly two of seven households. Moreover, Germany has a well-defined corps of civil servants. Their mark of distinction is that the state is their boss. To be a *Beamter* (civil servant) in Germany has always conveyed a special aura of authority and of loyalty and obligation to the state, in return for which that state offers privileged treatment not accorded ordinary citizens. With roughly one in seven a civil servant in Germany, this group covers people not usually accorded this rank elsewhere, such as teachers.

While the self-employed and professionals, along with many holding white-collar and civil service jobs, form West Germany's large middle class, skilled blue-collar workers predominate in the working class. These *Facharbeiter* have successfully completed an apprenticeship and received a certificate of skill. Government in Germany has always emphasized the technical training of its workforce and has tightly regulated it. The technical

Figure 19.2   The Occupational Structure of West German Society (Percent of Heads of Households)

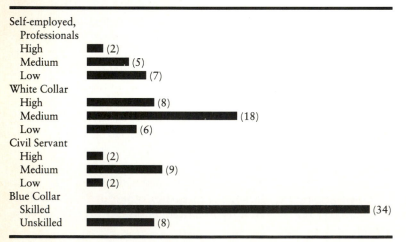

SOURCE: *Forschungsgruppe Wahlen* surveys, August 1982–March 1983; number of cases: 5,196.

proficiency of skilled labor has turned "made in Germany" from stigma to trademark. Politically speaking, since the late nineteenth century skilled workers have formed the backbone of the union movement and the Social Democratic Party. This working class has hardly ever approximated the wretched, impoverished,, and dispirited proletariat depicted by social critics.

The pay earned by members of the four broad occupational groups does not reveal shocking gaps. In 1985, the median net income per month for the self-employed was DM 2,400; for civil servants, DM 2,200; for white-collar employees, DM 1,700; and for blue-collar workers, DM 1,500.[9] To be sure, some self-employed earn far more than the median, with one in four making over DM 4,000 net a month. Even after taxes, with a top bracket of the income tax at 56 percent, the distribution of income in West German society remains skewed. Yet apart from a small layer at the top, the median incomes of the four key social "classes" diverge surprisingly little from each other. These figures do not portend a society torn apart by bitter strife between haves and have-nots.

EDUCATION

Virtually all schools in West Germany, from elementary schools to universities, are run by the state—in more than one sense. "State" here refers to state governments. Education is *Ländersache,* not federal responsibility. Private schools exist, but many of them operate just like public schools, charging no fees and being subject to strict state supervision. Under the common roof of the state, however, the German school system allows for sharp differentiation.

For only four years, from age six through

ten, Germans share the same schooling experience. At ten, their educational paths diverge (Figure 19.3). One path is the *Gymnasium,* a place for much mental, but little physical, exercise. It offers the longest, riskiest, but also the most prestigious of three alternatives. And it promises the surest route to upward social mobility. The chief mission of this vaunted institution has always been, and still is, to prepare youths in their teens for university study in their twenties. It's college-preparatory high school, in other words, but with a nine-year curriculum. Graduation at age 19—at the earliest—confers the right to seek admission to a university. The graduation diploma, the *Abitur,* however, is no longer a ticket to the university of your choice or to your most preferred major.

Entering a Gymnasium at age 10 used to be a rite of passage, with the child's parents making the key decision. For the student, caught between parental expectations and the pressures of a demanding and not too

Figure 19.3   The Educational System of West Germany
SOURCE: *Facts about Germany,* p. 334.

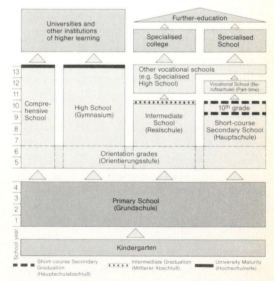

[9] *Statistisches Jahrbuch 1986,* p. 102.

forgiving scholastic environment, this was a moment filled with anxiety. Much of that has changed as the gates of this institution have swung more widely open since the 1960s. Still, by no means everyone enters a Gymnasium at age ten. A large number attend a *Hauptschule,* the second stage of what used to be called the *Volksschule,* the "school for the masses." This educational track teaches basic skills and leads to blue-collar and some white-collar jobs. *Hauptschule* graduates, at age 15 nowadays, proceed to a three-year apprenticeship accompanied by part-time vocational schooling. This combination culminates in an examination that bestows an official certification in a recognized job designation such as car mechanic, electrician, or carpenter.

This educational track, to be sure, has always supplied Germany with recruits for a highly skilled workforce (*Facharbeiter*), and instilled in them an appreciation for getting a job done well and on time. The state gives its stamp of approval, but it is the private sector that is doing the on-site training, continuing an apprenticeship tradition dating back to pre-industrial days. All told, the private sector made available some 700,000 apprentice slots for just as many graduates from *Haupt-* and *Realschulen* in 1985, though not always in the occupations desired the most. The *Realschule* represents a school type between Hauptschule and Gymnasium that is geared more to middle-level white-collar occupations.

It is not surprising that the three separate educational tracks, housed in different buildings and spawning their own social cultures, reinforce and transmit from one generation to the next some fundamental divisions of German society. For many years, upper-middle-class parents would send their offspring to the Gymnasium as a matter of course, while many a blue-collar worker would not think of it—not so much because

it would cost a lot of money but because the Gymnasium belongs to another social world. To them it loomed like an impregnable fortress.

The class bias of the Gymnasium has irritated liberal reformers and Social Democrats. The most radical reform proposal aimed at dissolving the Gymnasium by creating a unified type of secondary school, the *Gesamtschule*—an American-style high school, in other words. The Gymnasium survived this onslaught, but at a price. It is easier now to enter this track as well as to survive the first few critical grades. As a result, a much larger and more diverse student body nowadays attends the Gymnasium. One in four West Germans in their teens go there, as opposed to roughly one in 20 attending twenty years ago.

As one would expect, the destination of this educational track, namely the university, has filled up too. Long renowned for quiet places of academic study, tucked away in quaint towns like Heidelberg, Freiburg, or Münster, West German universities now strain to accommodate a student body that swelled from only 100,000 in the 1950s to 1.3 million at present. Entrance into a particular university and enrollment in a specific field of study, a *gratis* passage for a Gymnasium graduate in the old days, is now a matter of admission. But this is not handled by each university individually. Instead, a centralized bureaucracy for all universities in the Federal Republic handles admissions. In making decisions this office largely goes by the arithmetic of the high school grade point average. Little else matters.

So, with opportunities expanded, Gymnasium graduates are often getting a bitter taste of equality and competition. Many of them find their favored major closed out. Moreover, a rejection slip from the central admission office means being rejected not just by the favored university, but by every single one within the Federal Republic. This is true especially for those seeking admission to medical school. The expansion of university enrollment has raised expectations that have gone unfulfilled. The most popular majors of West German university students remain, in this order, law, medicine and business administration.

For many admitted to their favored major, the bitter taste may come after university graduation. In particular, students who now graduate with a degree in German literature or political science will find the door closed where they hoped to find employment: in the educational system, especially the Gymnasium. The state is not hiring. A shrinking population fills fewer classrooms—which require fewer teachers to staff them.

So, after years of uninterrupted growth, the Federal Republic is learning to cope with shrinkage. Its population is declining, its industrial sector is contracting, and job openings in the public sector are scarce. Still, this is not a society in turmoil. West Germany does not strike one as a society obsessed with the prospect of decline. At the very least, the country is shrinking gracefully. The economy is thriving enough to keep social tensions from turning nasty. Immigrant workers remain a foreign group in West Germany, but they have not provoked a political backlash among the Germans. Religion has lost much of its bite in politics, and so have class divisions, softened by the overhaul of the once rigidly stratified educational system. At long last, the social basis seems right for democracy to prosper too.

References and Suggested Readings

CRAIG, GORDON A. *The Germans.* New York: G. P. Putnam's Sons, 1982.

GUNLICKS, ARTHUR B. *Local Government in the German Federal System.* Durham, N.C.: Duke University Press, 1986.

LAQUEUR, WALTER. *Germany Today: A Personal Report.* Boston: Little, Brown, 1985.

LÖWENTHAL, RICHARD and HANS-PETER SCHWARZ, eds. *Die zweite Republik.* Stuttgart: Seewald Verlag, 1974.

MARKOVITS, ANDREI S. *Political Economy of West Germany: Modell Deutschland.* New York: Praeger, 1983.

20

I confess to be deeply convinced that the German people will never love political democracy.

— THOMAS MANN (1875–1955), *Reflections of a Nonpolitical Man*[1]

Democracies have ever been spectacles of turbulence and contention . . . and have in general been as short in their lives as violent in their deaths.

— JAMES MADISON, *The Federalist Papers*, No. 10

Acquiring a Taste for Democracy

Germany, the saying goes, has no democratic tradition. Its political thinkers did not pioneer or popularize liberal ideals as Locke, Montesquieu, and Jefferson, for example, did for England, France and the United States. Germany does not have a successful revolution to celebrate as its national holiday. Its people, it seems, never once defied political authority and won. Whatever advances liberal democracy made in that country came by way of grants from above or pressure from outside. It was whatever the rulers conceded or what foreign powers, having defeated Germany in war, mandated. Democracy, as one of her most celebrated writers of this century, Thomas Mann, said in 1918, was not made for Germany.

THE AUTHORITARIAN TRADITION

To many observers, German politics has a strong authoritarian flavor. This is the land of the *Obrigkeitsstaat,* a state of authority with little interference from the citizenry. Philosophers, historians, politicians, columnists, and

nonpolitical writers can be cited by the dozens to exemplify this political tradition, from Hegel, through Treitschke to Thomas Mann in his younger days. In Germany, the might of the state commanded more respect than the rights of citizens.

Strangely enough, in the nineteenth century in Germany this "illiberalism" is said to have conquered the social class that elsewhere led the fight for liberal values: the educated and prosperous middle class. Why this bizarre twist in Germany? The answer, according to the historian Fritz Stern and the sociologist Ralf Dahrendorf, is that this class was intoxicated with nationalist fervor, on one hand, and frightened by a vocal working class, on the other. The German middle class sought salvation in the national-conservative state dominated by the feudal class. Middle-class Germans either retired from politics altogether (the apolitical German) or ardently embraced the authoritarian state. One way or the other they surrendered the ideals of liber-

---

[1] Thomas Mann, *Betrachtungen eines Unpolitischen* (Berlin: S. Fischer Verlag, 1922), p. xxxiv.

alism and democracy. What spread instead was a political culture depicted as "averse to public virtues, prefering the rigidity of the cartel to lively competition, anxiously avoiding all conflicts, seeking a hierarchical world of fundamental inequalities."[2]

But how deeply this culture soaked through German society is not easy to verify in retrospect, nor whether it really did so in Germany any more than elsewhere. The appeal to strong leadership above the fray of divisive group conflict is certainly no German peculiarity, nor is it by itself a sign that the democratic ethos is missing. It is also a cornerstone of the presidential systems in the United States and France as well as of the British parliamentary system. Furthermore, German critics of "democracy" often seemed to be attacking an extreme version of this ideal, which was a far cry from the actual practice in Western nations. Wherever democracy took hold, constitutional checks and balances, restrictions of the right to vote or nonliberal and nondemocratic traditions have served, to varying degrees, to inhibit popular rule. In reality, there was far more *Obrigkeitsstaat* in the United States, France and Britain than those critics seemed to notice, mistaking flights of rhetoric for the real thing. By the same token, in extolling the virtues of an apolitical Germanic "culture" as superior to Western political "civilization," they overlooked the silent revolution that had spawned one of the liveliest party systems right under the nose of the *Obrigkeitsstaat*.

Liberal-democratic ideals, though not invented in Germany, nevertheless left a strong mark there. That they did not get their way in 1848 did not mean the defeat of those ideals. Where indeed has a violent revolution led to a stable liberal-democratic state with one stroke? The Germany formed in 1871 by no

means denied those ideals altogether but allowed them to be heard quite freely, especially after 1890, the year of Bismarck's dismissal as chancellor by Kaiser Wilhelm II. People took ample advantage of the right to vote in national elections. The press was remarkably vigorous, and membership in voluntary organizations was high. From 1900 on, the parties that favored democratic ideals or were amenable to them together commanded a clear majority of the German electorate. In 1919, the German people elected a national assembly that overwhelmingly endorsed a democratic constitution.

POPULAR ATTITUDES TOWARD DEMOCRACY

What cannot be safely ascertained for days past, namely what kind of political ideals and regime the German public favored the most, can certainly be done nowadays, with the help of frequent soundings of public opinion. In the early 1950s, a third of West Germans still favored a monarchy; by the mid-1960s only one in ten did.[3] At the same time, support for having just one political party shrank from 24 percent in 1950 to barely 5 percent by 1978. There is now a virtual consensus in the West German public that "the democracy we have in West Germany is the best form of government."[4] To a considerable degree, this appreciation is an acquired taste. In 1951, hardly any German named the Federal Republic ("at present") in response to the question, "When in this century do you feel things have gone best for Germany?" The democratic Weimar Republic also enjoyed negligi-

[2] Dahrendorf, *Society and Democracy* (Garden City, NY: Doubleday, 1967), p. 362.

[3] Elisabeth Noelle and Erich Peter Neumann, *The Germans: Public Opinion Polls 1947–1966* (Allensbach: Verlag für Demoskopie, 1967), p. 196.

[4] Noelle-Neumann, *The Germans 1967–1980*, p. 132.

Table 20.1　Opinions of West German Public about the Time in This Century When Things Have Gone Best

	1951 (%)	1959 (%)	1963 (%)	1970 (%)	1980 (%)
At present	2	42	63	81	80
Between 1933 and 1939 (Third Reich before World War II)	42	18	10	5	3
Between 1920 and 1933 (Weimar Republic)	7	4	5	2	2
Before 1914 (Kaiser Reich)	45	28	16	5	4
Don't know	4	8	6	7	11
	100	100	100	100	100

SOURCE: Elisabeth Noelle-Neumann, *The Germans—Public Opinion Polls 1967–1980* (Westport, CN : Greenwood, 1981).

ble support. By contrast, nine of ten named either the pre-1914 Empire or the pre-World War II Third Reich (Table 20.1). What an indictment of the political consciousness of Germans, it may seem: the authoritarian state beats democracy.

In both cases, of course, the authoritarian state delivered prosperity and national strength whereas the democracy of Weimar failed in that respect; the democracy of Bonn had yet to prove itself in 1951. One may wonder how, pressed to choose between good times under a dictatorship and bad times under a democracy, people elsewhere would decide. About the West German public one can say at least that the preference for authoritarian regimes recorded in that survey could not have derived from deep-seated values. Barely 10 years later, in 1959, the Federal Republic alone beat both the pre-1914 monarchy and the Nazi regime in the estimation of the German public; a few years later it was no contest anymore.

To be sure, this was not a vote on the abstract merits of democracy versus an authoritarian state. What Germans witnessed in the 1950s was an economic "miracle" and a no-less-miraculous return of (West) Germany to the ranks of major powers. Furthermore, the government in Bonn showed an impres-sive staying power and resolve in handling the postwar issues. All of this must have dis-pelled the fear that democracy would deliver neither (a) prosperity nor (b) international respect, nor (c) authoritative government. It was a set of lessons apparently not lost on Germans.

Studies of political attitudes have noted a special sensitivity of Germans to economic performance. Almond and Verba found that in response to the question of what they were proud of regarding their country, Germans in 1959 picked the "economic system" far more often (33%) than their governmental system (7%), in stark contrast to British and Ameri-can respondents.[5] Germans are seen as "output-oriented," which is to say they judge the value of the political system by how well it delivers key goods. A strong streak of op-portunism colors the political culture, to the point where an authoritarian regime, then a totalitarian regime, and finally a democracy may receive popular applause in rapid suc-cession. This is also the moral of many novels by Heinrich Böll, one of Germany's best known postwar writers.[6]

[5] Gabriel Almond and Sidney Verba, *The Civic Culture* (Boston: Little, Brown, 1965).

[6] Heinrich Böll, *Billiards at Half-Past-Nine* (New York: Avon Books, 1975).

Support for democracy may then be expected to wane again once the economy runs into a crisis. So far, three economic recessions have occurred, though none was even remotely comparable to the Depression of the 1930s. In the mid-1960s the economic setback coincided with a brief revival of right-wing extremism in some quarters whereas in the mid-1970s no similar reaction was felt. In the early 1980s, the recession was accompanied by the rise of new social movements and the Green party, but that seemed to have more to do with ecology than economy.

Still, the attitudes of the German public toward democracy have shown some wear. From 1972 to 1980, eight of ten West Germans typically expressed "satisfaction" with the democracy of the Federal Republic, according to *Forschungsgruppe Wahlen* surveys. In the next three years, as the West German economy suffered its worst recession since the 1930s, that support level began to slip toward the 50 percent mark. Since then it has stabilized between 65 and 70 percent. Half a century ago, the economic collapse paralyzed government and sapped what little popular support the Weimar Republic may have enjoyed. By contrast, the early 1980s raised small clouds of doubts but failed to ignite a thunderstorm.

THE CITIZEN IN POLITICS

Meanwhile the "apolitical German," extolled as a model by some and decried by others, is fast becoming an endangered species. Interest in politics has risen dramatically since the lukewarm reception of the Basic Law by the West German public in 1949. In 1952, barely one of four Germans reported to be interested in politics, while 20 years later

. . . the politically interested in the Bonn Republic are the most emphatic opponents of a reemergence of the totalitarian past . . . [and] far more likely to perceive a need for legislative institutions . . . The increases in political interest over time are related to increasing support for the political system's key values and institutions.

SOURCE: David P. Conradt, "Changing German Political Culture," in *The Civic Culture Revisited*, eds. Gabriel Almond and Sidney Verba (Boston: Little, Brown, 1980), pp. 239–41.

one of every two did.[7] Likewise, the inclination to talk about politics has surged, to a point where by 1972, during the election campaign, 85 percent reported discussing politics at least occasionally.[8] And what is most reassuring, the spreading interest in politics does not spell trouble for the democratic order.

Germans have also acquired a greater sense of civic competence—the feeling that citizens can do something about influencing political decisions at the top. In 1959, 38 percent indicated that they felt they could do something about an unjust national regulation; by 1974, 59 percent said so.[9] The gap that separated Germans from Britons in this regard has been virtually closed. If anything, Germans under 30 years of age have moved ahead of their contemporaries abroad. The young, after all, are being brought up in a thoroughly democratic climate that tolerates not the slightest espousal of authoritarian alternatives.

[7] Noelle-Neumann, *The Germans 1967–1980*, p. 150.

[8] Kendall Baker, Russell Dalton and Kai Hildebrandt, *Germany Transformed: Political Culture and the New Politics* (Cambridge, Mass.: Harvard University Press, 1981), p. 40.

[9] Almond and Verba, *The Civic Culture*, p. 142; Samuel Barnes and Max Kaase, *Political Action: Mass Participation in Five Western Democracies* (Beverly Hills, Calif: Sage, 1979).

Protest against Nuclear Weapons, West Berlin, 1982.
SOURCE: German Information Center.

As a result, Germany today represents an exception in reverse. Whereas the United States and Britain have witnessed a decline of such attitudes as civic competence, political efficacy, and trust in government, the trend line for those attitudes in the Federal Republic has pointed upward. Whatever deficits may have afflicted the German political culture have been largely erased. In the domain of group activity, the deficit was always more apparent than real.

GROUP MEMBERSHIP

While perhaps striking foreign observers as lacking in spontaneity in everyday social situations, Germans certainly are a nation of joiners, of non-political but also of political organizations. In a country that won the quadrennial Soccer World Cup in 1954 and 1974, a staggering 4.7 million belong to soccer clubs; and a country boasting of a Grand Slam winner in tennis with Steffi Graf counts 1.7 million members of tennis clubs; even more belong to gymnastic clubs.[10] *Schützenvereine* (rifle clubs), with their colorful attire, their parades and local festivals, are the heart of social life in small towns and in the countryside. Aloofness from social groups certainly is no characteristic of German society. Group activity pervades everyday life in

[10] *Statistisches Jahrbuch 1986*, p. 380.

West Germany to a remarkable degree even though the school system does little, by American standards, to foster the group spirit through extracurricular activities.

At work, nearly one of every three West Germans belongs to a labor union. This share has been achieved without the coercive benefit of the "closed shop" and has not changed much in recent years. The typical labor union in West Germany is one that encompasses a whole industry and commands a sizeable membership roll, with the largest, the steelworkers union, enrolling 2.5 million. Nearly all unions belong to the *Deutsche Gewerkschaftsbund* (German Labor Federation), which has no formal organizational connection with any political party. As a matter of practical politics, however, union ties with the Social Democratic Party are far more cordial than with any other party.

Not quite a match of soccer clubs or labor unions, the political parties nevertheless enroll large numbers of dues-paying, card-carrying members (Table 20.2). Almost a million each belong to the Social Democrats and the Christian Democrats. While mass membership has a long tradition in the Social Democratic party, it is of more recent vintage among Christian Democrats. Party members are entitled to participate in regular meetings of the precinct organization and take part in the nomination of candidates for office

and the formulation of party proposals. Of course, as in soccer clubs, many party members are content to sit back and watch the game rather than play in it.

PARTISANSHIP

Apart from those that carry a party card (actually a book in Germany), many Germans nowadays wear a party tie of a more psychological sort. They feel attached to a particular political party. This "party identification" serves as a guide for political opinions and electoral choice. In the aggregate, voter identification with political parties constitutes a critical built-in stabilizer of the democratic order. Without it, new and possibly anti-democratic parties would be able, in times of crisis, to mobilize large segments of the public behind their banner and thus undermine the ability of existing parties to govern. Just recall the breathtaking electoral surge of the Nazi party between 1928 and 1933. In those elections, voter support of parties eroded in direct relationship to the instability of their vote in the past. That is to say, parties that had cornered a share of the electoral market by 1928 lost little in the political crash following the economic collapse; on the other hand, those with loose or no electoral roots lost nearly all of their vote shares.

By the standard measure of party identification used in Germany ("Do you lean toward a party for a considerable time even if voting for another one now and then?"), seven of ten Germans identify with one of the two major parties, according to *Forschungsgruppe Wahlen* surveys. If anything, during the turbulent 1970s, when electoral commentary in the United States and Britain focused on partisan dealignment, the curve of party attachment pointed upwards in the

Table 20.2 Party Membership (in 1,000) in the Federal Republic

Year	CDU/CSU	SPD	FDP	Greens
1968	361	732	57	—
1972	530	954	58	—
1976	798	1,022	79	—
1980	865	987	85	18
1984	914	916	71	32

SOURCE: Bundeszentrale für politische Bildung (ed.), *Parteiendemokratie* (Bonn, 1985).

Federal Republic.[11] That is not to say that the German electorate is immune to dealignment. As in the United States and Britain, profound dissatisfaction with the performance of governing parties may spell a weakening of party identification.

NATIONAL FEELINGS

Where political attitudes remain most vulnerable in Germany is on the national question. The Federal Republic represents an incomplete nation-state. Its constitution exhorts the politicians to strive for unification. How burning is the desire in the West German public for reunification? Among the pressing political issues volunteered in opinion polls, reunification is not found anymore.[12] Only a tiny minority believes that Germany will be unified in the foreseeable future. Yet, in 1976 six of ten still favored reunification. It appears that the West Germans respond to this issue with a sense of resignation. They increasingly equate the Federal Republic with "Germany," as the nationality sign on their cars tells them to, and refer to the other Germany in the East as the DDR (German Democratic Republic).[13]

Compared with most other countries, West Germany is short on national pride. The results of an international poll conducted for the *New York Times* showed that 87 percent in the United States, 58 percent in Britain, and 42 percent in France said they were "very proud" of being citizens of their respective nation; in the Federal Republic only 21 percent did.[14] Pride is especially low among the educated young, that is, Germans under 30 with *Abitur*.

Growing up in the Federal Republic has meant growing up in a national vacuum or with a profound aversion to anything national. German schoolchildren do not recite something like a pledge of allegiance. When the German colors fly they are mostly at half staff, more to mourn than to celebrate. Sports events do not commence with a singing of the national anthem unless the national team is playing.

To raise the question of a national holiday is to stir a hornets' nest. It is true that neither Bismarck nor the liberals of 1848, neither Frederick the Great nor Wilhelm II, and no politician of the Weimar Republic represents a unifying historical figure akin to the Founding Fathers for the contemporary German public. The Nazi regime, if anything, serves as a negative foil, as the embodiment of everything to be avoided. And at age 40 the Federal Republic is too young to have a hallowed tradition of its own.

For a country where nationalistic fervor has turned to hubris before, and where the past raises painful questions rather than providing comforting answers, nationalistic abstinence may be welcomed. At the same time, some fear that this abstinence deprives the Federal Republic of an emotional attachment among its citizens that is common in other countries. If the United States may serve as proof, a democracy with strong national feelings is no oxymoron. To see a country as successful and powerful as West Germany feel ill at ease with its national identity may not be altogether reassuring, all professions

[11] See Helmut Norpoth, "The Making of a More Partisan Electorate in West Germany," *British Journal of Political Science*, 14 (1983):53–71; also his "Party Identification in West Germany: Tracing an Elusive Concept," *Comparative Political Studies*, 11 (1978): 36–61.

[12] Noelle-Neumann, *The Germans 1967–1980*, p. 127.

[13] See Gebhard Schweigler, "Normalcy in Germany," paper presented at the Wilson Center European Alumni Association Conference, Dubrovnik, May 20–27, 1988.

[14] E. J. Dionne, "Government Trust: Less in West Than U.S.," *New York Times*, Feb. 16, 1986.

Franz-Josef Strauss Addressing Meeting of the Christian Social Union (CSU), Schongau, Bavaria, 1983. SOURCE: German Information Center.

of Europeanism notwithstanding. It reveals an underdeveloped sense of self-confidence that renders the country vulnerable to external pressures, which in turn may trigger an unwelcome backlash at home.

Some have lately called for a more unabashed expression of German identity. The most vocal among these has been Franz-Josef Strauss, the long-time prime minister of Bavaria, who died in 1988. To play its part in the heart of the Western defense, the Federal Republic needs to end "the blockade of its return to historical normality," he declared. "We don't want totally fanatical nationalists . . . but instead we don't want a nation of 60 million nihilists either!"[15] Chancellor Kohl

has made it a point to appeal to national symbols, frequently invoking the "Fatherland" in his speeches, and calling for a "normal patriotism."

Others, however, shudder at these sounds of national revival. In the words of one, the renowned social philosopher Jürgen Habermas, "The only patriotism that does not alienate us from the West is a constitutional patriotism," not a "conventional form of national identity."[16] What disturbs critics like him is that nationalist tones often accompany calls for closing the book on Germany's Nazi past or removing its moral stains. In particular, the work by Ernst Nolte about the relationships between Bolshevism and National

---

[15] As quoted in *New York Times*, Jan. 13, 1987.

[16] As quoted in *New York Times*, Sept. 6, 1986.

Socialism struck a raw nerve and touched off a heated controversy in 1986 known as the *Historikerstreit* (historians' dispute), although it was by no means limited to the historical profession.[17]

A few popular movies have boldly addressed issues of national pride without the proverbial "chip on the shoulder." *Das Boot,* for example, depicts a German submarine crew in World War II, their boat being chased by Allied forces and ultimately blown up. The intriguing point is that it is the Germans who play the role of the victim in this movie, even though they fight Hitler's war. The movie portrays them as decent men who express considerable sympathy for their Allied adversaries and less than total devotion to the orders of their commander-in-chief (Hitler). Commenting on the success of the movie in West Germany, the movie's director said: "Germany somehow needs to come to an idea of its own identity . . . It has been living with guilt for 40 years."[18]

A similarly strong resonance greeted a 15-part television series entitled "Heimat," that untranslatable German expression connoting "area where one feels at home," where the land and the people are familiar and sweet. It is the saga of life in a fictional village, poor but picturesque, near Koblenz on the Rhine. It portrays its characters leading their daily lives through this century with political fallout from the Weimar to the Federal Republic raining on them like a faint drizzle. Yes, the Nazi regime also intrudes in their lives, but it is just one among many other events. Moreover it passes through without leaving much of a trace. The Nazis remain an alien force that fails to diminish the basic goodness of the people in "Heimat." It is a world of ordinary people living according to an apolitical rhythm. Governments come and go. They exact their price from those people and bestow some blessings upon them but the personal concerns prove vastly more important to those people than does politics.

Even at the present time, with citizens more heavily involved in politics, it is sobering to remind oneself that politics is not the all-consuming aspect of the average citizen's life, not in Germany or anywhere else. Full-time preoccupation with politics is a domain of activists in parties. It is here where the political alternatives that compete for the average citizen's attention take shape.

References and Suggested Readings

BURDICK, CHARLES, HANS-ADOLF JACOBSON, and WINFRIED KUDSZUS, eds. *Contemporary Germany: Politics and Culture.* Boulder, Colo.: Westview Press, 1984.

GREIFFENHAGEN, MARTIN AND SYLVIA. *Ein schwieriges Vaterland: Zur politischen Kultur Deutschlands.* München: List, 1979.

NELKIN, DOROTHY, and MICHAEL POLLAK. *The Atom Besieged: Extraparliamentary Dissent in France and West Germany.* Cambridge, Mass.: The MIT Press, 1982.

NOELLE-NEUMANN, ELISABETH, and RENATE KÖCHER. *Die verletzte Nation.* Stuttgart: Deutsche Verlags Anstalt, 1987.

SCHWEIGLER, GEBHARD. *National Consciousness in Divided Germany.* Beverly Hills, Calif.: Sage Publications, 1975.

STERN, FRITZ, *The Politics of Cultural Despair.* Berkeley: University of California Press, 1961.

---

[17] For an overview of this controversy, see Konrad H. Jarausch, "Removing the Nazi Stain? The Quarrel of the German Historians," *German Studies Quarterly* (1988):285–301; also see the documentation, "*Historikerstreit*" (no editor), München: Piper, 1987.

[18] As quoted in *New York Times,* April 24, 1985.

21

The political parties participate in the forming of the political will of the people. They may be freely formed. Their internal organization must conform to democratic principles. They must publicly account for the sources of their funds.
— BASIC LAW, ARTICLE 21, 1

The State of Parties in a Party State

In 1953, with the Bonn Republic barely four years old, the Christian Democrats won 45 percent of the vote in the federal election. With that, they captured a majority of seats in parliament. No German party had ever before accomplished either feat in competitive elections. In the last election before the onset of the Depression, in 1928, the largest party captured less than 30 percent of the vote. It needed help from three other parties for a workable majority.

That was rather typical for the German party system that had sprung up in the middle of the nineteenth century.[1] From 1871 to 1933, when the Nazis abolished all parties but their own, no single party ever came close to winning a majority of votes. Even two parties combined rarely did; and if so, they were as compatible with each other as fire and ice.

The nation that Bismarck unified in 1871, the parties divided. Divisions ran along constitutional, economic, social, religious and regional lines. Or to put it positively, imperial Germany was an idyll of interest representation. Virtually every imaginable issue spawned a political party. As some of those issues grew stale, however, no realignment disposed of obsolete parties. Weakened perhaps, they lingered on. The extreme fragmentation, nay, the wonderful diversity of political offerings, put a premium on ideological differentiation. It encouraged the parties to insulate each other against hostile competitors while thwarting their quest for executive power. No matter what the formal arrangements said about forming a government, and no matter how earnest or skilled the party leaders might have been, the snarled party system tied them in knots they were powerless to cut.

By contrast, the Federal Republic has been blessed with a party system that places a single party only a stroke away from majority control. A massive party realignment created broad-based and ideologically diffuse mass parties. To govern—that so-elusive goal of

[1] See Gerhard Loewenberg, "The Development of the German Party System," in *Germany at the Polls*, ed. Karl H. Cerny (Washington, D.C.: American Enterprise Institute, 1978).

German political parties—now comes so naturally to them that critical observers fear that the state has been turned over to the parties. The Federal Republic has been dubbed a *Parteienstaat*, a party state. The parties do not just play a part in forming the popular will; they run things.

THE CHRISTIAN DEMOCRATS

The strongest party in electoral terms is the CDU/CSU alliance (The Christian Democratic Union and, in Bavaria, the Christian Social Union; see Figure 21.1). Founded right after World War II, it is not simply a revival of one of those parties that went under in 1933. On the contrary, it was a calculated gamble to forge something new. To be sure, old hands of the former Catholic Center, like Konrad Adenauer, played leading roles in this venture. But their aim was to break the denominational mold that had stunted the old Catholic party. What the founders of the CDU/CSU did *not* want was another party that served as the "political action committee of German Catholicism," that would repel

non-Catholics. Instead they set their sights on rallying what they envisioned as the non-socialist majority of the German electorate behind a single party banner.

The conditions for such a venture to succeed were probably uniquely favorable in the immediate postwar years. In a perverse way, even the Nazi regime played a helpful hand. By wiping out all German parties in 1933 it gave attempts to work from scratch a fighting chance. What is more, the partition of Germany in the wake of World War II deprived the major conservative party of its (Eastern) strongholds. And Allied licensing stipulations checked any resurgence of nationalist-authoritarian parties. Voters leaning that way found themselves without a partisan home after 1945. Thus, an historic opportunity presented itself to political entrepreneurs willing to gamble on a political party with a broad enough appeal to attract a majority of German voters. None seized this opportunity more eagerly than Konrad Adenauer.

The "Christian" label permitted the fledgling party to adopt broad segments of the Protestant population now left in a state of political orphanage. At the same time, that label also allowed it to woo the Catholic clientele of the former Center party. The result was a marriage of political Catholicism with Protestant conservatism. In political colors, this was a "black-blue" configuration. Whatever its internal shades, the party was stamped by Adenauer and Ludwig Erhard, his long-time economics minister

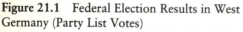

Figure 21.1   Federal Election Results in West Germany (Party List Votes)

SOURCE: Forschungsgruppe Wahlen, Mannheim.

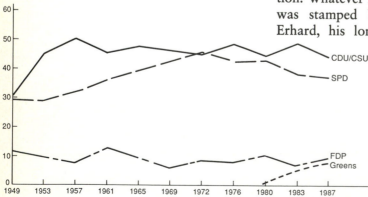

The CDU/CSU in the Early Days

. . . socialist and radical in Berlin, clerical and conservative in Cologne, capitalist and reactionary in Hamburg, and counterrevolutionary and states-rights in Munich.

SOURCE: As quoted in Heino Kaack, *Geschichte und Struktur des deutschen Parteiensystems* (Opladen: Westdeutscher Verlag, 1971), p. 172.

(1949–63), in several distinctive ways: free enterprise in the market place, conservative values in the home, strong aversion to Communism in the East, and close partnership with the West.

In foreign policy, the CDU/CSU's overriding goal has always been an unambiguous tie to Western Europe and the United States. The Federal Republic was to seek its role as a part of an integrated Europe instead of teetering between East and West. Reconciliation with France was a special priority for Adenauer, whose home base, the Rhineland, was often seen as pro-French. When the attempt to form a European army failed in 1954, the CDU/CSU became a strong advocate of the Federal Republic's joining NATO. It supported the rearmament of West Germany, though as an integrated part of NATO. While not opposed to German reunification, the CDU/CSU was not prepared to cut the ties with the West for the sake of that goal. Nationalism has not been one of the drawing cards of the CDU/CSU.

The domestic equivalent of its Western orientation is a strong advocacy of free enterprise. The CDU/CSU favors a market economy over socialism. At the same time, it is no anti-government zealot. The party tolerates and, in some instances, has initiated far-reaching social legislation. This pragmatic balancing of conflicting goals is aptly captured by the expression popularized by this party: the "social market economy." To be sure, the popularity of this concept owes less to its ideological appeal than to the "economic miracle" of the 1950s and 1960s. Nonetheless, the "social" modifier makes it possible for an avowedly Christian party to embrace capitalism without pangs of guilt.

On many other matters, however, the CDU/CSU is more comfortable with traditional orientations, be it on questions relating to the family, education, public morality, individual liberties or the place of religion in public life. No friend of strict church-state separation, though no mouthpiece of the churches either, the CDU/CSU will rise to the defense of the churches against their challengers. Overall, this is not a party that would win a prize for ideological purity, but that seems to be the price for being Germany's first democratic mass party.

The CDU/CSU has reaped ample rewards for that. From 1949 until 1969, it dominated federal governments, virtually transforming itself into a state party. And since 1982, under Chancellor Helmut Kohl, the party is at the helm in Bonn again. In all but one federal election, the CDU/CSU captured the largest share of the votes; once (in 1957) it actually exceeded the 50 percent mark. Since 1953, the CDU/CSU has never dropped below 44 percentage points in federal elections, a share no other German party ever exceeded nationwide until then.

Like any mass party, the CDU/CSU must accommodate the demands of a variety of interest groups. In this case, the list of groups ranges from big business to small business, from Catholic groups to Protestant ones, from industry to agriculture, from employer associations to labor groups active in the party, and more. Scanning this panorama of potential social conflict one cannot help but admire, grudgingly perhaps, the balancing act performed by the CDU/CSU. How impossible such a feat appeared in the pre-1933 German party system!

Of course, strictly speaking, the CDU/CSU is not one, but two parties. There is no CDU in Bavaria, and no CSU outside Bavaria; there is no such thing as a federal chairman of the CDU/CSU. But there is no electoral competition between CDU and CSU either. Where it counts at the federal level, the two "sister" parties act like a pair. They form a single parliamentary caucus in the Bundestag, just as southern and nonsouthern Democrats do in the U.S. Congress. And like them, they join forces behind a single candidate for the top political office in federal election campaigns.

All the while, very much in the vein of fratricidal warfare among U.S. Democrats, it is not beyond them to rub each other the wrong way. Under the leadership of the ebullient Franz-Josef Strauss, the CSU occasionally toyed with schemes of bolting the alliance and going federal. In 1976, Strauss briefly took the CSU on such a course over what he considered the wimpish campaign of the CDU. But when the CDU threatened retaliation by raising the possibility of a Bavarian CDU, and with rumblings of protest among the CSU rank-and-file, Strauss quickly relented and agreed to rejoin the parliamentary alliance. Talk of separatism in the CSU subsided. When the CDU/CSU returned to power in Bonn in 1982, it was without Strauss as either chancellor or cabinet minister, and without much help from him. Yet even on the sidelines of federal politics, governing his state with the longevity and public reverence of a Bavarian king until his death recently, Strauss had lost none of his bile or guile in riling his party cousins outside Bavaria.

Grown accustomed to the role of governing party, the CDU/CSU was late in assembling an organizational apparatus outside of parliament to match that of its main opponent, the SPD. For all its electoral successes,

the CDU/CSU did not become a "membership" party in the 1950s and 1960s. That is to say, it did not enroll a large number of dues-paying, card-carrying members, who would be entitled to take part in local party meetings and help mobilize the voters in election campaigns. Because of that, some observers were quick to dismiss the CDU/CSU as purely an electoral association. They viewed it as the personal following of Chancellor Adenauer. His departure from the political scene, they predicted, would prove fatal to the CDU/CSU. It did not turn out that way. What the exercise of power did not accomplish, the loss of power at the federal level in 1969 apparently did. Both CDU and CSU turned to organization-building. Membership rolls nearly tripled between 1968 and 1984 and supplied the CDU/CSU with a combined membership base rivaling that of the SPD.

At the same time, the leadership of the CDU shifted to the generation of Adenauer's grandsons and has rested for the past decade with someone who made his political mark in state government, not in Bonn: Helmut Kohl. Born in 1930, and elected party leader while premier (governor) of Rhineland-Palatinate, he took over a CDU that had been crushed by its defeat in the 1972 election. The joint parliamentary caucus of CDU and CSU chose him as their candidate for the chancellorship in the 1976 election. The CDU/CSU narrowly missed winning that election, and Kohl did not become chancellor. Yet he managed to retain his position as CDU party leader. With the expanding party apparatus behind him, Kohl was able to weather the stretch of lean years for the CDU/CSU in the federal capital. What is more, he also won the position as chairman of the CDU/CSU Bundestag caucus, thus becoming the leader of the Bundestag opposition.

Kohl's strategy for capturing political power in Bonn was to forge a coalition with

The Parties Speaking with Their Own Voices

The CDU: Christian Democratic policy continues to be based on . . . the social market economy, integration into the West, German-American friendship, Franco-German reconciliation, efforts aimed at European unification, as well as reconciliation of interests and mutual confidence between the East and the West. . . . In contrast to the Greens and to parts of the SPD, the CDU does not advocate dropping out of industrial society. . . . The Federal Republic must continue to be a modern, competitive, and welfare-oriented industrial country. . . . As an industrial country, it must be able to sell its technical products on world markets.

The SPD: The main goals of the party's peace and security policy are: a change in the structure and armament of NATO forces toward a more "defensive" deployment of weaponry . . . an agreement between NATO and the Warsaw Pact to renounce the first use of force; removal of the missiles stationed in East and West. . . . Top priority of social democratic economic policy is the fight against mass unemployment. . . . An SPD government would pass a modern working hours law that would encourage a shortening of the workday. . . . The SPD is determined that a withdrawal from nuclear power and dismantling of nuclear energy facilities . . . be carried out in the medium term.

The FDP: . . . aims at promoting private initiative . . . while at the same time reducing state intervention and various rigidities in the economy. . . . A liberal domestic policy aims at the maintenance and extension of individual freedom for all citizens. Civil rights, although guaranteed in the constitution, can never be taken for granted. . . . Safeguarding the constitutional state and thereby civil rights lies at the heart of the FDP's domestic policy. . . . The FDP also wishes to encourage citizens' active participation in environmental planning and decision making. . . . Protection of the environment needs more elements of a free market economy.

The Greens: . . . apply themselves against irresponsible waste of natural resources, whose creation required millions of years; against an economic policy which is possessed by a mania for growth and which is ready, in a shameless way, to push through its own economic advantages against the interests of millions of persons in the Third World; against a discriminatory policy by which women . . . continue to be repressed in the family, at work and in society; and against the continuation of a policy of heavy armament, which is quite obviously ready to jeopardize the survival of the entire human race.

SOURCE: Robert G. Livingston (ed.), *West German Parties* (Washington, DC: American Institute for Contemporary German Studies, 1986).

---

the third party, the Free Democrats (FDP). That party, however, was in power since 1969 with the Social Democrats. Unless and until that coalition collapsed there was no prospect for Kohl to succeed. In view of that uncertainty and his deep-seated animosity toward the FDP, Strauss advocated an all-or-nothing alternative for the CDU/CSU: either win a majority outright or stay in opposition, but no coalition with the FDP. That was his line as chancellor candidate of the CDU/CSU

in the 1980 election. The defeat in that election led the CDU/CSU to embrace the Kohl-strategy once again. Kohl was handed his long-sought opportunity when the SPD-FDP coalition did finally collapse in late 1982 and the FDP signaled its availability. Kohl quickly seized that opportunity. The CDU/CSU returned to government with him as the new chancellor through a parliamentary coup called the "constructive vote of no-confidence." (See page 318 of this text.)

THE SOCIAL DEMOCRATS

Of all the parties making claims to shape the politics of postwar Germany, none felt to be more justified than the *Sozialdemokratische Partei Deutschlands* (SPD). This is a party that demonstrated its democratic credentials with its heroic "No" in 1933 against the law that paved the way for Hitler's total takeover of power. Some 20 years earlier the SPD also proved that it was second to none in patriotism when it voted "Yes" to support Germany's entry into World War I. Having stood up for nation and democracy, with its leaders hounded, tortured or killed by the Nazis, the party proudly reestablished itself in 1945. It saw little reason to revise its party concept and reached for the reins of power with more confidence than ever before.

Yet oddly enough, at the moment of its greatest readiness, it found itself outmaneuvered by a shrewd and more daring partisan adversary in the form of the CDU/CSU. The SPD was slow in grasping the opportunities for party realignment after 1945. The party held on to its one-third of the electorate, a dependable clientele but no recipe for growth. Crushed by one electoral defeat after another, the SPD finally shed its "class appeal" and tried out "mass appeal." Gradually the strategy paid off and the SPD became a serious rival of the CDU/CSU for power in the Federal Republic.

The party's roots extend as far back as the early 1860s. The SPD is one of the world's oldest political parties still operating. By 1900 the SPD had already garnered the largest vote share in national elections, though far below a majority. The party held on to that rank until 1930. The SPD pioneered the modern type of "membership" party, what with more than one million card-carrying and dues-paying members enrolled before 1914.[2] It was a party of and for the

[2] Stephen Padgett and Tony Burkett, *Political Parties and Elections in West Germany* (New York: St. Martin's Press, 1986), p. 33.

"Workers of All Nations: Unite!" Social Democratic Poster, ca. 1900.
SOURCE: SPD, 1863–1986: Für Freiheit, Gerechtigkeit und Solidarität, Bonn 1976.

industrial working class. While closely allied with labor unions, the SPD never operated as the political action committee of the unions.

Two patron saints have inspired the party's faithful, but have also torn them in opposite directions: Karl Marx, on one side, preaching the doctrine of proletarian revolution and Communist utopia; and Ferdinand Lassalle, organizing worker associations and seeking more immediate changes through political action. From the outset, disputes between revolutionary and reformist wings have afflicted this party. After World War I, some of the revolutionary members broke away and formed the Communist party. The split deprived the SPD of one-quarter of its electoral support and kept this party looking nervously over its left shoulder.

But the split underscored that the SPD was not predominantly a revolutionary party, its strident pronouncements of ideology and Marxist rhetoric notwithstanding. The party did not hesitate, in fact, to suppress Bolshevik uprisings in the early years of the Weimar Republic. The SPD instead championed the cause of parliamentary government and behaved like a model citizen of pluralist democracy. When in power, its policies have been moderate and pragmatic, to the chagrin of its more radical activists and the hateful contempt of the Communists. Its espousal of socialism has always carried the qualifier "democratic." In all fairness, this party never was a friend of the "socialism" practiced by one-party Communist regimes.

Yet no matter what kind, socialism was definitely no winning card in the game of politics played in the Federal Republic. With the "economic miracle" giving the West German public a taste of unprecedented prosperity in the 1950s, pleas for socialism fell on deaf ears. With its foreign policy proposals the SPD fared no better. The party initially opposed the Western orientation pursued by the CDU/CSU. It was not that the SPD was in

any way enamored of Eastern Communism, but it feared that Western integration would jeopardize German reunification. At the time when the issues were being decided, the SPD said "No" to membership in the Atlantic military alliance, "No" to rearmament, and "No" to the European Economic Community.

As a party proud of its programmatic heritage, but also capable of dramatic shifts, the SPD underwent a wrenching ideological self-examination in the late 1950s. Fittingly, it was in the affluent and scenic resort town near the new federal capital, in Bad Godesberg, where the party took an ideological bath in 1959. The party congress unveiled a new policy platform. The SPD announced, in effect, the great policy compromise with the CDU/CSU. Out went the rhetoric of the class struggle, the goal of nationalizing industries, state planning of the economy, and other Marxist-inspired schemes of socialist transformation. Instead, private initiative and economic competition were praised, and the party reached out to be recognized as a people's party rather than as the party of the working class.

The SPD subsequently also endorsed the Federal Republic's ties to the Western alliance, including its military contribution to NATO. Still, the party did not stifle all its reformist zeal. The SPD kept up its demands for more equality in the educational system, more extensive worker participation in company management (*Mitbestimmung*), and more flexibility in dealing with the other Germany and the Soviet Union.

For the 1961 election, the SPD took a leaf from the book on campaigning American-style. It built its campaign on a young and attractive personality: Willy Brandt. As the popular mayor of West Berlin, then an embattled place in the East-West conflict, Brandt was also a figure in world politics and had impeccable credentials in opposing

Soviet-style communism. Brandt was also un-blemished by the Nazi past, having spent those years in exile in Scandinavia. Alto-gether the SPD hoped that he could do for them what John Kennedy had done for the Democratic party a year earlier. With its "people's party" look and personality-centered campaign, the SPD made substantial gains in the federal elections of 1961 and 1965, but fell short nonetheless of displacing the CDU/CSU as the leading party. For all its efforts, the SPD was still in opposition and likely to remain there until it could solve one more problem: enlisting one of the other par-ties as a partner in a coalition government.

In 1966, the SPD found itself in the envi-able position of being able to choose either the CDU/CSU or the FDP as its partner. It went for the safe choice, then a grand coali-tion with the CDU/CSU, but after the elec-tion of 1969 switched to the FDP. That elec-tion was widely read as *Machtwechsel,* a sweeping change of power. Willy Brandt be-came chancellor, the first Social Democrat to hold that office since 1930. But SPD and FDP together commanded only a slim majority in parliament. The tenure of this coalition gov-ernment turned into a political thriller as key measures came up for votes during the next few years. Undaunted, the SPD and FDP em-barked on an ambitious policy of détente with the other Germany and reconciliation with Eastern Europe.

The SPD also proposed bold programs of domestic reform, especially in the area of ed-ucation. The rigidly stratified German educa-tional system had long irked Social Demo-crats, who accused it of blatantly favoring the well-to-do. Access to higher education, they felt, ought to be a civil right for the sons and daughters of all families instead of a privilege, in effect, of those born to affluent families. Likewise, large industrial companies ought not to be controlled exclusively by owners and executives. Though eschewing national-

ization, the SPD pushed for a scheme of equal partnership between stockholders and em-ployees on the supervisory boards of compa-nies (*Mitbestimmung*). This was a key con-cern of the labor unions, the core supporting group of the SPD.

In the early 1970s, a new generation began entering the ranks of the party. Many had college degrees and a taste for radical ideas. Driven by a desire for social "transfor-mation," not just piecemeal corrections of consensus politics, this "new class" revived the Marxist spirit that the SPD had foresworn in Bad Godesberg. Radicals captured control of many local party branches, especially in cities like Munich and Frankfurt, where mainstream Social Democrats were eased out of their positions. The most receptive forum was the party's youth organization, the Young Socialists. They cared little for Helmut Schmidt, who succeeded Brandt as chancellor in 1974, or his all too moderate brand of social democracy. But they found a sympathetic ear in Brandt, who stayed on as party chairman. In fact, the longer he stayed as leader of the SPD—he did not resign until 1987, when he did so under a cloud—the more receptive he grew to new issues and movements. A beloved figure among the par-ty's left, Brandt often spoke warmly about the Greens and the prospect of a new major-ity to the left of the CDU/CSU.

One issue, in particular, aroused dissent within the SPD in the early 1980s: the defense policy of their own Chancellor Schmidt. Hav-ing lost power in 1982, the SPD promptly repudiated Schmidt's policy. Since then, the party's foreign policy proposals have sounded more and more critical of the United States, with neutralist and pacifist tones gain-ing strength, while its domestic proposals have taken on a Green coloration.

In the last two federal elections the SPD has fared poorly, wiping out much of the gain scored since the Bad Godesberg reforms.

How will this party make a comeback to power? All by itself, as it tried vainly in 1987? Or with an ally? If so, will it be with the FDP once again, now that the hard feelings over its "treason" have softened, or perhaps with the newcomer, the Green party?

THE FREE DEMOCRATS

It is perhaps the most remarkable paradox of West German politics that the third strongest party, the *Freie Demokratische Partei* (FDP), has been in power longer than either of the major parties. Within the West German party system, the FDP occupies a "position that is at once so fragile and so advantageous."[3] This party has been married to the CDU/CSU and to the SPD—and has divorced each of them. Both partners, have, on occasion, been mad and jealous enough to contemplate political murder. But the FDP has been shrewd enough to prevent the two from ganging up on it—or perhaps just lucky enough in an age of easy divorce and frequent remarriage.

Still, the FDP has teetered at the brink of extinction several times. To gain seats in the Bundestag, a party must win at least five percent of the votes. Never a "mass membership" party like the SPD or, in recent years, the CDU/CSU, this party has always had only a narrow social appeal. Its electoral pool has been largely confined to the better-educated and better-off.

The FDP claims the heritage of Germany's "liberal" tradition, whose roots reach back to the early nineteenth century. That liberalism is not the New Deal liberalism associated with the Democratic party in American politics. Instead, it is the liberalism of the Ameri-

can Revolution: popular sovereignty, limited government, individual rights, separation of church and state, free enterprise, and nation-building. In 1848, German liberals were near triumph, having shaken the old monarchical order and laid the groundwork for a constitutional system of government in a German nation-state. But they did not prevail, and the liberal movement soon split into rival partisan formations. The National Liberals would accept the Empire founded under Bismarck's leadership in 1871, whereas the Progressives opposed it for not meeting the liberal ideals.

Under new names, both kinds of liberals resumed their rivalry during the Weimar Republic. The successor of the Progressives helped inaugurate the Weimar constitution, while the national-liberal successor balked at first; later on, however, it participated in governments. Regardless, neither one of the liberal parties was especially good at what counts most for political parties: winning votes. By 1932, the voters had abandoned both of them as the Nazi party surged. Liberal parties, it seems, never captured a loyal clientele in the electorate, one that would stay with them in hard times as well as good times.

Yet, with their special talent to shrug off defeat, liberals rose from oblivion after 1945. This time they huddled under a single partisan roof, called the *Freie Demokratische Partei* (FDP)—a remarkable achievement for such a fractious bunch. Almost miraculously, the FDP alone captured as much electoral support in the first Bundestag election, in 1949, as its predecessors did combined in the last "normal" Weimar election, in 1928, before they went under. True to liberal form, the FDP stood for free enterprise and against government tutelage—in other words, for a market economy without any modifiers.

That made the FDP compatible, though not perfectly, with the CDU/CSU, and kept the SPD at arm's length. An SPD wedded to socialism was plainly unacceptable for the

[3] Christian Soe, "The Free Democratic Party," in *West German Politics in the Mid-Eighties,* eds. H. G. Peter Wallach and George K. Romoser (New York: Praeger, 1985), p. 120.

FDP. On the other hand, the FDP's anti-church attitude and its nationalistic tone in matters of foreign policy irritated the CDU/CSU. On the whole, the FDP found much to criticize in the CDU/CSU and proved to be a prickly and fickle partner for that party.

The FDP rationalized its government participation with claims of being the "liberal conscience" of the CDU/CSU. The FDP would serve in government, but also act as an opposition within government when the CDU/CSU trampled on liberal principles. There was always the risk that this strategy would land the FDP out of power, as happened in both the 1950s and the 1960s, or even worse, out of parliament altogether.

While in the political wilderness during the late 1960s, the FDP cleaned its political house. Out went the "liberal conscience of the CDU/CSU" principle and in came the notion of a "third force." That is to say, the FDP would be open to either side, depending on where the liberal prospects looked brighter. The party also adopted a "social-liberal" platform, emphasizing social reform more than economic *laissez-faire*. Party chief Erich Mende, whose face bore an uncanny resemblance to that of Kaiser Wilhelm II, gave way to the easy-going Walter Scheel. Even the party name underwent modernization. American-style dots were added to the initials, so technically it is now the F.D.P. instead of just FDP.

To those paying close attention to the body language of politics in the late 1960s, it was clear that the FDP under Scheel was signalling its availability to the SPD. The crux was that the FDP could not guarantee that it would be on hand to enter into that political liaison after the next election, in 1969. After all, when eyeing a new partner the FDP can no longer count on supporters of its marriage to the old one, no matter how bitter the marital strife. As it turned out, the FDP in 1969 cleared the 5 percent hurdle by less than one percentage point. But clear it did. And the FDP embarked with the SPD on a new coalition alignment in Bonn.

Having chosen a new partner, the FDP would henceforth serve as its "liberal conscience": partner of the SPD but also a check on that party's suppressed instinct for socialism. The strategy proved successful in the next three elections (1972–80), which rewarded the FDP with comfortable margins above the 5 percent minimum. German politics was set for a long "social-liberal" era under Chancellor Schmidt, who seemed more than happy with the FDP for helping him keep the more radical elements in his own party on a short leash.

Yet, the coalition snapped in 1982 as the economic crisis confronted the government with grim choices on which SPD and FDP failed to agree. The coalition collapse evoked memories of the breakup of the CDU/CSU-FDP coalition in 1966 and of the four-party coalition in 1930, the last one with a majority before Hitler came to power, which included the two liberal parties along with the Social Democrats and the (Catholic) Center. Each time, economics seemed to seal the fate of the government. But unlike the earlier instances, in 1982, the liberal party was quick, adroit and bold enough not to be left out of the next government. Under the leadership of Hans-Dietrich Genscher, also the foreign minister, the FDP forged a new coalition with the opposition party, the CDU/CSU, at the very moment that it severed its tie with the SPD. The FDP swiftly endorsed Helmut Kohl (CDU) as the new chancellor and kept all of its posts in the new government. The *Wende* (U-turn) in Bonn had been carried out smoothly. But would the FDP survive it outside Bonn? Would it now be credible to the public as the "liberal conscience" of the CDU/CSU, or would it suffer the punishment meted out for traitors?

The election of early 1983 proved surprisingly reassuring to the FDP, and the 1987 election even more so. The FDP clearly benefits from a spreading appreciation for coalition politics among West German voters. These voters do not want to see one party control the government. Even when supporting a major party themselves, they tend to approve of the presence of minor parties like the FDP. What had made the FDP long attractive in the eyes of many CDU supporters is that it could be counted on to check Franz-Josef Strauss, the late CSU leader, and keep him out of the federal government. For nearly a quarter century the FDP and Strauss were locked in a blood feud, ever since the FDP forced Strauss to step down as minister of defense. A Strauss in the cabinet would have been reason enough for the FDP not to join, or to quit. Many suspect that Chancellor Kohl did not mind. The FDP helped him stand his ground against Strauss and the more extreme elements in the CDU/CSU.

In coalition with the CDU/CSU the FDP has pressed more strongly than its partner for cuts in taxes and public spending, and for a policy of détente. In the immediate future the FDP may have little alternative but to stick with the CDU/CSU. An SPD-FDP coalition does not appear to be a winning hand in the foreseeable future anyway. The SPD, in turn, is far more concerned at this moment about the new party on its left side, a thorn but also perhaps a blessing.

THE GREENS

Stability is the hallmark of the West German party system. For nearly 30 years since 1953 not a single party made it into the Bundestag that was not in then. Something major must have happened in the Federal Republic to overturn that iron law. One key is certainly the growing concern with the environment; another is opposition to nuclear power.

Moreover, the debate over the stationing of intermediate missiles in the late 1970s gave a boost to the peace movement, which had been dormant since the advent of détente. Ecology and peace became popular rallying cries that challenged the existing political parties. Their recipes for dealing with those issues, it is fair to say, were not palatable in the late 1970s and early 1980s to a growing segment of the West German public. Discontent began to be vented through an array of "citizen initiatives." They bypassed the established political parties and tried out new forms of "unconventional" political participation.

A Green party was formed nationwide in 1979 as a partisan offshoot of initiatives concerned with the environment, nuclear power, disarmament, urban housing, gay and lesbian rights, Third World politics, and more. Among the Green founding fathers were veterans of the student movement and the "extraparliamentary opposition" of the late 1960s. Some Green activists had gone with the SPD for a while, but had found the march to positions of influence within that institution too long and frustrating. Others had developed a taste for politics in left-radical fringe groups on college campuses but felt the Communist label was too stigmatizing outside the perimeters of college politics. Still others had long dropped out of organized politics and sought an alternative life-style in the counterculture.

The Green party, in the eyes of many social scientists, represents the coming of age of the "post-materialist" value revolution,[4] with its emphasis on self-realization and participation. The Greens have taken charge of the "New Politics" agenda.[5] Others see the rise

[4] See Ronald Inglehart, *The Silent Revolution* (Princeton: Princeton University Press, 1977).

[5] See Baker, Dalton, and Hildebrandt, *Germany Transformed*, ch. 6.

The Greens
SOURCE: *Facts About Germany* (Lexikon-Institut Bertelsmann), p. 117.

of the Greens against the background of West Germany's weakening ties to the United States. Since the 1950s, a postwar generation has matured more in the wake of *Ostpolitik* than in an atmosphere of Soviet threats to the West.[6] No doubt, the Greens are a protest party against Western industrial society. Green activists abhor the idea of economic growth and the profit motive; they dispute the need for military defense and West Germany's NATO membership; and they judge the West guilty of exploitation, in the broadest sense, of the Third World. The rhetoric and style of Green politics remind those with long historical memories of the Youth Movement. Some 80 years ago in Germany that movement arose, filled with pessimism about the modern age, hostile to the spread of technical, urban life, and seeking refuge in a romantic idealism.[7]

[6] See Stephen Szabo, ed., *The Successor Generation* (Boston: Butterworths, 1983), ch. 3.

[7] See Laqueur, *Germany Today,* 1985, ch. 3.

Aside from matters of policy, the Green party also aspires to a new format of politics. It wants to take "democracy" seriously and literally: as grass-roots rule, in the fashion of mass meetings of campus politics. Leadership is frowned upon. This is not supposed to be a party run by an elite, but by its membership. To ensure that this is no empty promise, the party does not vest the top leadership in any single person, and mandates frequent changes of any such positions. Green deputies in the Bundestag are not to run for reelection, and at one time had to make way even before their term was up (the "rotation" principle). Thus the Green party represents an assault on the bureaucratization of conventional party politics and a desire to promote citizen participation beyond the perfunctory act of voting every four years and the largely passive membership in large organizations.

The Green party, to be sure, is no monolith but a patchwork of groups capable of noisy intramural bickering. Green party conventions typically feature the clash between the "fundamentalists" and the "realists." While the "fundis" see the Green party primarily as a vehicle of protest and eschew assuming governmental responsibility by formal coalitions, the "realos" are less averse to the governmental route. The only coalition alternative being debated by the Greens is the "red-green" kind, one with the SPD. In Hamburg and Hesse, the Greens tried it but without lasting success. For the federal election of 1987, the Green party convention narrowly approved a resolution that signalled a willingness to forge a "red-green" coalition in Bonn. Yet soon after the 1987 election, which failed to make such a venture at least mathematically possible, the anti-coalition "fundis" captured the leadership positions of the Green party.

Nonetheless, the arrival of the Greens has jolted the West German party system. The SPD now finds itself outflanked on the left of the political spectrum for the first time in over 30 years. The general public perceives the Greens as situated to the left of the SPD, with the SPD seen as left of center, while the FDP ends up right of center and the CDU/CSU to the right of the FDP[8] Unlike many other Socialist parties in Europe, the SPD had long been lucky enough not to be challenged by an electorally potent Communist party. The SPD's move toward the center in the late 1950s, curiously, failed to ignite any partisan explosion on its left. In the 1980s, however, the SPD lost that advantage. It has been anxiously looking over its left shoulder ever since. How have these changes affected the parties' electoral standings? How are the voters responding to the parties' appeals? How do their decisions translate into party shares and the distribution of governmental power?

References and Suggested Readings

BRAND, KARL-WERNER, DETLEV BÜSSER, and DIETER RUCHT. *Aufbruch in eine andere Gesellschaft*. Frankfurt: Campus Verlag, 1983.

BRAUNTHAL, GERARD. *West German Social Democrats, 1969–1982: A Profile of a Party in Power*. Boulder, Colo.: Westview Press, 1983.

BEYME, KLAUS VON. *Political Parties in Western Democracies*. New York: St. Martin's Press, 1985.

BÜRKLIN, WILLY. *Grüne Politik*. Opladen: Westdeutscher Verlag, 1984.

MARKOVITS, ANDREI S. *The Politics of West German Trade Unions*. Cambridge: Cambridge University Press, 1986.

WILDENMANN, RUDOLF. "The Party Government of the Federal Republic of Germany: Form and Experience," in Richard S. Katz (ed.), *Party Government: European and American Experiences*. Berlin and New York: Walter de Gruyter, 1987, ch. III.

---

[8] See Russell Dalton and Kendall Baker. "The Contours of West German Opinion," in *West German Politics in the Mid-Eighties*, eds. H. G. Peter Wallach and George K. Romoser (New York: Praeger, 1985), p. 36.

22

"Carry on, Germany!"
"Germany Needs a Chancellor Again It Can Trust!"

— CAMPAIGN SLOGANS OF CDU/CSU AND SPD IN 1987

The Act of Voting: Complicated but Decisive

Elections have given rise to great moments of hope but also despair in German history. It was a popularly elected assembly in 1848 that gave Germany its first democratic constitution, but the venture proved short-lived. Elections helped integrate the masses into the Empire of 1871, but their representatives did not govern. A popularly elected assembly in 1919 gave Germany a more democratic constitution, but voters in 1932 handed the Nazis the leverage to extinguish that same order. Nowadays an election is a commonplace event, at least in the Western half of Germany. It is no longer a life-and-death question. What difference do elections make in West Germany? What opportunity do they offer the electorate to decide who governs the Federal Republic?

THE ELECTORAL SYSTEM

To begin with, it must be noted that West Germans do not vote for chancellor or president. All they choose in federal elections are members of the lower house of the federal parliament, the *Bundestag*. But to elect them each voter is allowed to cast two votes. Take a look at the ballot shown in Figure 22.1. On the left side, where it says *Erststimme* (first vote), the voter is asked to choose a candidate from his or her district. On the right side, where it says *Zweitstimme* (second vote), the voter is asked to mark his or her preference for a party. Let us consider this second vote first.

Whatever percentage of these votes a party obtains entitles it to a commensurate share of seats in the Bundestag. Thus a party having obtained 10 percent of the party votes will get roughly 10 percent of the Bundestag seats. However, not every party on the ballot will be rewarded with seats. In order to enter the seat-allocation sweepstakes, a party must garner at least 5 percent of all party votes cast in the Federal Republic. Rounding won't help; 4.99 percent is as much a miss as is 0.001 percent.

The 5 percent hurdle was purposely installed to forestall the splintering of the party system that had afflicted Germany. No doubt there would have been more parties in the

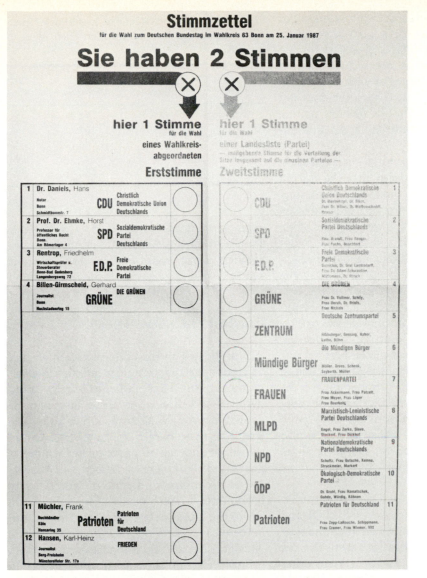

Figure 22.1   Federal Election Ballot: 1987 Election, 63rd District, Bonn.
SOURCE: German Information Center.

Bundestag with, say, a 1 percent hurdle; the National Democratic Party (NPD), a neo-Nazi party, would have made it in 1969 with its 4.3 percent of the votes. However, the 5 percent hurdle has not kept out the Green party, which cleared it with its 5.6 percent in 1983. The FDP has trembled in several elec-

tion campaigns about its prospects of surpassing 5 percent, but in the end always did so in federal elections.

Having cleared the 5 percent hurdle, how does a party decide who in particular will take the seats allocated to it? This is not a simple matter, and most Germans would be hard pressed to explain it to a foreigner. For one thing, in voting for a party a voter endorses a list of candidates prepared by that party. The ballot does not actually itemize that list; only the names of each party's top war horses are printed. The voter does not have the option of adding or deleting names, or of altering the rank order. It's a straight-ticket vote.

Say a party is entitled to 50 seats based on its vote share. That means that the top 50 people on its list can enter the Bundestag. Many of those candidates, however, also run in local districts, where voters cast their first vote. Remember the left side of the ballot where voters choose someone to represent their district. This part works exactly the same way as electing a member of the U.S. House of Representatives. Whichever candidate wins the most votes, not necessarily a majority, will go to Bonn for that district. Two hundred forty-eight members of the Bundestag are chosen from as many districts, making up half of the membership of the legislative body. The other half, and possibly a few more, is assigned from the party lists.[1] A candidate who wins a district and is also entitled to a seat based on the party share makes room for another candidate on the party list.

This embarrassment of riches afflicts only the big parties. Small parties like the FDP and the Greens do not carry any districts and thus fill their entire seat allocations from lists, as can be gathered from Table 22.1. In other words, the first-past-the-post method would produce a pure two-party system in the Ger-

Table 22.1 District Races vs. List Allocation: How the Parties' Candidates Won Their Seats in 1987

Party	District Races	List Allocation	Party Total
CDU/CSU	169	54	223
SPD	79	107	186
FDP	0	46	46
Greens	0	42	42
TOTAL	248	249	497

man parliament, just as it does in the U.S. House of Representatives. And as there, the majority party would take the lion's share of seats.

CANDIDATE NOMINATION

All candidates on the ballot with any chance of getting elected owe their nomination to a political party. That applies to district candidates no less than to list candidates. To become a party's candidate in a Bundestag district you must obtain the nomination from the district branch of a party. The local party guards this privilege jealously and frowns on interventions from state or federal party headquarters. Technically, the nomination lies in the hands of all the members enrolled in the district party organization. But neither one of the big parties conducts anything like a primary election among those members to select the party's favorite to run for the Bundestag. Instead, it is by small party committees that district candidates are typically chosen. Party regulars dominate the process. The ordinary member, who rarely attends local party meetings in the neighborhood and may be delinquent in dues payments anyway, takes little if any part in this process.

The local party activists, on the other hand, do not like to play rubber stamp. It is not

---

[1] The reason for the additional seats (*Überhangsmandate*) is that a party may actually win more seats in districts than it is entitled based on its overall percentage of the vote. In 1987, as can be seen in Table 22.1, there was one such additional seat. Thus the total membership came to 497 instead of 496. This total does not include the deputies from West Berlin, who hold a special status and are not popularly elected.

unheard of for an incumbent seeking another term to be challenged for renomination and lose. Almost one in ten incumbents have been deposed in some elections.[2] Most celebrated in recent years have been some bitter fights of big-city Social Democratic incumbents with district organizations in which the left wing gained the upper hand in the early 1970s. In the several such instances, mainstream SPD incumbents decided to quit rather than risk being dumped by their own party.

The choice of candidates for a party's list is not in the hands of local organizations, but neither is it in the hands of the national organization, which plays a quiet role in the whole nomination process. The lists are drawn up by the state (*Länder*) party organizations. They decide who gets on the party list, and in which order. Only the better-placed candidates have any chance of entering the Bundestag, so it is for those places that competition is fiercest. Much behind-the-scenes bargaining takes place among party factions as well as among organized groups supporting the party. Drawing up a party list always tests the party's balancing skill.

It is a common practice for candidates to get a place on their party list and be nominated in a district as well. All leading party figures buy themselves electoral insurance, so to speak, with highly placed positions on the list. Chancellor Kohl, for example, does not carry his local district in Ludwigshafen. He owes his Bundestag seat to his top place on the CDU's list in his state of Rhineland-Palatinate. He suffers no shame for not winning his district. Of course, Kohl could seek nomination in a district that is safe for the CDU. Instead, he prefers to run in his *Heimat*

(home place), the district where he grew up and feels at home even though he does not win there.

ELECTION CAMPAIGNS

No sooner have the local and state organizations of a party settled the business of candidate nomination than the federal headquarters of each party takes over the campaign for office. Without much doubt, Bundestag campaigns are fought over which party or party coalition should run the federal government, not who should serve in the Bundestag. These are not 248 local races or 10 state races that are conducted with local or state considerations or much emphasis on the personal qualifications of local and list candidates. These are national party campaigns, conducted under the same party banners, colors and slogans throughout the Federal Republic. Just about the only personal flavor comes from the party leaders, especially the incumbent chancellor and the chancellor candidate put forward by the major opposition party. And, of course, the CSU will emphasize some nuances in contrast to the CDU and prominently display its blue-and-white (Bavarian) colors.

The recent election in January of 1987 took place some four years after the CDU/CSU, with the help of the FDP, had taken over governmental power in Bonn from the SPD. In that interval the big issue of missile deployment was settled and the economy recovered from recession, although unemployment refused to drop below the 2 million mark. As the major party in government, and confident of its performance in office, the CDU/CSU ran a typical incumbent campaign: *Weiter so, Deutschland!* (Carry on, Germany!). It sounded like an echo of the party's motto 30 years ago: *No Experiments!* It was not a campaign of bold visions or

[2] See Gerhard Loewenberg, *Parliament in the German Political System* (Ithaca: Cornell University Press, 1966), p. 73. This work is a classic in the literature on German politics, indispensable for understanding the workings of parliament.

sharp attacks, but one that emphasized what the CDU/CSU saw as a return (*Wende*) to normalcy, steadiness, and reliability in domestic politics as well as in Germany's situation between East and West. With Chancellor Kohl the CDU/CSU had the perfect personality for such an appeal in the 1980s.

The SPD retorted: *Deutschland braucht wieder einen Kanzler, dem man vertrauen kann* (Germany needs a chancellor again it can trust). The motto aimed at raising doubts about the incumbent chancellor, about his competence as well as his integrity. It also encouraged voters to compare Kohl with his predecessor, Helmut Schmidt, and find Kohl wanting. Papering over its ideological cracks, the SPD in 1987 keyed its campaign on the chancellor question. The party picked a proven vote-getter, not an ideologically provocative figure, as its chancellor candidate. With Johannes Rau, it chose one who had proved his mettle in the SPD heartland. Rau's home base is North Rhine-Westphalia, West Germany's most populous state with a heavy concentration of old industries. It is a state having all the problems of the "rust belt" but also the time-welded party loyalties of the industrial working class. Rau's promise and the party's hope was that he would accomplish across the Federal Republic what he had done in his state: secure an outright majority for the SPD. No coalition strategy this time, neither with the FDP nor with the Greens. A centrist within a party strongly backed by the labor unions, Rau ruled out a coalition with the Greens. The FDP, of course, was unavailable as a partner for the SPD in 1987.

For the FDP, an electoral campaign always turns into a high-wire balancing act. On one hand, the FDP must prove its worth by emphasizing where it differs from the bigger partner in government; why bother voting for a copy of the original? On the other hand, the FDP cannot go too far in drawing distinctions lest it raise questions about its loyalty to its partner. Ironically, it always helps the FDP to be attacked by someone in the bigger party. Nobody could do this better than the late Franz-Josef Strauss (CSU)—the FDP's "best campaign weapon," as the jestful saying went. His nationalistic rhetoric, his tough talk of confrontation and his striving for a CDU/CSU majority in the Bundestag allowed the FDP to plead its case for restraint, détente and a check on immoderate majority rule. So long as Hans-Dietrich Genscher continued as foreign minister, so went the FDP's message, foreign policy would not be shaped by Strauss.

Electoral survival dictates that the FDP make a special appeal for the second vote, the party vote; the first vote is for the big parties to contest. Having made a coalition commitment to the CDU/CSU, the FDP can unabashedly ask for supporters of the CDU/CSU to split their ballots: Go ahead and vote for the Christian Democrat in your district, but "lend" the FDP your party vote! Since the government is run by coalitions anyway, don't worry so much about which particular party to support but make sure your most preferred coalition wins!

For the Greens, the 1987 campaign was a free play, as it were. The SPD had officially disavowed any coalition with them. So without much hope of capturing governmental power, the Greens were free to parade their ideas, parody the other parties, and make their mark with provocative campaign posters and happenings. Furthermore, two events not of their doing amplified their concerns more than anything they could have devised themselves: the Chernobyl nuclear accident with its fallout, and then, closer to home, the poisoning of the Rhine river following a spill by a chemical company in Switzerland. The Greens' gloomiest prophecies were about to be confirmed. And it did not take a single campaign speech to drive home the point.

MASS MEDIA

Electoral campaigns in West Germany are still geared to large partisan crowds, assembled in party strongholds. Larger-than-life pictures of Kohl, Strauss, Rau and Genscher, with their party autographs, adorn billboards across the country. Yet, television offers the parties a far more convenient and less expensive vehicle for reaching far greater numbers. By law, the two major networks, public corporations operating like PBS in a way, are required to make air time available to the parties for their campaign broadcasts, free of charge. The parties may use the time allocated as they please. They may feature interviews with their leading figures or commercials produced by public relations firms. In return for the free allocation, the parties may not purchase any additional air time, although they are not barred from taking out paid advertisements in the print media.

Aside from their deliberate use of the mass media for campaign purposes, the parties also benefit to a varying degree from the way the media cover them. While professing nonpartisanship and political independence, many newspapers and weeklies are not too shy to make their case for one party or another. They do so through the tone of their stories and the tenor of their editorials. It is uncommon, however, for them to endorse a particular party or candidate.

The *Frankfurter Allgemeine Zeitung,* widely regarded as first among Germany's prestige papers, minces few words about the benefits of a CDU/CSU-FDP government and the dangers of an SPD in government, with or without the Greens. So does *Die Welt.* By comparison, the *Süddeutsche Zeitung* takes a less charitable view toward the CDU/CSU, and the *Frankfurter Rundschau* leans toward the SPD and the Greens. Most Germans, of course, read none of these four prestige papers but prefer dailies like *Bild* that dwell

more heavily on more titillating fare than politics.

Where politics is extensively covered is on television (Figure 22.2) The political coverage by this medium frequently arouses the ire of the CDU/CSU. This party feels that especially the first network (ARD) puts a leftist spin on the news and in so doing hurts the electoral prospects of the CDU/CSU. In the election of 1976, when SPD and FDP won reelection by an exceedingly narrow margin, the charge was heard that television had "stolen" the election from the CDU/CSU. It was no secret that the political sympathies of television journalists lay with the SPD-FDP coalition rather than the CDU/CSU. Their political preferences, it was argued, colored their reporting of who was likely to win. That, in turn, created an "opinion climate" unfavorable to the CDU/CSU. Public opinion was swayed to expect that SPD-FDP would win, even though the heat was still dead even at that time.[3]

One of the staples of media coverage in the Federal Republic is a television debate a few days before election day. The two West German networks broadcast it jointly, as they

[3] See Elisabeth Noelle-Neumann, *The Spirale of Silence* (Chicago: Chicago University Press, 1984), pp. 157–69.

Figure 22.2   What West Germans Rate as Most Important for Forming Their Political Opinions
SOURCE: Noelle-Neumann, *The Germans.*

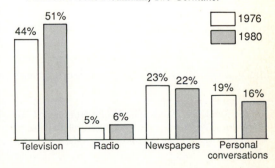

have done since 1972. However, these debates have never featured a straight duel between the two chancellor candidates. Instead, those two have had to share the limelight with the leaders of the other parties in the Bundestag, including the Greens in 1987. West Germany does not, after all, have a two-party system, and when it comes to television, the CSU proudly hoists its won partisan colors.

With four, or now five, participants and only two moderators in charge, these debates tend to turn into verbal free-for-alls, with participants interrupting one another and much questioning of each other's good manners—altogether an unruly spectacle, lacking in the supposedly German virtues of discipline and self-restraint. This is the participants' last chance to settle, on behalf of their parties, the accumulated campaign grudges; to test the thickness of the opponents' political skin in their presence; and to tag them as liars, crooks and incompetents in front of a national audience bereft of something else to watch. Even the best prepared and most attentive viewers probably despair of discerning shades of policy differences among the various parties to the debate. But what one cannot fail to notice is the visceral animosity between the leaders of the government and those of the opposition. These debates appear to be waged on the strategic premise not to win converts but to hold on to one's supporters, keep them in line and cheer them on.[4]

CAMPAIGN FINANCES

Campaigns cost money, even with generous allowances of free time for advertisement

on television. By dues, donations, and debts, German parties have long tried to finance their own operations. A mass-membership party like the SPD traditionally relied on the dues paid by its members. On the other hand, a party with few but wealthy backers, like the FDP, would depend more on donations. Yet neither dues nor donations have kept up with the ever-growing financial appetite of political parties. State subsidies nowadays cover more than a quarter of party expenditures. These subsidies are justified in legal terms as "reimbursements" of the parties for their electoral expenditures. Operationally, this means that a party bills the government a specified amount for every vote the party gained in the last election—proportional representation, financially speaking. Curiously enough, it is the Greens whom public financing has greatly benefited, an utterly unintended consequence.

Donations to parties nonetheless continue to be made on a grand scale and occasionally spice German politics with scandal. In recent time, the donations made by a gigantic but obscure company, the Flick concern, have given Germany a case of "Flick-gate." Two former economics ministers, and Chancellor Kohl almost, landed in court on charges ranging from bribery and perjury to tax evasion. The ministers Friedrichs and Count Lambsdorff were charged with granting lucrative tax waivers in return for Flick contributions to their party, the FDP. Indicted, they were found guilty in early 1987, but only on the lesser charge of evading taxes on the donations. Kohl was accused by a prominent Green legislator, Otto Schily, of having accepted Flick donations that were never reported, and lying about the channeling of donations through dummy party foundations. No indictment against the chancellor was handed up, however, because of "insufficient evidence." With no more court action or Bundestag investigations pending, talk

[4] See Kendall L. Baker and Helmut Norpoth, "Candidates on Television: The 1972 Electoral Debates in West Germany," *Public Opinion Quarterly*, 45 (1981): 329–45.

of Flick-gate subsided while a smell of impropriety lingered.

VOTING TURNOUT

In 1987, 84 percent of voting-age West Germans went to the polls. In Britain or France this would be an admirable turnout, and in the United States it would be unprecedented in this century. But in West Germany it was derided as "only" 84 percent. In fact, not since 1949 had so few Germans gone voting. In the 1970s, voting turnout surpassed 90 percent. It has been traditionally high in Germany, dating back a hundred years to the days of the Empire. Universal suffrage was given to men in 1871 and extended to women in 1919. How is it they have made such heavy use of the right to vote? Are Germans so much more concerned with politics than others, so much more convinced that their vote matters? Are the parties so much better at mobilizing their followers? If so, how did the notion of the "apolitical German" ever catch on?

Studies of voting turnout have shown that the decision to vote largely derives from a sense of civic duty. Even rational-choice models of turnout acknowledge this duty factor. Admittedly, the sense of duty may be stronger in Germany than elsewhere. The prevailing national stereotype certainly points in that direction. It is bad form in West Germany not to vote—in the views of some, even a disloyal act toward the state. But more important, a German need not make a special trip to register to vote. The residence registration, which Germans must by law file, takes care of that, probably unbeknownst to most. Voting, moreover, is always on a Sunday, in a polling station close enough to walk to, and does not take long, since there are only two votes to be cast. The inconvenience costs of voting to a German are truly minimal.

VOTE CHOICE

When going to the polls most German voters take a strong sense of partisanship with them. The symptoms of partisan behavior are unmistakable in West Germany. Each major party commands a sizeable voting bloc. Since 1961, with the postwar party realignment completed, CDU/CSU support has varied from 44 to 49 percent, SPD support from 36 to 45 percent.

The partisanship of German voters does not come out of thin air, but is nourished by a steady diet of group attachments. Being a Catholic, and especially a Catholic attending church regularly, spells "CDU/CSU" in the dictionary of electoral choice, just as it spelled "Center," the name of the Catholic party, until 1933. A Catholic going to church on election day, a Sunday of course, would be exhorted from the pulpit to vote for candidates favoring Christian principles. Seven of ten Catholics with a strong church tie (attending church every Sunday) voted CDU/CSU in 1987 (Table 22.2). Likewise, for more than a century, to be a blue-collar worker with a union card has spelled "SPD," though apparently less clearly. Six of ten such workers voted SPD in 1987.

Church-going Catholics and unionized workers define the respective electoral bedrocks of the two major parties. They guarantee each a base of support and ensure against electoral extinction. But they do not encompass the full sweep of electoral support each of those parties enjoys. The CDU/CSU could not win 20 percent of the vote with only regular Catholics, and the SPD could not do so with unionized workers only.

The recipe of success for the CDU/CSU has been its ability to attract Catholics while not repelling Protestants. Among Protestants with at least some tie to their church, the CDU/CSU draws roughly even with the SPD. The SPD's recipe, in turn, has been its appeal

Table 22.2   Portrait of the West German Electorate, 1987

Group (Cases)	Percent of Group Voting for			
	CDU/CSU	SPD	FDP	Greens
All (1,732)	43	38	9	9
Self-employed (174)	57	15	22	6
White Collar/Civil Service				
high (114)	45	28	18	8
low and middle (618)	47	33	9	10
Blue Collar				
skilled (516)	35	52	4	9
unskilled (151)	37	55	5	3
Union-Household				
blue collar (300)	29	60	1	9
white collar/civil service (168)	36	51	5	7
Non-Union (1,204)	48	31	11	9
Catholic (818)	55	30	7	6
Non-Catholic (914)	32	45	10	12
Catholics with				
strong church tie (306)	70	19	6	4
moderate church tie (255)	53	35	7	4
no church tie (257)	40	40	7	10

SOURCE: Manfred Berger, Wolfgang Gibowski, Matthias Jung, Dieter Roth, and Wolfgang Schulte, "Die Konso-lidierung der Wende: Eine Analyse der Bundestagswahl 1987," *Zeitschrift für Parlamentsfragen*, 1987, pp. 253–84.

to the growing ranks of white-collar and civil-service voters.[5] The unionized in those ranks preferred the SPD to the CDU/CSU by a 3-to-2 margin in 1987, while the non-union households gave the CDU/CSU the edge.

Both major parties, moreover, face the problem that their core constituencies are shrinking. In 1987 only one of three Catholics reported attending church regularly, compared to nearly two in three in 1953; and the ranks of blue-collar workers have dwindled from one-half of the electorate in 1950 to four-tenths by 1985. The West German electorate in the late 1980s is one in which most voters neither go to church regularly, nor hold a blue-collar job or a union card.

[5] See Baker, Dalton and Hildebrandt, *Germany Transformed*, ch. 7.

Thus, both major parties have to be adept at building electoral coalitions. An exclusive appeal to each party's traditional core constituency is a recipe for defeat and enhances the prospects of the FDP or the Greens. No doubt, the SPD has ceded electoral ground in recent elections, but the CDU/CSU has no reason to be smug. In 1987, both major parties lost ground for the first time in the Federal Republic. Their combined vote share was the lowest since 1953.

THE GREENING OF THE ELECTORATE

The Greens, who entered party politics in the late 1970s, captured enough votes in 1983 to enter the Bundestag. In 1987, they expanded their reach. The electoral profile of this party can be quickly drawn: the educated young. One of every five first-time voters in 1987 voted Green.[6] Few Green voters are older than 35.

Green support is most concentrated among those under-35 voters who have *Abitur,* that is, the diploma from a *Gymnasium.* Many of them are attending college or have recently graduated from it. Among highly educated young Germans, the Green party edges the SPD as the number-one party. This must rankle the SPD as a cruel reward for the party's devotion to educational reform, which made it possible for many of those voters to go to college in the first place. What is more, many Green voters who are employed are educators themselves. Not a few of them get their paychecks from SPD-run governments.

Small university towns with entrenched student subcultures and little industry prove most receptive to the Green appeal. Take a picture-book case like Freiburg, nestled in the Black Forest, for example. There the Greens scored a record 21 percent in 1987. What helps them, too, is the acute local concern over *Waldsterben,* the blight of forests suffering from acid rain, and over a nuclear plant nearby. The right issues for the Greens, nuclear power and environmental destruction, thus meet the right social habitat in places like Freiburg.

Green voters are distinguished from other voters by their high concern with the environment and disarmament, and their low concern with matters like inflation and social security. However, it is also worth noting that Green voters in 1987 were not oblivious to the issue of unemployment. They expressed as much concern about this problem as the supporters of the CDU/CSU. After all,

unemployment is no idle threat to many young people, including some highly educated ones looking for careers in the public sector.[7]

CANDIDATES AND ISSUES

Even though West Germans cannot vote for chancellor, the candidates for that office dominate the campaign limelight. Both major parties try to choose their nominees with an eye on the electoral bottom line. In rating the two candidates for chancellor, the West German public has typically given the incumbent chancellor a decided edge (Table 22.3). This is true even for incumbents who trailed far behind when they headed the opposition in earlier campaigns, like Brandt in 1961–65 and Kohl in 1976. Every chancellor, if Germans could have voted for that office, would have handily won reelection except one, Helmut Kohl in 1987.

In that election, the challenger, Johannes Rau of the SPD, drew even with the incumbent, actually outdrawing him in early polls. Kohl thus became the first incumbent to lack the *Kanzlerbonus* (Chancellor's edge) and to trail his party-plus-ally (CDU/CSU and FDP). A key reason: Kohl's support among FDP voters was lukewarm, with one-third of them preferring Rau to him. Contrary to his own no-Green-deal appeal, Rau was favored by Green voters almost as strongly as he was by SPD voters. Still, he was apparently unable to win either those Green supporters or FDP supporters more enamored of him than of Kohl over to the SPD. No doubt, the electoral appeal of chancellor candidates is limited. Most analysts would agree that German citi-

[6] *Forschungsgruppe Wahlen,* January 1987 survey; all subsequent data cited in this section on the 1987 election come from that survey.

[7] See Willy Bürklin, "Governing Left Parties Frustrating the Radical Non-established Left: The Rise and Inevitable Decline of the Greens," *European Sociological Review,* 3 (1987):109–26.

Table 22.3   Whom West Germans Prefer as Chancellor (Pre-election Opinion Polls)

Year	Incumbent	Challenger	Percent for Incumbent	Percent for Challenger
1961	Adenauer (CDU)	Brandt (SPD)	47	34
1965	Erhard (CDU)	Brandt (SPD)	57	33
1969	Kiesinger (CDU)	Brandt (SPD)	55	22
1972	Brandt (SPD)	Barzel (CDU)	61	27
1976	Schmidt (SPD)	Kohl (CDU)	53	40
1980	Schmidt (SPD)	Strauss (CSU)	61	29
1983	Kohl (CDU)	Vogel (SPD)	53	42
1987	Kohl (CDU)	Rau (SPD)	46	46

SOURCE: 1961–76: Helmut Norpoth, "Kanzlerkandidaten," *Politische Vierteljahresschrift*, 18 (1977): 563; 1980–87: Forschungsgruppe Wahlen surveys.

zens do not so much vote their feelings about chancellor candidates as they do their judgments of party performance and promise.

The key to such partisan judgments is often the state of the economy. In 1987, the governing parties (CDU/CSU and FDP) enjoyed a substantial lead over the opposition parties (SPD and Greens) in popular judgments concerning the all-important question of the economy. An economic record showing growth with inflation vanquished made the expected electoral impression, much as it gave Ronald Reagan the edge over Walter Mondale in 1984. High unemployment did little to help the opposition parties in West Germany. This problem, it seems, was still associated too closely with the SPD, the leading party in power until 1982.

Where, however, SPD and Greens topped the coalition of CDU/CSU and FDP was on the issues of environmental protection and disarmament. Here German voters expressed greater confidence in the "red-green" combination. Had the election turned into a referendum on just those two issues, SPD and Greens would have won the 1987 election. Unfortunately for them, that was not how voters made their choices.

COALITION VOTING

German voters are not accustomed to being governed by single parties and have grown comfortable with government by party coalitions.[8] Even many supporters of the big parties nowadays would not want their party to go it alone. In 1987, eight of ten CDU/CSU voters favored a coalition of their party with the FDP—that is, the continuation of the governing coalition. Among FDP voters, seven in ten were so minded. In effect, whether they voted CDU/CSU or FDP, those voters endorsed the Christian-liberal coalition led by Chancellor Kohl.

Among the opposition parties the pattern was less clear. SPD voters were deeply divided over the coalition question, an academic question more than a political one in 1987, to be sure. Only four of ten Social Democrats wanted a red-green combination.

[8] On the question of how German voters rank their preferences for the various parties, see Helmut Norpoth, "The Parties Come to Order! Dimensions of Preferential Choice in the West German Electorate, 1961–1976," *American Political Science Review*, 73 (1979):724–36.

The rest preferred one either with the FDP or with the CDU/CSU, though none of those alternatives topped the support for the red-green alternative. Green voters, on the other hand, embraced the SPD with surprising warmth. Nearly nine of ten would be happy with a red-green coalition and would vote SPD if no Green party was on the ballot. That does not mean they are ready to forsake the Green party for the SPD soon. What they would like to see formed is government with an SPD chancellor, checked by his Green partner.

In the mid-1980s German voting behavior was jelling into a two-bloc pattern, with one voting bloc loyal to CDU/CSU and FDP and another bloc loyal to SPD and Greens. If this were to hold firm it would deprive the FDP of its pivotal role in the West German party system. A *Machtwechsel* (change of the guard) would then be more difficult to engineer, but would prove far more sweeping if it did come about. Until now, one of the parties always remained in power during such changes. The ouster of a CDU/CSU-FDP government by an SPD-Green government would represent the first instance of a full turnover in power.

No federal election has yet been able to accomplish such a turnover. In some in-stances, however, elections gave rise to changes in the party composition of government (e.g., 1961 and 1969) or served to ratify changes made prior to the election (e.g., in 1983). Other elections simply confirmed the respective governing coalitions for another term (e.g., in 1972 and 1987). Still the initial composition of a government is not a decision made by the electorate but by party leaders in the halls and meeting places of the Bundestag.

References and Suggested Readings

CERNY, KARL H. (ed.) *Germany at the Polls*. Durham, N.C.: Duke University Press, forthcoming.

DALTON, RUSSELL, *Citizen Politics in Western Democracies*. Chatham, N.J.: Chatham House, 1988.

JESSE, EKKEHARD. *Wahlrecht zwischen Kontinuität und Reform*. Düsseldorf: Droste Verlag, 1985.

KAASE, MAX and HANS-DIETER KLINGEMANN (eds.) *Wahlen und politisches System*. Opladen: Westdeutscher Verlag, 1983.

KLINGEMANN, HANS-DIETER and MAX KAASE (eds.) *Wahlen und politischer Prozess*. Opladen: Westdeutscher Verlag, 1986.

They shall be representatives of the whole people, not bound by orders and instructions, and shall be subject only to their conscience.

— BASIC LAW, ARTICLE 38, 1

23

The People's Representatives: Partisan but Not Too Fractious

THE PLACE

Neither politically nor architecturally has the parliament ever been the jewel in Germany's crown. The Bundestag, as the popularly elected one of the two houses of the West German parliament is called, meets in a plain looking building, a former teachers' college. During a lengthy period of a much demanded renovation, the deputies found temporary refuge in, well, the city's waterworks. An unprepared newcomer to Bonn looking for the Bundestag may be forgiven for mistaking city hall, with its baroque style, or some university building for the site of the West German parliament.

The floor chamber of the Bundestag is as spacious as it is austere. The only concession to ornament is the gigantic emblem of an eagle. Members are assembled in a semicircle around the podium, and there is an unmistakable lecture-hall atmosphere (Figure 23.1). Each member of the Bundestag, or MB, has a seat and a desk along with it. The Bundestag comprises approximately 496 popularly elected MBs as well as 22 non-voting representatives from West Berlin. A regular Bundestag term runs to four years; early elections, however, may be called under certain circumstances. It is rare for a single parliamentary party to control a majority of seats in the Bundestag, although the CDU/CSU is never far away from it (Table 23.1). Only once, in 1972, did the SPD outpoll the CDU/CSU, but it still missed a majority. Throughout, the FDP has held on to a small share of seats. Though small, it was big enough between 1961 and 1983 to supply either one of the major parties with the winning margin.

A visitor attending a session on an important issue will also notice that the podium seats not only the presiding officer but also the "federal government"—namely, the chancellor along with the other members of the cabinet. The chancellor needs no special dispensation to attend the meetings of the Bundestag. He is free to speak up. No strict

316

Figure 23.1 The German Bundestag (as it looked until renovations were begun that have not been completed yet as of October 1989).
SOURCE: German Information Center.

separation-of-power doctrine keeps him at arm's length. In fact, he would be chastised for missing sessions where important issues are debated or voted on. Of course, the price for taking part in meetings of the Bundestag is being needled and grilled about his government's policies by the opposition.

THE CHANCELLOR VOTE

The Bundestag need not be content with verbal criticism. It has the option of taking action against the chancellor. It can remove the head of the federal government from office by means of a no-confidence vote. It is the

Table 23.1 Distribution of Seats by Party in the Bundestag

	1949	1953	1957	1961	1965	1969	1972	1976	1980	1983	1987
CDU/CSU	139	244	270	242	245	242	225	243	226	244	223
SPD	131	151	169	190	202	224	230	214	218	193	186
FDP	52	48	41	67	49	30	41	39	53	34	46
Greens	—	—	—	—	—	—	—	—	—	27	42
Others	80	44	17	—	—	—	—	—	—	—	—
TOTAL	402	487	497	499	496	496	496	496	497	498	497

SOURCE: Peter Schindler, *Datenhandbuch zur Geschichte des deutschen Bundestages 1980 bis 1987* (Baden-Baden: Nomos, 1988), p. 989.

Bundestag that has the constitutional authority to choose the chancellor in the first place. And what it giveth, it can taketh away. No impeachable offense need be demonstrated. It is a simple matter of what a majority of the Bundestag decides. The chancellor, in other words, serves at the pleasure of the majority of MBs. The Federal Republic thus meets the key criterion for a "parliamentary system." By contrast, the monarchy (1871–1918) did not, since it vested the authority to choose a chancellor in the Kaiser. The Weimar constitution of 1919 made the chancellor responsible to parliament by giving the latter the device of a no-confidence vote. The Reichstag could now bring down a chancellor. Little, however, was said about the Reichstag's role in installing one.

The selection of the chancellor ranks foremost among the roles assigned to the Bundestag, but it is not an everyday activity. Our visitor would have to pick a lucky day to witness it. A sure bet would be a session of the Bundestag soon after a federal election. At that time the newly elected Bundestag would take a vote—by secret ballot, that is—on who will be chancellor. Never mind that the incumbent chancellor may have led his party-*cum*-ally to a victory in that election. The Bundestag will not be denied taking a vote on the chancellor question. Kohl, for example, has been chosen chancellor three consecutive times by the Bundestag by now. The first instance, however, was quite special, a unique event, in fact, thus far in the history of the Federal Republic.

In September 1982, in the middle of the Bundestag's term that was supposed to run until late 1984, the governing coalition of SPD and FDP collapsed, as we have seen in Chapter 21. Having lost majority support in the Bundestag, Chancellor Schmidt could have decided to resign. He did not, however, but instead challenged the opposition to remove him by a no-confidence vote in the

Winners and Losers: Newly Elected Chancellor Helmut Kohl (CDU/CSU) Being Congratulated by the Defeated Incumbent Helmut Schmidt (SPD), October 1, 1982.
SOURCE: UPI.

Bundestag. He could be so bold since such a vote would only force him out of office if a majority of the Bundestag managed to select someone else as chancellor. Well, the Bundestag did just that on October 1, 1982, when 256 deputies, seven more than the required 249, voted for Helmut Kohl to take Helmut Schmidt's place as chancellor.

That motion was in accordance with what is called the "constructive-no-confidence" rule of Article 67 of the Basic Law. This rule ranks as the most celebrated constitutional invention of the Republic's founding fathers. It says to parliament, in effect, that you cannot beat somebody with nobody. There can be no more votes of no-confidence that leave a vacuum in government. Agree on a successor before dumping the incumbent, or else don't bother. The drafters of the Basic Law meant to spare the Bonn Republic the follies of the Weimar Republic, when chancellors rarely stayed in office longer than nine months. As it turned out, the chancellors of the Federal Republic have averaged almost that many *years* in office after their initial election: over seven years, approximating the tenure of a two-term American president.

The Bundestag has tried but twice to force out an incumbent chancellor by electing a successor: unsuccessfully in 1972 against Chancellor Brandt, whose social-liberal majority had eroded below par, and successfully against Chancellor Schmidt in 1982. What set the stage for the successful use of Article 67 in 1982 was a rare coalition realignment in the Bundestag. With the SPD-FDP coalition in a shambles, the FDP decided to align itself with the CDU/CSU. To be sure, this was a decision by the Free Democrats in the Bundestag, not the party organization outside parliament. Behind closed doors, the FDP caucus debated the coalition question and voted 2–1 in favor of the switch.[1] The two-thirds support for a new coalition with the CDU/CSU was enough to guarantee Kohl a majority in the Bundestag.

The constructive vote of no-confidence in the Bundestag legalized, as it were, the new liaison of CDU/CSU and FDP in parliament. It was obviously legal by the standards of constitutional law but smelled not quite legitimate. As a result, the new government resolved to call early elections, in March of 1983, to let the voters have the final word. In other words, a parliamentary license was not enough to operate a government; popular approval was needed as well.

Once the West German voters have spoken and a coalition of parties has obtained a majority of seats in the Bundestag, the suspense is gone from the Bundestag's chancellor vote. On that vote the coalition parties can count on enough discipline in their ranks to pull their chancellor candidate through. Those

who like to bet on things would be hard pressed to get any odds on most chancellor votes in the Bundestag.

OVERSIGHT

To control the everyday work of the government, the Bundestag needs more finely tuned devices than the no-confidence vote. One of them is the *Anfrage* (interpellation), which compels the officials named to address the issues raised in the Bundestag and leads to a discussion on the floor of the Bundestag. More than a thousand interpellations were handled by the tenth Bundestag (Table 23.2).

Table 23.2 Report Card for the 10th Bundestag: 1983–87

Meetings	Number
Floor	256
Committees	1,724
Party Caucuses	900
Controlling the Government	
Interpellations	
Big	175
Small	1,006
Questions	
Oral	7,028
Written	15,836
No-Confidence Motions	0
Disapproval Motions against Chancellor	3
Motion to Dismiss a Cabinet Minister	6
Legislation	
Introduced by (Passed)	
Government	280 (237)
Members of Bundestag	183 (42)
Bundesrat	59 (32)
Meetings of Conference Committee	6
Average Time Required for Passage of Legislation (Days)	259
Roll Call votes	128

SOURCE: Peter Schindler, *Datenhandbuch zur Geschichte des deutschen Bundestages 1980 bis 1987* (Baden-Baden: Nomos, 1988), pp. 993–1001.

[1]See Soe, "The Free Democratic Party," pp. 153, 185.

These exchanges are seen as tests of the mettle of officials and questioners. At the end, the Bundestag may conclude the exchange with a vote of approval or disapproval. While it can request the dismissal of a cabinet minister it cannot compel the chancellor to do so. Interpellations serve the opposition in the Bundestag as a device to engage the government in debates over basic policy issues.

Individual MBs, interested in specific and often technical items, may avail themselves of "oral questions," which in most cases will be answered by civil servants and in front of empty benches. In many such instances MBs act as errandboys for their constituencies, to settle a matter with the federal bureaucracy arising in their districts. The device of the oral question may also suit the purpose of raising issues not scheduled for parliamentary discussion, especially in instances where something happened literally overnight as in the celebrated *Spiegel* affair in 1962.

Special investigative committees have been set up by the Bundestag on occasion to probe charges of corruption. This was done recently in a case involving financial contributions to party treasuries that put even Chancellor Kohl and his predecessor, Helmut Schmidt, on the spot. To be sure, the government parties control those committees as they do the Bundestag as a whole, and their representatives are not likely to reach conclusions that would embarrass the government; to do so would be a form of political suicide. Still, an investigative committee provides the opposition with an opportunity to file a minority report and see its findings publicized in the media, especially in the *Spiegel* magazine.

LAWMAKING

The West German Bundestag has to share parliament's birthright, the making of laws, with another parliamentary body. This other body, the *Bundesrat* (Federal Council), is composed of representatives of the *Länder*. This suggests a similarity with the U.S. Senate. However, the members of the Bundesrat are not elected, nor are they free to decide matters as they see fit. Instead, the Bundesrat is composed of state officials acting in the name of their respective state governments. What some call the upper house of parliament in Germany turns out to be an extension of state governments.

Any legislation affecting the states requires approval by the Bundesrat, or else there is no law (Article 77). In the event of conflict between Bundestag and Bundesrat, a conference committee can be called to iron out the difference. On matters not affecting the states, the Bundesrat need not fall silent. Should it object in such a case to a bill passed by the Bundestag, the latter can override the veto by majority vote. However, a Bundesrat protest by two-thirds of its members requires an overrule by two-thirds in the other house as well.

Thus, should the opposition somehow muster a two-thirds majority in the Bundesrat, it could block any proposal put forward by the federal government, which almost never commands a two-thirds majority in the Bundestag. No opposition has yet been so fortunate. From 1972 to 1982, however, the CDU/CSU did control the Bundesrat while being in opposition in the Bundestag. Divided control became a thorny fact of life for the SPD-FDP government. On matters requiring Bundesrat agreement, the governments headed by Brandt and Schmidt had no choice but to compromise with the CDU/CSU opposition.

Bills to be considered by parliament are largely introduced by the federal government. Of the 522 bills submitted during the 1983–87 Bundestag term, 280 originated that way (Table 23.2), with 183 coming from members of the Bundestag, including the opposition, and 59 from the Bundesrat. Government bills are first considered by the Bundesrat, but can be taken up by the Bundestag after a certain period regardless of whether the Bundesrat has taken action on them.

As may be expected, member bills have a far lower chance of being enacted than government bills, and rare is the passage of a bill submitted by members of the opposition. Yet, the West German parliament is no rubber stamp for government bills. During the tenth Bundestag, 237 of the 280 bills introduced by the government were passed, which equals the 85 percent rate of passage for such bills since 1949.[2] And during the 1970s many that passed only did so after an eventful passage through conference committees.

The biggest and most important "bill" introduced by the government each year, of course, is the annual budget. In West Germany, the government does not have to contend, the way an American president may have to, with alternate budget proposals coming from parliament. Any proposal by MBs to spend more than provided by the government budget is futile, since the government can veto the request and the Bundestag cannot override that veto. But the Bundestag, especially in the budget committee, takes a close look at increases in proposed spending and not infrequently slashes them in incremental fashion.[3]

Like the U.S. Congress, the Bundestag rarely completes action on the budget in time for the new fiscal year. In that event, however, no special parliamentary action is required to avoid a shutdown of the government. Instead, the finance minister alone can authorize expenditures necessary to meet fiscal obligations. Most budgets are passed four to five months late. It is also worth noting that the constitution stipulates that the budget must be balanced (Article 110). However, an escape clause permits borrowing up to a specified limit. Still, the Bundestag is in no position to take advantage of that provision against the objections of the government.

COMMITTEES

To a considerable degree, the Bundestag is a parliament of committees. The roughly 20 standing committees have well defined jurisdictions, attract stable memberships and are often chaired by MBs who make a career out of that job. The individual MB spends as much time in committee meetings as on the floor of the house. After a bill has had its "first reading" on the floor, it is taken up for detailed discussion in one of the standing committees. Here, in a much more confidential setting, without the public intruding, the individual MB can make a difference. Expertise, specialization and hard work count. This is also the place where members of the opposition have a chance to affect the shape of legislation, and where much give-and-take appears to occur across party lines. Note that the Bundestag majority does not claim all committee chairs, but allocates the opposition its fair share of those posts, even on key committees.

Once a committee has concluded its work on a bill assigned to it and reports it back to the floor for final considerations, floor debate is dominated by members of the reporting committee. The Bundestag approximates what is called a "working" parliament far more than a "debating" parliament. In the latter type more time is spent on addressing big issues of policy for the general public than on settling the details of legislation in com-

[2]See Schindler, *Datenhandbuch*, p. 996.
[3]See Renate Mayntz and Fritz W. Scharpf, *Policy-Making in the German Federal Bureaucracy* (New York: Elsevier, 1975), p. 124.

mittees. Observers enamored of the ideal of the British parliament typically find the Bundestag wanting.

PARTY DISCIPLINE

Unlike most other constitutions, the Basic Law takes account of political parties. It recognizes their role in the political process (Article 21), but also endorses principles that seem to collide with the notion of party influence. According to Article 38, MBs are supposed to represent the *whole people,* not specific groups; to make decisions based on their *conscience,* not on orders or instructions. In reality, of course, the individual MB gets into the Bundestag by virtue of a party label and once there, belongs to a party caucus. Much of an MB's legislative life is spent in activities of the respective party caucus. It underscores the prominent role of party caucuses in the Bundestag that leading party figures serve as caucus chairmen. It is not unusual to find an MB with chancellor aspirations take on the job as caucus chairman. Until becoming chancellor in 1982, Helmut Kohl led the CDU/CSU inside the Bundestag, aside from being the federal chairman of the CDU organization outside the Bundestag as well. Hans-Jochen Vogel has been holding the same two jobs in the SPD since 1987.

Party caucuses meet often, and the average MB spends nearly as much time in caucus meetings as on the floor of the Bundestag or in its committees. It is in meetings of the whole caucus and of caucus committees that each party attempts to fashion a party consensus on all key issues to be taken up by the Bundestag. The caucus leadership prepares the agenda and steers the discussion. To be sure, these are meetings behind closed doors. Internal disagreements can be freely voiced and various organized groups within the parties can plead their case on legislation affect-

> The persistence of a high level of party unity . . . is above all a consequence of the high degree of party organization, which permits the parties to negotiate their internal differences in private and to reach a caucus decision which its Members are willing to support in public.

SOURCE: Gerhard Loewenberg, *Parliament,* p. 360.

ing them specifically. No doubt, the line adopted by the caucus will not please all caucus members, at least not equally. But so long as the caucus had the opportunity to discuss the matter, each member knows what is expected on the floor: to vote for the line adopted by the caucus. Not everyone always does, but overall the percentage of party-voting averages in the upper 90s, just a shade short of a perfect 100.

Party discipline is a well understood norm in the Bundestag. It is the glue that holds each party together and, if the coalition partners in government stick together, assures the chancellor a secure tenure in office. For an MB of a governing party to vote with the opposition is to jeopardize that tenure. Repeated acts of such disloyalty will not endear the rebels to their leaders or colleagues. It will jeopardize their political careers, and they had better look for another party or quit parliamentary politics altogether.

One famous rebel within the CDU/CSU, Gustav Heinemann, switched to the SPD in the 1950s and later became federal president, but this is an exceptional case. More common is the fate suffered by rebels within the FDP in the early 1970s. Strongly opposed to their party's coalition with the SPD, those dissenters in the end left the FDP. Some sought a new partisan home with the CDU/CSU. But for most of them the defection was a ticket to political oblivion. The new party was as wary of the defector as the former was unforgiving. The lesson is that party rebellion (usually) does not pay. How compatible is that lesson with the constitutional guarantee of free representation of the whole people?

Well, nobody has ever filed suit over this issue. If someone did, much would depend on how the party in dispute went about establishing its party line and how it enforced it. Say a party made you deposit, at the beginning of the term, an undated but signed letter of resignation of your Bundestag seat. This device, which was common in the Communist Party (KPD), would certainly be ruled unconstitutional. In fact, the whole party was so ruled in 1956 by the Constitutional Court of the Federal Republic.

The truth is that the leaders of party caucuses in the Bundestag have few penalties to impose on rebels within their ranks. It is not up to those leaders, for example, to decide on an MB's renomination. They may, on the other hand, see to it that he does not receive a ministerial position, a choice committee assignment or other perks at their disposal. Seldom is a rebel expelled from the party caucus. Only MBs who make a big spectacle out of their dissent and rub their party's nose in it have to fear expulsion.

Article 38 is not meant as a guarantee of tenure and promotion in parliamentary politics. It does not compel a party to give out rewards regardless of what a member does for the party. What is also important to recognize is that each party recruits candidates for the Bundestag that profess support for basic tenets of the party's values and goals to begin with. For most MBs a vote with the party is more a matter of instinct than of an agonizing struggle to reconcile one's conscience with party dogma.

With party discipline being as strong as it is, one might think that the Bundestag is an arena of merciless enmity between governing and opposition parties. That is certainly not so. Oddly enough, both sides more often than not agree with each other. It is quite rare to

witness all members of the CDU/CSU voting one way and all Social Democrats voting the opposite way. In the first Bundestag (1949–53), for example, which charted the postwar course of the Federal Republic, the opposition SPD voted with the CDU/CDU on 84 percent of the bills, its public furor over many key measures and its socialist ideology notwithstanding.[4]

Likewise, the CDU/CSU voted for 93 percent of government bills during the first Bundestag in which it was the opposition (1969–72).[5] Compared to the "adversary model" of parliamentary politics, as practiced in Britain, the West German case contains strong elements of a "cooperative model." A "grand coalition" between the two major parties is an important fact of everyday political life. Still, on the big-issue votes those parties do go their separate ways. The debates over such issues as Western integration in the 1950s, the *Ostpolitik* in the 1970s, and missile deployment in the 1980s exposed a deep antagonism between CDU/CSU and SPD.

BACKGROUND OF MBs

Being an MB nowadays is a full-time job. In fact, it's more like holding two or three full-time jobs. No doubt, the pay is attractive: the equivalent of $80,000 a year (at the rate of two Deutschmarks to the U.S. dollar).[6] Few members are able to devote any time to the non-parliamentary job they held before entering the Bundestag. The dominant occupa-

---

[4]See Wolfgang Kralewski and Karlheinz Neunreither, *Oppositionelles Verhalten im ersten deutschen Bundestag, 1949–1953* (Opladen: Westdeutscher Verlag, 1963).

[5]See Hans-Joachim Veen, *Opposition im Bundestag* (Bonn: Eichholz-Verlag, 1976).

[6]See *Week in Germany*, Nov. 14, 1986.

tional background of MBs, curiously, is the civil service. Germany is one of the few countries in which a civil servant may serve in parliament without having to resign from the service. He or she may take an extended leave of absence without any loss of perks that would accrue if the person did not venture into parliamentary politics. Running for and serving in the Bundestag is a no-risk proposition for German civil servants. In other words, they can eat their cake in parliament and have it too in the civil service.

In the Bundestag elected in 1983, 122 of 255 MBs of the CDU/CSU were civil servants.[7] That included 36 who served as cabinet ministers or as state secretaries, and a handful of salaried state employees. Among Social Democrats, even without the benefit of having MBs serve as ministers or state secretaries, civil servants nonetheless numbered 101 out of 202. Lawyers were rare among both parties, 19 in the CDU/CSU and 7 in the SPD, clearly outnumbered by employees of political parties and interest groups. At the same time, MBs with law degrees were not so rare, but their career paths typically crossed the civil service. All in all, private-sector oc-

cupations have never dominated the ranks of parliamentarians in Germany; in 1983, at most one in three MBs came from such a background.

Other than civil servants, nobody seems happy with this skewed recruitment of MBs. Politics already is bureaucratic enough to give civil servants a headstart in the parliamentary race as well. Whatever happened to the separation of powers? To the idea that parliament ought to be the place where "representatives of the whole people" meet and serve as an effective check against, well, the bureaucracy?

[7]See Schweitzer, *Basic Documents,* pp. 399–400.

References and Suggested Readings

BRAUNTHAL, GERARD. *The West German Legislative Process.* Ithaca, NY: Cornell University Press, 1972.

FRAENKEL, ERNST. *Deutschland und die westlichen Demokratien,* 7th ed. Stuttgart: Kohlhammer, 1979.

FROMME, FRIEDRICH KARL. *Gesetzgebung im Widerstreit,* 2nd ed. Bonn: Bonn Aktuell, 1980.

SCHINDLER, PETER. *Datenhandbuch zur Geschichte des deutschen Bundestages 1980 bis 1984.* Bonn: Nomos, 1986.

24

A prince, therefore, should always take counsel, but when he wants, and not when others want it. . . . But he should be a very broad questioner, and then, in regard to the things he asked about, a patient listener to the truth.

— MACHIAVELLI (1469–1527),
The Prince

Who Governs?

As is common in parliamentary systems, the Federal Republic distinguishes between a "head of state" and a "head of government." One is called the federal president, the other the federal chancellor. The makers of the Basic Law tried hard to sort out the relationships between those two offices. Without leaving room for any ambiguity, they designated the chancellor as the country's chief executive officer. They did not want to see the chancellor fall into the clutches of the president, as happened during the Weimar Republic. In those days, the president had a free hand in hiring and firing chancellors, who also could be deposed by parliament. The federal chancellor would be spared such a thankless job. The founding fathers of the Bonn Republic endeavored to create a strong chancellor, protected both against the whims of the president and the capriciousness of parliament. The political arena of the president would be closely circumscribed.

THE FEDERAL PRESIDENT

The federal president is a poor descendant of the monarch of the old days, but has to fill a monarch's shoes nevertheless—within the limits of constitutional government, that is. He shall reign but not rule, yet without the authority that derives from monarchical tradition. At the same time, he is also a poor descendant of the Weimar president, for the federal president has no popular mandate. The people do not elect him; an electoral college composed of MBs and an equal number of representatives from the states does that. He thus cannot claim to be the only public official directly chosen by the "whole people."

Not popularly elected, the federal president is also *not:* the chief policymaker, the chief lawmaker, the chief maker of governments, or the commander-in-chief of the armed forces. What is he then? In a formal sense, the president is the chief of state, "represent[ing] the Federal Republic in its international relations" (Article 59, 1). Still, do not mistake him for the chief foreign policymaker. He is not invited, for example, to the annual summits of the Western industrial nations. The chancellor is. The president's "representation" has more a social than a political ring, like being on hand to receive ambassadors and chiefs of state from other countries and visiting them in return.

In domestic politics, he lacks a veto against legislation passed by parliament, although his objections have occasionally prompted the government to withdraw a bill. Furthermore, he may neither dissolve the Bundestag nor hire or fire a chancellor on his own initiative. His authority is limited to "proposing" a chancellor candidate to the Bundestag. But the Bundestag is free to elect someone else if the president's choice does not receive a majority. Whomever the Bundestag elects, the president *must* appoint. No ifs and buts. A refusal to do so would precipitate impeachment proceedings against the president unless something was clearly suspect about the vote in the Bundestag.

It is easy, then, to dismiss the presidential office as insignificant altogether. Some actually advocated its abolition during the deliberations of the Basic Law draft in 1949. But they did not prevail. The key effects of the West German presidency are rather subtle. Even though it is no popular contest, the election of a president is often an historic event. It has served as an uncanny telltale of political winds gathering force. In 1949, the election of a Free Democrat (Heuss), with CDU/CSU

support, set the tone for the Christian-liberal era to follow. Similarly, the election in 1959 of a Christian Democrat known for his leaning toward the SPD (Lübke) raised the stock of a grand coalition. In the moment of crisis, in 1966, Lübke did his utmost to help along such a configuration.

Most prophetic was the election in early 1969 of a Social Democrat (Heinemann) with the support of the FDP, and against a Christian Democrat. This took place at a time when the CDU/CSU governed with the support of the SPD. Many read Heinemann's election as a dress rehearsal for the new social-liberal play to be staged in the federal government after the Bundestag election later that same year. Ten years later, the recapture of the presidential office by a Christian Democrat (Carstens) hinted that the days of that social-liberal coalition were numbered. Three years later it fell, and a Christian Democrat took over as chancellor again.

Among his formal responsibilities, the chancellor-nomination role does hand the president a potential trump card. West Germany, after all, is not Britain in that a single party typically winds up with a majority in the Bundestag. Someone must probe to find out who can command the support of a majority. In the Weimar Republic this was a demanding chore, given the hopelessly splintered party system and the deep cleavages dividing the key parties. It was the coalition uncertainty that gave the president sweeping leverage. Regardless of what the Basic Law says, such uncertainty would do so today as well. As it turned out, the parties of the Bonn Republic, for the most part, have proved adept and agreeable enough to form majority coalitions without presidential assistance.

That fact, more than any stipulation of the Basic Law, often relegates the federal president to the role of a messenger. He relays to the Bundestag what everyone who can read and count knows: the name of the person

---

The Federal Chancellor shall be elected . . . by the Bundestag on the proposal of the Federal President. . . . The person elected must be appointed by the Federal President.

SOURCE: Basic Law, Article 63, 1,2.

whom the parties in the majority coalition have agreed on to be the next chancellor. Were the president to forward any other name, he would suffer the embarrassing rejection of his nominee. The Bundestag would elect the majority candidate, and the president would then have to swallow hard and appoint that person. No president, in fact, has ever submitted a chancellor candidate to the Bundestag that was not subsequently elected. In 1961, however, when Adenauer's quest for a fourth term as chancellor met with opposition from the FDP, President Lübke asked for, and received, the result of a secret poll of FDP deputies that showed Adenauer with enough support to be reelected by the Bundestag.[1] It is not beyond presidents now and then to probe the bounds of their conventional influence.

Beyond their formal duties, federal presidents have made an invaluable contribution by serving on key occasions as the (good) memory and (bad) conscience of their people. That is to say, they have taken on the difficult task of addressing issues connected with the abominable deeds of the Third Reich done in the name of Germany. In so doing they face the dilemma of striving for explanations without sliding into exculpations; of assigning responsiblity without implying collective guilt; of avoiding blame that might be construed as self-serving partisanship. And they must appeal for forgiveness without asking for forgetfulness. How difficult that task can prove, even for a well-meaning speaker devoid of any personal responsibility, was recently illustrated by the fate of Bundestag Speaker Philipp Jenninger. His speech on the fiftieth anniversary of *Kristallnacht* (the Nazi pogrom of 1938) touched off such a furor that he was forced to step down as speaker.[2]

By contrast, President Weizsäcker's speech on the fortieth anniversary of Germany's defeat in 1945 was widely hailed as a bold exhortation not to forget. He chided his people for closing their eyes when there were unmistakable signs of the holocaust, and hailed the defeat of his country 40 years earlier as "a day of liberation."[3]

THE CHANCELLOR

While the president, for the most part, stands above politics and parties, but wields little power, the chancellor exercises power but is vulnerable to politics. Constitutionally, he is the head of the federal government, entrusted with the authority to make policy.

At the same time, he is singled out as being "responsible" for that policy. That says, in plain English, that he can be fired, by the Bundestag that is, for purely political reasons. The chancellor needs to maintain support of a majority in the Bundestag in order to keep his job. In making government policy, he cannot avoid politics, neither party politics nor coalition politics.

The support of his party is perhaps the key resource of any chancellor. Lose that support and a chancellor will not be able to govern effectively or much longer. It is an article of faith, though not of the Basic Law, that chancellors be the chiefs of their respective party organizations. This was true for Adenauer and Brandt, and presently holds

[3]Also note the recent address by President Weizsäcker to the congress of German historians. See Serge Schmemann, "Facing the Mirror of German History," *New York Times*, Oct. 22, 1988.

The Federal Chancellor shall determine, and be responsible for, the general policy guidelines.

SOURCE: Basic Law, Article 65.

---

[1]See Loewenberg, *Parliament*, p. 227.
[2]See Serge Schmemann, "Bonn Speaker Out after Nazi Speech," *New York Times*, Nov. 12, 1988.

for Kohl, but Erhard and Schmidt left the top party job to others. Whatever the formal arrangement, a chancellor must constantly work to nurture and secure support in his party for his policies and leadership. A chancellor cannot afford to let opposition within his party accumulate and gain momentum, nor can he afford to sow doubts as to whether he possesses the necessary personal qualities to do the job as chancellor. It would show poor judgment for a chancellor, just having won election, to take his party for granted until the next election. For it is not beyond the chancellor's party, fearful of its electoral prospects, to pressure its own man in the chancellor's office to make way in midstream.

To complicate matters, since his own party typically does not control an outright majority in the Bundestag, a chancellor also must maintain the support of his coalition partners. Coalitions are marriages of convenience between contentious spouses. To satisfy both your own party and your partner is easier said than done. It is almost like squaring the circle. Each coalition government contains the seeds of its own destruction, from differences between the coalition parties over policies, to personal rivalries, to barely suppressed suspicions of each other's fidelity. To maintain a coalition among distinct political parties in domestic politics is not unlike preserving peace among sovereign nations in world politics.

THE FORMATION OF GOVERNMENTS

For all the details of government that the Basic Law tries so earnestly to regulate, it is surprisingly mute on one essential: coalitions. You won't find the word "coalition government" in that constitutional document. This oversight notwithstanding, coali-

tion governments in the Federal Republic take shape and dissolve with law-like precision. Let us take the normal case where an election has just taken place and the various leading political actors eye their government prospects. Their actions typically unfold according to the following script:

1. Two or more parties (CDU and CSU are counted as one party) decide to negotiate the formation of a government coalition.
2. The negotiators try to fashion the policy agenda of the prospective government and to distribute the cabinet posts (Which party and which politician gets what federal department?).
3. A "coalition contract" is drafted and submitted for approval to each party's executive committee.
4. The president is consulted on the progress of the coalition negotiations.
5. The president nominates the chancellor candidate agreed upon by the coalition partners.
6. The Bundestag votes on that nominee; no vote is required for the would-be ministers in the cabinet.
7. The chancellor-elect presents the names of ministers agreed on during the coalition negotiations to the president, who formally appoints them and the chancellor.

This script has been enacted without a hitch after each federal election. The parties who initiate the coalition bargaining after a given election have never failed to connect, First down and touchdown. Moreover, they have always come up with a coalition commanding majority support in the Bundestag, although the margin of some (1949, 1969, 1976) has been breathtakingly slim (Table 24.1).

In fashioning coalition governments, the partners have reached agreement on the prospective chancellor, the policy agenda and the allocation of ministries. Of these three items, the chancellor question has always provoked

Table 24.1 Chancellors, Coalitions, and Bundestag Support

From	*To*	*Chancellor (Party)*	*Coalition Partners*	*Seat Margin*
1949	1953	Adenauer (CDU/CSU)	FDP, DP	+6
1953	1957	Adenauer (CDU/CSU)	FDP, DP, GB/BHE	+89
1957	1961	Adenauer (CDU/CSU)	DP	+38
1961	1962	Adenauer (CDU/CSU)	FDP	+59
1962	1963	Adenauer (CDU/CSU)	FDP	+59
1963	1965	Erhard (CDU/CSU)	FDP	+59
1965	1966	Erhard (CDU/CSU)	FDP	+45
1966	1969	Kiesinger (CDU/CSU)	SPD	+198
1969	1972	Brandt (SPD)	FDP	+5
1972	1974	Brandt (SPD)	FDP	+22
1974	1976	Schmidt (SPD)	FDP	+22
1976	1980	Schmidt (SPD)	FDP	+4
1980	1982	Schmidt (SPD)	FDP	+22
1982	1983	Kohl (CDU/CSU)	FDP	+30
1983	1987	Kohl (CDU/CSU)	FDP	+28
1987		Kohl (CDU/CSU)	FDP	+20

SOURCE: Adapted and updated from Helmut Norpoth, "Coalition Government at the Brink of Majority Rule," in Eric C. Browne and John Dreijmanis (eds.), *Government Coalitions in Western Democracies* (New York: Longman, 1982), pp. 12, 13.

Note: The 1953 government lost the support of the GB/BHE (the All-German Bloc-Federation of Refugees and Expellees) in 1955 and the support of the FDP in 1956, but neither defection jeopardized Adenauer's majority in the Bundestag. "Seat margin" indicates the number of Bundestag seats held by the coalition above the requirement of a bare majority.

the least controversy, and the filling of cabinet posts the most. While the prospective chancellor has the last word on who joins his cabinet, he has to weigh not only the requests of the coalition partner, but also the requests from various groups in his own party. Even more than the party lists in federal elections, the assembly of cabinet lists requires an uncanny sense of balance.

Furthermore, since 1957, no coalition has included more than two parties (counting CDU and CSU as one party). The coalition parties are always the ones who before the election agreed to forge a coalition afterwards, although SPD and FDP, admittedly, were quite coy, even devious, about their plans in 1969. The typical coalition is truly an odd couple, to be sure. It seems to pair a giant (CDU/CSU or SPD) with a dwarf

(FDP). What the dominant partner treasures the most is the chancellorship, while the small partner is content with exercising selective vetoes, be it on a matter of a policy or personnel that the small party finds objectionable. For the FDP, the coalition deal has always been quite generous, providing it with more cabinet posts than its seat share would require, and with choice selections as well, especially since 1969. Under Helmut Kohl as chancellor, the FDP controls, among others, the Foreign Office and the Economics Ministry. And Franz-Josef Strauss (CSU), its nemesis, was kept out of the cabinet.

It is rare nowadays for a government to collapse before reaching the electoral finish line. But when this happens, the president, the Bundestag, the parties, the old chancellor and would-be chancellors, the electorate, and even the country's constitutional court face some rare moments of suspense as well as tantalizing choices.

In the event that a chancellor has lost majority support in the Bundestag and no successor has yet been chosen, the president *may* dissolve the Bundestag and call new elections. Still, he may only do so "on the proposal of the chancellor." Such an opportunity arose in September of 1982, for example, but Chancellor Schmidt did not call on the president. His call was preempted when the CDU/CSU, with the support of the FDP, ousted him. By way of the constructive vote of no-confidence, as detailed above in Chapter 23 (pp. 317–19), the deputies of those two parties elected Kohl to take Schmidt's job as chancellor.

Some time after that vote, however, the president did get the call to dissolve the Bundestag. The call came from the chancellor who had just been installed with a clear majority in the Bundestag, Helmut Kohl. The purpose was to submit the new government for voter approval. For obvious partisan reasons, CDU/CSU and FDP had avoided seeking new elections before forging their coalition. But to do so now was not easy, given the constitutional rules governing the dissolution of the Bundestag. What had to be demonstrated, strictly speaking, was that "a motion of the Federal Chancellor for a vote of confidence is not assented to by the majority of the Bundestag" (Article 68, 1).

And so, in accordance with the letter of this article, Chancellor Kohl asked the Bundestag for a vote of confidence and managed to lose

The Federal Constitutional Court shall decide: (1) on the interpretation of the Basic Law in the event of disputes concerning the extent of the rights and duties of a highest federal organ. . . .

SOURCE: Basic Law, Article 93, 1.

it, on purpose, by the wholesale abstention of CDU/CSU deputies. The president, informed of the outcome of that vote, obliged, though reluctantly, and called new elections. But he certainly would have been in his right to call the vote a charade and refuse the request. In the end, even the Constitutional Court, an institution exclusively concerned with reviewing the constitutionality of government acts, had to rule on the matter. The court rejected the challenge by a 6–2 verdict, though not without a tongue-lashing from the bench. This was altogether a case where well-intentioned constitutional measures proved more constricting than constructive, forcing the political actors to play a charade everyone could see through.

MAKING POLICY

The chancellor together with the ministers of the cabinet constitute the federal government. In selecting the ministers, the chancellor needs no formal vote of approval from the Bundestag. And the president, who appoints them formally, exercises no "advise and consent" role either, though he may grumble about certain appointees. Each minister has the constitutional authority (Article 65) "to conduct the affairs of his department autonomously and on his own responsibility." But unlike the chancellor, the ministers need not worry about no-confidence votes in the Bundestag.

The cabinet, with the chancellor presiding, meets approximately once a week to discuss policy matters and reach decisions. In particular, the cabinet agenda includes bills to be introduced in parliament, the annual budget, defense and foreign policy measures, and senior appointments in the bureaucracy. It is in meetings of the cabinet that disagreements among ministers are to be resolved. The cabinet is no rubber stamp for the chancellor, his

Ministers . . . have invariably identified more with their roles as heads of departments than with their cabinet functions. It is as promoters of department policies that they will eventually be judged successful or unsuccessful. . . . Thus, the cabinet should be understood primarily as an assembly of heads of departments which must formally ratify important policy proposals originating from the departments.

SOURCE: Mayntz and Scharpf, *Policy-Making in the German Federal Bureaucracy* (New York: Elsevier, 1975), p. 43.

"guideline" authority notwithstanding. For one thing, cabinet ministers are chief executives in their own right, backed by the expertise of their respective departments and dependent upon their loyalty.

It is rare for the cabinet to settle matters by majority vote. A government in which, for example, the CDU/CSU ministers plus the chancellor were to line up and outvote the (minority) FDP ministers would not last long. The "guidelines" that matter for cabinet decisionmaking are not the chancellor's pet ideas but the provisions of the coalition treaty, that is, the items on which the coalition partners agreed at the outset.

While it is a routine operation that a cabinet undergoes every year, the preparation of the annual budget preoccupies much of its time and cannot fail to remind the government of its political mortality. Recall that the two chancellors forced out in midstream, Erhard in 1966 and Schmidt in 1982, fell over disagreements between the coalition parties over the budget. The finance minister holds special status in the cabinet because he is in charge of the budget preparation. He is supposed to arrive at agreements with the various departments in the federal government on their spending proposals. Most of his work is done before the full cabinet ever meets on the budget. In those meetings, the

finance minister is in a strong position to block attempts to reinstate cuts unless the chancellor deserts him.

In the Chancellor's Office, the chancellor has a formidable apparatus to assist him. At present that office, with its 500 or so staffers, rivals a mid-size government department with its employees in Bonn. It mirrors the organization of the federal bureaucracy in miniature format and allows the chancellor to keep up with the work of federal departments. The office grew rapidly in the early years of the social-liberal coalition but fell short of turning into a policy-planning superdepartment. It has not succeeded in taking command over the activities of the various government agencies, but acts more like a brokerage house mediating between them.

For a parliamentary system with coalition governments, the Federal Republic has enjoyed a surprising stability in the chancellor's office. West German chancellors have managed to stay in office nearly as long as two-term American presidents. Some of them have stamped the politics of the Federal Republic with a lasting imprint.

THE CHANCELLORSHIP OF ADENAUER (1949–63)

At the outset, the first federal chancellor was a most unlikely bet to last long. He was already 73 years old and was elected by a one-vote majority (his own vote, of course, as he always insisted). But despite his narrow base and post-retirement age, not to mention the enormous task of rebuilding Germany from the rubble of World War II, the new republic's first chancellor commanded the chancellorship for nearly 14 years. Of all German chancellors since 1871, only Bismarck governed longer. Note that Adenauer held office nearly as long as all 12 chancellors of the Weimar Republic (excluding Hitler) combined.

The Federal Republic Joins NATO: Chancellor Konrad Adenauer Taking His Seat at NATO Meeting, Paris, 1955.
SOURCE: UPI/Bettman Newsphotos.

On Konrad Adenauer as Chancellor

Even Adenauer's outward appearance had something suggestive. 6'3" tall, the lean, ramrod stiff Old Man towered over most of his compatriots. He exuded a natural authority and dignity, and possessed a tension that even much younger people could not match.

SOURCE: Peter Koch, *Konrad Adenauer: Eine politische Biographie* (Rheinbeck: Rowohlt, 1985), pp. 386–87.

Like Bismarck, the Empire's first chancellor, who left office when Adenauer was already a 14-year-old, the first chancellor of the Federal Republic was noted for a "will to power" and a sure hand at playing *Realpolitik.*

His style of governing became the stuff of legends in his own lifetime. His system of government was quickly dubbed "chancellor democracy." In meetings with his cabinet or party, it was said, Adenauer neither put up with much dissent nor suffered fools gladly. He was fond of quoting Article 65 of the Basic Law, the "guideline" power, and cheerfully taunted his opponents to try Article 67, the no-confidence vote, against him.

Few would deny that Adenauer was a master of the political game. But he also had to prove his mettle in the electoral arena. Adenauer led the CDU/CSU to the most resounding electoral victories a German party has ever scored, providing himself with a secure parliamentary base enjoyed by no other chancellor. Adenauer introduced party government as much as he did chancellor democracy. What is more, his government succeeded, aided by the Western powers, in quickly achieving prosperity and international respect for West Germany. In 1955, the Federal Republic rejoined the world of sovereign nations with full employment at home.

A man of traditional values in his personal life and commonly derided as a staunch conservative politically, Adenauer nonetheless broke with several molds of old politics. In the realm of party politics, he abandoned the Catholic-Center concept and gambled on a mass-party venture; in domestic policy, he took his chances with a free-market economy; in foreign policy, he dared abandon the national ambition. A successful innovator far more than a follower of conventional formulas, he put a stamp on the new republic that has not faded yet.

THE CHANCELLORSHIP OF ERHARD (1963–66)

Adenauer's successor was his long-time economics minister, Ludwig Erhard. Erhard's moon face and perennial cigar epitomized the contentment of a prosperous West Germany. By contrast to the cunning, flinty Adenauer, however, Erhard appeared, and largely was, a man without guile; warm-hearted, likeable, but unaccustomed to and uncomfortable with political trench warfare. The CDU/CSU chose Erhard because he was an enormously popular figure. Erhard was expected to ensure electoral triumphs for the CDU/CSU in the post-Adenauer era; the governing would be handled by others. He lived up to the electoral expectation in 1965, but soon afterwards faltered when West Germany's first postwar recession in 1966 undermined the public's faith in his economic wizardry and his approval ratings plummeted.

Unlike Adenauer, Erhard did not bother with party politics and was not adept at coalition politics, either. The CDU/CSU in the Bundestag practically took over the helm of government from the hapless Erhard. As the FDP quit his government in 1966—over budgetary issues—the CDU/CSU Bundestag caucus began negotiating a coalition with the SPD, the main opposition party since 1949. The CDU/CSU agreed on a new chancellor while Erhard still held the office. "Chancellor democracy" was dead, it seemed; long live "party government"! Rarely have the Bundestag caucuses, especially that of the CDU/CSU, played their hands so forcefully as in those days. But as they did, an eerie sense descended that Bonn, after all, might turn into another Weimar.

THE CHANCELLORSHIP OF KIESINGER (1966–69)

In an atmosphere of a floundering economy and faltering political leadership, the two major parties forged a grand coalition in late 1966 under Chancellor Kurt-Georg Kiesinger. Not a member of the Bundestag

at that time, Kiesinger was the premier of Baden-Württemberg, situated in the southwest of Germany; however, he had earlier served in the Bundestag and risen to stardom as his party's foreign policy expert. A convivial figure with a penchant for flowery oratory, the new chancellor presided over an unlikely combination. He himself had belonged to the Nazi party, whereas his foreign minister Willy Brandt had fled Germany as a foe of the Nazis and spent those years in Scandinavia. There was also Franz-Josef Strauss, making his government comeback as finance minister, joined by Conrad Ahlers, formerly a reporter for the news magazine *Der Spiegel*. In 1962 Ahlers had written an article on military policy that landed him in jail on charges of treason. It was the then minister of defense, Strauss, who instigated the action against Ahlers and *Der Spiegel*. The furor over those actions forced Strauss to resign.

Nonetheless, the grand coalition operated with remarkable harmony and effectiveness. Perhaps it was not all that remarkable. After all, the SPD had long adopted the role of a cooperative opposition. On many matters of economic and social policy, the CDU/CSU had long found the SPD to be more congenial than its previous coalition partner, the FDP. The new government applied some Keynesian medicine to the ailing economy and quickly restored full employment. With the German public, the grand coalition was a huge success. No West German chancellor has yet topped Kiesinger's approval ratings. For SPD voters the grand coalition was a dream come true. And CDU/CSU voters quickly embraced it with enthusiasm, having grown sick and tired of the uppity FDP.[4]

This, however, was not the way the leading cast saw the play. To them, the grand coali-

[4]See Helmut Norpoth, "Choosing a Coalition Partner," *Comparative Political Studies*, 12 (1980):424–40.

tion was a limited partnership, limited in time. Both parties' leaders hoped to end it on the stronger note and to take outright command of the government after the next election. For that reason, they agreed to reform the electoral system in such a way that either of them would be able to govern alone; no more prickly and fickle coalition partners. In the end, however, the big parties flinched. The fear of ending up the loser under the new system squelched the desire to win.

THE CHANCELLORSHIP OF BRANDT (1969–74)

Willy Brandt became chancellor in 1969 as the result of one of the most adroit coalition maneuvers witnessed in the Federal Republic. While still in the grand coalition with the CDU/CSU, the SPD found itself in the enviable situation of being wooed by the refurbished FDP, led by Walter Scheel. As the returns came in, showing a narrow seat majority for an SPD-FDP coalition in the Bundestag, SPD leaders quickly accepted the advances of the FDP and abandoned a dumbfounded CDU/CSU.

The first Social Democratic chancellor since 1930, Brandt was inaugurated with all the pomp and circumstance of a new era. This was to be the dawning of a modern Germany. "To dare more democracy," was a memorable rallying cry; *Ostpolitik,* that is, a more neighborly rapport with the other Germany, Eastern Europe and the Soviet Union, was another. For the first time, a West German chancellor met with his East German counterpart. Brandt also visited Warsaw and paid homage to the victims of German atrocities in World War II by kneeling in front of a memorial to the Warsaw Ghetto. Warmly applauded by one half of the West German public, this gesture infuriated the other half.

The reactions to this event sharply illuminated the new battle lines of conflict in the Federal Republic. Outbursts of partisan acrimony not heard since the early 1950s over Adenauer's Western policy now shattered the era of good feelings fostered during the 1960s. The new policy toward East Germany and Eastern Europe met with ferocious opposition from the CDU/CSU. It was denounced as a national sellout and as acceptance of German partition. As his Bundestag majority

First German-German Summit: Chancellor Willy Brandt Greets East German Premier Willi Stoph, 1970.
SOURCE: UPI/Bettmann Newsphotos.

On Willy Brandt as Chancellor

A talent for new things—places, people, roles. Always appearing to be firmly rooted. All in all, Lübeck [his birth place]. Then, equally firmly, Scandinavia [his exile]. In the 1950s and 1960s, Berlin [where he was mayor]. Later, through and through, Bonn: from top to bottom the statesman. . . . Afterwards, the number-one leading Social Democrat in Europe, a protagonist for the world-wide accommodation between North and South. And yet, one gains the impression in retrospect that he was always only a guest, just passing through, a life-long outsider. . . . And thus, the weeklong bouts of melancholy, the regular plunges into depression, resignation. Willy Brandt was nearly overwhelmed by feelings of total failure of his own efforts. . . .

SOURCE: Arnulf Baring, *Machtwechsel: Die Aera Brandt-Scheel* (Stuttgart: Deutsche Verlags-Anstalt, 1982), p. 745.

began to buckle, with a handful of FDP deputies defecting to the opposition, Brandt became the first chancellor to face the scourge of Article 67, the constructive vote of no-confidence.

Just barely and amidst charges of vote fraud, Brandt weathered this challenge. He won the Nobel Peace Prize for his *Ostpolitik* and led the SPD-FDP coalition to a triumphant victory in the Bundestag election of 1972, called one year ahead of schedule. Yet as he appeared safely in control, Brandt faltered. Domestic problems proved less tractable and captured Brandt's interest less than did the more grandiose task of international reconciliation. Never known for pounding the table or twisting arms, he grew visibly tired of reining in his squabbling cabinet. Brandt, it seemed, had lost his appetite for governing. When a Soviet spy was unmasked on his personal staff, Brandt immediately resigned, in a way that suggested that he was glad to have an opportunity to give up a burdensome office and turn to a new challenge.

THE CHANCELLORSHIP OF SCHMIDT (1974–82)

The parties in Brandt's government, however, stayed together and, without a hitch, elected Helmut Schmidt, the SPD's consensus candidate and eager heir, to succeed Brandt. A veteran of Bundestag politics and at one time leader of the SPD's caucus, he also distinguished himself as minister of finance as well as minister of defense. Known for his *Durchsetzungskraft* (resoluteness) and political savvy, and not bashful about his accomplishments, he was a sharp contrast in political temperament to Brandt. As chancellor, he displayed a muscular leadership and an ease in wielding power not seen since Adenauer departed. "Chancellor democracy" was definitely back in fashion.

With Schmidt at the helm, the West German government began to sound more self-confident than ever, arrogant to many foreign ears. It was not beyond Schmidt to upstage other heads of government on matters of economic and defense policy. Jimmy Carter probably was the first American president to suffer such upstaging at the hands of a West German chancellor. To his reputation for being a big mouth ("Schnauze") and a "Macher" (can-do man) were added "Schmidt the schoolmaster" and "Schmidt the paymaster of Europe." At the series of Western summits beginning in 1975, Schmidt, though short in size, stood out as a dominating and domineering figure. He acted as the leader of an economic giant, not as a self-doubting representative of a defeated nation with a guilty conscience. He was a chancellor that had the "right stuff" in the eyes of most Germans, including many who would never vote for his party. He took some chances and most of the times he won, as in the bold rescue operation of German hostages far away from home in Somalia in 1977.

Yet closer to home Schmidt fought a losing

Helmut Schmidt, Chancellor of West Germany, 1974–1982.
SOURCE: *Facts About Germany* (Lexikon-Institut Bertelsmann), p. 99.

battle to keep his own party on the political course he had charted as chancellor. Never on good terms with his party's left wing, he had little patience with the concerns of the "new social movements." Especially his policy of seeking the deployment of intermediate missiles met with mounting criticism. He was barely able to prevent his own party from rebelling against that policy. This was one of those instances where the SPD in government found itself under siege from its activists outside. And Brandt, still the party chairman, benignly smiled on the activities of the new generation. Someone less resolute and resourceful than Schmidt might have given up at that point or been deposed by his party.

The bubbling turmoil within the SPD made the FDP nervous about its partnership with that party. No doubt, Schmidt could count on the FDP. But some key figures in the FDP did not count on the SPD anymore, and began to scout for an alternative. What is more, the economic recession of 1981–82, the most severe postwar downturn, confronted the Schmidt government with some grim choices. The two governing parties sharply disagreed over the best way to handle the economic crisis: The SPD wanted to raise taxes, especially on higher incomes, and spend more on jobs; the FDP, led by Count Lambsdorff, preferred supply-side solutions like cutting taxes. Amidst bickering and mutual recriminations, SPD and FDP parted government company in September of 1982. Suddenly, Schmidt was a chancellor without a majority.

THE CHANCELLORSHIP OF KOHL (1982–)

Through the revolving door of the constructive vote of no-confidence, Helmut Kohl entered the chancellorship while Helmut Schmidt was tossed out. Leader of the CDU for almost a decade and chancellor candidate in 1976, Kohl assumed office with as firm a party backing as only Adenauer enjoyed in the mid-1950s. Kohl's immediate tasks were formidable: revive a flagging economy and

Chancellor Helmut Kohl Visiting German Troops During Exercises, 1983.
SOURCE: In-Press/AP.

steer the country through a wrenching battle over the stationing of Pershing II missiles. But more than prosperity and security was expected of the new government—the revival of a public spirit grown sullen and *ängstlich* (fearful).

That was a lot to expect from someone whom many critics contemptuously dismiss as an intellectual midget, despite his Ph.D. in political science. Indeed, Kohl is strong on expounding about homey values, but weak on articulating ideas; a bumbler in public appearances; a provincial man without a fluent command of English. With his massive body, Kohl towers over the other leaders at Western summits, but he is not seen as dominating those meetings politically. Often written off as mediocre and as a sure bet to fail, Kohl has relished his adverse image. On the eve of the 1987 election, he remarked that "I have been underestimated for decades. . . . I've done very well that way."[5] In fact, what makes his

detractors, like the magazine *Der Spiegel,* wince and howl may be exactly the source of his success.

Unlike Reagan and Thatcher, Kohl has not thrust his country into a different gear. He has not abandoned *Ostpolitik* or détente; and he has not rushed to dismantle the welfare state. In particular, Kohl has dedicated himself to the daunting task of reconciling Germans to their troubled past. His visit with Ronald Reagan to the Bitburg cemetery in May of 1985, 40 years after World War II, was undertaken with that goal in mind.

On Helmut Kohl as Chancellor

His real strength is touching the ground and having that feeling of the ground—and appealing to the man who wants simple home truths. In this way his petit bourgeois background, and even his gaffes, help him. He is regarded as a real human being, authentic.

SOURCE: Michael Stürmer, as quoted in the *New York Times,* January 21, 1987.

[5]As quoted in *New York Times,* Jan. 21, 1987.

The exercise of governmental powers and the discharge of governmental functions shall be incumbent on the Länder insofar as this Basic Law does not otherwise prescribe or permit.

SOURCE: Basic Law, Article 30.

While provoking outcries in the American public, that decision was widely applauded by the West German public.

Table 24.2 Public Sector Employment (×1,000) in West Germany, 1985

Federal level	
Government (excl. soldiers)	330
Railroads	297
Postal Service	536
Labor Office	62
Social Security	181
State (*Länder*) governments	1,914
Local governments	1,221

SOURCE: *Statistisches Jahrbuch 1986,* p. 436.

THE BUREAUCRACY

West Germany being a federal republic, the administration of federal laws lies largely in the hands of the states. Few federal departments have much of an infrastructure beyond the Bonn city limits. Instead they depend on the departments in the Länder to carry out federal policies. Rare are agencies wholly owned and operated by the federal government, such as the Foreign Office, the Defense Administration, the Federal Railroad System, the Postal Service, and the German equivalent of the Internal Revenue Service. In most areas the federal departments simply serve as the upper deck of an administrative ship anchored in the various Länder. Altogether, the federal bureaucracy in the narrow sense—excluding railroads, post, social security, and armed forces—only employs a little more than 300,000 people (Table 24.2). The Länder employ nearly six times as many and the localities four times as many as the federal government in a narrow sense. All in all, however, not a few Germans earn their paycheck in the public sector: close to one in five.

A federal department (ministry) is headed by a minister, who is invariably a member of the Bundestag and a member of one of the parties forming the government. The nonpartisan, non-political minister is an extinct species in the Federal Republic. Ministers have made their careers in party and legislative politics. They are not expected to leave all that behind once the chancellor puts them in charge of a ministry. They retain their seat in parliament and had better maintain a close rapport with their party as well. Ministers are political appointees, through and through.

The highest ranking civil servant in a ministry is the *state secretary*. He is part bureaucratic fish and part political fowl. Along with a few other high-ranking civil servants he can be removed (albeit at full pay) for such reasons as not getting along with the new minister or the new government. Below that level, tenure is a bureaucrat's best friend. In the late 1960s, the *parliamentary secretary* British-style was introduced. Like his minister, this kind of secretary also holds a seat in the Bundestag and belongs to one of the governing parties. He serves as the minister's temporary understudy and probable successor. Still, compared with the United States or even Great Britain, the slots that can be filled by bureaucrats in a new government are few and far between in West Germany. In other words, a new government inherits the bureaucracy from its predecessor and must be prepared to work with it.

Bureaucrats, especially in Germany, are supposed to be professional, non-partisan,

German civil servants frequently advise Bundestag committees, especially in connection with legislation that involves much technical detail. A community of interest between German civil servants and parliamentarians is nourished in these committees and fostered by the large number of former civil servants in parliament. . . . Our evidence indicates that German civil servants are more favorably inclined to politics and political advocacy than any other sample where comparable data exist.

SOURCE: Joel D. Aberbach, Robert Putnam, and Bert Rockman, *Bureaucrats and Politicians in Western Democracies* (Cambridge, Mass.: Harvard University Press, 1981), pp. 231–32.

apolitical, impartial and impersonal hands of the state; reliable implementers of policy, but neither critics nor initiators of policy. However applicable this ideal type may have been in the past, it certainly misses the point in the Federal Republic today. The distinction between the politicians and the bureaucrats has blurred.

Their favorable inclination toward the political game accords well with the reality that much of what West German civil servants do is *not* implementation of policies decided by politicians. Instead, what preoccupies the civil servants' time and attention far more is the formulation of policy—formulation and revision of existing policy by way of federal legislation and federal spending programs, to be precise.[6] Odd as it may sound, the federal bureaucracy is more involved in shaping policy than in carrying it out. The detailed proposals that fill the agenda of cabinet

meetings, and then become the grist of government bills introduced in parliament, are largely the work of bureaucrats.

Despite the image of a top-down command structure, most policy proposals within West German departments are initiated by their most basic organizational units, composed of not more than half a dozen civil servants.[7] These sections operate with considerable autonomy and responsibility. They are inclined to tackle problems they can handle by themselves and avoid those that raise cross-sectional rivalries. The section heads need good political antennas to sense opposition at higher levels of their department, in the cabinet and the Bundestag. Sections tend to shy away from narrow partisan politics but in order to operate successfully cannot avoid playing the political game.

Bureaucratic politics is not generally known for levity and humor, though bureaucratic snarls and excesses of "red tape" occasionally provide comic relief. In Germany everything seems possible in the bureaucracy, even the appointment as a civil servant of, well, a three-hundred pound, furry female called Luise, who speaks not a word of German, never passed a written examination, but emits an uncanny grunt when sniffing narcotics and high explosives. Luise happens to be a pig. Yes, a pig, but not an ordinary one. Her astonishing sense of smell has helped the West German police locate drugs and explosives smuggled into the country in suitcases. Her performance has earned her a civil service job in the state of Lower Saxony. After two years on active duty, the "sow in service" has been retired at roughly $60 a month, enough apparently to raise a pig family.

[6]See Renate Mayntz and Fritz W. Scharpf, *Policy-making in the German Federal Bureaucracy* (New York: Elsevier, 1975), p. 63.

[7]See Mayntz and Scharpf, *Policy-making*, p. 67.

References and Suggested Readings

HANCOCK, M. DONALD. *West Germany: The Politics of Democratic Corporatism.* Chatham, NJ: Chatham House, 1989.

KATZENSTEIN, PETER. *Policy and Politics in in West Germany: The Growth of a Semisovereign State.* Philadelphia: Temple University Press, 1987.

KOMMERS, DONALD P. *Judicial Politics in West Germany: A Study of the Federal Constitutional Court.* Beverly Hills, Calif: Sage Publications, 1976.

OLSON, MANCUR. *The Rise and Decline of Nations.* New Haven: Yale University Press, 1982.

SCHWARZ, HANS-PETER. *Adenauer: Der Aufstieg, 1876–1952.* Stuttgart: Deutsche-Verlags-Anstalt, 1986.

25

Germany will show its strength not in making, but in not making, choices that East or West might care to extract from it.
— NICHOLAS COLCHESTER AND
JONATHAN CARR,
— *The Economist*, Dec. 6, 1986

Less Butter and Fewer Guns? Issues of the 1980s

The 1980s have confronted West German governments with a score of thorny issues. Some of them, in fact, punctured the social-liberal government headed by Chancellor Schmidt. Those issues also put the subsequent government headed by Chancellor Kohl to the test. How did his government handle them? Did they strain the coalition between the governing parties? How did the opposition respond? The public at large? What do those actions and reactions tell us about the working of the West German polity? Two issues, one dealing with domestic policy, the other with foreign policy, have been chosen for a closer examination of those questions.

THE CRISIS OF THE WELFARE STATE

In the 1980s Germans had an occasion to celebrate one of the few continuities of their political existence: the 100th anniversary of the welfare state. It was, of all people, Chancellor Bismarck who in the 1880s introduced such pioneering social programs as health insurance and workman's compensation. No socialist at heart, Bismarck took those steps in large part, as he did with universal (male) suffrage, to build mass support for the new Germany and to drain support from his adversaries. While meeting demands of the socialists, the German welfare state was set up by conservatives, and rarely turned into a political football between the political right and left.

Nowadays the state provides practically womb-to-tomb coverage for almost every German: from maternity benefits, child allowances through tuition-free university education, with stipends for living expenses, to medical costs, unemployment payments, old-age pensions, all the way to subsidies for burial costs. By most standards, this is a generous package that, of course, is not "free" for the taxpayer. Payroll deductions, with matching contributions by employers, fi-

341

Günter Kundruhn is enjoying a generous retirement. . . . Today he and his wife get two pensions—one for his mid-level government job, the other the standard state pension. Together the pensions total almost $30,000 a year at present exchange rates, and . . . the Kundruhns pay virtually no tax on their income. As a result, the couple's net income is about equal to what it was when Mr. Kundruhn was working full time. . . . Mr. Kundruhn says he is able to save money and reckons that he is better off financially than three of his four children. He still helps support his youngest child, a 27-year-old daughter, giving her about $300 each month. "I'm pretty fortunate," Mr. Kundruhn says, "but quite a few of my colleagues are well off."

SOURCE: Thomas O'Boyle and Peter Gumbel, "Bonn Now Faces Task Of Finding A Solution For Its Welfare Crisis," *The Wall Street Journal*, Jan. 28, 1987.

nance most of those benefits. Deductions for old-age pension and health insurance, for example, come to three of every ten deutschmarks of gross earnings.

In West Germany, as in other Western industrial countries, social spending by government has been consuming an ever-growing share of the fiscal and economic pie. While in the early 1950s, two of ten Deutschmarks of the gross domestic product went for social expenditures, by the mid-1970s, it was one of three. The SPD has eagerly championed this trend, seeing it as a crucial means to alleviate inequality and foster social peace. The CDU/CSU, for the most part, has tolerated the growth of social spending, but has changed its tune in the early 1980s. In his inaugural address, Chancellor Kohl proclaimed: "We need a breather in social policy."

One reason for this change of mind is the growing mismatch between escalating costs and a shrinking population. With the lowest birthrate in the world—despite generous child allowances—West Germany faces a

prospect where fewer and fewer wage earners have to take financial care of more and more beneficiaries, many of them old and in need of expensive medical care. For the next century it is projected that for every German over 60, an age at which the average German retires, there will only be two working Germans.

In the short term, the fiscal pinch caused by the economic setbacks of the late 1970s and early 1980s compelled the government to take action. It was the Free Democrats and Count Lambsdorff, the outspoken economics minister, in particular, who took the lead in urging retrenchment of social spending. Lambsdorff maintained that West Germany could only hope to climb out of the recession and enjoy sustained prosperity again by cuts in social welfare. In line with this Reaganesque prescription, the Kohl government proposed specific measures, such as:

Unemployment benefits:	reduced from 68 percent to 63 percent
Maternity benefit maximum:	reduced from DM 700 to DM 510
Student grants:	from cash benefit to loan
Social security increases:	no longer pegged to inflation

The SPD and the Greens denounced these and other measures, which tightened eligibility for many benefits and taxed others, as tearing "holes in the social net" and "tearing down the welfare state." Critics claimed that those cuts would spawn a "new poverty." The labor unions and groups affected by the specific measures rallied to protest against their enactment. But with CDU/CSU and FDP agreeing on the changes, and controlling both houses of parliament, the cutbacks in social programs were adopted against the "No" of SPD and Greens.

In the 1987 election the SPD tried to make social policy a major issue of the campaign, promising the restoration of all cuts. But on matters of social security, the electorate professed more faith in a CDU-led government than in an SPD-led government, according to a *Forschungsgruppe Wahlen* survey taken in January of 1987. On the whole, the measures adopted to curb social spending resulted in slight savings for the government. When adjusted for inflation, social spending in 1983 amounted to 414 billion Deutschmarks as compared to 421 billion in 1981; for 1975 the figure was DM 370 billion.[1] Thus, it appears that the main effect was the reining in of what might have grown—would have grown under an SPD government. What the Kohl government wound up doing was to halt the growth of social spending. It stabilized such spending in real terms (minus inflation). But the safety net neither shrank nor was torn. If anything, certain threads were reinforced in subsequent years. The handling of the much trumpeted "crisis of the welfare state" in West Germany illustrates a cautious, though far-reaching and detailed, approach rather than a bold and drastic stroke. For all the sound and fury of partisan battle, the outcome did not signal a sharp reversal of policy. While Kohl made good copy for jokes (his name, after all, means "cabbage"), his policies had neither enough bark nor bite to earn him an "ism." If any-

thing, they made less of a dent than those enacted by the government of Social Democratic chancellor Helmut Schmidt a few years earlier.

FROM DOUBLE-TRACK TO DOUBLE-ZERO

With one half of Germany a part of the North Atlantic Alliance and the other half part of the Soviet bloc, international politics is no foreign matter in the Federal Republic. On the two sides of the German-German border more troops are stationed than in any other part of the world. The West German armed forces number 495,000 in peacetime, half of whom are draftees. In addition, the Federal Republic hosts armed forces of seven other NATO countries with a total of 400,000 of which more than half are Americans. What is more, a majority of the nuclear weapons for NATO forces are stored in West Germany. This country is part and parcel of the Atlantic Alliance, its army fully integrated into the Allied command structure and geared for only one military purpose: the defense of the West against a Soviet attack, not the pursuit of any purely West German objective.

In the 1970s the deployment of a new class of missiles by the Soviet Union aroused deep

---

[1]Jens Alber, "Der Wohlfahrtstaat in der Wirtschaftskrise," *Politische Vierteljahresschrift* 26 (March 1986): 28–60.

In historical perspective one cannot help but conclude that the long-term trend of public spending was broken in the mid-1970s under the social-liberal government rather than at the beginning of the 1980s under the Christian-liberal government.

SOURCE: Alber, "Wohlfahrtsstaat," p. 34.

All public transport facilities in the Federal Republic of Germany have been designed in the light of military requirements, i.e. roads, railways, airports and bridges. Freeways can be used as alternate landing strips for combat aircraft; around 90 percent of them are earmarked for troop movements and military supply use. Bridges, freeways and tunnels have been built with shafts for demolition munitions.

SOURCE: German Press and Information Office, *The German Contribution to the Common Defense*, 1986, p. 21.

concern in the Federal Republic. These were nuclear missiles with an intermediate range (SS-20s); their targets: Western Europe. The Schmidt government pressed for NATO action to respond to this threat. In 1979, NATO approved a course of action whereby offsetting missiles would be stationed in Western Europe, with most of them in the Federal Republic, should superpower arms negotiations fail to scale down the Soviet buildup. That decision came to be known as the "double-track decision." The deadline was set as 1983, after which deployment would commence.

Far from assuaging fears of the Soviet threat among the West German public, the NATO decision stirred the peace movement in an unprecedented fashion. Pacifist groups, with their sweeping demands for unilateral disarmament, were now able to capitalize on an immediate issue, something on their doorstep, that deeply divided the public. No matter the exact proportions of public opinion in favor or opposed, opposition was far more passionate and vocal than support for possible deployment of new missiles. The missile issue rattled West Germany more than any other in recent memory. Opposition in the SPD, Schmidt's own party, weakened his political influence. Even though that alone cannot be said to have driven him from office, it put much strain on the coalition with the FDP.

With Schmidt deposed as chancellor in late 1982, it fell to his successor to face up to the issue in 1983, when U.S.-Soviet negotiations in Geneva failed to reach an accord. To be sure, the major governing party, the CDU/CSU, favored deployment in no less certain terms than did former Chancellor Schmidt of the SPD. On the other hand, with Schmidt no longer chancellor, the SPD now firmly voiced its opposition. So did, far more vehemently, the Greens. In this charged political atmosphere, and with most opinion polls pro-

viding little comfort, the Kohl government of CDU/CSU and FDP in 1983 formally accepted the deployment of Pershing II and cruise missiles as part of a NATO plan to offset Soviet SS-20 missiles. The Bundestag vote revealed a sharp division between the two major parties on a key issue of foreign policy. Some saw it as the end of the foreign policy consensus that had prevailed, with some interruption over Ostpolitik in the early 1970s, since the late 1950s.

Then, as the issue appeared settled and the new missiles began arriving in West Germany, the new Soviet leader Gorbachev reopened it. In the spring of 1987, he expressed his willingness to dismantle the Soviet missiles that had given offense to the West, in exchange for a scrapping of the American missiles being deployed then. What this offer signalled was Gorbachev's belated acceptance of an offer made in 1981 by President Reagan. Ronald Reagan had then proposed what came to be known as the "zero option": no intermediate missiles on either side. But Gorbachev put a fresh twist on this plan in 1987. He offered also to get rid of missiles with a shorter range. His package was quickly dubbed the "double zero," and in the battle for international publicity it was delivered as the Gorbachev plan.

The plan put the West German government in a quandary. It was clear that the United States wished to conclude a deal with the Soviets along the lines of a "double zero." Most of the NATO countries were eager, too. At home, German public opinion favored it strongly, and the SPD and the Greens ardently embraced it. The peace movement, still smarting from its defeat in 1983, revived. Huge Easter demonstrations raised the prospect of a new season of protest. Within the West German government, it was Foreign Minister Hans-Dietrich Genscher and his party, the FDP, that pleaded for taking up the Gorbachev initiative:

If there should be a chance today that, after 40 years of East-West confrontation, there should be a turning point in East-West relations, it would be a mistake of historical dimensions for the West to let this chance slip by just because it cannot escape a way of thinking that invariably expects the worst.[2]

At the same time, the defense minister, a Christian Democrat, and leading figures in his party, as well as Strauss (CSU), intoned a chorus of disapproval (Fig. 25.1). They argued that the removal of short-range missiles especially would accentuate the Soviet advantage in conventional forces; and that it would also restrict the range of remaining battlefield nuclear weapons to German territory. They also worried that it would be a signal of United States uncoupling from the defense of Europe.

Chancellor Kohl echoed those concerns, though in a way that would not offend the foreign minister and the coalition partner, the FDP. Whatever his own feelings, Kohl had to move to a solution without provoking a rift in the governing coalition or his own party. Strategic considerations made Kohl lean toward the defense minister, his instinct for political survival, toward the foreign minister. Commenting on the disappointing showing of the CDU in two state elections at the height of the new missile debate in 1987, Kohl remarked:

> The elections are one piece of information . . . and the Federal Republic's strategic interests are another, and a more important one.[3]

If he meant it, Kohl acted coalition-wise and strategy-foolish, when it came to the showdown of the two parties in government. On June 1, the government agreed to support the

The Partisan Debate Over the Missiles in the Eyes of a Cartoonist
SOURCE: *German Tribune,* Sept. 6, 1987, p. 1.

Soviet-American "double-zero" plan, though with the proviso that West Germany maintain control over some short-range missiles (Pershing 1A). With the governing parties in accord, the debate shifted to the Bundestag. On "double-zero" alone, the government could count on the support of the opposition parties, SPD and Greens, but would take heat from its own ranks. Much of the parliamentary debate, however, got bogged down over the side issue, the Pershing 1As. SPD and Greens strongly opposed their retention, but lost the vote 239 to 163. Having failed on this point, the opposition also voted against the whole government proposal, but lost here again, 232 to 189.

Its parliamentary victory elicited little joy among the CDU/CSU, however. Many leading figures of the party felt they had given in to pressures from all sides, against their better instinct. What was most galling was the pressure coming from West Germany's foremost ally, the United States. West Germany's most prestigious paper, the *Frankfurter Allgemeine Zeitung,* known for its pro-American as well as pro-government lean-

[2]As quoted in the *New York Times,* Feb. 18, 1987.
[3]As quoted in the *New York Times,* May 19, 1987.

ings, scolded both the United States and Chancellor Kohl:

> If Government policy speeches are supposed to reflect the facts, the Chancellor could have kept it short today: He only needed to say he had been raped, which happens a lot in politics. And to be quite clear in this case, the victim should have explained that it happened with his consent.[4]

Call it rape, call it compromise, call it politics. While the winners may weep and the losers may gloat, a vexing issue was solved, for the moment at least. On the bright side, it can be noted that the government did not fall, the opposition got much of what it wanted, and public discontent was not going to explode over missiles. In the end, with the Soviets insisting on the dismantling of Pershing 1As as a condition of a Soviet-American treaty on intermediate missiles, the Kohl government gave way on that point as well.

The way in which the West German government handled the missile issue demonstrates that on key foreign policy matters, the Federal Republic is not Britain or France, free to say "No" to the United States, or even to the Soviet Union when super-power agreements are at stake. West Germany's vulnerable position in the middle of Europe, with

[4]As quoted in the *New York Times,* June 5, 1987.

Soviet troops right across its Eastern border, simply does not give it that degree of freedom. A West Germany brusquely claiming that freedom and turning up its nose at friends and foes would shake the international order to its foundation.

References and Suggested Readings

DOMKE, WILLIAM K., RICHARD C. EICHENBERG, AND CATHERINE M. KELLEHER. "Consensus Lost? Domestic Politics and the 'Crisis' in NATO." *World Politics,* XXXIX (April 1987): 382–407.

FLORA, PETER, AND ARNOLD J. HEIDENHEIMER. *The Development of Welfare States in Europe and America.* New Brunswick: Transaction Books, 1981.

HANRIEDER, WOLFRAM, ed. *West German Foreign Policy, 1949–1979.* Boulder, Colo.: Westview Press, 1980.

HELLWIG, MARTIN, AND MANFRED J. M. NEUMANN. "Economic Policy in Germany: Was There a Turnaround?" *Economic Policy* (Oct. 1987): 103–145.

RATTINGER, HANS. "The Federal Republic of Germany: Much Ado about (Almost) Nothing." In Gregory Flynn and Hans Rattinger (eds.), *The Public and Atlantic Defense.* Totowa, N.J.: Rowman & Allanheld, 1985.

SCHWEIGLER, GEBHARD. *West German Foreign Policy: The Domestic Setting.* New York: Praeger, 1984.

26

On the prosperous side of a sundered Germany, in a nation that still lowers its voice because of the Nazi crimes, that is reluctant to translate its economic might into political clout and that is geographically and psychologically vulnerable to blandishments from the Communist East, a search for an acceptable homeland goes on.

— JAMES MARKHAM, *New York Times*, Aug. 2, 1987

German Prospects

At age 40, the Federal Republic has many reasons to celebrate. The country has achieved unheard-of prosperity as well as social peace, with no blatant signs of urban squalor or visible pockets of poverty. Parliamentary democracy has worn well, as even critics of German society admit. To some, the suit feels a little tight in certain places, but no extremist party or movement threatens the constitutional fabric. The political parties that designed the constitutional order have taken root in the West German electorate. Their leaders have learned to wield political authority with a firm hand while forging durable coalition arrangements. Meanwhile the citizens of the Federal Republic express great satisfaction with their democracy.

As a country in the world of nations, the Federal Republic leads the life of a quiet neighbor. It is a loyal and respected member of both the European Community and the North Atlantic Alliance. Its borders with other countries of the European Community obstruct trade and travel hardly any more than do the borders of the West German Länder. In 1992, when the European Community removes its final barriers, the widely acclaimed moment will most likely prove to be an anticlimactic event for the Federal Re-

public. For all the military preparation against a Soviet attack, the country conducts its relationship with the Soviet Union in a business-like fashion. Soviet leader Gorbachev has an extremely good press in West Germany and a glowing image in public opinion.

It is the best that Germany ever had, at least in the West; so people believe. It almost sounds too good to be true. What about those "incomprehensible, contradictory, surprising and frightening Germans"? If anything may be incomprehensible it is how easily the democratic order has settled in the Federal Republic, given how insurmountable the obstacles appeared in the past and how dire the predictions had sounded; how agreeably the Federal Republic fits in with the rest of the world; how averse it is to power politics. What is startling, however, is how little West Germans are proud of their country. They are satisfied without being proud. They value the status quo but feel ill at ease defending it. Risk aversion runs deep and wide in West Germany.

This aversion can be seen in such diverse manifestations as the country's negative reproduction rate—the Federal Republic is the country with the lowest birthrate in the

West Germany is becoming more self-confidently German—a force for democracy, for capitalist wealth with a social conscience (now with Green cleanliness added), for peaceful coexistence and contact with neighbours whatever their ideology.

SOURCE: Nicholas Colchester and Jonathan Carr, *Economist,* Dec. 6, 1986.

world; or the widespread refusal among Germany's young people, especially the educated, to serve in the armed forces. Is the Federal Republic not worth defending militarily in their eyes? The new social movements and the Green party resonate with fear of risks, be it the risk of nuclear annihilation or ecological destruction.

But mainstream politics has its protectionist streak as well. "Stability" and "reliability," rather than challenges to entrenched interests and sharp departures from familiar paths, are the keywords of the Center-Right government of Chancellor Kohl. But as so often, one person's safeguard is another one's obstacle. Laws and regulations designed with the noblest intention to protect the jobs of the employed make it tough for the unemployed to get jobs. Rigid closing hours for shops stifle the growth of the service sector as the industrial sector shrinks and the public sector does little hiring, especially in the teaching field. Despite record surpluses in international trade, a rock-hard currency, vigorous economic growth again, and a declining population, nearly two million remain out of work. Still, those numbers did not provoke a "throw out the rascals" reaction in the 1987 election. Instead the Kohl government was comfortably reelected.

Predictability, safeguards and protection of accrued rights and privileges have emerged as the guidelines and catchwords of the 1980s.

SOURCE: Josef Joffe, *Süddeutsche Zeitung,* May 21, 1988.

In dealing with governments of other countries, West German leaders have learned the art of speaking softly while carrying a big stick, albeit a carefully wrapped one. More often they balk at requests from others to take certain actions—like stimulating their economy—than press them to accept German initiatives. All in all, the Federal Republic acts as if it were more comfortable in the shadow than in the sun of world politics.

There is no question that this is a nation haunted by its pre-1945 past, especially the gruesome 12-year Nazi period. The consequences of that past tie the hands of the republic in no uncertain way. For West Germany, the price of economic recovery and political rehabilitation after World War II was the forsaking of the national ambition. The Federal Republic would play (Western) group politics. It would swear off any go-alone kind of policy and thus avoid ending up standing alone one day. For the Federal Republic to assert German interests in a way that would cut itself off from the West, especially the United States, is nearly unthinkable.

Until now the country has been quite willing to pay the price. But will it do so forever? On one hand there is the temptation to escape from the perils of world politics by turning the Federal Republic into a neutral and arms-free zone; to play, in other words, a German hand by not playing at all anymore. On the other hand there is the temptation to play a German hand with all the cards at one's disposal, regardless of what the other players might do; in other words, to claim an influence in pursuing German interests commensurate with the power of the Federal Republic. While the first alternative enjoys vocal support among Greens and a good number of Social Democrats, the second alternative lies dormant, thus far. But it would be naive to believe that, given the economic and military clout of the Federal Republic, such an alternative is forever dead and buried. Cracks in

East Germans start hammering the Berlin Wall while waiting for a mechanical shovel to make a new crossing point in November 1989.
SOURCE: Reuters/Bettmann Newsphotos.

the Western Alliance, a disengagement of the United States from Europe, atrophy of the European Community, could all spark a German drive to take the country's destiny into its own hands.

The changes introduced or tolerated by Soviet leader Gorbachev in the Eastern bloc also open new and tantalizing vistas for the Federal Republic. The move toward democracy, especially in Poland and Hungary, has sparked a mass flight of East Germans to West Germany via those two countries. "The stark images of the extraordinary exodus— East Germans clambering over fences, besieging trains, rushing embassies and finally clenching in ecstasy on reaching West Germany—have served a brutal indictment on [Honecker's] Government."[1]

[1] Serge Schmemann, "Sour German Birthday," *New York Times,* October 6, 1989.

It is questionable how far East German leaders can go in dismantling Communism without dissolving a state that lacks a well-defined national base and has to live face to face with a free and prosperous neighbor of the same nationality. Granting political freedom in East Germany may very well spell the freedom of its people to demand union with West Germans under a joint political roof, lest the exodus to the West bleed East Germany dry. Once again, the national question is on the agenda, this time with active participation by the Federal Republic; nevertheless, West Germans seem as much bewildered as gratified by the joy with which the newcomers from the East embrace them. Once again, of course, the national question is an issue that Germans will not be able or allowed to solve by themselves. But this time, many Germans in the West do not appear too unhappy about that constraint.

IV

THE SOVIET UNION

> The steppe is vast and man is small.
> — CHINGIZ AITMATOV, *The Day Lasts More Than a Hundred Years*

27

Overview

In virtually every significant dimension that affects the governing of modern society, the Soviet Union looks quite different from the three other major countries examined in this book.

SIZE

Whoever is in charge in Moscow has responsibility for ruling a land area that covers one-seventh of the earth's surface. Consider that 20 Frances, 20 West Germanies and 25 United Kingdoms could all fit into the territory of the USSR *at the same time*.

While such a territory holds within it a substantial portion of the world's key energy and mineral resources, it also presents staggering problems of utilization of those resources. The USSR contains within its borders 20 percent of the world's coal, 10 percent of its oil, and one-third of the world's natural gas and iron ore. But just getting the oil, for example, from Siberia, Central Asia and the Far East, where most of it is found, to European Russia where most of it is used, or to markets in Eastern and Western Europe, requires more than 50,000 miles of pipeline.

Further, possessing a land area of 8,650,000 square miles does not automatically mean that this land will be productive enough to feed the country's population. Roughly three-quarters of the land area of the Soviet Union lies above 50° north latitude (about that of Winnipeg, Canada). In fact, only 27 percent of the land is considered usable for agriculture, with only 10 percent arable.

Being such a large country also means having lots of neighbors. The Soviet Union borders on 12 other countries and, looking only at its recent history, has engaged in military conflict in or with eight of them. Modern governments of all types—and those of communist countries are no exception—take it as their responsibility to provide for the security of their country—and of course of their own place in power. For the Soviet Union this task is not only huge, given the country's size, but very real, given its history.

POPULATION

With nearly 287 million people as of 1989, the Soviet Union ranks third in population among the world's states. While the country thus has less than one-fifth more people than the United States, they live in a territory two and one-half times as large. The population is unevenly dispersed in the country, with roughly 75 percent of the population living in the European—that is, Western—parts of the country. On the other hand, the population is growing much faster in the Soviet central Asian republics than in the European regions, which poses the problem of how to get this new group of job seekers together with the industries that provide the jobs. A much higher proportion of the population (20 percent) works in agriculture in the USSR than in the United States (5 percent). But as in the United States, the Soviet population is an aging one. The number of people in retirement pensions jumped from under one million in 1950 to nearly 60 million by 1989. This presents the government with pressing policy issues related to health care and labor force that are not unlike those in the West.

Equally pressing problems derive from the ethnic diversity of the population. Containing more than one hundred different national groups, the Soviet Union is one of the most ethnically diverse countries in the world (see Table 27.1). Ethnic Russians constitute the largest single group, just over one-half of the population, but will by most estimates fall below a majority by the year 2000. For the Soviet government this diversity and the relatively slow growth of the Russian and almost all other European populations in the country creates critical questions of economic and cultural policy, problems of staffing and representation in government, and even of language incompatibility—Soviet sociologists estimate that one-third of the country's population is not fluent in Russian.

POLITICAL SYSTEM

The governing system of the Soviet Union stands in equally sharp contrast to those in Britain, France, and West Germany. These states are characterized by systems of parliamentary democracy, competing political parties, politically vulnerable leadership and an established tradition of direct citizen involvement. The USSR, on the other hand, is a one-party state. Political competition takes place within the ruling party, the Communist Party of the Soviet Union, and the leaders of this party are the leaders of the country. In general they are vulnerable only to the wishes and power of the other top members of the party. Citizen participation, while not absent, has until recently been strictly limited.

Institutions familiar to students of Western democracies, such as parliaments, do exist in the Soviet Union, but the governing power does not reside there. While the public is encouraged to get involved in the business of running the country, this involvement has typically been channeled in very specific ways, with freedom of action and choice sharply limited. In political science terms, autonomous political organizations, such as parties or political action committees, or other organizations that might have political aims, such as independent trade unions, have not been tolerated. The creation and control of such organizations in the Soviet system is the sole prerogative of the governing party, which utilizes this power for the interests of the state. Those interests are themselves defined for the most part by political battles within the party.

Leadership selection in the Soviet system is, therefore, the sole privilege and responsibility of one party. While there may be multicandidate elections at the lowest level, there are no primaries and relatively little independent input from the general public. Top leaders are less known to the public than in the West, less

Table 27.1 Ethnic Composition of the Population of the USSR*

	1970	1979	1989	Percent of Total Population	Percent Change 1979–89
Total population of the USSR	241,720,134	262,084,654	285,688,965		9.0
Russians	129,015,140	137,397,089	145,071,550	50.8	5.6
Ukrainians	40,753,246	42,347,387	44,135,989	15.4	4.2
Uzbeks	9,195,093	12,455,978	16,686,240	5.8	34.0
Belorussians	9,051,755	9,462,715	10,030,441	3.5	6.0
Kazakhs	5,298,818	6,556,442	8,137,878	2.8	24.1
Azerbaijanis	4,379,937	5,477,330	6,791,106	2.4	24.0
Tatars[†]	5,930,670*	6,185,196	6,645,588	2.3	7.4
Armenians	3,559,151	4,151,241	4,627,227	1.6	11.5
Tajiks	2,135,883	2,897,697	4,216,693	1.5	45.5
Georgians	3,245,300	3,570,504	3,983,115	1.4	11.6
Moldavians	2,697,994	2,968,224	3,355,240	1.2	13.0
Lithuanians	2,664,944	2,850,905	3,068,296	1.1	7.6
Turkmen	1,525,284	2,027,913	2,718,297	1.0	34.0
Kirgiz	1,452,222	1,906,271	2,530,998	0.9	32.8
Peoples of Dagestan[‡]	1,364,649	1,656,676	2,072,071	0.7	25.1
Germans	1,846,317	1,936,214	2,035,807	0.7	5.1
Chuvash	1,694,351	1,751,366	1,839,228	0.6	5.0
Latvians	1,429,844	1,439,037	1,459,156	0.5	1.4
Bashkirs	1,239,681	1,371,452	1,449,462	0.5	5.7
Jews	2,150,707	1,810,876	1,449,117	0.5	−20.0
Mordvins	1,262,670	1,191,765	1,153,516		−3.2
Poles	1,167,523	1,150,991	1,126,137		−2.2
Estonians	1,007,356	1,019,851	1,027,255		0.7

* Includes peoples numbering one million or more.
† Includes Crimean Tartars in 1970 but not 1979 or 1989.
‡ Includes the following: Avars, Lezgins, Dargins, Kumyks, Laks, Tabasarans, Nogai, Rutuls, Tsakhurs, Aguls
SOURCE: From data presented in Ann Sheehy, "Ethnic Muslims Account for Half of Soviet Population Increase," in *Report on the USSR,* Vol. 2 (1990), pp. 16–17.

visible to them and, most importantly, less vulnerable to being removed by them either directly or indirectly.

But Soviet leaders are vulnerable, as we shall see. Though they do not have to stand for national election as individuals as in France or through their party as in Britain, they must satisfy those who put them in power; the highest echelons of the Communist Party.

Moreover, public dissatisfaction with a deteriorating economic situation, or even political grievances, can have resonance within the party and undermine elite support for a

political leader. One of the ironic aspects of the Soviet system of governance is that the leader typically considered "most powerful" can actually fall at any time. Because until 1988 the tenure of the leader of the party was not limited by statute or custom, it could be very long; Joseph Stalin was head of the party for nearly 30 years, Leonid Brezhnev for 18. But because a Soviet leader can be removed by the elites without waiting for an election, his term can also be short; Khrushchev became party first secretary in 1953 and was removed in 1964. This peculiarity of the Soviet system places certain substantial constraints on the power of Soviet leaders that might not be revealed by an initial glance at the powerful Communist Party system.

ECONOMIC SYSTEM

One of the questions for modern parliamentary governments and capitalist economies, as seen in the previous chapters, is how much the government should be involved in running the economy. Should it only set the guidelines for the economy and let private initiative provide the goods and services? Should the government provide these goods and services itself or should there be some mix, and if so, what is the proper mixture? In the Soviet Union, roughly ten years after the Bolshevik revolution, the private-public question ceased to be an issue until it became one again under Mikhail Gorbachev.

The economy is *socialist,* meaning that in theory the things the economy produces and the means it has to produce them are collectively rather than individually owned and operated. The Soviet government, meaning in practice the Communist Party leadership, determines the form and functioning of the economy. Questions such as how much is to be spent on what industries, how much on producing industrial machines as opposed to housing, on oil extraction instead of dresses, are decided by the party leadership. Production schedules, employment practices, prices, rights and duties of enterprises in the Soviet economy, business practices in general, are determined not by private owners or those they hire, but by the Communist Party acting on behalf of collective owners, the Soviet working class.

This does not mean that in such a system the Politburo decides how many pairs of red shoes are to be made in a particular year and how many white. But it does mean that until recently in the USSR virtually all economic decisions were government decisions at one level or another. In political science terms, the political and economic systems are more nearly *co-terminous.* Again somewhat ironically, this means that even more than in Western Europe, the success or failure of the economic system is the responsibility of government officials and can be a determining factor in their political careers.

Recently, under the prodding of Mikhail Gorbachev and his economic team, moves have been made to reduce this level of involvement and to make more of the economy operate autonomously rather than in response to government plans and directives (see the discussion of economic reforms in Chapter 33).

IDEOLOGY

If you were asked what the difference is between the Soviet Union and most of the states of the West, you would most likely reply that the USSR is a "communist" country. What does this term mean? The growing number and diversity of countries labelled "communist" renders this term less useful as a description by itself.

Communism has its roots in the social and economic philosophies of Karl Marx and other socialists writing in the nineteenth century. Marx argued that societies were divided into classes according to their relationship to the "means of production" (factories, commodities, money). The *bourgeoisie* owned property and capital while the working class, who owned nothing but their own labor, were obliged to sell this labor in order to survive. The existence of private property, Marx argued, allowed some people to exploit the labor of others for their own gain. Marx, Friedrich Engels, and others who followed believed a new system would emerge in which private property would be abolished. Under capitalism, Marx believed, the workers' situation would get progressively worse until they became a revolutionary *proletariat* and overthrew the whole economic system. With it would go the exploitation of people, since the factories and the financing would now belong to all workers. Since in Marxist terms any government or state only existed to enforce the domination of the ruling class, as exploitation disappeared, so would the governing state. The state would, in Engels' expression, "wither away." Instead, under communism workers would enjoy the fruits of their own labor in a classless society.

While Marx expected a revolution in which the workers would overthrow the ruling capitalists, he was not very specific as to what exactly would come next. Various theories as to how the revolution would take place were spelled out by Marxists throughout Europe at the end of the nineteenth century, but it was not until later, after World War I, that Marxists actually took and held power anywhere. In Russia, radical Marxists led by Vladimir Ilich Lenin and Leon Trotsky seized the opportunity to build and expand the ideological framework for governing a socialist system.

In his writings before taking power, Lenin had argued for a tightly organized, highly centralized revolutionary communist party that would be the "vanguard" of the proletariat. Once in power, Lenin wrote in *State and Revolution,* the workers would take over the existing state and use it to suppress the bourgeoisie and create the necessary conditions for communism. After a transitional period labeled "socialism," during which the guiding principle would be "from each according to his abilities, to each according to his work," a higher "communist" stage would emerge in which the principle would be "from each according to their abilities, to each according to their needs." Only then

would the state no longer be necessary and wither away.[1]

Of course the state has not withered away in the Soviet Union, nor has the Communist Party. Indeed, today some 18 million people work in the massive state bureaucracy. How does Soviet ideology account for this failure to achieve a key Marxist goal?

Lenin recognized that Russia had not yet developed the economic or social conditions necessary for the creation of socialism, much less communism. The country's capitalist industry and its proletariat were too small. Russia's people were overwhelmingly peasant and in any case preferred their own ownership of the land to state control. Drawing on Marx's notion of a revolutionary dictatorship of the proletariat, Lenin said a state was still necessary to direct the country toward the building of socialism and communism, to suppress the displaced bourgeoisie who would try to destroy the revolution, and to prepare society to be ready for communism.

In political terms, then, a "Leninist system" came to mean the use and dominance of the state by the Communist Party. While differences could and did exist within the party, under the guiding principle of *democratic centralism,* once decisions were taken all party bodies and members were to obey and implement the decision without question. More broadly, the party's rule over society and the economy—the *dictatorship of the proletariat*—could not be challenged. As will be seen in Chapter 28, Lenin was willing to modify Marxist tenets and his own orientations in attempting to create socialism in the USSR, but the dominance of the party was non-negotiable.

Under Joseph Stalin the dominance of the Communist Party over the state and society

---

[1]Vladimir Ilich Lenin, *State and Revolution* (New York: International Press, 1971; orig. pub. 1917), pp. 78–79.

yielded ultimately to the dominance of Joseph Stalin over the party. Like Marx and Lenin, Stalin believed that the Soviet Union needed to build a modern industrial base such as existed under capitalism, in order to bring about the transition to communism and at the same time make the USSR a more powerful country. Thus, in the late 1920s and the 1930s, Stalin and the people who supported him drove the country to an extremely rapid period of industrial growth and ended the independent existence of peasant farmers, who were replaced by collective or state farms.

In order to enforce such changes and to satisfy his own desire for absolute power, Stalin built a powerful and repressive state that eliminated people who were suspected of opposing his political power or the direction or pace of the country's transformation to socialism. One such target during the drive to collectivize in the early 1930s were better-off peasants, known as *kulaks*. But kulak or not, during this period and in an even broader terror of the late 1930s, millions of people suspected or accused of opposing Stalin's policies were deprived of their land, put into prison, or simply killed.

After Stalin died in 1953, the country's new leaders modified the brutality of Communist Party rule, ended the mass terror unleashed during Stalin's time, and began to modify the role of the party in the economy. But no one suggested changing the fundamentally dominant position of the party over the country's economy or its people. In 1956, Nikita Khrushchev condemned Stalin for his excesses, and suggested that the country was no longer a "dictatorship of the proletariat" but an "all people's" state. He tried to put this notion into practice by encouraging greater local involvement in economic and political governance, relaxing political control of culture somewhat, and replacing local party secretaries in great numbers. The vic-

tory of socialism in the country was declared in 1959 and a new party program in 1961 affirmed that the transition to communism would be achieved by 1980. Khrushchev's attempted reforms so unsettled those holding power in the party and state, however, that he remained a weak leader throughout his brief tenure, and was removed in 1964.

Under Leonid Brezhnev the ideological theme struck was that the Soviet Union was in a state of "developed socialism." According to this view, the growing complexity of socialism, especially in terms of scientific and technological advancement, continued to require the preeminence of the Communist Party for guiding the country to higher stages of socialism. The state, of course, remained necessary—it would even grow—for administration in this new situation; but its form would need to be continually "perfected" in order to be as effective as possible. In 1977 the ideological basis of Communist Party rule became codified in the Soviet constitution where for the first time the predominant role of the party was spelled out (see Chapter 32).

The major contribution of Mikhail Gorbachev and his leadership team to ideological developments is the rejection of the Stalinist system and its total state control as not being true socialism. Gorbachev sees socialism as represented more by the creative application of Marxism such as was seen during the period of the New Economic Policy of Lenin. While Gorbachev's reforms have not been based on an elaborate ideological framework, the goals of restructuring the economy (*perestroika*) and of applying "new thinking" (*novoe myshlenie*) to contemporary problems suggests—and Gorbachev explicitly states—that Marxism should not be seen as an unchanging dogma but as a flexible approach to solving modern problems of governance.

For the individual citizen of the Soviet Union, communist ideology subordinates in-

General Secretary Mikhail Gorbachev presides over the 19th All-Union CPSU Conference in June 1988.

SOURCE: Sovfoto.

dividual rights to collective or state goals, which are defined by the ruling party. In this view, the pursuit by a citizen of political or economic liberty cannot be done in such a way as to jeopardize what is seen as the greater good, that of society as a whole. This gives a Soviet government great leeway and control over the rights and liberties of its citizens. On the other hand, Soviet ideology holds that for an individual, full democracy has an economic component as well, one that only socialism can secure. Therefore people in the Soviet Union have some constitutional rights not provided for in Western countries, such as the right to work, to free medical care, and to free education at all levels. In this respect, Soviet ideology places a somewhat greater burden on its governments than is common in the West, where governing ideologies typically do not offer every citizen a job and free health care as a political right.

INTERNATIONAL ORIENTATION

The international situation of the Soviet Union is also fundamentally different from that of Britain and France. Though they all emerged out of World War II as victors over Nazi Germany, the Soviet Union's aim in the period following that war was to change as much of the world around it as possible. Having survived the interwar period as the world's only socialist state, with relatively little power to control events on either its European or Asian borders, the USSR was determined after the war to have a strong say in world affairs. In this it was to be challenged by the other state that decided to take on a global role, the United States.

In the immediate postwar period, the British and the French, supported by the United States, devoted their resources to preserving as much of the existing order as possible, complete with empires. But the Soviet Union was eager to see the power of the capitalist countries erode and to have as many communist countries emerge as possible. Where it

The Official Soviet View of Its System

The third program of the Communist Party of the Soviet Union, adopted in 1986, describes the essence of socialist society:

Socialism is a society on whose banner are printed the words "Everything in the name of man, everything for the sake of man." This is a society in which:

—The means of production are in the hands of the people and an end has been put forever to man's exploitation of man, social oppression, the rule of a privileged minority, and the poverty and illiteracy of millions of people;

—very broad scope has been opened up for the dynamic and planned development of productive forces, and scientific-technical progress entails not unemployment but the steady improvement of the entire people's prosperity;

—an equal right to labor and its just reward in accordance with the principle "from each according to his abilities, to each according to his labor" is guaranteed and the population enjoys social goods like free medical services and education and housing for a minimal payment;

—the indestructible alliance of the working class, kolkhoz [collective form] peasantry, and intelligentsia has been affirmed, men and women have equal rights and guarantees of their implementation, a reliable path into the future has been opened up for the younger generation, and social security for labor veterans has been guaranteed;

—national inequality has been eliminated and the legal and juridical and actual equality, friendship and fraternity of all nations and ethnic groups have been affirmed;

—genuine democracy—power wielded for the people and by the people themselves—has been established and is being developed and the citizens' increasingly broad and equal participation in the management of production, social, and state affairs has been ensured;

—the ideas of freedom, human rights, and the dignity of the individual have been filled with real content, the unity of rights and duties is being ensured, and the same laws and moral norms and the same discipline operate for one and all, and increasingly favorable conditions for the all-around development of the individual are taking shape;

—a truly humanitarian Marxist-Leninist ideology rules, the national masses have been given access to all sources of knowledge, and a progressive socialist culture has been created, absorbing all that is best from world culture;

—a socialist way of life based on social justice, collectivism, and comradely mutual aid has formed, giving the working person confidence in the future and spiritually and morally ennobling him as the creator of new social relations and of his own destiny.

Socialism is a society whose thoughts and actions in the international arena are aimed at supporting the peoples' desire for independence and social progress and are subordinated to the main task—preserving and strengthening peace.

SOURCE: *Programma Kommunisticheskoi Partii Sovetskovo Soyuza* (Moscow: Izdatel'stvo politicheskoi literaturi, 1986), pp. 10–11.

could, as in Eastern Europe, the Soviet Union facilitated the creation of subordinate or friendly governments. For both ideological reasons and those of national protection, the USSR also supported the creation of communist governments in China, Korea and Vietnam, while the United States and Western European countries opposed them.

However, in the decades since World War II, while Western empires in Africa and Asia dissolved into independent states, the new Soviet empire in Eastern Europe had remained intact, for the most part. Roles became reversed. The USSR still challenged Western and U.S. influence around the world but sought to keep its own family of "fraternal socialist allies" unchanged. This of course led to significant conflict in various parts of the world, and to the use of force by the Soviets in Eastern Europe. In areas outside Europe, especially the Middle East and Asia, competition for influence and control has often been fierce and has involved arming allies to the teeth. But direct armed conflict between the USSR and the world's Western powers has been avoided. On balance, while the ability of Britain and France to protect their power in other regions of the world steadily receded, that of the Soviet Union grew along with the attendant complications.

But this points to a final and very significant distinction between the Soviet Union and the major capitalist countries of Western Europe, which might be called the *disparity quotient*. Internationally there is no question that the Soviet Union is a superpower. It possesses a nuclear strike force that dwarfs that of the British and French combined, and a conventional military force that is the largest in the world. But in terms of economic power, the military giant is a dwarf. The Soviet Union accounts for just over 4 percent of world trade—less than one-third of the United States share—and outside of raw materials such as oil and gas, its exports (and

imports) are a blip on the screen of the world economy. This means that in playing its desired role in international affairs, the range of instruments available to the USSR is quite narrow, in contrast both to the power of the economies of the West and its own domestic governance. Soviet policies in Africa illustrate this disparity. The Soviet Union was capable of helping Marxist guerrilla movements take power in Mozambique and Angola during the 1970s, but it could do very little after that to help them manage or improve their economies.

This unevenness of power poses certain severe problems for the USSR in its attempt to achieve a more friendly and secure world for itself. Trying to do so almost inevitably provokes a challenge from the United States and its allies, whose vision of a more friendly and secure world is usually quite different from that of the USSR.

For the Soviet Union the problems of domestic governance and international influence at the end of the twentieth century are being tackled by a political system established on principles quite different from those of the parliamentary democracies, and influenced by a history equally different. To see how these factors affect soviet governance, we turn first to that historical legacy.

References and Suggested Readings

BIALER, SEWERYN. *The Soviet Paradox*. New York: Vintage Books, 1986.

COHEN, STEPHEN F. *Rethinking the Soviet Experience*. New York: Oxford University Press, 1985.

COLE, J. P. *Geography of the Soviet Union*. London: Butterworths, 1984.

Congressional Quarterly, Inc. *The Soviet Union*. Washington, DC: Congressional Quarterly, 1986.

MELLOR, ROY E.H. *The Soviet Union and its Geo-*

graphical Problems. Atlantic Highlands, NJ: Humanities Press, 1982.

SHIPLER, DAVID K. *Russia: Broken Idols, Solemn Dreams.* New York: Penguin Books, 1984.

SMITH, HEDRICK. *The Russians,* rev. ed., New York: Ballantine Books, 1984.

TREADGOLD, DONALD W. *Twentieth Century Russia.* Boulder, CO: Westview, 1987.

28

Historical Antecedents

RUSSIA BEFORE THE REVOLUTION

The modern Soviet Union has roots in both Europe and Asia, and its territory has had conquerors from both regions. In what is now European Russia and Ukraine, various nomadic empires ruled before the birth of Christ: the Cimmerians, Scythians, Sarmatians. A brief period of Greek influence was then destroyed by the emergence of the successive power of the Goths and, from central Asia, the Huns, Avars, Khazars and Magyars. One of two European forerunners of modern Russia was the state known as Rus which was formed around Kiev near the end of the ninth century and lasted until the mid-thirteenth century. It was during its dominion that the Slavs were converted to orthodox, or eastern, Christianity, forcibly by decree of their ruler Vladimir, at the end of the tenth century.

Kievan Rus was to disappear as an independent entity in the thirteenth century under the onslaught of the Mongols, who at the same time also conquered the area around Moscow. It was in this latter area that the core of the later Russian empire and the USSR developed. The medieval state of Muscovy was able to gradually expand its power against a weakening Mongol empire and eventually, by the end of the sixteenth century, defeat and replace the power of the Khans in Europe.

But Muscovy's enemies were as numerous as the drive of its successive leaders for power was strong. Ivan IV, better known as Ivan the Terrible, was the first to take the title of *Tsar*, possibly derived from the Roman title of *Caesar*, in 1547. But he was only one of many autocrats whose power to determine the fate of his subjects was challenged by internal rebellion or external foe, not by political institutions or culture. For the next three centuries wars and campaigns continued against Poland, Sweden, and Lithuania in the west, the Tartars and Turks in the south, and the remains of the Mongol empire in Siberia and the far east. By the beginning of the eighteenth century Russia was officially an empire, the title having been taken by Peter the Great in 1721. By the end of that century, with the final partition of Poland, the territo-

363

rial base of the empire extended from central Europe to the Pacific.

Social, economic, and political development did not match the pace of territorial expansion, however. The power of the Tsar grew and covered all key aspects of the lives of his subjects, from labor to faith. Though advisory councils and assemblies existed from time to time—even under Ivan the Terrible there was a *zemskii sobor* or landed council—their powers were limited and frequently changed by the ruler. The overwhelming mass of the population, which was the peasantry, had no effective representation and under various forms of serfdom, little personal or economic freedom. Reforms could and did take place during the imperial period, with those of Peter the Great (1694–1725), Catherine II (1762–96), Alexander I (1801–25) and Alexander II (1855–81) being most significant. Such reforms were important for modernizing the military, administration, and education of the empire; but they did little to increase the influence of the *narod*, or people, on government policies. Moreover, reforms could be and often were reversed—sometimes by the same autocrat who had decreed them. By the end of the nineteenth century, there had developed in the Russian empire no effective institutional structures of the types seen in England or the United States that could counter the power of the Tsar or, just as crucial, provide a legal forum or moderate alternative for reform movements or individuals.

Economically, the empire was behind the states of Western Europe at the end of the last century but was gaining fast. Coal extraction tripled between 1890 and 1905, at which time Russia was the world's fifth largest producer. At the outbreak of World War I the empire produced more steel and cotton than France and nearly as much pig iron. Though well behind the industrial powers of Germany, Great Britain and the United States,

Russia was still among the world's top five industrial powers.

But the core of the country's economy lay in agriculture. Progress in this sector was hurt by the continued economic oppression of peasants, who had been emancipated from serfdom in 1861 but who were made to pay massive compensation for the land given them. Redistributed land was usually of the poorest quality and in allotments that were too small to be economical. In addition, rapid population growth, the fastest in Europe, increased pressure on the land and in the cities. Desire was strong among the peasantry for more and better land; among the workers for better working conditions; and among various political groupings for a different, more responsive form of government.

An additional critical difference between Russia and France or Germany at this time was the absence of an industrial or commercial middle class, what historian Richard Pipes calls "the missing bourgeoisie." In Western Europe such groups were interested in stronger civil administration, political rights for people with property, and less arbitrary dictatorial rule by the king. They had been central in the struggle to reduce the power of the monarch. In Russia such a group was still tiny, owing to the economic monopoly exercised by the Tsar, the continued power of the nobility, and the fact that most of the vigorous sectors of the rapidly growing industrial economy were foreign-owned.[1]

In addition, even among those who wanted to change things in Russia, not everyone favored imitation of instutitions found in Western Europe. A strong strain in Russian thought during the nineteenth century was "Slavophilism," a glorification of the

[1]Roger Muntig, *The Economic Development of the USSR* (New York: St. Martin's Press, 1982), p. 34; Richard Pipes, *Russia under the Old Regime* (New York: Charles Scribner's Sons, 1974), pp. 191–98.

uniqueness of Russia and its people. Adherents to this view felt that the country should seek a return to its own values of rural, collective life and the Orthodox religion and reject the bureaucratic states and individualism of the West. Politically, such views took the form of conservative or even reactionary political groups.

Opposing this view were several different lines of thought, held by people considered "westernizers," or those who felt Russia could advance only by borrowing institutions and ideas from the West including, for some, socialism.

Some reform-minded groups argued that Russia could develop along the lines of the Western parliamentary democracies. But the country lacked a strong force for moderate reform or any historical precedent for it. Through the centuries opposition to the Tsar or his policies had tended to take the form of outright rebellion, such as that of Pugachev against Catherine II in 1773–74, conspiracy, such as that of the Decembrists against Nicholas I in 1825, or radical actions such as the terrorism of the "People's Will" group which in 1881 assassinated Tsar Alexander II.

Marxism thus came to a country which in the late nineteenth century looked quite different from that described in Marx's *Capital*. It was overwhelmingly (87%) rural and peasant, without a dominant bourgeoisie, a large proletariat or the type of political system—parliamentary democracy—Marx had insisted would exist as the handmaiden of the ruling propertied class and precursor to the final, workers' revolution.

In Germany, for example, the dominant strain of Marxism at this time was social democracy. Adherents of the philosophy of "evolutionary socialism" ran for office in the *Reichstag,* developed programs for modifying the worst excesses of capitalism, and formed through parties and trade unions a representative political force for a growing working class. In Russia, faced with an unmodified autocratic system and the absence of such representative opportunities, Marxism tended toward a more radical revolutionary form. There were those such as Georgii Plekhanov, considered the father of Russian Marxism, who argued for some similar form of social democracy and for supporting in Russia the bourgeois revolution that had occurred in Western Europe, only then bringing about the proletarian revolution that Marxism said would inevitably occur. But Vladimir Ilich Ulianov, born in 1870 and better known by his revolutionary name, Lenin, favored a more radical line. He argued in a booklet published in 1902 entitled *What Is To Be Done?* that what was needed was a small secret party of "professional revolutionaries" who would strive not for parliamentary representation or the improvement of working conditions—an approach labeled "economism"—but for the overthrow of the entire system.

Adherents of the two approaches split the Russian Social Democratic Party at its 2nd Congress held in Brussels in 1903. Those who supported Lenin's views were declared by him to be "bolsheviki" or the majority, even though they had been outvoted at the congress on several key issues; those supporting the less radical line were termed "mensheviki," the minority.

There were also other groups opposed to the way the Russian autocracy was operating. There were the liberals, such as Paul Miliukov, who favored the establishment of a system of government more like that of a western parliamentary democracy; anarchists, such as Mikhail Bakunin, who opposed a strong state of any kind; and there were Socialist Revolutionaries, whose program derived more from the needs of the peasantry than those of the industrial working class.

Slowly some changes did occur in the Tsarist government. In 1906 the first quasi-parliamentary institution, the *duma,* met. Though representation as well as the power of the body was severely restricted, it did represent the first institutional form by which society could possibly limit the discretion of government.

Even this limited step had been forced by revolution. In 1904, with economic grievances mounting on the side of both the peasants and the industrial workers, a disastrous war with Japan put even more pressure on Russian society, which had to finance the war and fill the Tsar's armed forces. In St. Petersburg (now Leningrad), which was then the capital of imperial Russia, workers marching to present their grievances to the Tsar on January 22, 1905, were attacked by palace guards. Many people were killed and "Bloody Sunday" proved a stimulus to revolution.

The attempt was ultimately unsuccessful due to the low level of organization of revolutionary forces and the fact that the Tsar's armed forces remained loyal. But the revolution of 1905 had galvanized a broad base of opposition among workers and peasants and

On the morning of January 9, 1905, a procession led by the priest George Gabon marched to the Winter Palace of the Tsar. During the resulting confrontation, over 1,000 people were killed. This "Bloody Sunday" ushered in the first Russian Revolution.
SOURCE: Novasti from Sovfoto.

it did force the Tsar to convene the new *duma*. Though this institution remained relatively weak—and grew weaker when electoral laws reduced representation of the peasantry even further—significant land reforms were undertaken by Prime Minister Peter Stolypin and the situation for industrial workers improved somewhat.

But the fundamental problems of autocratic Russia that had taken centuries to come to a head could not be solved speedily enough. Most peasants remained in desperate straits, and they as well as industrial workers still had influence over public policy only through radical action and only if the Tsar accepted it. For example, two successive *dumas* were dissolved by the Tsar when they proved uncooperative. Opposition to reforms was strong among conservative forces; and when Stolypin was assassinated in 1911 and a reputed "holy man," Grigorii Rasputin, began to have influence in the royal family because of his ability to ease the pain of the Tsar's hemophiliac son, movement toward solving Russia's difficulties stopped altogether.

The outbreak of World War I in 1914 was to prove the last straw. A peasantry eager for land and prosperity was instead conscripted to fight, and sent to do so poorly fed, clothed, equipped, trained and led. And the numerically small but strategically located industrial workers were, in William Chamberlain's words, "sufficiently literate to grasp elementary socialist ideas, sufficiently wretched to welcome the first opportunity to pull down the temple of private property."[2] Economic and political reform was put off by the exigencies of the war, which dragged on with little hope of victory by Russia or its allies (Britain and France) against Austria-Hungary and Germany.

Revolutionary Marxists, especially Lenin, had tried to use the war as a rallying cry to get the world's proletariat to fight against their own governments instead of each other. Lenin saw the war as a battle among monopoly capitalists to divide up the world; the role of the workers was to oppose such a war and use it to bring down rather than support their governments[3]. But Lenin's call was not heeded and socialist parties throughout Europe chose to support their governments. In Russia, though, as the situation worsened, the opportunity arose for putting revolutionary words into practice.

THE BOLSHEVIKS COME TO POWER

The end of the autocracy did not come at the hands of Lenin or the Bolsheviks but as a spontaneous chain reaction begun in Petrograd (as St. Petersburg was called after 1914) as a demonstration for bread, joined by rebellious troops and ending in the abdication of the Tsar on March 15, 1917. The new provisional government, headed by Prince George Lvov, was welcomed by Russia's allies and attracted the support of several non-socialist political parties. But substantial power was also held by the *soviet* (or council) of workers' and soldiers' deputies, which was dominated by the socialist parties. The government favored and promised reform, but on the key issues troubling Russian society—an end to the war, land reform, and social welfare for workers—little movement was evident. Some of the socialist parties, such as the Mensheviks, cooperated with the new government, and in July a Socialist Revolutionary, Alexander Kerensky, became

[2]William H. Chamberlain, *The Russian Revolution*, 2 vols. (New York: Grosset & Dunlap, 1965), 1:275.

[3]Vladimir Ilich Lenin. *Imperialism: The Highest Stage of Capitalism* (New York: International Press, 1939) [orig. pub. 1917].

prime minister. Lenin, however, counseled against such cooperation and instead, in his famous "April theses" delivered upon his return to Russia from exile, called for continuing the revolution and handing "all power to the soviets." Indeed during the summer of 1917 a system of "dual power" developed with the provisional government exercising some authority, the workers' *soviets* some, and in much of the country no one exercising much authority at all.

In July another uprising occurred, this time against the provisional government, taking it and the revolutionary Marxists by surprise. Uncoordinated and lacking strong leadership, the movement was crushed by armed forces remaining loyal to the government. No sooner had this danger been defeated than a threat to the government arose from the armed forces themselves. General Lavr Kornilov, the commander-in-chief, tried to march on the capital in August and destroy the powerful Petrograd *soviet*. However, the government relied on parties of the Left and armed workers to defeat the coup attempt.

But the war dragged on, land reform was delayed and the soldiers began to "vote with their feet"—they deserted their posts and the provisional government. Lenin, who had fled to Finland after the July uprising, returned to Russia in October and stunned his followers by proclaiming that the time was right to take power from the weak provisional government. The Bolsheviks were a tiny party and even among socialists they were a distinct minority except in Petrograd and Moscow, where they finally persuaded the local *soviets* to their views that autumn. Lenin's view on immediately taking power was supported by the Bolshevik central committee in a vote on October 10. On October 25 by the old calendar (now November 7) soldiers and sailors supporting the insurrection occupied key parts of the city, the provisional government collapsed and, at least in Petrograd, the Bolsheviks were in power.

Having declared themselves in power, however, did not mean that Lenin and the Bolsheviks actually ruled the country. In November 1917, in the only national multiparty elections in the country's history, a Constituent Assembly was elected. This body, promised by the provisional government and supported by all the parties, was to determine the form and policy of the new state. But the majority of delegates were Socialist Revolutionaries; the Bolsheviks had received just under 10 million of the nearly 42 million votes cast and roughly one-fourth of the seats. When the Constituent Assembly met early the next year and refused to accept the Bolshevik program, it was dispersed by force. The new government moved to suppress opposition parties and remnants of the provisional government. Within a month after taking power it signed an armistice with Germany. In March 1918 a peace treaty was signed ending Soviet involvement in World War I and bringing down on the new state the wrath of its former allies. British, French, American and Japanese troops landed in northern and southern European Russia and in the Far East between 1918 and 1919. With the help of the Czech legion, a group of soldiers who had been fighting against Germany and were trapped inside Russia when the war ended, this intervention almost succeeded in "strangling the Bolshevik baby in its cradle," as Winston Churchill put it. The Bolsheviks managed to survive, however, but soon faced a much tougher test in a vicious civil war against various groups, referred to as "Whites," who opposed the "Red" government. This civil war lasted until 1921. During it (1920) an additional brief war was fought against Poland, sparked by Polish attempts to regain territory held before its dismemberment and continued by Soviet attempts to spread the revolution westward. At one point

Lenin in his office in the Kremlin, 1918.
    SOURCE: TASS from Sovfoto.

the soldiers of the Polish state, itself a republic reborn after 1918, held Kiev. Ultimately, the success of the new communist government against such an array of enemies can be attributed as much to the disarray and differences in political designs among its enemies (western democracies, White supporters of everything from the monarchy to peasant rebellion, restive nationality groups) as to its own strength. Still, by the end of the civil war the Soviet government was in control of most of the old Russian empire.

POLITICS AND POLICIES BETWEEN THE WARS

In the face of its many crises, the Bolshevik approach was to try to establish virtually to-

tal control of the country's productive forces. Under what came to be known as "war communism" the government nationalized every form of production in the country and tried to exercise total state control over all citizens under what Trotsky characterized as the "mobilization of labor." The state became the sole sanctioned buyer and seller of all goods. The program was a reaction to the country's extreme emergency filtered through the radical ideology of the Bolsheviks. The effect was disastrous. The historian E. H. Carr describes it:

A catastrophic decline in industrial production, due in part to the destruction of plant, in part to the disorganization of labour, in part to the cumbrous system of centralized administration represented by the glavkj [chief committees which directed the economy] had been followed by a virtual breakdown of state or state-controlled distribution of commodities at fixed prices, leading to a rapid growth of illicit private trade at runaway prices and a wild currency inflation; and this in turn had prompted the refusal of the peasant, in the face of a goods famine and a worthless currency, to deliver necessary supplies of grain to the towns, so that population was progressively drained away from the industrial centres, and industrial production brought still nearer to a standstill.[4]

In 1921, after demonstrations in Petrograd and a brief rebellion among sailors in Kronstadt, a "New Economic Policy" (NEP) was declared. The new policy allowed a mixture of capitalist and socialist institutions to grow in the country. The regime retained what Lenin called "the commanding heights" of the economy: banking, foreign trade and large industry. State control in most other areas was reversed, a market was allowed to operate again and most important, the pressure on the country's peasantry was eased. Instead of having grain requisitioned, for example, farmers were allowed to pay a "tax in kind" after which they could sell their products on the open market. Private enterprise flourished, especially in the retail area; for example, in Moscow in 1922, 83 percent of all retail trade was private.[5]

Industry began to recover during this period—steel production increased nearly tenfold between 1921 and 1925—but investment capital was scarce, the price of industrial goods rose much faster than that of agricultural goods (the so-called "scissors" effect) and by most indicators the industrial development of the country was still well behind where it had been before World War I. At the same time, a political struggle was beginning among those who would succeed

Lenin, who had suffered a stroke in 1922 and died in 1924. Lenin left no clear heir. But in a letter regarded as his last testament, he spoke affectionately of Bukharin and critically about Stalin (see box). Nevertheless, through a combination of manipulation of party personnel, political adroitness and exploitation of the character of his opponents—Trotsky, for example, was reluctant to lead a full-scale challenge to Stalin after Lenin's death[6]—Stalin was able to outmaneuver first Trotsky and other leaders from the revolution, Grigorii Zinoviev and Lev Kamenev, and then Nikolai Bukharin, to assume dominant leadership of the party by the time of the 15th Party Congress in 1927. In a major ideological pronouncement Stalin enunciated the policy of building "socialism in one country"; that is, concentrating on strengthening the one socialist country that then existed, as revolutions had by then failed throughout Europe and, in the most bloody fiasco, in China.

Economically, this policy meant pushing the country forward much more rapidly. Like Lenin before him, Stalin believed that for socialism to be possible a modern industrial economy had to be built. Unlike the policies seen in the NEP, however, Stalin as well as many others in the party favored a much more rapid and state-controlled process. At the end of the 1920s, Stalin pushed the Soviet Union into what has been called a second revolution, one directed from above. Gradually at first and then abruptly, the mixed economy policies of NEP were replaced by more and more state control. In 1929 the first five-year plan was announced, setting extremely ambitious quotas for rapidly and broadly industrializing the country. Coal and oil production were to double in the five

[4]E. H. Carr, *The Bolshevik Revolution*, 3 vols. (London: Penguin Books, 1970), 2:271–72.

[5]Muntig, p. 49.

[6]Leonard Schapiro, *The Communist Party of the Soviet Union* (New York: Vintage Books, 1971), pp. 302–6.

In December 1922 Lenin dictated a letter evaluating his potential successors. Though published in the West soon after, its existence remained a party secret until Khrushchev quoted from the letter at the 20th Party Congress in 1956. Of his colleagues Lenin said:

> Comrade Stalin, having become General Secretary, has concentrated an enormous power in his hands; and I am not sure that he always knows how to use that power with sufficient caution. On the other hand, Comrade Trotsky, as was proved by his struggle against the Central Committee in connection with the question of the People's Commissariat of Ways and Communications, is distinguished not only by his exceptional abilities—personally he is, to be sure, the most able man in the present Central Committee—but also by his too far-reaching self-confidence and a disposition to be too much attracted by the purely administrative side of affairs.
>
> These two qualities of the two most able leaders of the present Central Committee might, quite innocently, lead to a split; if our party does not take measures to prevent it, a split might arise unexpectedly.
>
> I will not further characterize the other members of the Central Committee as to their personal qualities. I will only remind you that the October episode of Zinoviev and Kamenev [when they voted against and publicly opposed the Bolshevik takeover] was not, of course, accidental, but that it ought as little to be used against them personally as the non-Bolshevism of Trotsky.
>
> Of the younger members of the Central Committee, I want to say a few words about Bukharin and Pyatakov. They are in my opinion, the most able forces (among the youngest) and in regard to them it is necessary to bear in mind the following: Bukharin is not only the most valuable and biggest theoretician of the party, but also may legitimately be considered the favorite of the whole party; but his theoretical views can only with the very greatest doubt be regarded as fully Marxist, for there is something scholastic in him (he never has learned, and I think never has fully understood, the dialectic).
>
> And then Pyatakov—a man undoubtedly distinguished in will and ability, but too much given over to administration and the administrative side of things to be relied on in a serious political question.
>
> Of course, both these remarks are made by me merely with view to the present time, or supposing that these two able and loyal workers may not find an occasion to supplement their knowledge and correct their one-sidedness.
> December 25, 1922

Ten days later Lenin added a pointed postscript about Stalin:

> *Postscript:* Stalin is too rude, and this fault, entirely supportable in relations among us Communists, becomes insupportable in the office of General Secretary. Therefore, I propose to the comrades to find a way to remove Stalin from that position and appoint to it another man who in all respects differs from Stalin only in superiority—namely, more patient, more loyal, more polite and more attentive to comrades, less capricious, etc. This circumstance may seem an insignificant trifle, but I think that from the point of view of preventing a split and from the point of view of the relation between Stalin and Trotsky which I discussed above, it is not a trifle, or it is such a trifle as may acquire a decisive significance.
> January 4, 1923

SOURCE: "Lenin's Testament," *The Crimes of the Stalin Era: Special Report to the 20th Congress of the Communist Party of the Soviet Union* (New York: The New Leader, 1962), pp. 566–67.

years, iron ore to more than triple, and campaigns were orchestrated to fulfill the plan in only four years. Millions of new workers were mobilized—employment in the state economy grew 55 percent between 1927 and 1932—largely from peasants driven off their land into collective farms.[7] This industrial policy, referred to as "the great turn," was matched by a complete reversal of agricultural policy. Private trading and especially better-off peasants, referred to as *kulaks,* were eliminated, and through various measures, including taxation, coercion and widespread terror, peasants were forced to merge their land into collective farms. As in the cities, the state assumed full control of the rural economy in a breathtakingly short time. In September 1929, 7.4 percent of the land was collectivized; by December of the same year, 59.3 percent of the land had been collectivized. After a brief pause in early 1930, during which Stalin declared that those implementing the program were "dizzy with success," pressure on the peasant farmer resumed and collectivization was completed by the mid-1930s.

The economic mobilization of the country both in the cities and in the countryside was accompanied by an immense rise in the power of the state over all aspects of the society and the economy. Spheres of public and private activity not controlled by the state disappeared in a fashion not seen since before the "great reforms" of Alexander II. While the legal freeing of the serfs by that Tsar might be termed emancipation without development, this period is referred to by Moshe Lewin as "development without emancipation."[8]

Politically, the 1930s saw the rise to personal preeminence of Joseph Stalin. While the campaign to transform the country's economy and society was continuing, foes real and imagined were also eliminated by arrest, deportation, imprisonment and execution. In 1934 Sergei Kirov, the party secretary of Leningrad and reported to be an opponent of Stalin's policies, was assassinated under circumstances that were never fully revealed. Using this as evidence of a broad conspiracy, Stalin and those supporting him launched a purge of the leadership of the party and other key institutions. Of 139 full and candidate members of the party central committee in 1934, 98 were arrested and shot by 1938, according to Nikita Khrushchev, who ought to know. In the army one-half the officer corps were purged, including three of five marshals, more than half of all brigade, division, corps, and army commanders, 90 percent of all generals and 80 percent of all colonels.[9] In some cases show trials were staged during which one-time political opponents were forced to confess that they had tried to undermine the system or that they were working for the country's enemies. After one such trial in 1938, Nikolai Bukharin was executed along with several other prominent "Old Bolsheviks." Leon Trotsky had long since been exiled from the country; but when he was murdered in Mexico in 1940, it was widely believed to be on Stalin's orders.

The purges and associated terror spread throughout society and reached their peak during 1936–38. The exact number of those displaced, arrested or executed is the subject of some debate and may never be known, but estimates range from hundreds of thousands to a staggering ten million.[10] Their "crimes"

[7]Mikhail Heller and Aleksandr M. Nekrich, *Utopia in Power: The History of the Soviet Union from 1917 to the Present* (New York: Summit Books, 1986), pp. 225–26.

[8]Moshe Lewin, *The Making of the Soviet System: Essays in the Social History of Interwar Russia* (New York: Pantheon Books, 1985), p. 273.

[9]Schapiro, p. 424.

[10]Jerry F. Hough and Merle Fainsod, *How the Soviet Union Is Governed* (Cambridge: Harvard University Press, 1979), pp. 170–78. The most prominent critical historian in the Soviet Union, Roy Medvedev, estimates that between labor camps, forced collectivization, famine and executions, some 20 million people died. *New York Times,* February 4, 1989, pp. 1, 4.

may have been economic; for example, profiting under the NEP system; or political, being associated with one of the losing party leaders; or nonexistent, simply being the unfortunate victims of a local leader's desire to settle a score or secure the job of a purged superior. According to Stalin himself, one-half million people moved up in the party and state during this period. Whatever the national or local motives, the human misery unleashed was of staggering dimensions and transformed the USSR.

Economically the accomplishments were significant. By the end of the first five-year plan, gross industrial production (as measured in 1926–27 prices) more than doubled and national income increased by nearly 90 percent. These figures more than doubled again by the end of the second five-year plan, 1937, by which time coal production was more than three times what it had been in 1928. Oil production more than doubled, steel and pig iron output increased by a factor of four and electricity capacity by a factor of seven.[11] But the upheaval in the countryside caused by the forced collectivization and return to compulsory deliveries, as well as a lack of investment in agriculture, produced retrograde results. In resistance to collectivization, peasants slaughtered their livestock by the millions. Between 1928 and 1932 the number of horses and cattle in the country fell 42 percent, the number of pigs by more than one-half, and sheep and goats by nearly two-thirds. Grain production fell, and during 1931 and 1932 widespread famine and related diseases killed an estimated five million people.[12] Grain production did not equal 1928 levels again until 1937, and most production still had not recovered by the outbreak of World War II.

[11]Muntig, p. 93.
[12]Heller and Nekrich, pp. 237–42.

THE IMPACT OF WORLD WAR II

If the great turn, forced collectivization and the terror of the 1930s were a homemade shock to the people of the Soviet Union, the effects of World War II were an externally generated catastrophe. As noted in Chapter 34, the Soviet Union tried to buy time by signing nonaggression pacts with its most dangerous enemies, Germany (1939) and Japan (1941). Given Hitler's ambitions and his view of the proper role in the universe for all Slavic peoples (slaves) and for communists especially (dead), it was simply a matter of time before he got around to attacking and invading the USSR, which he did in June 1941.

During the initial period of the war that Soviet historiography refers to as "The Great Patriotic War," the Soviet Union yielded vast lands to German invasion—a territory equal to the size of France in the first six weeks. The military's retreat involved "scorching the earth" behind it so as to leave nothing of value for the approaching enemy. When in 1942 the country was able to mount a counterattack and then an offensive against the invader, more lives were lost and land and industry suffered again. From 1941 until the middle of 1944 the Soviet Union faced Hitler's armies virtually alone in continental Europe. Though supplied by Allied lend-lease and aided eventually by the Allied landing at Normandy, France, in June 1944, the price of driving out and defeating the aggressor was immense (see box).

During the war the political system of the Soviet Union became less ideological, more nationalistic. Citizens were asked to fight the invader for the *rodina*, the motherland, not for socialism or the revolution. Cultural repression that had accompanied the political terror of the 1930s was eased a bit as the regime sought to replace its previous war

Wartime Destruction of the Soviet Union

HUMAN COST:

20,000,000 dead, of which:
    7,000,000 soldiers killed (4,000,000 in POW camps)
    6,000,000 died in Nazi occupied zone
    4,000,000 died in Nazi labor camps
    3,000,000 died in unoccupied zone (of war-related injuries)
1 out of every 8 Soviet citizens in 1939 died during World War II
97 percent of the males ages 17 to 20 (in 1941) died
Millions wounded, handicapped, severely weakened physically
In 1959, there were only 4 males for every 7 females ages 35–50
50 Soviet citizens died for every American who died

PHYSICAL DAMAGE:

1,710 towns wholly or partly destroyed
70,000 villages wholly or partly destroyed
25,000,000 homeless in 1945
    50 percent of all urban living space destroyed
    75 percent of all rural living space destroyed
30 percent of national wealth destroyed
2/3 of wealth in occupied zone destroyed

Industrial Destruction:

    31,850 industrial enterprises destroyed (formerly employed 4,000,000)
    40,000 miles of railroad track destroyed
    4,100 railroad stations destroyed
    13,000 bridges destroyed
    15,800 locomotives destroyed
    428,000 railway cars destroyed

Agricultural Destruction:

    98,000 *kolkhozi* (collective farms)
    1,876 *sovkhozi* (state farms)
    2,890 machine-tractor stations
    137,000 tractors (=30% of 1939 total)
    5,000,000 pieces of mechanical equipment
    7,000,000 horses (=34% of 1939 total)
    17,000,000 cattle (=30% of 1939 total)
    20,000,000 hogs (=71% of 1939 total)
    27,000,000 sheep and goats (=29% of 1939 total)
    110,000,000 poultry
In 1953, the number of horses, cattle, sheep and goats was less than that in 1928.

SOURCE: Compiled by William Chase, Department of History, University of Pittsburgh.

against society with as close a union as possible in order to defeat the enemy.

When the war ended, the Stalinist system of political and economic management returned. Five-year plans with high quotas, imbalance of investment favoring heavy industry at the expense of consumer goods and agriculture, and even political terror returned. Soldiers who had been in German prison camps during the war, for example, were routinely sent to labor camps, which one again became filled with those accused or suspected of disloyalty. The secret police under Lavrenty Beria resumed its role as guarantor of the political dominance of Stalin over the party and the entire society. With a country to rebuild and new communist nations installed throughout Eastern Europe (see Chapter 37), the ideological heat was turned up again both domestically and in foreign policy. Externally, this was a period of the "cold war" with the West, as both the USSR and the United States struggled to secure allies for their vision of how the postwar world should look. At home the country made a rapid recovery in the targeted industrial sectors, such as steel, oil production and electrical energy. Production (as measured in constant prices) doubled by 1950. Once again, though, agriculture did not do as well, and in this sphere production in 1950 had not even returned to 1940 levels.[13]

CHANGE OF DIRECTION UNDER NIKITA KHRUSHCHEV

Soviet politics during the period after Stalin's death are distinguished by a shift away from what can be called a "totalitarian" phase of mass mobilization, personal dictatorship and widespread use of terror against both political opponents and the public. Under Nikita Khrushchev politics were still dominated by the elite of the Communist Party; but new directions were attempted in both domestic and foreign policy, and battles among elites over power and policy emerged into the open.

When Stalin died in 1953, his replacement as party leader was Nikita Khrushchev, who had been party head in Ukraine, while Georgii Malenkov, another of Stalin's lieutenants, became prime minister. Malenkov began to articulate a "new course" for the Soviet Union that would include reducing the traditional economic emphasis on heavy industry, investing more in things the population needed—such as housing—and in agriculture, and, most important, returning to "socialist legality" by ending the use of terror. He also suggested that there could be peaceful resolution of conflicts between the USSR and the West.

At first, Khrushchev opposed these notions and allied with the more orthodox members of the leadership. He held to a more hostile foreign policy position *vis-à-vis* the West and suggested dealing with the country's chronic agricultural problem by opening up for cultivation vast new lands in Siberia and elsewhere, the so-called "virgin lands" program. In April 1955 Khrushchev, with the support of the more conservative forces such as Lazar Kaganovich and Vyacheslav Molotov, succeeded in removing Malenkov from the premiership. He was replaced by Nikolai Bulganin.

But soon Khrushchev adopted many of the very policies he had previously denounced. Most significantly, he pressed the attack against the personality and policies of Stalin. In an extraordinary speech to the 20th Party Congress in February 1956, Khrushchev bluntly attacked Stalin for betraying the Leninist legacy, for ignoring the party, subordinating it to the will of one person and terrorizing it with the secret police. Khrushchev named names, gave dates and statistics

[13]Muntig, p. 126.

The Question of Responsibility

The joke is told that in 1956 when Nikita Khrushchev was giving his speech to the 20th Party Congress condemning Stalin for persecuting and executing real and imagined opponents and for the widespread use of terror, a voice from the back of the hall yelled, "Comrade Khrushchev, where were you when all of this was going on?"

Khrushchev looked up sharply, "Who said that?" he demanded

No hand was raised or person stood to acknowledge the question.

"That's where I was," said Khrushchev.

---

and pronounced Stalin "sickly suspicious." He accused him of developing a "cult of personality," seeking-self glorification, and virtual treason in the face of the enemy. When the country needed him most, Khrushchev said, during World War II, Stalin virtually collapsed. "After the first severe disaster and defeat at the front," Khrushchev said, "Stalin thought that this was the end. . . . Even after the war began, the nervousness and hysteria which Stalin demonstrated, interfering with actual military operation, caused our Army serious damage."[14]

By enumerating Stalin's crimes, Khrushchev was not telling the party elite anything they did not know. Rather, he was declaring war on the old elite by detailing these horrors before the party and giving hope to new party cadres and the population that things would be different. For this reason, Khrushchev had to defeat more than one counterattack aimed at weakening his power, and in 1957 he removed Malenkov, Molotov and Kaganovich, whom he labelled the "antiparty group," from the party's ruling body. Replacing peo-

ple wholesale at the Central Committee level and, after 1957, at the level of the *Presidium* (as the Politburo was then called) protected Khrushchev and his new policies, but he remained a vulnerable leader and ultimately aroused sufficient opposition to cause his downfall in 1964.

During his tenure as first secretary, Khrushchev made moves aimed at reducing the dominant central control of the economy held by the government and stimulating more local control through the party and the *soviets*. In 1957 economic councils or *sovnarkhozi* were created throughout the country to run the economy on a regional basis instead of by the powerful ministries from the center. This reform engendered the opposition of those who enjoyed power under the ministry system, and it had the additional disadvantage of not working well for the economy either. In 1963 the effort was cut back and the number of councils reduced. After Khrushchev's departure the ministries were restored to power.

Khrushchev also favored increasing local participation both within the party and from the public. In 1962 the party was divided into industrial and agrarian branches with the aim of making the party more responsive to and involved with the economic needs of local enterprises. The machine tractor stations, which held the equipment for the collective farms and were a hallmark of the collectivization effort, were abolished in 1958, and collective farms were entitled to have their own equipment. Citizen involvement in the *soviets* was encouraged and Khrushchev made bold promises about "catching and overtaking" the United States in the quality of life. Though it wasn't called it at the time, Khrushchev also encouraged a limited amount of *glasnost* or voicing of problems, and allowed publication of previously banned writings. In 1962, reportedly at his personal intervention, Aleksandr Solzheni-

---

[14]Nikita S. Khrushchev, "The Crimes of the Stalin Era," in *The Crimes of the Stalin Era: Special Report to the 20th Congress of the Communist Party of the Soviet Union* (New York: The New Leader, 1962), p. 540.

tsyn's *One Day in the Life of Ivan Deni-sovich,* an explicit description of life in a Sta-linist labor camp, was published.

As with the *sovnarkhozi,* these moves stirred opposition: from those whose po-sitions were threatened; from those like most of the upper echelons of the party—including Khrushchev himself—who had come to power under Stalin; and from those who feared that discussing forbidden subjects like the recent past might lead to attacks on the current system. In addition, Khrushchev's foreign policy failures and embarrassments weakened his position. Despite a visit to Yu-goslavia in 1955 and declaration of support for the idea of "many roads to socialism," Khrushchev was unable to woo that country back into the Soviet camp. Indeed, the next year Hungary had to be kept there forcibly. Worse than that, the leaders of the world's other major communist country, China, be-gan attacking what they called "revisionism" in domestic policy and Soviet moves to im-prove relations with the United States in the early 1960s. Their attacks soon provoked an open break, taking tiny Albania with them. In relations with the West, despite the summit with the United States, including the first visit ever by a Soviet leader to the United States in 1959, Khrushchev was unable to restrain the growth of American power. In 1961 an at-tempt to force the western allies out of Berlin (still occupied by the four victors in World War II) produced fruitless tension and a So-viet failure. This was followed in 1962 by an even more dangerous gambit, the placing of medium-range nuclear missiles in Cuba. In this case, the United States responded with a naval blockade of Soviet ally Cuba and a public demand that the Soviet Union remove the missiles. The world was literally taken to the brink of nuclear war, and after heated internal debate the Soviet Union agreed to remove the missiles in return for a U.S. pledge not to invade Cuba. The incident proved an international embarrassment and a domestic blow to Khrushchev.

By 1964, with the country's economy do-ing poorly, with policy administration in tur-moil and a foreign policy going backwards, Khrushchev was removed and replaced as party leader by Leonid Brezhnev and as prime minister, an office Khrushchev had assumed in 1958, by Alexei Kosygin.

THE BREZHNEV ERA

The ensuing period of Soviet politics was gen-erally one of increasingly conservative even immobile domestic policy combined with an active but not always successful foreign pol-icy. Leonid Brezhnev, himself an associate of Khrushchev, was able to remove political ri-vals such as Nikolai Podgorny, who became chairman of the Presidium of the Supreme Soviet in 1965. He was eventually replaced by Brezhnev himself, who assumed what was essentially the presidency of the Soviet Union in 1977. Though Alexei Kosygin did remain prime minister until he was replaced by Nikolai Tikhonov in 1980, by the beginning of the 1970s Brezhnev was the most powerful political leader.

In contrast to the Khrushchev period, the top leadership during Brezhnev's tenure was characterized by what Brezhnev himself called "stability of cadres." For example, at Nikita Khrushchev's last party congress (1961), two-thirds of the central committee elected had not been full members four years before. At the time of the 1971 party congress under Brezhnev, 81 percent of the full mem-bers had held the posts five years before, and nearly 90 percent were reelected at the next party congress (1976).[15] Changes in the Politburo—so renamed in 1966—were few

[15]Hough and Fainsod, *How the Soviet Union Is Gov-erned,* pp. 232, 262.

and served mostly to make the top leadership older and more secure for Brezhnev. In 1973, for the first time in 10 years, the head of the KGB, Yuri Andropov, became a full Politburo member, as did two other leaders who had made their careers chiefly outside the party apparatus, foreign minister Andrei Gromyko and defense minister Andrei Grechko. When Brezhnev became party leader (1964) the average age in the Politburo was 60; by the time of his death (1982) it was 67.

Broader domestic developments reflected this conservatism. The economic reforms Khrushchev had championed were undone and criticized; the ministries returned to full power and their number expanded. Reforms in prices and enterprise control that were announced in the mid-1960s were evaded, put off and undone by the powerful bureaucracies. As Ed Hewett characterizes it, "the reform, never a terribly vibrant affair, was dead by the early 1970s."[16]

While under Khrushchev a certain "thaw" had occurred allowing the voicing of critical ideas and a more varied cultural scene, the policy under Brezhnev was one of relentless repression. In 1966 Soviet writers Andrei Siniavsky and Yuli Daniel were tried, convicted and sentenced to hard labor for publishing works *abroad* that were critical of the Soviet Union. Other trials and imprisonments followed and were complemented in some cases by forcing dissidents and uncompliant writers, such as Aleksandr Solzhenitsyn, to emigrate. While pursuing détente with the West and officially recognizing its obligation under its own constitution, of which a new version was published in 1977, and international treaties such as the Helsinki Accords of 1975, the Soviet regime nevertheless continued to crack down on political and human rights dissenters of all types. Groups set up to monitor Soviet adherence to international standards on human rights were smashed and their leaders sent to psychiatric hospitals or labor camps.

Without attendance to fundamental problems, the economy began to experience difficulties. The high growth rates of the 1960s and early 1970s gave way to slowing growth and stagnation. Agriculture turned in successive bad harvests and millions of tons of grain had to be imported. The living standard for the average Soviet citizen did improve but remained far behind those not only of the United States and Western Europe but of some Eastern European countries as well.

Though committed to little change at home, Leonid Brezhnev pushed an active policy of improving relations with the West, especially the United States. In this respect the Brezhnev period was a logical continuation, rather than a reversal, of the Khrushchev period. The nuclear test ban treaty of 1963 was followed by treaties banning nuclear weapons from outer space (1965), from the seabed (1970) and from being spread by the superpowers to other countries (non-proliferation, 1968). Negotiations began in 1969 for a strategic arms limitation treaty (SALT I) that was eventually signed and ratified by both sides (1972).

Despite the increased involvement of the United States in Vietnam during the 1960s and the Soviet invasion of Czechoslovakia in 1968, U.S.-Soviet relations improved. Summit visits were exchanged, and a treaty establishing the principles of relations between the two states was signed in 1972, in acknowledgment of the USSR's status as a world power and an equal of the United States. Trade expanded in the early 1970s and in implicit response to U.S. concerns, Jewish emigration from the Soviet Union increased, reaching 35,000 in 1973.

[16]Ed A. Hewett, *Reforming the Soviet Economy* (Washington, DC: The Brookings Institution, 1988), p. 238.

But from the Soviet point of view, détente with the United States did not mean giving up its goal of securing more politically reliable friends worldwide. Preventing a nuclear holocaust or engaging in a mutually beneficial exchange of goods and ideas did not, in the Soviet view, mean that competition between the two systems would cease or that the USSR would stop helping revolutionary groups achieve power where they could, especially in the Third World. Soviet efforts to this effect in Africa, and their continued heavy investment in defense—especially nuclear weapons—contributed to disenchantment in the West over détente. In addition, in some areas progress was slowed or even reversed. The USSR's leaders rejected the Jackson-Vanik amendment (named after the two senators who sponsored it) to the 1974 trade law that explicitly linked the extension of economic benefits to the Soviet Union with its willingness to pose no barriers to free emigration. While the Soviet Union had eased emigration restrictions, as noted, they rejected the idea of letting the U.S. Congress annually review its behavior as a price for improved economic ties. Beyond that, continued repression of its own writers, artists and political and religious dissenters eroded the basis of détente.

In 1979, NATO decided to install medium-range nuclear missiles in Western Europe in response to a massive Soviet buildup of such weapons in the western USSR. The presence of missiles in Europe that could hit the Kremlin in 10 minutes provoked a massive—but unsuccessful—Soviet campaign directed against this decision and at stirring Western European opposition to accepting the missiles. Though negotiations on the SALT II treaty were completed and the treaty was signed in 1979 by Brezhnev and U.S. President Jimmy Carter, after the Soviet invasion of Afghanistan at the end of that year the president was obliged to withdraw the treaty

from Senate consideration for fear it would be rejected. Détente was dead.

The last years of the Brezhnev regime saw a return to much harsher rhetoric, reminiscent of the early cold war. The election of Ronald Reagan (1980), Soviet pressure on Poland to end the activity of the independent trade union Solidarity, and the infirmity and uncertainty evident in the Brezhnev Politburo meant that the great centerpiece of Brezhnev's international policy, détente with the United States, had been undone. Nor were there successes in Soviet relations with China, where hostility had not ceased with the death of Mao Zedong and was only increased by the Soviet invasion of Afghanistan; or with Eastern Europe, where the rise of Solidarity in Poland trumpeted profound disaffection and the economic figures throughout the whole region told bluntly of economic stagnation; or with the Middle East, where Soviet influence seemed to reach its nadir after the Israeli invasion of Lebanon in 1982 and the dispersal of the Soviet-supported Palestine Liberation Organization.

Thus, in terms of domestic and international policy, the legacy of the Brezhnev regime was one of serious problems whose solution had been put off too long. Worse, the bequest of the Brezhnev years to the country was a narrow, aging leadership that could not even attend immediately to its difficulties. When Brezhnev died in November 1982, his immediate successor, Yuri Andropov, did attempt some reforms. Campaigns were launched against corruption, which had grown to epidemic proportions under Brezhnev, and for greater labor discipline and efficiency. But at 68 Andropov's own poor health rendered him a weak leader, and his death in early 1984 ended this brief attempt to shake things up. International relations continued to deteriorate, with no ongoing negotiations with the United States on nuclear weapons. More spectacularly, the USSR was condemned virtually throughout the world in September 1983 when its defense forces shot down a Korean Airlines passenger jet that had strayed over Soviet territory, killing 269 people.

Nor was Andropov's successor in any better position to revive either the Soviet economy or its international policy. Konstantin Chernenko was even older (72) than Andropov when he became general secretary in February 1984 and, evidently, even sicker. Few policy initiatives were taken, but in early 1985 feelers were extended about beginning new negotiations on nuclear weapons once again. Chernenko was not to live to see them come to fruition, as he died in March 1985 and was replaced by General Secretary Mikhail Gorbachev.

THE PAST IN THE PRESENT

Throughout the following chapters and especially in Chapter 33, reference is made to Mikhail Gorbachev's attempts to "restructure" the Soviet economy and its necessary accompaniment, to reshape the way the Soviet government works. While he brings great political power to the task and the need to effect change for the future is clear, neither he nor the country is free from the bequest of centuries of Russian and, more recently, Soviet, history. As this review indicates, some themes have persisted in this history. Certainly autocratic rule, rule from the top down, has been the dominant mode. When autocracy became oppressive, the absence of moderate alternatives or effective opportunities for popular involvement in making changes was evident. Along with the violent upheavals this situation often produced, the very notion that the great mass of people have a legitimate status apart from their role as resource for the rulers to manipulate is a fairly recent one.

It should also be clear that popular images of Russia or the Soviet Union as an immobile, unchanging society having a fixed and immutable government are false. Just in this century alone this country has gone from a largely peasant, rural-based empire, through revolution and civil war to forced urbanization, industrialization and collectivization of agriculture, two world wars, two recoveries, and emergence into a position as world superpower. What is interesting also about these changes and those throughout Russian history is the persistence of change directed "from the top," that is, by the rulers. Gorbachev is not the first leader to try to make the system work better. Changes widespread enough to call them revolutions were instituted by Peter the Great, Alexander II, by the first Bolshevik leaders and by Stalin. And both contemporary and earlier history show numerous examples of the "top" wanting subsequently to stop the changes once started, or even reverse them. Often the consequences, for example, of broadening the education of the population or of ending serfdom, proved unexpected or dangerous. But just as often they were irreversible. Whether the changes initiated by Mikhail Gorbachev will prove as momentous as those of Peter the Great or Alexander II remains to be seen. But our comprehension of the situation must begin with analysis of how the Soviet system operates now.

References and Suggested Readings

CARR, E. H. *The Bolshevik Revolution*, 3 vols. London: Penguin Books, 1966.
———. *Socialism in One Country*, vol. 1. London: Penguin Books, 1970.
COHEN, STEPHEN F. *Bukharin and the Bolshevik Revolution*. New York: A. A. Knopf, 1973.
CONQUEST, ROBERT. *The Great Terror: Stalin's Purge of the Thirties*. New York: Macmillan, 1968.

DMYTRYSHYN, BASIL. *A History of Russia.* Englewood Cliffs, NJ: Prentice-Hall, 1977.

DOBB, MAURICE. *Soviet Economic Development since 1917.* New York: International Pub., 1966.

GETTY, J. ARCH. *Origins of the Great Purges: The Soviet Communist Party Reconsidered, 1933–1938.* New York: Cambridge University Press, 1985.

GOLDHURST, RICHARD. *The Midnight War: The American Intervention in Russia.* New York: McGraw-Hill, 1978.

HALMSON, LEOPOLD H., *The Russian Marxists and the Origins of Bolshevism* (Boston, MA: Beacon Press, 1966).

LENIN, V. I. *Imperialism the Highest Stage of Capitalism.* New York: International Pub., 1939 (orig. pub. 1917).

———. *State and Revolution.* New York: International Pub., 1971 (orig. pub. 1917).

———. *What Is to Be Done.* New York: International Pub., 1943 (orig. pub. 1902).

McCAULEY, MARTIN, ed. *Khrushchev and Khrushchevism.* Bloomington: Indiana University Press, 1987.

MEDVEDEV, ROY A. *Let History Judge: The Origins and Consequences of Stalinism.* rev. and exp. ed. New York: Columbia University Press, 1989.

SCHAPIRO, LEONARD. *The Origins of Communist Autocracy.* Cambridge, MA: Harvard University Press, 1987.

SOLZHENITSYN, ALEKSANDR. *The Gulag Archipelago,* 2 vols. New York: Harper & Row, 1974 and 1975.

———. *Letter to the Soviet Leaders.* New York: Index on Censorship, in association with Harper & Row, 1974.

TUCKER, ROBERT C. *Stalin As Revolutionary, 1879–1929.* New York: W. W. Norton, 1973.

———. *The Marx-Engels Reader.* New York: W. W. Norton, 1972.

You are born a human being and you become an official.
Repentance

— SOVIET FILM BY TENGIZ
ABULADZE

29

Political Culture: The View from Above and Below

In any complex modern society it is risky to try to offer summary assessment of "the" political culture. If we define political culture as the attitudes and behavior of individuals directed toward their political institutions, most countries will show evidence of many such orientations, as can be seen in the discussions of France in this volume, for example. In the Soviet Union, a society and economy of a different sort, with quite a different type of political system, this is also true. In addition, at present in the Soviet Union key aspects of the dominant political culture, including the ideas on the nature of socialism, are undergoing reconsideration and reformulation. Moreover, our analysis of the political culture of the society is made much more difficult by the tight control traditionally exercised over the flow of information, such as public opinion surveys. This does not mean such information does not exist; numerous surveys, especially of workers' attitudes, have been done, and more are being reported now than previously. But the wealth of data such

as is available to students of Western democracies about how people feel about their government or its policies is not readily available for the Soviet Union. Therefore, analysts must often rely on secondary or incomplete sources, on learning what they can from those surveys that are reported, and from studies of limited specific populations, such as emigrés.

THE TWO POLITICAL CULTURES: I—THE OFFICIAL VIEW

In the Soviet Union, views of the political system held by society, what might be called the "political culture from below," coexist with the official political culture, or "the view from above." Before assessing the popular political culture, or what people seem to think about key aspects of the system, it will be useful to review what the official view of the system is. This can be done in terms of four key themes: (a) Soviet socialism; (b) the situation of the workers; (c) the issue of nationalities; and (d) the international role of the country.

Under Leonid Brezhnev the Soviet Union was officially designated a "mature" or "developed" socialist society. In such a society, Soviet theorists explained, there still exist different classes, such as workers, peasants, intelligentsia. But all accept the working class's interests as their own and support the Communist Party as the interpreter of those interests and the guide to further development. In political terms, and in policy pronouncements, this means that pushing other interests that might challenge those of the workers (as interpreted by the party) are restricted. This includes interests based on religion or on private control of property. It also means the interests of state, which claims to represent and act for the workers, take precedence over the desires of individuals. Mikhail Gorbachev's formulation has taken this somewhat further, to argue that diversity of economic interests under socialism are possible, can even include different forms of property ownership and can be "harmonized."

But in order to accomplish this and to advance the economic progress of socialism, a broad "democratization" of the state and party is necessary, though not to the extent of allowing alternative political parties. Popular political activity is sought and indeed encouraged. But, as will be seen in the section on participation, such activity still must take place within the channels and in directions that are deemed beneficial to the socialist society.

The benefits of the system accrue to the toilers, according to the official political culture. At every party congress, the advancements made by Soviet workers are chronicled: their gains in standard of living, health care and housing. At the 24th Party Congress (1971), for example, Leonid Brezhnev reported:

In the past five years, real income per capita increased by 33%, as against the 30% envisaged in the Directives of the 23rd Party Congress and the 19% in the preceding five-year period.

As you know, comrades, in this five-year plan the minimum wage of workers and office employees was increased to 60 rubles a month. The average wage of workers and office employees for the country as a whole increased by 26%. The incomes of collective farmers from the communal sector increased by 42%. Guaranteed pay has been introduced, the pension age has been lowered, and the payment of sickness and disability allowances has been established for collective farm members. . . .[1]

Similarly, in 1988 Gorbachev reported to a party plenum:

Counting all sources of finance, about 130 million square metres of housing were built in 1987, or almost 2.5 million square metres of floor living space more than planned and 10 million square metres more than in 1986. This is more than in any previous year. During the past year alone the construction of general educational schools went up by 18 percent, childcare centres by 7 percent, vocational schools by 61 percent, outpatient clinics by 17 percent, and clubs and community centres by 36 percent.[2]

But unlike his predecessors, Gorbachev has been just as forceful in pointing to the need for renewal or *perestroika* to allow the full

[1]"Brezhnev: Central Committee Report," in *Current Soviet Policies, VI, The Documentary Record of the 24th Congress of the Communist Party of the Soviet Union* (Columbus: American Association for the Advancement of Slavic Studies, 1973), p. 16.
[2]"Revolutionary Perestroika and the Ideology of Renewal," Speech by Mikhail Gorbachev, General Secretary of the CPSU Central Committee, at the Plenary Meeting of the CPSU Central Committee on February 18, 1988. [mimeo, in English]

Mikhail Gorbachev, President of the USSR Supreme Soviet, votes at the
Congress of the People's Deputies, on May 26, 1989.
SOURCE: TASS from Sovfoto.

flowering of the economic power of socialism. (See the discussion in Chapter 33.)

Beyond these material gains, the official
view is that the Soviet Union, by virtue of its
emergence as a socialist society and the dominance of working-class interests, has overcome clashes of interest based on differences
in nationality. In the Soviet constitution it is
stated that the USSR is home to

a society of mature socialist social relationships
in which, on the basis of the rapprochement of
all classes and social strata, of the legal and
factual equality of all nations and nationalities,
and of their fraternal cooperation, a new his-

torical community of people—the Soviet
people—has taken shape.[3]

The official view is that the rapprochement or
drawing together (*sblizhenie*) of the different
nationalities under socialism overcomes ethnic antagonisms; and while national cultures
and heritages are preserved, social cooperation predominates over narrow nationalism.

Internationally, the USSR portrays itself as

[3]The text of the Soviet constitution can be found in
F. J. M. Feldbrugge, *The Constitutions of the USSR and
the Union Republics: Analysis, Texts, Reports* (Alphen
aan den Rijn, The Netherlands: Sijthoff and Noordhoff,
1979), p. 73.

The Soviet National Anthem (1977)

Linked up eternally, Republics standing free,
Surviving for ever, great USSR.
Children of Russ-i-a, strong in adversity
Born of a people entrenched near and far.

Chorus
Fame's flame long burning, sustaining our
    Motherland,
Friend to all nations, strong bulwark of right;
Forceful and fearless in the spirit of Lenin,
Speeding the victory of Communist might.
Freedom's sun never dimmed, while we survive
    ever on
Led through the tempest time by Lenin the Great;
Rousing up nations, making the blindest see,
Marking the open path to freedom's broad gate.
All clear, far ahead, see our fortune and future
Unperished and safe in our Communist hands,
Faithful and steadfast, through pain and
    endurance,
Behind the Red Banner as proudly it stands.

SOURCE: David Lane, *Soviet Economy and Society* (Oxford: Basil Blackwell, 1985), app. C.

---

a country that stands for social justice, peace and progress and supports other movements and countries that do the same. The natural adversaries of such states are the imperialist countries, that is, the developed capitalist states of the West, within which there are reactionaries and monopolies whose desire for world domination threatens international peace. Lenin had seen conflict between imperialism (which he called the ultimate stage of capitalism) and socialism as inevitable, a view Stalin had only partly modified after World II, by indicating that the camp of socialism would grow strong while the imperialists fought among themselves. Nikita Khrushchev, however, revised this notion in 1956. In the presence of growing nuclear arsenals, he argued that war between the two systems was no longer "fatalistically inevitable." Moreover, he recognized the existence of other forces, such as newly independent states and national liberation movements, that could be enlisted in the struggle against imperialism. The new party program, adopted in 1986, reiterates this view. Since Khrushchev, Soviet leaders have generally pursued various forms of "peaceful coexistence," continuing to try to exert influence and contesting the influence of the West where they can, chiefly in Third World arenas, while avoiding direct military conflict between the nuclear superpowers. Seeing the greatest danger as that posed by nuclear weapons, the official Soviet view is that while it is necessary to have such weapons for national defense, the USSR is eager to enter arms control agreements that would eliminate them (see the discussion, Chapter 34).

The official political culture is not divorced from the past, either that of the Soviet or of the pre-revolutionary period. The party's revolutionary heritage holds an important place in the party's conception of itself and its presentation to the public. The party's key role in bringing about the revolution and the great transformation of the country from backward autocracy to modern socialist society is a dominant theme in Soviet historiography and education.

More specifically, the role of Lenin as interpreter of Marx, revolutionary strategist, and political leader is glorified and invoked as justification for contemporary policies. It is not accidental, as the Soviets might say, that Mikhail Gorbachev's attempt to revitalize the national economy is consistently linked by him to the New Economic Policy instituted by Lenin in the early 1920s after the civil war had ended. Tying current policies to revered actions of the past demonstrates that such policies and the leader espousing them are in the tradition of "the great Lenin." This lends legitimacy to actions that might appear to some comrades as revisions of Marxism.

Other aspects of the Soviet Union's tumultuous and trying history are constantly put before the population in education and popular culture. Episodes are depicted in the struggle against enemies of the revolution at home and abroad, in the building of socialism and, especially, of the Soviet suffering, battles and victory in World War II. Every village and town has its monument to those who died either in battle or under German occupation. Books, films and television shows about the war, which is referred to as "The Great Patriotic War," abound, serving both to imbue Soviet youth with respect for the price paid for the country's defense and liberation and to link the current party and system to the sacrifices and struggle endured at that time.

Despite the transformation engendered by the Communist Party, some aspects of the pre-revolutionary political culture remain, even if they are not officially acknowledged. The desire for tight control of society exercised by the political rulers, for example, is no less strong among some of the leaders of the CPSU than it was among the Russian tsars. Indeed, many of the mechanisms of social control that the Bolsheviks themselves railed against, such as the internal passport, have been used by the party to maintain control. Some analysts link this to a traditional Russian fear of disorder or anarchy, a feeling held by both leaders and led that, left to itself, society and the country would disintegrate.[4]

In the international sphere, Soviet communists guard the country's sovereignty and domestic and international prerogatives as jealously as any of the imperial foreign ministers and armed forces did. While the present definition of who is friend and who is foe may be based on a view of the world different from that of the autocracy, and the instruments available to implement Soviet foreign policy may be more varied and powerful (for example, including nuclear weapons), the Soviet leadership's desire to play an active and, where possible, dominant role in key regions such as Eastern Europe, and on global issues of vital interest such as arms control, are as evident as they were before the revolution.

THE TWO POLITICAL CULTURES: II—POPULAR POLITICAL CULTURE

To what degree have these aspects of official political culture (the view from above) become part of the popular political culture (the view from below)? As noted, it is impossible to determine this in great detail or, in some cases, at all, because of the relative scarcity of reliable information. But evidence from several careful observers, combined with partial measures, gives us some picture of the degree of congruence or disparity between these two political cultures.

One source is a survey of Soviet emigrants, undertaken in 1983–1984. People were asked about all aspects of life in their former country, about things they liked and did not like about it and what they would change or keep if they could change things. One of the most interesting results of this survey was that despite the fact that the people interviewed had left the Soviet Union permanently, most did not condemn Soviet socialism wholesale. When asked, for example, which parts, if any, of the economy they felt should be under state rather than private control, nearly two-thirds of the respondents were in favor of keeping medical care under state control rather than in private hands, and roughly half felt that way about heavy industry. On the other hand, on the question of collective versus individual rights, three-fifths of the respondents felt that the right to

---

[4]Frederick Barghoorn and Thomas F. Remington, *Politics in the USSR* (Boston: Little, Brown, 1986), pp. 43–44. On the persistence of this and other themes from traditional political culture, see Edward L. Keenan, "Muscovite Political Folkways," *The Russian Review* 45(1986):115–81, and the debate this provoked in "Discussion," *The Russian Review* 46(1987):157–210.

strike should be a private right, and nearly four-fifths felt that the question of where a person should live should be decided by the individual and not by the state.[5] In other words, the survey results suggest that some aspects of the official political culture, in particular those relating to economic control and social welfare, are accepted by the Soviet population, but some aspects are not, such as those involving individual civil rights. In a recent poll conducted in Moscow by the new Institute of Sociological Research, just over one-half of the respondents supported the idea that a one-party system could promote democracy.[6] In another public opinion poll in 1989, most respondents were reported to oppose private ownership of large enterprises, even though most did favor private ownership of small businesses.

Other parts of the emigré survey show that in general the regime had succeeded in creating public satisfaction with the standard of living. Here the official view and the popular view for a time did not substantially diverge. For example, the survey of emigrants found that nearly two-thirds of the respondents said they had been somewhat or very satisfied with housing; roughly half expressed this level of satisfaction with regard to their job, the overall standard of living, and medical care. In fact, when people were asked what the United States could learn about from the Soviet Union, the health care system was often cited in response.[7] Creating this level of

satisfaction is important for the regime politically, since this and other surveys have shown that those with a higher level of material satisfaction tend to be those most supportive of the government and its policies.

This link poses a problem for public policy, however. What happens when the regime does not or can no longer provide the improvements in material standard that create those feelings of satisfaction and some degree of political support? Mervyn Matthews's extensive study of poverty in the Soviet Union produces an estimate that some two-fifths of all Soviet workers and their families live below the official poverty level.[8] A recent Soviet study reported that one-fifth of the Soviet population lived at or near the official poverty line, a group consisting mainly of families where the main earner brings home too little, young couples with children, single mothers and retired people.[9] While the situation for most workers has indeed improved since World War II, the earnings in some industries, such as trade, catering, health and social services and education, has lagged well below the average. But even when a basic level of satisfaction has been achieved, how can the system ensure loyalty and better performance in economic sectors if it cannot keep supplying a better and better standard of living? New Soviet polls, taken under conditions of *glasnost* but also of economic difficulty, document a very low level of popular satisfaction with living standards. Soviet sociologists in their own studies of workers' attitudes have found that it is not enough to provide high wages and to praise the "social value" of labor. Increasingly, workers' satisfaction with their own jobs and their attitudes toward work in general are found to be a function of work conditions, such as the

---

[5]Brian D. Silver, "Political Beliefs of the Soviet Citizen: Sources of Support for Regime Norms," in *Politics, Work and Daily Life in the USSR: A Survey of Former Soviet Citizens*, ed. James Millar (New York: Cambridge University Press, 1987), p. 110.

[6]*New York Times*, May 27, 1988, pp. 1, 7; Tass (in English), December 22, 1989.

[7]James R. Millar and Elizabeth Clayton, "Quality of Life: Subjective Measures of Relative Satisfaction," in *Politics, Work and Daily Life in the USSR: A Survey of Former Soviet Citizens*, ed. James Millar (New York: Cambridge University Press, 1987), p. 33.

[8]Mervyn Matthews, *Poverty in the Soviet Union* (Cambridge: Cambridge University Press, 1986), p. 32.

[9]Aaron Trehub, "Poverty in the Soviet Union," *Radio Liberty Research*, June 20, 1988.

location of the job and the amount of stress associated with it, and of longstanding and family attitudes which the regime's incessant glorification of labor has not succeeded in erasing. One Soviet study of students' attitudes toward work, for example, found that on a scale of ten, workers' occupations (as opposed to those of professionals) rated less than a five.[10] Perhaps the most influential Soviet sociologist today, Tatiana Zaslavaskia, wrote in 1984:

> A low level of labor and production discipline, indifferent attitudes toward the work being done, low quality of work, social inertia, low importance of work as a means of self-realization, strongly pronounced consumer orientations, and low level of morality are traits common to many workers, which have been shaped during recent five-year plans.[11]

Soviet studies report increasing difficulties in finding people to take managerial positions in factories, and economic statistics show falling worker productivity. Overcoming this particular disjunction between the official political culture and the attitudes actually held by people is the focus of at least one aspect of the economic reform under Mikhail Gorbachev, referred to as activating the "human factor."

What about the "national question"? Do the Soviet people feel like "the Soviet people" of official repute? That is, has the socialist system muted or removed the internationality differences that the official view blames on previous systems of exploitation?

Apparently not totally. Evidence for this is sometimes spectacular. In February 1988 an estimated one million Armenians marched through the capital of that republic demanding that a predominantly Armenian part of

the neighboring Azerbaijan Republic, called Nargoko-Karabakh, be joined instead with the Armenian Republic. In the aftermath of some demonstrations inside the disputed region, and in Azerbaijan and Armenia, riots occurred in which scores of people were killed and thousands fled their homes in both directions. Order was restored in these regions only when Soviet troops were put on the streets. At the beginning of 1990 violence between Azerbaijanis and Armenians escalated into virtual civil war. Thousands of Soviet interior ministry and army troops were again sent to the region. Between 1988 and 1990 it is estimated that more than six hundred people died in interethnic violence in this region as well as in Georgia, Uzbekistan, Kazakhstan, and Tajikistan.

One of the most pervasive forms of ethnic tension in the Soviet Union is that between the indigenous population of a republic, say the Kazakhs in Kazakhstan or the Estonians in Estonia, and the numerous Russians who have come there. Since in most cases the Russians have come as representatives of the ruling center, socialist or not, they are resented. Rasma Karklins's study of nationality feelings reports that the immigration of official Russians, accompanied by substantial pressure on the local population to learn and use the Russian language, has created widespread fears of loss of identity. Fears of "Russification" are especially strong in two of the Baltic republics, Latvia and Estonia, where the ratio of the indigenous population to Russians declined sharply between 1959 and 1979.[12] With greater latitude for expression under Mikhail Gorbachev, national feeling has sometimes taken unprecedented form in this region. During 1988 and 1989 in all three republics massive demonstrations oc-

---

[10]Vladimir Shlapentokh, "Evolution in the Soviet Sociology of Work: From Ideology to Pragmatism," *The Carl Beck Papers in Russian and East European Studies,* no. 404 (Pittsburgh, PA: University of Pittsburgh, Center for Russian and East European Studies, 1985), p. 31.

[11]Cited in *ibid.,* p. 65.

[12]Rasma Karklins, *Ethnic Relations in the USSR* (Boston: Allen & Unwin, 1986), ch. 1 and p. 232 (table); Ann Shehy, "Russian Share of Soviet Population Down to 50.8 Percent," *Report in the USSR,* Vol. 1, No. 42 (1989), pp. 4–5.

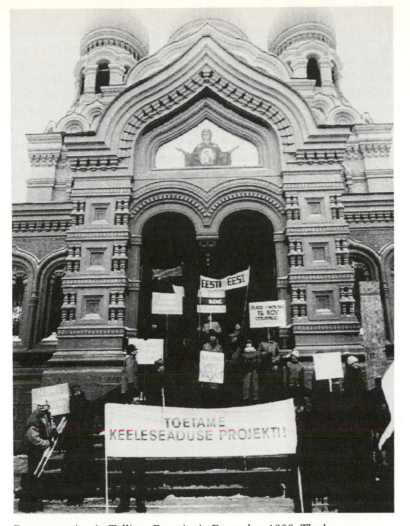

Demonstration in Tallinn, Estonia, in December 1988. The banner
proclaims: "We support the language law project."
SOURCE: AP/Wide World Photos.

curred, national flags were displayed for the first time since World War II, and at one point Estonia even declared itself "sovereign" to the extent that it could apply Soviet laws and practices as it saw fit, a position rejected by the government in Moscow. If learning to use one another's language is any indication, *sblizhenie* is going slowly. Soviet studies show that outside of Byelorussia and the Ukraine, an average of 39 percent of the local people know Russian. Conversely, apart from these same two republics, only 12 percent of the Russians know the local language. Judging from such figures and the forceful appearance of national feeling under Gorbachev, it seems that there is some divergence between the official culture and the popular political culture on the question of nationality relations. Recognition of this was demonstrated by the holding, in September

1989, of a special Central Committee plenum devoted to the nationalities question. The first such meeting in more than sixty years, it adopted a platform reaffirming both the federal character of the country and the need for the party to do a better job at combating interethnic strife and nationalism.

This issue poses another difficult dilemma for Soviet public policy. As noted above, Soviet workers do seem to accept the basic norms of socialism, with acceptance more prevalent, it seems, among those who are doing well. Following this logic, one way to deal with potential nationality tensions would be to adopt a policy of increasing the status and power of nationalities; to give them more control over their own affairs. Under existing Soviet nationality policy, the major national groups already have their own republics and a good deal of autonomy in local affairs; for example, primary and secondary education is usually in the local language. But to extend any more real power to the republics would be to weaken the control of the center and threaten the achievement of the Communist Party's key national goals, not to mention its very power. Providing the economic satisfaction needed to create political support can, under the right circumstances, be stimulated by switching investment plans and thus allowing the production of more goods and services and presumably more support for the regime. But in dealing with the country's many nationalities, what can be done to improve their feeling of control, reduce their resentments and strengthen support for the regime while not at the same time eroding the political and economic controls that are central to the Soviet system of socialism? For the Soviet system and for Mikhail Gorbachev, "the national question" may prove the most vexing dilemma.

As with the leadership's policies, in the popular view of government several traditional elements more associated with the country's history than the present appear to persist. Reference has already been made to the evident preference among many Soviet people for a "strong hand" ruling from Moscow. During the Brezhnev years, a substantial amount of nostalgia for the order of the Stalin period was evident. In fact, during Brezhnev's rule public attacks on Stalin's crimes ceased and a certain degree of "rehabilitation" of his reputation occurred. Reinforcing this feeling among some members of the population is a tendency to personalize the ruler of the country, whether it is the tsar or the Soviet leader, seeing him as representing the individual's shield against the tyrannies of local bosses. As one Soviet worker put it,

> The intelligentsia may dream of democracy but the huge mass of people dream of Stalin—his strong power. They are not reactionary but they are being mistreated by their petty bosses, who cheat and exploit them, suppress them. They want a strong boss to "put shoes on" the petty bosses. They know that under Stalin [economic] conditions were not as good, but the state farm directors and other officials were not robbing them under Stalin, were not mocking them. There was a check on local authorities.[13]

Autocratic rule is a persistent feature of the history of the Russian empire, of the medieval

[13]Hedrick Smith, *The Russians* (New York: Ballantine Books, 1976), p. 327.

In a letter attacking *perestroika* and *glasnost* published in March 1988 (see box, p. 405) a teacher from Leningrad expressed just this point of view: "There is no question that this period was extremely harsh. But it is also true that personal modesty bordering upon asceticism did not feel ashamed of itself and that potential Soviet millionaires were still afraid to peck away in the quiet of minor offices and trading centers" (Nina Andreyeva, "Letter to the Editorial Office From a Leningrad VUZ [institution of higher education] Lecturer," *Sovetskaya Rossiya*, March 13, 1988, p. 3 [Foreign Broadcast Information Service, *Daily Report*, Soviet Union, March 16, 1988, pp. 50–51]).

states of Muscovy and Kievan Rus that preceded it, and of the period of Mongol domination that lasted three centuries. This does not mean there are no instances of limitations on the personal rule of the leader or even of limited participation by certain groups of the governed. The *zemskii sobor* (Landed Assembly) of the sixteenth and seventeenth centuries, the *boiarski duma,* and other executive councils established under Peter the Great and Catherine II often wielded enormous influence. The tsar himself was chosen by election, not dynasty, until the eighteenth century. But especially after Peter the Great, the representativeness and power of such assemblies and councils—including that of the first broadly elected *duma* established after the Russian revolution of 1905—were a product of regime design rather than popular will. Neither those groups who held power, which before the revolution usually went with property, nor the ruler himself were effectively limited by these weak institutions. When the last tsar of Russia (Nicholas II) was faced with a more troublesome *duma* than he liked, he dissolved it. The electoral law was changed and a more manageable assembly elected.

Russian history has few examples of institutions that afforded opportunity on a regular basis for public influencing of the policy process. Instead it has numerous instances of state-directed campaigns aimed at increasing the public's contribution to, rather than determination of, state goals. And in the absence of a regularized legitimate vehicle for public input into policies affecting them, the history of the country has included numerous instances of public insurrections, violence against the government—some four thousand officials were killed by revolutionaries in 1906–07 alone—and revolution. While such a history does not of course predetermine that a population is forever locked into a choice between subordination and revolution, it does mean that as a part of contemporary political culture, people cannot harken back to earlier periods of broad popular influence. Such periods do not exist.

While the ethos of autocratic rule may set Russian political culture apart from that of Britain or France, the prevalence of public support for defending the country's interests abroad—even if it means intervening in a fellow socialist state as the USSR did in 1968—is a more familiar aspect of Soviet political culture. Many observers have commented on the widespread and unselfconscious expressions of patriotism Soviet people display both in public and in private. It is not known to what degree the Soviet military involvement in Afghanistan that began in full strength in late 1979 was shortened by fear of the erosion of this support. But some evidence of dissatisfaction among the Soviet population with the length and cost of this involvement—an acknowledged 15,000 dead and 35,000 wounded—did surface as that war dragged on for eight years.

There have been those who publicly reject in whole or in part the official political culture and try to suggest an alternative for Soviet society. Referred to as "dissidents" in the West, such people comprise several groups holding a range of views as to how the Soviet Union should change. The opposition of some people is issue-specific: They challenge the restrictions on emigration, on the right to write or speak freely or to practice their religion. Groups known as the Helsinki Monitoring Groups were formed in the mid-1970s as autonomous observers of Soviet adherence to the Helsinki accords (1975) obliging governments to protect certain human rights of their citizens. They published a record of violations known as the *Chronicle* that earned them international support and regime suppression.

Some challenges come from within the family, so to speak. Historian Roy Medvedev

For the Soviet population the policy of *glasnost* has meant that the party's political debates and disagreements, heretofore hidden from public view, are presented for all to see. In this respect the party conference in June 1988 proved "extraordinary" not just in the sense of "unscheduled." While it met the public could read, for example, the bitter attack of Boris Yeltsin (who had lost his position as Moscow party chief but was still a candidate member of the Politburo) on the Central Committee in the pages of its own newspaper, *Pravda:*

In a number of countries a practice is established: the leader goes—the leadership goes. In ours we are used to blaming the dead for everything. Especially since they do not hit back. Now it turns out: only Brezhnev is to blame for stagnation. But where were those who were then in the Politburo for ten, fifteen, twenty years and are still there? Each time they voted for various programs. Why were they silent, when one man was deciding on the say-so of the Central Committee apparat, the fate of the party, of the country of socialism? They kept on voting until one man had five stars [Orders of Lenin] and society as a whole was in crisis. Why did they appoint the sick Chernenko? Why was the Party Control Committee, punishing relatively small deviations from the norms of party life, afraid and is still afraid to call to account major leaders of republics, of *oblasts* for taking bribes, for damage to the state in millions and so forth?

They read Yeltsin's criticism of Ligachev, which he had delivered in interviews to foreign television services:

There was such a question: Do you think that, if in place of comrade Ligachev there were some other person, *perestroika* would go faster? I answered "Yes."

On Moscow radio they heard Ligachev respond:

Dear comrades! Perhaps it is more difficult for me than for anyone in the leadership to speak in connection with the speech by Boris Nikolayevich Yeltsin. And not because it referred to me. The time has simply come to tell the whole truth. . . .

I cannot be silent, because Communist Yeltsin has taken the wrong road. It has turned out that this person has not a constructive but a destructive force. His evaluation of the process of restructuring, his approaches and methods of work have been recognized by the party as groundless *and* mistaken.

. . . Incidentally, when he was a secretary of the party *gorkom* [city committee], he never once attended a sitting of the secretariat. And I would like to mention something else to you. It's hard to believe, but it's a fact: As a member of the Politburo and attending its sittings—and they last for 8, 9, or 10 hours—he took hardly any part in discussions of the country's vitally important problems or in the adoption of decisions awaited by the people. He kept silent and bided his time. It's monstrous, but it's a fact. Does this really signify party comradeship, Boris?

On the evening news they were treated to unprecedented scenes of delegates disagreeing with each other, exchanging views with Gorbachev, and even naming names.

[V. I. Melnikov, first secretary of Komi Autonomous Republic] Whoever in former times actively conducted the policy of stagnation should neither be nor work in the central party and local soviet organs. Everyone must be called to account, and personally! [applause]

[Gorbachev] Perhaps you have some specific suggestions to make? [laughter in the audience] Otherwise, we are just sitting here without knowing whether this refers to me or to him.

[Melnikov] Mikhail Sergeyevich knows, I think. I was referring here to Comrade Solomentsev, in the first place, Gromyko, Afanasyev, Arbatov, and others. [applause]

SOURCES: *Pravda,* July 2, 1988, p. 8; Moscow Domestic Service, July 1, 1988 (Foreign Broadcast Information Service, *Daily Report,* Soviet Union, July 5, 1988, pp. 31, 101, 103).

has been fierce in condemning Stalinism but insists that socialism is not itself at fault and can be democratic in the USSR, a position now embraced by Gorbachev. Others, such as Aleksandr Solzhenitsyn, reject totally not only Marxism-Leninism, which Solzhenitsyn calls "a grim jest of the twentieth century," but the "myth" of eternal progress. He sees the salvation of the country as residing in Russia's own traditions, such as those of village life and the family and Christian Orthodoxy, which he describes as "the only living spiritual force capable of undertaking the spiritual healing of Russia."[14] For his opposition, Solzhenitsyn was forced to emigrate in 1974. In the late Brezhnev period in particular, many groups emerged that based their opposition on nationalism, both that of nationalities such as Ukrainians and Latvians and that of the dominant Russians.

Until very recently, the Soviet government's response to dissent of all types has been to repress it. Attempts to form free labor unions or political groupings, whether based on alternative views of the country as a whole or in support of specific causes, were smashed, and leaders were imprisoned in labor camps, psychiatric hospitals or ordinary prisons. At the very least such persons usually lost their jobs and were subject to various other forms of pressure. Even forms of repression used by the tsars, such as exile, were employed against dissidents, the best known of whom was nuclear physicist Andrei Sakharov, who was sent to the city of Gorky from 1980 to 1987.

Under Mikhail Gorbachev the clash between notions of civic culture defined by the elite and those defined by others has become less severe. More varied debates on key issues have been tolerated in the press, and most of those imprisoned or repressed for earlier political offenses have been released. Some, such as Andrei Sakharov, have even been given official status, their support for *perestroika* welcomed even though they may remain critical. Since Gorbachev's ascension to party leadership, dozens of prominent Jewish dissidents as well as hundreds of "refuseniks"—those refused permission to leave—have been allowed to emigrate.

This new approach is part of the policy of *glasnost,* which translates roughly as "openness" or "frankness." Its application has meant a greater willingness on the part of the leadership to delve into the problems involved in the ongoing development of socialism. It does not represent the abandonment of the idea of building society according to Marxist-Leninist principles, much less weakening the party's political monopoly. Rather it can be seen as an attempt to improve the governing process by adding to the top-down nature of the elite culture more elements of genuine participation and input from the population. Through this process the government will be better informed—for better or worse—as to the nature of the view from below. Whether the regime can react effectively on issues that are raised in this way is another question, as indicated in the discussion of economic reform (Chapter 33).

---

[14]Aleksandr Solzhenitsyn, *Letter to the Soviet Leaders* (New York: Index on Censorship, in association with Harper & Row, 1974), p. 57.

References and Suggested Readings

BROWN, ARCHIE, AND GRAY, JACK, eds. *Political Culture and Political Change in Communist States.* New York: Holmes and Meier, 1979.

FRIEDBERG, MAURICE, AND ISHAM, HEYWARD, eds. *Soviet Society under Gorbachev.* Armonk, NY: M. E. Sharpe, Inc., 1987.

GORBACHEV, M. S. *Speeches and Writings.* New York: Pergamon Press, 1986.

HERLEMANN, HORST, ed. *Quality of Life in the Soviet Union.* Boulder, CO: Westview Press, 1987.

MILLAR, JAMES R., ed. *Politics, Work and Daily Life in the USSR: A Survey of Former Soviet Citizens.* New York: Cambridge University Press, 1987.

TUCKER, ROBERT C. *Political Culture and Leadership in Soviet Russia.* New York: W. W. Norton, 1987.

YANOV, ALEXANDER. *The Russian New Right: Right-Wing Ideologies in the Contemporary USSR.* Berkeley, CA: Institute of International Studies, 1978.

30

> "Today many will vote for the first time in their lives. Let them remember this day and also that they are new citizens of the country, fulfilling their duty according to democratic law. However, we are all also today voting again for the first time."
>
> — *Pravda*, March 26, 1989, on the occasion of the first contested multicandidate elections in more than seventy years.

Socialization and Participation

At a minimum, all governments need in one way or another to secure the acquiescence of the citizenry under their rule. They have to be sure that opposition to their rule is kept to a minimum or, in some systems, destroyed. This kind of goal is often secured by terror or intimidation of the population, or in other cases by providing some people with enough material satisfaction or power that they are co-opted or persuaded to abstain from opposition to the government's existence or policies.

While this sort of minimum goal may be sufficient for simply preserving a regime in power, if the rulers have broader goals, such as changing or developing their society and economy, something other than simply holding power will be necessary. In this case, the population must become a citizenry; the individual who under a terroristic regime wants merely to survive and thus refrains from opposing the government must be persuaded to do more than that, to come forth and offer his or her contribution to society, to take an active part in making the changes the rulers have in mind. Whether it is passive obedi-

ence or active participation the government wants, a key role in the process is played by political socialization.

POLITICAL SOCIALIZATION

The socialization process involves imbuing individuals, beginning as early as possible in their lives, with a clear idea of what the proper norms of behavior are—in this case, political behavior. Ideally, politically socialized citizens accept the dominant norms, act in ways that contribute towards keeping the prevailing political system strong, and ultimately take an active part both in that system and in the socialization of others. In other words, they become mobilized into participating in the system. All political systems rely on a socialization process to create support, and on mobilization of part of a population, such as a ruling elite or a greater part of the mass public, to keep the system functioning. When American children stand and salute the flag in their elementary schools they are being socialized into important political values, pa-

395

triotism and loyalty, and they are taught to have respect for an important political symbol, the flag of the United States. When as adults they vote, help political candidates or even run for office themselves, they have become mobilized into taking part in the political system.

In the Soviet Union, the need for socialization and mobilization is the same, even if the goals and parameters of the process are somewhat different. As the Soviet Union is based on the ideal of a collective rather than an individualistic society, the aim of much of the socialization that occurs, especially at early ages, is toward building in individuals a sense of the importance of the group or collective, and instilling a sense of subordination of the individual to the goals of that group,

whether it is a school class or society as a whole.

Early socialization along these lines takes place within the schools of the Soviet Union. While there is an extensive system of day care and kindergartens, most Soviet children spend their earliest years at home, cared for by relatives, often the grandmother. They enter primary school at age six or seven, and the values imparted there are more general and behavioral than explicitly political. Students are taught to be well-behaved, punctual, cooperative and respectful as one might expect in any school system. But in the Soviet schools the class itself, as well as the teacher, becomes the instrument for teaching and enforcing appropriate behavior. Students are taught to conform and are brought into line

The 1,175 young residents of Druzhba learn in a new school in the city.
SOURCE: Fotokhronika TASS.

by their fellow students to a much greater degree than in the United States, where the teacher would assume this responsibility almost totally. In many schools the class is divided into small teams in which children perform their tasks together and help each other but also act to keep each other in line.[1] While not explicitly political, this approach to learning conveys to students the very political message that the collective takes precedence over the individual; and while the group can be supportive and helpful, it can also be the source and method of control and punishment.

As with any school system, the education itself contains both explicit and implicit socialization. Lessons involving the imperial and Soviet past and, especially, the life of Lenin pass on the desired orientation to the country's history, while submersion in the rich heritage of art and literature is designed to reinforce pride in the national culture. Soviet students typically memorize long portions of the works of Pushkin, Mayakovsky, Gogol and Tolstoy. More broadly, Soviet schools try to instill a "love of labor" in students, designed both to acquaint students with work outside of school and to counter a "love of things" as well as a rather persistent social preference, somewhat embarrassing in this case, for white-collar or non-manual labor.

At the same time, patriotism and military training are predominant values present throughout the educational system. In addition to joining the Pioneers (see below), boys in secondary schools have required military classes and training in the summer in preparation for military service. In the Soviet Union this is still compulsory for young men, through either active duty or the reserves. Needless to say, service in the armed forces

[1]David K. Shipler, *Russia: Broken Idols, Solemn Dreams* (New York: Penguin Books, 1984), pp. 79–80.

Filling in Some Blank Spots . . .

Among the changes Mikhail Gorbachev urged as part of the policy of *glasnost* or voicing of issues, was the filling in of "blank spots" in official Soviet history. Many subjects which had either been ignored or treated only in the "proper" way were reconsidered. These included: some of Lenin's actions, especially in utilizing the secret police against opponents; the views and actions of previous "enemies of the state" such as Nikolai Bukharin, Grigori Zinoviev, Lev Kamenev and even Leon Trotsky; the methods and human cost of collectivization, and the full scope of the Stalinist terror. One Soviet historian, describing the official descriptions of World War II, said, "We do not have histories of World War II, only histories of our victories." By 1988 so many changes were needed in standard histories that the final written history exams of students leaving secondary school had to be cancelled and be replaced by ungraded oral exams.

. . . and Blanking Out Some Others

In late 1988, "in response to letters and public appeals," the Soviet government decided to remove the name of Leonid Brezhnev—the Soviet ruler for 18 years—from all public buildings, including places where he once lived.

SOURCE: *Financial Times*, June 10, 1988, p. 2, and December 30, 1988, p. 3.

itself provides further opportunity for the government to instill ideals of patriotism, respect for the sacrifices made by past generations for the defense of the homeland, and obedience to the common good.

Children's activities are guided from a very early age. In the first three grades, ages 7–9, they usually become *Octobrists*, which introduces them to the idea of organized group activity and prepares them to join the *Pioneers*. This virtually universal group is for children ages 10–14, through the eighth grade, and is designed to instill in all children the values of patriotism, respect for the coun-

Students in a secondary school in Frunze, the capital city of Kirghizia, Central Asia, now get computer software specialists' certificates of competence in addition to their general education certificates. They are taught computer technology and software by specialists invited from Frunze's polytechnic institute, who first organized a computer hobby group in that school, and now has introduced regular classes.
SOURCE: Fotokhronika TASS.

The Law of the Pioneers (ages 10–14)

The Pioneer adheres to the motherland, the party, communism.

The Pioneer prepares to become a Komsomol member.

The Pioneer emulates the heroes of struggle and labor.

The Pioneer reveres the memory of the fallen fighters and prepares to become a defender of his motherland.

The Pioneer is persistent in studies, work, and sports.

The Pioneer is an honest and true comrade and always stands for the truth.

The Pioneer is a friend and leader of the Octobrists [members of an organization of younger children]

The Pioneer is a friend to other Pioneers and to the children of workers of all countries.

SOURCE: David K. Shipler, *Russia: Broken Idols, Solemn Dreams* (New York: Penguin Books, 1984), p. 119.

"palaces" provide the site for cultural, artistic and sports activities, as well as more explicitly political activities such as classes on contemporary topics or demonstrations on national holidays.

From age 15 on young people are eligible to join the *Komsomol* (the acronym for *Kommunisticheskii Soyuz Molodezhi*, the Communist League of Youth). This organization is devoted much more specifically to political direction of the young generation and recruitment of people into the ranks of the Communist Party. Like other groups, the organization provides the services and activities youth want, such as summer camps and, more recently, rock concerts. Membership in Komsomol is more selective than in the Pioneers, comprising roughly half the population of 15–28 year olds, and initiates this age group into both the rewards and demands of being social activists. For example, in addition to the many activities run by the Komsomol,

try and its system, and self-discipline. With elaborate ceremonies and distinctive red scarves, children are brought into this organization by promising to obey the "Laws of the Pioneers" (see box). Pioneer groups organize after-school activities, summer camps and team competitions with a strong military flavor. In every city Pioneer "houses" or

Young Pioneers at Artek—show their peace movement posters.
SOURCE: Photo by V. Repik, Fotokhronica TASS.

admission to a university or a good job usually requires a recommendation from the candidate's Komsomol committee. At the same time, Komsomol members are expected to contribute their free time to socially useful labor, such as working in the fields or on construction projects, or aiding veterans groups, and to take political education classes.

Such an organization performs several functions for the ruling party. It teaches the political and social values most desired by the party: self-discipline, respect for the will of the group, the willingness to contribute to the common good, patriotism. Beyond that it provides a source of "volunteer" or very cheap labor needed for the immense tasks involved in keeping the country running or expanding its capacities. Third, and equally critical, the Komsomol provides a recruitment and training field for the country's ruling elite, the members and leaders of the Communist Party. The current Soviet leader, Mikhail Gorbachev, had the opportunity to exercise substantial authority in the Komsomol organization before moving over to the party itself in the 1950s (see box, p. 415).

Political socialization is carried on in other forms as well. The media in the Soviet Union have traditionally performed the vital function of presenting to the public the preferred view of society. This is accomplished by including the treatment of some subjects, such as criticism of life in the West, and excluding others, such as (until 1988) how many soldiers died in Afghanistan. But in addition to simple censorship, it is the way a particular subject is treated that is supposed to contribute to creating the appropriate attitude. Soviet newspapers and television have for years carried articles and material about life in the West and in the United States in particular, but virtually always with a critical point of view, the message being that socialism is indeed preferable and enables Soviet society to avoid the evils of capitalism, which are underlined. Such an approach can backfire, however. In studying the Soviet media, Ellen Mickiewicz reports that the biased treatment of international news and in particular of the West created a strong demand among the Soviet public for more—and more accurate—information precisely about the outside world and the West in particular.[2]

The government's dominance of information is ensured through the ubiquitous publication of official newspapers, more than

[2]Ellen Mickiewicz, "Making the Media Work: Soviet Society and Communications," in *Soviet Society Under Gorbachev*, ed. Maurice Friedberg and Heyward Isham (Armonk, NY: M. E. Sharpe, 1987), pp. 141–42.

8,100 in 55 languages throughout the country, in all fields, as well as magazines, books, and plays and films with approved treatment of themes. As in the United States, however, the dominant medium is television. This was not always the case. As late as 1960 only 5 percent of the population had access to television; by 1986 this figure was 93 percent.[3] Unlike newspapers, which tend to be read more by the better educated strata of the population, television has the capacity to reach people of all levels of education and all ages. This has created what Mickiewicz terms "the first mass public in Soviet history."

Ironically, however, just as the capacity has been achieved to reach almost everyone in the country with the same message, the era of *glasnost* has struck at the media's ability to maintain control of information. Since the death of Leonid Brezhnev and especially since the emergence of Mikhail Gorbachev, many topics that had been taboo began to be discussed openly in Soviet media sources, press conferences, and even phone-in television and radio shows. Jamming of the broadcasts of The Voice of America and Radio Liberty was stopped. In 1988 U.S. President Ronald Reagan was given uncensored access to the media by having a New Year's message broadcast directly to the Soviet population. At the same time numerous television "space bridges" brought unfiltered contact between the societies directly into people's homes.

While this degree of openness may under-

[3]*Ibid.*, p. 132.

SOURCE: *Christian Science Monitor*, November 17, 1988, p. 15.

WHAT? JUST COMRADE GORBACHEV WALKING HIS DOG, "GLASNOST"

DANZIGER

A Sign of the Times

Indications of the new political environment in the USSR are numerous. In the field of public education two journals that for years conveyed the party's message were eliminated. One was called "Political Education," the other "Agitator." Their replacement? A journal called "Dialogue."

mine the task of socializing the Soviet public to an explicit message, it can strengthen support for the regime by improving the credibility of the media. Instead of being widely scorned or ignored as presenting distorted or incomplete news, the Soviet press and television are increasingly seen as fulfilling their

SOURCE: *Krokodil* (Moscow), September 26, 1988, p. 3.

function of informing the public and earning their trust. While it is clear that many Soviet leaders are uncomfortable with this particular method of building trust—the Soviet defense minister in 1988 explicitly complained that critical articles were hurting the Soviet military—it may be that opening up the media, as well as film and other vehicles of cultural expression, will prove a more effective method of socialization than trying to present a censored and "sanitized" universe.

PARTICIPATION

While socialization of the governed is essential to the stable rule of those who govern because it creates acceptance of the rulers' goals, values and norms among the population, all but the most simpleminded dictatorships will also need some participation by the public. People have to be persuaded to do more than simply conform. Those who rule need people to play active roles in administering their society, especially if, as has often been the case in the Soviet Union, the aim of government policy is to make changes in the way things are done.

In western democracies we are accustomed to considering participation as meaning involvement by people in the process of deciding or affecting public policy; for example, by voting in elections, running for office, petitioning elected officials, supervising them through the medium of public interest "watchdog" groups, and so on. The actual degree of influence exercised by these forms of participation varies, of course, but its legitimacy, the right of individuals to play such a role, is, in general, not questioned.

Public participation in the Soviet Union, however, involves stimulating activism much less on the policy-determining side of government and much more on the implementation side. Public choice and influence are limited—

though not absent—when it comes to deciding what policies will be applied, and much broader, though still limited, when it comes to putting those policies into practice. In political science terms, participation in the Soviet Union is generally *elite-determined* and *mobilized,* rather than *mass-determined* and *autonomous.*

Under Stalin, those people terrified into submission, imprisoned or physically eliminated could hardly be called participants in the massive social and economic transformation unleashed at the beginning of the 1930s. Indeed, historian Roy Medvedev, in his study of the conditions that allowed Stalinism to occur, points to the relatively low level of resistance to the widespread terror of the 1930s. He attributes this in part to the success of the Stalin cult of personality and the stifling of a free flow of information, but also to the belief held by many of the victims that this was all somehow a mistake that would be rectified, ironically, as soon as Stalin himself got wind of it. Medvedev relates the case of the former head of Gosplan (the state economic planning agency) who, when arrested, continued to work at his job from his cell, even writing a memo on planning before his execution.[4]

But there also had to be people to carry out the policies, to enforce, for example, the industrial labor quotas, to prosecute "spies and wreckers," and to administer the forced collectivization of farms. As Medvedev acknowledges, "It is an unavoidable fact that Stalin never relied on force alone. Throughout the period of his one-man rule he was popular."[5] During the worst of his excesses people were willing to carry out the repression and execution of their fellow citizens not simply because of fear for their own lives but because many of them believed the Soviet Union was besieged by external and internal enemies, that the unprecedented success of the Bolshevik revolution had demonstrated that the party leadership was correct and its survival justified repression of its enemies. Many of course also profited directly from the removal of hundreds of thousands of bosses and leaders in the party, in the bureaucracy, in industry and in the countryside. Sheila Fitzpatrick called this process the creation of "a new elite."[6] As Arch Getty put it, "the cataclysm had beneficiaries." Getty goes even further to argue that the widespread terror was less a product of Stalin's master plan than of the chaotic, uneven and conflicting utilization of his ideas by central and local leaders for their own purposes. In this view "participation" got somewhat out of control.[7] Whether or not such people carried out Stalin's will uniformly, the Soviet system, even during the period of mass terror, still needed active participation to implement its policies. Since Stalin's death, when the needs of the Soviet Union became more complex and diverse, if less dramatic, the system and its leaders needed more effective public or mass participation and less passive submission.

Securing participation of both elites and the public is of course a key task of the Communist Party. Since the party is the dominant governing force, it oversees, either directly or through public organizations, the recruitment and selection of its future leaders. Such people are identified through their professional work or trade, or through their activism in Komsomol, trade unions or other

[4]Roy A. Medvedev, *Let History Judge: The Origins and Consequences of Stalinism* (New York: Vintage Books, 1973), pp. 355–432.

[5]*Ibid.,* p. 362.

[6]Sheila Fitzpatrick, "Stalin and the Making of a New Elite, 1928–1939," *Slavic Review,* 30 (1979): 377–402.

[7]J. Arch Getty, *Origins of the Great Purges: The Soviet Communist Party Reconsidered, 1933–1938* (New York: Cambridge University Press, 1985).

social organizations. After a probationary period of one year, with the sponsorship of party members, they are brought into the party.

The demands on party members can be substantial, involving agitation and propaganda (*agitprop*) in support of government policies, petition drives for government-approved causes, elections, rounding up people for holiday demonstrations, and volunteer labor. In addition, attending to such tasks is for most party members an extra responsibility, unpaid and in addition to their regular employment. Barghoorn and Remington estimate the number of full-time paid party workers at less than 200,000. For mobilizing the country of more than 160 million adults, this is hardly sufficient. Hence the party relies heavily on mobilizing part-time activists.[8]

Of course, not all of the party's 20 million members will attend to their tasks with equal vigor. In fact, one of the problems the party has derives from its broad social power. Because many people view party membership as necessary for advancement in their careers, the party attracts a number of people who join for these reasons and thus lack the proper amount of *partiinost,* or party-mindedness. The corps of active party people in any one sphere, say education or ideology, known as the *activ,* form the backbone of the party's involvement with society. This group, estimated at one quarter of party membership, has the most frequent contact with the public, forms the core of other mass organizations, and supports public administration; and it is these members who presumably reap the greatest benefits from party membership, such as access to higher decision-makers and to scarce goods and opportunities, such

as foreign travel. Periodically, however, the party conducts an exchange of party cards in which members turn in their cards and have their activism judged. In this way thousands of members are purged from the party's ranks and thousands of others get the message that party membership must be more than a formality.

Outside the party itself, Soviet public life includes numerous other methods of mobilizing public participation. Among the most important are the *soviets* or councils that are elected locally up through the region to the national level (see Chapter 32). Selection for candidacy in the election for deputy to the *soviet* is dominated by the party. According to changes implemented under Gorbachev, elections to the *soviets* now usually involve multiple candidates, though nomination will still reflect party influence. This is directed at ensuring election of people who support current policies. In the past the party leadership has also tried to secure appropriate representation of key groups, such as workers, women or particular nationalities. Part of the *demokratizatsia* favored by Mikhail Gorbachev involves a greater role for the *soviets* and through them, greater involvement of the public. Deputies have the most direct contact between the public and the decision-makers higher up in the government and party who determine policy. In this way the *soviets* play an important role in both directions of governance. They must implement "down" policies determined by the regional *soviet* and more importantly, the party. But they also pass "up" the complaints and problems of the people in their district and thus perform what Theodore Friedgut calls a "signalling" function, alerting higher authorities to problems.[9] Since in the Soviet Union "ev-

[8]Frederick Barghoorn and Thomas F. Remington, *Politics in the USSR* (Boston: Little, Brown, 1986), p. 220.

[9]Theodore H. Friedgut, *Political Participation In the USSR* (Princeton, NJ: Princeton University Press, 1979), p. 228.

erything counts," that is, there are few aspects of life beyond the purview of the government, such a signaling is critical to effective administration.

Electing deputies under circumstances in which people have little real influence over the choice of candidates may seem to be an empty exercise. Even under *demokratizatsia* alternative political parties are not permitted in most of the Soviet Union. Compared to the multiple choices typically offered in, say, a French election, the process may seem an expensive sham. But the aim of election, as with other forms of participation in the Soviet system, is to affirm rather than determine policy choice, to build public support for policies determined by the party rather than to allow alternatives. Speaking of the local *soviets* at the 27th Party Congress (1986), Gorbachev said: "Today they can and must become one of the most effective links for mobilizing the masses for the effort to accelerate the country's socioeconomic development."

Even so, some public influence is possible, at least over deputy selection to the local *soviets*. Local workers' groups can and have made known their opposition to a particular candidate, and sometimes nominees are rejected and candidates defeated in local soviet elections (see page 420).

Being nominated for local office, taking part in a campaign and running for local office, and the act of voting itself do serve a broader purpose more akin to that of elections in the West: They build the legitimacy of the system. Particularly in the Soviet case, elections offer the government one more opportunity to push its program, to trumpet its successes, to involve people in supporting it and to build local identification with national goals and leaders. Recalling the importance of the collective over the individual, elections serve as a reaffirmation of the national collective and a reminder to the individual of his or her role in supporting that collective.

The actual governing of the country in all its aspects is supported by a vast system of mobilization of the public through volunteer organizations. Local street patrols, known as *druzhini,* for example, supplement the local police in helping secure public safety. "Comrades' courts" act as a kind of arbitration panel to help settle disputes and ease the burden on the state court system. And numerous professional, veteran and other welfare and social support groups offer services to the community that the government might otherwise have to provide. All of this is supplemented by a widespread ethos of volunteer labor, an expectation that everyone from students to retirees will give free or very cheap labor on the weekends, evenings or during the summer to help finish a railroad line, harvest crops or provide day care for children. Since all of these and most other activities are, in the Soviet system, the responsibility of the government, it is essential that such volunteer labor supplement government activity. Not only does it save the government millions of rubles every year, but such mobilization provides to the local citizens services that might otherwise not be provided at all, and by their own neighbors who know their needs best.

While this kind of participation at the receiving rather than the determining end of policy clearly affords the government support, labor and skills, it is not without its "risks." The government needs the public to get involved to help implement social and economic policy, to help administer cities, regions and collective farms. But to do so people have to be given some amount of responsibility and access to information and resources. And citizens must be free to do their jobs without excessive interference. But because such a "hands off" approach involves relinquishing some power or control, conflict will often occur between the leaders of the central administration and local gov-

Not So Fast, Comrade. . . .

As Mikhail Gorbachev and his supporters frequently point out, there remain many opponents to his policies, especially that of *glasnost* or voicing of previously unspoken issues. In March 1988 a long letter was published in *Sovetskaya Rossiya* complaining about the "excesses" of the new situation, especially as it related to education and the country's past. The writer, a teacher from Leningrad named Nina Adreyeva, was particularly exercised about the treatment of Stalin:

> I have been reading and rereading sensational articles. For example, what can young people gain— disorientation apart—from revelations about "the counterrevolution in the USSR in the late twenties and early thirties," or about Stalin's "guilt" for the advent in power of fascism and Hitler in Germany? Or the public "reckoning" of the number of "Stalinists" in various generations and social groups? . . .
>
> The industrialization, collectivization, and cultural revolution which brought our country to the ranks of great world powers are being forcibly squeezed into the "personality cult" formula. All this is being questioned. Matters have gone so far that persistent demands for "repentance" are being made of "Stalinists" (and this category can be taken to include anyone you like). . . .
>
> It is the champions of "left-wing liberal socialism" who shape the tendency toward falsifying the history of socialism. They try to make us believe that the country's past was nothing but mistakes and crimes, keeping silent about the greatest achievements of the past and the present.

The letter was reportedly personally embellished by conservative opponents of Gorbachev and praised by Yigor Ligachev, a member of the Politburo. It was taken as an attack on the whole Gorbachev approach, and after some delay, supporters of reform rallied to defend *perestroika* and *glasnost*. In the fall [of 1988] Ligachev's responsibilities in the secretariat were reduced.

SOURCE: *Sovetskaya Rossiya,* March 13, 1988, p. 3 (Foreign Broadcast Information Service, Soviet Union, *Daily Report,* March 16, 1988, pp. 49, 50, 52).

ernment or party leaders, and between those in the party with the formal responsibility for guiding society and those in the government and economy responsible for making it work. Attempts under Mikhail Gorbachev to move the economic reform forward and erode the substantial but often corrupt power of local leaders, for example, have led to trouble. In 1986 the removal of the leader of the Kazakh republic and party, a Kazakh, and his replacement by an ethnic Russian led to public demonstrations and even rioting in Alma Ata, the capital of the republic. In all, 6 of 14 republican first secretaries were replaced in the first two years of Gorbachev's leadership.

The party-government-economy issue has been a continuing one in Soviet governance,

revolving around the question of how much the party should be involved in actually administering things, especially the economy, and how much of this task it should leave to the very people whom it has mobilized to work in government or run factories and farms.

Under Nikita Khrushchev an attempt was made to increase party involvement, especially in economic activity at the local level. The party itself was divided into industrial and agricultural branches, and the economic administration was taken from central ministries and given over to the control of regional economic councils (*sovnarkhozi*). This proved economically unsuccessful and politically dangerous to the powerful bureaucracies. After Khrushchev was overthrown, the party was reunited and the *sovnark-hozi* abandoned. While Khrushchev's "hare-brained" schemes were denounced, the problem remains of just how extensively the party should be involved in the day-to-day economic affairs of the country, as opposed to acting as a leader and guide.

More broadly, mobilizing the population into activity does not always mean that such participation can be controlled. As successive Russian tsars discovered, improving the education of the population so they might better serve the state can have unintended consequences. Once people learned to read, for example, they could read "dangerous" things, as well as the tsar's orders. The Russian historian Kliuchevsky referred to this dilemma of both needing and fearing the increased capacity and involvement of the population as "trying to square the circle." In the contemporary USSR the problem persists. Studying the activism of Soviet citizens who have emigrated, William Zimmerman reports that it was precisely those people who were mobilized into involvement in Soviet politics who were more likely to read *samizdat* (self-published, uncensored) material and listen to foreign radio broadcasts. Conversely, those who indicated a high level of conformity in their behavior before they emigrated were also less likely to be mobilized into politics. Unfortunately from the Soviet point of view, these also tended to be the less well-educated, less technically skilled people.[10] Under the

prodding of Mikhail Gorbachev local activism within the communist party began snowballing to the point that within the first two months of 1990 more than a dozen local party leaders were forced to resign.

Squaring this modern circle, both creating and guiding the activism and participation of the public, is a problem for all governments. But it takes a unique form in the Soviet case because of the dominant ideology of socialism and, especially, the one-party control of the political process. Looking at how the party attempts to carry out its self-proclaimed goals and ensure its control is our next task.

___

[10]William Zimmerman, "Mobilized Participation and the Nature of the Soviet Dictatorship," in *Politics, Work and Daily Life in the USSR: A Survey of Former Soviet Citizens*, ed. James Millar (New York: Cambridge University Press), 1987.

References and Suggested Readings

FRIEDGUT, THEODORE H. *Political Participation In the USSR*. Princeton, NJ: Princeton University Press, 1979.

GROSS, NATALIE. "*Glasnost*: Roots and Practice." *Problems of Communism* 36, 6 (November-December 1987):69–80.

LANE, DAVID. *Soviet Economy and Society*, Oxford, England: Basil Blackwell, 1985.

McCREA, BARBARA P., JACK C. PLANO, AND GEORGE KLEIN. *The Soviet and East European Political Dictionary*. Santa Barbara, CA: ABC Clio Information Services, 1984.

SCHULZ, DONALD, AND JAN S. ADAMS, (eds.) *Political Participation in Communist Systems*. New York: Pergamon Press, 1981.

ZWICK, PETER R. "Soviet Nationality Policy: Social, Economic, and Political Aspects." In *Public Policy and Administration in the Soviet Union*, ed. Gordon B. Smith. New York: Praeger, 1980, pp. 142–71.

31

Parties and Elections

A very high concentration of power has always been characteristic of our society. The majority of representatives of the top group hold responsible places in several ruling organs simultaneously. CPSU Central Committee members have become Supreme Soviet deputies, republican leaders have become CPSU Central Committee members, and ministers have joined the Supreme Soviet and the Central Committee. In brief, a powerful ruling nucleus subordinate to no one has always taken shape. The centralist principle always dominated drastically over the democratic principle.

— TATIANA ZASLAVASKIA,
PRESIDENT OF SOVIET
SOCIOLOGICAL ASSOCIATION

It might be useful to think of the governing system of the Soviet Union as a human body. The most evident parts of the body—the skin, the face, the hair—provide the body's overall appearance and establish its superficial impression. The direction, skill and force of that body, however, is provided by the brain, which, through the nervous system, controls the motor force produced by the muscles and skeleton.

In the Soviet system, the institutions of governance, the forms most apparent and familiar to us, present the government's face to the people. There are institutions not unlike those seen in the West: for example, a parliament, a council of ministers. But behind these bodies, providing their political orientation and direction, the brain and nervous system of the Soviet system is the party, the Communist Party of the Soviet Union (CPSU).

This should not be taken to mean that the "governing face," the parliamentary and ministerial institutions, are mere façades. They are not. Real decisions affecting the lives of Soviet citizens are made in these institutions every day, and the way they operate

in governing and allowing participation in governance merits attention. The point to remember is that these institutions take their cues from, operate within parameters established by, and are themselves staffed by the Communist Party, which, in contrast to Western counterparts, cannot be voted out of office. This means that to a large extent the *politics* of governing the Soviet Union, the battles over what Lenin called *Kto kovo,* who does what to whom, take place *within* the governing Communist Party rather than between a governing party and an opposition. But such battles directly affect the actual governing of the country, which for the most part is the responsibility of the Soviet *government*. The forms and agents of that government— the skin and hair, to return to our analogy— will receive our attention after we first explore the brain and nerves of the system, the Communist Party of the Soviet Union.

THE ROLE OF THE PARTY

In the USSR the role of the political party is both broader and narrower than in Western

407

parliamentary democracies. The first point to be noted is that it is *the* political party that is being discussed. The Communist Party of the Soviet Union has been the only legal political organization since the end of the civil war, when Lenin and the Bolsheviks proscribed and suppressed opposition political organizations. This monopoly has been justified on ideological grounds, since the party is the guardian of the interests of the working class, in whose name the country is governed. It alone is the purveyor and interpreter of the guidance provided by Marxism-Leninism on building socialism and communism. Other political parties would, by definition, represent interests hostile to those of socialism.

In one sense, then, the party's role is narrower than that of parties in the Western parliamentary democracies. Unlike competitive parties in Britain, France or Germany, the CPSU has not needed to submit policy positions or particular individuals to contests for public approval, that is, elections. Other mass political organizations have not legally been entitled to seek public support, and the CPSU did not fear being voted out of office. All members of the *Supreme Soviet,* the parliament of the USSR (see discussion pp. 419–23), have been approved by or actually are members of the CPSU.

The Soviet Union is, in T. H. Rigby's terms, a "mono-organizational society," one in which all of the country's social, economic and of course political activities are subject to the directives of one dominant organization— the Communist Party.[1] This means, therefore, that the Soviet Communist Party has much *more* to do than does a typical political party in a Western capitalist democracy. Its roles and duties permeate society and the economy, and despite its dominance of politi-

cal activity, it does face challenges. This chapter will consider first the party's vast responsibilities, then the organizational structure through which it seeks to discharge these responsibilities, and then offer a brief description of the size and composition of the party.

More so than in Western political systems, the party in the Soviet Union is what one might call a *definer*. The party's leaders and their ideology offer an interpretation of the country's past and present and define what the society should look like in the future, even if it does not look that way yet. They describe the nature of the future toward which the society as a whole is moving: in this case, communism. This vision changes, of course. In 1961 the party program adopted under Nikita Khrushchev declared that with the building of socialism complete, the country was now constructing communism, and that the current state structure was not a dictatorship of the proletariat, which carried with it the need for repression, but an "all people's state" in which greater public involvement was encouraged.[2] Under Leonid Brezhnev this view was modified somewhat to hold that the Soviet Union was in a state of "mature" or developed socialism, and the attainment of full communism was by omission put off again to the uncertain future. The third party program, adopted in 1986 under Mikhail Gorbachev's guidance, accepts this premise but goes on to link more specifically the achievement of full communism to improving the country's economic performance.

Communism's material-technical base presupposes the creation of production forces which open up opportunities for the full satisfaction of the sensible requirements of society and the in-

---

[1] T. H. Rigby, "Politics in the Mono-Organizational Society," in *Authoritarian Politics in Communist Europe,* ed. Andrew C. Janos (Berkeley, CA: Institute of International Studies, 1976).

[2] Jerry F. Hough and Merle Fainsod, *How the Soviet Union Is Governed* (Cambridge: Harvard University Press, 1979), pp. 226–27.

dividual. All production activity under the conditions of communism will be built on the use of highly effective technical means and technologies, and the harmonious interaction of man and nature will be ensured.

. . .

At the same time the CPSU proceeds from the premise that it is impossible to allow sluggishness in implementing urgent transformations and resolving new tasks. The party believes that in the seventies and early eighties, in the development of the country alongside the undoubted successes which were achieved, there were definite unfavorable tendencies and difficulties. In significant measure they are connected with the fact that changes in the economic situation and the need for in-depth improvements in all spheres of life were not promptly and properly assessed and due persistence was not displayed in their implementation. This prevented the fuller utilization of the opportunities and advantages of the socialist system and held back our advance.[3]

The country's past, like its future, is written and rewritten by the party, not always for the sake of historical accuracy but to serve a current political purpose. For example, for nearly 50 years after his execution under Stalin, Nikolai Bukharin and the ideas he propagated about allowing more individual and private enterprise under socialism were anathema to the Soviet party leadership. But in 1987 Mikhail Gorbachev himself spoke favorably of the man and his ideas and in 1988 Bukharin was formally "rehabilitated" by a party commission. This act had political significance as an example of the party now being willing to leave "no blank pages," in Gorbachev's words, in the country's history. As party of the policy of *glasnost* or openness the party was trying to show by example that problems in the system could be examined and corrected.

[3] *Programma Kommunisticheskoi Partii Sovetskovo Soiuza* (Moscow: Izdatel'stvo politicheskoi literatury, 1986).

But in more specific terms, by rehabilitating Bukharin and placing his policies in a more favorable light, the party leadership was indicating that such ideas could and should be considered now, as a way of dealing with current problems. This points to what might be called "the uses of the past" by the party leadership as a way of defining the parameters of permissible behavior in the present. For example, in the economic realm, the party determines whether small private business has any role to play in a socialist economy and if so, how much of a role. Since the end of the New Economic Policy in the 1920s this role has been defined extremely narrowly—private enterprise being restricted to small family farm plots. But under the prodding of Mikhail Gorbachev, a redetermination was made, and in a Central Committee plenum in 1987 greater latitude was given to private enterprise. The Soviet system differs from Western parliamentary democracies in that such a fundamental decision is still virtually the sole prerogative of the government. But it also differs in that the political maneuvering surrounding such a decision—the battle between those who favor and those who oppose it—takes place within the single political party, usually away from public view.

In the area of politics, both the party's ideology (described in Chapter 27) and the desire to retain dominant power led it to suppress for seventy years the formation of autonomous political organizations, such as other parties that might compete with it for control of the country. Beyond that, the party's pervasive role in society, its view of itself as mobilizer and guide of the country's development, not to mention its jealousy of power, led it to control and limit, through the state apparatus, the formation and behavior of *all* independent organizations, whether or not they have an ostensible political purpose. Except for a brief period under Nikita Khrushchev and currently under Mikhail

Gorbachev, the party has seen itself as needing to be everywhere at once, "guiding" activities in all areas of political, social and economic life. This has meant that activities of the type seen in the parliamentary democracies which reflect public participation in the governing policies of the country, like the formation of political action committees, contested elections or the use of referenda, have been strictly controlled by the Communist Party.

This does not mean that political competition does not exist in the Soviet political system. Rather, such competition takes place within the party itself and, most importantly, at its highest echelons. The party tried to eliminate such competition at its 10th Congress in 1921 by banning factions, and under Stalin opponents were arrested, sometimes tried, and usually put into prison camps. Still, as the historical review indicates, differences over policy, combined with personal desires for power, have ensured that political struggle among party leaders has continued, even when it was less subject to public input and less visible to the outside world than in the West. In 1990, for example, in response to the changes and reforms pushed forward by Mikhail Gorbachev and the revolutionary changes that swept East Europe, a formal faction of the party was formed. Called the Democratic Platform, this group declared itself in favor of rapid, thorough democratization of the Communist Party and for making the party one of several competing for political influence, rather than the only one through constitutional monopoly.

The party also has responsibility for the overall direction and health of the economy. Because it is acting in the name of the workers, peasants and intelligentsia and because its goal is to create an effective, productive, prosperous socialist society, it is the party that has both immediate and ultimate responsibility for how the economy is running. This responsibility runs from the very top of the party, where members of the Secretariat (see page 415) have responsibility for certain sectors of the economy, down through regional first secretaries who oversee developments in their own *oblast* or *krai,* to party leaders in the factories and enterprises. In the United States, if a large automobile factory in, say, central Michigan is performing poorly, the local Democratic party chairman does not have to answer to the president. In the Soviet Union, however, one of the local party secretary's key functions is to ensure the productive functioning of the economic units in his area. His own career advancement could depend on such performance.

The party also defines the nature of the country's relationship with the outside world. In this the party leadership is guided by ideological concerns, in particular the desire to support movements and states that espouse some adherence to socialist principles, as well as by the needs of the Soviet state, the desire to create a nonthreatening, physically secure, politically supportive, and economically beneficial external environment. The general secretary of the party, as the most internationally visible and politically powerful individual, has usually tried to reshape this relationship in accordance with his view of Soviet foreign policy. Mikhail Gorbachev, for example, has clearly tried to imbue Soviet foreign policy with "new thinking" (*novoe myshlenie*), which includes in large part an effort to reduce international tensions in order to make domestic economic restructuring possible.

Because neither he nor his party has had to stand for public reelection the party leadership usually does not have to worry about public reaction to foreign policy moves. While this may be changing now, the persistence of political competition at the top has always meant that a party general secretary in his foreign policy role, as in domestic affairs, must satisfy his most immediate and powerful constituency: the other members of the highest party organs.

Related to all of these functions is the party's role as a *mobilizer* of society. In pursuit of the party's goals, people must be persuaded to make their contribution, to work productively and to play their supporting role in the political system. This is an especially important and tricky task in a system where working for personal profit is supposed to take a back seat to the collective good, and where political activity of only certain types is sanctioned. How can the party motivate people in such a situation?

Under Stalin the method of choice was terror; suppressing real or imagined opponents of the system through arrest, imprisonment and execution, and frightening everybody else into passivity. Since Khrushchev, widespread use of this type of terror has not been practiced, and the party's task is somewhat more complex. Khrushchev recognized, as Gorbachev apparently does also, that the passivity of the population hinders the achievement of national goals, that running a modern complex economy and ensuring that political stability does not become stagnation requires a degree of public participation and involvement, especially by the most highly trained and well-educated members of society. For example, to accomplish the multitude of tasks it sets for itself, the party always needs committed and qualified new members. Therefore, it must provide the proper mixture of rewards and incentives that convince people to act on the party's behalf in the factories and on the collective farms, or to explain a new party policy to their communities. Beyond that, the party must replenish its own leadership ranks at both the regional and national levels.

The rewards the party can offer, precisely because of its control of both the government and the economy, are considerable. People can achieve career advancement, and gain improved access to scarce goods, travel within and beyond the borders of the USSR, the possibility of influence with higher authorities, and some authority of their own.

People will join the party for many reasons, of course, and there are no reliable surveys to indicate the precise breakdown of motives, but at last count some 20 million people were members of the Communist Party, an estimated 200,000 of them being full-time paid party workers, or *apparatchiki*.

The party in the Soviet Union also performs an *integrative* function much broader than that of a political party in a competitive political system. First, the dominant organization responsible for the political, social and economic dynamics of the country, the party seeks to control all of these various aspects of modern life either directly or through subordinate organizations, such as government ministries or trade unions. In the Soviet Union, the spheres of a person's life—for example, one's job, political activity, education, family life, or recreation—areas which might in another society be kept separate from each other—are seen as spheres not only in which the party should play a role directly or indirectly, but which should be shaped to support the goals of socialist society.

Second, the party seeks to integrate the country nationally, by acting as the overarching political organization exercising power throughout the country. The party's organization, discussed below (pages 412-16), is designed to keep decision-making power near the top and to try to see to it that the country's various regions and provinces, not to mention nationalities, are guided by the party's vision and rules. There are of course separate party units in different regions, but they all exercise influence and retain power—which can be strengthened or weakened—through the central apparatus of the national party.

LEGAL STATUS AND ORGANIZATION OF THE PARTY

The Soviet constitution of 1977 enshrines the Communist Party as "the leading and guiding force of Soviet society and the nucleus of its political system and of state and social organizations." In the previous constitution of 1936, the party had been listed as one of many social organizations, though it was described as "the vanguard of the working people" and the "leading core" of all organizations. The newer postulation, coming at the very beginning of the constitution, made clear its political predominance.

However, in 1990 a plenum of the Central Committee, over the objections of party conservatives, voted to recommend that the party give up this entitlement and begin to act as one party among others. The change in the constitution has to be implemented by the Congress of People's Deputies (see pp. 420–21) but under the pressure of events in East Europe (see Chapter 37) and within the party itself (the Democratic Platform group), the CPSU leadership took the first step in the direction of forming a parliamentary democracy.

The Communist Party of the Soviet Union is organized at the national level, at the republic, regional and city, town or rural district level, and into what are called primary party organizations.

At the national level the party is in theory directed by the will of its members, which is expressed at the nationwide *party congress*. This is a gathering of representatives indirectly elected from the regional parties with the task, in principle, of determining the policies and practices of the party and country.

In practice, such a meeting is a cumbersome method of determining policy. In addi-

[4] F. J. M. Feldbrugge, *The Constitutions of the USSR and the Union Republics: Analysis, Texts, Reports* (Alphen aan den Rijn, The Netherlands: Sijthoff and Noordhoff, 1979), p. 79.

The 27th Congress of the CPSU, held at the Kremlin Palace of Congresses in March 1986.
SOURCE: Fotokhronika TASS.

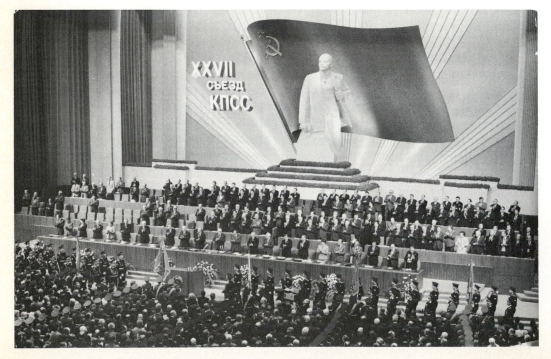

tion to its size—the 27th Party Congress in 1986 had 5,000 delegates—the party congress meets usually only once every five years. In the first years after the revolution, party congresses were more frequent and included significant debates and decisions. As that became less practicable, and the control of the party leadership under Stalin became more stringent, party congresses were held less often. Since then they have become more like political rallies, significant mostly for what they reveal about the leadership's domestic or foreign policies and about personnel at the top. It was at the 20th Party Congress in 1956 that Nikita Khrushchev denounced the policies and practices of Stalin and also offered a significant revision of standard doctrine on Soviet foreign policy (see pp. 375–76 and 385). In 1986 at the 27th Party Congress Prime Minister Nikolai Ryzhkov and General Secretary Mikhail Gorbachev outlined serious criticisms of the country's economy and their plans for its renovation. The party leadership may also on occasion call for a party *conference,* a national meeting of delegates like a congress but which meets for a specific purpose. In 1988 the first party conference since 1941 was called to strengthen Mikhail Gorbachev's campaign for economic and political change in the country.

In the period between congresses, the authority of the party formally rests with the *Central Committee.* This body, now numbering 249 full and 146 candidate (or non-voting) members, is made up of the key political and economic elites in the Soviet Union. For example, most government ministers and high military leaders are members of the Central Committee, along with regional party secretaries and important officials in the security apparatus and heads of cultural, youth and trade union organizations. The Central Committee serves as a kind of national pool of political and economic leaders as well as the formal authority for party actions. The Central Committee typically holds a full session, called a *plenum,* twice a year,

and leaves the continuous management of the country's affairs to the two most important political bodies: the *Politburo* and the *Secretariat.* However, since it formally instructs these higher bodies, it can be used to strengthen a general secretary's position. By demanding a full Central Committee plenum in 1957, Nikita Khrushchev was able to prevent his own removal, and in 1988 Mikhail Gorbachev called an emergency session of the Central Committee to implement several changes in party personnel and structure. The next year the General Secretary secured the removal of 110 Central Committee members, including 74 full members, most of whom had held important positions under Leonid Brezhnev. At the February 1990 plenum that recommended the changes in the party status, the Central Committee also agreed to ask the next party congress to change its own size, to around 200, which will also allow Gorbachev to build a Central Committee more to his liking.

The *Politburo* (called the *Presidium* from 1952 to 1966) constitutes the very top leadership of the Soviet Union. A body that has ranged in size from 7 elected in 1917 to 11 full and 7 candidate members under Mikhail Gorbachev, it officially acts in the name of the Central Committee. In fact, as the center of political power in the country, it is the Politburo that determines policy direction and key actions that the Central Committee and ultimately the party congress usually ratify. The mono-organizational nature of the Soviet system ensures that the very top leadership posts in all areas of Soviet governance are subordinate to the Politburo or actually held by its members. In 1989, for example, the country's prime minister, president (chairman of the Presidium of the Supreme Soviet), foreign minister and head of state security were full members of the Politburo, while the first deputy chairman of the Council of Ministers, the defense minister, and the premier of the Russian Republic were candidate members of the Politburo.

The Politburo is a collective leadership body, though the power and influence of particular members will vary. At times, such as under Stalin, even this body became subordinate to the will of one person. More recently, it appears that some members, because of their control of key parts of the party apparatus or key policy areas, or their associations with the general secretary, are more powerful than others. At present those party secretaries who head the Central Committee's six commissions (see box, p. 416) with responsibility for various policy sectors would fall into this category.

The party leader, the *general secretary* (called the *first secretary* from 1953 to 1966), is the most powerful person on the Soviet political scene, even though his formal position in the government may be quite modest—Mikhail Gorbachev, for example, was until 1988 a deputy of the Supreme Soviet. Once in power, the general secretary has the opportunity to try to implement his vision of what the country should look like and what its relations with the outside world should be. But achievement of this vision is now far from automatic. While Stalin's personal power was nearly absolute, since his death the power of this office has depended more on the general secretary's ability to generate support for his policies and to control personnel than it has on simply holding this office.

Tenure in office can vary greatly, and the Politburo that chooses a general secretary can in principle remove him at any time, if his policies are deemed unsuccessful or if political support deserts him (there and in the Central Committee) for whatever reason. Stalin was general secretary for more than 30 years, and Leonid Brezhnev for 18. But after Brezhnev's death in 1982 there were no less than three general secretaries in the next three years (Chernenko, Andropov and Gorbachev). Gorbachev's career (see box) enabled him to have both personnel and policy experience and to secure a base for assumption to the top leadership position. Once in power he was able to change both the size and composition of the two key bodies, the Politburo and the Secretariat.

Between 1985, when he became general secretary, and 1988, Mikhail Gorbachev was able to replace or remove all but two full Politburo members, all candidate members of that body, and all but one member of the Secretariat (while doubling its size). In the course of this changeover Gorbachev removed people who were considered both more cautious (Grigorii Romanov, the party leader in Leningrad) and more impatient for change (Boris Yeltsin, the Moscow party leader) than he was.

Since usually very little is revealed publicly about Politburo discussions or procedures, analysts must spend a great deal of time putting together clues about what is happening and who is taking what position on policy issues. One of the best known instances of such "Kremlinology" occurred soon after the death of Stalin in 1953 when observers noticed that all the members of the Politburo went to the Bolshoi Ballet but that the head of the secret police since 1938, Lavrenty Beria, was not among them. The conclusion drawn, which proved to be correct, was that Beria had been removed from the Politburo. (This was accomplished by arresting and later executing him.)[5]

The Politburo is reported to meet once a week and to arrive at decisions by consensus, that is, without formal votes, though occasionally votes are reported. Because the Politburo is formally the agent of the Central Committee, on rare occasions its actions can be overturned. In 1957, by demanding a session of the full Central Committee, Nikita Khrushchev was able to reverse a Politburo decision that had been taken to oust him from power. Proposals accepted by the Cen-

---

[5] Ernst Kux, "Technicians of Power Versus Managers of Technique," in *The Soviet Political Process*, ed. Sidney I. Ploss (Waltham, MA: Ginn, 1971), p. 171.

Gorbachev's Career: Moving Fast Across Thin Ice

Mikhail Gorbachev is the first of a new generation of Soviet leaders to reach the top. Unlike all previous party leaders since Stalin's death, Gorbachev's is a post-World War II career. Born in Privolnoye of the Stavropol region of the Russian Federation, he was only ten when World War II came to the USSR. He worked on a collective farm and graduated from secondary school with good enough performance to enter the law faculty of prestigious Moscow State University in 1950. He joined the party in 1952, too late in the Stalin era to bear responsibility for the excesses of the purges. Nor can he be said to have advanced in his career over the graves of purged officials, as did Khrushchev and Brezhnev.

While Gorbachev received his law degree in 1955—making him the first leader of the party since Lenin with higher education—his entire professional career has developed within the party. After working in the Komsomol at Moscow State, he returned to the Stavropol region in 1955 and worked in the agitation and propaganda department of that organization. He rose quickly to become Komsomol first secretary of the region in 1958.

Gorbachev moved to the party apparatus in 1962 and there moved up just as fast: from head of the party organizational department in 1962 to first secretary for the city of Stavropol in 1966, to first secretary of the entire region in 1970, at the age of only 39. Along the way, Gorbachev devoted special energy to agricultural issues and by correspondence received an additional degree in agronomics from the Stavropol Agricultural Institute in 1967.

By the time he was 40, Gorbachev was a full member of the CPSU central committee and in 1978 was appointed a Central Committee secretary with special responsibility for agriculture. Though agricultural difficulties continued and even grew worse, Gorbachev was neither blamed nor demoted. In fact he sped up to the politburo, spending only one year as a candidate (or nonvoting) member before becoming a full member in 1980. At 50, Gorbachev was 20 years younger than the average politburo member. In the Andropov and Chernenko interregnum, Gorbachev's responsibilities grew and eventually included the economy, foreign affairs, ideology and party cadres. In essence during this period of infirm Soviet leadership it appears that Gorbachev was a shadow general secretary. In 1985, within 24 hours of the death of Konstantin Chernenko, he formally assumed the top position.

In 1988 Gorbachev was elected chairman of the Supreme Soviet under the old system and then to the same, but much stronger, post by the new Congress of People's Deputies in 1989. In 1990 he put forth proposals to strengthen further the powers of the presidency.

SOURCES: Congressional Quarterly, *The Soviet Union* (Washington, DC: Congressional Quarterly, Inc., 1986); Christian Schmidt-Hauer, *Gorbachev: The Path to Power* (Topsfield, MA: Salem House, 1986).

tral Committee in 1990 envisage a new politburo which would return to using the name presidium and be expanded to include representatives from all Soviet republics, something which is by no means guaranteed and does not occur at present.

The other critical body atop the Soviet system is the *Secretariat*. A body of varying size, it grew from 6 at the time of the death of Leonid Brezhnev to 14 under Gorbachev. Like the Politburo, it is formally subordinate to the Central Committee. The exact relationship between the Secretariat and Politburo has not been spelled out in party rules and has varied depending on power holders. One analyst argued in 1987 that under Gorbachev the Secretariat came close to replacing the Politburo as the party's most powerful body.[6] Membership in these bodies usually overlaps. In 1989 five full and one candidate member of the Politburo were also party secretaries. As the statutory and organizational arm of the party, the Secretariat, through its control of the Central Committee's six commissions (see box), has responsibility in key

[6] Jerry F. Hough, "Gorbachev Consolidating Power," *Problems of Communism* 36 (1987):21–43.

Central Committee Reorganization

In September 1988, the way in which the Central Committee of the CPSU supervises the country's affairs was reorganized. Six commissions were created, each with a specific area of responsibility and each chaired by a person who is both a member of the Secretariat and at least a candidate member of the Politburo. Each commission is also headed by someone who came to a leading position in the party after Mikhail Gorbachev became General Secretary.

Central Committee Commission	Chair, as of Fall 1989
Party building and cadre policy	Georgi P. Razumovsky
Ideology	Vadim Medvedev
Social and economic policy	Nikolai Slyunkov
Agriculture	Yegor Ligachev
International policy	Aleksandr Yakovlev
Legal policy	Unfilled

SOURCE: *Pravda,* October 1, 1988, p. 1.

policy areas such as personnel, agriculture, and social and economic policy.

The Secretariat's role in particular is enhanced by the activities of what is known as the *central party apparatus.* That is a vast network of officials whose job it is to provide the Central Committee, and thus the Politburo and Secretariat, with the information they need to run the country. From 22 departments the Central Committee apparatus was reorganized into six commissions in October 1988. Each of these headed by a party secretary whose appointment is clearly a key lever of power for the general secretary. For example, in 1988 four of these commissions were headed by people considered to be strong supporters of *perestroika.*

Below the national level, the party is organized along lines similar though not identical to the national level. Union republics such as Estonia or Kazakhstan have their own party congresses, central committees, *buros* (the equivalent of the national Politburo) and secretariats. This is true also at the *oblast* (regional) and *krai* (rural/provincial) level and at the district (*raion*) or city (*gorod*) level. While all of these bodies are subordinate to the central party hierarchy and have their leaders appointed by them, the party organi-zation in some regions such as Ukraine, or in cities such as Moscow, have become powerful political figures in their own right and have held concurrent positions at the very top of the national party structure.

At the bottom rung are the most numerous and in some ways most critical actors in the CPSU, the *primary party organizations.* The PPO is the unit of the party that has the most direct and continued contact with the population and daily life and thus is the most direct link between the dominant organization and the society it dominates. It is a small group, usually with less than 50 members, formed at the workplace or school or in some cases organized by residences, with a structure similar to that of higher party bodies. It is this group that must see that goals the party leadership sets are met on the shop floor and on the street and that the public understands and supports government policy. Beyond that, this group must continually identify and recruit skilled energetic people who will want to contribute to the immense task of running the country. At last official count there were nearly one-half million such PPOs throughout the country.[7]

[7] Ronald J. Hill and Peter Frank, *The Soviet Communist Party* (Boston: Allen & Unwin, 1986), pp. 47–55.

PARTY COMPOSITION

Soviet figures indicate that the party's 20 million members are made up of workers (43.7 percent), peasants (12.6 percent), and what might be termed intelligentsia (43.7 percent). As Ronald Hill and Peter Frank point out in their analysis, the rising education levels and changing occupational and geographic distribution of the Soviet population—more technical workers, more urbanization—make it likely that this is a far cry from the image of the party of the "toilers," if that is taken to mean manual laborers. As the vanguard of the working class it is not in the party's interest to have too few "workers" among its rank and file, and therefore recent recruitment drives have concentrated on increasing the number of those classified as workers. Similarly, the number of women recruits to the party has increased; but women remain greatly underrepresented in the party as a whole (28.8 percent as of 1986), and are almost absent from its top ranks (currently one candidate Politburo member is a woman).[8]

Reflecting their dominance of the political process, ethnic Russians are overrepresented in the party (59.1 percent to 51 percent of the population) while most other nationalities, especially Muslim peoples such as the Uzbeks, Azerbaijanis and Kazakhs, are substantially underrepresented. While the party as a whole is growing older, the top leadership shows a declining average age. At the time of Brezhnev's death the average age of Politburo members was 68. But since then, with the average age of Politburo entrants declining—Gorbachev himself was 54 when he became general-secretary—the average age in the Politburo has fallen to under 65. Both the party rank and file and the Politburo are now filled by people whose political activism and socialization came *after* World War II. This

presents a challenge to the party to keep the "heroic spirit" alive in the dominant and popular political culture (see Chapter 29). But it also represents an opportunity for the party to overcome some of its own excesses, such as those of the Stalinist period, since this new generation does not bear responsibility for those mistakes.

It is worth recalling that we still have not even begun a discussion of institutions and actors we commonly refer to in a Western context as the "government," e.g., the prime minister or Parliament. These institutions do exist in the Soviet Union and have some power over the internal and external affairs of the country. But they exist alongside of and for the most part subordinate to a vast party structure which in some instances duplicates and in most instances dominates and directs them.

THE ROLE OF ELECTIONS

There are elections in the Soviet system, but they serve a very different purpose from that in competitive party systems. In the Soviet system the role of elections has been to ratify and support the political choices made by the Communist Party. Elections outside the party, such as for the Supreme Soviet or local councils, have usually had a single slate of candidates, determined by the local or national Communist party. The public's choice thus has been to support this candidate or either abstain or somehow indicate a rejection of the candidate (usually not a wise course of action). Thus, election returns typically showed near unanimity in support of the candidate. Recently, though, multicandidate elections were held for a new Congress of Peoples' Deputies (see pp. 420–22) and Gorbachev secured acceptance of this principle for elections within the party itself. Moreover, according to reforms enacted in 1988, party officials will be limited to two terms of office of five years each. Aimed at

[8] At the top echelons workers apparently fare no better: as of 1990 only 29 or 249 members of the Central Committee were industrial or agricultural laborers (Reuters, February 4, 1990).

improving the performance and responsiveness of Soviet government, this will also act to weaken the position of those who might be opposed to Gorbachev's plans for reforming the Soviet system.

Within the party, the electorate is of course smaller, being made up only of party members or particular party bodies who then elect their representatives to higher bodies. But even here the slate of candidates is typically determined by the higher party bodies and elected unanimously. In this process the role of the Central Committee and especially the Secretariat is key. In essence elections are ratifications of the central and higher party bodies' choices for the personnel throughout the party. Since these lower office holders then send delegates to the party congresses and formally elect the Central Committee, this process also serves to reproduce the party in accordance with the leadership's wishes.

The actual process of "staffing" elections and thus the posts they fill is part of a system known as *nomenklatura*. This refers to the party's naming of people for lower posts in the party itself, in all government agencies, in the economy, and in fact in all key institutions of government. The privilege of *nomenklatura* embodies the party's authority and is the vehicle of its penetration of both political and what we might consider nonpolitical areas of life in the Soviet Union. It is estimated that some two million managerial and influential posts inside and outside the party are filled through the *nomenklatura* system.[8] While the spread of multicandidate elections both inside and outside the party might serve to dilute the influence of the *nomenklatura* system, party leaders will still exercise enormous influence over the nomination of candidates as well as the even more numerous choices of non-elective posts. Thus the withering away of the *nomenklatura* is probably a few months off.

[8] T. H. Rigby and Bohdan Harasymiw, eds., *Leadership Selection and Patron-Client Relations in the USSR and Yugoslavia* (London: George Allen & Unwin, 1983), p. 3.

References and Suggested Readings

BIELASIAK, JACK. "Party Leadership and Mass Participation in Developed Socialism." In *Developed Socialism in the Soviet Bloc,* ed. Jim Seroka and Maurice D. Simon. Boulder, CO: Westview Press, 1982, pp. 121–54.

HAMMER, DARREL P. *The USSR: The Politics of Oligarchy.* Boulder, CO: Westview Press, 1986.

LAIRD, ROY D. *The Politburo: Demographic Trends, Gorbachev, and the Future.* Boulder, CO: Westview Press, 1986.

SMITH, GORDON B. *Soviet Politics: Continuity and Contradiction.* New York: St. Martin's Press, 1988.

32

All power to the soviets.
— V. I. LENIN

We are talking today about the need to review the power of the soviets as Lenin interpreted it.
— M. S. GORBACHEV

National and Subnational Government

THE ORGANIZATION OF THE SOVIET STATE

Article 70 of the Soviet constitution of 1977 states:

> The Union of Soviet Socialist Republics is a unitary, federal, multinational state, formed on the basis of the principle of socialist federalism, and as the result of the free self-determination of nations, and the voluntary association of equal Soviet Socialist Republics.[1]

Easier said than done. This clause reflects all by itself the contradictory dimensions and the problems of governing the modern Soviet Union. To begin with, the state is defined as both unitary *and* federal, as both unitary *and* multinational. It is described as socialist, suggesting that this philosophy will rule, but also as a federal system resulting from self-

[1] F. J. M. Feldbrugge, *The Constitutions of the USSR and the Union Republics: Analysis, Texts, Reports* (Alphen aan den Rijn, The Netherlands: Sijthoff and Noordhoff, 1979), p. 109.

determination and equality. Does this mean that republics in the Soviet Union can differ in the amount of socialism they employ? Does it mean that they have equal power to or more power than the central government? And if the system is multinational and federal, where does the unity come from?

These questions of Soviet *politics* should be kept in mind as the formal Soviet *government* structure is described from the top down.

THE OLD AND NEW PARLIAMENT

Until 1989, the Supreme Soviet had been both the national legislature and the highest state body—at least in theory. This *soviet,* or council, represented the people of the Soviet Union in decision-making. Like the U.S. Congress it had two chambers, a Soviet of Nationalities and a Soviet of Unions.

The Soviet of Nationalities represented the country's constituent regions and therefore many of its nationalities. Different subnational units (see pp. 425–26), depending on their level in the hierarchy, sent different

419

numbers of deputies. The Soviet of Unions represented Soviet citizens on the basis of elections in single-member electoral districts of equal size. In the old parliament each chamber had 750 members, with candidates for seats chosen by the local party. The voter in most cases was relieved of the burden of choice, having the option only to approve or strike out the name of a candidate. Choice was not critical, however, since this parliamentary body was more symbolic than powerful. It met only twice a year for two or three days and virtually always unanimously supported party policy.

A key aspect of Mikhail Gorbachev's plans for reform involved infusing the system of *soviets* with greater power and responsibility. In his speech to a party plenum in February 1988 he said it was necessary

> to take a better look at how the Soviets are formed. This means upgrading our election system so that the process of forming the bodies of power makes for active involvement of the people and for a careful selection of persons capable of ensuring the soviets' activities with respect to the goals of perestroika.[2]

Accordingly, the CPSU, at a special national party conference called for the purpose in June 1988, approved plans to reform the Soviet state government. In December the first part of the plan was approved by the Supreme Soviet. The new "supreme organ of USSR state power" is the Congress of People's Deputies. This body, elected through multicandidate, secret-ballot elections, consists of 2,250 people. One-third are elected from districts of equal size (257,300 voters for each deputy), and one-third are elected from national units (32 from each union re-

[2] "Revolutionary Perestroika and the Ideology of Renewal," Speech by Mikhail Gorbachev, General Secretary of the CPSU Central Committee, at the plenary meeting of the CPSU Central Committee on February 18, 1988 [mimeo, in English].

public, 11 from each autonomous republic, 5 from each autonomous *oblast,* and one from each autonomous *okrug*). The remaining third are elected by local party organizations, trade unions, and veterans and youth groups. Figure 32.1 shows the new structure of the Soviet government.

In the first elections for this large body, held in March and April 1989, the party received a rude shock when many of its key regional officials—including the first secretaries of Riga, Minsk, Kiev, Kishiniev, and Alma Ata and the first *and* second secretaries in Leningrad all lost. Many party candidates lost in districts where they ran unopposed, because they did not get the required majority of "for" votes. (People could vote both "for" and "against" candidates.) Overall, many outspoken supporters of *glasnost* and *perestroika,* including former dissidents such as historian Roy Medvedev and physicist Andre Sakharov won seats to the Congress.

The Congress itself does not serve as the legislature but instead elects a new, smaller Supreme Soviet which, according to the amended constitution, is the "standing legislative, administrative, and monitoring organ of USSR state power." Unlike its predecessor, it is supposed to remain in session long enough to actually debate and legislate. The new Supreme Soviet still has two chambers, 271 members each, all of whom are elected not directly by the population but from the membership of the Congress of People's Deputies. In the Soviet of Unions members are chosen from those elected to the Congress from the equal electoral units. In the Soviet of Nationalities, each union republic sends eleven deputies, each autonomous republic four, each autonomous *oblast* two, and each autonomous *okrug,* one.

While the aim of this change is clearly to make the Supreme Soviet a more active parliament, it is evident that the Communist Party still wields predominant influ-

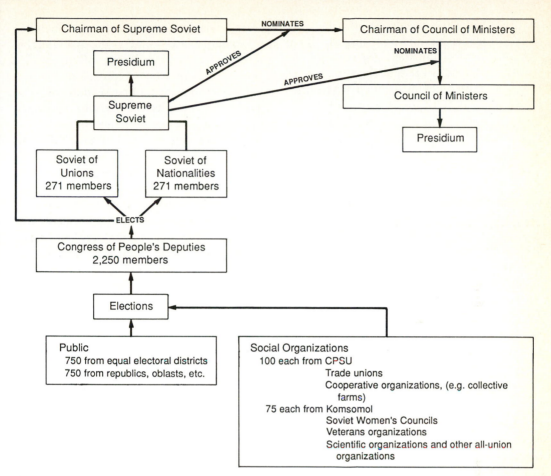

Figure 32.1   The New Soviet State and Government

ence: through the nomination of candidates; through its role in the related organizations that have the right to elect one-third of the deputies to the congress; through republican and regional governments; and because the Supreme Soviet itself is not elected directly but from the Congress.

Notwithstanding the electoral success of many reformers, the Congress of People's Deputies still contained more than 85 percent party members.[3] This Congress then elected a

[3] Dawn Mann, "The Congress of People's Deputies: The Election Marathon Ends," *Report on the USSR*, Vol. 1, # 22 (June 2, 1989) p. 4.

Supreme Soviet which excluded many of the country's most prominent exponents of radical reform.

In addition, the wishes of the party leadership are critical in helping the Congress make another of its key decisions, the election of the *chairman of the Supreme Soviet*. The person holding this position, currently Mikhail Gorbachev, is the "highest official of the Soviet state," commonly referred to as the president. He is elected by the Congress for a maximum of two terms of five years each and can be recalled by the Congress. This new president has substantial formal power, including the right to initiate legislation, the responsibility for leadership and reporting on all important matters, and the right to nominate the first deputy chairman of the Supreme Soviet, the chairman of the Council of Ministers (the prime minister), the chairman of the Supreme Court, and of other bodies. He heads the Defense Council, the country's supreme military authority, and represents the Soviet Union internationally. Apart from this impressive array of institutional powers, the person holding this office continues to derive the greatest measure of his power from being designated by the leader of the CPSU—or by being the leader himself.

The Supreme Soviet's executive committee is the *Presidium,* which organizes and coordinates the activity of both the Congress and the Supreme Soviet. In the old system, when the Supreme Soviet was not in session—which was most of the time—the Presidium exercised legislative power as well. Now its potentially most significant role lies in its power to declare states of emergency and "special forms of administration" in the country, or parts of it, in emergency situations. Membership in the Presidium is made up of the chairman of the Supreme Soviet, a first deputy, the 15 chairmen of union republic supreme soviets, and the chairmen of other key bodies in the national legislature.

In the past, Supreme Soviet deputies have not been full-time legislators, but either party members or those chosen by the party to be candidates, often as representatives of particular subgroups of society: workers, women, and so on. Given the added duties but low returns in terms of power or influence, there was a high rate of turnover among those deputies who did not simultaneously hold an important office in the Communist Party. Central Committee members and other important party officials, military officers and heads of large enterprises were routinely elected and reelected to the Supreme Soviet, thus ensuring party leaders' control of both the process and the outcome. The new Supreme Soviet is likely to continue to be filled with familiar faces—and as the first selection indicates, strongly reflective of the preferences of the senior CPSU leadership.

Nevertheless, in the first sessions of these new bodies the effect of *glasnost,* contested elections and the new frankness of the leadership in discussing problems in the USSR combined to produce the most vigorous and lively debates since the 1920s. Gorbachev himself and his appointees were challenged; previously taboo subjects such as the military budget and role of the KGB were openly discussed. In June 1989 several key ministerial appointments were blocked by the legislature, either in committee or, in one case, by vote of the full Supreme Soviet.

Even when it does not act as a deliberative or autonomous legislative body, the Supreme Soviet and its Presidium do fulfill several key functions common to all governments. For one thing, these institutions provide a *symbolic* public center for Soviet government actions. They are the legal embodiment of power even if that power is mostly exercised elsewhere. In this role, the legislature acts as a national forum for explaining Soviet government action, for getting across the party's point of view, and for criticizing the views and actions of the country's adversaries. The role of the president is important to this symbolic function and has been an indicator of the degree of power or confidence held by a Soviet party leader. Nikita Khrushchev, for example, though he was party leader from 1953 to 1964, was never state president. He was, however, able to install his close associate, Leonid Brezhnev, in the position from 1960 to 1964, until Brezhnev replaced Khrushchev as party leader. In 1977, as a reflection of the growth of his own power, Brezhnev was elected president of the Presidium of the Supreme Soviet. Assuming this position allowed him to act formally as head of state in the country's international affairs, something he had already been doing in fact as head of the CPSU. Going beyond this,

Andrei Sakharov's View of Constitutional Changes Secured by Mikhail Gorbachev

In political terms, his recent strategy can be fairly accurately described as a campaign to achieve democratic change through nondemocratic means. The way I see it, it is an extremely dangerous strategy, threatening to bring forth unworkable antidemocratic structures we'll have to contend with for a long time. I mean the constitutional reform, the plan of instituting indirect elections to the Supreme Soviet, with all power vested in the person of the head of state who doubles as the General Secretary of the Party—and let me emphasize, it is the only political party in the country. The new draft constitution never so much as mentions even the possibility of political pluralism and has no constitutional provisions for a multiparty system.

SOURCE: Statement at meeting of Woodrow Wilson International Center for Scholars, Washington, DC, November 14, 1988.

Mikhail Gorbachev simultaneously became president and also succeeded in strengthening the power of that office. Apparently finding this unsatisfactory and perhaps wanting to strengthen the state in relation to the party, Gorbachev in early 1990 succeeded in having the party accept both the end of its own political monopoly and the idea of a stronger presidency, possibly to be elected directly by the population. Under these proposals, the president would be able to veto legislation and declare states of emergency, powers that an American president has, for example.[4] These changes must still be enacted by the Congress of People's deputies and, like most of those proposed, are controversial. Several critics of the reforms, including Andrei Sakharov (see box), pointed to the potentially dangerous concentration of power in the hands of one person—something the country has seen quite often.

The changes insisted on by Gorbachev illustrate the role of the Supreme Soviet as an *instrument* of party power. By dominating selection of its membership and the chairmanships of the standing commissions and through the powers of the Presidium and now the presidency, the Communist Party can see that its policies and ideas—in this case, *perestroika*—are not only publicly applauded but also rendered into laws and regulations. This applies also to the military. The Defense Council, the country's highest military body, was placed under the Presidium by the 1977 constitution and is chaired by the president.

The Congress of People's Deputies and the Supreme Soviet also serve an *interactive* function between government and society. The process of selecting and electing deputies provides the party with the direct contact with the general public. Standing for election, even if it is only for a body that then elects another, is the closest thing the Communist Party does to having its members or those chosen by it submit to public approval. By the same token, finding people to serve as deputies to either the national or the regional *soviets* is part of what the party needs to do to involve the Soviet citizenry in supporting, ratifying and implementing the governing decisions made by the party.

Finally, the Congress and, to a lesser extent, the Supreme Soviet act as *participatory* agents by encouraging citizen participation, though on a somewhat limited and indirect basis (see Chapter 30). As debate in both new bodies shows, criticisms of various aspects of Soviet governance can be frank and directed right at the leadership. In addition, the office of the Presidium in Moscow hears direct citizen complaints about the functioning of Soviet government and thus allows a certain amount of access to influential actors.

THE GOVERNMENT

The aims and orientations of the country and its laws are decided on by the Communist Party leadership. The formalities of state are observed by the Supreme Soviet and its chairman. But it is the ministries and state committees that have the responsibility for the actual governing of the country—that is, executing the policies and putting decisions into practice. At the top of this system is the *Council of Ministers*. Membership in this body is formally approved by the Supreme Soviet upon recommendation by the chairman of the Council of Ministers, commonly referred to as the *prime minister*. The prime minister is himself appointed by the Supreme Soviet, upon nomination by the Soviet President.

Currently numbering nearly 90, the Council of Ministers is virtually a mini-legislature of its own, being made up of the heads of most important administrative and economic agencies in the country. Some of these are *ministries*, such as defense, foreign affairs or agriculture as well as less publicized ministries such as mineral fertilizer production or the ministry for the meat and dairy industry. Some ministries are what is known as *all-union*, meaning that they administer their sphere of activity directly from the national level and are not further subdivided into subordinate agencies at the republic level. The ministries for chemicals and petroleum are all-union ministries, as are defense and some special construction ministries. Others, such as education, culture, foreign affairs and justice, are known as *union-republic* ministries and operate at the republic level through counterparts or subordinate branches.

Of equal importance are the *state committees*, which are also created by the Supreme Soviet and which also have national responsibilities, usually in ways that cut across the sectoral responsibilities common to the ministries. Prices, for example, are the responsibility of the State Committee for Prices. The national plan for the economy, which until recently has been the key directive controlling the allocation of the country's resources, is created and administered by such a committee, known as *Gosplan* (for *Gosudarstvenni planovii komitet*). Perhaps the best known of these committees is the committee for state security or *Komitet Gosudarstvennoi Besopasnosti*, better known by its initials, KGB.

The council of Ministers also includes representatives from agencies, such as the state bank (*Gosbank*), that have ministerial status, and some agencies, such as for foreign tourism, that do not have such status. Finally, the council also forms its own commissions designed to improve coordination in particularly important areas such as energy or agriculture. One of these, created in 1987, was the State Foreign Economic Commission, a kind of super-ministry with the responsibility for improving the cooperation and efficiency of foreign trade. In 1988 this commission was combined with the Ministry of Foreign Trade to form a new Ministry of Foreign Economic Relations covering all areas of international economic involvement. With all this, the Council of Ministers is itself too large to act as a cabinet—it reached 106 in 1987—and much of its decision-making is accomplished by its own *presidium* made up of the chairman of the Council of Ministers, first deputy chairmen and deputy chairmen. Because of the presidium's more continuous supervision of national policy, and its role as a kind of

Stability = Stagnation

One of the most commonly repeated phrases of the Gorbachev era has been the reference to the Brezhnev period as one of "*zastoi*" or stagnation. For the ministries, the "stability of cadres" of this period meant virtually assured tenure. In mid-1988 the Soviet journal *Ogonyok* published a study of 45 ministry and department heads who had served under Brezhnev. For these people the *average* time of service in their position was eighteen years! Within the first three years of Gorbachev's rule more than 70 percent of top ministry and department officials were replaced.

SOURCE: Pavel Levedev, "What Do We Know about our Ministers?" *Ogonyok*, No. 31 (July 1988):6–8 (*Current Digest of the Soviet Press*, 40, 39 (1988):17).

inner core of Soviet government, people in this body can be considered among the most powerful in the Soviet government. Not surprisingly, several of these people also hold positions in the Politburo of the Communist Party. Prime Minister Nikolai Ryzhkov, chairman of the Presidium, is a full Politburo member, and Anatoly Lukyanov, the first deputy chairman, and Yuri Maslyukov, head of Gosplan, are candidate Politburo members.

The Council of Ministers as a whole and the ministries, state committees and agencies are subject to the direction and domination of the party. Through *nomenklatura* (see p. 418), the party secretariat staffs all key positions. Through a process known as *kontrol* it monitors the work of the ministries. This domination is not always complete, nor is the involvement of party officials in the running of the economy always welcome or beneficial. The country's economy is of course the party's concern. But the party is also a political organization and therefore worries about mobilizing the population and keeping domestic and international threats to a minimum. A ministry official can thus be put in something of a bind. Suppose, for example, in an attempt to produce the most and best quality trucks, he wants the factories under his jurisdiction to reduce the pay of workers who do not show up or who do not produce. This may move him closer to his goal of improved, efficient production, but the party leadership in a region of some of his factories may complain that firing and cutting the pay of workers causes political problems and is in any case contrary to socialism. Or even worse for the ministry official, suppose the local party leader, responding to demands from higher up, decides he can run the enterprises better? Political goals and economic goals may conflict. In a capitalist economy the owner of a factory does not need political permission to fire workers; on the other hand, the workers have little protection

against unemployment. In the Soviet system, the law of the land and the doctrine underlying it guarantee the worker a job, but the degree of political involvement needed to enforce party goals may be detrimental to an efficient running of the economy. Indeed, one of the most serious concerns of those around Mikhail Gorbachev is the number of money-losing enterprises, estimated at 24,000 in 1988, which cost the state billions of rubles in subsidies.

Beyond the question of economic performance, this situation exemplifies the chronic problem of control of the economy. If, for example, the factory or enterprise director were able to make his or her own decisions about hiring, firing, buying supplies and selling products, what would be the role of the primary party organization and of the ministries? Would they simply become advisory bodies, reduced essentially to stating goals and offering guidelines? But if ministry officials or regional first secretaries still have to report to the political leadership on the health of their region or economic sector, how can they keep "hands off" the day-to-day running of the economy? Hence, when people argue for reform in the Soviet economy, invariably they run up against the fears of loss of control and position by those who are currently controlling things. In the Soviet Union this means the ministries and, ultimately, the party. Reform of the economy, as Mikhail Gorbachev recognizes, must include reform of the party itself (see discussion, chapter 33).

SUBNATIONAL GOVERNMENT

The "Union" in the name Union of Soviet Socialist Republics refers to the joining of fifteen legally sovereign but functionally subordinate units, known as *union republics* all of which have the formal right to secede (article 72 of the constitution) but, of course, choose not to. The largest of these units is the Russian Soviet Federated Socialist Republic

(RSFSR). By its sheer size (roughly 75 percent of the Soviet Union's territory), by the dominance of ethnic Russians in the party and government, by having its government located in Moscow and by having its party functions handled until 1989 by the apparatus of the Central Committee of the CPSU itself, not a regional party, this republic and its leaders tend to be the most influential in the Soviet system.

Some union republics were formed from previously independent countries, such as Lithuania, Latvia and Estonia, which were independent between World Wars I and II and were taken over by the Soviet Union in 1940 (an absorption still unrecognized by the United States). Union republics constitutionally have the right to engage in their own foreign relations, but in only one area is this right put into practice. The Byelorussian and Ukrainian SSRs are treated as separate countries in the United Nations, an arrangement agreed to at the founding of the organization in order to offset the substantial U.S. influence among the original membership.

All of the union republics have a nationality base; that is, they are derived from and give institutional form to a predominant nationality group, such as the Uzbeks or Armenians. In practice, however, the prerogatives of the union republics, as with all other units of the system, are restricted by the central government. Leaders of republics and party and state organs are formally elected, but in practice are appointed by the central party apparatus through *nomenklatura*.

Within the largest union republics are smaller governing units, such as regions (*oblasti*) and areas (*krai*). All union republics (except the Russian Republic) and all the various subunits have party organizations with a structure similar to that of the national party. Thus, each area has its own party committee; for example, an *oblast* has an *oblastni komitet* or *obkom*. All but the smallest regions

have a party governing *buro*, a secretariat and a conference or congress duplicating that of the country as a whole. The Russian Republic gained its own intermediary party unit only in 1989, due in part to the growing influence of Russian nationalism.

Four union republics also contain within their territory *autonomous* soviet socialist *republics*. As in the union republics, these have formal legislatures, *soviets*, councils of ministers, and prime ministers. Within the Russian Republic there are 16 such autonomous republics; there are two in the Soviet republic of Georgia, and one each in Azerbaijan and Uzbekistan. The autonomous republics are subordinate to the union republic and do not have even the formal right to secede. Like the union republics, their existence is representative of a nationality.

Within republics may also be found *autonomous oblasts*. These subunits of union republics do not have their own constitution but they do of course have their own party organizations. Five of the eight autonomous oblasts are in the Russian Republic. Below the *oblast* level is the autonomous *okrug* or region, which represents relatively small groups of people; all ten of these are within the Russian Republic.

Can such a governing system actually be all the things that article 70 of the Soviet constitution aspires to? Can it be both unitary and federal, both socialist and self-determined? In theory, yes; in practice, no. When these goals have conflicted in Soviet governance, the unitary has won out over the federal and the socialist over the self-determined. For example, while the various levels of government are formally tied to nationality, some curious anomalies exist. There are more than six million Tartars, and their representative administrative unit is an autonomous republic within the Russian Republic. There are only one million Estonians, however, yet they have a full union republic of their own, ostensibly because they are in a border region while other more numerous nationalities are not. The Jewish Autonomous Oblast is an artificial creation of some 36 million square miles in the remote Soviet Far East, where few Jews ever lived. Created before World War II, the region's formation was evidently designed to offer Jews a territorial "homeland" conveniently located thousands of miles from the center of Soviet power—and of Soviet Jewry. The region still contains very few Jews—roughly 20,000—and acts mostly as official recognition of the existence of one of the more numerous peoples living in the USSR. Even this shell is more than some other groups have, with more or nearly as many people. Neither Germans, for example, who number nearly two million in the USSR, nor Poles, just over one million, have representative units of any kind. The former in fact were exiled and dispersed from their traditional homelands along the Volga River because of their alleged collaboration with the Nazi invaders during World War II.

December 1988: A demonstrator waves the national Soviet flag in front of a crowd with clenched fists, in the Azerbaijan capital of Baku.
SOURCE: AP/Wide World Photos.

Recently the status of one region was challenged publicly. Nagorno-Karabakh, lying within the predominantly Muslim union republic of Azerbaijan, is largely Armenian ethnically and Orthodox in religion. In February 1988, taking advantage of the era of *glasnost* instituted by Mikhail Gorbachev, Armenians began to demonstrate in favor of transferring this autonomous *oblast* from Azerbaijan to Armenia. Some of the demonstrations were massive—a million people marched in Yerevan, the capital of Armenia—and violence flared between Armenians and Azerbaijanis, taking more than 80 lives by official report. The *soviet* of Nagorno-Karabakh voted to secede from Azerbaijan in July 1988, but the supreme soviet of that union republic refused to agree. For almost two years the region was under special administrative control from Moscow. In the fall of 1989 the central leadership had to intervene forcefully to lift a virtual blockade of Armenia by Azerbaijainis, and in 1990 troops were sent in to try to halt the intercommunal violence. The central government has rejected changing republican boundaries, fearing an explosion of other such demands throughout the country. The emergence of this issue into public view 65 years after the annexation of the Nagorno-Karabakh region (1923) demonstrates the persistence of internationality tensions despite the complex federal structure and social policies designed to mitigate them.

In the economic sphere, despite 70 years of socialism, substantial differences exist in levels of economic development between the regions of the USSR. For example, national income per capita in the five central Asian republics at the beginning of the 1980s was less than half that in the Russian Federation and just over 40 percent of that of Latvia and Estonia.

Over the years the Soviet government has tried various schemes for economic governance of the country. The most radical change was the creation, under Nikita Khrushchev, of *sovnarkhozi* or regional economic councils. Under this arrangement, direction of the economy became the responsibility of over one hundred regionally based councils in an attempt to make the economy more efficient and responsive to regional strengths and needs. The aim was also to weaken the power of the ministries to the benefit of local party leaders and *soviets*. In practice, the decentralization, fragmentation and political conflict this produced tended to benefit the larger and better-off regions even more, and after Khrushchev's downfall in 1964, this system was undone. Currently the USSR is divided into 18 regions for economic purposes of planning, but it is the national state committee for planning (Gosplan) that is the key actor, not regional planning bodies.[4] Ultimately politics within the party dominates the governing process. In the presence of so many different national groups, with so many different levels of development, it is the party that aims to provide both the unity and the control within the overall goal of building a modern socialist economy and country. At all of these levels, the regional *soviets,* executive *buros* and councils of ministers would quite likely diverge in direction, pace and level of political, social and economic development even more, were they truly "self-determining." Instead, it is the central party and the government that do the determining and, using both policy and personnel, exercise power over regional actors.

Even apart from the role of the party, the central government is dominant. The formal powers of subnational units are relatively weak and ill-defined. In the debates on the recent changes in the constitution, representatives of some republics—chiefly those in the Baltics—wanted to strengthen the powers of the republics to accept or reject

[4] Alec Nove, *The Soviet Economic System* (Boston: Allen & Unwin, 1986), pp. 54–55.

national legislation. Though some accommodations to these sensibilities were made in the amendments—stating, for example, that the Supreme Soviet lays down "general principles" but not "basic guidelines" for subnational governments—the fundamental relationship did not change. The Supreme Soviet, for instance, has the power to repeal orders of republican ministries if they are "inconsistent" with the USSR constitution and laws. In January 1990 a new Constitutional Compliance Committee, established by the Supreme Soviet over the objections of many Baltic deputies, came into being. The Committee will review all laws and offer opinions as to their conformity with Soviet constitution. One analyst concluded that, as presently constituted, republics are essentially "regional branches of the national government," a situation that stands in some contrast to that in Germany.[5]

Further eroding the power of the republics and other lower units are the economic levers held at the center. It is the national government that allocates most investment funds to the different regions. The country's national plan governing economic activity is formulated at the national level, and republics and provinces are obliged to carry it out. In these respects the ministries act as the national government's arm, and in the economic sphere, stronger all-union ministries predominate over union republic or local ministries.

This does not mean that actors below the central level have no input or influence. Indeed, because regional and local leaders are usually more aware of specific conditions and needs, their involvement is critical to formulating national policy. In developing the national economic plan, for example, republican and ministerial officials at the regional level have an important impact by virtue of the information they supply to the central planning agency (Gosplan) and their ability to push for their local or regional interests in the plan.[6]

Moreover, regional party first secretaries wield potentially enormous power in their home areas because of the pervasiveness of party responsibilities in virtually all aspects of public life. Because the local party heads, along with agents of the ministries, are the ones who allocate the country's resources most directly, implement decisions made at the top, and report back to the center on the effect of actions, they can build a local power base while satisfying the demands of the center. This combination of governing "down" and influencing "up" can give a regional secretary significant power as the intermediary between a strong central government and the governed people.

On the other hand, popular demands for greater regional control, such as those that emerged after 1988 in the Baltic republics, in the Transcaucasus and Ukraine, call into question both the legitimacy of the local leader and the very structure of the relationship between the governing center and the governed regions.

[6] Nove, pp. 49–53; Gordon B. Smith, *Soviet Politics: Continuity and Contradiction* (New York: St. Martin's Press, 1988), pp. 122–131.

References and Suggested Readings

BARGHOORN, FREDERICK, and THOMAS F. REMINGTON, *Politics in the USSR*. Boston: Little, Brown, 1986.

SIEGLER, ROBERT W. *The Standing Commissions of the Supreme Soviet: Effective Co-optation*. New York: Praeger, 1982.

SMITH, GORDON B., ed. *Public Policy and Administration in the Soviet Union*. New York: Praeger, 1980.

[5] Peter B. Zwick, "Soviet Nationality Policy: Social, Economic, and Political Aspects," in *Public Policy and Administration in the Soviet Union*, ed. Gordon B. Smith (New York: Praeger, 1980).

33

History will not forgive us if we miss our chance. An abyss must be crossed in a single leap—you can't make it in two."
— VASILY SELYUNIN,
SOVIET ECONOMIST

Policy Case I: Mikhail Gorbachev and Economic Reform

As noted earlier, the Soviet Union was a relative latecomer to both political and economic modernization. Industrial production had grown rapidly during the last part of the nineteenth century and then again between 1907 and 1914. By the outbreak of World War I, Russian production of key industrial commodities was comparable to that of France but still well behind that of England, Germany and the United States.[1] Being Marxists, the Bolsheviks were committed to pushing forward the industrialization of the new Soviet Union. They saw this as indispensable to the building of a new socialist society. After the period of war communism and civil war had given way to relative internal peace, a period of new economic policy, or NEP, was tried utilizing more incentives to peasants instead of forced requisitions, and less central control of the country's economy. Small-scale and consumer goods industries recov-

ered fairly quickly, but the main industrial base of the country still sputtered. By the time of the 12th Party Congress of 1923, industry as a whole was still working at less than one-third capacity.[2] The real industrial spurt and rapid development of the country did not occur until the late 1920s and 1930s under the relentless pressure of Stalin's "revolution from above." The gains, as described earlier, were substantial, as was the cost.

Beyond the economic growth, however, the Stalinist period fused onto the Soviet economy a model of economic control that was to last in its basic form into the present era. While this system performed the task of transforming the country from a primarily rural, peasant-based economy into a twentieth-century economic power in a remarkably short period, it also left the country's present rulers with significant problems. The economic tasks for the USSR at the end

[1] Roger Muntig, *The Economic Development of the USSR* (New York: St. Martin's Press, 1982), p. 33.

[2] E. H. Carr, *The Bolshevik Revolution,* 3 vols. (London: Penguin Books, 1966), 2:310.

of the twentieth century are not the same as those after World War I or even those of the reconstruction period immediately after World War II. The country's period of *extensive* economic development has given way to the need for *intensive* development. An economy with, as Charles Lindbloom put it, "strong thumbs and no fingers" has to develop those fingers. The attempt by Mikhail Gorbachev and the people around him to deal with this crucial policy area reveals much about the way the ideological, political, governmental and personal aspects of the Soviet Union intertwine.

THE NEED FOR REFORM

By the mid-1980s the evidence was clear that the Soviet economy was slowing down and, in some instances, stagnating. Growth rates, which had averaged more than 4 percent between 1960 and 1975, declined to just over 2 percent between 1976 and 1985. Critical areas of the economy were not performing. Oil production, overall energy production and other indicators of achievement—for example, industrial growth and agricultural production—lagged to below half of what they had been in the 1960s and 1970s.

Qualitatively the economy was also soft. Labor productivity, a measure of how much one worker produces, is currently roughly half the level of the United States. Investment in new machines and equipment, which had grown at more than 10 percent per year during 1960–65, grew at less than 5 percent annually during 1981–85.[3] Consequently, some 35 to 40 percent of Soviet industrial equipment is between 15 and 20 years old, and repair of aging plants and equipment absorbs the efforts of six million workers and costs 35 billion rubles per year.[4] Soviet Prime Minister Nikolai Ryzhkov has said that less than 30 percent of the Soviet Union's manufactured goods could meet world standards.

[3] U.S. Congress Joint Economic Committee, *Gorbachev's Economic Plans* (Washington: U.S. Government Printing Office, 1987) vol. 1, p. 151.
[4] Timothy Colton, *The Dilemma of Reform in the Soviet Union,* rev. and exp. ed. (New York: Council on Foreign Relations, 1986), p. 40.

Moscow: A new shipment of shoes immediately attracts a long line of people.
SOURCE: UPI/Bettmann Newsphotos.

In the work place, growing absenteeism, apathy, lack of ambition and lost work due to abuse of alcohol has been documented by Soviet sociologists. With the consumer goods sector continually starved by the emphasis on heavy industry, workers have found there is little to buy with their wages, which they receive regardless of how well or how often they work. By 1987 13 percent of Soviet enterprises were operating at a loss, according to official Soviet estimates.

While the USSR is as close to a self-sufficient economy as exists in the modern world, this seeming advantage has also meant a degree of isolation from the advances seen in more dynamic economies. Technological innovation, including the use of imported equipment, has proceeded only slowly. Enterprise managers have had no incentive or power to try to buy and adapt the latest technology for their production. Everything they make has been purchased at fixed prices on the domestic market, and losses have been made up by the state. And as they have not been encouraged or allowed to sell internationally, there has been little need to worry about world standards.

But the leaders of the Soviet Union have discovered that the country does need to buy some things from the rest of the world—for example, grain. Since Soviet currency, the ruble, is not convertible, that is, it does not have a market-generated value in relation to other currencies of the world, the USSR must earn "hard" currency, such as dollars, to be able to buy what it needs on the world markets. As harvests were especially poor in the later Brezhnev years and continually failed to keep pace with demand, Soviet agricultural purchases began to take more and more of the country's precious hard currency earnings.[5]

Then, at the beginning of the 1980s, the major item the Soviet Union could sell to the West, oil, began to bring lower prices on the world market, even as it was costing more to extract it from places such as Siberia and the Arctic regions.

THE FACETS OF THE ECONOMIC PROBLEM

There are reasons for these difficulties. The economic system of the Soviet Union is a creation of and is tightly bound up with the political domination of the Communist Party. Some of the problems are derived from that domination, some from the ideology that underlies it, and some from phenomena seen elsewhere in the world, such as bureaucratic power.

Some of the problems of the Soviet economy are *structural;* that is, they have more to do with fundamental and less malleable factors than with particular policy mistakes. The Soviet economy is much more labor-intensive than those in the West, taking many more people to do a job, especially where up-to-date technology is lacking. This is not a problem as long as the labor force is growing, as a result either of population growth or of movement of people from the country to the city. At present, however, the Soviet labor force is not growing fast enough to provide the numbers of laborers needed. Moreover, the areas where it is growing, such as central Asia and the Caucasus, are not the major industrial areas of the country. In the European republics, where most Soviet industry is located, families average just over two children each; in central Asia the average is 4.4. As in other industrialized countries, the Soviet work force and population overall are aging. In 1950 just over 10 percent of Soviet population was of retirement age; by 1990 this figure reached 17 percent. These fac-

---

[5] U. S. Congress Joint Economic Committee, *Gorbachev's Economic Plans* (Washington, U.S. Government Printing Office, 1987) vol. 2, p. 478.

tors mean that the USSR cannot turn around economic growth simply by employing more people, unless it steals from one part of the economy to support another.

The huge size of the country and its poorly developed infrastructure—bridges, roads, telecommunications—also contribute to the stagnation of the economy. In the beginning of the 1980s there were fewer telephones in the USSR than in France or West Germany—countries with roughly one-fifth the Soviet Union's population; a fraction of the number of cars, trucks and busses; and fewer paved roads in the whole country than there are in Texas.[6] This aspect is especially critical for the energy sector, where the natural resources are now more remote from the industrial plants that use them. In the agricultural sphere the poor performance of the Soviet Union is made somewhat more understandable when one realizes that though the country is two and one-half times the size of the United States, it actually has less high-quality growing land. The climate, soil conditions and water supply in most Soviet territory are not naturally conducive to productive agriculture.

Many of the problems of the economy are the direct result of the way it is set up to operate. Since the time of the Bolshevik revolution, the determination of economic policy for the country has been a tightly held monopoly of the Communist Party leadership. Though the party leadership has allowed more or less freedom for decisions at lower levels over the years, fundamental economic power, for example, over allocation of resources and responsibility for their use, has remained a prerogative of the very top of the political structure. Complete control was attempted by the Bolsheviks during the mobilization period just after the revolution, referred to as "war communism," but actually achieved only under the central planning and collectivization instituted under Stalin. In an ironic reversal of the Marxist axiom, in the Soviet Union politics dominates economics.

This means that an astonishing number of specific and concrete economic decisions, as well as the determination of central policy direction, are made at the top of the political system. As Edward Hewett's study of Politburo agendas indicates,

> In the four meetings that normally occur every month, the Politburo can hear reports and issues decrees relating to the Yamburg natural gas pipeline, the preparation of livestock for winter, the development of the television industry, changes in selected retail prices, and the rational use of the various bus fleets in the USSR. The development of a particular town, the state of shoe production, and the use of a Soviet-developed technology in assembly lines, techniques for stock-breeding, the management of the Chernobyl' disaster, and the fall harvest are additional, fairly random samples of what Politburo members discuss and make the subject of decrees.[7]

In a country as vast as the USSR, with a complex industrial and agricultural economy to oversee—not to mention other annoyances such as arms control and a war in Afghanistan—it is to be expected that not all decisions made by a ruling body of a dozen or so individuals will be timely or correct.

Of course the Politburo does not work out every detail of the economy. That has usually been the job of the government, especially Gosplan and its subordinate units and the various ministries. This has given rise to an immense bureaucracy that must decide not only about the production and distribution of

---

[6] Seweryn Bialer, *The Soviet Paradox* (New York: Vintage Books, 1986), p. 63.

[7] Ed A. Hewett, *Reforming the Soviet Economy* (Washington, DC: The Brookings Institution, 1988), p. 164.

millions of products but also about the resources necessary for the millions of others needed to produce those. As in any organization with such responsibilities, battles occur over the allocation of resources, battles in which control over the raw materials, technology, and information become valuable weapons. In such a situation, where no market or competition "corrects" for poor choices, and where the requirements for information are immense, the decisions that emerge may reflect the results of political battles more than the economy's real needs. Even were such battles not present, such a complex of administrative decisions from the top down restricts the flexibility of an economy and its ability to respond to changing needs. While such a system may have been appropriate for the forced-march type of industrialization the country went through in the 1930s or in wartime, and though it may have some benefits for consumers (see page 435), it has proved a drag on efficient economic performance, especially after the economic "base" is established and more complex needs are evident.

Without a market to set prices, competition to encourage innovation, or the possibility of bankruptcy, a factory manager has no incentive to improve a product or even to try to sell more of it than the year before. It is only necessary to fulfill the state-set quota. Indeed, if a Soviet manager wanted to produce more of a product by introducing new technology or offering workers higher wages, such decisions would usually not be his or hers to make. Since prices are controlled by the government and since not profit but production—meeting or surpassing quotas—is the key to success, enterprise managers have strong incentives to hoard resources, both material and human. Thus, the resources necessary to expand or improve production are not likely to be available unless a high-level decision is made in favor of investment in that particular sector.

Finally, the Soviet economy is beset by a huge amount of duplication of economic effort. Because it is, as Hungarian economist Janus Kornai terms it, a "shortage economy" in which enterprises and ministries are answerable essentially only to those above them—they do not have to compete for real "customers"—there is a strong incentive for ministries and enterprises to control all aspects of whatever it is they produce. Thus, instead of buying from a supplier the electronic components or raw materials that go into making, say, a truck, the Soviet ministry of automotive industry will produce much of its own components and materials. More than that, because production is the key to success, factory managers and ministries will try hard to attract workers and keep them satisfied by making sure they receive the things they need most. Hence consumer goods, housing, and even food will typically be produced through enterprises and ministries that nominally have nothing to do with those sectors. Control of resources is the name of the game, but this kind of ministerial autarchy without countervailing pressure to reduce costs (no competitors, prices set by the state) creates immense duplication of effort and inefficient use of already scarce resources.

These difficulties are compounded by an ideological favoritism on the part of the leaders toward heavy industry, as opposed to consumer goods. This emphasis is partly derived from Marxism, which stresses industrial development and an emphasis on the "means of production." It is reinforced by a Soviet desire to become and remain a world industrial power. For the Soviet economy this has meant that building new plants and equipment for heavy industry has had first claim on the investment budget, while funds for agriculture, transportation or consumer goods receive smaller pieces of the pie. Industries devoted to "consumption" or "nonproductive" services, that is, those that relate to people instead of goods, are last to get supplies and new technology, and they receive a consistently lower share of investment. In 1980, for example, of more than 1.7 billion rubles of investment, two-thirds went into "productive" capital, and of that, fully one-half went to industry—especially, machine building, metals, and fuels and power—and only 20 percent into agriculture.[8] In the Soviet system these are essentially political decisions and reflect the long-standing policy preference for developing the industrial base of the country. In addition, the country's immense military needs and establishment have made a constant claim on some 20 percent of the country's productive capacity. Most developed countries share this desire to develop and keep a strong industrial economy, but few governments have the kind of political power needed to force their own economies in this direction, as the Soviet government does.

Changing such an emphasis in the economy thus runs up against both ideology and politics. Introducing any form of independent decision making at the factory level—allowing enterprise managers to determine the size of their labor force or the price of their product, for example—means taking this power away from the party and government, which currently make and implement these decisions. Moreover, from the ideological point of view, if such decisions are removed from the party's direction, how can society be protected from the abuses common to capitalism, such as unemployment, in-

flation, and the stark differences between rich and poor that exist in such systems?

The dominant mass political culture also tends to support keeping things as they are because of what has been called a "tacit bargain" between the government and the population.[9] After the passing of Stalinism and the crises of the 1930s and the war years, the Soviet population at long last began to enjoy a degree of personal security, an end to mass arrests and totalitarian terror, and some economic progress. In return for satisfying those basic human needs, the Soviet rulers enjoyed a degree of public political acquiescence and a low likelihood of the kind of social upheaval seen in Hungary or Poland.

After the hardships of the collectivization and rapid industrialization period and the suffering of the war years, there is no doubt things did improve for the Soviet populations. Living standards improved, access to apartments and appliances expanded, food supply became more assured and varied, and educational and employment opportunities grew. Overall, per capita private consumption—a measure of how much of what the country produces is consumed by individuals—grew during 1953–70 by an average of 4.1 percent annually (in comparison, the figure for the United States during this period was 2.2 percent).[10]

However, with the onset of economic difficulties in the past decade, the regime's ability to keep its end of the bargain eroded. The continued emphasis on heavy industry and neglect of investment in agriculture or consumer goods meant that beyond basic needs, the economy could not keep the standard of

---

[8] U.S. Congress, *Soviet Economy in the 1980's: Problems and Prospects,* part 1 (Washington, DC: U.S. Government Printing Office, 1982), p. 131.

[9] Colton, *The Dilemma of Reform,* pp. 47–50.

[10] Gertrude Schroeder, "Soviet Living Standards in Comparative Perspective," in *Quality of Life in the Soviet Union,* ed. Horst Herlemann (Boulder, CO: Westview Press, 1987), p. 21.

Comparing Costs

How many minutes (unless otherwise noted) of work time it takes an average industrial worker in Washington and Moscow to purchase various goods and services.

	Washington	Moscow		Washington	Moscow
One loaf of rye bread	18	11	A bar of soap	3	17
One chicken	18	189	Bus fare for two miles	7	3
One grapefruit	6	112	Baby sitter per hour	44	279
One liter of milk	4	20	First class postage stamp	2	3
One liter of red wine	37	257	Men's haircut	62	34
One head of cabbage	7	7	A pair of jeans	4 (hours)	56 (hours)
Three ounces of tea	10	36	A pair of men's shoes	6 (hours)	37 (hours)
Car wash	40	139	Washing machine	46 (hours)	177 (hours)

Note: Study conducted in October 1986

SOURCE: *New York Times,* June 28, 1987; Radio Free Europe/Radio Liberty.

living growing. The rate of annual growth of per capita private consumption fell to 2.6 percent during 1970–81 and was less than 2 percent in the last part of the 1970s. The standard of living for the average Soviet worker remained far behind that of his counterpart in the West, as it always had been (see box), but it also lagged behind the standard achieved in other communist countries. In 1981, for example, Soviet consumers ate less meat and more grain and potatoes than their comrades in most of Eastern Europe. Consumers in Hungary, Poland, East Germany, and Czechoslovakia had more home appliances and many more private cars than people in the USSR. Urbanization of the country put increased pressure on an already inadequate housing stock and educational system. Health care provision proved inadequate. The infant mortality rate increased. For the first time since World War II, a modern industrial country showed a marked *decline* in life expectancy.[11] The gaps in the standard of living caused by stagnating and uneven growth were exacerbated by the politics of the Brezhnev regime, which tolerated corruption and privilege for members of the elite and those connected with them.

ADDRESSING THE PROBLEM OF ECONOMIC REFORM

While the economic indicators can flash warning signals, actually reversing the pattern of economic stagnation means addressing both the economic and the political aspects of the problem.

The approach of Mikhail Gorbachev and those around him to this complex problem has been to try to tackle all its key dimensions: political, economic, and ideological.

Politically, Gorbachev and his supporters took a major step by publicly identifying the problems affecting the economy and labeling them for what they were. This in itself represented a significant change in a political system in which leaders had only spoken of success. At the 27th Party Congress in 1986, Gorbachev said:

[11] Trevor Buck and John Cole, *Modern Soviet Economic Performance* (Oxford: Basil Blackwell, 1987), p. 60.

The situation today is such that we cannot limit ourselves to partial improvements. A radical reform is needed. Its meaning consists in truly subordinating the whole of our production to the requirements of society, to the satisfaction of people's needs, in orienting management towards raising efficiency and quality, accelerating scientific and technological progress, promoting a greater interest of people in the results of their work, initiative and socialist enterprise in every link of the national economy, and, above all, in the work collectives.

In this speech and several others, Gorbachev went on to outline specific problems that needed to be addressed, such as producing not simply more of something but better somethings more efficiently, improving the fit between scientific research and the needs of the economy, improving planning, finance, the system of prices and supply and strengthening basic Soviet enterprises against "the petty tutelage" of ministries and departments.

The willingness to address frankly the system's problems has been part of a policy of *glasnost* or "voicing" of real issues. Newspapers and journals as well as radio and television began to feature discussions, exchanges, even call-in shows on all sorts of previously restricted subjects, such as the war in Afghanistan, or missing subjects, such as crime, drug addiction or AIDS. Relaxation of strictures in cultural areas brought back to society the contributions of poets and writers such as Vladimir Vysotsky and Boris Pasternak, whose work had been banned in the USSR, and even those of Aleksandr Solzhenitsyn exiled under Brezhnev, as well as new writings, plays, and films with critical themes.

With regard to economic reform, *glasnost* facilitated criticism of poor performance and identification by Gorbachev of those who might try to block reform to protect their own prerogatives. One of the aims of *glasnost*

was to alert those responsible for the performance of the economy that their shortcomings, their simply doing what had always been done, or their blocking or undermining needed reforms would become public knowledge. Those with knowledge of such shortcomings have been encouraged to speak out without fear that they would be penalized. But *glasnost* in the economy serves a broader political purpose as well. For the average citizens, who were aware of the system's failings even if these were not acknowledged by the leadership, it validates what they already knew. It thus improves the credibility of the regime and provides the public with a symbolic payoff—especially important if economic payoffs will be some time in coming.

In addition, *glasnost* speaks specifically to a very important sector of society, the *intelligentsia,* or well-educated, highly trained people. Urbanization and rapid modernization of the Soviet Union, especially since World War II, has created a new generation of urban professionals who are desirous of greater freedom as well as better living conditions.[12] Gorbachev needs such people to be willing to work and contribute their talents and ideas to the improvement of the economic and social situation. To do so these people will require a more open environment in which to work and exchange ideas. They have to feel that if they speak out, criticize poor performance or specific policies or offer alternatives, they will not suffer the fate of Andrei Sakharov, who was exiled to Gorky in 1980 for criticizing Soviet policy and supporting human rights activists. The release of Sakharov from exile in 1987 and the more tolerant treatment of dissidents since then were part of *glasnost* and were important signals to the intelligentsia that Gorbachev wanted their contribution.

[12] Moshe Lewin, *The Gorbachev Phenomenon* (Berkeley: University of California Press, 1988).

Dissident and academician Andrei Sakharov gives a press conference at the USSR Foreign Ministry, June 1988.
SOURCE: V. Kuzmin/TASS.

At the elite level, Gorbachev moved to ensure his political power by removing opponents, both those who might have been more conservative, such as Politburo member and party chief of Leningrad, Grigorii Romanov, and those who seemed to want to go too far too fast, such as candidate Politburo member and party leader of Moscow, Boris Yeltsin. In the changing of the guard, Gorbachev was aided by nature (the death of several key holdovers) and circumstance (the unimpeded flight into Moscow in 1987 of a small private plane piloted by a young West German, which provoked a housecleaning in the defense ministry). In the Politburo, in the Central Committee, in the central government and throughout the republics, a purge took place, beginning in 1985, and accelerating after a Central Committee plenum in January 1987. By the beginning of 1988, virtually the entire Politburo had been replaced or removed (leaving the Politburo at 12) and the Secretariat had been expanded from 4 to 14 and filled with Gorbachev appointees. Gorbachev appointed his own prime minister, defense minister, KGB head and foreign minister. Andrei Gromyko, who had held this last post for 28 years, became president of the Presidium of the Supreme Soviet for a short time and then was replaced as president by Gorbachev himself and removed from the Politburo. In Gorbachev's first three years as party leader, 11 of 13 deputy chairmen of the Council of Ministers and three-quarters of the Council itself were replaced. Six of 14 republican party chiefs were replaced, as well as roughly half of all secretaries (including first secretaries) of *oblast,* city and district party committees.[13] Gorbachev did not make himself unassailable by these actions, but he did lessen the chances that his program of economic reform would be cut off at the top. Still, judging from Gorbachev's own criticism of the bureaucracy, the program ran into opposition lower down.

The actions taken on the economy amounted to nothing less than the most far-reaching attempts since the New Economic Policy to change the way the system operates. In 1987, a law was passed making some 60 percent of the economy "self-financing." That is, enterprises are now supposed to be able to find their own suppliers, determine wage levels in accordance with employee performance, and raise their own financing. Put into effect at the beginning of 1988, the new system still involves substantial restrictions. The ministries remain responsible for the overall performance of enterprises in their sectors, and enterprises will still have to rely overwhelmingly on centrally determined sources of supplies and prices. In fact, state orders still account for roughly 90 percent of industrial production.[14] As a spur to efficient performance, a specifically capitalist device has been introduced. In 1987 the first enterprise went bankrupt, a construction firm in Leningrad, and 2,000 workers were switched to other jobs.

The pressures and constraints at the factory level illustrate the political aspects of economic reform. Those who are currently making economic decisions and exercising

control—in the party and ministries—are loathe to give up this power. On the other hand, it is very clear that better performance is necessary, and the top leadership of the country is pressing for change. Several leaders have acknowledged the fact that very little of what is manufactured in the Soviet Union meets world standards. Most of that is produced in a wasteful and costly manner (see box). In 1986 a new ministry, Gospriomka, was set up to inspect the output of many factories to ensure that quality as well as quantity was produced.

But putting this policy into practice creates other problems. In one bus-producing factory in Likino, near the Ural mountains, old equipment was being used in 1987 to produce the same model of bus as had been produced in 1970. When Gospriomka began inspecting—and rejecting—production, workers' salaries, which are tied to production norms, fell. As one worker explained, "The number of buses coming off

---

An appreciation of the inefficiency of the Soviet economy can be gained by comparing the amount of energy and steel used to produce the equivalent of $1,000 of gross domestic product in several countries.

	Energy used per $1,000 of GDP	Steel used per $1,000 of GDP
Eastern Europe		
Poland	1,515	135
Soviet Union	1,490	135
East Germany	1,356	88
Hungary	1,058	88
Western Europe		
France	502	42
West Germany	565	52
Britain	820	38

Figures for 1979–80. Energy in kg of coal equivalent. Steel in kg.

SOURCE: *The Economist,* May 30–June 6, 1987.

---

[13] Jerry F. Hough, "Gorbachev Consolidating Power," *Problems of Communism* 36:34; Thane Gustafson and Dawn Mann, "Gorbachev's Next Gamble," *Problems of Communism* 36(1987):10.

[14] *Financial Times,* March 16, 1988, p. 2.

the conveyor belt decreased. Instead of 33–34 a day we were making 20–25 so we were not getting our bonuses any longer. I used to make an extra 100 rubles. Everybody lost at least 60–70 rubles."[15] As this situation was duplicated across the country, worker dissatisfaction and strikes spread, illustrating one aspect of the political fallout from trying to reform the Soviet economy. In September 1989 a group called the United Front of Workers of Russia was formed to coordinate and focus action against reforms which some workers saw as detrimental to their situation.

Other reforms have extended new opportunities for private economic activity. Until recently virtually the only legal private economic activity was the working of small private plots by peasants after their labor on the collective farm. Though constituting less than 2 percent of the land, these produced 60 percent of the country's fruit, 28 percent of its meat and 23 percent of its milk.[16] Trying to capitalize on this productivity, new policies essentially privatized part of the output of collective farms by allowing farms to sell their surplus—the amount not delivered to the state—on private markets or to the government at double the regular state price. Gorbachev himself supports moving away from the system of collective farms and has endorsed the idea of giving long-term leases on the land to individual farmers. In 1989 the government began offering farmers convertible currency for their output, but with little to buy with it, few took the offer.

Also in 1987 the government moved to make legal the operation of individual private enterprise in most services (for example, taxis). Under this law, an individual can run a repair shop, for instance, as a private business but cannot employ anyone outside his or her own family. Other new policies encouraged the development of small cooperatives that can hire employees and operate in various sectors of the economy. This reform was aimed at harnessing individual initiative in traditionally backward sectors of the economy, such as services, and thus provide some improvement in the standard of living for the average citizen. In a very short time the number of cooperatives expanded rapidly. By 1989 there were already an estimated 100,000 operating in the country.

But legalizing individual private enterprise also brings into the legal—and thus more controllable—economy many of the services that were being performed already *na levo* (on the side). As with other aspects of reform, this action reflected the regime's sometimes contradictory desire for improvement in key aspects of the economy but also for continued or even expanded control of the economy. Politically such reform actions are not without their risks. Legalizing private services and small businesses and tying workers' bonuses to performance, instead of appearance, on the job will increase economic stratification in the society; some people will do better than others, some a lot better. While this is a common situation in capitalist countries such as the United States, in the USSR it runs counter to the widespread value of egalitarianism (confirmed by recent Soviet studies) and may further provoke public unhappiness and political opposition. During a central committee plenum in 1988 Gorbachev responded to such criticisms

No sooner do people in pay-your-own-way collectives get pay rises through better final results, than protests and irritated voices come to be heard, complaining that those people are allegedly earning too much.

Under socialism, however, the question can only be whether the wages have been earned or not, rather than whether they are high or low.

[15] *Financial Times,* October 16, 1987, p. 3.
[16] Ed A. Hewett, "Reforming the Economy," *The Nation,* June 13, 1987, p. 803.

During the summer of that year the cooperative movement and its supporters mounted what would be called in the West a lobbying campaign to kill a finance ministry plan that would have heavily taxed the profits of cooperative enterprises. Still, in December 1988 the Council of Ministers announced new restrictions on the business activities of cooperatives and the next year a bill in the Supreme Soviet to outlaw cooperatives was only narrowly defeated.

When it comes to foreign economic questions, the reformers have begun to resolve the conflict between efficiency and control more in favor of efficiency. Recognizing the need for foreign trade and technology, the Gorbachev regime in 1987 and again in 1988 attacked the state monopoly on foreign trade

Grappling with the Consequences of Perestroika

The difficulty of dealing with the possible effects of ending subsidies to enterprises was evident in this interview with L.I. Abalkin, a leading economist in the Soviet Union.

Interviewer:
Nonetheless, is the bankruptcy of enterprises possible under conditions of financial autonomy? Will it not lead within certain limits to the appearance of unemployment?

Abalkin:
I do not think that it is necessary to use the word "bankruptcy." Closure, or the liquidation of unprofitable enterprises, is better. After all, unprofitability is a phenomenon alien to the nature of the socialist economy. If there are hopelessly sick enterprises that are essentially living off society, living at the expense of other people's work, and if no measures can help, then the enterprise must be liquidated and closed and its property must naturally be sold. That also benefits socialism.

At the end of 1989 the Soviet government acknowledged unemployment for the first time— some 3 million people.

SOURCES: *Sovetskaya Rossiya*, July 19, 1987, p. 3; *Financial Times*, January 26, 1990.

by extending to enterprises and cooperatives the right to engage in their own foreign trade; to deal with their foreign suppliers and customers directly, and to buy and sell the foreign currency they need to do business. While the new Ministry of Foreign Economic Relations still retains supervision over these activities, such decentralization is unprecedented in Soviet history.

Other new laws allowed direct foreign investment in the Soviet Union for the first time, and scores of foreign businesses making everything from plastics to pizza began joint ventures. Though some areas of the economy, such as mining, were off limits to foreign investors, within a short time the laws and practices were being modified further to encourage investment—for example, by allowing majority ownership by Western partners.

Action or inaction on prices illustrates a key political aspect of economic reform, that of regime-society relations. Soviet economists as well as political leaders recognize that price reform is one key to making the economy more efficient, responsive and productive. Especially in the food and consumer goods areas, retail prices do not reflect real costs, and the government makes up the difference between, for example, what it costs to raise livestock and the price of meat in the market. In this particular case, the price is estimated to reflect only 40 percent of real costs. In a capitalist economy a meat company would likely go bankrupt in such a situation. But in the Soviet Union, the government is the meat company and it cannot simply go out of business. Overall, it is estimated that subsidies consume 19 percent of the state budget. Allowing prices to find a level that better reflects costs would presumably bring more and better quality goods to market and allow prices to act as an economic "signal" to tell producers what is needed.

But Soviet workers *as consumers* have gotten used to low prices for their goods. In the

Moscow, 1988: The van-cafe "Astro Pizza" of the joint Soviet-American venture "Dialog".
SOURCE: SOVFOTO.

USSR rents have not changed since 1928, utility prices since 1946, and state-regulated food prices are as they were 20 to 30 years ago. As workers' salaries have increased, this has created a huge amount of surplus capital (accumulated savings in 1987 equalled more than 75 percent of all retail sales)[17] and shortages of many goods (known as "hidden inflation"). But low prices have helped avoid the kind of upheaval seen in Poland, and have contributed to giving the Soviet worker a sense of economic security that is uncommon in the West. Housing costs for the average Soviet family, for example, take only 6 percent of the family budget. To raise prices enough to make them reflect costs strikes directly at this sense of security. It means telling Soviet workers that not only are they now going to have to work harder and produce better goods or else find their pay cut or

maybe even their factory closed, and not only are consumer goods going to continue to be scarce until the economy improves; now workers will be told that the price of those goods that are available will go up, probably by quite a bit. Offering workers a package like this in the name of economic restructuring makes even the most secure regime nervous. Already the prices of some—many say the best—agricultural produce have increased as farmers sell their surplus on private markets. Faced with this particular bind between the needs of production and consumption, and lacking capitalist devices or ideology to help find a balance, Soviet leaders have opted for some delay on this issue. Price reform is to be introduced gradually, first in the wholesale sector and then in the retail sector.

Added into this mix is the ideological aspect. Economic reform in the Soviet Union must contend not only with officials in the planning sector who will lose power in a re-

[17] Schroeder, "Consumer Malaise in the Soviet Union: Perestroika's Achilles Heel?" *PlanEcon Report*, vol. IV, no. 11 (March 18, 1988), p. 5.

SOURCE: *Moscow News,* No. 14 (1989), p. 5.

The Ecological Issue: Not a Capitalist Monopoly

As the world learned dramatically in April 1986 when the Soviet nuclear reactor at Chernobyl exploded, ecological devastation is a risk which knows no boundaries. With the blossoming of *glasnost,* the breadth and depth of environmental deterioration and disasters in the USSR have become more subject to public discussion. River, sea, and air pollution and misuse of land and other of the country's vast natural resources have been shown to be a major problem.

In the early spring of 1989 more than one third of the population of the small village of Muzhichya Pavlovka in Siberia had to be completely and permanently evacuated because of the accumulated effects of having hundreds of thousands of tons of toxic gas deposited on them by the nearby Orenburg gas works.

form, but with politically powerful conservatives who feel that movement in the direction Gorbachev is taking is movement away from socialism. After all, introducing private economies might allow for exploitation, especially in the countryside. Allowing farmers to sell their surplus runs the risk, in the eyes of some, that some peasants could get rich, a phenomenon the country endured a bloody upheaval to remove in the 1930s. Cutting back or even whittling away the state monopoly in the economy inevitably alarms those who equate the Stalinist command economy with socialism, even with the "developed socialism" of Brezhnev. To change things significantly, Gorbachev must give an ideological justification for what he is doing, as well as a purely economic one.

Gorbachev and the people around him have addressed this aspect of reform by first stressing the creative aspects of Marxism and rejecting its use as an unchanging straightjacket. Speaking on the 70th anniversary of the Soviet revolution, for example, Gorbachev said:

> As a creative teaching, Marxism-Leninism is not a collection of ready-made recipes and doctrinaire instructions. Far from being narrow-minded dogma, Marxist-Leninist teaching provides an active interaction between innovative theoretical thinking with practice and with the course of revolutionary struggle itself.

It is important for Gorbachev to link his reforms to the party's historical and revolutionary roots, in order to prove their purity. Indeed, Gorbachev insists that it was the system built under his most notorious predecessor, Stalin, that was the deviation. While acknowledging the necessity of the accomplishments achieved under forced industrialization and collectivization, Gorbachev rejects the continued application of such a system. In his intellectual autobiography, *Perestroika,* Gorbachev writes:

> The management system which took shape in the thirties and forties began gradually to contradict the demand and conditions of economic progress. Its positive potential was exhausted. It became more and more of a hindrance, and gave rise to the braking mechanism which did us so much harm later. Methods for extreme situations were still being used.

In supporting ideologically what he describes as a "revolution" in Soviet management, Gorbachev explicitly links the new measures to the period of NEP under Lenin.

> We are now turning increasingly often to Lenin's last works and to the Leninist ideas of the

NEP and are striving to take from that experience everything that is valuable and necessary for us today.

Since Lenin is the highest god in the Soviet pantheon and his policies are revered, this is an important link to make.[18]

Making such an ideological pitch is important in the Soviet context, and it has been pursued vigorously. But it would not be effective without the pragmatic political actions taken by Gorbachev to remove or weaken possible opponents of reform. And neither the ideological nor the political moves will be sufficient to keep him in power or keep reform going if the economic results do not bear sufficient fruit to warrant the costs of changing a system that had not been revised in more than fifty years.

References and Suggested Readings

BUCK, TREVOR, and JOHN COLE. *Modern Soviet Economic Performance.* Oxford: Basil Blackwell, 1987.

DELLENBRANT, JAN AKE. *The Soviet Regional Dilemma.* Armonk, NY: M. E. Sharpe, Inc., 1986.

GOLDMAN, MARSHALL I. *Gorbachev's Challenge.* New York: W. W. Norton, 1987.

GORBACHEV, MIKHAIL. *Perestroika: New Thinking for Our Country and the World.* New York: Harper & Row, 1987.

HEWETT, ED A. "Reforming the Economy." *The Nation,* June 13, 1987, pp. 802–804.

————. *Reforming the Soviet Economy.* Washington, DC: The Brookings Institution, 1988.

KORNAI, JANOS. *Economics of Shortage.* 2 vols. Amsterdam: North Holland, 1980, Vol. A.

NOVE, ALEC. *The Soviet Economic System.* Boston: Allen & Unwin, 1986.

[18] Some proponents of reform go even further. When asked what he though the "criteria of socialism" were, Soviet economist Leonid Abalkin answered, "Well, I can ask you the following: If the food problem has not been solved has socialism been built?" Moscow TV, October 17, 1988 (FBIS, October 24, 1988, p. 55).

No question of any significance can be decided without the Soviet Union or in opposition to it.

— ANDREI GROMYKO, SOVIET FOREIGN MINISTER, 1957–85

34

Policy Case II: Managing Soviet International Relations

For the USSR a second critical area of policy management lies beyond its borders. In the late twentieth century, all nations must deal with the outside world, no matter how strong they are or how they order their domestic society and economy. For the Soviet Union, sharing borders with twelve different countries, lying two-thirds in Asia and one-third in Europe, and having suffered invasion and occupation twice in this century alone, managing the country's international relations poses special problems.

Managing foreign policy is not like dealing with other aspects of public policy, which take place largely within the domestic arena. One critical difference is that the government cannot exercise as much control as with domestic issues. If, for example, the political leadership of the CPSU does not want its own public to hear of certain events or be allowed to engage in non-approved political activities, it can utilize censorship and control public political action. This is not possible internationally, where the "global public"

can be lobbied all the time by the USSR's adversaries and where those adversaries and all other actors are less subject to restrictions on their political behavior.

Second, the resources necessary to carry out effective foreign policies are not necessarily those available to the Soviet leadership. Militarily, there is no question that the Soviet Union is a superpower, with both a nuclear and a conventional force second to none. Economically, however, the Soviet Union is what economists call a "price taker": a weak and marginal actor due to the inefficiency and backwardness of its economy in many key areas and the relatively narrow range of its internationally tradeable goods. The muscular military aspects of Soviet foreign policy allow it to help a friendly group come to power, even far from the Soviet borders; but puny economic power offers precious little with which to help a new regime succeed—or for that matter, to help the USSR obtain what if needs for its own economy.

Third, in international relations the outcome of a policy decision, or non-decision, can have momentous consequences. A domestic policy action may be wrong or ineffective in the domestic setting, but in most cases such mistakes will not threaten the existence of the country or the regime in power or even the lives of its citizens. An inability to manage foreign affairs, however, where situations of potential and real conflict—including armed conflict—are common, can lead to the nation's destruction.

THE HISTORICAL LEGACY

The modern history of Russia, from the time of the emergence of the medieval state of Muscovy from Mongol domination (fourteenth century) until the Soviet period, has been one of continual struggle to gain governing control over its own territory and to expand the definition of what "its own territory" means. During the sixteenth and seventeenth centuries, while the growing country suffered many grievous defeats and intrusions at the hands of more powerful European neighbors in the west and the Ottoman Empire in the south, Moscow's rule did expand into central Asia and the Far East. By the end of the eighteenth century, with the weakening of both the Polish commonwealth and the Turkish empire, Russia was able to reverse its fortunes, gain territory and influence and become the largest and most populous country in Europe.

Wars and rebellions in the Russian empire continued, however, and after the defeat of Napoleon's invading forces in 1812, the nineteenth and early twentieth centuries were not times of foreign policy successes. As the Ottoman empire decayed in the Balkans and new states were emerging, Russia showed a keen interest in spreading its own influence into this region, in the Black Sea and over the narrow straits separating this body from the Mediterranean Sea. But repeatedly Russian interests in the region were blocked by a combination of Austria-Hungary, Prussia and, especially, Great Britain. Defeat in the Crimean War (1856) at the hands of a European coalition led by England was followed by embarrassment at the Congress of Berlin in 1878. After securing major gains in a war against Turkey in 1877–78—including Romanian independence, occupation of a large Bulgaria and substantial Russian influence elsewhere in the Balkans—Russia was obliged to give back many of these gains and acquiesce to continued British predominance in the Turkish straits and the Black Sea. The empire was simply not strong enough to challenge the major European powers. Its other rival for influence in the Balkans, the Austro-Hungarian Empire, was handed administration of Bosnia-Herzogovina at the 1878 conference, a territory which it annexed in 1908, again over futile Russian objections.

Russia's most spectacular humiliation of the period was its defeat by Japan in the Russo-Japanese war of 1904–05. In the space of ten months both the Russian Pacific and Atlantic fleets were destroyed, and major Japanese gains in the Far East were ensured. The costs and results of fighting this war contributed to domestic upheaval of the 1905 revolution. Similarly, the strain on the empire and its ineffectiveness in World War I contributed directly to the final collapse of the autocracy and the emergence of the Soviet Union.

Though the new regime's goals were different—promoting world revolution, for example—it was no more successful in foreign relations than its predecessor had been. Forced to sue for peace to prevent further German advance (the treaty of Brest-Litovsk of 1918), the new socialist republic surrendered the share of Poland it had held since the eighteenth century, along with substantial portions of territory in Ukraine and Byelorussia. The Baltic republics of Latvia, Estonia, and Lithuania became independent, and in the south, Bessarabia (which had gone back and forth in the nineteenth century) was lost to Romania. Though some Bolsheviks, such as Nikolai Bukharin, argued for continuing the war in order to spread the revolution, Lenin stressed the need to safeguard the new home of socialism and secure peace, however unpleasant the terms.

Between 1918 and 1920 the regime did succeed in holding off a combined intervention by the United States, Britain, and France in European Russia and (along with Japan) in the Far East; and in 1920, in the brief Polish war, Russian armies did save Kiev and drive back Polish forces until a treaty established the eastern boundary with that reborn state. But despite the expansion of Bolshevik control into most of the old empire and the establishment in 1919 of the *Comintern,* or Communist International, revolutions failed to take and hold power elsewhere. Such upheavals, which Bolsheviks had expected, might have meant a less hostile world for the USSR. As it was, Soviet interwar diplomacy followed dual and in fact contradictory tracks. On the one hand, to protect the Soviet state and try to gain for it what benefits could be derived from international involvement, the government signed agreements and established relations with countries such as Great Britain and even its former enemy, Germany. On the other hand, through the instrument of the Comintern, the CPSU supported the world revolution its leaders expected and hoped would come, even in those states with whom it was officially conducting friendly relations.

By the end of the 1920s, though, with failures of revolutions in Germany, Hungary, Finland, and especially, China (where communists were massacred in 1927), the promise of world revolution had faded. At the same time, the self-absorption and upheaval that accompanied rapid industrialization and collectivization kept the USSR as weak as it had always been in affecting affairs outside its borders.

In 1938 this weakness was made starkly clear in its own front yard. Faced with growing German power and the successful moves of Adolf Hitler in reoccupying the Rhineland, rebuilding and equipping his army and forcing union with Austria, the leaders of Great Britain and France met with Hitler in Munich in September. There they agreed to the German demand to hand over from the new state of Czechoslovakia—created after World War I—the extreme western and mostly German part of Czechoslovakia known as the Sudetenland. Agreeing to this demand crippled Czechoslovakia, and was soon followed by its total absorption by Germany. For the Soviet Union, the Munich agreement had broad and frightening implications. The acquiescence of the West in the dismemberment of Czechoslovakia proved to the USSR that the Western capitalist powers would do nothing to restrain Hitler as long as he moved toward the East, that the Western powers could not be trusted, and that their long-standing hostility toward the Bolsheviks, evident in the intervention in the civil war, still prevailed. From the Soviets' point of view, territories on their own border had been handed over to a mortal enemy, and they had been powerless to prevent it.

Faced with such a situation and fearing the rising power of *both* Germany and Japan, which was already engaged in a full-scale war in China, the USSR moved to avoid or put off its most dreaded nightmare, war on both western and eastern fronts. Nonaggression pacts were signed with Germany in 1939 and Japan in 1941. The former, known as the Molotov-Ribbentrop Pact after the names of the respective foreign ministers, also contained secret protocols by which Germany agreed to allow the Soviet Union to occupy

Glasnost and Foreign Policy

Under Mikhail Gorbachev criticism of the way things have been managed in the Soviet Union extends also to foreign policy. Reexaminations of past policies in particular have come in for scrutiny and fuller disclosure. In August 1988, as nationalism began to take on wider expression in the Baltics, the secret protocols signed between the Soviet Union and Germany in August 1939, which had never before been published or even officially acknowledged in the USSR, were published by an Estonian newspaper. Though brief and phrased in bland diplomatic language, they signified the end of the independence of the Baltic states and territorial changes at the expense of Poland and Romania, all of which remain in effect to this day.

The text of the protocol reads as follows:

On the occasion of the signing the nonaggression treaty between the German State and the Union of the Soviet Socialist Republics, the undersigned, fully authorized representatives of both sides, have discussed, in strictly confidential talks, the delineation of their respective spheres of influence in Eastern Europe.

These negotiations lead to the following result:

1. In case of a territorial and political reorganization of the area belonging to the Baltic states (Finland, Estonia, Latvia and Lithuania), the northern border of Lithuania will also mark the boundary between the German and the USSR spheres of influence. In this connection, both sides will recognize the interests of Lithuania in the region of Vilnius.

2. In case of a territorial and political reorganization in the area belonging to the state of Poland, the approximate boundary between the German and the USSR spheres of influence will run along the line of the Narew, Vistula and San rivers.

The question of whether or not preserving an independent Poland will serve the interests of both sides, and what should be the boundaries of that state, can finally be settled only in the course of future political development.

In any case, both governments will settle this question by way of an amicable agreement.

3. In southeastern Europe, the Soviet side asserts its interests in Bessarabia. The German side declares a complete lack of political interest in that region.

4. Both sides will keep this document in strict secrecy.

SOURCE: Rahua Haal (Tallinn), August 10, 1988 (FBIS, September 16, 1988, p. 69).

---

nearly one-third of what was then Polish territory, as well as Finland, Estonia and Latvia, and to retake Bessarabia from Romania (see box). Except for Finland, which fought Soviet armies to a standstill during the "Winter War" of 1939–40, all these territories as well as Lithuania and additional territory in northeastern Romania (northern Bukovina) were occupied by the USSR in 1940.

None of this prevented invasion by Germany, which began in 1941 and was not halted until later that year in Moscow and in 1942 in Stalingrad (now Volgograd). It was only Germany's defeat and dismemberment and the occupation by the Soviet Union of most of Eastern Europe that gave the country for the first time the power to set things up in this region the way it preferred. For the USSR the lessons of the late Tsarist period and the interwar period were clear: The West could not be trusted except on a temporary basis as necessary; only the Soviet Union's own involvement could ensure that dangers would not develop in regions that were considered vital to national security; military power was the ultimate guarantor of that involvement and in all cases must be kept at a level sufficient to ensure the defeat of the country's attackers and adversaries.

THE FOREIGN POLICY APPROACH OF THE POSTWAR PERIOD

After World War II, achieving these goals proved easier in some respects but more complicated, expensive and dangerous in others. Old enemies, such as Germany and Japan, were defeated, occupied and, in the case of Germany, divided. Soviet troops were in occupation from Berlin to Asia, and even former Western adversaries such as Britain and France were economically and militarily exhausted. Moreover, within five years after the end of the world war, the number of states that were communist and allied with the Soviet Union grew to ten and included half of Europe as well as the world's most populous state, China. The Soviet Union was now a superpower, and its major adversary was now the world's other superpower, the United States.

Thus, foreign policy management for the USSR after World War II became an attempt to achieve persisting goals under new circumstances. The old ideal of unchallengeable protection against foreign invasion, especially from Germany, remained prominent, and was ensured through the existence of a substantial conventional armed force both inside the USSR itself and in Eastern Europe. To this was added the need for alliance management, as the Soviet Union tried to ensure conformity and support from the new communist states in Eastern Europe and China. But beyond this historical legacy, protection after World War II meant insuring that the only state really capable of doing great harm to the USSR or its new international situation, the United States, be prevented from doing so.

Alliance management proved difficult from the first. Differences as to how socialism was to be applied in Eastern Europe combined with old-fashioned nationalism and internal Soviet politics to create upheavals in Hungary, Poland, and Czechoslovakia. Yugoslavia and Albania, each for their own reasons and at different times, broke with the Soviet Union altogether. Others such as Poland and Romania began in the 1960s to pursue external policies that were in significant ways quite at variance with those of the Soviet Union. The USSR used various means to try to keep the "socialist commonwealth" in line, including bilateral diplomacy, military pressure and force, and the mechanism of multilateral alliances, the Council for Mutual Economic Assistance (1949) and the Warsaw Pact (1955).

The most significant loss to the new Soviet international position was the break with China in the early 1960s. The roots of the dispute extend back to the prewar period when the Soviet party, then the only ruling communist party, seemed not to appreciate the differences between its situation and that of the Chinese, and gave often inappropriate advice to its Chinese comrades (such as to cooperate with the noncommunist Kuomintang in a rebellion in 1927—which ended in a massacre of Chinese communists). Soviet support for the Chinese communists fighting for control after World War II was decidedly restrained, evidently to forestall Western fears and involvement. At the end of World War II, the Soviets even signed a treaty with the then-ruling noncommunist government of China under Chiang Kai-shek, while continuing to help the communist forces militarily in Manchuria. After the Chinese communists' victory in 1949 and throughout the 1950s, the two states did cooperate extensively. But differences appeared, especially over foreign policy and specifically over how to deal with the United States. When domestic reform under Nikita Khrushchev was combined in the early 1960s with a more conciliatory approach toward the United States and some progress on arms control, the regime of party leader Mao Zedong unleashed a torrent of criticism of Soviet policies, accused Moscow of "revisionism," capitulating to the United States and not supporting the rule of the Chinese Communist Party. What became known as "the Sino-Soviet split" burst into view.

Since that time, though leaders have changed in both countries, the two communist giants have contested with each other—sometimes violently—over a range of issues both domestic and international. For Soviet foreign policy this has meant that in addition to a powerful global adversary in the form of the United States, it faces an additional, vigorous and often very active opponent in China. While much weaker militarily, the Chinese have challenged the Soviet influence in various parts of the world, including Africa and especially Asia. Ideologically, the Chinese break sundered Soviet claims of being the leading communist party and the spiritual center of communism. In the 1960s and early 1970s, the Chinese accused the Soviet leadership of abandoning the revolution at home and of joining with the United States in a division of the world between two "hegemonies," that of imperialism (United States) and "social-imperialism" (USSR).

In the late 1970s and the 1980s, as the Chinese themselves modified their views and practices—encouraging private enterprise and engaging in a wide variety of international diplomatic and economic ties—the ideological aspects of the Sino-Soviet conflict receded. But the traditional aspects of interstate conflict remained. The Chinese oppose the extension of Soviet influence into Asia and have been very concerned about the substantial Soviet military buildup in southeast Asia. They have countered Soviet support for the Vietnamese invasion and occupation of

Cambodia, begun in 1978, by sending arms of their own to Khmer Rouge guerillas fighting there. The Soviets' own invasion in 1979 of Afghanistan, which borders both countries, presented, in the Chinese view, a second serious obstacle to any improvement in Soviet-Chinese relations. Finally, the presence of some one million Soviet troops along their common 4,500-mile border and inside the Soviet-allied People's Republic of Mongolia represents a military threat to China. The exact specifications of much of this border are in dispute, and armed clashes have occurred between Chinese and Soviet forces. In opposing Soviet power, the Chinese have forged a virtual alliance with the United States. Thus the Soviet Union finds itself with the political equivalent of a two-front war: military and political adversaries in both East and West.

While China is not really a military threat to the USSR, the United States is. Hence the centerpiece of Soviet foreign policy since the end of World War II has been its relations with the United States. In managing this complex and dangerous relationship, Soviet aims have been to: (a) ensure the physical security of the USSR; (b) attach to itself as many political and military allies as possible while ensuring that the United States does not wean away any of its existing allies; (c) erode U.S. and, more recently, Chinese influence wherever possible; and (d) secure from the global economy the wherewithal to allow the Soviet economy to function as effectively as possible, while ensuring that the ideological and structural bases of socialism are not threatened.

Since Khrushchev, Soviet leaders have realized that the greatest international threat to the continued existence of their state and socialism is a nuclear war, in which all of their gains would be lost. To protect the Soviet Union from what it sees as an American threat, and to support its own pretensions to global power, Soviet policy has been to try to match or exceed the development of the American nuclear arsenal. The United States exploded a nuclear device in 1945; the Soviet Union did so in 1949; the United States exploded a hydrogen bomb in 1950, the USSR in 1953. Both the United States and the USSR have developed new and more sophisticated ways of depositing these bombs on each other, including intercontinental ballistic missiles, multiple warhead missiles, missiles launched from land, submarines and supersonic aircraft. While the United States held clear nuclear superiority through the 1960s, by the end of the 1970s the two sides had what was described as "parity" in nuclear forces. Determining exact equivalence or who is "ahead" is exceptionally difficult because of the difference in weapons systems and in the mix of each side's nuclear force (see box).

Soviet nuclear weapons policy aims at building a force adequate to threaten the United States (and anyone else) while also negotiating where possible to limit or even reduce the nuclear arsenals. Not surprisingly, Soviet arms control proposals have aimed at stopping the development of or removing those weapons systems in which the United States has the lead, such as cruise missiles or strategic defense, while U.S. proposals usually call for cuts in those areas where the Soviet Union has a preponderance, such as in heavy missile launchers. Nuclear arms negotiations deal with the most dangerous and, to say the least, explosive part of the U.S.-Soviet relationship, and they are almost always long, difficult, and technically and politically complex. Moreover, they are not separate from the overall status of U.S.-Soviet relations. A very limited Strategic Arms Limitation Treaty (SALT I) came into force in 1972,

Who's Ahead in the Strategic Nuclear Arms Race?

The *Soviet Union* has more land-based *missiles*:
   The USSR has deployed 1,398 intercontinental ballistic missiles (ICBMs).
   The US has deployed 1,010 intercontinental ballistic missiles.
   The USSR has deployed 944 sea-launched ballistic missiles (SLBMs).
   The US has deployed 640 sea-launched ballistic missiles.

The *United States* has more *warheads*:
   At sea the USSR has 336 SLBMs with multiple warheads and a total of 3,216 sea-launched warheads.
   At sea the US has 640 SLBMs with multiple warheads and a total of 6,656 sea-launched warheads.
   The USSR has 160 strategic bombers carrying 1,080 nuclear bombs and missiles.
   The US has 260 strategic bombers carrying 4,080 nuclear bombs and missiles.
   Total bombs and warheads (land-, sea-, air-launched) for USSR: 10,716.
   Total bombs and warheads for US: 12,846.

The *Soviet Union*'s force has more "heavy" missiles:
   The USSR has deployed 308 missiles with a throwweight of nearly 17,000 pounds; the largest US missile is roughly half that size.

The *United States* has a more accurate force:
   All US sea-launched missiles have a radius of probable landing significantly smaller (1/2 or 1/3 the size) than most Soviet sea-launched missiles.

SOURCE: *The Military Balance, 1986–1987* (London: International Institute for Strategic Studies, 1986).

putting a cap only on land- and sea-based missiles and leaving out bombers and qualitative improvements, such as adding more warheads to a missile. The second treaty on strategic weapons, SALT II, took nearly seven years to negotiate. Signed in 1979, this treaty did affect multiple warheaded weapons and bombers but still only limited, rather than cut, the size of each side's arsenal. By the end of the 1970s, however, the U.S.-Soviet détente that had spawned the negotiations had badly eroded because of conflicts over trade, the deployment in Europe of intermediate-range nuclear missiles, and Soviet involvement in Africa and especially Afghanistan. The SALT II treaty thus stood little chance of being ratified by the U.S. Congress when President Carter withdrew it from consideration after the Soviet invasion of Afghanistan in December 1979. Though each side pledged to uphold the terms of the treaty if the other did, the "new cold war" in the early 1980s found the United States and the Soviet Union no longer willing or able to engage in fruitful arms control negotiations. Amidst angry rhetoric, events multiplied that poisoned the negotiating atmosphere: During 1980–81 the Soviet Union exerted military and political pressure on Poland to crush *Solidarity,* the region's only independent trade union; in 1983 the United States invaded Grenada to oust a Marxist regime there; the Israeli invasion of Lebanon in 1982 brought Israel and Soviet ally Syria into direct conflict, and U.S. marines to Lebanon; NATO determination to proceed with installation of its own medium-range missiles in Europe to counter a huge Soviet preponderance in that area prompted Moscow to break off negotiations on intermediate-range missiles in 1983—at the time, the only negotiations going on. Finally, in late 1983 the low point was reached when Soviet air defense forces shot down a Korean civilian airliner that had strayed over Soviet territory in the Far East,

killing all 269 people on board, including a U.S. congressman.

When relations began to improve somewhat in the second administration of Ronald Reagan and under the new regime of Mikhail Gorbachev, prospects for arms control improved. Arms negotiations were resumed and finally in 1987 a treaty eliminating one class of weapons, short- and intermediate-range missiles, from Europe and Asia was achieved.

At the end of the 1980s a clear strategic goal for the Soviet Union was to restrain or eliminate the development by the United States of a strategic defense system. Suggested by President Reagan in 1983 and the target of significant investment as well as controversy since then, the strategic defense initiative (SDI), popularly referred to as "Star Wars," would, in theory, provide the United States with a defensive shield against Soviet missiles. The USSR sees this as potentially an offensive system, however, since it would give the United States the ability to launch a nuclear strike against the USSR without itself being vulnerable to a counter-strike. The system of "mutual assured destruction," in which each side's vulnerability presumably prevents Armaggedon, would be violated. As before, the Soviet approach has been to try to prevent the construction of such a system through a treaty while working on developing its own strategic defense system.

This same combination of international diplomacy and action—including military action if necessary—characterizes Soviet attempts to create a world in which there are more states favorable to them and fewer friendly toward its adversaries. For the USSR, fulfilling this broad aim means, in specific cases, using the means of international power—political, military and economic—to try to bring about events the leadership wants to occur and prevent those it does not want to occur in situations of often substantial uncertainty and incomplete control. Perhaps because of the relative weakness of its other options, the military method has often proved attractive to the USSR. In 1956, for example, the Soviet Union invaded Hungary to prevent changes and the possible overthrow of the communist regime there. In 1968 the USSR and all of its allies except Romania invaded Czechoslovakia to put an end to reforms there which, though started by the Czechoslovak Communist Party, would have profoundly altered the form of that regime and possibly others in the region. In 1979, after failing in every other way to create and secure an effective regime in Afghanistan, on its southern border, the USSR invaded that country also; but it found that in this case the military option did not succeed, and Soviet troops began to withdraw in 1988. In none of those cases was the foreign policy of the target state the major issue; but in all cases the leadership in the Kremlin feared that Soviet political interests would suffer a setback in that a less controllable government might take over, which could lead to a weaker military position and at the least, a gain for adversaries of the USSR.

On this basis the Soviet Union has also supported the use of force by its allies, or has created allies by providing the wherewithal for them to use force on their own. This was done successfully in Angola where, in 1975, revolutionary groups supported by the USSR and Cuba became the government. This approach has been less successful in the Middle East, where military force alone has proved insufficient to bring Soviet allies victory over their adversary, Israel, while Soviet diplomacy has been unable to bring about the kinds of settlement or exert the influence in the region that the USSR desires.

In the Middle East and elsewhere, the Soviet Union, like the United States, takes an *instrumental* view of regional conflicts. That is, it sees such conflicts not so much on their own terms but in terms of how they affect the overall struggle for influence between the Soviet Union and its adversaries, the United States and China. Thus, while one might expect the Soviet Union to always support communist groups or states against those that are not communist, this expectation is not always a good guide. In Angola, several different groups fighting for power in 1975 claimed adherence to Marxism, and in southeast Asia, Moscow supported the invasion of one socialist state, Cambodia, by another, Vietnam. While ideological concerns are not absent, sides are often chosen by the USSR, as they are by the United States, on the basis of "whatever he's for, I'm against."

This poses certain problems for management of foreign relations. First, one's local ally fighting for power or influence in a country or region may have a more direct, limited view of the conflict than the supporting superpower, in this case the USSR, which may see the conflict in broader global terms. In Africa, for example, the Soviet Union supported the seizure of power by revolutionary groups in both Mozambique and Angola. It provided military advisers and logistical support to Cuban troops which, in the case of Angola, actually fought alongside the Popular Movement for the Liberation of Angola (MPLA) against two other groups in a civil war, making a critical contribution to the success of the MPLA. Once conflicts in these two states were over, however, the quite limited ability of the Soviet Union to provide economic as opposed to military assistance became clear, and both Angola and Mozambique moved to improve relations with the West. Most ironic of all, in Angola the quintessential capitalist device, the multinational corporation (Gulf Oil), resumed production and had its oil fields guarded by Cuban troops, flown there by the Soviet Union!

Second, the Soviet Union, like the United States, has found allies difficult to manage. One of the reasons the Soviet Union invaded

Afghanistan in 1979 was that previous attempts to make the Marxist regime there effective—by getting it to modify radical policies that were stimulating rebellion, for example—did not succeed; nor did economic aid or the use of military advisers in support of the ally's own forces. Concerned about having a friendly regime on its border, and having committed itself to creating one, the USSR wound up trying to protect its investment with its own military.

In the Middle East, Soviet support of allies such as Egypt (until 1972), Syria and Libya has often put the country in the position of supporting military actions and risking conflict with the United States. When that has happened and Soviet allies have been defeated, as with Syrian forces in Lebanon in 1982, the USSR has rather consistently chosen to forgo the danger of all-out support for its allies. But in the 1973 Yom Kippur War, a confrontation with the United States did occur when Israel surrounded an Egyptian army and was in a position to annihilate it. The Soviet Union put some troops in the southern Ukraine on alert and threatened Israel. In response, the United States put its forces on full military alert worldwide. Israel responded to both American and Soviet pressure and did not destroy the surrounded Egyptian army. But no one can assume that such confrontations, derived from supporting one's allies, can always be avoided.

Finally, because of the inadequacies of the Soviet economy (discussed in Chapter 33), management of Soviet foreign relations also means seeking for the country what it cannot produce itself in sufficient quality or quantity, especially technology and manufactured goods, but also food. To pay for these goods the USSR must sell its own commodities, chiefly oil and natural gas. But being dependent on selling such commodities means the country will earn less when the price of oil falls, as it did in the beginning of the 1980s.

By Soviet estimates, the falling price of oil cost the Soviet Union $66 billion between 1985 and 1988.

Pursuing its own economic health can also conflict with the goal of keeping its friends and allies happy. The USSR sells oil and natural gas, as well as other raw materials, to the Eastern European countries—at special "friendship" prices. During the late 1970s these were below world prices. Though the prices have recovered, these states for the most part do not pay in convertible currencies such as dollars, that can be used to buy things on the international market, but in their own commodities. Thus the USSR incurs a substantial *opportunity cost* because it cannot sell this part of its oil and gas to the West for usable currency. Moreover, since many of the manufactured goods it buys from the Eastern European states are overpriced and of poor quality, the USSR in effect subsidizes these economies. One analysis suggests this subsidy cost the Soviet Union more than $87 billion between 1960 and 1980.[1]

The Soviet Union must also try to accomplish things in the international market without being part of the mainstream of the world capitalist economy, which is dominated by the United States, Japan and Western Europe. It is not a member of the International Monetary Fund (IMF) or the General Agreement on Tariffs and Trade (GATT), and, as noted in Chapter 27, it is not a significant actor in world trade. Its economy is based on socialist, collective, state-dominated planning principles rather than those of the market, competition, and private trade. For this reason, part of the economic reform introduced in 1986–1988 was designed to increase Soviet contacts with foreign economies by decentralizing control of foreign trade and by al-

[1] Michael Marrese and Jan Vanous, *Soviet Subsidisation of Trade with Eastern Europe* (Berkeley, CA: Institute of International Studies, 1983), p. 3.

lowing joint ventures with capitalist partners. Moscow has also explored the possibility of joining the IMF and GATT, but the Western countries have been cool to the idea.

Such actions illustrate the intertwining of politics and economics that makes management of foreign relations tricky. With regard to the West, Soviet economic needs will often pull foreign relations one way, say, toward improving and expanding ties in order to improve trade and overall economic cooperation. On the other hand, political aims, such as the need to support an ally or dominate a situation the Soviet Union sees as dangerous, will pull the other way, toward conflict with the United States. For example, when, with substantial Soviet involvement, martial law was declared by the Polish government in 1981 in order to crush the independent labor union *Solidarity,* the United States placed economic sanctions not only on Poland, but also on the Soviet Union, and encouraged the Western allies to do the same. These measures, such as forbidding the sale of various oil pipeline technologies, were designed to economically punish the Soviet Union for putting political and military pressure on the Polish regime to crack down.

The Soviet approach to this dilemma is similar to that seen in arms policy (build and negotiate): Continue supporting groups and states favored by Moscow while trying to achieve progress in both economic and arms control spheres by keeping them separate from the overall course of U.S.-Soviet relations. The West, however, and particularly the United States, does not always view developments in this light. A worsening of U.S.-Soviet political relations usually is accompanied by an economic "cold war" as well. After the invasion of Afghanistan, President Carter imposed an embargo on trading several classes of goods with the Soviet Union, including grain.

The foreign policy of Mikhail Gorbachev

has demonstrated the most explicit linking of domestic economic needs and Soviet international behavior. His approach to securing physical and political security has been to try to resolve as expeditiously as possible the most dangerous issues and wherever possible, to reduce international tensions that might derail his leadership and the economic restructuring it is determined to achieve. His initiatives have included direct and specific overtures to China, involving a withdrawal of forces from the Far East, the withdrawal of Soviet forces from Afghanistan and direct negotiations with Afghan rebels, the acceptance of the Chinese position on one key border dispute, and a visit to Beijing by Gorbachev himself—the first trip to China by a Soviet leader in thirty years. The result was a return to full party and state relations between the two communist adversaries. Attention has also been devoted—less successfully—to improving relations with Japan, which was one of the first places visited by Edward Shevardnadze, the Soviet foreign minister, and the noncommunist nations of Southeast Asia.

In the Middle East Soviet interest in improving and possibly someday reestablishing diplomatic relations with Israel (broken after the 1967 Six-Day War) has been evident, as has attention to former Soviet ally Egypt and several other states with whom the USSR had not previously had relations, such as Oman and the United Arab Emirates. Since coming to power, Mikhail Gorbachev indicated his interest in seeing reform succeed in East Europe and during 1989 he demonstrated his willingness to tolerate its consequences (see Chapter 37). Equally dramatic was the reversal in Afghanistan, from which the Soviet Union withdrew its troops during 1988–89 after nearly nine years of fighting, with the fate of their ally, the government in Kabul, very much in doubt.

The Gorbachev approach to the United

Changing Soviet Views on
International Relations

In mid-1988 *Moscow News* conducted a poll of more than 100 Soviet foreign policy experts, including diplomats, scholars and other public figures. The results revealed a wide range of views, including a high degree of support for a less ideological, more open Soviet view of the world.

On the question of ideology, those polled were asked, "To what extent will ideological contradictions between the USSR and the U.S.A. hamper the normalization of Soviet-American relations?" One-half of the respondents said to a small extent or not at all.

When asked if restrictions on western books, periodicals and other information should be kept or changed, 92 percent favored reducing or eliminating them altogether.

One-third of the Soviet experts on international relations said there was no American threat (43 percent said there was) and just over half said that political means were the best way to ensure the USSR's security. More than 90 percent of the respondents accepted the idea that criticism of a nation's human rights practices is legitimate.

SOURCE: *Moscow News*, no. 32, August 14–21, 1988.

States has been to try to achieve progress on arms control questions, while removing the most contentious issues—like Afghanistan—which poison the negotiating atmosphere. The release of most human rights activists from prison and an easing of political and cultural repression are contributions in this direction, as is the increase in the number of Jews allowed to leave the country, after years of declining emigration. In the critical area of arms control, Gorbachev has made the most far-reaching and comprehensive proposals for cutting strategic arms, such as that at the Reykjavik summit in 1986, which among other things envisaged a 40 percent cut in nuclear warheads within five years. These proposed cuts were rejected by the United States because they included restrictions on development of SDI. The treaty on intermediate-range nuclear weapons, signed in 1987, was made possible by repeated Soviet acceptance of U.S. terms, including the elimination of all Soviet weapons of this type while the British and French retained theirs, the elimination of short-range weapons and of intermediate-range weapons in Asia where the United States had none, and for the first time, the acceptance of on-site inspection of weapons plants inside the USSR itself. In 1988 at the United Nations Gorbachev announced a unilateral cut of 10 percent in Soviet conventional forces as well as varying cuts in numbers of tanks, planes and artillery.

The aim of all of this movement by the new Soviet leadership has been to try to make the world somewhat less dangerous for the USSR, and to provide for Gorbachev and the country the stability and "normalcy" in international ties that will allow economic restructuring and progress to return. As Gorbachev himself put it before a conference on peace and disarmament:

> Before my people, before you and before the world, I state with full responsibility that our international policy is more than ever determined by domestic policy, by our interest in concentrating on constructive endeavors to improve our country.[2]

Because the Soviet Union is not the only powerful actor in the international field as it is in the domestic setting; because it must deal with adversaries as well as friends; because the stakes —including national survival—are so high; and because achieving goals like fruitful economic contacts and political support often means pursuing conflicting policies, the management of foreign policy for the Soviet Union presents as daunting a challenge as does that of economic reform.

[2] *New York Times*, February 17, 1987, p. 1.

References and Suggested Readings

BIALER, SEWERYN. *The Soviet Paradox*. New York: Vintage Books, 1986.

HOUGH, JERRY. *Russia and the West: Gorbachev and the Politics of Reform*. New York: Simon and Schuster, 1988.

KENNAN, GEORGE. *Russia and the West under Lenin and Stalin*. Boston: Little, Brown, 1961.

MENON, RAJAN. *Soviet Power and the Third World*. New Haven: Yale University Press, 1986.

ULAM, ADAM. *Expansion and Coexistence: The History of Soviet Foreign Policy, 1917–1967*. New York: Praeger, 1968.

VEEN, HANS-JOACHIM, ed. *From Brezhnev to Gorbachev: Domestic Affairs and Soviet Foreign Policy*. Leamington Spa, Great Britain: Berg, 1987.

ZAGORIA, DONALD. *The Sino-Soviet Conflict 1956–1961*. Princeton, NJ: Princeton University Press, 1962.

V

LATIN EUROPE, SCANDINAVIA, AND EASTERN EUROPE

35

To entrust to one person, no matter how able and trustworthy he may be, the whole future of a collective undertaking is not politically advisable.

— Antonio de Oliveira Salazar

The Countries of Latin Europe

It is traditional to group the countries of southern Europe together: Italy, Spain, and Portugal, and France on the borderline.[1] Such a classification is both helpful and misleading. It is helpful because, as we shall see, there are many similarities between the politics of these countries. It is misleading because there are many differences among them as well. Broadly, France, Italy, Spain, and Portugal share many similarities of language and culture, but differ considerably in terms of their economies and political institutions. Economically, Portugal and southern Italy have significantly lower levels of economic development. Spain has been growing rapidly in the past two decades and northern Italy has been so dynamic as to make Italy the third largest economy in Western Europe, surpassing Britain by some measures (although British economists dispute this). Politically, Spain and Portugal have relatively fledgling democracies, while Italy has not moved beyond the politics of fragile coalitions reminiscent of France during the Third and Fourth Republics.

POLITICAL DEVELOPMENT

Spain

As might be expected, the countries of southern Europe have had varied pasts. From the feudal period, Spain most resembled France. Spain developed an absolutist monarchy much like that of its neighbor to the north. In fact it was the first great absolutist monarchy in Europe, growing out of the kingdoms of Castille and Aragon, which

[1] Greece is often grouped with these countries as a "Mediterranean democracy." While Greece shares many characteristics with Latin Europe, some cultural and historical dissimilarities, as well as economy of space, have led me to omit discussion of this country, although it is part of southern Europe. For linguistic reasons, of course, Greece is not "Latin." For a discussion of the notion "Mediterranean democracy," see Arend Lijphart, Thomas C. Bruneau, P. Nikiforos Diamandouros and Richard Gunther, "A Mediterranean Model of Democracy? The Southern European Democracies in Comparative Perspective," *West European Politics,* 11, 1 (January 1988):7–25.

461

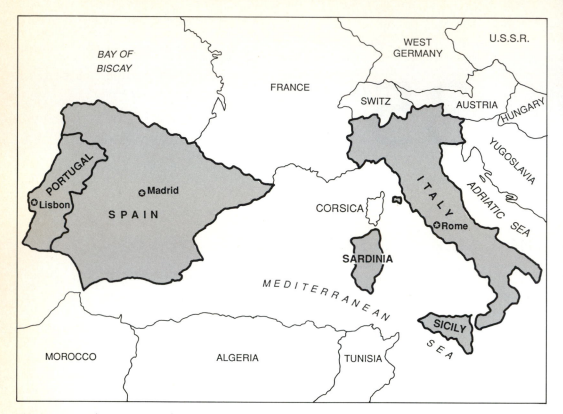

Figure 35.1   The countries of Latin Europe.

were united by the marriage of Ferdinand and Isabella in 1469.[2]

Spain's early success as a mercantilist empire, however, impeded its evolution. Wealth from the Americas disinclined the king to encourage the development of commerce within Spain. The growth of commercial classes interested in modernizing the Spanish political system simply did not occur in sufficient strength to influence authority structures before the intrusion of Napoleon in 1808. Moreover, the agricultural policies of absolutism created large, inefficient estates (*latifundia*) in the south, while protecting sheep-herding to the detriment of the small holdings in the north. The Inquisition led to the expulsion of Moors and Jews in 1492, leaving the country with a decimated financial sector. To the extent that entrepreneurial activity occurred at all, it was largely in the periphery, especially in the Catalan and Basque regions (north and northeast of Madrid). Eventually, industrialization, such as it was, would become associated with regionalism.[3] All in all, the heritage of absolutism and the regimes that followed it in the nineteenth century would be a stagnant economy and an underdeveloped political system.

[2] Perry Anderson, *Lineages of the Absolutist State* (London: Verso, 1979), chap. 3.

[3] This argument relies heavily on Donald Share, *The Making of Spanish Democracy* (New York: Praeger, 1986), chap. 1.

Change, although hardly improvement, came with Napoleon's imposition of his brother Joseph on the Spanish throne in 1808. Shaky from the beginning, Joseph Napoleon's regime became the target of traditional Spanish elites and the few Spanish liberals that could assemble in the *Cortes*, or Parliament, of Cadiz (1810–12). The revolt against Napoleonic domination was successful by 1812, but it ushered in a period of instability that would characterize the entire century.[4] According to one author, "Between 1815 and 1875 Spain experienced six different constitutions, one royal charter, 35 *pronunciamientos,* or coups (eleven of these successful), one republic, two periods of military regency, and two protracted civil wars!"[5] The end of the century saw the reestablishment of authoritarian royal rule under Alfonso XII, whose son, Alfonso XIII, was overthrown by the general Primo de Rivera in 1923. The latter was a figure not unlike Italy's Benito Mussolini, but he lacked the Italian's mass base of support (see page 466).

The authoritarian rule of Primo de Rivera was undermined by the Depression. In 1931 the Second Republic was declared. In the words of one political scientist:

> The Second Republic was Spain's first genuinely democratic regime, but it was plagued by the misfortune of being born within the context of the volatile and highly mobilized society of post-World War I Spain. It tried to graft parliamentary democracy onto a society experiencing rapid social change, but still characterized by elitism, class division, and semifeudal agrarian conditions. The result was a chaotic and fragmented party system, polarized from the start.[6]

The problems of the Depression compounded the difficulties of forming stable governing coalitions. The electoral system exaggerated the results of minute shifts of voters, and the policies of Spain shifted dramatically with the rise and fall of governments.[7] This climate of instability and frustration encouraged the military to revolt against the left-wing Popular Front government of 1936. Jumping off from North Africa, General Francisco Franco led the major portion of the army and sympathizers of the traditional Right into an attack on the Spanish Republic. Even with the aid of Hitler, Mussolini, and most of the regular Spanish army, it took Franco until 1939 to subdue the Loyalist defenders of parliamentary democracy and to ensconce his authoritarian regime. Originally established with the trappings of fascism—a single party, corporatist interest organization, repression of unions

[7] Richard Gunther, Giacomo Sani, and Goldie Shabad, *Spain after Franco* (Berkeley and Los Angeles: University of California Press, 1988), pp. 17–20.

General Francisco Franco, whose authoritarian regime ruled Spain for more than thirty years.
SOURCE: AP/Wide World Photos.

[4] Pierre Vilar, *Histoire de l'Espagne* (Paris: Presses Universitaires de France, 1947), p. 50; Share, p. 8.
[5] Share, p. 8.
[6] Share, pp. 12–13.

and a consequent low-wage, pro-capitalist economy—the Franquist regime gradually reverted to traditional authoritarianism. Franco was supported by the historic bloc of conservative landowners, clerics and businessmen that had backed previous dictatorships, but he did not seek to mobilize the masses, as Hitler and Mussolini had done, so much as to depoliticize public life. The later stages of Franquism were characterized by a regime of technocrats which, in fact, facilitated the transition to democracy after Franco's death in 1975.

Spain was able to negotiate a smooth transition to democratic government thanks to the political skills of King Juan Carlos I, Franco's designated successor, and Adolfo Suarez, the king's prime minister. The latter ably included both Franquist and opposition figures in reorganizing the *Cortes* (parliament) as a constituent assembly. A new constitution was adopted with the participation of all groups of Spanish society, legitimating the new institutions as products of broad consensus. The democratic constitution was approved by 87.8 percent of Spanish voters (with 7.8 percent opposed) December 6, 1978. Spain has had a Socialist government since 1982.[8]

Portugal

Portugal, though much smaller, followed a path of political development similar to that of Spain, of which it had formerly been a part. Traditionally, Portugal dates its inde-

pendence to the year 1140, and except for an interregnum from 1580 to 1640, when the kingdom fell under Spanish Hapsburg rule, it has remained (at least nominally) independent ever since.[9] Like France and Spain, Portugal experienced a period of absolutism dating from the sixteenth century reconquests of territory from Moorish and Castillian occupiers. While political authority remained highly centralized throughout Portugal's history, regionalism never developed along the lines of that in its Iberian neighbor.

Portugal's integration into the world economy, like Spain's, inhibited economic development, but for different reasons. Whereas Spanish mercantilist success diverted attention from developing a dynamic bourgeoisie at home, Portugal's dependent trade relationship with Britain had a similar effect. According to one author, "The Anglo-Portuguese relationship which emerged from this economic arrangement was one of strong dependence by Portugal on England, although it reinforced the [royal] Braganza House and the landed interests, and thus the aristocracy and church."[10] The incoming wealth from the Portuguese Empire, like Spain's, disguised the fundamental weakness in the metropole's domestic economy for some time.

A weak bourgeoisie in a society dominated by an agricultural elite proved a formula for authoritarian rule into the dawn of the twentieth century.[11] The First or "Demo-

---

[8] On the transition to democracy, see Gunther, Sani, and Shabad, pp. 34–36; Share, pp. 198–217; and Kenneth Maxwell, "Spain and Portugal: A Comparative Perspective," in Stanley G. Payne, ed., *The Politics of Democratic Spain* (Chicago: Chicago Council on Foreign Relations, 1986), pp. 256–73. On the constitutional referendum, see Demitri-Georges Lavroff, *Le Régime Politique Espagnol* (Paris: Presses Universitaires de France, 1985), p. 6.

[9] For a brief introduction to the history of Portugal, see Richard Robinson, *Contemporary Portugal* (London, George Allen and Unwin, 1979), chap. 1; and Thomas C. Bruneau, *Politics and Nationhood: Post-Revolutionary Portugal* (New York: Praeger, 1984), chap. 1.

[10] S. Sideri, *Trade and Power: Informal Colonialism in Anglo-Portuguese Relations* (Rotterdam: Rotterdam University Press, 1970), p. 5, quoted in Bruneau, p. 14.

[11] See especially, Barrington Moore, Jr., *Social Origins of Dictatorship and Democracy* (Boston: Beacon Press, 1966), chap. 8.

cratic" Republic inaugurated in 1920 probably had more in common with the brief French Second Republic and Napoleon III's Second Empire than with the truly democratic French Third or Spanish Second Republic. Elections were manipulated, politicians motivated by spirit of *enrichissez-vous* ("help yourself to riches"); and the short-lived parliamentary regime was unsurprisingly dotted with military coups. The Democratic Republic ended when quasi-fascist elements in the Lisbon Barracks, influenced by Primo de Rivera in Spain, seized power in 1926. Military incompetence gradually made them dependent on their civilian minister of finance, Antonio de Oliveira Salazar.[12] Salazar gradually created a regime extraordinarily similar to the one Franco would establish in Spain.

Like the Franquist regime, Salazar's "*Estado Novo*" ("New State") was a personalistic dictatorship with the outward trappings of fascism. The system was corporatist and clerical, justified by reference to Pope Leo XIII's *Rerum Novarum,* which envisioned a society of hierarchically organized non-conflictual interest groups. Like Spain, only a National Movement, rather than political parties, was permitted to link citizen and state. In fact, like Franco, but unlike Mussolini and Hitler, Salazar had no interest in mobilizing the citizenry.

Salazar became incapacitated by a stroke in 1968 and died two years later, succeeded by Marcelo Caetano, a Salazar *apparatchik.* Caetano was less adept at manipulating the enormous bureaucracy devised by his predecessor, but his ultimate undoing proved to be his mishandling of the uprisings in Portugal's African colonies. Guerrilla activity had begun as early as 1961 in Angola, Mozambique, and Guinea-Bissau. By the early

1970s no end was in sight, and disaffection grew with the prosecution of colonial wars that seemed only to claim scarce national resources and much of the nation's youth. It was the armed forces that eventually revolted in 1974. For the first time in Portuguese history, the army intervened from the Left.

While the stolid General Antonio Spinola as titular head of the regime gave the Portuguese revolution conservative credentials, the leftist orientation of the junior officers who masterminded the coup soon brought the country to the brink of radical social change. The officers were divided, however, and a counter-coup on November 25, 1975 by Colonel Antonio Ramalho Eanes halted the leftward movement of the revolution and established political institutions well within the mainstream of West European democracy.[13]

Italy

Unlike the other countries of Latin Europe, Italy never experienced a period of absolutism. The early development of merchant capitalism in the city-states of the north undercut the landed aristocracy whose support was necessary for full-blown absolutism.[14] Instead, lacking a unifying force, Italy remained divided into a number of petty principalities. In the south the Kingdom of the Two Sicilies, an outpost of Spanish Bourbon rule, preserved a feudal system based on *latifundia.* The middle of the peninsula harbored the repressively administered Papal States. The north was composed of smaller principalities dominated by Austria in the northeast and Piedmont in the northwest, as the previously free city-states of the Renaissance fell to external domination.

In many ways the political history of Italy

---

[12] For a detailed look at this period, see Robinson, chap. 2.

[13] For a conservative appraisal of this period see Maxwell, pp. 256ff.

[14] Perry Anderson, *Lineages,* pp. 143–72.

parallels that of Germany: a divided, economically backward set of principalities with a weak bourgeoisie and a conservative landed aristocracy. Liberal republics failed in the abortive nationalist revolutions of 1848 in Italy just as in Germany. As Germany was united under Bismarck and the Prussian Junkers, so Italy gradually became consolidated under the conservative regime of Victor Emmanuel II, King of Piedmont. Bourgeois nationalist aspirations took the form of the *Risorgimento* (national resurgence) whose heroic representative was Giuseppe Garibaldi, an enterprising general who captured the south from the Spanish Bourbons. Garibaldi and his followers were outmaneuvered by Victor Emmanuel's prime minister, Cavour, and this heterogeneous group eventually accommodated to the conservative, but constitutional, *Piemontese* monarchy. Partially by conquest, partially by diplomacy, Italy was gradually united by 1870.

Italy, like the other countries of Latin Europe, was a late developer. Especially in the north, economic growth was a rapid and alienating process. The rise of radical trade unions and left-wing political activists, responding to the stresses of industrialization, provoked anxiety in the urban middle classes and suspicion among the very large peasantry. This proved to be fertile ground to nourish fear of democracy, liberalism and socialism, and the solution to these fears for many was a former socialist journalist named Benito Mussolini. A demagogue of considerable skill and few principles, Mussolini saw his opportunity to attract a constituency on the far Right, quickly abandoning his earlier ideals. He and thousands of followers, uniformed in black shirts, marched on Rome in October 1922. Frightened conservative politicians threw their support to the Fascist party which, after manipulated elections in 1924, acquired a large majority in the parlia-

ment. By 1925 the country was ruled by dictatorship.[15]

Like the Iberian regimes, Mussolini's Italy was loosely based on the fascist ideas of turn-of-the-century Europe. Interest groups were organized along corporatist lines, and a concordat was reached with the Catholic church. Democracy was scorned, elitism and hierarchy were praised, and the regime was guarded by the repressive apparatus of the state. Unlike the Iberian countries, but like Nazi Germany, popular support was mobilized around an expansionist foreign policy and the virtues of war.

The imperial aims of the fascist regime proved to be its undoing. The very term "fascist" was taken from the *fasci* (rods that surround an axe) that formed the symbol of power in ancient Rome. Mussolini aimed at conquering a new empire, essentially in Africa, to recapture lost glory and to divert attention from domestic political conflict. The latter, according to fascist theory, did not exist for the nation was idealized as a smoothly functioning integrated whole in much the same way as Pope Leo XIII's *Rerum Novarum* envisioned a society as composed of nonconflictual interests. But denying conflict did not dispel it, and Mussolini's imperial drive led him into an alliance with the other fascist powers and ultimately into defeat. Not only was Mussolini defeated by the Allies in 1943; his regime was undone from within by Italian partisans (many of them Communists) who never shared the fascist vision of an organic nation captained by a dictatorial state.

A new, democratic constitution was completed by 1947. Italy gained a strong parlia-

[15] This account draws heavily on Stephen Hellman, "Italy," in Mark Kesselman and Joel Krieger, et al., *European Politics in Transition* (Lexington, MA: D.C. Heath, 1987), pp. 320–43.

ment that looked very much like that of the French Fourth Republic, or indeed, the parliament of Spain established thirty years later. What is important to recognize is that democratic institutions were established by indigenous groups with wide popular support.

CULTURE

Certainly, the most evident similarity among the countries of Latin Europe is linguistic. As the name implies, the citizens of France, Spain, Italy, and Portugal all speak languages based on Latin. To some extent similarities of language bespeak a common culture. Similar words often mean similar visions and concepts; similar ways of viewing the world. One should not, however, push this too far. Significant populations of France have historically spoken Celtic (*Breton*) or Germanic (*Alsacien* languages (see Chapter 11). France

---

. . . I sometimes find it difficult to communicate directly the value and certain aspect of our Constitution. And this is because there are, around our Constitution, certain intangibles that have to be explained in historical terms, and for that reason you have to go back to the beginning of democratic Italy, which is very recent . . . [Y]ou have the problem of having [Americans] understand that we, the old country, Italy of so many centuries of civilization is the recent, new, young democratic country, and . . . young America, has the oldest democratic constitution in the world . . . America is the old country of freedom and liberty and individual rights, and ours is the country in which individual rights, freedom, liberty and the values of democracy were discovered recently . . .

SOURCE: Prof. Furio Colombo, President of FIAT, USA; quoted in "The Fortieth Anniversary of the Italian Constitution," *Italian Journal*, 2, 4 (1988).

and Spain both have significant populations that speak Basque, a language totally unrelated to Latin. Even within Italy, diverse dialects are often mutually incomprehensible and "standard" Italian is viewed by many of the country's citizens as an artificial invention, an imposed vehicular language. By contrast, English and German both have many Latin borrowings, while neither Britain nor the Federal Republic have ever been considered "Latin" countries. Linguistic similarities do, however, bear witness to at least some elements of a common history.

Another similarity, politically much more important, has been the role of Catholicism in all four countries. The vast majority of the citizens of Latin Europe are, at least nominally, Catholic. In all of these countries the historic role of the Church has been similar. As in France, the Church has tended to be associated with political conservatism in Italy, Spain and Portugal. In all four countries the Church historically allied with oligarchies resistant to the forces of change. This took on especially tragic proportions in Spain when the cleavage between Left and Right ultimately led to a long and bloody civil war (1936–39) with conservative clerics lining up clearly with the "Nationalist" forces of General Francisco Franco in his rebellion against the short-lived Spanish Second Republic.

In fact, the clerical-versus-secular conflict that motivated so much of French politics during the Third Republic was mirrored equally in Italy and Spain (and in a somewhat more constrained way in Portugal, where secular forces were weaker). The political result, however, was different in the four countries. In France the issue seethed continually, but more or less nonviolently, until it gradually faded. In Spain the church-state issue was part and parcel of a hecatomb that no one wished to repeat after Franco died in 1975. Church influence became formalized in Italy.

Pope John Paul II address an overflowing audience of worship-
pers at St. Peter's Basilica.
    SOURCE: Reuters/Bettmann Newsphotos.

The nineteenth-century statesman Cavour
argued that Italy should have "a free church,
a free state," but a clear separation of church
and state was not to be. Mussolini signed a
concordat with the Holy See in 1929 (not
unlike Napoleon's in 1802 or Spain's under
Franco), and the persistence of a powerful Christian Democratic party after 1945
preserved the influence of the Church in such
issues as education, divorce and abortion.
While the Church was also associated with
political conservatism in Portugal, the left-
wing revolution in 1974 that brought democracy to that country also brought secular government.

These countries, owing to their delayed
economic development, have all had very significant peasantries whose views of central
authority have been similar. Peasants have
traditionally been suspicious of the forces of
modernization, especially as the latter came
from the city. Even when not aggravated by the
existence of ethnic minorities who felt threatened by the national culture based in the capital, peasant resistance to the demands of the
modern secular state have provided the raw
materials for reactionary movements. It is not
an accident that France, Spain, Portugal, and
Italy have all had conservative, authoritarian
experiences. Hitler himself recognized the
peasantry as a pillar of his own fascist revolution:

Our revolution would not have been possible at all if a certain part of the nation had not lived on the land. If we review the revolution soberly we must admit that it would not have been possible to accomplish this revolution from the cities. In the urban communities we could not have reached a position which gave to our policies the weight of legality.[16]

ECONOMIC ANTAGONISMS

Related to the religious cleavage, class cleavages in the Latin countries of Europe have

[16] Quoted in Alexander Gerschenkron, *Bread and Democracy in Germany* (Berkeley and Los Angeles: University of California Press, 1943), p. 3.

Portuguese Political Culture

One of the salient features of Portuguese society—and one which does not differentiate it in kind from any other south European society—is the prevalence of networks of kinship and patronage. Lengthy and complicated laws and regulations may be constantly drawn up, promulgated and revised to settle the rules by which society is to operate, but in practice every Portuguese knows that such rules are there to be bent or circumvented as one's own needs dictate and insofar as means can be found to achieve this. For historical reasons, including the political instability of the last two centuries, it can be said that no concept of objective legitimacy of law or government has ever taken root in Portugal. It is assumed that those who make law or government do so to further their own interests rather than those of society as a whole, and therefore the taking of countermeasures in self-defense is a natural and legitimate activity. From time to time there is a breakdown of the governmental system, a change of political regime and new laws result, but these changes do not usually make much impact on the substructure of social relationships.

SOURCE: Richard Robinson, *Contemporary Portugal* (London: George Allen and Unwin, 1979), pp. 22–23.

been roughly similar. Just as in France, issues of secularization reinforced class antagonisms. Those siding with the Church have tended to be the bourgeoisie or peasantry, while anticlerical sentiment has run highest among the working classes and urban intellectuals. Landless agricultural workers in all four countries have tended also to be anticlerical and left-wing. Proportionately, this group has been especially important in Portugal, particularly in the Alentejo region.

As in France, the coincidence of class and religious cleavage separating the same groups meant that levels of trust between these groups would be especially low. Because of this lack of "overlapping memberships," the conditions for democratic stability were not auspiciously present. In Spain social cleavages were so deep as to erupt in civil war (1936–39), which in turn provided the Franco regime (1939–75) with an excuse to suppress democracy entirely. Even without civil war, when feuding segments of society were represented in democratic parliaments, the result was often political immobilism, which invited dictatorial coups. Italy, Spain and Portugal all experienced long periods of authoritarian rule because democratic forces were divided and weak.

Corporatism

One solution offered by the conservative governments of Latin Europe to the problems of class antagonisms was corporatism. The ideology of corporatism preached a vision of society as an organic whole with each group making a specific contribution, and benefitting from its particular place in a rigid hierarchy.

Rather than projecting a society of self-interested individuals whose free interactions would maximize prosperity—the liberal ethos of the United States and Britain—

Corporatism in the Ibero-Latin Tradition

If modern political analysis in the Northern European and Anglo-American tradition was to lead to the glorification of the accomplished fact and of political pragmatism, to materialism and the success theory, was also derived principally from the experiences of these nations, then Iberic-Latin culture can surely claim as its basis a moral idealism, a philosophical certainty, a sense of continuity, and a unified organic-corporate conception of the state and society. This conception derives from Roman law (one can still profitably read Seneca for an understanding of the Iberic-Latin tradition), Catholic thought (Augustine, Aquinas), and traditional legal precepts (the *fueros* or group charters of medieval times, the law of the *Siete Partidas* of Alfonso the Wise). In comprehending the Iberic-Latin systems, one must think in terms of a hierarchically and vertically segmented structure of class and caste stratifications, of social rank orders, functional corporations, estates, juridical groupings and *intereses*—all fairly well defined in law and in terms of their respective stations in life—a rigid yet adaptable scheme whose component parts are tied to and derive legitimacy from the authority of the central state or its leader.

SOURCE: Howard Wiarda, "Toward a Framework for the Study of Political Change in the Iberic-Latin Tradition: The Corporative Model," in Ikuo Kabashima and Lynn T. White, eds., *Political System and Change* (Princeton: Princeton University Press, 1986), pp. 253–54; originally published in *World Politics* 25, 2 (January 1973).

corporatism preached value by identification with an hierarchy. Groups were perceived as not inherently in conflict, but, rather, naturally in harmony, provided each stayed in its place. This ideology of group interaction made all the societies of Latin Europe susceptible to fascist demagogues who preached inherent hierarchies and organic nationalism.

Radical Politics

If the countries of northern Europe were largely able to develop a kind of consensual politics where the fear of revolution rarely menaces any of the political bargaining, the same cannot be said for southern Europe.

The deep class antagonisms and religious conflict polarized Left and Right. Alienated workers turned to radical parties in all of Latin Europe. While Italy and Spain had strong anarchist traditions, the emphasis of Communists on strong organization, well-adapted to clandestinity, made them the most durable opponents to the fascist regimes of southern Europe. (But only in Italy did the Communists remain influential after fascism was defeated.)

As in France, the radicalized workers' movements were partially the product of late industrialization. Firms in all these countries were relatively small and, therefore, less likely to be unionized. Thus, left-wing political parties developed without the support of a more pragmatic trade union movement. Because unions were small and too weak to support long strikes, labor strategy turned to short strikes, meant to be symbolic and to underline *political* demands rather than economic ones.

Fear of a radical Left drove the peasant and middle classes into the arms of the Right. Since the latter were more numerous, conservative government has tended to be the norm in southern Europe, at least until the 1980s.

Dirigisme and Politically Oriented Interest Groups

Late development has also reinforced the tendency toward a significant state role in the economies of Latin Europe—the concept of *dirigisme* discussed in Chapter 9. The lack of entrepreneurs and the small size of firms in these countries meant that the job of amassing large sums of capital necessary for industrialization fell to the state. While this began to change in the 1980s (for reasons outlined in Chapter 9 for France), a long history of state intervention has marked the political and economic terrain of all the countries of the region.

This, in turn, has reinforced the political orientations of interest groups. It has been necessary to influence the state in order to achieve their economic goals, which has often meant aligning with political parties. For labor, competing trade union organizations developed in Spain, Italy, and Portugal. In Italy, the CGIL labor confederation aligned primarily with the Communists, the CISL with the Christian Democrats, and the UIL with the center-left parties. In Portugal, the CGTP aligned with the communists, the UGT with the Socialists. In Spain, the UGT and *Commissiones Obreros* reflected the political positions of Socialists and Communists respectively. There were, of course, no independent trade unions permitted during the periods of fascist rule.

Business groups have consistently been in an easier position in southern Europe. Long periods of conservative government were conducive to their general interests, but over-long government protection made businesses stodgy and uncompetitive. Here, Italy is a notable contrast, where, in the north especially, businesses are highly competitive. Uncompetitiveness of Spanish and Portuguese

Thousands of Italian workers march in Rome during a strike to protest the Christian Democratic government's economic and social policies—January 1980.
SOURCE: UPI/Bettmann Newsphotos.

A Matter of Rank

. . . The Italian economy has caught up with, and possibly surpassed, Britain's. That appears to be true both in terms of sheer size, as measured by the Gross Domestic Product yardstick, as well as per capita income. Some economists and politicians, in Italy and Britain alike, have been quick to point out that exchange rate distortions may be responsible for Italy's promotion to fifth place among the world's industrial democracies, and Britain's demotion to sixth. There is no denying, however that over the the last few years the country that used to be dubbed "Europe's sick man" and "NATO's soft underbelly" has undergone momentous changes.

SOURCE: "Special Report: Italy," advertising supplement to the *Washington Post,* March 25, 1987.

businesses led to especially high unemployment as these countries entered the Common Market in 1986. The Spanish economy has grown rapidly ever since its entry into the European Community, but while profits rose rapidly, unemployment continued at over 18 percent. This failure of the majority of Spaniards to share in the new wealth led to a general strike in December 1988, and to growing tensions between the nominally Socialist government and the trade unions.

REGIONAL DISPARITIES

All of the countries of Western Europe are troubled by regional disparities, but these are especially severe in southern Europe. Italy, perhaps, offers the greatest problem in strictly economic terms. The north of Italy is a fabulous success story. Per capita income in the north is among the highest in the world, making Italy by some estimates the third largest economy in Europe, after Germany

and France, and, in 1987, ahead of Britain.[17] This performance is all the more impressive when one considers the backwardness of the *Mezzogiorno,* the half of the country south of Rome. It is a tragic fact that southern Italy has more in common with the Third World than Western Europe. While economically the backward *Mezzogiorno* has provided the north (and much of Europe) with a reservoir of cheap labor, politically this largely rural area has served to keep the Christian Democrats in power.

Regional disparities have had a different impact in Spain. The culturally distinct areas of Catalonia and the Basque country have traditionally been suspicious of Madrid. The democratic government that succeeded Franco in 1975 devolved considerable autonomy onto the local governments of these regions to placate separatist sentiments and rising terrorism on the part of the Basque ETA.[18] Whereas Italy's south had never industrialized, the Basque and Catalan regions of Spain were among the most developed in the country. Since the 1970s, however, it is precisely the industries in these regions that have been in decline, and the diminishing prosperity has aggravated traditional tensions.

The Alentejo region of southeastern Portugal, a region of *latifundia* (large estates), was the area of the country most sympathetic to communism. Initially, the radical left government that replaced the conservative dictatorship in 1974 divided the area into col-

[17] The Italians called their bypassing of Britain *il sorpasso.* See "A Matter of Rank," above.
[18] "Euskadi ta Askatasuna," an ultra-nationalist group seeking total independence for the Basque region. For an analysis of Spanish separatist movements, see Goldie Shabad, "After Autonomy: The Dynamics of Regionalism in Spain," in Stanley G. Payne, ed., *The Politics of Democratic Spain* (Chicago: The Chicago Council on Foreign Relations, 1986), pp. 111–80.

lective farms. After 1975, as the radical Left was defeated in Lisbon, the parliament retracted the reforms and lands were returned to their former owners.

POLITICAL STRUCTURES AND PARTIES

All the government of southern Europe are essentially parliamentary in character. That is, there is a fusion of executive and legislative power, where the prime minister and his cabinet must enjoy the confidence of the parliament. The president of Italy and the king of Spain hold positions that are essentially ceremonial, although they may exert some influence in terms of whom they pick as candidates to form a government. Usually, however, they merely ratify the decisions of party leaders. Portugal, after 1975, chose to create a presidency somewhat closer to the French model, although weaker than that of France. The president of Portugal enjoys greater flexibility, especially in foreign affairs, than does the chief of state of Italy or Spain. In 1982, however, the power of the presidency was somewhat weakened in Portugal, but the country still has a stronger chief of state than the other countries of southern Europe.

There are, however, significant differences in the nature of parliamentary politics in these countries. Portugal, Spain and France have all known stable majority parties, whereas Italy has never had a majority party. Italian politics resemble those of France during the Third and Fourth Republics. Coalitions are fragile and governments rarely last out a year. The persistence of a large Italian Communist party commanding a consistent 30 percent of the vote limits the room for maneuver of the non-communist parties and has led to the *de facto* dominance of the Christian Democratic party, necessary for any non-communist coalition.

Like Fourth Republic France as well, unstable Italian coalitions in parliament are complemented by a stable pool of elites from which cabinet ministers are drawn, consistently representing the five major non-communist parties.[19] Italy also has a powerful, clientelistic bureaucracy. Different ministries are controlled by different parties, and bureaucratic careers are determined by patronage. The pattern even filters down to the large nationalized industries that are often dominated by this politics of patronage. Sometimes, however, the pattern reverses: Enrico Mattei, long-time entrepreneurial president of ENI, the state-owned oil company, used financial contributions from his company to play off one party against another.[20]

Government stability is a harder issue to judge in Portugal and Spain, which have only known democracy since the 1970s. The Portuguese parliament has been especially unstable, reflecting the deep problems of that benighted land and the lack of consensus on how to approach them. In 1987, the country for the first time elected a majority of center-right Social-Democrats to manage their entrance into the European Community. The policies advocated by this relatively conservative party, including significant reductions in the public sector, represent a dramatic shift from the political ideas of the 1974 revolution. The effect of this new majority remains to be seen.

After the death of dictator Francisco Franco in 1975, Spain cautiously adopted democratic government under the leadership

[19] Christian Democrats, Socialists, Social Democrats, Liberals, and Republicans.

[20] Paul Frankel, *Mattei, Oil and Power Politics* (New York: Praeger, 1966).

of King Juan Carlos. Whereas in Portugal the army pushed the country to the left, in Spain Juan Carlos had to navigate between an influential army on the far Right and separatists on the far Left. The failure of an abortive coup in 1981 may, however, indicate that the Spanish army is no longer as deeply conservative as it was under Franco.

A relatively conservative socialist party, the PSOE, dominated Spanish politics throughout the 1980s, after gaining the majority for the first time in 1982. The party was, in fact, so conservative that its associated labor confederation, the UGT, disavowed the alliance, and in fact called a general strike against the government. Like the Italian Socialists and the Portuguese Social Democrats, the PSOE have pushed for a roll-back of the state. Unlike the French situation, there was simply much more of the state to roll back in Spain and Portugal, largely because both countries have only recently emerged from fascist-style state-directed economies. It is not so much that the public sectors were larger, but rather that years of fascist bureaucracy had made them much less dynamic than in France.

THE ROLE OF THE EUROPEAN COMMUNITY

France and northern Italy are perhaps most starkly different from their Iberic neighbors in terms of their levels of economic development. While France and Italy are among the seven richest countries in the capitalist world, Spain and Portugal lag far behind. Portugal is especially underdeveloped and industrially weak. Spain, considerably more developed than Portugal, is, nevertheless, industrially backward, with over a quarter of its population still involved with agriculture.

Both countries (along with Greece) saw the solution to their underdevelopment in the Eu-ropean Community. Europe would offer tremendous new markets for their agricultural produce, and the cheap labor would be attractive to European industries that could then sell Spanish- and Portuguese-assembled goods to the rest of the EC without worrying about tariffs. The Spanish economy has done especially well for these reasons.

From the perspective of those countries already members of the EC, the new members were an additional burden. Not only would the agricultural production of the new members compete with the farmers of France and Italy, but the huge subsidies paid by the Community through the Common Agricultural Policy would become a monumental burden on the industrial producers of Europe. This led many in the developed part of the Community to advocate *l'Europe à deux vitesses* (Europe with two speeds): a different set of rules and subsidies for Spain, Portugal and Greece.

Moreover, the somber example of southern Italy stood as a caution to the advantages of economic integration. Clearly, there are disadvantages as well. Economic integration with the highly industrialized parts of Europe meant "infant industries" in the south could not be protected from the efficient competition of the north. Free movement of capital might just as easily mean capital flight *from* as well as *to* Spain and Portugal.

CONCLUSION: LATIN EUROPE IN COMPARATIVE PERSPECTIVE

This all too brief survey of Latin Europe offers us an additional perspective from which to view the nature of comparative politics. Most importantly, the quick overview of these countries underlines the need for caution when we try to suggest explanations for the development of Europe's political and economic institutions. Max Weber suggested, in his *Protestant Ethic and the Spirit of Capitalism,* that culture explains the level of economic development.[21] But a look at Latin Europe weakens his argument. The cultures of these countries are quite similar, while their levels of economic development are vastly different.

Politically, however, the intense segmentation characterizing the cultures of these countries is instructive. The deeply divided and frequently unstable parliaments and party systems of Latin Europe are, in many ways, explained by their divisive cultures. Parliaments that represent the people represent their divisions as well.

Yet, the experience of Spain, Portugal, and France, demonstrates that these divisions are not insurmountable. Moreover, the case of Italy suggests that the divisions need not be overcome: Prosperity can be achieved *without* solving the problems of cultural conflict.

Finally, these countries illustrate the great variety of political arrangements produced by cultures and circumstances that are broadly similar. Similarities at one level yield

differences at another. By studying the mechanisms that produce the convergences and divergences in political systems, we learn something more about the nature of politics in general. Not only is this a study that is enriching, but in a disquieting world, the comprehension of politics is a requisite for survival.

References and Further Readings

GUNTHER, RICHARD, GIACOMO SANI, AND GOLDIE SHABAD. *Spain After Franco.* Berkeley: University of California Press, 1988.

HAYCRAFT, JOHN. *Italian Labyrinth.* Harmondsworth: Penguin, 1985.

KAYMAN, MARTIN. *Revolution and Counter-Revolution in Portugal.* London: Merlin Press, 1987.

LANGE, PETER, and SIDNEY TARROW, eds. *Italy in Transition: Conflict and Consensus.* London: Frank Cass, 1980.

LA PALOMBARA, JOSEPH. *Democracy Italian Style.* New Haven: Yale University Press, 1987.

PAYNE, STANLEY G. *The Politics of Democratic Spain.* Chicago: The Chicago Council on Foreign Relations, 1986.

ROBINSON, RICHARD. *Contemporary Portugal.* London: George Allen and Unwin, 1979.

SHARE, DONALD. *The Making of Spanish Democracy.* New York: Praeger, 1986.

---

[21] Max Weber, *The Protestant Ethic and the Spirit of Capitalism* (New York: Charles Scribner's Sons, 1958), first published in 1904–05.

36

Scandinavia

MUCH ADO ABOUT A THIRD WAY

Political events in Scandinavian countries rarely make headlines in the American press. It takes such news as the decision of the Swedish authorities to send juvenile delinquents on a Caribbean cruise to draw our attention to those countries.[1] For the most part, they remain in a dead spot of American awareness. Their domestic politics seem to lack drama, and in world politics those countries have long ago relinquished any ambition of playing a main role. The combined population of Sweden, Norway and Denmark barely approximates one quarter of West Germany's population. In short, Scandinavia is neither a big wheel, nor a squeaky one in need of oil. So why bother with its politics?

The Scandinavian Appeal

In a world of politics that often approximates Hobbes's account of the state of nature

as "war of all against all," Scandinavia presents a welcome contrast as an oasis of civility, reason and compromise, almost like a place in a Hans Christian Andersen tale. The Scandinavian countries entered the modern age of industrialization and mass democracy without political revolution, terror, civil war, authoritarian backlash, threats of coups, fascist uprisings or other kinds of violence. The last 200 years witnessed a steady textbook progression from undisputed monarchical rule to a political order premised on the principles of equality, liberty and parliamentary responsibilility.

How did the Scandinavian countries manage to engineer such a smooth passage through the turbulence of modernization? Why did they adapt so successfully to conditions that elsewhere proved so upsetting and perilous for the ideal of democratic government? To find answers to this set of questions alone should make a study of Scandinavian politics worth the effort. But there are further reasons.

Modern Scandinavia is synomous with "welfare-state." Economic adversity, illness

---

[1] See Steve Lohr, "Swedes Scuttle Cruise for Young Delinquents," *New York Times,* June 6, 1989.

or other misfortunes of life have lost their sting with the provision of "womb-to-tomb" services by the government. To many outside observers this smacks of socialism. But at the same time, the Scandinavian countries have achieved fabulous prosperity, with standards of living at a par with that enjoyed by Americans and ahead of most other Europeans. The fact is that the "wealth-and-welfare" states of Scandinavia have done little to impede the workings of a free-market economy. Businesses are run by businessmen, not government bureaucrats. In other words, the goose that lays the golden eggs has not been slain.

To many observers the Scandinavian countries represent a middle way between unfettered *laissez-faire* capitalism and dictatorial socialism. This middle way is seen as achieving extensive equality in the economic and social standing of citizens without infringing on their political liberties. It is a model of economic and social progress without curbs on the exercise of democracy. It reveals the benefits of historic compromises between opposing social forces like agrarian and urban interests, or business and labor.

Politically speaking, Scandinavia has proved uniquely hospitable to a phenomenon virtually unknown in the United States, though quite familiar in Britain, France, and especially Germany: *social democracy,* the governing by a political party that arose out of the working class with strong ties to labor unions and a breath of Marxist ideology. In Sweden, a party called the Social Democratic Labor Party has governed for over 50 of the past 60 years; in Norway and Denmark an equivalent party did so for most of those years, too. Neither Britain nor France nor Germany—nor, certainly, the United States—have experienced social democratic government for such extended periods.

The dominant role of social democratic parties thus is a feature that also sets Scandinavian politics apart from the rest of the

Social democracy offers to the world one of the most durable and successful labor movements ever, and Scandinavian social democracy stands out as the international model.

SOURCE: Gosta Esping-Andersen, *Politics Against Markets: The Social Democratic Road to Power* (Princeton: Princeton University Press, 1985), p. 312.

world, and begs our attention. How did these parties manage to come to power so early and hold on to it so long? How did they handle their socialist impulses of overthrowing capitalism and bourgeois rule? Has the enjoyment of their lengthy stay in power robbed them of any socialist zeal? How have they dealt with some of the troubling issues that have recently driven left-wing parties from power in many Western democracies?

A Legacy of Blessings

Scandinavia no doubt has enjoyed several advantages. Geography is certainly one of them. For all practical purposes, Norway and Sweden form an island—an island, moreover, whose climate and mountainous terrain combine to deter invasions by other powers. Except for the Germans in World War II, no foreign power has occupied any of the Scandinavian countries in 1,000 years, if not longer; and Sweden was spared even the German occupation.

The outside world has not intruded much in the domestic development of Scandinavia. In turn, Scandinavia has stayed aloof from the rest of Europe for long stretches of history. The Viking invasions of England and the Swedish expansion in the seventeenth century remain exceptional. The Scandinavian countries were fortunate enough to stay out of World War I, which brought down a tsar in Russia, an emperor in Austria-Hungary and a kaiser in Germany, with far-

Table 36.1 Vital Statistics on Scandinavia

	Sweden	Norway	Denmark
Population (millions)	8.4	4.1	4.9
Area (thousand square miles)	174	125	17
GNP/capita	$12,400	$13,800	$11,490
Workforce in (%)			
agriculture	5	7	7
industry	34	37	35
services	61	56	58
Real economic growth (annual rate 1973–82)	0.8	3.2	1.2
Population growth (annual rate 1973–82)	0.2	0.4	0.2
Defense spending (% of GNP)	3.3	3.4	2.4

SOURCE: *Der Fischer Weltalmanach '87* (Frankfurt: Fischer, 1986).

reaching consequences for the political regimes of each of those three countries.

Left to and by themselves, the Scandinavian countries have each emerged as highly homogenous societies with a firm sense of national identity. Ethnically, all but perhaps one percent of the population of Sweden is of Swedish stock; and the same goes for the Norwegians in Norway and nearly the same for the Danes in Denmark. As for religion, nearly all belong to the (Lutheran) Protestant church of their respective country. And with regard to language, only Norway is less than perfectly uniform, with *Riksmal,* a Danish version of Norwegian, being challenged by *Nynorsk,* a more indigenous one. Even with that complication, one is hard pressed to find countries in the world with a lower potential for ethnic strife, religious turmoil or linguistic disputes than in Scandinavia. Much of what makes politics dramatic but also violent is

simply missing there. Scandinavia has been spared the traumatic and often bloody clashes arising in the process of nation-building.

It would not be difficult, of course, to imagine a more violent course—if, for example, one of the three countries had seriously attempted to forge a Greater Scandinavia; and if that power had tried to impose its religion and language on the others. While at one time or another the Danes and later the Swedes may have harbored pan-Scandinavian ambitions, neither of them sought to achieve that goal with "blood and iron" during the past century and a half. As compatible as the three were with each other, they wound up as separate states in the twentieth century, feeling secure and content with their modest role in world politics.

It is no accident that each of the three Scandinavian countries remains a monarchy. They are among the few nations left with an established crown. The Scandinavian "royal democracies," like Britain, are living proof that monarchy and democracy are by no means mutually exclusive political principles; that democracy requires neither a republican form of state nor a revolution. The monarchs of today, of course, do not rule in the sense of making policy, but serve as heads of state. Most important, they are seen as a symbolic thread connecting the present with a past of nearly 1,000 years. They are a tribute to the willingness of dominant forces in the Scandinavian countries to accommodate newly aspiring forces within existing traditions. No doubt, not all traditions have survived, and power has shifted, but the old rulers were not deprived of life or liberty, and many of the old institutions stayed in place. Scandinavia appears to be both very traditional and very modern, the oldest monarchies run by the most entrenched socialist parties.

The Countries of Scandinavia

FROM ARISTOCRATIC MONARCHY TO ROYAL DEMOCRACY

Nation-Building

Of the three Scandinavian countries, it is little Denmark that can look back at the long-est tradition as an independent country. It boasts the oldest kingdom in Europe, dating back to A.D. 900, if not earlier. Moreover, the same dynasty has occupied the Danish throne for over 500 years by now. At times, Denmark played aggressive power politics, invading and occupying parts of England, Norway, Sweden, and Germany. As late as 1864, Denmark tangled with a Prussia bent on unifying Germany; it lost that tussle as well as a province called Schleswig. Whatever wars Denmark fought it managed to do on the territory of other countries. Except for the German occupation in World War II, the Danes have not been conquered by foreign powers.

At the same time, Denmark has not shied from conquering its Scandinavian neighbors. It is curious to note that Sweden established—better perhaps, re-established—its national independence in a fight against Denmark in the 1520s. The leading figure of that struggle for independence was Gustav Vasa, Sweden's "founding father" and first king (1523–60). Clearly, not all politics in Scandinavia happened peacefully and by mutual accommodation, but one has to go back nearly 400 years to find instances of violent clashes.

Norway also gained its modern-day national independence from a fellow Scandinavian country—actually, from two. For centuries going back to 1380, it was under Danish influence, which almost succeeded in extinguishing any Norwegian sense of national identity. With the redrawing of Europe's political map in the wake of the Napoleonic Wars in 1814, the Danes were deprived of their centuries-long control over Norway. That, however, did not mean full independence for Norway. Instead, Norway was handed to Sweden—to compensate the latter for its loss of Finland to Russia.

Norway did not look kindly on its new Scandinavian ruler and tried to resist this new imposition in a brief "war" that ended with an amicable compromise: near political autonomy for Norway, but with recognition of the Swedish monarch as supreme ruler of what was called the "union" between Sweden and Norway. Even though Swedish rule, unlike the Danish rule before, was benign and did not greatly impinge on Norway's domes-

tic political life, nationalistic fervor grew in Norway and full independence was demanded. Without bloodshed, Norway finally obtained it in 1905 from a Sweden resisting the temptation to maintain the union by force. The prospect of a civil war was averted.

Of the three Scandinavian countries, Norway could have been perhaps the one to experience violent upheavals, driven by resentment against its fellow Scandinavians. Only in Norway did the process of nation-building even remotely resemble the kind of struggle that many other nations underwent, notably Germany in the period from 1848 to 1871. Still, the last 200 years did not witness in Norway a traumatic struggle that cost the lives of thousands of people in a civil war or in battle with the armies of other countries.

Constitution-Building

Modern democratic government arrived in the Nordic countries without revolution or much domestic strife. And it did not cost them the monarchy. Traditional institutions redefined their roles through reform and managed to survive. The dominant forces made enough concessions at the right time to forestall violent changes. This is especially true for Sweden, a country with a vigorous parliamentary tradition that dates back, some say, as far as the 1350s. Most agree that the *Riksdag* was firmly established as the Swedish parliament by the time of the rule of King Gustav Vasa.

The Organic Law of 1617 spelled out the powers of the four estates that made up the Riksdag. These estates were the nobility, the clergy, the burghers, and the peasants (see box). Note the unusual fact of the peasantry being recognized as a separate estate. It was a tribute to the considerable economic importance of this group and bore historical wit-

The Swedish Parliament ca. 1750

The distribution of power within the Riksdag can be partly gauged from the numbers in the different Estates. About 300 nobles, representing approximately 1,000 families, ususally attended the Riksdag sessions. The clergy numbered 75, including all the bishops, with the archbishop presiding *ex officio.* Some 100 members represented the burghers. The peasantry (or rather the freeholders and crown tenants only) numbered around 150 who were usually selected by district on the basis of indirect elections. Obviously, the nobles enjoyed disproportionate influence through sheer numbers; if needed they could mobilize close to 1,000 members. Moreover, by virtue of their control of high administrative offices, the nobles could lay special claims to representing the Establishment.

SOURCE: Kurt Samuelsson, *From Great Power to Welfare State: 300 Years of Swedish Social Development* (London: Allen & Unwin, 1968), p. 118.

ness to its leading role in the fight for Swedish independence from Denmark.

At the beginning of the seventeenth century, the Riksdag was securely institutionalized in the Swedish monarchy. Its existence was not a matter of royal grace but of laws backed by the weight of tradition. The Swedish king was no absolute monarch, but one who learned to deal with the representatives of the four estates in the Riksdag. In fact, the king was supposed to govern through a council that was responsible to the Riksdag. The members of the council, in turn, were subject to dismissal by the Riksdag.

In Sweden's Age of Liberty (1720–72), the ideas of the Enlightenment spread among the educated, and economic change of the pre-industrial era created a growing class of wealthy merchants, shippers and manufacturers. The Riksdag, as constituted along estate lines, afforded them insufficient influence. Pressure for reform coalesced in a group called the Caps, whose antagonists were called the Hats. In the best spirit of the Enlightenment, the Caps opposed any form of privilege and favored equal rights, free elections, parliamentary rule and economic *laissez-faire.*

Against the backdrop of growing pressure for political reform, as well as a war with Russia, King Gustav III (1771–92) struck a curious deal with the Riksdag. On one hand, he asserted the principle of royal absolutism in matters of war and peace. But on the other hand, he went against his traditional ally, the nobility, in meeting the demands for reform by strengthening the position of the burgher estate and the peasantry. By taking the side of the newly aspiring forces, the king ensured the continuity of the monarchy in Sweden.

In the aftermath of the French Revolution of 1789, yet without a revolution of its own, Sweden formally adopted a "constitution" in 1809. Until the mid-1970s, when it was to adopt a new constitution, Sweden enjoyed the distinction of having the oldest constitution in Europe. The 1809 document defined a monarch with strong executive powers checked by an independent judiciary and legislature. It also provided for an *ombudsman,* an investigator of citizen complaints about official misconduct.

Without the revolutionary turmoil afflicting most European countries in 1848, Sweden proceeded with its course of political reform. The demands by the growing middle class for more political influence led to a sweeping reform of parliament in 1866. The four-estate institution gave way to a bicameral legislature, but the name, Riksdag, remained. The upper chamber was to be indirectly elected, thus ensuring the continued influence of the nobility, while the lower house was to be elected by the "people." Property and income requirements were set such that approximately 25 percent of adult males were eligible to vote at the time.

The elections resulted in a lower house dominated by rural and agricultural interests, that is, well-to-do farmers without noble title. Still, urban and commercial interests had a voice, too, in this body. On the other hand, Sweden's vast majority then, the less-well-off agrarian population, lacked both the vote and parliamentary representatives; and so did the growing industrial working class. All in all, the pace of political change in nineteenth-century Sweden must be considered slow and deliberate. It was certainly too slow for ardent advocates of democracy, though always too fast for the nobility. More important, it was apparently just right to avoid inciting one side to revolution and the other to reactionary backlash.

On Toward Mass Participation

It was not until 1909 that mass democracy, in the sense of the right to vote, arrived in Sweden, at least for adult males; women were granted suffrage in 1918. Technically, executive power still lay largely in the hands of the king who chose the prime minister. However, the choices made by the newly enfranchised electorate at the polls soon rendered this a hollow prerogative. Any attempt to exercise that prerogative in a manner contrary to the dominant sentiments of the lower house would most likely provoke a political crisis that might jeopardize the monarchy. By appointing a prime minister enjoying the support of Liberals and Social Democrats in 1917, the king tacitly recognized the principle of parliamentary responsibility of the government. Without much upheaval or a formal amendment to the constitution, Sweden had become a parliamentary monarchy as well as a mass democracy.

While starting further back, the other two Scandinavian countries, if anything, moved more briskly toward modern democracy. Despite its semi-colonial status, Norway adopted a far more progressive constitution in 1814 than what Sweden chose in 1809. Sweden allowed Norway to retain its constitution at the price of recognizing the Swedish monarch as the supreme ruler of the union, which Norway did until 1905. Denmark meanwhile installed a two-house parliament with the adoption of the 1849 constitution. The right to vote was vastly expanded in 1901, ushering in the parliamentary system and ending conservative rule.

If you can't beat 'em, let 'em join you.

The ease with which the three Scandinavian countries transformed themselves from feudal monarchies in the seventeenth century to mass democracies in the twentieth century is truly remarkably. This was not simply a matter of nature-like evolution, but a matter of conscious choices of political actors. Elites, groups with political power, face the decision at crucial moments whether or not to share some of their power with groups demanding a greater share or any share at all. If they refuse, they risk revolution and loss of their power altogether. In the three Scandinavian countries, the behavior of the "haves" demonstrated an ability and willingness to make concessions to "have-nots" without surrendering power altogether. Over the past 200 years the institutions of the monarchy have proved adaptable enough to accommodate the demands for reform before the revolutionary storms could gather force.

The inherent pluralism of the four-estate order with the monarch as the supreme broker must be credited in large part with that success. It created a political situation where no single group could expect to dominate the political process. There was simply no homogeneous elite that wielded all the power. Even in the estate of the nobility there was an element of pluralism, owing to the considerable stratification of titles. Three hundred years before the advent of party competition and the ascent of the mass public, politics in Scandinavia was a process of competition (although among elites, to be sure), which was understood and accepted by the privileged few allowed into the game.

In such an established pattern of orderly competition for power, some parts of the elite, in an effort to strengthen their side, will try to enlist additional support from outside, and those outside, strong enough to voice demands, will look toward some on the inside to do their bidding and facilitate their inclusion. What is important to realize is that such a process lends itself to change by adaptation. Once competition was regularized on the inside, the circle of participants could be widened without abandoning the old system.

COLLECTIVE ACTION IN A COMMUNAL SOCIETY

The account of Scandinavian politics thus far has a familiar ring. It is bound to recall accounts of British politics. There, too, we find evidence of piecemeal and peaceful adaptation to new economic circumstances and political demands under the umbrella of a monarchy prepared to facilitate change. Yet, as we come to the main actors of democratic politics we are forced to take note of startling differences in their roles and relationships.

Poor but Free

One of the distinctive characteristics of Scandinavia has been the role of an independent peasantry. In Sweden, especially, the nobility typically did not own the vast amount of arable land, but instead controlled the administration and the military. The peasants on the land typically were not serfs, that is, subject to the jurisdiction of a local lord, tilling his land, and without political voice. In Sweden, royal policy encouraged the ownership of land by freeholding peasants, often to the chagrin of the nobility that would have liked to claim such lands. It was not unusual for the Swedish king to enlist the peasantry as his ally against the nobility.

During the seventeenth century through what became known as the Great Reductions the peasants gained possession of half of all arable land. Many plots, to be sure, were not especially efficient economically, but owning your own land meant representation in one of the four estates of the Riksdag. Thus a large part of the Swedish population had a political voice and was able to select leaders that could play the political game with king, nobility and the other estates. Viewed this way, the politics of that era may not seem to be such a far cry from contemporary politics.

With the political reforms of the late eighteenth and nineteenth centuries, agrarian influence reached its peak. The directly elected houses of parliament typically witnessed the dominance of independent farmers, not of urban-commercial interests. Meanwhile the nobility, with its entrenched position in the administration, held on to control of the upper house. This did not change until the reforms of the early twentieth century that recognized belatedly the consequences of industrialization.

Late but Not Little

Industrialization in Scandinavia arrived later than it did in Britain, France or Germany; not any sooner, actually, than in Russia. Agriculture still employed over 70 percent of the Swedish population by 1870. Sweden did not really begin to industrialize in earnest until after 1880. But then it did so at a furious pace. By 1910 less than half earned a living from the land. Meanwhile the population also grew rapidly, and so did the productivity of agriculture, one of the side effects of industrialization being the rationalization of agricultural production.

A heavy flow of emigration helped alleviate some of the resulting hardship. From 1860 to 1910, nearly one million Swedes settled in the United States, at times as many as half the natural increase of the population and far more than migrated from the countryside to towns. For Norway the figures are similar. It was a case of "flesh and blood in America" rather than "skin and bones at home."

Many of the goods produced by the rapidly churning industrial machine in Sweden went for exports, from paper and wood products to steel ingots. Industrialization fed on two plentiful natural resources in Sweden, trees and iron, which also proved helpful for the building of railroads. Given the wide geographical dispersal of the key natural resources, industrialization in Sweden did not lead to a heavy concentration of the working class in urban ghettos. Most industrial enterprises were of modest size and situated in small communities.

Like many new things, industrialization holds out a promise and a curse. It promises an escape from the poverty and confinement of village life but it also deprives people of a sense of security nourished nearly undisturbed in village communities over the centuries. Although village life was by no means idyllic and bountiful, it endured on the strength of a communal spirit bolstered by a common religion. Industrialization turned the countries of Scandinavia into affluent societies, but it somehow did not destroy the communal spirit. That spirit still thrives in the urban societies that the Scandinavian countries have become, although religion has little to do with it anymore.

The Organized Society

To an astonishing degree, citizens of the Scandinavian countries are organized in groups. The classic economic interests—farmers, business and labor—have longstanding organizations that leave few members uncovered. In Sweden, over 90 percent of blue-collar workers belong to a labor union, the highest percentage in western democracies; Denmark and Norway lag somewhat behind that level, but still exceed Britain, France, and West Germany as well as the United States (Figure 36.1). Blue-collar workers belong to unions within the labor federation called the *Landsorganisationen* (LO), founded at the end of the nineteenth century.

In recent years, unionization has also caught up with the growing white-collar ranks in the workforce, though largely outside the LO orbit. In Sweden, again the most advanced case, over 70 percent of white-collar workers belong to a union, most of whom are affiliated with the TCO federation (Central Organization of Salaried Employees).

The key class-related groups maintain close ties to political parties, their patrons in the political arena. The tie between the LO and the Social Democrats is institutionalized in Sweden by means of "collective affiliation" of a union with the party. In plain English that means the union members are all members of the party as well. However, unlike in Britain, the union leaders cannot influence party politics through a bloc vote of their respective membership. Farmers' associations maintain a close though less formalized, rapport with agrarian parties; and business associations, with conservative parties. There is no pretense of any of those groups being independent of party politics.

Settling Class Warfare Swedish-style

Even in Scandinavia, the arrival of labor organizations was not greeted warmly by business. Industrial relations until the mid-

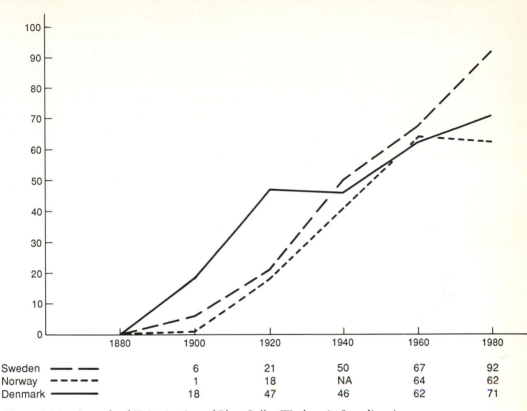

		1880	1900	1920	1940	1960	1980
Sweden	— — —		6	21	50	67	92
Norway	- - - -		1	18	NA	64	62
Denmark	————		18	47	46	62	71

Figure 36.1   Growth of Unionization of Blue-Collar Workers in Scandinavia
SOURCE: Esping-Andersen, *Politics Against Markets,* p. 64.

1930s were known more for strikes and lock-outs than for the social peace one now associates with these countries. To forestall government regulation of business-labor relations, in the 1930s the leaders of the LO and SAF (Swedish Employers' Federation) arranged to meet in the Baltic resort of Salts-jöbaden. It took them nearly two years to reach the famous Saltsjöbaden Agreements in 1938. The event deserves to be noted not only for the rules it laid down for collective bargaining and for the far-reaching effect on industrial unrest, but also for the ability of social adversaries to transform a relationship of distrust and animosity into one of trust and compromise (see box).

The Saltsjöbaden Agreements laid the foundation for a system of collective bargaining between business and labor that was centralized and did not permit government interference. Both sides guaranteed that their respective rank and files would abide by deals reached at the top. They also agreed on provisions regarding layoffs and rehirings. Many observers believe that the Saltsjöbaden Agreements ushered in an age of unprecedented labor peace in Sweden.

MANY (PARTIES) ARE CALLED . . .

While their political development seems to have much in common with Britain, the Scan-

Recalling Saltsjöbaden

We had our first meeting in the SAF offices in Stockholm, but soon realized that we had to be able to get away from everyday political and labor disputes, telephone calls and the rest. . . . We settled on the Grand Hotel in Saltsjöbaden because it was close enough to be able to send people in to get material and yet far enough so we would spend our leisure time out there. . . . It was absolutely necessary to create an atmosphere that was free from politics and ideology, a business-minded atmosphere that concentrated on practical and reasonable solutions. . . . We grew together out there. Of course, there were one or two on both sides who had difficulty adapting themselves. I remember at the beginning one of our men came up to me. He felt ill at ease and worried to see that his colleagues had apparently dropped titles with the labor delegates and were calling them by their first names. After he got over this initial uncertainty he fitted in just fine.

SOURCE: Gustaf Soderlund, president of SAF in the 1930s, as quoted in Frederic Fleisher, *The New Sweden: The Challenge of a Disciplined Democracy* (New York: McKay, 1967) pp. 80–81.

dinavian countries have spawned party systems more like the ones of France and Germany of an earlier era. In Denmark, the array of parties is downright bewildering, and the names of many parties are more confusing than enlightening to outsiders. Yet, the Scandinavian countries have not been known for the paralysis and instability of government typically associated with multi-party systems. This raises some intriguing questions about the conditions of political stability. But before engaging in that discussion let us sketch the background of the Scandinavian party systems.

Electoral System

No doubt, the use of proportional representation as an electoral system has some-

thing to do with party diversity. Unlike Britain or the United States, none of the Scandinavian countries uses the first-past-the-post system of electing one representative per district. Instead, when universal and equal voting rights were granted in the early twentieth century, those countries all adopted some method of allocating seats in parliament to the political parties in proportion to the votes cast for them.

It may come as a surprise that it was the established forces who pressed for the proportional method, not the newly aspiring forces demanding political rights. The adoption of proportional representation in conjunction with mass voting thus marks another one of the historical compromises of Scandinavian politics. It calmed the fears of the ruling forces of being swept aside in the new era of mass participation, while guaranteeing the forces on the outside a share of parliamentary representation commensurate with their popular strength.

The party system that took shape in the aftermath of that compromise some 80 years ago has survived remarkably well to this day. Some names have changed, to be sure, and so have ideological positions as well as electoral constituencies, but the parties have preserved much of their original identities. What is more, in none of the three Scandinavian countries has a new party succeeded in becoming the dominant one. Proportional representation has proved to be a good preservative of the party system of the early 1900s. It has allowed those parties to adapt deftly to new issues.

Main Cleavages of Party Conflict

While electoral systems may magnify or compress political divisions, they nevertheless do not create them. What prompts the creation of parties are social cleavages that upset or excite significant groups of people at a time when people get the right to vote and leaders forge organizational machines. Political parties position themselves in such a way as to capitalize on support for one side of a particular conflict. Scandinavian political parties are often placed at the intersection of two dimensions of conflict.

One of these seems distinctively Scandinavian: the center-periphery cleavage, pitting the peasantry in the countryside against the political elite in the nation's capital city. It is rooted in the struggle between the peasant estate and the nobility, with echoes from the battles between the dominant forces of the two houses of the nineteenth-century parliament. The two political groupings—proto-parties—arising out of that conflict adopted the labels Right and Left. While partly economic, their conflict goes to the heart of cultural concerns, including even religion and language in Norway (see box).

Cutting across this center-periphery axis is

the social class dimension, pitting working class against middle class. This cleavage realigns the party system in the wake of the suffrage extensions in the early twentieth century. It gives rise to Social Democratic parties in all three Scandinavian countries, and rearranges the existing parties. To emphasize the essential feature of the new party system (in a way that oversimplifies the complex partisan changes), let us view it as a triangular competition (Figure 36.2).

Industrialization and the rise of a powerful Social Democratic party did little to close the gap between the Right and Left of yesterday—far from it. The adoption of proportional representation did not help fuse some erstwhile adversaries and create a single "bourgeois" (non-socialist) counterweight to the emerging Social Democrats. Instead, the largely agrarian Left underwent several splits, too complicated to relate in detail here. Suffice it to say that the Scandinavian party systems of the early 1900s comprised the following political parties: Conservatives, Agrarians, Liberals, Social Democrats and (in the wake of the 1917 Bolshevik Revolution in Russia) Communists. None of these parties has vanished in the seven decades since. Their orientations *vis-à-vis* one another and their shares of electoral support have shown remarkable staying power.

The Parties

Among the Scandinavian countries, Sweden is the one with the most compact party system. We will use it here as an example to delineate the basic divisions of party conflict and the identities of the parties. It is simplest to view Sweden's party politics as a battle between a socialist bloc and a bourgeois bloc, with the Communists and the Social Democrats forming the one bloc and the Agrarians, Liberals, and Conservatives the other. Note, however, that this is more a shortcut to sim-

---

The Center-Periphery Cleavage in Norway

The provinces resented the dominance of the capital. The awakening rural communities resisted the influence of an alien and foreign-oriented urban culture. The peasantry found it more and more difficult to accept the standards set by the officials and the patrician establishment; the urban language, the *riksmal*, so remote from the inherited dialects of the countryside, the rationalist Lutheranism of the State Church, the foreign manners, the tolerant morals, and the convivial drinking prevalent in the open urban society. . . . Mobilization did not lead to cultural integration; instead it produced a widespread breakdown in human communication and generated a number of "countercultures" essentially hostile to the established standards and models of the original elite.

SOURCE: Stein Rokkan, "Norway: Numerical Democracy and Corporate Pluralism," in Robert Dahl (ed.), *Political Opposition in Western Democracies* (New Haven and London: Yale University Press, 1966), pp. 76–77.

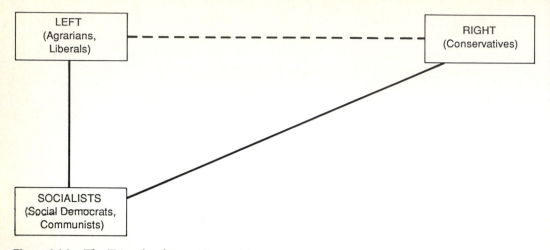

Figure 36.2   The Triangle of Party Competition

plify a complex world than an indication of party behavior in practice. Old rivalries and distinctive clienteles keep the "bourgeois" parties at arm's length from one another.

The Conservatives. Known since 1969 as the Moderates (and in Norway literally as the "Right"), the Conservatives have their roots in the nobility of the pre-industrial society. They were the ones who controlled the upper house of parliament in the second half of the nineteenth century as well as the country's administration. Their main historical adversary was the peasantry, which then gained control over the lower house of parliament. Officially the Conservative party was founded in 1904. Formed in defense of an essentially aristocratic monarchy, the party nevertheless accepted political reform such as universal suffrage, and has survived remarkably well in the age of democracy.

It subsequently became the adopted party of the entrepreneurial middle class and today is identified primarily as the party of business and free enterprise. This is more remarkable than it may seem, for the old Conservatives, through their dominance of the state bureaucracy and army, were quite favorable to state intervention. Indeed, the party is at present "conservative" in the sense of the word familiar to American ears. And that goes for its Danish and Norwegian counterparts as well. Conservative leaders are nowadays maligned for their ideological kinship with "foreign villains" like Margaret Thatcher and Ronald Reagan.

The Liberals. Currently known as the People's Party in Sweden, the Liberals derive from the old Left. Organizationally, the party took shape during the struggle for parliamentary rule and suffrage extension late in the nineteenth century. It was officially founded in 1902. The key adversary of the Liberals then was the conservative elite, which was resisting such change and organized its political party two years later. But with the big issue of the constitutional order long settled, that animosity is barely a historical reminiscence.

Both are now parties of the better-off middle class, with the Liberals perhaps more instinctively prone to proposals of reform, "new ideas," to use a cliché of American electoral politics. While sometimes favorable toward Social Democratic policies, the Liberals can be counted on to raise their voice to defend individual rights and to challenge sweeping state intervention in the economy. In that regard, they are not primarily "liberal" in the American sense of the term. Of all the parties, the Liberals lack a clear interest group connection and a distinctive electoral profile. In Denmark, the party actually comes in two versions, one of which better fits the mold of the agrarian parties in Norway and Sweden.

The Agrarians. Now officially known as the Center, this party has deep roots in the Left. It goes back to the representatives of the independent peasantry that constituted the fourth estate of the old Swedish parliament and controlled the lower house of the bicameral parliament of 1866. Back then its main adversary was the establishment dominated by the nobility. This antagonism was rooted in the "center-periphery" cleavage, an urban-rural division with overtones of cultural chasms that have never been entirely overcome. It has proved most troublesome for Norway, where some resentment over the long domination by Denmark and later Sweden still lingers.

Formally founded in 1921 through a merger of existing parties with agrarian appeals, the Farmers' Party, as it was then known, could count on a firm group foundation in the electorate. This has allowed the party to survive but not exactly to thrive. Its natural base, after all, has been shrinking inexorably; fewer than one in ten now live off the land. What has helped the party remain a considerable force and even attract the political spotlight is its espousal of new issues such as the environment and decentralization. In particular, this party took a determined stand on an issue alarming Western publics in the 1970s: nuclear power. Under the leadership of Thorbjörn Fälldin, the Swedish Center party embarked on a crusade against an energy source viewed by others as the panacea for a Sweden overly dependent on foreign oil (see box).

True to its roots as the party of the simple life in the periphery and of protest against heavy-handed bureaucrats and sophisticated technocrats in the capital, the party went to the Swedish voters with an absolute "No" on this issue. More than any other existing party, the Center was uniquely positioned to take advantage of the "greening" of politics, given the party's concern for its ecology and aversion to large-scale technology. In the 1970s, the Center improved its electoral showing to the point where, together with the other two non-socialist parties, it finally ousted the ruling Social Democrats in 1976. Yet however helpful the nuclear issue may have been for displacing the Socialists, it proved too fissionable for the "bourgeois" coalition, which soon afterwards exploded. Swedish politics entered into an era of middling government trying to muddle through.

The Social Democrats. In Sweden, as in the other Scandinavian countries and almost everywhere else (except in the United States), industrialization spawned viable socialist parties. In Scandinavia, moreover, the message of Karl Marx fell on receptive ears, and the working-class party established in Germany, called the Social Democratic Party, seemed a model worth emulating. To end the exploitation and misery of the proletariat under capitalism and to create a socialist society certainly defined the original misssion of the

---

No government post is so important to me that I will hedge on my conviction in this matter. . . . I will not take part in a government that starts one more reactor.

SOURCE: Thorbjörn Fälldin, leader of Swedish Center Party; quoted in Hugh Heclo and Henrik Madsen, *Policy and Politics in Sweden: Principled Pragmatism* (Philadelphia: Temple University Press, 1987), p. 42.

Swedish Social Democratic Labor Party when it was founded in 1889.

Yet, whatever its goals, the party at that time lacked the key prerequisite of a political party: voters. It appealed to a group of citizens that were almost entirely shut out of politics, given the restrictions on the right to vote in force then. That might actually have been a blessing in disguise for the newly formed socialist party. Why? Because it meant that none of the existing parties made serious attempts to woo the working class. That clientele remained to be tapped.

The socialist party thus pressed for universal voting rights, a goal that was also endorsed by the Liberals, who were attempting to displace the conservative elite. A general strike by an increasingly well-unionized working class raised the stakes of the suffrage struggle and hinted at threats of revolution. With the gates for (male) electoral participation fully opened in 1909, it did not take the socialist party ten years to win the largest share of votes in elections. That put the party in a position, with help from the Liberals, to effectively institute parliamentary rule and by 1918 extend voting rights to women.

There can be little doubt that the extension of suffrage so close on the heels of rapid industrialization gave the young socialist party—which was actually older than the non-socialist parties—maximum advantage in rallying what it considered its natural constituency. The other parties proved neither willing nor able to compete effectively for this vast new electoral resource. For the rest of the twentieth century they would pay the price for this lack of will or ability. True, they had managed to survive the entry of the working class into the political arena, but they would have to sit on the sidelines for the most part from now on.

Like the Democrats in the United States, Sweden's Social Democrats happened not to be in power at the time of the Depression, and thus in the fortunate position to take advantage of the ruling parties' misfortune. In Sweden 30 percent of the labor force were out of work in 1932. The election that year put the Social Democrats in office in Sweden, as it did the Democrats in the United States. In Sweden this was the beginning of over 50 years of nearly uninterrupted rule. In the United States, it was the beginning of an equally long control by the Democratic party of the U.S. Congress and the American electorate, though not of the presidency.

Sweden's Social Democrats thus have had plenty of opportunity to put their ideological stamp on policy. In appraising that record, it is as important to note what they did *not* do , as well as what they did. They did *not*: nationalize private industry; introduce state planning of the economy; precipitate a political or social revolution. True, their control of parliament was tenuous, often requiring support from others. But even when the party held a solid majority, it did not attempt to usher in a brave new socialist world overnight.

Instead the party concentrated on achieving full employment while striving for an ever more perfect welfare state. These were the ingredients of Social Democratic success at the polls. More than anything else, the party engineered Sweden's recovery from the hardships of the Depression. Since that time, Social Democracy has spelled "prosperity" in Scandinavia.

This is not a party inspired by socialist dogmas and sounding the call of class warfare, but a party of pragmatic reform with a Scandinavian twist. Its long-time leader and prime minister (1932–46), Per Hansson, identified the party's mission with the vision of a "people's home," to provide the individual in today's society with the same sense of security and belonging that an (ideal) family does for its members. However appealing this vision may be, it entails a commitment to

In the Social Democratic vision, politics is a kind of therapeutic exercise. Its mission is the slow, careful eradication of disease and the establishment of a regimen of good health in society. It is always to be done with the patient's consent, but also with the recognition that some unpleasant medicine and restrictions may need to be accepted because they are good for people.

SOURCE: Heclo and Madsen, *Policy and Politics in Sweden*, p. 27.

government intervention that at every step may look innocuous but that reaches far and deep when allowed to accumulate unchallenged for more than half a century (see box).

Whatever the appeal of its ideals, the Social Democratic party has ensured better than any of its rivals that it can win where it counts most in a democracy: at the polls. Thanks to the collective affiliation of unions with the Social Democrats (see page 484), this party can rely on roughly one million members, almost one of every five Swedish voters. At election time, thousands of office holders in the labor unions (LO) and government bureaucracy provide active help. A score of party newspapers sound the party message, while numerous private associations affiliated with the party disseminate it among their members. To be sure, not every member is an active one; in fact, many resent their union's collective affiliation with the party, but it provides the Social Democratic party with a core constituency unmatched by any of its competitors.

The Communists. A significant force to the left of the Social Democrats in Sweden is the Communist Party (called Left Party Communists since the late 1960s). Like other Communist parties, the one in Sweden is a legacy of the Bolshevik Revolution of 1917 in Russia. Those segments of Socialist parties everywhere that accepted the Soviet Union as

a model for the future moved to constitute the Communist parties in their respective countries. Long toeing the Moscow line, the Swedish Communist party began to sound more independent in the late 1960s. The party joined the chorus of the New Left and welcomed student radicals and activists of the new social movements proliferating in the 1970s.

Now the voice of educated discontent, the party has shed much of its blue-collar image. In so doing, the Swedish Communists avoided the fate of their counterparts in the other Scandinavian countries. In Norway and Denmark, left-wing socialist parties captured much of the new left ideology. As a result, they relegated the Communist parties in their respective countries to insignificance. That, however, came as little relief to the Social Democrats, who found it no easier to accommodate the left socialists than the communists before.

The Voters' Choices

Scandinavians are avid voters. In Sweden, which again leads the field, voting turnout now hovers above the 90 percent mark. Like so many other things, the turnout curve shows a steady upswing since the 1920s. With present rates in the upper and lower 80 percent range respectively, Denmark and Norway are not far behind Sweden. This high level of electoral mobilization, one suspects, is not so much a matter of excitement with the candidates and issues of the specific campaigns as a matter of so many individuals belonging to social groups with a political and partisan flavor. It is evidence of successful collective action, especially among social strata that otherwise would be much less inclined to go to the polls.

In all three Scandinavian countries the respective Social Democratic parties (called the Labor Party in Norway) capture the lion's share of electoral mobilization. They gain more votes than any other single party. That has been the "law" of electoral politics in Scandinavia for more than 50 years, although the law has come under increasing challenge in the past 25 years. The story of Scandinavian voting since then has been the erosion of Social Democratic strength. The party finds itself squeezed between more radical parties on its left and centrist and revitalized conservative parties on its right (see Figure 36.4).

Especially in Denmark, something has been "rotten" with the party's electoral performance. Here the Social Democrats have lost much ground in fierce competition with left-wing rivals. Those prickly thorns in their left side have stung the Social Democrats especially painfully over foreign policy issues such as Denmark's NATO membership. The issue of NATO membership has also cut into the support of the party's counterpart in Norway. Not being a member of this Alliance, Sweden has been spared the fallout from that issue.

In Denmark and Norway, the debate over joining the European Community further scrambled the party system in the 1970s. Opposition to such a move grew so strong in Norway that a referendum was called resulting in Norway's withdrawal from the Community. In Denmark, moreover, disenchantment with the cost of the welfare state led to the formation of an anti-tax party under Mogens Glistrup (the share of that party is included under the "conservative" column in Table 36.2). Sweden, in turn, experienced

Table 36.2   Voter Support for Four Parties (Blocs) in Selected Elections in Sweden, Denmark, and Norway (Percent)

	Left Wing	Social Democratic	Liberal/ Center	Conservative
		SWEDEN		
1948	6%	46%	35%	12%
1960	4	48	31	16
1973	5	44	36	14
1985	5	45	27	21
		DENMARK		
1947	7%	40%	39%	12%
1960	7	42	29	21
1973	11	26	38	25
1984	15	32	25	27
		NORWAY		
1949	6%	46%	30%	18%
1961	5	47	28	20
1973	11	35	30	22
1985	5	41	18	34

SOURCE: Ole Borre, "Critical Electoral Change in Scandinavia," in Russell J. Dalton, Scott C. Flanagan, and Paul Allen Beck (eds.), *Electoral Change in Advanced Industrial Democracies* (Princeton: Princeton University Press, 1984) pp. 333, 363; *Der Fischer Weltalmanach '87* (Frankfurt: Fischer Verlag), pp. 304, 426, 454.

a sharp rise of support for the (agrarian) Center party in the 1970s over such issues as nuclear power. For a number of reasons, some quite diverse, the 1970s offered gloomy prospects for the future of social democracy in Scandinavia.

The performance of the economy did little to help. While less affected than many other western countries, Scandinavia also experienced economic setbacks during the worldwide recessions of the mid-1970s and early 1980s. Economic growth slowed, while inflation and unemployment both rose. As in Britain and the United States, conservative parties scored significant electoral gains with their promises of new recipes for dealing with economic stagnation and decline. Their gains in Scandinavia, however, seem to have come largely at the expense of Center-Liberal parties, as Social Democratic parties have recovered some ground.

One of the remarkable features of change in the parties' electoral foundations is the blurring of the class division. The Social Democratic parties used to have the nearly undivided attention of the working class. A vote for this kind of party was a reflex of class identification, unimpeded by concerns about either the personalities at the head of the parties or political issues. By the same token, the non-socialist parties together enjoyed a monopoly over the middle class, however fiercely they fought with each other over different chunks of that class.

Until 1960, over 70 percent of the working class typically voted Social Democratic, as compared to less than 20 percent of the middle class (including white-collar employees). That 50-point gap in class voting has shrunk in half by now. For the Social Democrats that is partly good news, partly bad. The bad news for the party is the loss of support in the working class, which is also shrinking in size. The good news for the party is the gain in the middle class, especially among the growing ranks of white-collar voters. The Swedish Social Democrats show the most favorable balance sheet, while their Danish cousins have done least well in this type of transaction.

For the party system the loosening of the old class alignment spells increasing volatility. The parties cannot count anymore on their hard core, their strongholds, to deliver comfortable returns regardless of the particular circumstances of each election. This gives more leverage to short-term forces connected with new issues and leading personalities. Furthermore, evaluations of party performance in critical areas like the economy, social security and foreign policy are not likely to be reflexes conditioned by a voter's party identification. The electoral verdict no longer carries the clear group message it did before.

Still, it is important to emphasize that the old alignments have not been obliterated, nor are they close to extinction. Except perhaps for the Popular Socialists in Denmark, no new party has caught on with large segments of the electorate, however spectacular its early showing (e.g., Denmark's anti-tax party). While much has changed, the Social Democrats are still the single largest party in all three of the Scandinavian countries; and the non-socialist parties have not "realigned" into a cohesive alternative to them. They are as jealously distinctive as ever, mired in divisions as old as great-grandparents. What is perhaps most astonishing is the parties' instinct for adaptation and survival, for making comebacks after setbacks.

. . . BUT ONE (USUALLY) CHOOSES TO GOVERN

In constitutional terms, politics in the Scandinavian countries is guided by the rules of the parliamentary system. The government is headed by a prime minister who is responsible to parliament. In the three countries considered here, parliament today consists of only one chamber, Sweden being the last to abolish its upper house in the 1970s. For all practical purposes, a prime minister can stay in power until and unless a parliamentary majority expressly registers its lack of support by way of a no-confidence vote. In case of a vacancy in the prime minister's office, it has been typically the right of the Monarch (the Speaker of Parliament in Sweden nowadays) to ask a promising candidate to form a government and then to appoint him or her. As always in such situations, practical considerations make it advisable to pick a candidate with a good chance of commanding enough support in parliament lest the appointee immediately be ousted by parliament.

At the same time, the choice of a prime minister is not necessarily a foregone conclusion. The reason is that in Scandinavian elections each party typically receives a share of seats in parliament proportional to its share of the votes cast in elections. This kind of electoral system does not easily reward a single party with a majority of seats for winning the most votes. When no single party emerges from elections with a seat majority, which would give that party an indisputable claim to govern, such a majority must be found by agreements among several parties. This can take the form of explicit coalitions, with each participating party getting control of some ministries and a say in cabinet deliberations. Or else it can be done in a more informal way, by letting one party form the government, even though it lacks a majority, while other parties pledge support without claiming portfolios or a say in cabinet deliberations.

For over 60 years now, the Social Democrats have won a plurality of votes in Scandinavian elections, but not typically a majority of seats. Nevertheless, they have been the party to govern for the most part (see Table 36.3). Only in Norway have they enjoyed a lengthy stretch of majority control. The

Danish Social Democrats came to power in 1929 with support from (radical) Liberals, while their Swedish cousins did so in 1932 with help from the Agrarians. Both renewed their respective connections occasionally in the 1950s and 1960s. And even when not in formal coalition agreements with those allies, social democracy in both countries could count on their tacit support—or at least, on the assurance that they would not join the opposition on a no-confidence motion. So long as that was the case, the notion of a "bourgeois" coalition remained a fiction.

Norway

It was only in Norway that under the solitary, though long, rule of the Social Democrats (Labor) the non-socialist parties found common ground in their poor and brutish life out of power. In 1965, they won the election and a majority of seats in the *Storting*, the Norwegian parliament. They proceeded to form a government that endured until the next election, but soon afterwards split in the middle of the parliamentary term, less from the hammer blows of the out-of-power Social Democrats than from the corrosive effect of internal bickering.

Since the historic turnover of power in 1965, Social Democrats have traded places with non-socialist governments five more times in Norway. But elections rarely precipitated the move. More often, issues arising with special vehemence, like the debate over membership in the European Community in the early 1970s, wreaked havoc on the parties in the middle of their term in government. One thing was sure: No gilded age of "bourgeois" rule would supplant the iron age of social democracy. While no longer fiction, bourgeois coalitions were quite fragile and fissionable. The political pendulum had begun to swing frequently but uneasily.

When the Social Democrats returned to

Table 36.3   The Governing Parties in Scandinavian Governments

Year	Sweden L	Sweden S	Sweden C/L	Sweden K	Norway L	Norway S	Norway C/L	Norway K	Denmark L	Denmark S	Denmark C/L	Denmark K
1946		x				x					x	
·		x				x					x	
·		x				x				x		
·		x				x				x		
1950		x				x				x		
·		x	x			x					x	x
·		x	x			x					x	x
·		x	x			x					x	x
·		x	x			x				x		
1955		x	x			x				x		
·		x	x			x				x		
·		x	x			x				x	x	
·		x				x				x	x	
·		x				x				x	x	
1960		x				x				x	x	
·		x				x				x	x	
·		x				x				x	x	
·		x				x				x	x	
·		x				x				x	x	
1965		x				x				x		
·		x					x	x		x		
·		x					x	x		x		
·		x					x	x			x	x
·		x					x	x			x	x
1970		x					x	x			x	x
·		x				x					x	x
·		x				x				x		
·		x					x			x		
·		x				x					x	
1975		x				x					x	
·		x				x				x		
·			x	x		x				x		
·			x	x		x				x		
·			x			x				x	x	
1980			x	x		x				x		
·			x			x				x		
·			x					x		x		
·	x						x	x			x	x
·	x						x	x			x	x
1985	x						x	x			x	x
·	x					x					x	x
·	x					x					x	x
·	x					x					x	x

Key: L = Left-wing parties, S = Social Democrats, C/L = Center/Liberals, K = Conservatives.

SOURCE: Alastair Thomas, "Denmark: Coalitions and Minority Governments," in Eric Browne and John Dreij-manis (eds.), *Government Coalitions in Western Democracies* (New York: Longman, 1982), p. 118; Keesings Contemporary Archives.

power they typically formed a minority government. Their margin of security came from a party on the left sideline. The Left Socialists would not formally join the Social Democrats in government, but neither would they add their weight to the "bourgeois" opposition. Their dissatisfaction with the "moderate" tone of social democracy (lack of radicalism in overcoming capitalism, and pro-Western orientation in foreign policy) precludes a formal coalition. Yet at the same time these left-wing socialists shrink from lending a hand to attempts by the opposition to oust the Social Democrats from power. Rather a Social Democratic government that they can harass and hold to the fire than a non-socialist government that they cannot blackmail.

Sweden

In Sweden, the seemingly perennial rule of the Social Democrats came to a temporary halt in 1976. The election that year gave the combination of Center, Liberals and Conservatives a majority of seats. Like their counterparts in Norway a decade earlier, they proceeded to form a government, with the prime minister coming from the Center party. And just as in Norway, the coalition soon disintegrated, first over the inability of the participants to come to grips with the nuclear power issue, and then over how to deal with the economic crisis of the early 1980s. The spectacle of the indecisive and incompetent non-socialist alternative boosted the public stock of the out-of-power Social Democrats

The Session Hall of the Parliament Building—Sweden.
SOURCE: The Swedish Institute/Lasse Hedberg.

more than anything they could have devised themselves. "We told you so," was all they had to say. The memory of the Social Democrats rescuing Sweden from the scourge of the Depression in the 1930s contrasted sharply with the economic deterioration under the present-day "bourgeois" government.

And so, in the 1982 election the Social Democrats beat their three-party replacement and returned to power. But as in Norway, they also required some outside help to govern. The party on their left, the rejuvenated Communist party, has provided that assistance, and very much under the same terms—no formal participation in government—thus leaving the Social Democrats technically with only a minority in parliament, but without the threat of an ambush of the government in parliament either.

Denmark

The task of government formation has proved more formidable in Denmark than in Sweden or Norway. Governments in Copenhagen change hands more frequently and stay in office less long than their counterparts in Oslo and Stockholm. Still, the Social Democrats managed to form governments for most of the time until 1982. Often, however, they did so as a single party without a majority. In the early 1960s their hold on government weakened as gains by left-wing socialists eroded electoral support for the Social Democrats.

The rise of left-wing socialists poses a strategic dilemma for the Social Democrats. If they try to accommodate this new Left, they risk the loss of the old Left, that is, the (radical) Liberals, on whose support they have come to rely. Unlike their counterparts in Norway and Sweden, the Danish Social Democrats have lost so much electoral ground since the early 1970s that even tacit support from the left-wing socialists no longer provides them with a majority, nor does support from the (radical) Liberals. Liberal support, in any event, is not forthcoming as long as the Social Democrats continue their courtship of the left-wing socialists. The prospects for Social Democratic rule in Denmark appear gloomy indeed.

Since late 1982, the first Conservative prime minister in 80 years, Poul Schluter, has headed the Danish government. His own party joined with three liberal-centrist parties to form what has been dubbed the "four-leaf clover coalition." Nevertheless the coalition requires outside help from supportive parties in parliament who decline to join the government formally. The Schluter government has confronted serious challenges over its attempts to trim the sprawling welfare state and inject more free enterprise into the economy.

After several coalition reshuffles and with a changing cast of outside supporters, the Schluter government is on its way to becoming the longest serving non-socialist government in Scandinavia. Its record may go to prove that in Denmark "coalition government" is no contradiction in terms. In Norway and Sweden that has yet to be shown. There the Social Democrats have retained enough strength to claim control of government with just a little help from "friends" in parliament; and their non-socialist adversaries have proved unable to bury old rivalries or keep new ones from wreaking havoc on their joint attempts at governing.

[Conservative Prime Minister Poul] Schluter has said that Karl Marx is dead. I know that. He died in 1883. But what Schluter is presenting is Adam Smith's philosophy of the free market packed in cellophane and presented with charm.

SOURCE: Anker Jorgensen, Social Democrat and former prime minister of Denmark (quoted in *New York Times*, Sept. 7, 1987).

Government by party coalitions is not congenitally a part of Scandinavian politics. The disdain the British have for that kind of politics appears to run deep in Scandinavia, even though the lack of a (parliamentary) two-party system makes that luxury hard to afford. But perhaps that does not matter much, since parliament and the parties are, as some claim, a sideshow anyway in Scandinavia.

Harpsund Democracy

It is a widely heard refrain of political commentary that parliaments in Western democracies have lost influence and that even governments no longer control policymaking. Instead, key interest groups—business, labor and farmers—are said to have gained a foothold in important domains of policy.

In Sweden they call this kind of government "Harpsund democracy." Harpsund is a retreat for the prime minister, where top-level meetings with leaders of interest groups take place away from the capital. Political scientists refer to "corporatism" or "neocorporatism," meaning that government policy is effectively made outside the formal channels through bargaining with the leaders of labor,

---

The crucial decisions on economic policy are rarely taken in the parties or in Parliament: the central area is the bargaining table where the government authorities meet directly with the trade union leaders, the representatives of the farmers, the smallholders, and the fishermen, and the delegates of the Employers' Association. These yearly rounds of negotiations have in fact come to mean more in the lives of rank-and-file citizens than the formal elections. In these processes of intensive interaction, the parliamentary notions of one member, one vote and majority rule make little sense.

SOURCE: Rokkan, "Norway: Numerical Democracy and Corporate Pluralism," p. 107.

There are many ways in which structured consultation sanctions and rigidifies approved behavior. Conflict becomes channeled in predictable forms. Political aspirations for reform become merged with issues of technical detail. Those recognized as having a stake in an issue are offered a sense of due process in the making of policies.

SOURCE: Heclo and Madsen, *Policy and Politics in Sweden*, p. 15.

---

business and other powerful groups. To put it bluntly, the parties, the members of parliament and even the cabinet are presented with *faits accomplis.* They find themselves reduced to rubber stamps.

No doubt, the key economic interests are well organized in the Scandinavian countries, firmly connected with political parties and deeply entrenched in the process of policymaking. Scandinavia puts much stock (and faith) in the consultation of interests affected by a prospective policy. "Commissions of inquiry" are an everyday feature of political life. Before embarking on a major new policy initiative the government assembles a commission from representatives of interested parties (including also political parties), civil servants, experts, and so on. The commission's report then goes to government agencies as well as interest groups for *remiss,* that is, comments. Only after digesting this multi-course diet of suggestions will the government decide whether to proceed at all and what kind of legislation to propose to parliament. Some observers, however, suspect that this politics of patience may conceal more than it reveals. The form is consultation, to be sure, but the spirit may not always be compromise.

The Wage Earner Fund Issue

As a case of Scandinavian policymaking, let us consider the handling of an issue that

The Wage Earner Fund Debate: Pros and Cons

PRO: THE UNIONS	CON: THE EMPLOYERS
Power over people and production belongs to the owners of capital. With wage earner funds the labor movement can repeal this injustice. If we do not deprive capital owners of their ownership, we can never fundamentally alter society and carry through economic democracy.	The wage earner funds only serve the purpose of transferring the power and the ownership of commercial and industrial life to the union organization.
Wage earner funds should be owned and administered collectively. An individually based profit sharing system would not involve anything like increased worker influence.	Wage earner funds lead to fund socialism: In the long run, all large companies in the country will have one and the same owner: the union organizations.
Through investment decisions of high-profit firms, a large and essential part of social development is determined. These decisions should be democratized.	The market economy is abolished and is replaced by a "union planned economy."
	Sweden's economy has been built through free enterprise and private ownership. That foundation would be destroyed if wage earner funds are introduced. The alternative to wage earner funds is a preserved market economy and dispersed ownership.

SOURCE: LO newspaper Fack, no. 19, 1975 (reprinted in Heclo and Madsen, p. 298).

Pamphlet of Swedish Employers' Federation (SAF), 1982 (reprinted in Heclo and Madsen, p. 304).

created much political heat in Sweden in the 1970s. It concerns a proposal that one side touted as the transition to economic democracy while the opposition condemned it as the end of economic freedom. The proposal, which originated with the Swedish LO, the blue-collar labor federation, in the 1960s, envisioned the creation of funds fed by company profits but controlled by workers for purposes of investment in the economy. In this way, so the justification went, workers would gain influence over the decision-making of private companies. The plan would redress what after a half-century of welfare-state expansion remained a grossly uneven distribution of economic power in Swedish society.

The "Meidner report," which was drafted by the leading LO economist, Rudolf Meidner, spelled out the details of the plan in 1975 and prodded the partisan allies of labor, the Social Democrats, to take up the cause and

put it into policy. The Meidner plan quickly aroused the ire of the business confederation (SAF), which denounced it as creeping socialism and a power grab by labor. Not only the Conservatives, but also the Liberals and the Center, echoed those objections. The gauntlet had been tossed for full-fledged class-party warfare, except that the Social Democrats did not immediately assume their role as the partisan advocate of labor's plan. The party leadership instead took evasive action. It neither endorsed nor rejected the plan. Then-party leader Olof Palme emphasized the complexity of the issue and pointed out that the unions as a whole had not fully resolved the matter.

The Swedish Social Democrats were obviously caught in a quandary: endorse the plan and jeopardize the carefully fostered image of a moderate party comfortable with capitalism; or reject the plan and affront your key clientele, your historic ally. It was a classic dilemma between policy and politics. While policy dictated taking the unions' side, politics dictated the opposite.

Their defeat in the 1976 election took the Social Democrats off the hook as far as immediate policy action was concerned. In the meantime, a government commission on wage earner funds proceeded with its work. But its attempts to compromise the opposing positions of business and labor failed to win the support of both groups. While profit sharing, in principle, proved acceptable to business, labor would not accept any form of individual ownership of the fund. Yet business, in turn, would have none of the collective ownership of the fund. At heart, collective ownership and management of business profits was the key to labor's demand, just as much as it was the key to business' opposition. The commission, headed by a series of chairmen, was unable to paper over, let alone resolve, that profound disagreement. What it finally produced in 1981 was a mass of data but no policy recommendation of any use to the political antagonists.

In the interim, however, one gap closed, though not through the efforts of the commission. By late 1981, the Social Democrats found a *modus vivendi* with the LO on their cherished plan. The party endorsed the principle of collective ownership but did not cede to the unions clear-cut control over the funds to be established. By that time, too, the Social Democrats no longer had as much to fear in electoral terms. The government formed by three non-socialist parties in 1976 had done more to self-destruct than to accumulate a glowing record for reelection in 1982. Popular attention then focused more heavily on the negatives of the governing parties than on the proposals of the out-of-power Social Democrats.

Back in power after the 1982 election, the Social Democrats proceeded to turn the plan into policy with a minimum of fanfare, playing down any implication that it would radically transform Sweden's mixed economy or enhance worker control over the economy. Instead the emphasis was placed on increasing the supply of venture capital. The three non-socialist parties pledged to dismantle any such plan once they returned to power. The business federation, in turn, refused even to participate in the formalities of consultation.

While the legislation that ultimately established the wage earner funds did not fulfill the original dreams of the labor movement, the way in which it was passed left little doubt that it was not by consultation or compromise. Instead it was adopted through the superior power of one party, which was little restrained by its adversaries. That party, perhaps with some reluctance, accepted the demands of its key clientele and ultimately delivered a policy acceptable to it. It was the display of a party able to control its own ranks (while enjoying the benign neutrality of the Communists) and in no need or mood to accommodate its partisan opposition on the right.

THE MIDDLE WAY: THE VASASHIP OF THE 1980S?

In early 1986, the Swedish prime minister, walking home after watching a movie in downtown Stockholm, was assassinated. In any country, the assassination of a political leader is a shocking event, but for Sweden it was nearly incomprehensible. Had not political violence, like smallpox, been eradicated in that country? With fewer than 100 homicides a year, compared with over 1,500 in New York City, which has roughly the same population, Sweden is not accustomed to daily stories of murder and mayhem.

Palme's death at the hands of an assassin nonetheless was a brutal reminder that paradise was still postponed in Scandinavia. Politics in that region had long won acclaim for solving the problems of modern life, but the 1970s raised serious doubts as to whether that record could be sustained. Palme himself had lost the premiership in 1976, although he regained it six years later; and his counterparts in Oslo and Copenhagen experienced similar political turbulence in office. In Denmark, in particular, new parties with agendas challenging the Social Democrats from left, right and center rendered Hamlet's kingdom virtually ungovernable in the 1970s.

"The Middle Way"—that was supposedly the recipe of the Scandinavian success story. In a nutshell, the middle way referred to key partnerships and compromises, among political parties, among interest groups, between such groups and government, between rival doctrines like free enterprise and communal values, and between individuals making money and a government caring for people (see box).

But the prosperity sustaining the ever-expanding welfare state could not be taken for granted in the rough climate of international competition; nor did the welfare state, for all its accomplishments in making life secure, abolish economic inequality. A sputtering economy revived public interest in non-socialist alternatives fashionable among conservatives, whereas persistent inequality gave impetus to demands for "economic democracy," fashionable on the left. While one side demanded tax cuts for individuals and program cuts by government, the other demanded more say by workers collectively over the profits and decisions of private companies.

The Social Democrats, the long-time navigators of the middle way, who were now being pulled in opposite directions, decided to veer to the left. To secure enough support to govern they began relying on the parties on their left instead of the agrarian/liberal par-

The Middle Way

The socialist-agrarian partnership [of the 1930s] was the solid foundation on which the reforms of future years were based. . . . The political partnership between the socialists and the farmers was paralleled by an economic partnership between labor and industry, underwritten by the pact of Saltsjöbaden. . . . Here was a mutual recognition of the accepted roles of the two principals in the economic process, each motivated by a sense of well-being of a country dependent on sales abroad to live. . . . So long as the international competitiveness of industry, privately owned up to 90 or 95 percent, continued to increase, with prosperity thereby sustained, the growing scope of welfarism could be supported through taxation that tended to keep pace with welfare benefits. A highly disciplined and comprehensive labor movement . . . was an important element in the stability of the country.

SOURCE: Marquis W. Childs, *Sweden: The Middle Way on Trial* (New Haven and London: Yale University Press, 1980), pp. 18–19.

ties on their right. Meanwhile, proposals for wage earner funds gravely strained the partnership between business and labor. What is more, the numerically strong, but for years politically feeble, gathering of non-socialist parties grew bolder in its challenge of social democracy.

As a result, politics in Scandinavia has discovered the principle of government turnover, with power now changing hands frequently in a party system polarized between a still formidable Social Democratic party on the left and an assortment of Centrist-Liberal and Conservative parties, bent on reining in welfare state expansion, on the right. The fabled middle way appears to be turning into a deserted road. Will it be another Vasaship? That is to say, a formula that for all its elegant appeal proved not to be politically seaworthy?

A keener sense of political competition

The Ship Called Vasa

Sweden's newest, most expensive and most elaborately outfitted warship, the *Vasa,* set out across Stockholm harbor with five hundred persons aboard for her maiden voyage. It was the evening of a balmy Sunday [August 10, 1628]. Thousands of Swedes watched proudly as the tall, 64-gun man-of-war moved slowly away from the Palace of the Three Crowns. And then a strong but quite ordinary breeze billowed the topsails. The great ship keeled over and sank ignominiously to the bottom. The *Vasa* remained there until she was raised in 1961, three and a third centuries later, and put on display in a special museum.

SOURCE: Donald Connery, *The Scandinavians* (New York: Simon and Schuster, 1966), p. 281.

does not spell the end of stability for Scandinavian countries. Past accounts have probably erred in underestimating the extent of that competition. As long as Social Democrats held firm control of the government and their non-socialist opponents tied themselves in knots, it was easy to mistake socialist rule for consensus government of the middle way. Now with a shrunken Social Democratic base and an emboldened opposition, the middle way looms more clearly as the no-man's land separating political adversaries.

References and Suggested Readings

BORRE, OLE. "Critical Electoral Change in Scandinavia." In Russell J. Dalton, Scott C. Flanagan and Paul Allen Beck (eds.), *Electoral Change in Advanced Industrial Democracies.* Princeton: Princeton University Press, 1984, ch. 11.

CASTLES, FRANCIS G. *The Social Democratic Image of Society.* London: Routledge & Kegan Paul, 1978.

CHILDS, MARQUIS W. *Sweden: The Middle Way on Trial.* New Haven and London: Yale University Press, 1980.

CONNERY, DONALD. *The Scandinavians.* New York: Simon and Schuster, 1966.

CONVERSE, PHILIP, AND HENRY VALEN. "Dimensions of Cleavage and Perceived Party Distances in Norwegian Voting." *Scandinavian Political Studies* 6 (1971);107–52.

DAMGAARD, ERIK, AND JERROLD RUSK. "Cleavage Structures and Representational Linkages: A Longitudinal Analysis of Danish Legislative Behavior." *American Journal of Political Science* 20 (May 1976);179–206.

ECKSTEIN, HARRY. *Division and Cohesion in Democracy.* Princeton: Princeton University Press, 1966.

ESPING-ANDERSEN, GOSTA. *Politics Against Markets: The Social Democratic Road to Power.* Princeton: Princeton University Press, 1985.

FLANAGAN, ROBERT, et al. (eds.) *Unionism, Economic Stabilization, and Incomes Policies.* Washington, DC, 1983, chs. 4, 6, and 8.

FLEISHER, FREDERIC. *The New Sweden: The Challenge of a Disciplined Democracy.* New York: McKay, 1967.

HANCOCK, M. DONALD. *Sweden: The Politics of Postindustrial Change.* Hinsdale: Dryden Press, 1972.

HECLO, HUGH, AND HENRIK MADSEN. *Policy and Politics in Sweden: Principled Pragmatism.* Philadelphia: Temple University Press, 1987.

KORPI, WALTER. *The Democratic Class Struggle.* London: Routledge & Kegan Paul, 1983.

ROKKAN, STEIN. "Norway: Numerical Democracy and Corporate Pluralism." In Robert Dahl (ed.), *Political Oppositions in Western Democracies.* New Haven and London: Yale University Press, 1966, ch. 3.

SAMUELSSON, KURT. *From Great Power to Welfare State: 300 Years of Swedish Social Development.* London: Allen & Unwin, 1968.

THOMAS, ALASTAIR. "Denmark: Coalitions and Minority Governments." In Eric Browne and John Dreijmanis (eds.), *Government Coalitions in Western Democracies.* New York: Longman, 1982, ch. 4.

VALEN, HENRY, AND DANIEL KATZ. *Political Parties in Norway.* London: Tavistock, 1964.

37

Eastern Europe

I think that this hopeful aspect of our situation today has two main reasons. Above all, man is never merely a product of the world around him, he is always capable of striving for something higher, no matter how systematically this ability is ground down by the world around him. Secondly, the humanistic and democratic traditions—which are often spoken about in such a hollow way—nonetheless lay dormant somewhere in the subconscious of our nations and national minorities, and were passed on quietly from one generation to the next in order for each of us to discover them within us when the time was right, and to put them into practice.

—VACLAV HAVEL, PLAYRIGHT AND DISSIDENT, ELECTED PRESIDENT OF CZECHOSLOVAKIA IN DECEMBER 1989

THE NEW EASTERN EUROPE

The states of Eastern Europe enter the decade of the 1990s in a greater state of flux and with more changes in politics and government than any other of the states or regions covered in this volume. After forty years, the ruling Communist parties of the region find themselves weakened, displaced or even destroyed as the dominant political force. The changes and revolutions of 1989 have changed the rules of the political game in the states of this region. How significantly can be seen by considering first the region's key characteristics before and during the period of Communist rule and then looking at what happened during the last year of the previous decade that will make the next one so interesting—and challenging.

OVERVIEW AND HISTORY

The common designation of a part of Europe as "Eastern Europe" is more a political description than a geographic one and, like most such designations, it is misleading. In terms of location, after all, Prague is farther west than Vienna; and Greece, a member of NATO and the European Community, is farther east than most of the "Eastern European" states. Politically, the region contains some states that have been closely aligned with the Soviet Union, like Bulgaria, and some, like Romania, that have followed quite distinct foreign policies. Two states, Yugoslavia and Albania, are not members of the Soviet-created alliance systems, the one having helped found the nonaligned movement and the other following a determinedly

Figure 37.1   The countries of Eastern Europe.

independent and at times isolationist course in world affairs.

The eight countries of the region usually referred to as Eastern Europe today contain some 140 million people, representing more than two dozen different nationalities. In the recent past the states were dominated by Communist parties, which came to power as a direct or indirect result of the Soviet victory over Germany in World War II. Each of these governments aimed for the development of a socialist economy, but each pursued a somewhat different path to that goal. Some of the states, notably those in the central and northern part of the region, are industrially developed, while others, such as those in the Balkans, are not. For example, the gross national product *per capita* (a rough measure of economic development) for Czechoslovakia is $11,860, while the figure for Romania is $6,358 and for Yugoslavia $6,302. (See Table 37.1. By comparison, the figure for the United States is $18,416.)[1]

In external affairs, six of the eight are members of the Warsaw Treaty Organization (WTO, referred to as the Warsaw Pact), but they vary greatly in the degree to which they

[1] Thad P. Alton, Krzsztof Badach, Elizabeth M. Bass, Joseph T. Bombelles, Gregor Lazarcik, and George J. Staller, "Economic Growth in Eastern Europe 1970 and 1975–1987," in Thad Alton et al., *Research Project on National Income in East Central Europe* (New York: L. W. International Financial Research, Inc., 1988), p. 26.

Table 37.1   Socialist Europe: Basic Data

Country	Size (Sq. Mi.)	Population[1]	GNP per Capita[2]
COMECON members			
Bulgaria	44,365	8,961,000	7,222
Czechoslovakia	49,371	15,582,000	9,715
German Dem. Rep.	41,612	16,610,000	11,860
Hungary	35,900	10,609,000	8,260
Poland	120,700	37,727,000	6,890
Romania	91,699	22,937,000	6,358
Others			
Yugoslavia	99,000	23,431,000	6,302
Albania	11,097	3,086,000	907[3]

[1]Dates of censuses vary.

[2]In constant 1987 dollars.

[3]1986.

SOURCES: Minton F. Goldman, *The Soviet Union and Eastern Europe* (Guilford, Conn.: Dushkin, 1988); Thad P. Alton, Krzysztof Badach, Elizabeth M. Bass, Joseph T. Bombelles, Gregor Lazarcik, and George J. Staller, "Economic Growth in Eastern Europe 1970 and 1975–1987," in Thad Alton et al., *Research Project on National Income in East Central Europe* (New York: L. W. International Financial Research, Inc., 1988), p. 25, 26.

contribute to the alliance. For example, Romania and Bulgaria spend proportionately much less of their GNP on defense than do other members, and rarely host military maneuvers. East Germany, Poland, Czechoslovakia, and Hungary have Soviet troops stationed on their territory, but there are none in Bulgaria or Romania. Six are members of the Eastern European economic group, the Council for Mutual Economic Assistance (CMEA or COMECON), but some, such as Hungary and East Germany, trade heavily with the West while others, such as Czechoslovakia and Bulgaria, do not.

Whatever their historical or contemporary diversity, developments in this region have long been of direct interest to the Soviet Union, and the United States. For the peoples of the region, the attention and involvement of powerful outside forces are not new.

The region has in modern times usually been the chess board of the great empires, with its peoples and their aspirations as pawns. It was not until the collapse of the three European empires at the beginning of the century that independence could be achieved, if only briefly. (See Table 37.2.) Virtually all of the socialist states of Europe began this century as part of one or even two of the empires that dominated Europe: the Ottoman, Hapsburg (Austro-Hungarian), and Russian. Poland, an empire once itself, had disappeared from the map of Europe at the end of the eighteenth century, divided among its neighbors Prussia, Austria and Russia. A Polish rump state created after the defeat of Napoleon in 1815 was dominated by Russia and virtually totally absorbed into the Russian Empire after an insurrection in 1830–31. It did not reemerge as an independent country until the collapse of the Russian autocracy at the end of World War I.

Central Europe was dominated until this century by the Austro-Hungarian Empire, which stretched from Krakow and Prague in the north to Dubrovnik on the Adriatic Sea. Parts of present-day Poland, Hungary, Czechoslovakia, Yugoslavia and Romania

Table 37.2   Evolution of the East European States

Current State	Pre-World War I Status	Date of Independence	Status Between World War I and World War II
Poland	Partitioned among: Russia, Prussia, Austro-Hungarian Empire	1918	G: parliament → dictatorship (Piłsudski, "colonels") T: reestablished and enlarged (USSR, Germany, Austria, Czechoslovakia)
Czechoslovakia	Austro-Hungarian Empire	1918	G: parliament T: established (Austria-Hungary, Poland, Germany); partitioned (1938, Germany, Hungary, Poland); absorbed (1939, Germany, Hungary)
Hungary	Austro-Hungarian Empire	1918	G: parliament → communist (Kun) → regent (Horthy) → parliament T: greatly reduced (Czechoslovakia, Romania, Yugoslavia)
Yugoslavia		1918	G: parliament → royal dictatorship (Alexander, Paul) T: established (Austria, Hungary, Bulgaria, Albania)
Slovenia	Austro-Hungarian Empire		
Croatia	Austro-Hungarian Empire		
Vojvodina	Austro-Hungarian Empire		
Bosnia-Herz.	Ottoman → Austro-Hungarian Empire		
Serbia	Ottoman Empire	1878	
Montenegro	Ottoman Empire	1878	
Kosovo	Ottoman Empire		
Macedonia	Ottoman Empire		
Albania	Ottoman Empire	1913	G: parliament → king (Zog) T: absorbed (1939, Italy)
Romania	Ottoman tributary	1878	G: parliament → royal dictatorship (Carol)
Wallachia-Moldavia	Ottoman tributary	1878	T: greatly enlarged (Hungary, Bulgaria, Austria, USSR)
Transylvania	Austro-Hungarian Empire	(1918)	
Bulgaria	Ottoman Empire	1908	G: peasants union (Stambolisky) → parliament → royal dictatorship (Boris) T: reduced (Greece, Romania, Yugoslavia)

Key: G = progression of forms of *government;* T = changes in *territory* and border states affected.

were all once under the control of the dual monarchy, being ruled from either Vienna or Budapest. For Hungary, then, the situation created after World War I meant the loss of virtually all of its share of the empire and adjustment from a role as ruler of some 20 million people to a land of under 8 million, with more than 3 million Hungarians left outside its new borders. To its north came a brand-new state formed by merging the

Czech lands of Bohemia and Moravia with Slovakia through a pact signed in Pittsburgh, Pennsylvania, in May 1918.

Also new on the twentieth-century map of Europe was Yugoslavia, an amalgamation of territories and peoples liberated from both the Hapsburg and Ottoman empires. To the Balkan state of Serbia, which had gained independence from Turkey in 1878, were added Croatia, Bosnia-Herzogovina and Slovenia in the west, and Vojvodina in the north, all from the defeated Austro-Hungarian Empire, and parts of Macedonia to the south and east, at the expense of Bulgaria. Thus was created a country of some 11 million people, of more than a dozen nationalities, 47 percent Eastern Orthodox (chiefly Serbs, Montenegrins and Macedonians), 40 percent Roman Catholic (chiefly Croats and Slovenes), 11 percent Muslim (chiefly Albanians and Bosnians).[2]

Romania too had been independent before World War I, having profited from the Russian defeat of Turkey in 1877. But the prewar state that embraced Moldavia and Wallachia more than doubled in size at the end of World War I by adding to its territory Transylvania, at the expense of Hungary, Dobrudja from Bulgaria, also a loser in World War I, and taking Bessarabia from the weak new Soviet state. For Bulgaria, such losses were only the latest in a string of humiliations dating back to 1878, when the country's victory over the Ottoman Empire on the battlefield was reversed by the major powers at the Congress of Berlin.

The boundaries and status of the states of this region had always been drawn for the advantage and convenience of controlling and usually opposing empires. Nothing illustrates this so much as the creation of Albania,

the smallest of the East European states, on the shores of the Adriatic Sea. When in 1878 Albanian nationalists petitioned the powers at the Congress of Berlin to establish a national state for them within the defeated Turkish Empire, they were rebuffed. Otto von Bismarck, the German chancellor and the inspiration behind the Congress remarked, "There is no such thing as the Albanian nationality." But 35 years later when the independent state of Serbia had profited from a new Balkan war against Turkey, the great powers feared that a powerful Serbian state would emerge. Hence they now assented to the creation of Albania to block Serbia's access to the sea.

After World War I the redivision of Eastern Europe into seven different—and some completely new—states left virtually all of them with disputes with their neighbors. Two of the states, Hungary and Bulgaria, emerged from the war with significant losses in territory and prestige and a powerful predisposition toward changing the consequences of that war. On the other hand, the "winners" in the new situation, Czechoslovakia, Romania, Yugoslavia and Poland, were concerned with keeping at least the status quo or improving it, if the opportunity arose. Most of these states were fearful of Germany, the biggest loser of all in World War I, and in some cases, such as in Poland and Romania, there was also the danger of possible territorial conflicts with the Soviet Union. Poland had in fact fought a brief but inconclusive war with the Soviet Union in 1920–21, at one point laying siege to the Ukrainian capital of Kiev. In all the new states except Czechoslovakia there was profound concern over the revolutionary goals and tactics of the new communist USSR.

Economically, interwar Eastern Europe depended heavily on agriculture, with only Czechoslovakia and some parts of Poland having significant industrial resources. In

---

[2] Joseph Rothschild, *East Central Europe Between the Two World Wars* (Seattle: University of Washington Press, 1974), p. 202.

most cases, but especially in the Balkans, the agriculture was still of a primitive and unproductive kind. For example, in Denmark the average wheat yield exceeded 8,000 lbs. per acre; in Yugoslavia the average was under 2,500 lbs.[3] At the same time the number of nominally free but poor and indebted peasants eager for loans was substantial. In Eastern Europe nearly 60 percent of the population depended on agriculture, while in the West the figure was 24 percent.

Nor was the region a fertile ground for the emergence of democratic institutions. Limited advisory councils or parliaments had operated in parts of the Austro-Hungarian Empire during the nineteenth century, and before its partition Poland had employed a representative system that was the most advanced of its time. But for the most part the leadership of these new states, with uncertain international security and in difficult economic straits, had little experience with or inclination toward the process or mechanics of parliamentary democracy. Most slid quickly into military or other forms of dictatorships.

In Hungary, a postwar liberal government was overthrown in 1919 by the first communist revolution outside the Soviet Union, led by Béla Kun. The regime, a curious mixture of radical socialism and nationalism directed against its neighbors, was itself undone before the year was out with the help of the victorious Allies, including troops from Romania. A conservative anti-democratic regime under Admiral Miklós Horthy led eventually to a full-scale dictatorship under Gyula Gömbös and later, alliance with Adolf Hitler, who promised to undo the consequences of World War I. Similarly, the radically pro-peasant rule of Alexander Stambolisky in Bulgaria was ended in 1923 by a military coup; the new military regime, with the support of King Boris, also pursued a nationalist line and also lined itself up with resurgent Germany.

In Poland the parliamentary experiment lasted a bit longer, but proved weak and ineffective in governing the country. The extremely popular Jozef Piłsudski, who had led the Polish armies against the Soviet Union, took power in 1926 and at his death in 1936 passed on virtually total control to a military dictatorship known as the "regime of the Colonels." Both Romania and Yugoslavia had similarly unrewarding experiences with representative legislatures that proved unable to resolve ethnic disputes, deal with the serious economic situation, especially the needs of the peasantry, or prevent the manipulation of the system by rival groups aspiring to power. In these two cases the monarchy, which had been preserved with constitutional limitations, violated these limitations and took full power by the end of the 1920s.

Only in Czechoslovakia was the process of representative democracy made effective. A two-chambered parliament based on universal suffrage and proportional representation gave expression and the opportunity to participate to a variety of political parties and national groups. In addition some effective economic measures were taken to help new landowners prosper. But Czechoslovakia, as the rest of Eastern Europe, was undone by its precarious situation, caught between disgruntled neighbors such as Hungary and even Poland, which made claims on the city of Cieszyn (Teschen), and Germany, which claimed the western part of the country, known as the Sudetenland. That pressure, in addition to the economic collapse that struck the entire industrial world at the beginning of the 1930s, hardly made for a stable governing environment.

The growth of protectionism against imports and the accompanying worldwide eco-

---

[3] F. B. Singleton, *Background to Eastern Europe* (London: Pergamon Press, 1965), p. 60.

nomic collapse devastated the already weak economies in Eastern Europe, cutting off trade possibilities and throwing millions out of work. In Czechoslovakia there had been fewer than 90,000 people unemployed in 1929; by 1932 that figure was more than 900,000. The Depression fueled the growth of militant nationalism, militarism and *fascism,* a movement to strengthen the powers of the state. This was especially true in Germany, where Adolf Hitler's Nazi Party dominated the elections of 1933, allowing him to become chancellor. Hitler was determined to change the map of Europe, to restore what he saw as Germany's rightful place and establish a "thousand-year reign" of Aryan rule over lesser peoples, including Slavs. After coming to power he was able to challenge the divided and apprehensive allies of Britain and France by rearming his country, reoccupying the Rhineland (1938) and forcing union with Austria (1938). Then, at a meeting in Munich in September 1938, Britain and France agreed to hand the Sudetenland from Czechoslovakia to Germany. Representatives of the Czechoslovak government, though present in Munich, were not even consulted or made party to the dismemberment of their country. With the loss of 30 percent of its population, one-third of its territory, and 40 percent of its national income, "the country ceased to be economically or strategically viable."[4] Within six months it was totally absorbed by Germany, and Slovakia, the country's eastern part, was set up as a puppet state. When Hitler, in August 1939, pressed claims on Poland and they were refused, the invasion of that country produced declarations of war from Great Britain and France and, in short order, World War II.

The war brought destruction and occupation to most of Eastern Europe, but no country suffered as did Poland. Already having

been struck a mortal blow by its division between the USSR and Germany in their 1939 Nonaggression Pact, it was quickly occupied by Hitler. Over the next five and a half years until its liberation, more than six million Poles were to die—more than one of every six people—including more than 3 million Jews, virtually annihilating what had been Europe's most numerous Jewish population. Other Eastern European countries either accommodated to Hitler's growing power, as did Hungary and Bulgaria, or were attacked and occupied, as was Yugoslavia in 1941. In some cases old scores were settled. With Hitler's blessing Hungary took back Transylvania from Romania, and in Yugoslavia the fascist puppet state of Croatia unleashed attacks against Serbs on its territory. Romania was able to keep Germany at arm's length by virtue of the vigor of its own fascist movement and its eagerness to cooperate in joining the German attack on the Soviet Union in 1941.

It was that attack that ultimately led to Hitler's defeat. But this did not occur for four more years, after the monumental battle of Stalingrad (now Volgograd) in which more than 200,000 German soldiers were killed and nearly 100,000 captured, and after the German armies were driven out of eastern (and western) Europe. In the East, except in Albania and Yugoslavia, the key military force was Soviet troops, usually aided by domestic anti-fascist groups. In one case, that of East Germany, the boundaries of what was to become a completely new state were set by the final battle lines.

The dominating presence of Soviet troops throughout the region meant that they would be the ultimate force in determining the postwar political situation in this area. At Teheran in November 1943, Winston Churchill and Franklin Roosevelt agreed to Soviet demands to retain the eastern third of Poland, and all three leaders agreed to throw

[4] Rothschild, p. 132.

their support in Yugoslavia behind the communist forces led by Josip Tito. "By the end of 1944," writes historian John Lukacs, "no power existed in East Europe that could effectively resist the Russian conquerors."[5] Churchill had already informally proposed to Stalin a division of influence in the region in which the USSR would have predominant influence (Churchill suggested 80–20 percent) in Bulgaria, Romania and Hungary and the British would retain power in Greece; Yugoslavia was to be divided "50–50." At a meeting in Moscow in 1944 Churchill wrote these numbers on a slip of paper and slid it across the table to Stalin, who indicated his approval by making a check in the bottom right-hand corner. This so-called "percentages" agreement was yet another division of the region by outside powers, and it also reflected the new reality of Soviet power. The agreements at Yalta in February 1945 essentially ratified this situation while extracting from the USSR pledges that free elections would be held in the Eastern European countries.

After the war such pledges were given short shrift, as in the Soviet view the key to its own security lay in establishing friendly, compliant socialist governments on its border, something it had never had before. As communist parties gained full control in the region and suspicion and hostility replaced wartime cooperation between East and West, the entire region became trapped behind what Churchill would call in 1947 an "iron curtain." Though the details differed in each country, the process and the end result were the same: coalition government was replaced by communist-led or all-communist rule; opposition parties and political activity were

banned; and by 1948, with the end of multiparty rule in Czechoslovakia, the new empire in Eastern Europe, this time a socialist Soviet-dominated one, was established.

THE PROBLEM OF GOVERNANCE UNDER THE COMMUNISTS

For the leaders of the Communist parties in Eastern Europe, who were the effective rulers of these various states since soon after the end of World War II, the fundamental dilemma was finding policies that would satisfy their countries' political, economic and social needs, as determined by that leadership, while also meeting their international obligations—that is, Soviet demands. In some cases the decision as to how to resolve this dilemma was made for them; Soviet power simply dictated what would be done in their state; a leader's choice was to comply or be removed. In other cases, public demand or the leaders' own desire for greater prerogative put them into potential or real conflict with the USSR. Sometimes, when Soviet concerns were not addressed sufficiently, full-scale military intervention occurred.

For the first five years after communist rule was fully established, the Eastern European states followed plans for economic development not unlike those that had characterized the Soviet Union during the "great turn" (see pp. 370–72). Investment was poured into heavy industry, and collectivization of agriculture was instituted. The result was tremendous social upheaval as societies were virtually transformed. A "new proletariat" was created as peasants deprived of private ownership of the land joined the urban industrial labor force. Nearly one-half million people made this transition in both Bulgaria and Yugoslavia, more than three quarters of a mil-

---

[5] John Lukacs, *A New History of the Cold War* (New York: Doubleday and Co., 1966), p. 47.

lion in Hungary and Romania, and almost two million in Poland.[6]

Apart from the defection of Yugoslavia (see box), the first significant variation in political and economic behavior did not occur until after the death of Joseph Stalin in 1953. While the leadership in the Soviet Union embarked in fits and starts on a new direction in economic policy and replaced the cult of personality with collective leadership, some of the states in Eastern Europe followed suit and some did not. For example, new leaders emerged in Bulgaria, Hungary and Poland but not in East Germany or Czechoslovakia, and in Romania the party leader at the time, Gheorghe Gheorghiu-Dej, used the de-Stalinization process to weaken his opposition and consolidate his own position.

ECHOES OF 1956 AND 1968

In two countries in particular the wave of change set off by de-Stalinization in the Soviet Union in the mid-fifties produced consequences with ramifications for governance up to the present day. In both Poland and Hungary popular anti-Stalinist leaders re-emerged into prominence. In Poland, waves of workers' strikes plus intellectual ferment and deep-seated opposition to collectivization led the party to turn to Władysław Gomułka, who had been purged as a "nationalist" in 1949 and kept under house arrest between 1951 and 1954. After 1956 some reforms were instituted in Poland; collectivization was ended, pressure was eased on the Catholic church, and workers' councils were established in the factories. But soon Gomułka began to strengthen his politi-

[6] Zbigniew Brzezinski, *The Soviet Bloc: Unity and Conflict,* rev. and enlarged ed. (Cambridge: Harvard University Press, 1971), p. 102.

cal power and to undo many of the social and economic changes promised. Though collectivization was not tried again, the private agricultural sector languished under a combination of neglect and restrictions—on size and sale of land, the possibility of loans, and so on. By the late 1960s the failure to reform the economy alienated workers eager for some return from the country's development; moreover, economic growth itself was slowing down. The lack of investment in private agriculture kept production down, and the poorly performing socialist agricultural sector could not compensate. Food was costing more to produce than it sold for because prices were kept low to forestall worker unrest. Thus subsidies consumed increasing amounts of the state budget. Just before Christmas 1970, the government announced immediate and substantial price increases. Worker demonstrations broke out; in Gdansk the party headquarters were attacked, and when the Soviet Union turned down a request for military assistance, Gomułka himself was replaced.

The new leader, Edward Gierek, faced the same dilemma as had his predecessors: how to get the economy to function more productively while keeping within the bounds of socialism and not taking any actions, such as decentralization, that would threaten the position of the party and, in that way, the interests of the Soviet Union. In an attempt to solve its problem, the Polish party followed what became known as the "Gierek strategy." The country began to vigorously import Western technology, licenses and sometimes whole factories to try to rapidly improve productive capacity. As Poland's own exports to the West—chiefly coal but also food—were insufficient to pay for all these imports, the government began to borrow. In the mid-1970s, Western governments were eager to build economic ties to

Yugoslavia: The First Heretic

When Soviet troops entered Yugoslavia in 1944 to assist in driving out the German invaders, they found that, unlike in Romania or Hungary, a strong, functioning and popular communist movement, led by Josip Broz Tito, was already in existence. Almost immediately the question of who would determine the country's future, the communists in Moscow or those in Belgrade, became inflamed into a conflict. Yugoslavs objected to Stalin's attempt to restructure the country's government and army along Soviet lines, to what they saw as exploitation of the country's resources and Soviet unwillingness to support full scale industrialization in the country. In addition, old-fashioned nationalism was not muted by common socialist inclinations. Tito publicly rejected any kind of great power agreement (such as "50–50") on the country's fate; there was resentment of Russian cultural arrogance—Vladimir Dedijer, a Yugoslav journalist and biographer of Tito, reports that in the first few years after the war the Yugoslavs published more than 1,800 Soviet books while "they published two of ours"—and at lack of Soviet support for Yugoslavia's dispute with Italy over Trieste or for the creation of a "Balkan federation," with Yugoslavia at the head.

After the foundation of the *Cominform* (the acronym for Communist Information Bureau) in 1947 the conflict became internationalized, with the Soviet Union and its Eastern European allies combining to try to pressure Yugoslavia to get in line. Yugoslavia was thrown out of the Cominform, all the Eastern European states cut economic ties with the country, and a massive propaganda campaign was unleashed against Tito and the leaders of the Yugoslav party. But the Soviet regime overestimated its power—Stalin said, "I will shake my little finger and Tito will fall"—and underestimated the cohesiveness of the Yugoslav party, forged in a guerrilla war against the Germans. Despite the economic boycott and increased military tension on its borders and almost complete political isolation, Yugoslavia did not return to the fold. In the early 1950s the country began to explore the possibility of relations with the West, expanded economic ties with the United States and Western Europe, and began to create its own form of socialism, known as workers' self-management. In the 1960s Yugoslavia became one of the founding members of the nonaligned movement.

SOURCES: George W. Hoffman and Fred W. Neal, *Yugoslavia and the New Communism* (New York: Twentieth Century Fund, 1962). Alvin Rubinstein, *Yugoslavia and the Nonaligned World* (Princeton, NJ: Princeton University Press, 1970); Robert L. Wolf, *The Balkans in Our Time*, rev. ed. (New York: W. W. Norton and Co., 1974).

strengthen East-West détente, and banks had billions in oil revenue deposits that they were eager to lend. From the Polish point of view, the plan was to use the new industrial capacity the country would build to expand exports to the West and thus pay for new machinery and the loans.

But there was another need driving the desire for new technology, one derived both from the Polish experience of 1956 and 1970 and the experience of Czechoslovakia in 1968. In that country economic stagnation in the early 1960s and long-delayed political reform—including the continuation of the Stalinist leadership of Antonín Novotný—finally produced a political and social movement for change. In January 1968, Novotný was removed, and the Czechoslovak party under Aleksandr Dubcek began easing control of the press and other media, rehabilitated former political prisoners, and issued an action program calling for full-scale economic and political reform. As discussion became more vigorous and independent political activity more a possibility, strong pressure to clamp down came from the Soviet Union and other Eastern European states, including Poland. But domestic social pressure on the Prague government was also strong; to move further and faster, to allow non-communist political activity, full and open discussion of all questions, and a stronger voice for the country's Slovak minority (19 percent of the population). The leadership of the Czechoslovak party was caught between what it saw as changes necessary to improve the governance of the country and Soviet desire to prevent what its leaders described as "counterrevolution."

When the Soviet Union became convinced that reforms were not going to be reversed and that an upcoming extraordinary (that is, scheduled before the usual five-year interval had elapsed) party congress would install reform-minded cadres throughout the party, a decision was made to intervene with force. On August 21, 1968, troops from the Soviet Union and all allied countries except Romania crossed the borders of this fraternal ally and quickly occupied the country.

Though reforms were systematically undone in Czechoslovakia, and party leaders who had instituted political and economic change were removed, the regime there and others throughout Eastern Europe realized that crucial to stable rule was the ability to provide at least economic satisfaction, in the form of more and better housing, automobiles, consumer goods and foodstuffs. Thus in most of the Eastern European states, attempts were made to improve the economic situation of the population while holding off political reform. This so-called "social contract" held throughout the 1970s, or as long as the relatively weak economies of those states could manage it.

In Poland, therefore, an additional component of the Gierek strategy was to produce more consumer goods to satisfy the popula-

tion and avoid the trauma of what had happened in Czechoslovakia in 1968 and what had already occurred in Poland in 1956 and 1970. For a while, the strategy worked. The situation for Poland's consumers improved. Real personal income grew by 50 percent in six years. Consumption of meat increased and that of cereals and potatoes declined. By 1976 twice as many people had refrigerators as in 1970 and sales of radios and television sets nearly doubled.[7] But the Polish economic system proved unable to fully absorb the new technology, and western imports of machines and licenses led to more western imports of spare parts and new equipment. Though exports grew, they were not enough to cover the growing import bill or the cost of interest and debt repayment. And loans spent on equipment that produced consumer goods for the politically important domestic market brought in no hard currency at all for loan repayment. In fact in some ways, such as the increase in the number of private automobiles, keeping the "social contract" began to cost the country even more hard currency, in this case for imported petroleum.

External events contributed to the difficulties. In the mid- and late 1970s, most of the Eastern European states, but especially those like Poland that were heavily involved with the western international economy, were hit indirectly by the effect of the quadrupling of oil prices. Most of the region—including Yugoslavia—bought their oil from the Soviet Union. But oil price hikes produced recessions in the major western economies, like the United States and those of Western Europe, leading them to lower their imports

[7] Thad Alton, Krzysztof Badach, Elizabeth Bass, Joseph Bombelles, and Gregor Lazarcik, "Money Income of the Population and Standard of Living in Eastern Europe 1970–1987," in Thad Alton et al., *Research Project on National Income in East Central Europe* (New York: L. W. International Financial Research, Inc., 1988), pp. 12, 25.

from Eastern Europe. With expected sales thus not being realized, Poland and several other Eastern European countries like Romania, Hungary and Bulgaria, needed to borrow even more. In 1976 Poland's net debt was $11.3 billion. By 1980 this figure had grown to $23.5 billion. Romania owed more than $9 billion and Hungary, with less than one-half Romania's population, nearly $8 billion. By the beginning of the 1980s most of the Eastern European economies were in trouble. But with concern rising about their ability to repay their debts and détente waning between East and West, the opportunity to go to the well one more time for new loans had passed.

It was in Poland once again that tight economic straits precipitated political crisis. An attempt in 1976 to raise prices had spawned worker riots, attacks on party headquarters, and government retreat on the economic issue. Unlike in 1970, the party leadership was not changed; but neither were economic reforms implemented. By 1980 the situation was desperate. The Polish economy showed a negative growth rate in 1979, debt payments were absorbing virtually all export earnings, and food subsidies alone were taking 20 percent of the state budget. The Polish people were no longer looking forward to a steadily improving situation, but they were no better informed as to the true seriousness of the situation and no more able to determine public policy than they had been before. When in the summer of 1980 price increases were once again announced, the result at first seemed the same: worker strikes, wage increases, government promises, talk of reform. But this time the Polish workers recognized the need for a more thoroughgoing transformation. With the assistance of groups such as the Committee for the Defense of Workers (KOR), they articulated demands for broader change, chiefly through formation of the first

non-governmental labor union, which became known as Solidarity.

From September 1980 until December 1981 the dilemma of all Communist parties in Eastern Europe was starkly illustrated in Poland: At home the party was faced with clear demands for change, including a major role in government for the workers, in whose name the state was supposed to be ruling. But the party did not want to relinquish its own monopoly of political power and, moreover, it had to assure the Soviet Union that its interests in the region were being protected. In the Gdansk Agreements of August 1980, Solidarity was grudgingly acknowledged, and other important concessions were made that suited Polish society. For the first time, for example, the country's 95 percent Catholic population could listen to Catholic mass broadcast live over the radio. But over the next year the party leadership fought the union on each specific aspect of reform, such as the demand for a farmers' union, and the workers' demand to put an end to Saturday work and for greater control over the key decisions regarding the country's economy. Though Solidarity recognized "the leading role of the Polish United Workers Party" (the Communist Party) and pledged adherence to Poland's existing "system of international alliances," Soviet pressure on Warsaw to crack down was intense and over the next sixteen months included massive troop movements and maneuvers, personal letters from Leonid Brezhnev, and several high-level visits. Ultimately the Polish party saved its nominal rule by declaring martial law on December 13, 1981. At that time the military, headed by Wojciech Jaruzelski, who was also party leader, took power.

Clamping down on Solidarity with military rule did not solve Poland's economic problems. Though martial law formally lasted until 1983, the effects of years of neglecting agriculture and of blocking real economic reform elsewhere came home to roost. Net national product fell by almost one-fourth between 1980 and 1982 and barely returned to 1978 levels by the mid-1980s. But though its situation was the most dramatic, Poland was not alone. Unbalanced over-investment and the growing debt burden, in addition to the lack of ability to quickly respond to changing international conditions, left most of the other Eastern European states with similar difficulties. Average growth rate for the Eastern European "six" for 1980–85 was a meager 1.4 percent, and after that all of them moved to cut international borrowing: By 1984 debt had been reduced by more than 20 percent, but growth remained quite uneven.

DIFFERENT APPROACHES: HUNGARY AND ROMANIA

In contrast to Poland, the situation in Hungary in 1956 moved beyond the control of the party leadership. Here too a popular leader, oriented toward the country's special needs, had come to power after the death of Stalin. Imre Nagy pushed the party toward putting more investment into consumer goods, ending the drive for collectivization, providing higher pay and lower quotas in industry, and tolerating broader intellectual freedom. During much of his attempt to dismantle Stalinism, Nagy had Soviet support. But opposition to these actions within the party leadership in Hungary and uncertain signals from the USSR as Moscow grappled with its own de-Stalinization weakened his control. By late 1956 popular demand for change outdistanced whatever reformers in the party leadership wanted to do and thoroughly alarmed conservatives. Soviet troops, stationed in the country under the terms

of the Warsaw Pact, were invited to restore control. When pitched battles broke out and overthrow of the communist system seemed imminent, a full-scale invasion was mounted and Imre Nagy was arrested and executed.

While the new party leadership of János Kádár completely reestablished control, by the beginning of the 1960s a political accommodation with the population was signalled by Kádár's statement that "he who is not against us is with us." In 1968 the leadership began wide-ranging economic reforms that reduced the authority of the central plan, allowed enterprises a greater degree of autonomy, and introduced some market mechanisms. Agricultural cooperatives, which account for most of the country's production, were also given greater freedom and incentives, which allowed Hungary to become not only self-sufficient but also a net exporter of grain and meat. Though reform slowed a bit in the mid-1970s, it regained momentum soon after. The government adopted a policy of providing more information about the country's situation so that when difficult decisions needed to be taken the public was not shocked and alienated. When in the late 1970s and early 1980s adjustment to changing and difficult international circumstances required some austerity, the Hungarian regime was able to avoid the upheaval and challenges that occurred so often in Poland.

In contrast to the Hungarian path of reform, the Romanian party, for example, determined that it would continue to strive for rapid broad industrial development even when the Stalinist period of Soviet domination of the region ended and even though its own base of natural resources, including raw materials and good land, made it more suited to a role as provider of primary products. But rejecting the role it had played before the war as the "gas station and breadbasket" of Europe, the regimes of

Gheorghe Gheorghiu-Dej and, after 1965, of Nicolae Ceauşescu began pursuing a broad range of contacts with western countries in order to secure in the West what it could not get in the East: machines and equipment to expand its manufacturing and technology base. In support of this policy, which was at variance with official Soviet aims of a high degree of specialization within COMECON, Romania followed a foreign policy often quite different from that of Moscow. In 1967 it established full diplomatic relations with West Germany without waiting for its allies to recognize this economically important state or insisting that Bonn formally recognize East Germany first. On the grounds that each party has the right to utilize policies most appropriate to its own situation, Bucharest did not cooperate in 1968 in pressuring Czechoslovakia to end its reforms and in fact condemned the invasion of that country. Romania maintained good party and state relations with China even after that country and the Soviet Union exchanged bitter accusations and split the world communist movement in the mid-1960s. This independent foreign policy earned Ceauşescu's regime the support of the United States and other western countries, and domestically it appealed to Romanian nationalism. It was not, however, accompanied by domestic reform. The economy remained totally controlled by the state and by the central planning apparatus. A nascent free trade union movement and occasional worker demonstrations, as well as the activities of those few dissidents who spoke out, were crushed.

As in Romania, both the Bulgarian and East German parties maintained tight political control of their countries. Unlike Romania, however, Bulgaria accepted a degree of specialization as an agricultural producer in the region and has over the years become the most efficient producer of crops in the region. Its foreign economic relations are dominated by the USSR, which by itself accounts for more than one-half of Bulgaria's trade. Bulgaria, too, began to expand western ties in the 1970s, but when its international debt became excessive the government quickly cut back on imports and borrowing.

Of all the states in Eastern Europe, probably the strongest economically is East Germany. Based not on reform but on a system of centrally controlled "industrial combines," the East German economy also benefits from being able to export its goods to West Germany without international tariffs because the Federal Republic (West Germany) considers this as intra-Germany trade. Moreover, the East German government has had access to special financing in West Germany, because of that government's desire to improve relations and contacts between people in the two states. On the other hand, West Germany creates a problem for the East German party that does not worry the other states as much: the presence of a flourishing "other Germany" which provides a counterexample of high living standards and greater personal freedom. When changes in Hungary, Czechoslovakia, Poland, and East Germany itself allowed virtually free emigration for the first time in nearly thirty years, the East German economy began to suffer a considerable drain of its human resources.

THE END OF COMMUNIST DOMINANCE IN EASTERN EUROPE

The ascension to power in Moscow of Mikhail Gorbachev and his push for *glasnost* and *perestroika* in the social, political and economic system of the USSR have had profound repercussions for Eastern Europe. Reform in the dominant state in the region made change easier in the smaller states by giving reform leaders and ordinary people alike the hope that Soviet pressure, which had stifled change so often before, would not do so this time. In Poland, the need for economic reform and a degree of political openness were formally recognized by the party after widespread strikes in 1988. In early 1989 the Communist government accepted the participation of Solidarity, once again legalized, in competitive elections and a new two-chambered legislature. The elections then proved disastrous for the Communist party, which managed to hold on only to those seats that it was allocated by law. Unable to form a working government, the party yielded control for the first time since World War II and a leading Solidarity advisor and editor of its newspaper, Tadeusz Mazowiecki, became prime minister.

Hungary, which began implementing reform more than 20 years ago, had already allowed the greatest range for private economic behavior, including a stock market. But the party tried to retain political control by changing its leadership, in the spring of 1988 and again in 1989. Neither move satisfied the public's growing desire for political pluralism and the Hungarian party was then also forced to sanction independent political activity and open elections. In the fall of 1989 the once dominant Hungarian Socialist Workers Party dissolved itself, changed its name (to the Hungarian Socialist Party) and found itself struggling for popularity and votes.

These changes in Poland and Hungary had a significant impact on the people and governments of the neighboring states. As people in the rest of the region learned of the democratic changes in Poland and Hungary through now freer media in these countries and greater access to western media in their own, pressure began to build. In May 1989 Hungary announced that it would open the border between itself and neighboring Austria, in places tearing down what had literally been an iron curtain between East and West.

The possibility of leaving this way attracted thousands of East German citizens, for decades penned up in their state by a regime fearful of losing its population. In September the Budapest government suspended an agreement with East Germany under which it was obliged to prevent the exit of East German citizens without valid visas. By November some 45,000 people had taken this route to the west, and back in East Germany itself public pressure grew to enact democratic reforms. For the first time since 1953 thousands of East German citizens took to the streets in Leipzig, East Berlin, and other cities demanding change. In October Soviet General Secretary Mikhail Gorbachev visited East Germany to help celebrate the state's 40th anniversary. He gave indirect but unmistakable public backing to those calling for change, urging the East German party to cooperate with "all forces in society." On October 18 long time party leader Erich Honecker resigned but his successor Egon Krenz lasted only long enough to remove one of the most hated symbols of the division of East and West: the Berlin Wall. On the night of November 9 all East German borders were opened including the Wall, and within weeks more than 5 million East Germans visited the West. But this was not enough—or perhaps it was too much since many East Germans were now stunned to find out just how far behind their Western cousins they were. At the beginning of December Krenz was replaced by Gregor Gysi, a lawyer best known for his defense of political dissidents. Here too the party was forced to yield its political monopoly: independent political activity was allowed, "round table" talks with opposition leaders were held, elections were promised, and the party's legally enshrined "leading role" was abandoned.

Now surrounded by countries in which reform was riding high, the Czechoslovak party found its days of dominance numbered. Huge

"This just in! . . . no, hold it . . . *this* just in . . . forget that . . .
this just in . . . !"

SOURCE: Bob Gorrell, *The Richmond News Leader,* North American Syndicate.

demonstrations and workers' strikes increased pressure on the regime to get in line with its neighbors. On the night of November 17 the government tried force, unleashing police on student demonstrators in Prague. The effect of this brutal action was the opposite of that intended as it brought even more people to political action. Within a week the Communist party leadership had resigned, with Karl Urbanek replacing Milos Jakes as party Secretary General. But with the party in disarray and on the defensive over its handling of the demonstrations—not to speak of its twenty-year commitment to conservatism—the leadership was obliged to change once again. At the end of December Ladislav Adamec, who had been Prime Minister from October 1988 until December 1989, became leader of the party.

But by this point such changes were almost irrelevant. With dizzying speed the party in Czechoslovakia, as in Hungary, had moved from the center and top of a political stage it once controled, to the wings, as parties and groups of all political persuasions began to take action. In Czechoslovakia as in East Germany and Hungary, elections were scheduled, the leading role of the party was dropped, and, as in Poland, a new government was formed with Communists, for the first time since 1948, in the minority. To complete the political circle, Alexander Dubcek, the man who had led the party into the "Prague Spring" in 1968, was elected Chairman of the Federal Assembly. Gustav Husak, who had directed the "normalization" of Czechoslovakia after 1968, resigned as President. Vaclav Havel, a reknowned playwright and dissident leader for more than twenty years who had begun the year in prison for taking part in public protests and whose works were banned in Czechoslovakia, became President.

What happened in Czechoslovakia has

New Situations, New Jokes

As Communist parties throughout East Europe found themselves in retreat before an aroused public and facing open elections, some retained their sense of humor. In Czechoslovakia a current joke has the party soliciting funds.

"If you donate 1,000 crowns to the Communist party, you become a member in good standing. If you donate 2,000 crowns, you receive a form saying you used to be a member in good standing. If you donate 3,000 crowns, you receive a form saying you never have been a member."

SOURCE: *Christian Science Monitor*, December 20, 1989.

been termed "The Gentle Revolution" because of the relative lack of violence.[8] Not so in Romania. As the nature of its Communist rule in this country had been so different, so too was its transition, which came upon the country suddenly and violently in the week before Christmas 1989.

As often happens in revolutions, the immediate catalyst was a seemingly isolated event, the attempt by the government of Nicolae Ceausescu to evict an outspoken Hungarian priest, Laszlo Toekes, from his home in Timisoara on December 15. Protest had been rare in Romania under Ceausescu but this time a small crowd gathered to try to protect their pastor. They were soon joined by many others and a now large demonstration move to the center of town. It was the regime's response to this demonstration which was to start its downfall. On the personal orders of Ceausescu heavily armed security forces opened fire on the crowd, even on those who

had put their children ahead of them thinking they would be safe. Hundreds were killed in this and further actions by the hated *securitate* (secret police). Confident of his absolute power, Nicolae Ceausescu called for a demonstration in Bucharest on December 21. This was to be one of the "old" type, orchestrated and carefully staged to show support for the government. The result was a revolution. Instead of showering Ceausescu with cheers, some in the crowd, mostly students, began to boo and jeer. The party and state leader was rattled and when the crowd could not be controlled, abruptly left off speaking. Emboldened, masses of people filled the streets of Bucharest demanding the downfall of Ceausescu. With breathtaking speed their wish was granted. At noon on December 22 Mircea Dinescu, a dissident poet and target of various attacks by the Ceausescu regime, spoke to the nation on Radio Bucharest: "Please remain calm. There are moments in which God has turned his face toward Romania. . . . The army is with us! The Dictator has fled![9] That day a group calling itself the National Salvation Front declared itself the new government in Romania.

But more tragic events were still to occur, as the security forces loyal to Ceausescu sought to quell the uprising in blood. Fierce battles raged in Bucharest in particular, especially for control of the radio and TV stations in the capital. In general the army sided with the revolution but this mostly conscript, poorly equipped and trained force was severely pressed. They were joined by groups of students and others ready to die to save the new government. On Monday, Christmas day, the National Salvation Front announced that Nicolae Ceausescu and his wife Elena, captured the day after they fled, had been executed after a summary trial. The trial and

[8] Jiri Pehe, "Czechoslovakia: An Abrupt Transition" in *Report on Eastern Europe*, Vol. 1, No. 1 (January 5, 1990), p. 11.

[9] Radio Bucharest, December 22, 1989.

their dead bodies were immediately shown on Romanian TV. The level of violence dropped, possibly because the security forces were now deprived of the possibility of restoring their leader. By year's end the country had a new government headed by Prime Minister Petre Roman, a 43-year-old engineer and professor of hydraulics. The National Salvation Front was expanded to nearly 150 people with members ranging from students and civil rights activists to former high Communist party officials such as Ion Iliescu, the president of the Front. The cost of this change had been fearful, with possibly as many as 10,000 killed in the brief but ferocious struggle, and thousands made homeless by the destruction.[10]

Not even Bulgaria, in general the most quiescent of the East European states, could escape the sweep of change in the region. At the beginning of November independent groups used the opportunity of an all-European conference on ecology in Sofia to acquire public support for their demands for change. Demonstrations grew and the response of the regime of Todor Zhivkov, anxious to avoid international criticism, wavered. On November 17 Zhivkov resigned as party and state leader and was replaced by Petar Mladenov, the country's foreign minister for the last 18 years. Soon after, as in the other states, round table talks began, elections were pledged, and the party's monopoly of power ended.

NONALLIANCE MEMBERS

Yugoslavia, the first to break away from Soviet domination, has followed a quite differ-

ent path of development. Since the 1950s Yugoslav party theorists, especially Edvard Kardelj, developed a framework for a system of "workers' self-management." Over the years a complex system of workers' councils and work organizations has grown up to try to run the economy on the basis of social, but not state, ownership. At the same time, the country's many nationality groups are represented in the governments of six republican and two autonomous provinces and, through them, to the national federal government. The heads of both the party, known as the League of Communists of Yugoslavia, and the collective state presidency rotate every year among the eight major nationality groups. Yugoslavia was not untouched by the major movements for change in East Europe during 1989. Pressure built in the country for the Yugoslav party to follow the lead of the East European parties and abandon its claim to political monopoly, something which finally happened at the beginning of 1990.

Internationally, Yugoslavia became a founding member of the Nonaligned Conference during the 1960s and has followed an independent foreign policy ever since, on different occasions criticizing either the United States or the Soviet Union or both and jealously guarding its prerogatives in both politics and economics. This became increasingly difficult at the beginning of the 1980s when its debt problem ($18 billion) and domestic economic stagnation required careful balancing of the demands of western creditors and the lure of easier but less profitable Soviet trade (its largest partner).

Albania, on the other hand, has, since the early 1960s, rejected broad international contacts and has been especially careful about relations with the major powers. After the war the leadership feared absorption by Yugoslavia and the party leader Enver

---

[10] See Michael Shafir, "The Revolution: An Initial Assessment," *Report on Eastern Europe,* Vol. 1, No. 4, 26 January 1990, p. 34–42.

Hoxha strongly supported the USSR in its dispute with Belgrade. The Albanian party also rejected the kind of economic reforms seen in Yugoslavia as well as any improvement in relations with the West. When the USSR then began to accommodate itself to Yugoslavia's "separate road to socialism," to dismantle Stalinism, and to engage in arms negotiations with the United States, the Albanians linked up with China, which at that time was following a radical economic policy at home calling for "a great leap forward" and maintaining fierce hostility toward the United States. When in the 1970s Beijing too began to modify its policies and improve relations with the West, Albania broke these ties as well. Only recently, after the death of Hoxha and his replacement by Ramiz Alia, has Albania begun to expand its international ties with a few select Western European countries. But Alia has explicitly rejected the political reforms that swept East Europe in 1989.

MULTILATERAL ALLIANCES

The two major alliance structures in Eastern Europe, the Warsaw Pact and the Council for Mutual Economic Assistance, were both begun to serve Soviet foreign policy interests, and both have been dominated by the superpower. The Warsaw Pact was formed in 1955 in response to the entry of West Germany, the successor state to the region's former invader, into the American-backed North Atlantic Treaty Organization (NATO). The Warsaw Pact is not an alliance of equals. The military commander-in-chief has always been a Soviet general, and the alliance as a group has served to support and reflect Soviet policy goals. At times, such as in 1968, the alliance has acted as an agent for pressuring members to defend socialism as the Soviet Union sees it

and as a vehicle to justify "fraternal aid" by the allies. The existence of an alliance formalizes and legalizes the stationing of some one-half million Soviet troops in Eastern Europe, mostly in East Germany opposite NATO's troops. Since 1973 negotiations have been going on about reducing the number of each side's forces. In 1988 Mikhail Gorbachev announced a unilateral cut in Soviet forces worldwide, and specified that some 50,000 Soviet troops and 5,000 tanks would be withdrawn from Eastern Europe. After the changes of government in 1989 Czechoslovakia, Hungary, and Poland announced their intention to negotiate a full withdrawal of Soviet troops from their territories. The members of the alliance have not always kept in step. In 1960 Albania stopped participating as part of its dispute with the Soviet party leadership, and in 1968 it withdrew in protest over the invasion of Czechoslovakia. As noted above, Romania often took positions that differed from those of its allies.

The Council for Mutual Economic Assistance (CMEA) was formed in 1949 but remained largely a paper organization until the early 1960s. At that time, in an attempt to respond to the growing movement toward Western European unity, as well as to competition from China for influence in the region, Soviet leader Nikita Khrushchev pushed to "further perfect" the organization through economic specialization of its members. Romania explicitly rejected this approach, and in general, integration of the organization has gone very slowly. In fact, trade among CMEA members is still done almost totally on what is known as a "clearing" basis. Balances are kept in "transferable rubles," an accounting device allowing for a yearly tally of surpluses and deficits. But since the currencies are not convertible and trade has been based solely on government agreements and quotas, using surpluses to buy more goods is difficult. Hence pressure to keep trade strictly balanced—even at the cost of economic advantage—is strong. In 1985, in an attempt to get the members' economies to become more integrated and efficient, an agreement was signed on scientific and technological cooperation to the year 2000. As with the Warsaw Pact, the events of 1989 have proven a stronger impetus to reform, as several East European members have called for immediate and far-reaching reforms.

THE SIGNIFICANCE OF CHANGE IN EAST EUROPE

Reviewing the extraordinary transformations that have occurred in East Europe, several central aspects emerge. First is the extraordinary speed of the changes. In less than one year regimes that had held power for more than four decades were radically transformed and in some cases destroyed altogether. Moreover, the pace of change accelerated. What had taken roughly a year in Poland took only two months in East Germany, only weeks in Czechoslovakia, and less than one week in Romania. This bore witness to the effect changes in one East European state had on the situation in others.

Related to this is the surprising fragility of these regimes. After all this time, after holding all the key reins of power for so long, none of them was in a position to withstand concerted public pressure without Soviet support. Even Nicolae Ceausescu, whose personal dictatorial control had seemed so total, was forced literally to flee from headquarters in the face of public opposition. That opposition may have been slow in coming, but when it did it was total and neither Ceausescu nor any of the other regimes in East Europe had much to rely on to keep them in power.

Such fragility existed mostly because these regimes had failed to create what political scientists call "legitimacy," the public belief that those in power have the right, not just the means, to be in power. The periodical upheavals in Poland, Hungary, and Czechoslovakia and the events of 1989 throughout the region dramatically show that despite these regimes' dominance of the political process, the economy, and the media, they had failed to eradicate the notion that Communist rule was alien to these countries' culture, history, and traditions, and that they represented only the desires of a narrow ruling elite and a powerful international neighbor. They had failed, in David Easton's terminology, to create "diffuse support". And, despite control of the economy, they had failed to create enough material satisfaction to have most people support them simply on the basis of the goods they received, which Easton terms "output support."

Even as the role of the Soviet Union was preponderant in putting these regimes in power, its forbearance in the face of the rapid and sweeping changes in the region was a key factor in the various revolutions. By accepting the change to non-Communist government in the summer of 1989, Moscow signalled that it would, for the first time since the end of World War II, accept the erosion and even elimination of the Communist party's political monopoly. This had been the guarantor of Soviet interests in the region since the war. By pushing forward with *perestroika* at home and indicating that reform was necessary in East Europe as well, Mikhail Gorbachev both provided the initial stimulus to change in East Europe, something which had happened before and, more importantly, redefined and in fact removed limits to such change, something that had not happened before.

THE FUTURE FOR EAST EUROPE

Several factors must be considered in assessing the prospects for new forms of government in Eastern Europe. One of these is the creation of a new relationship between citizenry and government in which people now have the opportunity and right to engage in the formulation, determination, and implementation of policies that affect them. People have seen that they can become the creators not just the objects, of public policy. The new governments in the new East Europe will have to take that into consideration or risk the fate of their predecessors.

This new situation relates to a second factor that will affect the future of these states: the active politicization of a much greater part of society than has been the case for the last forty years. Politics, both in and out of government, is not longer the sole preserve of the one legal and ruling party. The game is now open to all comers. The events of 1989 in East Europe have brought into direct involvement broad sectors of the population. This step was necessary to make the revolutions occur. Their continued involvement may be necessary to make them succeed.

They will, however, struggle against the background of some important continuing factors. First, several of these states face dire economic conditions, brought on by years of mismanagement and lack of accountability. Poland is $40 billion in debt, with an industrial base scathingly referred to as "the museum of the industrial revolution." Debts are high in Hungary and Bulgaria as well; in Romania the country's economy has been so distorted by various grand schemes of the Ceausescu period that the country, once an exporter of grain, may not be able to feed itself for years. And throughout the region, especially in its more industrial areas, the air, water, and soil have been polluted and contaminated by years of unrestricted development. For the citizens of these countries some hard tasks have been done, but some hard times remain.

At the same time it would be naive to assume that those who ruled for so long will simply slip into the dustbin of history. Throughout this region those who ran the countries on a day-to-day basis and whose jobs depended on the communist government, the people in the *nomenklatura* positions (see p. 418) remain in place. For the most part the new governments have no one to replace them with. In some cases, such as East Germany, Bulgaria, and Romania, formerly high-level officials in the Communist party still are in powerful positions and the party's long-standing network of influence and organization may allow them to remain influential even after they no longer rule from the top.

Finally, the future cannot be treated without reference to the past. The division and redivision of East Europe over the centuries has left a tangled web of ethnic and national knots that Communist party rule only subdued but did not eliminate: Hungarians in Romania, Turks in Bulgaria, competing claims to Transylvania and Moldavia, borders decided by the big powers. While it seems unlikely that such disputes will erupt into warfare in this region, the open politics that the revolutions of 1989 created will allow parties and people espousing causes of all stripes to make their appeals. Longstanding grievances between countries and long-denied demands for minority rights could well issue into immoderate statements or ill-conceived actions by governments eager for popular support. To ensure that rights are protected and grievances are alleviated without allowing a return to times of divisions and manipulation will be but one of the great struggles of the new politics of East Europe.

References and Suggested Readings

Brown, J. F. *Eastern Europe and Communist Rule*. Durham, NC: Duke University Press, 1988.

Dawisha, Karen. *Eastern Europe, Gorbachev and Reform: The Great Challenge*. Cambridge: Cambridge University Press, 1988.

Gati, Charles. *Hungary and the Soviet Bloc*. Durham, NC: Duke University Press, 1986.

Linden, Ronald. *Bear and Foxes: The International Relations of the East European States*. Boulder, Colo.: East European Quarterly, 1979.

"1989: A Year of Upheaval," *Report on Eastern Europe* 1, 1 (1990): 5.

Rakowska-Harmstone, Teresa, ed. *Communism in Eastern Europe*. Bloomington: Indiana University Press, 1984.

Ramet, Pedro. *Cross and Commissar: The Politics of Religion in Eastern Europe and the USSR*. Bloomington: Indiana University Press, 1987.

Rusinow, Dennison. *The Yugoslav Experiment, 1948–1974*. Berkeley: University of California Press, 1977.

Skilling, H. Gordon. *Czechoslovakia's Interrupted Revolution*. Princeton, NJ: Princeton University Press, 1976.

Staar, Richard F. *Communist Regimes in Eastern Europe*. Stanford, Calif.: Hoover Institution Press, 1988.

Wallace, William U., and Roger A. Clarke. *Comecon, Trade and the West*. London: Frances Pinter Publ., 1986.

Wolchik, Sharon, and Alfred G. Meyer, eds. *Women, State, and Party in Eastern Europe*. Durham, NC: Duke University Press, 1985.

Copyrights and Acknowledgments

PART I: ENGLAND

Page 4: Culver Pictures.

Page 5: New York Public Library.

Page 7: David Easton—American Political Science Association.

Page 7: Gabriel Almond—American Political Science Association.

Page 23: Sygma.

Page 26: Kenneth O. Morgan, ed., *The Oxford Illustrated History of Britain* (Oxford: Oxford University Press, 1984), p. 306.

Page 28: Cartoon from *Punch:* The Bettmann Archive.

Page 30: R. T. Wilson, *The Workhouse,* Plate 13.

Page 32: Kenneth O. Morgan, ed., *The Oxford Illustrated History of Britain* (Oxford: Oxford University Press, 1984), p. 516.

Page 43: *The Guardian,* July 25, 1986.

Page 49: Figure 3.1—*The Economist Diary,* 1988, p. 17.

Page 50: Figure 3.2—*The Economist Diary,* 1988, p. 42.

Page 53: Figure 3.3—*The Economist Diary,* p. 18.

Page 55: Table 3.1—Central Statistical Office, *Regional Trends* 22.

London: Her Majesty's Stationery Office, 1987.

Page 55: *The Guardian,* June 13, 1987.

Page 63: Table 4.1—The Audit Bureau of Circulations, September 1987, as reported by *The Guardian,* October 26, 1987.

Page 64: Hugo Young, *One of Us* (London: Macmillan, 1989).

Page 66: *The Guardian,* October 16, 1986.

Page 67: Sykes/Sygma.

Page 67: Cartoon—*The Independent,* May 5, 1987.

Page 70: Bernard Donoughue, *Prime Minister* (London: Jonathan Cape Inc., 1987).

Page 74: *The Guardian,* December 3, 1986.

Page 82: *The Guardian,* October 30, 1987.

Pages 86–87: Table 5.1—*The Guardian,* May 22, 1987.

Page 88: *The Guardian,* October 3, 1986.

Page 89: Table 5.2—*The Guardian,* October 29, 1986.

Page 90: Peter Jenkins, *Mrs. Thatchers's Revolution* (London: Pan Books, 1989).

Page 91: Table 5.3—Fred Ridley, "At the Bottom of the Democracy League," *The Guardian,* August 10, 1987.

Page 93: Figure 5.1—Helmut Norpoth, "Guns and Butter and Government Popularity in Britian," *American Political Review* 81 (1987): 951.

Page 93: Figure 5.2—Helmut Norpoth, "Guns and Butter and Government Popularity in Britain," *American Political Review* 81 (1987): 951.

Page 94: Reuters/Bettmann Newsphotos.

Page 95: Derek Hudson/Sygma.

Page 98: *The Guardian,* April 8, 1987.

Page 104: Peter Hennessy, *Cabinet* (Oxford: Basil Blackwell Ltd), cover. Copyright by Peter Hennessy.

Page 109: Peter Hennessy, *Whitehall* (London: Secker & Warburg), 1989.

Page 112: Bernard Donoughue, *Prime Minister* (London: Jonathan Cape Ltd., 1987).

Neumann, *The Germans—Public Opinion Polls 1967–1980* (Westport, Conn.: Greenwood, 1981).

Page 286: German Information Center.

Page 289: German Information Center.

Page 292: Figure 21.1 *Forschungsgruppe Wahlen* (Mannheim).

Page 296: SPD, 1863–1986: Für Freiheit, Gerechtigkeit und Solidaritat, Bonn 1976.

Page 302: *Facts About Germany* (Lexikon-Institut Bertelsmann), p. 117.

Page 305: Figure 22.1—German Information Center.

Page 309: Figure 22.2—Elisabeth Noelle-Neumann, *The Germans* (Westport, Conn.: Greenwood, 1981).

Page 312: Table 22.2—Manfred Berger, Wolfgang Gibowski, Matthias Jung, Dieter Roth, and Wolfgang Schulte, "Die Konsolidierung die Wende: Eine Analyse der Bundestagswahl 1987," *Zeitschrift für Parlamentsfragen,* 1987, pp. 253–287.

Page 314: Table 22.3—1961–1976 figures: Helmut Norpoth, "Kanzler-kandidaten," *Politisches Vierteljahresschrift,* 18 (1977): 563; 1980–1987 figures: *Forschungsgruppe Wahlen* surveys, Mannheim.

Page 317: German Information Center.

Page 318: UPI.

Page 319: Table 23.2 Peter Schindler, *Datenhandbuch zur Geschichte des deutschen Bundestages 1980 bis 1987* (Baden-Baden: Nomos, 1988), pp. 993–1001.

Page 329: Table 24.1—adapted and updated from Helmut Norpoth, "Coalition Government at the Brink of Majority Rule," in Eric C. Browne and John Dreijmanis (eds.), *Government Coalitions in Western Democracies* (New York: Longman, 1982), pp. 12, 13.

Page 332: UPI/Bettmann Newsphotos.

Page 334: UPI/Bettmann Newsphotos.

Page 336: *Facts About Germany* (Lexikon-Institut Bertelsmann), p. 99.

Page 337: In-Press/AP.

Page 338: Table 24.2 —*Statistisches Jahrbuch 1986,* page 436.

Page 345: *German Tribune,* September 6, 1987, p. 1.

Page 349: UPI/Bettmann Newsphotos.

PART IV: RUSSIA

Page 355: Table 27.1—Michael Ryan and Richard Prentice, *Social Trends in the Soviet Union from 1950* (New York: St. Martin's Press, 1987), p. 61.

Page 359: Sovfoto.

Page 366: Novasti from Sovfoto.

Page 369: TASS from Sovfoto.

Page 374: Data compiled by William Chase, University of Pittsburgh.

Page 384: TASS from Sovfoto.

Page 389: AP/Wide World Photos.

Page 396: Fotokhronika TASS.

Page 398: TASS from Sovfoto.

Page 399: By V. Repik, TASS from Sovfoto.

Page 400: *Christian Science Monitor,* November 17, 1988, page 15.

Page 401: *Krokodil* (Moscow), September 26, l988, p. 3.

Page 412: TASS from Sovfoto.

Page 427: AP/Wide World Photos.

Page 431: UPI/Bettmann Newsphotos.

Page 436: Data from the *New York Times,* June 28, 1987; and Radio Free Europe/Radio Liberty.

Page 439: *The Economist,* May 30 and June 6, 1987.

Page 438: Sovfoto.

PART V: LATIN EUROPE, SCANDINAVIA, AND EASTERN EUROPE

Page 463: AP/Wide World Photos.

Page 468: Reuters/Bettmann Newsphotos.

Page 471: UPI/Bettmann Newsphotos.

Name Index

Subject Index